COMMONLY USED SYMBOLS

Symbol	Term	Page Where Symbol Is First Introduced
Y	GNP (or income)	25
C	Consumption	25
I	Investment	25
G	Government spending	25
X	Net exports	25
F	Government transfers	39
T	Taxes	39
S_p	Private saving	40
S_g	Government saving	40
S_r	Rest of world saving	40
M	Money	42
B	Bonds	42
W	Wage	66
U	Unemployment	66
L	Labor force	66
t	Tax rate	75
R	Interest rate	97
P	Price level	101
N^*	Potential employment	128
K	Capital stock	129
N	Employment	129
Y^*	Potential GNP	130
π	Rate of inflation	139
π^e	Expected inflation	139
Z	Exogenous price shock	181
R^K	Rental price of capital	229
E	Exchange rate	262
RE	Reserves of the Fed	323
M_B	Monetary base	324
m	Monetary base multiplier	325
D	Deposits at banks	340
U^*	Natural unemployment rate	436

MACRO-ECONOMICS

Second Edition

To accompany this text

Study Guide, Second Edition, by David H. Papell
Study Guide with MacroSolve Exercises, IBM® version, Second Edition, by
 Stephen R. King, Rick M. McConnell, and David H. Papell
Study Guide with MacroSolve Exercises, Macintosh™ version, Second Edition,
 by Stephen R. King, Rick M. McConnell, and David H. Papell

MACRO-ECONOMICS

THEORY, PERFORMANCE, AND POLICY

Second Edition

Robert E. Hall
John B. Taylor

STANFORD UNIVERSITY

W · W · NORTON & COMPANY · NEW YORK · LONDON

To Donna, Christopher, Anne, Jonathan, and Andrew
R.E.H.

To Allyn, Jennifer Lynn, and John Andrew
J.B.T.

Contents

Part III   The Micro Foundations of Aggregate Supply and Price Adjustment

Preface

THE ENTHUSIASTIC response given to the first edition of this book heartened us, and was soon countered by the sobering responsibility of success. Nowhere in economics does research develop as rapidly as in macroeconomics, so our goal—to capture the spirit and content of the new work in a form that is manageable in the intermediate-level course—requires steady revision. Also, while our fellow researchers have given us major discoveries to contend with, the tens of thousands of students who have used the book have made many useful suggestions about how to fine tune the presentation. And because teaching the macroeconomics course at Stanford has benefited enormously from the MacroSolve software, we are pleased that with this edition our publisher makes it available to all our readers.

The late 1980s have seen the complete assimilation of the big idea of the 1970s: rational expectations. The results can be seen in every chapter of this book. Our discussion of consumption, investment, foreign trade, and money embraces rational expectations at many points. Even in areas—notably the sluggish adjustment of prices—where our model has properties disputed by leading rational expectations theorists such as Robert Lucas or Thomas Sargent, our analysis adopts rational expectations.

Recent years have seen an upsurge of interest in models where only real factors influence real variables. We devote more attention in this edition to the real business cycle view in its several forms, although the main thrust of our analysis is toward a view in which both real and monetary factors shape the economy in the short run.

With all this attention to new developments, however, it remains our conviction that there is much that is worth retaining in traditional Keynesian and monetarist macroeconomics. In particular, two key ideas remain important in our thinking. First, output, not prices, responds strongly in the short run to shifts in demand; in the long run, prices adjust, returning the economy towards its potential level determined by the supply of labor and capital. Second, as a consequence of this, the level of employment and hence of disposable income is a given to households in the short run, so it is useful to look at the propagation of spending through the consumption function. In other words, we have not banished the expenditure process of elementary macroeconomics, though we move beyond it early in the book.

Price adjustment, of course, is a basic fact of macroeconomics, and this book puts demand, supply, and price adjustment on an equal footing. There is more to the subject than IS-LM and aggregate demand, so we try not to spend so much time on the details of aggregate demand that aggregate supply and price adjustment become an addendum covered late in the course. Students get the basics of aggregate supply and price adjustment in the first few chapters of the book; later chapters uncover their origins in microeconomics and the stickiness of wages and prices that develops at the microeconomic level.

Chapters 4–7 constitute a complete macro model, capable of analyzing all the major concerns of macroeconomics including inflation. In the second edition, we have strengthened and augmented this mini-course. Now we have separate chapters—Chapters 4 and 5—on spending and on financial markets, which allow a fuller development of the IS-LM model. Another advantage of this change is that the crucial topic of foreign trade now appears earlier, as an integral part of the presentation of consumption and investment in Chapters 4 and 5.

Other significant changes are the streamlining of the investment model in Chapter 9, fuller treatment of trade in Chapter 10, simplification of monetary economics in Chapter 12, a more familiar treatment of the flexible-price IS-LM model in Chapter 13, and a discussion of real business cycle models in Chapter 14.

In almost every chapter, we have added topic boxes, a well-received feature of the first edition. They now include such new topics as "Does a Tax Cut Pay for Itself?" (Chapter 4), "Portfolio Investment and Macro Investment" (Chapter 5), "IS-LM in the Business Pages" (Chapter 5), "How the Real Business Cycle School Views Supply" (Chapter 6), "Three Oil Price Shocks" (Chapter 7), "Why Is the Saving Rate Higher in Japan Than in the U.S.?" and "Does Consumption Take a Random Walk?" (Chapter 8), "The Effect of the Tax Reform Act of 1986" (Chapter 9), "The Budget Deficit and the Trade Deficit" (Chapter 10), "Deficit Control: The Gramm-Rudman-Hollings Approach" (Chapter 11), "What Does a Union Contract

Look Like?" (Chapter 15), "What Would an Optimal Policy Have Been in 1979–86?" (Chapter 17), and "The Annual Economic Summits" (Chapter 18).

Distinctive Features at a Glance

What, in our experience, makes this book work well as a class text? A short list includes the following features, most of which set this book apart from others in the field:

- Development early on of a *complete working macro model* with aggregate demand, aggregate supply, and price adjustment.
- Treating the *price level as a predetermined variable* consistently throughout the book for expositional simplicity.
- Repeated use of *intertemporal budget constraints* that link savings to the accumulations of assets for consumers, firms, and government.
- Introduction to the *open economy* early in the book and integration of this into the macro model.
- A comprehensive treatment of the *microeconomic foundations of macroeconomic theory.*
- Careful exposition of the *empirical regularities* of the macroeconomy at the start of each chapter on micro foundations.
- Review of the *policy implications* of micro foundations for IS, LM, or price adjustment at the end of each chapter on micro foundations.

Pedagogical Features at a Glance

There are several strictly pedagogical features in the text that we have found enhance presentation of the material.

- *Summary boxes* draw together key ideas at appropriate places within each chapter. They serve a reinforcing function by allowing readers to check their understanding of one aspect of the analysis before tackling new material. And they also serve a review function, helping readers locate the building blocks of the analysis without rereading entire chapters.
- *Topic boxes* introduce special concepts related to the discussion in the text, including computing growth rates, quarterly GNP statistics, budget projections, indexing taxes, and the relationship between graphs and algebra. They also present discussion of historical examples, current policy issues, and other illustrations of points in the text.
- *Problems.* At the end of each chapter there are two types of problems: nu-

merical and analytical. The numerical problems require the use of a hand calculator and usually take more time. We have found these useful for special projects. The analytical questions can be done with graphs or simple algebra. In addition, there are short questions for review.

- *References.* We have tried to keep footnotes to a minimum. Footnotes are used mainly to document a specific statement or reference in the text.
- *Parallel graphical and algebraic presentation.* In most cases arguments are presented in both graphical and algebraic form. We have found that some students learn better with graphs and some learn better with algebra, especially if the algebra is presented in a way that does not intimidate. Graphical arguments are not necessarily easier for all students and the algebra is provided to help those with a preference for algebra. Of course, graphical presentation usually helps with the intuition and we would expect even the less graphically inclined students to learn basics such as the Keynesian cross or IS-LM. A special effort has been made to demonstrate that graphs and algebra are just two ways to describe the same economic concepts. See especially the topic box on page 75.
- *Real-world examples.* Showing how economic theory works in practice is the best way to learn. Too often, however, these lessons of experience are placed at some distance from the analysis, with the result that students often sense that a barrier exists between macroeconomic models and the real world from which they are drawn. We have chosen to make the performance of the economy an integral aspect of the exposition, with new concepts constantly illuminated by examples.
- *Teaching supplements.* An *Instructor's Manual* that we have prepared jointly with Gary W. Yohe of Wesleyan University is available from the publisher. This *Instructor's Manual* contains many teaching "tricks" to prompt students to become actively involved in the subject. These include macro-forecasting contests, policy projects on Federal Reserve monetary targeting and federal budget projections, debate formats for lectures, classroom skits to illustrate the forward-looking theory of consumption and other models, and class participation in financial decision-making. There are also references to more complicated material related to the text and a large number of test questions. An excellent *Study Guide* prepared by David H. Papell of the University of Houston to go with the text is also available. A *Test-Item File* of roughly 700 questions has been prepared by Gary W. Yohe and is available either in printed form as part of the *Instructor's Manual* or on diskette for most personal computers.
- *Computer software.* The MacroSolve package, written by Stephen R. King and Rick M. McConnell, embodies the IS-LM and price adjustment equations developed in the text. The user can shift curves on the graphical display and see immediately how the economy reacts.
- *Data sources.* Whenever possible the data in charts and tables are taken from the most recently available *Economic Report of the President.* This

makes it easy to look up additional related data, or to keep lectures up-to-date.

A Guided Tour

The book starts with a mini-course in macroeconomic analysis in Part I that covers many important topics. We review the basic facts of macroeconomic fluctuations and develop a simple but complete model of the macroeconomy. Our approach to aggregate demand is standard, through the IS-LM apparatus. We include trade even in the first development of the IS curve. We have chosen to use the term aggregate supply in its classical sense—a vertical line in the output-price diagram, showing the full-employment, or potential, level of output. The long-run equilibrium of the economy occurs at the intersection of aggregate demand and potential output.

The path to long-run potential is governed by the price-adjustment process. But the price level is unresponsive in the short run—output occurs where the aggregate demand curve intersects the predetermined-price level. We do not drop the predetermined-price assumption when we bring the supply side into the picture. IS-LM remains our theory of output determination in each period of the dynamic analysis. Price adjustment comes into play the period after a policy or other change has affected output.

The expositional simplification we achieve in this way is enormous. We do not feel that the empirical evidence justifies the complexity of simultaneous determination of prices and output in each period. There is certainly no contradiction to the predetermined-price assumption if the period is a quarter of a year, and the assumption is valid as a close approximation if the period is a full year.

The adaptation of price adjustment to inflation ranks high among the ideas that have evolved in macroeconomics over the past two decades. We avoid characterizing this adaptation solely as a matter of changing expectations. Even with rational expectations, price adjustment depends partly on recent inflation experience since contracts and other rigidities prevent quick adjustments. We discuss how the adaptation of expectations to inflation depends on how prices and wages are set.

After the short course in macroeconomic analysis, we go on to develop the micro foundations of aggregate demand in Part II. At the start of each chapter we present the key facts or puzzles that need to be explained. At the end of each chapter we look at the implications for IS-LM. The consumption chapter (8) develops a forward-looking theory of consumption based on the life cycle and permanent income formulations, emphasizing the role of rational expectations. By establishing an intertemporal budget constraint, we avoid present discounted values and forbidding summations. Chapter 9, on investment, focuses on Dale Jorgensen's model. The foreign trade chapter (10) focuses on flexible exchange rates, with a rational expectations model of the exchange rate as its centerpiece. Chapter 11, on government, contains more material on the deficit and government debt than is customary alongside a standard treatment of automatic stabilizers and related subjects. When the intertemporal budget constraint for the government is presented, the idea is already familiar to the student from consumption and investment. Chapter 12, on the monetary system, takes up money demand and describes the role of the Federal Reserve using financial balance sheets developed in Part I. We emphasize the credit, or intermediation, role of banks in addition to their role in determining the money supply.

Part III contains much that we think is novel for an intermediate text. It is here that we develop the micro foundations of aggregate supply and price adjustment. Chapter 13 sets the stage with perfect price flexibility, long-term growth, and inflation. An appendix deals with the algebra of rational expectations models. Chapter 14 takes a careful look at the real business cycle model and development in the area—the imperfect information model of aggregate supply developed by Robert Lucas. Chapter 15 deals with micro foundations and macro implications of overlapping wage setting. It also discusses markup pricing and the optimal contract model of Costas Azariadis, Martin Baily, and others. Chapter 16 discusses the implications of price adjustment for the dynamic behavior of the macroeconomy and compares these implications with actual experience.

Part IV pulls the analysis together into a comprehensive treatment of macroeconomic policy evaluation. Chapter 17 takes up general policy issues such as time inconsistency, multiplier uncertainty, targets and instruments, and the rational expectations critique of policy evaluation. The emphasis is on policy rules, rather than on one-time policy changes. The inflation-unemployment trade-off appears as a policy frontier between output stability and price stability. Chapter 18 then considers the problem of macroeconomic policy in the world economy including a review of how the international monetary system evolved from Bretton Woods and how policy works in countries with fixed exchange rates.

Acknowledgments

Early drafts of both the first and second editions were used in several intermediate macroeconomics courses at Stanford, and we thank the students and teaching assistants for their very helpful comments. We are deeply grateful to the many teachers and students at Stanford and elsewhere who wrote to us with comments on the first edition. This second edition is immeasurably better than it would have been without their feedback. In particular, we would like to single out the following:

Francis Ahking, University of Connecticut
Ugur Aker, Hiram College
Robert Barry, College of William and Mary
Ernst Berndt, Massachusetts Institute of Technology
Olivier Blanchard, Massachusetts Institute of Technology
Ronald Bodkin, University of Ottawa
Norman G. Clifford, University of Kansas
Wilfred J. Ethier, University of Pennsylvania
George Evans, Stanford University
Frederick Goddard, University of Florida
Pete Gomori, St. Francis College (New York)
Harvey Gram, City University of New York
Howard Gruenspecht, Carnegie-Mellon University
Joseph Guerin, St. Joseph's University
John Haltiwanger, University of Maryland
James Hamilton, University of Virginia
Daniel Himarios, University of Texas at Arlington
Takatoshi Ito, University of Minnesota
Demetrius Kantarelis, Assumption College
Stephen R. King, Stanford University
John Laitner, University of Michigan
Bennett McCallum, Carnegie-Mellon University
Basil Moore, Wesleyan University
Richard F. Muth, Emory University
Ian Novos, University of Southern California
Ernest H. Oksanen, McMaster University
David H. Papell, University of Houston
Edmund S. Phelps, Columbia University
Mikko Puhakka, Cornell University
Garey Ramey, Stanford University
Duane J. Rosa, West Texas State University
Michael Sattinger, SUNY Albany
Shinichi Watanabe, University of Kansas
J. Kirker Stephens, University of Oklahoma
Stephen Tomlinson, Stanford University
Michael Truscott, University of Tampa
Larkin Warner, Oklahoma State University

Finally, we would like to thank Drake McFeely, Donald Lamm, and Nancy Palmquist of W. W. Norton for outstanding editorial help and advice.

Stanford   R.E.H.
December 1987   J.B.T.

PART I

Fundamentals of Macroeconomics

1

◆━━━━━━━━━━━━━━━━━━━━━━━━━━━━━━━━━━━━━━━◆

The Macroeconomy

THE ECONOMY is always in motion. Most of the movement is upward. Production of cars, TVs, personal computers, and apartment buildings rises each year. Firms hire more and more workers to make these products. But in some years, production falls, workers are laid off, and unemployment rises.

As you read this book, the economy is at some stage of its ceaseless pattern of fluctuations. This year's upturn or downturn is temporary. And as it occurs, longer run, more slowly evolving forces—such as population growth and technological progress—are leading to more lasting increases in output as the economy grows over time. The current fluctuation is a temporary diversion from the longer run growth path.

Fluctuations in output and employment are among the most regular and persistent facts of economics. Although there are undoubtedly some new or special features of the current upturn or downturn in economic activity, such fluctuations themselves are not new. They have been recorded for hundreds of years. Economists have developed a branch of economic theory, called **macroeconomics,** to explain these fluctuations. This book is about macroeconomics. Macroeconomics seeks to explain why fluctuations happen and to investigate policies that can mitigate them.

The word **macro**economics was coined to distinguish the subject from **micro**economics. Microeconomics is the study of how individual consumers and firms behave, and how the market system allocates scarce resources. Microeconomics is not usually concerned with the temporary fluctuations in

3

the economy. But it is a mistake to isolate macroeconomics from microeconomics. When macroeconomists try to explain the fluctuations in the economy they must look at the behavior of consumers and firms, the organization of labor markets and industry, the workings of financial markets, and even the machinations of governments. They rely on microeconomics when they do so. Macroeconomics is only as good as the microeconomics that underlies it.

During the past 15 years economic fluctuations in the United States and other countries have been larger and more erratic than at any time since the Great Depression of the 1930s. Most people sense this and are therefore more concerned than ever with the ups and downs of the economy. A recession has substantial effects on our economic welfare. Layoffs during recessions and the inability to find work during periods of high unemployment create severe hardships. Poverty rises during recessions. Even for those who don't lose their jobs, lower incomes reduce what can be consumed; lower incomes also reduce what can be invested to increase the productive capacity of the economy in the future.

Other important variables also fluctuate as the economy goes through its ups and downs. Fluctuations in inflation, interest rates, and the international value of the dollar all accompany the fluctuations in the economy. These key economic variables move together in reasonably predictable ways. We will have a lot to say about the relationships among output, employment, interest rates, prices, and exchange rates. Indeed, macroeconomics has been more successful in predicting relationships among variables than it has been in predicting the levels of the variables. For instance, macroeconomists are not much better than anyone else in forecasting interest rates. But they can tell you that a fall in the value of the dollar will probably accompany a fall in interest rates, and they can tell you why.

The media give high priority to economic fluctuations, and this is some indication of their importance. Newspaper headlines like "UNEMPLOYMENT REACHES HIGHEST LEVEL IN FOUR YEARS," "INFLATION HITS FIVE-YEAR LOW," and "DOLLAR PLUNGES TO NEW DEPTHS" record the ups and downs in the economy. Economic fluctuations are also big items on the platform of any national political campaign. The incumbents usually try to claim credit for any good news, such as a drop in inflation, while the challengers blame them for the bad news, such as a high unemployment rate.

1.1 Recent Performance of the Macroeconomy

Figure 1–1 documents the fluctuations of the U.S. economy over the 20-year period from the mid-1960s to the mid-1980s. The colored line in the figure traces **real gross national product (GNP),** a concept we will examine in more detail in the next chapter. Real GNP is the actual, physical produc-

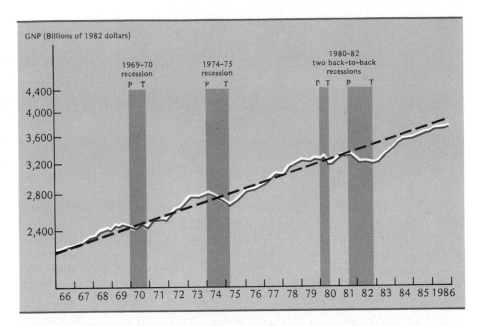

GNP (Billions of 1982 dollars)

Figure 1-1. REAL GNP IN THE UNITED STATES, 1966–86.
The colored line shows what has happened to real GNP. During the periods that are shaded, real GNP declined—these are recessions. The black line shows what real GNP would have looked like if it had grown smoothly during the period instead of fluctuating as it did. Source: *Business Conditions Digest,* February 1987, p. 19.

tion of cars, trucks, TV sets, rock concerts, Hollywood films, haircuts, and every other good or service that people in the United States prepare for trade with one another or with the rest of the world. We get real GNP by summing up the dollar value of production, and then adjusting for any price changes that have occurred from year to year.

The vertical axis in Figure 1-1 shows the values of real GNP in 1982 prices. The horizontal axis indicates the year. During this recent 20-year period, the U.S. economy has gone through four recessions—periods when real GNP declined. In the chart the recessions are shaded. The P at the start of each recession is the **peak,** and the T at the end of each recession is the **trough.** Between the shaded areas the economy is growing rapidly—these are the recoveries.

Note that GNP tended to rise during the 20-year period. There is a growth trend because of a growing labor force and increased capital stock, and because of technological improvements. The black dashed line in the chart indicates the steady upward trend that underlies the behavior of real GNP. This trend line is called **potential GNP.** Real GNP fluctuates around potential GNP as the economy goes through successive recessions and recoveries.

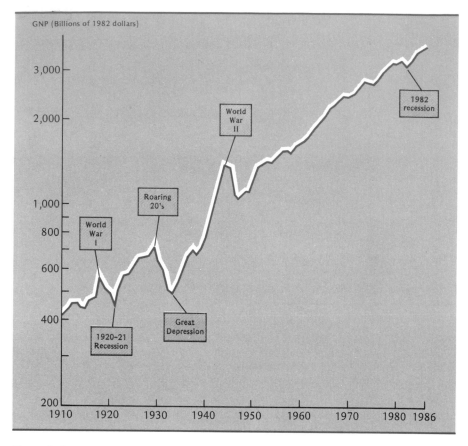

Figure 1–2.   REAL GNP, 1910–86.
The largest decline in real GNP occurred from 1929 to 1933, the years of the Great Depression. Another important contraction occurred in the early 1920s. Both were more serious than any recession since 1950. Source: *National Income and Product Accounts of the U.S.* (U.S. Department of Commerce) and *Economic Report of the President,* 1987, Table B–2.

Fluctuations do not occur at regular intervals. They certainly cannot be anticipated with great accuracy, and this is what makes macroeconomic forecasting both difficult and interesting. For example, the recovery that began in 1975 was relatively long, whereas the recovery that began in 1980 was very short.

Figure 1–2 gives a longer perspective on the fluctuations in economic activity, showing the ups and downs in the economy over the last 75 years. The most noticeable single fluctuation during this period was the downturn during the Great Depression of the early 1930s. Note, however, that the recession in the early 1920s and the subsequent boom in the late 1920s were also comparatively large in magnitude. Although economic fluctuations in the United States have not ceased, they appear to have diminished in magnitude compared to this earlier period.

EMPLOYMENT

Fluctuations in employment follow closely the fluctuations in real GNP. Figure 1–3 shows the ratio of employed workers to the working-age population for the same 20-year period covered by Figure 1–1. Employment fell rapidly as the economy went through each of the four recessions during this period. Firms laid off workers as the economy's production fell, and hired fewer new workers. As the economy began to recover after each downturn, employment again grew as firms called workers back to work and hired many new workers. This close association between production and employment as the economy fluctuates is one of the key facts of macroeconomics. Recurrent recessions are serious social problems, because they involve large-scale job losses.

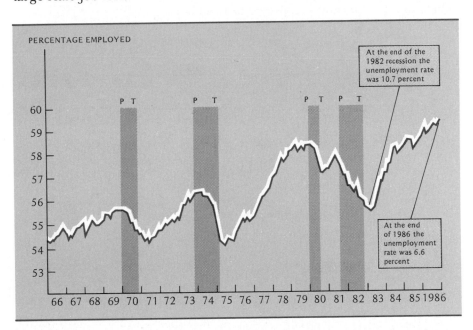

Figure 1–3.   EMPLOYMENT AS A PERCENTAGE OF WORKING-AGE POPULATION. Recessions are periods of declining employment, measured as a fraction of the working-age population. Because of the fluctuations in employment, recessions influence a large fraction of the public. As the economy fluctuates, the unemployment rate varies inversely with employment. Source: *Business Conditions Digest,* February 1987, p. 17.

Mirroring the fluctuations in employment are the fluctuations in the **unemployment rate,** which is the percentage of workers who are not working but who are looking for work. When employment falls the unemployment rate rises as workers are laid off. For example, during 1982 the unemployment rate rose to over 10 percent. By the middle of 1987 it had fallen to about 6 percent.

INFLATION

Another important fact of economic fluctuations is their correlation with the rate of **inflation**—the percentage change in the average price of all goods in the economy. In general, prices tend to rise faster when the economy is operating near its peak. Conversely, prices tend to fall, or at least rise less rapidly, when the economy is near a trough. These rises and falls lag behind the fluctuations in real GNP.

Figure 1–4 shows the rate of inflation. The chart demonstrates that almost all of the significant declines in the rate of inflation occurred just after recession periods. Are recessions a necessary part of the disinflation process? This is one of the central concerns of this book.

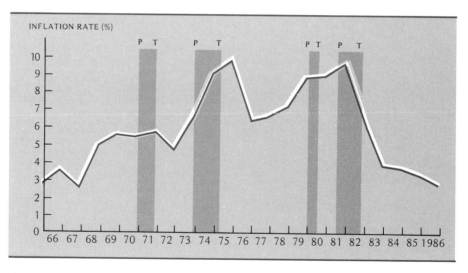

Figure 1–4.   THE RATE OF INFLATION.
Starting in the late 1960s, the rate of inflation rose. In the 1980s, it began to decline. Bursts of inflation have preceded or accompanied recessions. Typically, inflation subsides to some extent just after recessions. Source: *Economic Report of the President,* 1987, Table B–3.

INTEREST RATES

Interest rates also tend to fluctuate over the business cycle. The interest rate is the amount charged for a loan by a bank or other lender per dollar per year, expressed as a percent. For instance, if your roommate lends you $100, for which she asks you to pay her $110 a year from now, the interest rate is 10 percent. Figure 1–5 shows one representative interest rate, the Treasury bill rate, during the same four recessions that we previously considered. The Treasury bill rate measures how much the government pays to borrow. There was a general rise in interest rates starting in the 1960s as inflation rose. As we will see, interest rates usually rise with inflation to compensate lenders for the falling purchasing power of the dollar. The interest rate minus the expected rate of inflation is called the **real interest rate.**

However, the fluctuations of interest rates during the recessions are most dramatic. Interest rates are **procyclical;** they rise during recovery periods and fall during recessions. They are also one of the most volatile of macroeconomic variables, and the most difficult to predict. Nevertheless, as Figure 1–5 makes clear, these interest rate fluctuations are intimately related to the fluctuations in production and employment. A thorough understand-

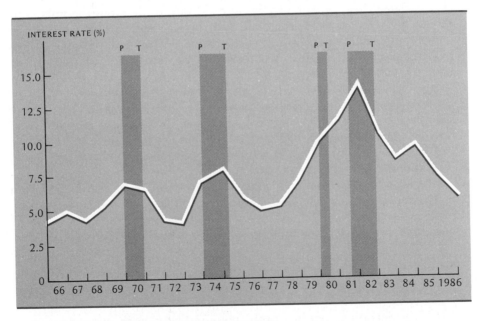

Figure 1–5.   THE TREASURY BILL INTEREST RATE.
Like other interest rates, the rate on Treasury bills reaches a peak just before a recession and then usually falls sharply. Source: *Economic Report of the President,* 1987, Table B–68.

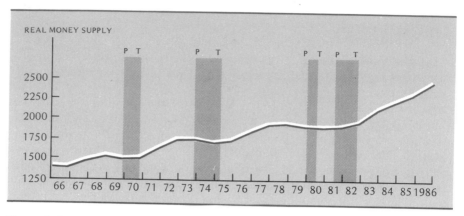

Figure 1–6. THE MONEY SUPPLY.
The money supply divided by the price level—real money—seems to decline before recessions. The general trend in real money is positive because the growth in the economy creates a need for more money to assist in buying and selling goods. Source: *Economic Report of the President,* 1987, Tables B–3 (GNP deflator) and B–64 (M_2).

ing of interest rate behavior is crucial to any explanation of economic fluctuations.

A variable closely related to the interest rate is the **money supply.** The money supply consists of currency and the deposits that people have at banks and certain other financial institutions. The money supply is controlled by the Federal Reserve Board, the governing body of the central bank of the United States.

The behavior of the money supply is shown in Figure 1–6. The chart shows the money supply divided by the price level, or **real money.** There seems to be a relationship between money and the timing of recessions and booms. The relationship suggests that changes in the money supply may be causing the fluctuations in the economy. In the theory that we develop in this book the money supply is a primary force in economic fluctuations.

The ideas, theories, and models we study in this book endeavor to explain why GNP and employment fluctuate so much. They will also try to provide reasons for the cyclical movements of inflation, interest rates, and the money supply as well as a number of other macroeconomic variables.

Macroeconomic Fluctuations

1. The economy undergoes recessions and recoveries at irregular intervals. Recessions are periods of contracting economic activity; recoveries are periods of above-average economic growth after a recession. Over the long haul the economy expands as population and technical progress increase output along the trend of potential GNP.

2. The physical volume of output—measured by real GNP—contracts in a recession and expands in a recovery.

3. Employment moves closely with output. Recessions are periods of job loss, that is, rising unemployment.

4. The period between World War I and World War II saw two very large contractions. Recessions have continued since World War II. In the early 1980s the overall contraction was the worst since the Great Depression.

5. Inflation generally subsides in the wake of a recession.

6. Interest rates usually reach a peak just before a recession starts and then fall considerably during the recession.

1.2 Explaining Fluctuations: Flexible or Sticky Prices?

At the core of any theory of macroeconomic fluctuations is an explanation of how the economy responds to economic forces. How does GNP adjust when a new technology is introduced? What if there is a sudden increase in demand for new factories and machines because of a massive buildup of defense spending? What if the price of oil is quadrupled because a cartel of producers cuts back on production? In constructing an explanation of how the economy responds to these forces, the macroeconomist constructs a **model.** A model is simply a description of how consumers and firms behave and how they interact with each other in markets.

The earliest economic theories about the determination of GNP went as follows: At a given moment, there is a certain amount of productive capacity in the economy. The level of the capacity depends on the number of factories and machines and the number of workers. Full employment will prevail in the economy, because if unemployment developed it would quickly disappear as wages fell enough to stimulate the demand for labor. The basic theory of supply and demand assumes that prices or wages would adjust quickly so that supply would equal demand. Analogously, early theories of macroeconomics supposed that wages and prices for the whole economy would adjust quickly to keep labor and machines fully employed. Prices were assumed to be *flexible* enough to bring about a complete and quick adjustment.

According to such a theory, a change in overall demand in the economy would result in a change in the price level, but not in the level of production. The workings of a macro model with flexible prices are shown in the simple macroeconomic supply-demand diagram in Figure 1–7.

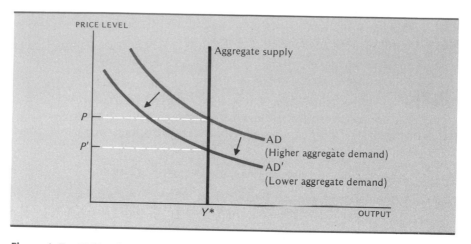

Figure 1–7. THE MODEL WITH PERFECTLY FLEXIBLE PRICES.
The level of output, measured by real GNP, is determined by the capital stock and the
number of workers, neither of which responds to the price level. Consequently, aggregate supply is a vertical line. Aggregate demand is a downward-sloping schedule, but demand does not influence the level of output. If the aggregate demand schedule shifts
downward, from AD to AD', only the price level changes; output remains the same.

The productive capacity of the economy is shown as a vertical line. The
productive capacity is determined by the volume of productive factors—
capital and labor—and is unrelated to the price level. In later chapters, we
will have much more to say about productive capacity, because it is a concept that retains an important role in modern macroeconomics. Productive
capacity determines **potential output,** labeled Y^* in Figure 1–7. Potential
output is the amount of output that can be produced from the existing capital stock and labor force.

Figure 1–7 also shows an **aggregate demand curve,** which slopes downward. Aggregate demand is the total amount of demand throughout the
economy. Demand depends on the price level—demand is higher if the
price is lower. The negative relationship is due to financial factors: A higher
price level increases the demand for money and credit and raises interest
rates. Higher interest rates then lower demand. We will have much more to
say in later chapters about aggregate demand, which has a central role in all
macroeconomic theories.

With perfectly flexible prices the economy always operates at the intersection of aggregate demand and aggregate supply. If the price level
happened to be too high, so that demand fell short of supply, and
unemployment threatened, then the price level would fall immediately by
just enough to stimulate demand and restore equilibrium.

What is interesting and important about this model is that demand influences only the price level, not the level of output. If a change in economic policy shifts demand downward, prices fall immediately. Output remains unchanged. With perfectly flexible prices, *shifts in demand cannot explain recessions and booms.* Shifts in demand explain only variations in inflation.

To explain the continuing pattern of major fluctuations in output and employment, this type of model has to say that potential GNP is shifting. But potential GNP depends on the amount of capital and the number of people available for work, neither of which seems likely to fluctuate much from one year to the next. The model seems an unpromising way to explain recessions and booms.

This type of model with perfectly flexible prices was essentially what economists in the early twentieth century used for analyzing the macro-economy. The Great Depression in the 1930s saw a drop in real GNP that was so large—30 percent from 1929 to 1933—that an explanation based on a drop in potential GNP seemed out of the question. A drop in demand seemed like a more plausible explanation. During the depression, John Maynard Keynes, the great British economist, created a new macroeconomic model where shifts in demand *could* influence the level of output. Keynes's ideas transformed macroeconomics, even though macroeconomists have since criticized Keynes's original theory and introduced many qualifications and improvements.

Keynes's idea was to look at what would happen if prices were "sticky"— meaning that they were not adjusted in response to demand. Productive capacity was ignored and instead the economy operated with a given, unresponsive price level. Figure 1–8 shows what happens in a model with an

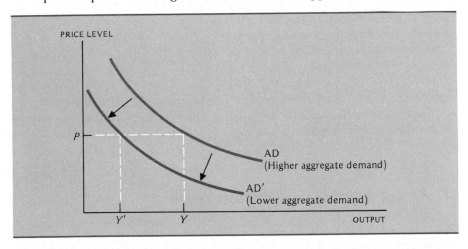

Figure 1-8. THE MODEL WITH STICKY PRICES.
In the model with sticky prices, output is not necessarily equal to potential. The economy operates on its aggregate demand schedule, at a given price level. If aggregate demand falls, the price level remains unchanged. Output falls instead.

unresponsive price level when the aggregate demand curve shifts downward.

The model with sticky prices allows us to explain fluctuations in output in terms of shifts in demand. The aggregate demand curve appears to be much less stable than is potential output. Each year, changes in government policy shift demand. Investment demand fluctuates. Consumers change their moods and spend less or more. The demand for exports shifts as conditions in other countries change. The model with sticky prices opens up a way for each of these demand shifts to influence output, whereas the model with flexible prices says that output can change only when potential output changes.

Models with Flexible Prices and Sticky Prices

THE MODEL WITH FLEXIBLE PRICES

1. The price level fluctuates immediately to keep the aggregate demand for output equal to potential output. Unemployment and other unused resources do not occur.

2. Potential GNP is determined by the capital stock and by the number of workers, neither of which is likely to shift very much from one year to the next.

3. Output is determined by the productive capacity of the economy. The demand schedule determines the price level.

THE MODEL WITH STICKY PRICES

1. Output does not necessarily equal potential GNP. The price level is fixed, and output is aggregate demand at the fixed price.

2. When demand shifts, output shifts.

3. Because aggregate demand seems to be less stable than is potential GNP, the model with sticky prices is more successful in explaining short-run fluctuations in output.

1.3 Recent Advances in Macroeconomics

Macroeconomics has undergone tremendous developments since the Keynesian revolution in the 1930s. These developments have led to important changes in actual economic policy. The changes in economic policy have in turn altered the nature of the fluctuations.

The acceptance of Keynesian ideas brought recognition of the importance of maintaining a steady growth of aggregate demand. After many years of research, the importance of controlling aggregate demand has now been well documented both theoretically and empirically, though there is still considerable controversy among macroeconomists about the best method of control.

One important school, the **monetarists,** usually identified with Milton Friedman, formerly of the University of Chicago, now of the Hoover Institution at Stanford University, holds that steady money growth will best stabilize the growth of aggregate demand.

Macroeconomists in the **Keynesian** school have argued that changes in taxes and government spending are also desirable. James Tobin of Yale University and Franco Modigliani of M.I.T. are macroeconomists usually identified with this school. They also favor the active use of monetary policy to offset other sources of instability, in place of the passive, steady growth policy of the monetarists.

In the 1960s, some Keynesians began to think that controlling aggregate demand could virtually eliminate economic fluctuations; for example, in 1969 Martin Bronfenbrenner entitled a book *Is the Business Cycle Obsolete?* and argued that it was. More recent research and the actual experience in the 1970s and 1980s have shown this to be a false hope. We now know that aggregate demand management will not eliminate economic fluctuations, or be able to bring unemployment permanently to very low levels.

In recent years, progress in macroeconomics has been substantial in two areas: price adjustment and expectations.

PRICE ADJUSTMENT

Price adjustment is the process through which firms adjust their prices in response to changing demand and supply conditions in their markets. The new theories of price adjustment attempt to fill in gaps in the simple model with sticky prices. First, the assumption of sticky prices might be reasonable for the short run but is clearly false in the long run. Second, in an inflationary environment many prices are continually increasing. Price-adjustment theories had to describe how price setting would incorporate the steadily rising trend in prices. Third, early theories of price adjustment were vague about the microeconomic reason for the slow adjustment. New theories of price adjustment have provided better explanations based on labor contracts and lack of information firms have about the nature of the changes in demand. All the newer theories about price adjustment show explicitly that potential GNP matters in the long run. In fact, in the long run, the economy returns to potential.

RATIONAL EXPECTATIONS

Expectations about the future are an important part of all macroeconomic theories. In *The General Theory of Employment, Interest and Money*, Keynes talked about expectations repeatedly. Keynes emphasized the erratic nature of expectations, that they could shift around randomly with no rational explanation. One of the most interesting recent theoretical developments is the hypothesis of **rational expectations.** The hypothesis has influenced macroeconomic thinking deeply, and many parts of this book show the influence. Consumption, investment, and price adjustment are areas where we have to deal forthrightly with the issues of how people form their expectations.

The principle of rational expectations holds that firms and consumers form expectations about the future "rationally." This simply means that they make the most of the information that is available to them. If they know from past experience that the Federal Reserve increases money growth in order to lower interest rates whenever there is an increase in unemployment, then they will expect the Federal Reserve to act the same in the future, unless information to the contrary is provided. Or, if they know that a 3-year tax cut has been passed, they will anticipate a reduction in their tax bill 3 years down the road and adjust their behavior accordingly.

The rational expectations assumption is used so much in this book—in the analysis of consumption, investment, and wage and price determination —that you may find the idea somewhat routine. But it is important to keep in mind that rational expectations has been the subject of considerable controversy. Frequently, rational expectations is taken as a shorthand phrase to stand for propositions that economic policy is ineffective and that inflation can be reduced quickly without a recession. We will explain later in the book how these propositions can be derived from strong, unrealistic assumptions and why we think the propositions are wrong. But it is not rational expectations that makes the propositions wrong.

With these new developments in macroeconomics, new schools of thought are emerging that have only loose connections with the older schools such as Keynesians and monetarists. Virtually all macroeconomists today accept the idea of rational expectations in one form or another, even though the idea was rejected initially by traditional Keynesians.

Today two broad schools of thought have been categorized by researchers. The **new classical** school includes economists such as Robert Lucas of the University of Chicago and Thomas Sargent of Stanford University. The new classicals accept the idea of rational expectations but maintain that prices adjust very quickly, like the classical economists assumed. A branch of this school, called the **real business cycle** school, including Edward Prescott of the University of Minnesota and Charles Plosser of the

University of Rochester, maintains that monetary factors or aggregate demand are relatively unimportant in explaining economic fluctuations.

The **new Keynesian** school includes economists such as Olivier Blanchard of M.I.T. and Edmund Phelps of Columbia University. The new Keynesians also accept the idea of rational expectations, but maintain that wages and prices adjust slowly and that this slow adjustment is the key to explaining economic fluctuations. There is a sense in which the new Keynesians could just as accurately be called new monetarists, for this school emphasizes the importance of money and also maintains that the economy eventually returns to some natural level of output.[1]

How Did Today's Macroeconomists Come to Study Economics?

Macroeconomists—whether traditional Keynesian, monetarist, new classical, or new Keynesian—began studying economics for many different reasons. Some got interested because the hardships of the Great Depression of the 1930s touched them personally. For others it was pure chance. But whatever the reason, they all liked it and stuck with it. Here are some answers to the question "How did you come to study economics?" from some macroeconomists whose work we will study in this book.[2]

Franco Modigliani

[Laughter] That's a good question. I'd say, by chance. I started my university years with the expectation that I would become a doctor, because my father was one. . . . At the last moment I realized that I wasn't cut out for that profession; I cannot stand the sight of blood. So I went into law, which is in Italy very general.

Then there was a national competition among university students to write an essay about the effect of price controls. I decided to participate. . . . I wrote my essay and won first prize. The judges said that I should pursue the study of economics and so I began.

James Tobin

I went into economics for two reasons. One was that as a child of the Depression I was terribly concerned about the world. It seemed then

---

[1] Of course no categorization can be complete for long because new research is always developing new ways of thinking. For example, a recent school of thought to emerge might be called the *market power school,* based on research by Oliver Hart of M.I.T., N. Gregory Mankiw of Harvard, and others. These researchers explain unemployment in recessions with models of oligopoly or monopoly in which firms or workers have some market power.

[2] The answers come from separate interviews published in Arjo Klamer, *Conversations with Economists,* Rowman and Allanheld, 1984.

that many of the problems were economic in origin. If you thought that the world should be saved, and I did, then economics looked like the decisive thing to study. The second thing was that you could have your cake and eat it too, because it was an intellectually fascinating subject.

Robert E. Lucas, Jr.

I have always liked to think about social problems. It may have something to do with my family. We always argued about politics and social issues. I studied history. . . . But I came around to the view that economic forces are central forces in history, and started trying some economics. It was a big shock to me to find books in English that were incomprehensible to me. . . . [Like] Keynes's *General Theory*. I still can't read Keynes. [Laughter] I realized I couldn't pick it up as an amateur. So I got into economics in a professional way and got my Ph.D. at Chicago.

Thomas J. Sargent

[Long pause and hesitation] I liked it when we studied it in college. But also I was truly curious, ever since I was a kid, about what causes depressions. The Great Depression had a big effect on me: a lot of people in my family got wiped out. My grandfather ran a quarry in the construction business, and he got wiped out. My other grandfather was in the radio business, and he got wiped out. It was the common story.

1.4 The Macroeconomic Model Used in This Book

Although many alternative theories are discussed, a main model appears throughout this book. This model combines the new theories of price adjustment, the new theories of rational expectations, and the earlier Keynesian ideas about aggregate demand and output determination. It is introduced first in a rudimentary, or "no-frills," form in Chapters 4 through 7, and then in a more complete form later in the book.

The basic ideas in the rudimentary model can be explained as follows: In the short run prices and wages do not adjust. Workers' wages are set at a particular level for about a year, and firms usually set their price and wait to see what the market will buy at that price. But eventually prices begin to adjust and reach their market-clearing level; aggregate demand will eventually equal potential GNP.

How does the economy move from a situation where output is greater or less than potential GNP to the situation where aggregate output equals potential GNP? The process of price adjustment does the job. The simplest expression of the idea of price adjustment is: *When output is less than potential GNP, there is pressure on prices to adjust downward. When output exceeds potential GNP, there is pressure on prices to adjust upward.*

The slow adjustment of wages and prices has important implications for macroeconomics. If a disturbance moves the economy away from its potential growth path, then the slow adjustment of prices will prevent the economy from returning to potential quickly. Prolonged departures of the economy from potential, such as we observed in Figure 1–1, will then occur. Moreover, if prices adjust slowly, then changes in prices or inflation will occur with a lag. As we will show in considerable detail, price rigidities are capable of explaining both the economic fluctuations and the price movements associated with these economic fluctuations.

The rest of the book is a systematic development of the interrelationships among these three factors: aggregate demand, aggregate supply, and price adjustment. In the short run, aggregate demand determines output because the price level is fixed. In the long run, the supply of productive factors determines output and aggregate demand determines the price level. The price-adjustment equation tells how the economy makes the transition from the short to long run.

Review and Practice

MAJOR POINTS

1. Output and employment expand and contract at irregular intervals.

2. Other measures of the state of the economy, like interest rates and inflation, also track fluctuations.

3. With flexible prices, output is set by supply conditions alone; output is always at its potential level. The model with flexible prices has problems explaining large movements of output.

4. The model with sticky prices says that output need not be equal to potential output. Output is determined by aggregate demand given a fixed price level. The price level does not change to equate demand with supply.

5. In the model with sticky prices, fluctuations in output are caused by shifts in aggregate demand.

6. The price-adjustment process describes the transition from the short run to the long run. Prices fall when output is below potential GNP and rise when it is above. The price movements move the economy in the direction of potential GNP.

KEY TERMS AND CONCEPTS

Fluctuations	Rate of inflation	Aggregate demand
Recession	Rate of interest	Sticky prices
Recovery	Unemployment rate	Flexible prices
Trough	Potential GNP	John Maynard Keynes
Peak	Procyclical	Keynesians
Gross national product	Model	Monetarists
Real GNP	Aggregate supply	Price adjustment
		Rational expectations

QUESTIONS FOR DISCUSSION AND REVIEW

1. Which of the following are procyclical?
   a. Interest rates
   b. Employment
   c. Inflation
   d. Money supply

2. Explain the difference between potential GNP and real GNP.

3. Describe a typical macroeconomic fluctuation, starting from a peak.

4. What are the determinants of potential GNP?

5. How have economic fluctuations changed during the last 75 years?

6. How does GNP respond to aggregate demand when prices are perfectly flexible?

7. How does GNP respond to aggregate demand when prices do not adjust?

PROBLEMS

Numerical

1. Real GNP in the United Kingdom from 1953 through 1982 is given below. All data are in billions of 1980 pounds.

1953	117.0	1968	181.6
1954	121.4	1969	184.4
1955	125.9	1970	188.3
1956	128.0	1971	193.3
1957	130.5	1972	197.1
1958	130.5	1973	212.0
1959	135.6	1974	209.8
1960	141.9	1975	208.4
1961	146.7	1976	216.0
1962	148.0	1977	218.7
1963	154.0	1978	226.8
1964	162.2	1979	230.5
1965	166.2	1980	226.2
1966	169.7	1981	221.6
1967	174.1	1982	225.0

a. Plot U.K. real GNP over the 30-year period. Put real GNP on the vertical axis of the graph and the year on the horizontal axis.

b. Estimate potential GNP by drawing a smooth trend line through the points on the graph. Identify any shifts in the trend of potential. By what percent did real GNP grow during this period?

c. Identify the fluctuations of real GNP around potential GNP. How many complete (peak-to-peak) economic fluctuations occurred during this period? How does the frequency of economic fluctuations during this period compare with that of the United States during the same period?

2. Suppose that the aggregate demand curve in a particular year is given by the algebraic expression $Y = 3000 + 1000/P$, where Y is output and P is the price level. Potential output is $Y^* = 4000$.

a. Draw the downward-sloping aggregate demand curve and the vertical aggregate supply curve to scale on a diagram with the price level P on the vertical axis and output Y on the horizontal axis.

b. Suppose that prices are flexible. Find the price level and show it on the diagram.

c. Now suppose that the following year the aggregate demand curve is given by $Y = 3000 + 1100/P$. In what direction has the curve shifted? If output remains at potential, what is the new price level? What was the rate of inflation between the two years?

d. If prices are instead assumed to be sticky, what will the new level of output be? Will there be pressure on the price level to move upward or downward? Explain.

3. We have the following data on interest rates and the price level (in the United States) for the years 1977–86:

Year	Price Level	Interest Rates
1977	67.3	—
1978	72.2	—
1979	78.6	—
1980	85.7	11.4%
1981	94.0	13.8
1982	100.0	11.1
1983	103.9	8.8
1984	107.9	9.8
1985	111.5	7.6
1986	114.5	6.0

a. Calculate the rate of inflation for the years 1978–86.

b. Calculate the expected rate of inflation for the years 1980–86 assuming (i) people expect the rate of inflation to be the average rate of inflation in the two previous years, and (ii) people have perfect foresight and expected inflation just equals actual inflation.

c. For each of the assumptions in Part b, calculate the real interest rate for the years 1980–86.

d. In light of this example, explain why economists have such a difficult time measuring the real interest rate.

Analytical

1. What explains the fluctuations in output in models where prices are flexible? In models where prices are sticky?

2. Comment on the following two explanations of the large drop in output in the early 1980s in the United States:

   a. "There was a decline in aggregate supply. Potential output declined because the number of people available for work declined."

   b. "There was a decline in aggregate demand. With very high interest rates, consumers and firms purchased fewer goods so that production and employment declined."

   Which statement seems more plausible? Which statement is consistent with the macro model with flexible prices and which with the model with sticky prices?

3. Explain how the debate between the current schools of macroeconomic thought resembles the macroeconomic debates of the 1930s. In what way is this debate different from those between the Keynesians and the monetarists?

4. Would Keynes have argued that prices in the 1930s were too low or too high? Explain.

5. Explain briefly the idea behind rational expectations. Why is the theory of expectations important when discussing the real interest rate?

2

Measuring Economic Performance: Output and Income

In chapter 1 we examined the behavior of several key macroeconomic variables—production, employment, inflation. In this chapter and the next we show how these and other important variables are defined and measured.

2.1 Gross National Product

We begin with gross national product (GNP). GNP refers to production during a particular time period, which we will usually take to be a year, or a quarter of a year. GNP is the *flow* of new products during the year or the quarter.

There are three different ways to think about and measure GNP. First, we can measure **spending** on goods and services by different groups—households, businesses, government, and foreigners. Second, we can measure **production** in different industries—agriculture, mining, manufacturing, and so on. Last, we can measure the total wage and profit **income** earned by different groups producing GNP. Each of these measures has its own special purpose, but they all add up to the same thing. We consider each in turn in the next three sections.

How do we know that the total amount of spending is equal to the total value of production, which in turn is equal to the total amount of income? Think about an individual firm. Suppose the value of its production is $1 million. It is unlikely that its sales are exactly $1 million in that year—suppose its sales are $900,000. For accounting purposes, we treat the remaining $100,000 as spending. It is the firm's investment in inventories of its own goods and is included as part of total investment. Both at the level of the firm and at the level of the whole economy, the equality of production and spending is the result of considering inventory investment as part of spending.

The equality of the value of production and income also derives from accounting principles. Our firm takes in $900,000 in one year. In addition, we add in the $100,000 value of its inventory accumulation as sales, for a total of $1 million. The firm pays out $450,000 in wages. That amount is counted in the incomes of the workers. The firm pays $50,000 in interest, which is counted in the incomes of whoever holds the firm's bonds. It pays $400,000 for its raw materials, which is counted in the incomes of the sellers of materials or of their employees, bondholders, etc. The residual, $1,000,000 − $450,000 − $50,000 − $400,000 = $100,000, is the profit earned by the owner of the firm, which counts as part of the owner's income. All of the receipts of the firm from its sales are paid out to somebody as income. The value of production and the total amount of income generated are the same.

As a result of the two accounting rules—including inventories in spending and computing profit as the residual between sales and expenses—it is always true that production, spending, and income are exactly the same. This kind of relation is called an **identity**—it is the inevitable outcome of the accounting system, not a statement about how the economy works.

The alternative measures of GNP are gathered together in the national income and product accounts (NIPA). Economists and statisticians at the Bureau of Economic Analysis (BEA), an agency of the United States government in Washington, D.C., are responsible for collecting the GNP data and publishing the NIPA. Many of the ideas behind GNP were developed by the late Simon Kuznets of Harvard University. He won the Nobel Prize in economics in 1971 for this work.

2.2 Measuring GNP through Spending

Total spending on goods and services produced by Americans during any period can be broken down as follows:

Gross national product = Consumption
+ Investment
+ Government purchases
+ Net exports (or exports minus imports).

Using symbols this key identity can be written on one line:

$$Y = C + I + G + X$$
where Y = Gross national product
C = Consumption
I = Investment
G = Government spending
X = Net exports (exports minus imports).

CONSUMPTION

Consumption is defined as spending by *households.* It includes purchases of (1) **durable goods,** such as washing machines, stereos, and cars, (2) **nondurable goods,** such as food, clothing, and gasoline, and (3) **services,** such as haircuts, medical care, and education. Spending on new houses is the only type of household spending that is not included in consumption. Instead it is included in fixed investment.

INVESTMENT

Investment consists of **fixed investment** and **inventory investment.** Fixed investment is the purchase of new factories, machines, and houses. Inventory investment is the change in inventories at business firms. We first discuss fixed investment.

Fixed Investment. Fixed investment is broken down into **nonresidential** fixed investment and **residential** fixed investment. Nonresidential fixed investment is spending on structures and equipment for use in business. Steel mills, office buildings, and power plants are examples of structures. Trucks, lathes, and typewriters are examples of equipment. Residential fixed investment is spending on construction of new houses and apartment buildings. The term "fixed" connotes that these types of investment goods will be around for a long time, and distinguishes fixed from inventory investment, which is much more temporary, as we will see below. The term "fixed" is conventionally dropped when the meaning is implicit from the context, and we will follow this convention.

Investment is a *flow* of new capital during the year that is added to the *stock* of capital. The capital stock is the total amount of productive capital in the economy—it includes all the buildings, equipment, and houses. The capital stock increases from one year to the next as a result of investment. However, because the capital stock is constantly wearing out, part of the investment reported in each year's GNP is actually devoted to replacing worn-out capital, not increasing the capital stock. What is reported in GNP is *gross* investment. This accounts for the term "gross" in GNP. Statisticians have a number of ways of estimating the loss of the existing capital stock from one year to the next. This loss is called **depreciation**. **Net investment** is defined as follows:

Net investment = Gross investment − Depreciation.

We have the following relation:

Capital stock at the end of this year = Capital stock at the end of last year
  − Depreciation during this year
  + Gross investment during this year.

By rearranging this equation and putting in the definition of net investment, we have:

Net investment = Capital stock at the end of this year
  − Capital stock at the end of last year.

These equations hold whether we are looking at total investment or separately at nonresidential and residential investment. An alternative to GNP is **net national product,** or NNP; it includes only net investment. GNP, on the other hand, includes this year's gross investment.

Inventory Investment. Now consider inventory investment, which is simply the change in the stock of inventories held at businesses.

Inventory investment this year = Stock of inventories at the end of *this* year
  − Stock of inventories at the end of *last* year.

For example, when a publisher produces and stores 10,000 copies of a newly printed book in its warehouse, the books are counted in GNP as inventory investment. Even though no one has yet purchased the books, they must be counted in GNP because they have been produced. If subsequently you purchase a book directly from the publisher, consumption is up by one book and inventory investment is down by one book; GNP does not change, nor should it since there is no new production. When the publisher sells a book to a bookstore, the publisher's inventory investment is down by one book and the bookstore's inventory investment is up by one book. Total inventory investment does not change, and neither does GNP.

Inventory investment is positive when inventories are increasing, and negative when inventories are decreasing. In 1981 inventory investment was 24.0 billion dollars. In 1982, a recession year, it was −24.5 billion dollars. If inventory investment were not added to spending when computing GNP, we would underestimate production when inventory investment was positive, as in 1981, because spending would be less than production; similarly we would overestimate production when inventory investment was negative, as in 1982, because spending would be more than production.

As the data for 1981–82 show, inventory investment adds to the fluctuations of GNP. **Final sales** is a measure that excludes inventory investment. Final sales is defined as GNP minus inventory investment. Final sales fluctuates less than GNP.

GOVERNMENT PURCHASES

Government purchases are the sum of federal government and state and local government purchases of goods and services. In 1986, state and local government purchases were 58 percent of total government purchases. Schools, road construction, and military hardware are examples of government purchases. Government purchases are only part of the total government *outlays* that are included in budgets. Government purchases exclude such items as welfare payments and interest payments on the public debt that are included in government outlays.

The distinction between consumption, investment, and government is based primarily on the type of purchaser rather than on the type of product that is purchased. If a Chevrolet is purchased by a household it goes into consumption—as a consumer durable. If it is purchased for use by a business, it goes into investment—as business fixed investment in equipment. If it is purchased by government, it goes into government purchases. The only exception to this rule is residential investment, which includes all housing purchases whether by households, businesses, or government.

IMPORTS AND EXPORTS

The United States has an open economy. An open economy is one with substantial interaction with other countries. The United States has experienced a growing volume of transactions with the rest of the world, and GNP has to take these into account. **Exports** are deliveries of goods and services from the United States to foreigners. Included in exports of services are the wages earned by American workers abroad and the profits and interest earned by American-owned assets abroad; these earnings are called **factor incomes. Imports** are deliveries of goods and services from foreigners to the United States. Included in services are the factor incomes of foreign workers and foreign assets in the United States.

Part, but not all, of United States exports represent goods and services *produced* by Americans. The other part has been imported to the United States and then sold abroad, perhaps as part of manufactured products. For example, General Motors might put a radio imported from Japan into a Chevrolet that is exported to Mexico. We want to subtract the radio from the exported car, if we are measuring goods produced by Americans. More generally, if goods are imported from abroad and purchased by United States consumers, businesses, or governments, the goods should not be counted in a measure of U.S. production. For these reasons imports are subtracted from spending and exports are added to spending when computing GNP. In other words, only **net exports,** that is, *exports less imports,* are added to the total volume of spending when computing GNP. Note that this decomposition of GNP does not tell you what part of consumption was imported and what part was produced in the United States. Nor does it break down investment, government purchases, or exports between domestic and imported components. The total of net exports is sometimes referred to as the **trade balance.** When net exports are positive there is a **trade surplus.** When net exports are negative there is a **trade deficit.**

THE RECENT RECORD

Table 2–1 shows how U.S. GNP broke down in 1986. Consumption is the biggest component—about two-thirds—of GNP. Services is the biggest component of consumption—about 50 percent. Services (restaurants, utilities, housing, transportation, medical care, and the like) have been growing as a share of consumption. In the early 1950s services accounted for less than a third of consumption. Medical services have grown most rapidly.

Fixed investment is about 16 percent of GNP. Nonresidential fixed investment is much larger than residential fixed investment. Government purchases are larger than investment, at about 20 percent of GNP. Exports and imports are each about 10 percent of GNP in normal years (imports were almost 12 percent in 1986). Foreign trade is now a much bigger factor in the United States than it was 20 or 30 years ago. In the early 1950s exports and imports each were about 5 percent of GNP.

These 1986 shares are fairly typical for consumption, investment, government purchases, exports, and imports in any recent year. Inventory investment and net exports fluctuate dramatically, and can be negative as well as positive; no year is typical. Since exports were much smaller than imports in 1986, net exports were large and negative. Final sales were slightly less than GNP in 1986 since inventory investment was positive.

Table 2-1.   GROSS NATIONAL PRODUCT IN 1986—THE SPENDING SIDE
(billions of dollars)

Gross national product	4,208.5
Consumption	2,762.4
Durables	388.3
Nondurables	932.7
Services	1,441.3
Investment	686.4
Fixed investment	675.1
Nonresidential	458.5
Residential	216.6
Inventory investment	11.4
Government purchases	865.3
Net exports	−105.7
Exports	373.0
Imports	478.7
Final sales	4,197.1

Note: Final sales is GNP less inventory investment. Details in the table may not add to totals because of rounding.
Source: *Economic Report of the President*, 1987, Table B-1.

Bringing Astronomical Numbers Down to Earth

Table 2–1 shows that GNP was $4,208.5 billion, or about $4.2 trillion, in 1986. With all the zeros this looks like $4,208,500,000,000. An astrophysicist would write it 4.2085×10^{12} dollars. How can we make intuitive sense of such large numbers?

The best way to bring numbers like these down to size is simply to divide by the population—that is, to calculate GNP per person, or GNP per capita. The population in the United States in 1986 was 241 million. GNP per capita in the United States is thus $17,463 (4,208,500,000,000/241,000,000 = 17,462.67).

U.S. consumption in 1986 was $2,762.4 billion. This amounts to about $11,462 per capita for food, clothing, transportation, and other consumer items. On average, every man, woman, and child in the United States consumed $11,762 of goods and services in 1986.

Government purchases of goods and services were $865.3 billion in 1986. This amounted to $3,590 per capita for national defense, schools, highways, police, and so on. The sum of private consumption plus public consumption per capita in the United States in 1986 was $15,052.

Net exports were −$105.7 billion in 1986, or about −$439 per capita. In other words, on average every person in the United States bought $439 more goods that were made abroad than they made goods that were sold abroad. Stated differently, on average every person in the United States borrowed $439 from foreigners in 1986.

WHICH SPENDING ITEMS SHOULD BE INCLUDED?

In deciding which spending items to include in computing GNP, we must be careful to avoid double counting. For example, the purchase of a 10-year-old house should not be counted; that house was counted 10 years ago when it was constructed. Similarly, the purchase of the assets of Gulf Oil by Chevron in 1984 should not be counted; the Gulf building in Pittsburgh and Gulf's offshore oil rigs were included in business fixed investment when they were built.

To avoid double counting, we also do not include the purchase of **intermediate goods.** These are goods that are converted into other goods in the production process (for example, steel is an intermediate good used in the production of cars). We only include purchases of the **final goods,** such as the cars themselves. The value of the steel is included in GNP as part of a car when someone buys the car. The purchases of steel by automobile manufacturers are not counted.

In computing GNP, we value different types of goods, such as apples and oranges, using the price of each good that is paid by the purchaser. The price includes sales and excise taxes. If apples cost twice as much as oranges, then each apple will contribute twice as much to GNP as will each orange.

REAL GNP

GNP is a dollar measure of production. In comparing one year to another, we run into the problem that the dollar is not a stable measure of purchasing power. In the 1970s especially, GNP rose a great deal not because the economy was actually growing rapidly but because the dollar was inflating. For comparisons across years, we need a measure of output that adjusts for inflation. We want *GNP in constant dollars,* or, as we will generally call it, **real GNP.** In contrast, the GNP that we have looked at so far is sometimes called **nominal GNP.** From 1972 to 1986 nominal GNP grew by about 255 percent from $1,212.8 billion to $4,208.5 billion. During the same period real GNP grew by about 41 percent. The conversion from nominal to real makes a big difference.

The concept of real GNP is straightforward. We want to measure consumption, investment, government purchases, and exports in physical rather than dollar units. Further, we want to subtract imports in the same physical units, so that real GNP is a measure of production by Americans.

To compute consumption in real terms, the national income statisticians gather data on the prices of consumption goods in great detail. They take the data on the corresponding detailed flows of goods to consumers and restate them in 1982 dollars. For example, suppose the retail price of a typical shirt rose from $10.00 in 1982 to $15.00 in 1988. The flow of shirts to consumers was $3 billion in 1982 and $5 billion in 1988. Consumption of shirts in real terms was $3 billion in 1982 dollars in 1982 and $3.3 billion in 1982 dollars in 1988. The $3.3 billion is computed as

[5 billion 1988 dollars] $\times$ [(10/15) 1982 dollars per 1988 dollar]
= 3.3 billion 1982 dollars.

The same type of adjustment for price change is applied to each detailed category of consumption, investment, government purchases, exports, and imports. Then real GNP is real consumption plus real investment plus real government purchases plus real exports less real imports.

Quarterly GNP Statistics and Recessions

The spending data reported in Tables 2–1 and 2–2 are *annual*. They give the flow of spending for a year. *Quarterly* GNP data are also available in the United States. These give the spending flows for a quarter of a year. Quarterly data are useful for understanding shorter-run movements of business cycles. Private forecasting firms and government agencies all use quarterly models of the economy. Quarterly data on real GNP are reported in the newspapers as soon as they are available, usually a few weeks after the quarter is over. The traditional rule of thumb for a downturn to qualify as a recession is two consecutive quarters of declining GNP. Some important conventions of the reporting of quarterly data are illustrated in the following comparison.

Year: Quarter	Real GNP	Year	Real GNP
1984:1	3,444.7	1984	3,489.9
1984:2	3,487.1		
1984:3	3,507.4		
1984:4	3,520.4		
1985:1	3,547.0	1985	3,585.2
1985:2	3,567.6		
1985:3	3,603.8		
1985:4	3,622.3		
1986:1	3,655.9	1986	3,676.5
1986:2	3,661.4		
1986:3	3,686.4		
1986:4	3,702.4		

The flow of GNP in each quarter is stated at an annual rate, which means that the actual flow each quarter is multiplied by 4. If you add up the four quarterly flows for each year, and divide by 4, you get the annual figure reported at the right.

Table 2–2 shows the breakdown of real GNP for the four-year period that spans the deep 1981–82 recession in the United States. This recession was preceded by record high interest rates in the summer of 1981. As we will see later, the high interest rates were the result of policy actions at the Federal Reserve Board. There are many figures in Table 2–2, but with some study they give a good account of what happened to the U.S. economy. With a close look, at least five interesting facts can be gleaned.

1. Real GNP fell from 1981 to 1982, and then rose again in 1983 and 1984 beyond the 1981 value. This decline and subsequent rise is the essential feature of an economic cycle. Each cycle begins with a contraction of real GNP, reaches a trough, begins an expansion, and then reaches a peak. The next cycle starts with the next contraction.

2. Real GNP fell by more than final sales in 1982, since inventory investment declined. In fact, inventory investment became negative—firms drew down their inventories because they anticipated lower sales during the recession. The decline in inventories made the recession worse than it otherwise would have been.

Table 2–2.   REAL GROSS NATIONAL PRODUCT, 1981–84 (billions of 1982 dollars)

	1981	1982	1983	1984
Gross national product	3,248.8	3,166.0	3,279.1	3,489.9
Consumption	2,024.2	2,050.7	2,146.0	2,246.3
Durables	250.8	252.7	283.1	318.9
Nondurables	764.4	771.0	800.2	828.6
Services	1,009.0	1,027.0	1,062.7	1,098.7
Investment	545.5	447.3	504.0	652.0
Fixed investment	521.7	471.8	510.4	592.8
Nonresidential	395.2	366.7	361.2	422.2
Residential	126.5	105.1	149.3	170.6
Inventory investment	23.9	−24.5	−6.4	59.2
Government purchases	629.7	641.7	649.0	675.2
Net exports	49.4	26.3	−19.9	−83.6
Exports	392.7	361.9	348.1	369.7
Imports	343.4	335.6	368.1	453.2
Final sales	3,225.0	3,190.5	3,285.5	3,430.7

Source: *Economic Report of the President,* 1987, Table B–2.

3. Consumption increased only slightly in 1982, as high interest rates made borrowing for automobiles, furniture, and appliances costly. Also, people postponed purchases of big-ticket items until better times.

4. Both residential investment and nonresidential investment fell sharply in 1982. The high interest rates made it difficult to borrow to finance both housing and factory construction. Both types of investment rose beyond the 1981 figure by 1984.

5. Net exports fell in 1982, but did not recover in either 1983 or 1984, as the U.S. trade deficit got worse. In fact, net exports continued to decline through 1986. The high value of the dollar through 1984 had much to do with this drop in net exports.

Computing Growth Rates

The growth rate of a variable between two periods, in percent, is defined as *the change in the variable divided by the value of the variable in the first period multiplied by 100.* Thus, the growth rate of real GNP from 1985 to 1986 is

$$100 \times (\text{real GNP in 1986} - \text{real GNP in 1985})/(\text{real GNP in 1985})$$
$$= 100 \times (3676.5 - 3585.2)/(3585.2) = 100 \times (91.3)/(3585.2)$$
$$= 2.5 \text{ percent.}$$

Growth rates are usually converted to "annual rates" because everyone is used to annual rates. For a change from one year to the next the growth rate is already at an annual rate. For the growth rate from one quarter to the next the annual rate is approximated by multiplying the quarterly growth rate by 4.

2.3 Measuring GNP through Production: Value Added

GNP can also be computed by adding up production of goods and services in different industries. As we observed on the spending side, we must avoid counting the same items more than once. Many industries specialize in the production of intermediate goods that are used in the production of other goods. If we want each industry's production to include the contribution of those industries to total GNP, then we want to take the production of intermediate goods into account.

The concept of **value added** was developed to prevent double counting and to attribute to each industry a part of the GNP. The value added by a firm is the difference between the revenue the firm earns by selling its products and the amount it pays for the products of other firms it uses as intermediate goods. It is a measure of the value that is added to each product by firms at each stage of production.

For General Motors, for example, value added is the revenue from selling cars less the amount it pays for steel, glass, and the other inputs it buys.

For a car dealer, value added is the revenue from selling cars less the wholesale cost of the cars. The value added to a car by a car dealer takes the form of a convenient showroom, ample selection, advice (for what it's worth), and final preparation and testing. The car dealer produces these services by hiring salespeople and car mechanics, renting showroom and garage space, borrowing money to hold a big inventory of cars, and keeping the profits. Wages, rents, interest, and profits are thus what make up value added at each firm.

GNP is the sum of the value added by all the firms in the United States. If a firm sells a final product, the sale appears in that firm's value added but does not appear anywhere else. On the other hand, if a firm sells its output as an input for another firm, that sale appears negatively in the other firm's value added. Products sold by one firm to another are called **intermediate products.** When the two firms are added together in the process of computing GNP, sales of intermediate products wash out. When a firm imports a product, the transaction appears negatively in that firm's value added, but does not appear positively in the value added of any U.S. firm.

A breakdown of real GNP in terms of the value added by various industries is given in Table 2–3 for 1985. These figures tell some interesting stories about the modern U.S. economy. We tend to think of the economy as producing goods—cars, machines, paper clips, and so on—but the sector that produces the most goods, manufacturing, contributes only one-fourth of

Table 2–3.   VALUE ADDED BY INDUSTRY IN 1985 (billions of dollars)

Gross national product	3,998.1
Gross domestic product	3,956.9
Agriculture	91.5
Mining	122.8
Construction	182.2
Manufacturing	795.8
Transportation and utilities	374.4
Wholesale and retail trade	652.5
Finance, insurance, and real estate	626.6
Services	639.4
Government	477.4
Statistical discrepancy	−5.5
Rest of the world	41.2

Source: *Economic Report of the President,* 1987, Table B-10.

GNP. The trade sector, whose only function is to take produced goods and make them available to the public, is almost as large as the manufacturing sector. The finance, insurance, and real estate sector is another large one.

Near the bottom of the list is a small item called **statistical discrepancy**. Although the value-added computation of GNP should give the same answer as total spending, in practice there are measurement errors that cause a slight discrepancy between the two.

One of the items in the list of value added by industry is something called *rest of the world*. How does the rest of the world figure in the computation of U.S. GNP, which is a national concept? The answer is that Americans contribute productive services to other economies. They work overseas, and they own capital used in other countries. The earnings of this type are counted as exports and the corresponding value added is assigned to the sector called the rest of the world. The result of including this item in GNP is to make GNP a measure of the output produced by American-owned factors of production, including factors that are actually used overseas. There is another concept, called **gross domestic product (GDP),** which omits net earnings from the rest of the world. GDP measures the output produced by factors in the United States.

2.4 Measuring GNP through Income

The Americans who produce GNP receive income for their work. This income provides a third way to compute GNP. To see the relation between GNP and income, think again about the value added of a car dealer. Value added is the difference between the revenue from selling cars and the wholesale cost of cars. That difference must be somebody's income. Part of the difference is the wages the car dealer pays to salespeople and mechanics. Another part is the rent that the car dealer pays to a landlord for the use of the showroom and garage. Another part is the interest that the car dealer pays to a bank for loans to finance inventory. The rest of the difference is profit, which goes into the income of the owner of the car dealership. Thus, all of the value added shows up in income, in the form of either wages, rent, interest, or profit. Since we know that the sum of all firms' value added is GNP, the sum of all incomes must also equal GNP.

Because of taxes and certain other complications, there are several concepts of income. The most comprehensive is **national income**. It is a broad measure of the incomes of Americans, including taxes and several other items that are deducted before people receive actual payments. The two important reasons national income is less than GNP are, first, that depreciation is subtracted to get national income, and, second, that national income is measured in terms of the prices firms receive for the products they sell, whereas GNP is measured in terms of the prices paid by purchasers. Prices received differ from prices paid by the amount of sales and excise taxes.

There are two other minor conceptual differences. Business transfer payments—such as business gifts—are deducted from national income. Subsidies paid by the government to the businesses it runs are added to national income.

Finally, there is the statistical discrepancy. Conceptually, the income calculation should be numerically the same as the spending calculation of GNP. But because of measurement errors, there is a small discrepancy. (This discrepancy is identical to the discrepancy in the calculation of value added, which attributes incomes to the various industries.)

The relation between GNP and national income is shown in Table 2–4.

Table 2–4.   THE RELATION BETWEEN GNP AND NATIONAL INCOME IN 1986 (billions of dollars)

Gross national product	4,208.5
less: Depreciation	455.1
equals: Net national product	3,753.4
less: Sales and excise taxes	348.7
less: Business transfers	23.2
less: Statistical discrepancy	5.4
plus: Net subsidies to government business	11.3
equals: National income	3,387.4

Source: *Economic Report of the President, 1987*, Table B–21.

A large amount of national income is diverted by the government and by businesses before it reaches wage earners or shareholders. But government and businesses also augment the income of some people by paying social security and other benefits. The NIPA contain two concepts of income that take account of these diversions and augmentations. **Personal income** is total income received by the public before income taxes, and **disposable personal income** is total income after income taxes.

For wage income, the social security tax is one of the important differences between wages paid by businesses and wages received by workers. The aggregate amount of social security tax, called **contributions for social insurance,** is subtracted from national income to get personal income.

All of the profits of corporations are included in national income, but only the cash payments of dividends by corporations are included in personal income. The difference between profits and dividends consists of **retained earnings** and the income taxes paid by corporations. These two items are excluded from personal income.

The public has two other important sources of income other than from

Table 2–5. NATIONAL INCOME, PERSONAL INCOME, AND PERSONAL DISPOSABLE INCOME IN 1986 (billions of dollars)

National income		3,387.4
less:	Contributions for social insurance	376.1
less:	Corporate retained earnings	218.5
plus:	Nonbusiness interest	180.5
plus:	Transfer payments from government and business	513.7
equals:	Personal income	3,487.0
less:	Income taxes	513.4
equals:	Disposable personal income	2,973.7

Note: Wage accruals less disbursements, a trivial accounting item, is omitted from the list of adjustments to national income.
Source: *Economic Report of the President*, 1987, Tables B–22 and B–25.

American production of goods and services. First, the government pays social security and other benefits. Second, the public receives interest from the government debt and from other nonbusiness sources. Both of these are included in personal income. Note that social security contributions by employers are taken out of personal income, but the benefits financed by the contributions are added back in to personal income.

The relationship between the three concepts of income is shown in Table 2–5. Disposable personal income was $2,973.7 billion, or $12,339 per capita. As mentioned above, consumption per capita was $11,762, so all but $577 of income per capita was consumed.

How much of national income is earned by workers and how much is profit? Table 2–6 shows the breakdown for 1986. About 74 percent of national income was earned by labor; this includes payments to workers in wages and salaries as well as fringe benefits. The profit share includes not only corporate profits, but also rental income, proprietors' income, and net interest income. Since labor plus profits exhaust income, the profit share was 26 percent in 1986. These relative shares are fairly stable from year to year. In 1970 the labor share of national income was also 74 percent.

Table 2–6. LABOR AND PROFIT SHARES OF NATIONAL INCOME IN 1986 (billions of dollars)

Compensation of employees	2,498.3	} Labor share 74 percent
Proprietors' income	278.9	⎫
Rental income of persons	15.6	⎪
Corporate profits	299.7	⎬ Profit share 26 percent
Net interest	294.9	⎪
National income	3,387.4	⎭

Source: *Economic Report of the President*, 1987, Table B–23.

The National Income and Product Accounts

1. Gross national product (GNP) is the production of goods and services by Americans. The spending, value added, and factor income measures of GNP are all equal. In particular the national income identity says that spending on GNP is equal to the income earned from producing GNP.

2. Consumption, investment, government purchases, and net exports are the four basic components of spending. Consumption is the largest component and investment is the most volatile component.

3. The investment component of GNP includes the replacement of depreciating capital. It is thus gross investment. Net investment is gross investment less depreciation. Net national product is GNP less depreciation.

4. Real GNP is a measure of production that is adjusted for the effects of inflation. It measures the physical volume of production. Nominal GNP measures the dollar volume of production.

5. Final sales is GNP less inventory investment. It fluctuates less than GNP.

6. To avoid double counting we measure the contribution of each industry by its value added and do not include any goods that were produced in an earlier year.

7. Disposable personal income is the amount of national income that is available for households to spend. It excludes retained earnings at corporations. It includes what is left of wage and salary income, fringe benefits, rents, dividends, interest, and small business income after all taxes are paid to governments.

2.5 Saving and Investment

Saving is defined as income minus consumption. An important, but sometimes confusing, fact is that *saving must equal investment*. To see this, consider first a closed economy with no government and therefore no taxes. Then,

$$\text{Spending on GNP} = \text{Consumption} + \text{Investment}.$$

Also, from the definition of saving,

$$\text{National income} = \text{Saving} + \text{Consumption}.$$

Since spending on GNP equals national income, we know that

$$\text{Consumption} + \text{Investment} = \text{Saving} + \text{Consumption}$$

or

$$\text{Investment} = \text{Saving}.$$

The equality of saving and investment follows from nothing but the definitions of GNP and income. As long as the statisticians adhere to these definitions, there is no possibility that investment can ever differ from saving. We don't have to say, "If our theories hold, saving and investment will be equal." No matter how investors and consumers behave, saving and investment will be equal.

The simple identity that saving equals investment becomes more complicated for an open economy interacting with other economies in the world. By borrowing, a country can invest more than it saves. By lending, a country can save more than it invests. The ability to borrow or lend permits investment to be undertaken at the most efficient place and time. Borrowing means accumulating financial liabilities. Lending means accumulating financial assets. These financial assets and liabilities have implications for macroeconomic behavior. An important example is the borrowing of the United States government to finance its budget deficit. As the stock of government bonds (liabilities of the government) grows, the interest payments on the debt may require increasing future taxes or printing more money, either of which has macroeconomic implications. Another important example is the growing indebtedness of the United States to the rest of the world as it must borrow to finance an excess of imports over exports.

SAVING AND INVESTMENT IN AN OPEN ECONOMY

We now look at saving and investment flows at the sector level. The economy is divided into three sectors: private (households and private businesses), government, and the rest of the world. Some more symbols will save space. Let

F = Government transfers to the private sector
N = Interest on the government debt
T = Taxes

S_p = Private saving (saving of the private sector)
S_g = Government saving
S_r = Rest of world saving

and recall that we previously defined

Y = GNP
C = Consumption
I = Investment
G = Government spending, and
X = Net exports.

Private Saving. From the definition of saving we know that private saving is disposable income $(Y + F + N - T)$ minus consumption (C):

$$S_p = (Y + F + N - T) - C. \qquad (2-1)$$

Government Saving. The NIPA use the convention of treating all government expenditures as government consumption. That is, investment is always assumed to equal zero for the government sector. Hence, government saving equals income (tax receipts, net of transfer payments, and interest payments) minus purchases of goods and services:

$$S_g = (T - F - N) - G. \qquad (2-2)$$

Government saving is also called the government **budget surplus** or **budget deficit**. The budget is in surplus when G is less than $(T - F - N)$ and in deficit when G is greater than $(T - F - N)$.

Rest of World Saving. The rest of the world saving vis-à-vis the United States is income received from the United States (from our imports) less spending on U.S. goods and services (our exports). Rest of the world saving is therefore equal to U.S. imports minus U.S. exports—net exports with the sign reversed $(-X)$:

$$S_r = -X. \qquad (2-3)$$

The rest of the world saving is used either to buy financial assets in the United States or to reduce foreign financial liabilities. Either is called a **capital inflow.**[1] Put another way, the United States finances any excess of im-

---

[1] Gifts and other transfers that Americans make abroad net of gifts they receive from abroad, as well as interest payments the U.S. government pays to foreigners, must also be financed by capital inflows from abroad. When these items are subtracted from net exports we get the current account surplus. More accurately, capital inflow from abroad is equal to the current account surplus with the sign reversed rather than only net exports with the sign reversed. For example, in 1986 net exports were minus $105.7 billion while capital inflow from abroad was $143.7 billion. Hence $38 billion was paid abroad as transfers to foreigners and government interest payments.

ports over exports by borrowing from abroad. Then rest of the world lending is equal to U.S. borrowing.

It is important to note that these equations do not imply that saving equals investment for any of the sectors individually. However, for the three sectors as a whole, saving must equal investment. The sum of the three sectors' saving is

$$S_p + S_g + S_r = (Y + F + N - T) - C + (T - F - N - G) - X. \qquad (2-4)$$

Everything cancels out on the right-hand side except $Y - C - G - X$, which from the income identity is equal to investment, I. Thus, private saving plus government saving plus saving from the rest of the world equals investment. This identity is of great importance in interpreting movements in investment and saving. Because of large shifts in the saving of these three sectors in recent years, the identity deserves particular emphasis, as is illustrated in Table 2–7.

Table 2–7. GROSS SAVING AND INVESTMENT FOR 1985 AND 1986
          (billions of dollars)

	1985	1986
Gross private domestic saving	687.8	680.5
plus: Government saving	−136.3	−143.7
plus: Capital inflow	115.2	143.7
plus: Statistical discrepancy	−5.5	5.4
equals: Gross private domestic investment	661.1	686.4

Source: *Economic Report of the President,* 1987, Table B–27.

Table 2–7 shows the movement in gross investment in the United States between 1985 and 1986. The 4 percent increase in investment occurred, despite the decline in private saving and government saving, because of the large increase in capital from abroad. The government deficit was a large negative factor in both years, but investment in new factories and equipment in the United States continued to grow because of the willingness of foreigners to invest in the United States. For example, several Japanese automobile companies were constructing factories along Interstate 75 between Detroit and Lexington, Kentucky, in 1985 and 1986.

SAVING AND CHANGES IN ASSETS

To illustrate how these saving and investment decisions relate to the accumulation of assets and liabilities, consider two types of financial assets: government bonds and government money (currency). Money and bonds are financial liabilities of the government and are financial assets of the private sector. We call bonds B and money M. Let the symbol Δ represent a change from one year to the next. Then ΔM means change in money and ΔB means change in bonds.

The excess of saving over physical investment can be used to increase assets or reduce liabilities. In the NIPA the government is treated as if it does not undertake any physical investment. The entire government saving can be used either to reduce the national debt or to reduce money. The relation between government saving and asset accumulation is thus summarized as

$$S_g = -(\Delta M + \Delta B). \tag{2-5}$$

Since the government deficit is $-S_g$, Equation 2–5 equivalently says that the deficit must be financed by issuing money or by issuing bonds. Sometimes Equation 2–5 is called the **government budget identity.** If the private sector restricts itself to money and bonds, then the excess of private saving goes into either money or bonds. That is,

$$S_p = I + \Delta M + \Delta B_p. \tag{2-6}$$

The subscript p on B means that this is the private holding of bonds. Finally, if the rest of the world invests only in government bonds, then we have

$$S_r = \Delta B_r. \tag{2-7}$$

The subscript r on B means that this is foreign holdings of U.S. government bonds. By adding the assets for these three equations together we find again that $I = S_p + S_g + S_r$, the saving equals investment identity for the economy as a whole. As is clear from these equations, a government deficit generates an increase in either money or government bonds or both. A capital inflow from abroad results in an accumulation of U.S. debt abroad. In this sense the U.S. trade deficit is used to help finance the government budget deficit.

2.6 Transactions with the Rest of the World: The Balance of Payments Accounts and the Exchange Rate

We have already discussed transactions with other countries: imports and exports of goods, factor payments from and to foreigners, and capital inflows and outflows with the rest of the world. These are part of the NIPA. In addition, there is a separate set of international accounts called the **balance of payments accounts,** tabulated by the U.S. Department of Commerce. Although there are no concepts in these accounts that we have not already discussed, you will frequently hear about various types of deficits using the terminology of these accounts. It is important to understand what these mean. In addition, transactions with other countries require that U.S. dollars be exchanged for foreign currency—Japanese yen, German marks, Italian lire, Canadian dollars, and more. The **exchange rate** is the price at which these exchanges of dollars for foreign currencies take place.

BALANCE OF PAYMENTS ACCOUNTS

The balance of payments accounts are divided into the **current account** and the **capital account**. The current account keeps track of net exports as well as government grants and interest payments from the U.S. government abroad.

The capital account keeps track of borrowing and lending. When an American lends to a foreigner, by making a loan, buying a bond, or some similar transaction, the lending appears with a negative sign in the capital account. When an American borrows by taking out a loan in another country or by selling stocks and bonds, the borrowing appears with a positive sign.

The current account is broken into the merchandise account and a number of smaller accounts. These accounts are illustrated in Table 2–8 using data for 1986. The **merchandise account** keeps track of trade in the usual sense—imports and exports of business products. The United States tends to import more of these products than it exports—since 1976, there has been a substantial merchandise trade deficit every year, and in 1986 the merchandise deficit reached over $140 billion.

Table 2–8.   UNITED STATES BALANCE OF PAYMENTS ACCOUNTS, 1986 (billions of dollars)

1. Merchandise trade balance	−148
Equals merchandise exports	222
Less merchandise imports	370
2. Investment income balance	22
Equals receipts	90
Less payments	68
3. Balance of other miscellaneous items*	1
4. Balance on goods and services	
Equals (1) plus (2) plus (3)	−125
5. Remittances and transfers abroad	−15
6. Balance on current account	
Equals (4) plus (5)	−140

* Military transactions, travel and transportation receipts, royalties
Source: *Survey of Current Business*, March 1987, Table 1–2, p. 44.

The current account also reports investment earnings. These are part of the factor incomes in the NIPA. Since World War II the United States consistently has had a surplus—we have earned more overseas from our investments than foreigners have earned from their investments in the United States. The **balance on goods and services** in the current account adds together the merchandise account, investment earnings, and a few other very small categories. The balance on goods and services, in concept, equals net exports in the national income and product accounts. However, differences in measurement techniques mean that the two can be somewhat different in any given year. The deficit in the balance of goods and services account was $125 billion in 1986.

The last item in the current account is remittances and transfers. The U.S. government and the U.S. public make gifts, pension payments, and other transfers to the rest of the world. These enter the current account with a negative sign.

An important principle of the balance of payments accounts is that the current account and the capital account should sum to zero. When the United States imports more than it exports, it must be borrowing from the rest of the world to finance its current account deficit. There should be a positive balance in the capital account equal in magnitude to the current account deficit. This principle is what underlies Equation 2–3. When Americans buy more than they sell they must borrow from abroad.

The current account and the capital account are measured independently in the balance of payments accounts. Thus, in practice, the sum of the two is not zero; there is a statistical discrepancy.

THE EXCHANGE RATE

The dollar exchange rate measures the *price of dollars* in terms of foreign currencies. For example, the exchange rate between the U.S. dollar and the Japanese yen in March 1987 was 150 yen per dollar. That is, one could go to a bank and get 150 yen with one dollar. The *price* of one dollar was 150 yen. When Americans purchase foreign goods—such as a cup of coffee in Tokyo—they must pay for these goods with foreign currency—such as yen. Hence, the exchange rate is important for international transactions. A cup of coffee that costs 300 yen in Tokyo would cost an American 2 dollars if the exchange rate is 150 yen per dollar. If the exchange rate rises to 300 yen, that same cup of coffee would cost "only" one dollar.

The exchange rate determines how expensive foreign goods are compared to American goods. When the exchange rate rises, foreign goods become cheaper compared to home goods. As we will see in Chapter 5, this causes Americans to buy more goods abroad and foreigners to buy fewer goods in the United States.

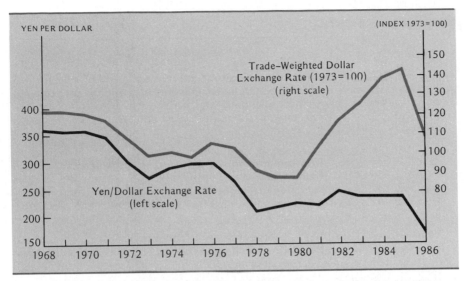

Figure 2–1.   YEN-DOLLAR AND TRADE-WEIGHTED DOLLAR EXCHANGE RATES.
The exchange rate has had large fluctuations during the last 10 years. Some of these fluctuations are associated with the movements in U.S. output. The dollar fell during the boom of the late 1970s and rose during the slump of the early 1980s. Other fluctuations seem unrelated to the state of the U.S. economy. Source: *Economic Report of the President,* 1987, Table B–105.

There is a dollar exchange rate for every foreign currency. Rather than keep track of all of these exchange rates, it is a useful simplification to consider an average of the different exchange rates. The **trade-weighted exchange rate** is an average of the exchange rates between the dollar and several different currencies, with those countries that trade more with the United States getting more weight.

The trade-weighted dollar exchange rate against 10 major currencies is shown in Figure 2–1, along with the dollar-yen exchange rate. Note that both exchange rates fluctuate by large amounts. Some of these fluctuations are associated with the fluctuations in real GNP in the United States. For example, the dollar fell during the boom in economic activity in the late 1970s, and rose during the slump in economic activity in the early 1980s. But there are many other movements in the exchange rate. During the period from 1967 to 1986 the dollar was generally falling relative to the yen. As we will see this was a result of the higher rate of inflation in the United States compared to Japan during these 20 years.

Review and Practice

MAJOR POINTS

1. There are three ways to measure and think about GNP: the spending side, the production side, and the income side. The components of spending are consumption, investment, government spending, and net exports. The components of production are the values added by each industry. The components of income are wages, profits, and interest.

2. Real GNP is the physical volume of production, after the effects of rising prices have been removed. Real GNP growth has averaged about 3 percent per year since the end of the Second World War, but there have been many fluctuations. Potential GNP is real GNP after the economic fluctuations have been removed. Nominal GNP is just GNP without adjustment for inflation or for economic fluctuations.

3. Value added is the difference between revenue and purchases of goods and services by a firm. It is the firm's contribution to GNP. GNP for the whole economy is the sum of value added across all producers.

4. Depreciation is the loss of capital from wear and tear. Net investment is gross investment less depreciation. Net national product is GNP less depreciation.

5. Conceptually, income and production are equal. All of value added is somebody's income. In the national accounts, there are various measures of income. National income is GNP less depreciation and less sales and excise taxes. Personal income is national income less social security taxes and corporate retained earnings plus transfer payments and interest paid by the government to consumers. Disposable personal income is personal income less income taxes.

6. The balance of payments accounts consist of a current account and a capital account. The two sum to zero except for the statistical discrepancy. The current account is in surplus when the United States is exporting more than it is importing. At the same time, the capital account is in deficit—capital is flowing out because the United States must be lending to the rest of the world if the United States is importing less than it exports.

7. The exchange rate is crucial for international transactions. It is the price of dollars in terms of foreign currency. When the exchange rate rises, more foreign currency can be bought with each dollar. This makes foreign goods cheaper in terms of dollars.

8. An important implication of the equality of income and product is the equality of saving and investment. It will always be the case that investment equals private saving plus the government surplus plus the capital inflow from abroad.

KEY TERMS AND CONCEPTS

Gross national product	Imports	Government saving
Value added	Exports	Real GNP
Consumption	Depreciation	Nominal GNP
Gross domestic product	Net investment	Balance of payments

Fixed investment	Net national product	Current account
National income	Final sales	Capital account
Inventory investment	Factor incomes	Exchange rate
Personal disposable income	Private saving	Trade-weighted exchange rate
Government purchases	Intermediate goods	

QUESTIONS FOR DISCUSSION AND REVIEW

1. Explain why spending on GNP is equal to income earned from producing GNP.

2. Identify which of the following are flows and which are stocks: consumption; government bonds outstanding at the end of last year; government purchases; inventories; inventory investment; depreciation; factories and equipment in the U.S. on December 31, 1985; the budget deficit.

3. Explain how real GNP is calculated.

4. Which components of spending fluctuate the most over the cycle?

PROBLEMS

Numerical

1. The following are data for the U.S. economy for 1986 in billions of dollars.

Rental income of persons	69.9
Depreciation	450.4
Compensation of employees	2428.6
Personal consumption expenditures	2618.2
Sales and excise taxes	340.1
Business transfer payments	19.3
Statistical discrepancy	−9.2
Gross private domestic investment	712.4
Exports of goods and services	406.5
Net subsidies of government business	16.1
Government purchases of goods and services	836.1
Imports of goods and services	480.5
Net interest	318.6
Proprietors' income	172.9
Corporate profits	318.0

    a. Compute GNP using the spending approach.
    b. Compute net national product.
    c. Compute national income two ways.

2. Fill in the blanks.
    a. If investment is $700 billion, private saving is $650 billion, and capital inflow from abroad is $100 billion, then the government budget deficit is _____ billion.
    b. If the stock of inventories in the economy is $500 billion at the end of 1985 and $520 billion at the end of 1986, then inventory investment for 1986 is _____ billion.

c. If production of U.S. GNP by Americans and American capital abroad is $50 billion and GNP is $4,000 billion, then GDP is _____.

3. (Warning: This problem is tough.) Data on the U.S. economy are given in the following tables (billions of dollars).

	Purchases of Intermediate Inputs from						
Industry	Agriculture	Mining	Manufacturing	Transportation and Utilities (T&U)	Trade	Finance, Insurance, and Real Estate (FIRE)	Services
Agriculture	—	1	19	14	7	7	18
Mining	8	—	21	4	18	18	8
Construction	21	21	22	23	18	15	5
Manufacturing	54	153	—	139	20	106	11
T&U	1	60	20	—	25	55	12
Trade	9	7	464	79	—	76	8
FIRE	0	13	24	36	14	—	7
Services	4	9	104	29	56	73	—

Industry	Purchases of Capital from		
	Construction	Manufacturing	Abroad
Agriculture	2	3	1
Mining	11	12	2
Construction	0	8	1
Manufacturing	21	132	14
T&U	8	17	3
Trade	27	25	0
FIRE	143	6	0
Services	19	15	1

Industry	Imports of Inputs	Sales to Government	Sales to Consumer	Exports	Wages
Agriculture	12	8	12	37	60
Mining	90	9	1	21	88
Construction	2	23	0	0	98
Manufacturing	181	188	21	206	315
T&U	5	5	101	13	132
Trade	2	6	935	15	287
FIRE	3	11	178	5	256
Services	6	4	583	21	195

Government wages: 337
Earnings of U.S. factors abroad: 49

Assume that consumer and government purchases from abroad are zero, and that there is no inventory investment.

a. Compute consumption, investment, government purchases, exports, and imports. Compute GNP from these.
b. Compute value added for each industry. Calculate GNP by summing all value

added. Is it equal to GNP from Part a? (Hints: Government value added is its wage payment. In calculating value added, do not subtract capital inputs.)

c. Compute profit for each industry as sales less purchases of current inputs (do not subtract investment). Compute national income as total profit plus total wages. Is it equal to GNP?

d. Compute net exports.

4. Consider a closed economy with expenditure totals for a year given by

Consumption	1,300
Investment	500
Government purchases	500
Government tax receipts	400
Depreciation	200

Suppose that the financial assets in the economy consist of money and bonds. Assume that money equals 500 at the start of the year, and that government bonds equal 700 at the start of the year.

a. Assuming that 90 percent of government deficits are financed by bonds, calculate the new levels of bond and money holdings for the private sector and for the government.

b. Show how the total change in government liabilities—money (M) + bonds (B) —can be computed in two ways.

Analytical

1. Identify which of the following purchases is counted as part of GNP. You purchase a used lawn mower at a garage sale. General Motors purchases tires from Goodyear to equip new Chevrolets. General Motors purchases tires from Goodyear to replace worn tires on executives' company cars. A neighbor hires you to babysit for an evening. You purchase a share of AT&T. A neighbor breaks your window with a golf ball, and you purchase a new window. You pay your tuition for the semester.

2. As part of its drive to replace welfare with workfare, the government decides to redesignate $100 billion in welfare benefits as government wages. The recipients become government employees.

a. For each of the methods used in calculating GNP, describe the effect of this policy change.

b. Suppose now that the workfare recipients are removed from the government payroll and are moved into the payroll of the newly incorporated Workfare, Inc. As part of its support for the workfare program, the government stands ready to subsidize Workfare, Inc., if its sales do not cover its costs. Since Workfare, Inc., has no products to sell, the subsidy ends up being the full $100 billion. How does this arrangement affect your answers to Part a?

3. Suppose that automobile purchases were to be treated like housing purchases in the national income accounts. How would that affect saving? Investment?

4. Determine whether the following statements are true or false, and explain why.

a. The trade deficit is equal to the government budget deficit plus investment less private domestic saving.

b. If GNP were measured at the prices firms receive for the products they sell, then sales and excise taxes would not be subtracted from GNP in computing national income.

c. The importance of different goods in GNP is determined by their relative price: for example, the production of one ounce of gold counts much more in GNP than the production of one ounce of steel.

5. In 1986, spending by Americans on personal consumption, private investment, and government operations totaled 104 percent of GNP. How is that possible?

6. Explain how the trade deficit in 1986 helped finance the large goverment budget deficit as well as the large increase in private gross investment in the United States. Should Americans care whether foreigners or other Americans hold the U.S. public debt?

7. Suppose initially that exports are zero and imports are $100 billion. Then assume that the government places a ban on imports. Assume that the spending habits of consumers, firms, and government remain the same (i.e., they spend the same amount but substitute domestic goods for imports).
   a. What happens to GNP?
   b. What happens to each category of savings (assume taxes remain unchanged)?
   c. Does total savings still equal investment?

8. Suppose that in a given year U.S. foreign trade consists of some consumer importing a single Honda Accord for $12,000 (1.8 million yen). Here are some possible financial transactions to accompany the purchase: (i) The consumer pays with $12,000, which Honda puts in its American bank account. (ii) The consumer pays with 1.8 million yen that he happens to have in a Japanese bank account. (iii) The consumer pays with $12,000; Honda invests the proceeds in U.S. Treasury bills. (iv) The consumer purchases 1.8 million yen on the foreign exchange market from some anonymous American foreign exchange trader, and then pays for the car.
   a. Is the United States running a current account surplus or deficit?
   b. For each of the financial transactions described above, explain the effect the transaction has on the U.S. capital account. What is the sum of the current account and capital account balances?

3

Monitoring the Economy: Inflation and Employment

THE NATIONAL income accounts and the related accounts discussed in Chapter 2 do not cover all of the important measures of economic performance. In this chapter we take up two measures—inflation and employment—that are not only more visible to unsophisticated observers, but have formed the basis of most policy initiatives of the past 25 years. In the first case, the cost of living is measured by a price index that is not part of the accounts, though it is closely related. As for the second case, employment and unemployment, while these are possibly the most important dimensions of performance, they are not part of the national income accounts at all.

3.1 Measuring Inflation

Almost everybody watches the rate of inflation. It is a major indicator of how the economy is doing, and changes in inflation are closely related to fluctuations in real GNP. The **rate of inflation** is defined as the percentage rate of change in the general price level from one period to the next. The general price level is a measure of the purchasing power of the dollar, or the amount of goods and services the dollar can buy. For example, one measure of the price level was 328 in 1986, which means that the same basket of goods that cost $100 in 1967 cost $328 in 1986. Much of the original economic research on measuring the general price level was done by Irving Fisher of Yale University in the 1920s. There are now two approaches to measuring the general price level: constructing **price indexes** directly from data on the prices of thousands of goods and services, and calculating **deflators** by dividing a component of nominal GNP by the same component of real GNP.

PRICE INDEXES

A price index is a ratio showing the price of a basket of goods and services in various years in relation to the price of the basket in a base year. The index is 100 in the base year and correspondingly higher in later years if the prices of the things in the basket have risen. The most conspicuous price index is the **consumer price index (CPI).** This index measures the cost of living for a typical urban family. The Bureau of Labor Statistics (BLS) of the Department of Labor computes it in the following way: Once every 10 years or so, the BLS makes a survey of the buying habits of American families. The survey covers not only the products they buy in stores, but other expenditures like the purchases of houses. Then the BLS makes a long list of goods and services whose prices they can determine once a month. From the survey of buying habits, they estimate the quantities of each item bought by the average family. The list includes tomato soup, for example. The amount of tomato soup in the CPI basket is greater than the fraction of income that the typical family spends on tomato soup. The price of tomato soup is considered representative of the prices of similar products that are not included in the index.

Every month, the BLS sends surveyors into stores to write down the actual prices of goods and services. When discounts are available, they take them into account. The BLS is particularly careful about new car prices because they have a large role in the price index and few people actually pay the sticker price for a new car.

Each month, the BLS computes the new level of the price index by using the detailed prices to compute the cost of the CPI basket. The basket is chosen so that its price was 100 in 1967, which means that the index had the value 100 in 1967. Almost all the prices going into the index have risen a lot since 1967. In 1986, the index was 328, so prices had more than tripled over 19 years. Some prices have risen more than others. The 1986 level of medical care was 434, while the level of clothing prices was only 208; both started at 100 in 1967.

Figure 3–1 shows the history of the U.S. price level as measured by the CPI since 1960. Inflation was moderate in the early 1960s, gained momen-

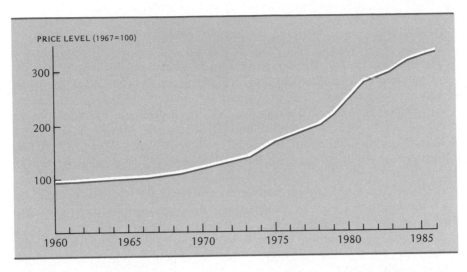

Figure 3-1. THE U.S. PRICE LEVEL.
The consumer price index measures the price of a bundle of goods and services representative of the purchases of a typical family. By construction, it has the value 100 in 1967. Because of inflation at varying rates since 1967, the index stood at 328 in 1986. Source: *Economic Report of the President*, 1987, Table B–55.

tum in the late 1960s and early 1970s, and reached two peaks in 1974 and 1980. Inflation moderated in the 1980s.

The CPI is the most widely used measure of the purchasing power of the dollar. When people make an agreement that is set in dollars and want to protect themselves against inflation, they can write in a provision that payments rise in proportion to the increase in the CPI. This practice is called **cost-of-living adjustment (COLA)** and is used for social security payments and in many collective bargaining agreements that spell out the terms of employment for unionized workers.

The government puts out another major price index in addition to the CPI. Formerly the wholesale price index, it is now called the **producer price index (PPI).** Instead of measuring the prices actually paid by consumers, it measures the prices charged by producers at various stages in the production process. There is no clear basis for the choice of weights for the PPI, comparable to the market basket that gives the weights for the CPI. As a result, there is much less interest in the monthly value of the PPI itself. However, the BLS reports all of the detailed prices going into the PPI and these prices and the price indexes computed from them are the best source of information about prices of crude materials and intermediate goods. Some economists think that the PPI for crude materials is one of the most sensitive early warning indicators of future inflation.

DEFLATORS

The construction of data on nominal and real GNP results in another type of price index. The purpose of measuring real GNP is to get rid of the price effects in nominal GNP. Thus, the ratio of nominal GNP to real GNP is a measure of prices. It is called the **GNP implicit price deflator.** For example, in 1986 nominal GNP was $4,209 billion. Real GNP was $3,677 billion 1982 dollars. The GNP deflator for 1986 was 100 × 4,209/3,677 = 115. That is, with a base of 100 in 1982, the price level according to the GNP deflator was 115.

Each component of GNP has a deflator. For example, the ratio of nominal consumption to real consumption is the **consumption deflator.** It is widely used as an alternative to the CPI as a measure of the cost of living.

Remember that GNP does not include imports. Correspondingly, the GNP deflator does not count the prices of imported goods. When the world oil price jumped in 1974, the GNP deflator did not rise by as much as the deflators for consumption, investment, and government purchases, which do include the prices of imports. The GNP deflator rose by 9.1 percent from 1973 to 1974. At the same time, the consumption deflator rose by 10.5 percent, the investment deflator by 10.3 percent, and the government deflator by 10.8 percent. The deflator for exports rose by 19.5 percent and the deflator for imports by 42.0 percent. Had it not been for the increase in export prices, the 42 percent increase in import prices caused by the oil price increase would have driven up product prices in the United States by even more compared to the GNP deflator.

Import price shocks have been sufficiently small that the GNP deflator and the consumption deflator tell pretty much the same story about the U.S. price level. Further, they largely agreed with the CPI until the mid-1970s. The CPI gives an unreasonably heavy weight to the costs of owning a home, which rose dramatically after 1975. The consumption deflator uses better weights and gives a more accurate picture of the cost of living. For this reason, economists have come to prefer the consumption deflator over the CPI. However, in 1983, the BLS made improvements in the weights for the CPI, so future divergences of the two indexes should be smaller.

Inflation, Price Indexes, and Deflators

1. Inflation is the rate of increase in the price level. The price level is an average of all prices in the economy.

2. There are two types of measures of the price level: price indexes and deflators. The consumer price index (CPI) and the producer

price index (PPI) are the two major price indexes. The weights on the individual prices in the CPI are based on a survey of consumer buying habits. The GNP deflator is the ratio of nominal GNP to real GNP. It is a measure of the prices of all goods and services produced in America.

3. The CPI is used for cost-of-living adjustments in many union contracts and in many government programs.

3.2 Measuring Employment, Unemployment, and Wages

Employment falls along with production during recessions, and rises again during recoveries. Over the long haul, employment grows along with potential GNP, as firms hire more workers to produce the growing output. Information on employment in the United States comes from two surveys, one of *households* and the other of *establishments*—the offices, factories, stores, mines, and other places where people work.

The household survey—called the Current Population Survey—is conducted each month by the Bureau of the Census, and the data are tabulated and reported by the BLS. About 100,000 adults are interviewed each month to find out whether they were employed during the calendar week that includes the 12th of the month. Everyone who worked an hour or more during that week is counted as employed for that month. The results are blown up by multiplying by about 1,000 so that they are good estimates of the total number of workers employed that month in the whole economy (each person in the survey stands for a little over 1,000 people in the population). Some other people who did not work—notably those on vacation—are also counted as employed.

Total civilian employment by this measure was 109.6 million in 1986, up by 2.4 million from its level of 107.2 million in 1985 and up by 10.1 million from its level of 99.5 million in the recession year of 1982. The long recovery and expansion of the mid-1980s involved substantial growth in employment, as expansions generally do. On the other hand, employment falls during recessions. Employment reached a peak of 100.7 million in July 1981 and then fell to a trough of 99.0 million in December 1982.

The establishment survey interviews employers to find out the number of people on the payroll at each workplace. The survey excludes farm employees. Because it is based on payrolls, it also omits people who are self-employed. Total non-agricultural payroll employment was 100.2 million people in December 1986.

HOURS PER WEEK AND TOTAL HOURS

The number of hours worked each week varies among workers and over time. Some people normally work part time for only a few hours a week and others work 60 to 70 hours. The average factory worker now puts in about 41 hours per week, while the average store worker puts in about 29 hours. Also, the number of hours per week falls during recessions and rises during expansions. When demand is booming many workers are asked, or choose, to work overtime. For example, in the 1981–82 recession, average weekly hours fell from 35.3 hours in July 1981 to 34.7 hours in November 1982, and rose again to 35.2 hours in December 1983. For many decades there has also been a downward trend in hours of work in some industries. For example, average weekly hours fell from about 40 hours per week for store workers in 1947 to about 29 hours per week now. Average weekly hours in manufacturing have remained steady at about 40 hours per week since 1947.

For all these reasons, employment by itself is not a complete measure of labor input to the economy. Total hours of work—the number of people working multiplied by the hours of work of the average worker—is a better measure. The BLS publishes an index of total hours for the business sector. This index is shown in Figure 3–2 for the period from 1963 to 1985.

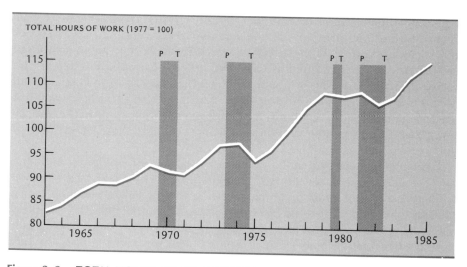

Figure 3–2. TOTAL HOURS OF ALL WORKERS.
The total amount of work performed in the United States, measured by the hours of all workers, fluctuates along with the business cycle. In each of the four recessions shown here—1969–70, 1973–75, 1980, and 1981–82—total hours declined. In general, total hours have been growing. Growth was particularly strong from 1975 to 1979. Source: *Economic Report of the President,* 1987, Table B–43.

When the level of real output of the economy declines, total hours of work decline. The work force feels the effects of a recession in the form of fewer hours of work per week, as well as in the possibility of being laid off. Their pay declines in either case even if the wage rate does not change.

UNEMPLOYMENT

One of the most important questions in macroeconomics is why the economy does not provide work for the entire labor force. Even in the best of times, people are unemployed. They are interested in working and are available for work, but have not found jobs. One of the principal purposes of the Current Population Survey is to determine how many people are unemployed each month. High unemployment is the single most important signal of distress in the economy.

The Current Population Survey counts you as unemployed if you did not work at all during the survey week and you were looking for work. In each survey, several million people are found to be unemployed. The **labor force** is defined as the number of persons 16 years of age or over who are either working or unemployed. The **unemployment rate** is the percentage of the labor force that is unemployed.

There are millions of people who are not working but who are not counted as unemployed. They are considered out of the labor force because they are retired, in school, at home looking after their own children, sick, or not looking for work for some other reason. The **labor force participation rate** is the percentage of the working-age population that is in the labor force. Whether one is in the labor force or not is sometimes a matter of opinion; this has lead some economists to look at other less subjective measures of labor market conditions. One example is the **employment/population ratio.** This is the percentage of the working-age population that is employed.

Table 3–1 shows the number of people in the population aged 16 or over along with the labor force, employment, and unemployment for four different years: in 1981 before the 1981–82 recession, at the trough in 1982, at the start of the recovery in 1983, and later in the recovery in 1986. The unemployment rate got up to 10.7 percent in 1982, a level it had not reached since the depression of the 1930s. The unemployment rate at the 1981 peak was higher than normal because the economy had not fully recovered from the 1980 recession when the 1981–82 recession began. The labor force participation rate sometimes falls during recessions, because some workers get discouraged looking for work and leave the labor force to retire early, go back to school, or do something else. This did not happen in the 1981–82 recession, because it was offset by other factors that increased the labor

Table 3–1.   UNEMPLOYMENT, LABOR FORCE, AND THE POPULATION

	1981	1982	1983	1986
Millions of people:				
(1) Aged 16 or over	170.1	172.3	174.2	180.6
(2) In labor force	108.7	110.2	111.6	117.8
(3) Employed	100.4	99.5	100.8	109.6
(4) Unemployed	8.3	10.7	10.7	8.2
Percentage:				
Labor force participation rate, (2)/(1)	63.9	64.0	64.0	66.8
Unemployment rate, (4)/(2)	7.6	9.7	9.6	7.0
Employment/population ratio, (3)/(1)	59.0	57.8	57.9	62.1

Source: *Economic Report of the President*, 1987, Table B-31.

force. The labor force participation rate for women has been increasing in the last few decades, and this continued during the 1981–82 recession. The labor force participation rates for teenagers and for males over 20 did decline during the recession, but were offset by the increased participation rate for women. Note that the employment/population ratio tells about the same story as the unemployment rate during this period.

Figure 3–3 shows how the average annual unemployment rate behaved during the period since the Second World War. Unemployment moves with the business cycle. When real GNP is high relative to the trend path of potential GNP, unemployment is low. When output is at low levels in the depths of recessions, unemployment is high.

Note that in normal times—when real GNP is equal to potential GNP—unemployment is not zero. Even in boom times there is some **frictional unemployment.** When workers enter the labor force for the first time or after a spell out of the labor force, they need some time to find a job. During this period they are counted as unemployed. Similarly, when workers quit their jobs, there will frequently be a span of time before they find new jobs. Movements from one job to another are particularly common for young workers as they find out what type of job they are best suited for. This is one reason why young workers have higher unemployment rates than older workers. In addition, there are some low-skilled workers who are frequently unemployed. Additional training for such workers would reduce the unemployment rate. The term economists use for the unemployment rate that prevails in normal times is the **natural rate of unemployment.** The natural rate of unemployment now seems to be about 6 percent. It was apparently closer to 5 percent in the 1960s. The reasons for the increase in the natural

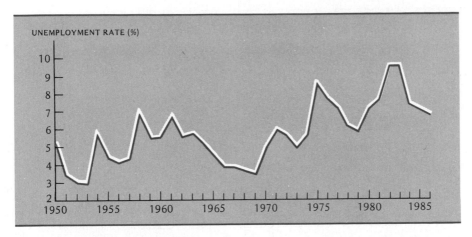

Figure 3–3.   THE UNEMPLOYMENT RATE.
The unemployment rate has fluctuated between 3 and 10 percent since 1950. Unemployment rises during recessions and falls during expansions. There has also been an upward drift in the unemployment rate. Source: *Economic Report of the President,* 1987, Table B–35.

employment rate in the past two decades are not well understood. Although the labor force was younger, on the average, in the 1970s in comparison to earlier decades, the labor force was also quite a bit better educated. The first factor may have increased the natural rate but the second should have lowered it.

OKUN'S LAW

There is a useful shorthand formula that closely approximates the cyclical relationship between unemployment and real GNP. It is commonly called **Okun's law,** after its discoverer, Arthur Okun, who used it to illustrate the effects of macroeconomic policy when he was on the staff of the Council of Economic Advisers during the early days of the Kennedy administration in the 1960s. Okun's law says that for each percentage point by which the unemployment rate is *above* the natural rate, real GNP is 3 percent *below* potential GNP. The percentage departure of GNP from potential is called the **GNP gap.** For example, if unemployment is 8 percent, 2 percentage points above the natural rate of 6 percent, then real GNP is 6 percent below potential. The GNP gap is minus 6 percent. The historical accuracy of the formula is illustrated in Figure 3–4.

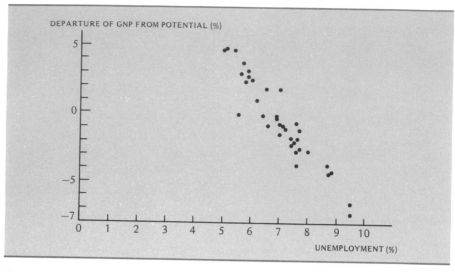

Figure 3–4. OKUN'S LAW.
The movements in unemployment are closely related to the movements in the percentage departures of real GNP from potential GNP. The slope of the relationship is roughly 3 percentage points of real GNP for each percent of unemployment.

The Labor Market in the 1960s and the 1980s

The 1960s and the 1980s both had economic expansions of unusual length. The middle years of these expansions show the labor market under more or less standard conditions—neither suffering from a recent recession nor enjoying super-heated conditions. In 1964 the unemployment rate for civilian workers was 5.2 percent. In 1986, the same unemployment rate was 7.2 percent. By that measure, unemployment was considerably worse in the 1980s than in the 1960s. Jobs seemed to be harder to find.

By another measure, the insured unemployment rate, the situation was the reverse. In 1964, 3.8 percent of workers eligible for state unemployment insurance benefits were unemployed. In 1985, the rate was only 2.9 percent. The job situation seemed much better in 1985 than it did in 1964; fewer insured workers were out of work in any given week.

A third measure, the volume of help-wanted advertising, tells a story partway between the two unemployment rates. Katherine Abraham of the Brookings Institution has created an index of help-wanted advertising that adjusts for the growth of the labor market and for other factors. Her index was 95 in 1964 and also 95 in 1985. Employers were placing about the same volume of help-wanted ads in 1985 as in 1964. The index is a sensitive indicator of labor market conditions—it reached an all-time low of 75 in the severe recession of 1982 and a high of 136 in the extreme boom of 1969.

Experts are still uncertain about why unemployment has risen in comparison to other indicators of how easy it is to find a job for a worker or how much effort it takes an employer to find a suitable worker. One important factor is that more of the unemployed are people who have not worked recently. These people are not eligible for unemployment insurance. That is why insured unemployment is so low compared to total unemployment.

WAGES

Remember that the income side of the national income and product accounts reports the total earnings of workers. Total annual earnings divided by total annual hours of work gives a measure of the average hourly wage paid to workers in the United States. The BLS calls this compensation per hour. Compensation per hour includes the value of fringe benefits as well as cash wages. Wages are the most important component of the cost of production.

Wages and prices generally moved together throughout the swings in inflation in the 1970s. The **real wage** is the hourly average wage divided by the cost of living. From the point of view of workers, it measures the purchasing power of the wage—the amount of goods and services that can be bought with one hour of work. From the point of view of employers, it measures the real cost of labor input. The real wage since 1950 is shown in Figure 3–5.

After steady growth through 1973, the upward path of the real wage was interrupted by increasing oil prices in 1974. Growth resumed in the late 1970s, only to be interrupted again by the second oil price shock in 1979–80. The real wage jumped upward in 1986 when oil prices declined. Oil is an important input to the U.S. economy. When the price of such an input rises, the prices of goods must rise relative to the wage. Thus, the real wage declines if oil prices rise and rises if oil prices fall.

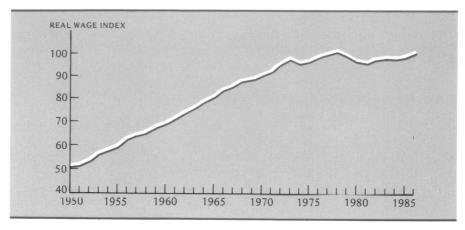

Figure 3–5.   THE REAL WAGE.
The real wage is the ratio of the dollar wage (compensation per hour) to the cost of living (the consumer price index). The real wage grew quite smoothly until the oil price shocks of 1973–74 and 1979. The real wage in 1982 was about the same as in 1973. Source: *Economic Report of the President,* 1987, Table B–43.

3.3 Productivity

Productivity is the amount of output produced per unit of input. Because labor is the most important input, the most popular measure of productivity is **labor productivity**, or output per hour of labor. When economists talk about productivity they usually mean labor productivity. A broader measure of productivity, called **total factor productivity**, is output per generalized unit of input (factor is a general term for an input like labor or capital). The generalized unit counts capital, energy, and materials as inputs in addition to labor. However, output per unit of labor and total factor productivity for the United States as a whole tell about the same story for recent years.

The BLS computes labor productivity for the economy as the ratio of real GNP originating in the business sector to the total hours of work in that sector. The recent history of labor productivity is shown in Figure 3–6. Productivity has generally been increasing as workers have become more efficient and have had more and better machines to work with. This increase in productivity underlies the growth in real wages that we saw in the previous section. But productivity is also procyclical. It rises in booms, and falls in recessions. Firms tend to keep skilled workers on the payroll and let them produce fewer items in slack times, rather than lay them off and run the risk that they will find jobs elsewhere. They make up for their low productivity in bad times with higher productivity in good times.

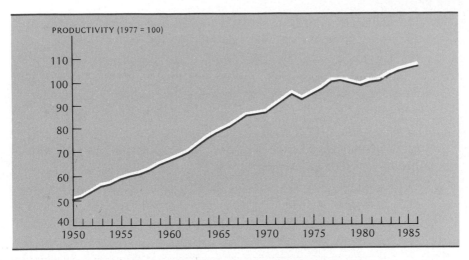

Figure 3–6. LABOR PRODUCTIVITY IN THE UNITED STATES.
Productivity is the amount of output produced per hour of work. The general trend in productivity has been upward. Productivity tends to drop or at least not grow as fast as usual in recessions. The drop in productivity was especially pronounced in the oil shock recessions of 1973–75 and 1980. Source: *Economic Report of the President,* 1987, Table B–43.

Productivity growth has been disappointing since 1973. It has declined in each of three serious recessions, but the intervening expansions have not been strong enough to bring productivity growth back to the normal trend. Economists disagree about the reasons for the post-1973 productivity slowdown. Some stress the role of the increases in oil prices. Others point to a reduction in expenditures on research and development and say that technical innovation has slowed down as a result. Still others say that we are not investing enough in new machines and factories. Of all the puzzles about the recent performance of the U.S. economy, the slowdown in productivity growth is perhaps the most difficult one for economists to solve.

Employment and Productivity

1. Employment data are collected in a household survey and in an establishment survey. Employment is closely related to output fluctuations.

2. The unemployment rate is the percentage of the labor force that is unemployed. The participation rate is the percentage of the working-age population that is in the labor force.

3. The unemployment rate is closely related to the deviations of real GNP from potential GNP. This relation is called Okun's law.

4. The wage rate is the amount paid to workers per hour, week, or month of work. The real wage measures the purchasing power of the wage payment. The real wage grew steadily in the United States until the early 1970s, when its growth slowed down.

5. Labor productivity is defined as output per unit of labor input. Labor productivity has been growing for a long time, though with fluctuations during business cycles.

6. In the United States productivity growth slowed down in the early 1970s. Growth of productivity permits the real wage to grow, and the slowdown in productivity is the main reason for the slowdown in real wage growth in the United States.

Review and Practice

MAJOR POINTS

1. The consumer price index is the number of dollars required to purchase a market basket of goods and services typical of the consumption patterns of Americans.

2. Price indexes called deflators can be calculated by dividing a component of nominal GNP by the same component of real GNP. The consumption deflator is widely used by economists as an alternative to the CPI. The overall GNP deflator is a measure of the price of domestic production; it does not include the price of imports.

3. The best measure of total labor input to the economy is the total number of hours worked by all workers each year. That measure tends to move in proportion to real GNP.

4. A good measure of hourly wages is total labor earnings divided by total hours worked. The real wage is the ratio of the hourly wage to the price level. The real wage in the U.S. grew smoothly until the oil price jumps of the 1970s, after which almost no growth occurred.

5. The unemployment rate is the percentage of the labor force that is actively looking for work but has not found work. Many people who are not working are not counted as unemployed because they are not looking for work. The unemployment rate has varied between 3 and 10 percent since 1950. Okun's law describes the relation between unemployment and real GNP: For every 3 percent by which real GNP departs from its trend path, the unemployment rate departs in the opposite direction from its normal level by 1 percentage point.

6. A simple measure of productivity is the ratio of real GNP to labor input. In the United States, productivity grew smoothly from 1950 until the oil shock recessions of the 1970s. Growth has continued since then, but more irregularly and at diminished rates.

KEY TERMS AND CONCEPTS

Price indexes

Consumer price index

Producer price index

Price deflators

Labor force

Unemployment rate

Participation rate

Rate of inflation

Frictional unemployment

Natural rate of unemployment

Okun's law

GNP gap

Real wage

Labor productivity

QUESTIONS FOR DISCUSSION AND REVIEW

1. What is the difference between high prices and inflation?

2. What is the difference between being unemployed and not working? Give some examples of people not at work who are not unemployed.

3. Explain why unemployment falls when output rises. In the process, mention what happens to employment.

4. Describe how the real wage, employment, and hours of work influence the purchasing power of earnings.

PROBLEMS

Numerical

1. Suppose that Okun's law between unemployment and GNP is given by

$$(Y - Y^*)/Y^* = -3(U - U^*),$$

where U is the unemployment rate, U^* is the natural rate of unemployment, Y is GNP, and Y^* is potential GNP. Unemployment is measured as a fraction. Suppose that the natural rate is 6 percent; that is, $U^* = .06$.

a. Calculate the GNP gap for each of the years in 1982–86 using the following unemployment data: $U = 9.5, 9.5, 7.4, 7.1,$ and 6.9 percent respectively.

b. GNP for these same years is as follows: $3,166, $3,279, $3,489, $3,585, and $3,676 billion. Using these data and your answers to Part a, calculate potential GNP for each of these years. What is the average growth rate of potential GNP?

c. Suppose that from 1986 to 1989, potential GNP continues to rise at the average rate of growth for the previous 5 years. By how much must actual GNP increase in that time in order to reduce the unemployment rate to 6 percent in 1989?

2. The consumer price index for the 1978–82 period and the GNP deflator are listed below. The CPI is equal to 100 in the base year 1967; the GNP deflator is equal to 100 in the base year 1982.

	CPI	GNP Deflator
1978	195.4	72.2
1979	217.4	78.6
1980	246.8	85.7
1981	272.4	94.0
1982	289.1	100.0

a. Calculate the rate of inflation according to both measures from 1979 through 1982. What might explain the differences between the two?

b. Suppose that the hourly wage rate for a group of workers that sign an employment contract for the 3-year period starting in 1979 is indexed to the CPI according to the formula

$$\Delta W/W = .03 + .5\Delta CPI/CPI.$$

Calculate the actual increase in the wage during each year of the contract period. If the wage was $12.00 in 1979, what was it in 1980, 1981, and 1982? What happens to the real wage measured in terms of the CPI?

c. Repeat your calculations with .03 reduced to 0 and .5 increased to 1. What indexing formula would the workers' employer have preferred? Is there any reason for the employer to have been happy with the other formula before the actual inflation experience was known?

3. The CPI is calculated for a fixed market basket. It measures the change in the cost of the market basket from the base year until the current year. An index with the market basket fixed in the first year—like the CPI—is called a Laspeyres index. An alternative index—called the Paasche index—is based on a market basket in the end year. It measures the change in the cost of a market basket fixed in the end year. Suppose that the base year is 1973. Suppose that the market basket contains only two items, peanut butter and gasoline, and that the quantities consumed in 1973 and 1974 are:

	Peanut Butter	Gasoline
1973	100 jars	50 gallons
1974	150 jars	45 gallons

Suppose that the price of peanut butter increased from $1.00 per jar in 1973 to $1.20 per jar in 1974, and that the price of gasoline increased from $.50 per gallon to $2.00 per gallon.

a. Calculate the rate of inflation for the Laspeyres (CPI) index and the Paasche index.

b. Will inflation calculated using the Laspeyres index always exceed inflation calculated with the Paasche index? (Hint: Use standard indifference curve analysis.)

c. Workers often receive an adjustment in their wages equal to only a fraction of inflation as calculated using the CPI. In view of the preceding analysis explain why workers would likely be better off than they were before if they were fully compensated for inflation. Would this also be the case if inflation was calculated using the Paasche index?

Analytical

1. Okun's law suggests that over the course of the business cycle a change in the unemployment rate of 1 percentage point will be accompanied by a 3 percent change in output. Using the formula:

$$Y = (Y/H)(H/N)(1-U)L,$$

where Y/H is output per hour worked, H/N is hours per worker, N is the number of employed workers, U is the unemployment rate, and L is the labor force, explain in what direction and why some of the factors other than Y and U might change. (Note that if $W=XYZ$, then for small changes, the percentage change in W

is given by the sum of the percentage changes in X, Y, and Z. Note also that $1-U = N/L$, and that a change in the unemployment rate of 1 percentage point corresponds to approximately a 1 percent change in N/L.)

2. An empirical regularity in the U.S. economy is that roughly 25 percent of output goes to capitalists in the form of earnings of capital, while 75 percent goes to workers in the form of wages.
   a. Using the formula given in Question 1, show that the increase in the average hourly wage will be given by the growth in productivity per man hour, Y/NH.
   b. From Figures 3–5 and 3–6 it appears that real wage growth slowed even more than productivity growth in the last 15 years. Does this imply that there has been a rise in the share of output going to the owners of capital?

3. Suppose that on January 1, 1989, the government creates a million new jobs. Only those currently without jobs may apply. The new jobs attract 3 million applicants, half of whom would not otherwise be looking for work in January.
   a. Is the labor force for January changed from what it would have been in the absence of these new jobs? By how much?
   b. Assuming that without the new jobs the labor force would have been 100 million and the unemployment rate 6 percent, what will the unemployment rate for January now be?

4

Spending Balance

MEASURES of income, spending, and employment, of the sort we have examined in Chapters 2 and 3, are the cornerstones of macroeconomics. But having established the evidence, how do we explain it? In the rest of this book we develop a system for analyzing macroeconomic fluctuations. The theory, or model, presented is used by economists for forecasting business cycles, for determining the size and timing of government policy action to mitigate the effects of recessions or to combat inflation, and for asking what went wrong in particular episodes such as the Great Depression in the 1930s or the "Great Inflation" of the 1970s. Such models are the "bread and butter" of macroeconomic analysis.

We begin, in this chapter and the next, by presenting the basic methods used by economists to analyze aggregate demand. We will use the ideas about aggregate demand to explain short-run fluctuations of GNP around the potential GNP path; that is, the movements associated with recessions and booms in economic activity. According to Okun's law, which we discussed in Chapter 3, the overall level of unemployment can be closely tied to the fluctuations of actual GNP around potential GNP. Hence, understanding the fluctuations in actual GNP relative to potential GNP will also provide an explanation for observed periods of unemployment.

Our first step is to explain the concept of spending balance. In the process, we will develop a simple model that explains the determination of GNP.

4.1 An Overview

In Chapter 2 we noted that GNP could be defined and measured in three alternative ways: as **spending** on goods and services, as **production** of goods and services, and as **income** received by workers and firms. It is a simple matter of accounting identities that these three alternatives will give the same answer for total GNP, aside from measurement error and statistical discrepancies. When we move beyond accounting identities to a theory of what determines the fluctuations of GNP, however, it makes quite a difference which one of these concepts is used. In practice, it has turned out to be useful to focus first on the spending side.

Firms produce goods because people have decided to buy them. Aggregate demand theory starts by examining spending decisions. For example, consider how a macroeconomist goes about projecting the growth of GNP for the upcoming year. The macroeconomist begins with a projection of the spending demands of consumers, firms, and governments. If a personal tax cut is coming up, then the macroeconomist will naturally anticipate a larger amount of demand for consumption goods by households. If interest rates are projected to rise because of a change in monetary policy, then investment demand from firms is likely to be lower. If there is a public clamor for decreased defense spending, then government demand is likely to fall. By adding up the spending demands of the various sectors of the economy the macroeconomist obtains an estimate of aggregate spending. This total then serves as the projection for GNP for the upcoming year. While it will be necessary to check whether these spending projections are consistent with incomes—in a way to be made clear below—the basic forecast is obtained from an analysis of the spending decisions in the economy. Because the total spending forecast is an aggregation of demand in all sectors of the economy, we refer to the total as **aggregate demand.** Implicitly the macroeconomist is making an assumption that aggregate demand determines the amount of goods produced in the economy. This assumption is central to our analysis of economic fluctuations.

A FIRM'S RESPONSE TO CHANGES IN DEMAND

To see why the macroeconomist's assumption that aggregate demand determines output is usually a reasonable assumption, we need to consider the typical behavior of business firms at the microeconomic level. Under normal conditions most business firms operate with some excess capacity, and respond to increases in demand by producing more goods. In the United States the average level of capacity utilization in manufacturing industries is about 86 percent. Some machines are left idle on standby; others are run for only two of three shifts. Hence firms have considerable leeway to produce more by increasing capacity utilization when demand increases. If additional labor is necessary to operate the equipment more intensively, it is usually possible to have some workers increase their hours per week, to recall some workers from layoff status, or even to hire additional workers. The natural rate of unemployment is about 6 percent, indicating that additional workers can be hired in the short run, even at full employment. Hence, for both capital and labor inputs to production, there is considerable short-run flexibility for firms to meet an increase in the demand for their products. And though we have been speaking entirely in terms of increases in demand, the same response occurs for declines in demand. A firm will produce less when the demand for its product declines. In sum, both increases and decreases in demand for a firm's product get translated into increases and decreases in production. In the economy as a whole, short-run fluctuations in aggregate demand result in similar fluctuations in GNP. In this sense, the assumption that "demand determines output" is a reasonable one for analyzing most short-run fluctuations of GNP from its long-run growth path.

Firms not only adjust their production in response to changes in demand, they also adjust their prices. When an increase in demand results in a firm producing at above-average operating levels, it usually increases its prices as well. Similarly, a decline in demand that brings the firm to below-normal operating levels will result in a price adjustment below what would have been appropriate otherwise. By adjusting its price in this way the firm can usually both increase its profits in the short run and encourage a shift in demand to a more desirable level from the firm's point of view.

There is a crucial difference, however, between the adjustment of production and the adjustment of prices in response to a change in demand: *Prices appear to be very "sticky" compared to production; the adjustment of prices occurs gradually, whereas the adjustment of production and employment occurs almost instantaneously.* Economists have only recently begun researching the reasons for this slow price adjustment on the part of firms, and we will summarize this exciting and important research in Part III. The implication of this slow price adjustment is that changes in aggregate demand first result in changes in production, much as described above, and only later in changes in prices. In fact, in the very short run it is usually a good approximation to ignore price adjustment and focus on the changes in production.

We have left out one important aspect of firm behavior in our discussion so far. Many firms maintain a stock or inventory of their finished products on their shelves, so that when there is an increase in demand the immediate response is usually to meet the demand out of the inventory. Conversely, a drop in demand can be matched by an accumulation of inventory. Clearly, changes in demand that are exactly matched by changes in inventory will not affect production or GNP. However, for the economy as a whole, increases in sales are met with increases in production. Thus, as an approximation it is possible to ignore inventory adjustments and assume that changes in demand are directly translated into changes in production. A full treatment of the process of inventory adjustment is given in Chapter 9.

AN EXAMPLE: GENERAL MOTORS

Production in the automobile industry rises and falls by large magnitudes in response to changes in demand, and automobile purchases are a very large part of total spending, so this is an important example. During the large downturn from 1929 to 1933, for instance, annual production of automobiles in the United States fell from about 5 million to about 1 million cars. In the downturn from 1979 to 1982 production of cars at GM plants in the United States fell from 4.8 million to 3.1 million cars per year.

Consider what happens at GM when there is a change in the demand for automobiles. Suppose, for example, that there is an increase in demand for automobiles as there typically is in a recovery period following a recession like the one that ended in 1982. In the short run this increase in demand results in more automobiles being produced; some workers are asked to work more hours, others are recalled from layoff, some new workers are hired, plants are worked an extra shift, and plants that were closed earlier are reopened. Employment and capacity utilization in the automobile industry are increased to correspond to the increase in demand.

In 1984, for example, the demand for cars was increasing rapidly in the United States, as the economy was recovering rapidly from the previous recession. People bought 4.6 million cars from GM dealers in 1984, up 13 percent from the 4.1 million purchased in 1983. As a result, production of cars increased and the number of workers at GM plants in the United States increased to 375,000 in 1984, up 12 percent from 336,000 in 1983. With more workers on the job for longer hours, wage payments to GM workers increased by 19 percent to $13.6 billion during the same period. GM profits also rose dramatically, and dividends paid to holders of common stock increased from $900 million to $1.5 billion. Bonuses to managers were increased. Some of the increased profits—about $282 million—were shared with workers under a profit-sharing plan instituted during the previous recession. GM workers, managers, and owners thus had more income to spend, and this added further to the demand for goods in the economy. By the end of 1984 GM was building about the same number of cars that it was in 1979, before the downturn.

4.2 Consumption and Income

From this simple microeconomic description of firm behavior, we now proceed to investigate **spending balance.** When the economy is in spending balance, spending decisions generate a level of GNP consistent with the income underlying the spending decisions.

THE INCOME IDENTITY

We presented the spending components of demand in Chapter 2 using the accounting identity

$$Y = C + I + G, \qquad \text{The Income Identity} \qquad (4\text{--}1)$$

where Y is GNP, C is consumption, I is investment, and G is government spending. We have left out net exports for now because we are focusing on an economy that does not trade with the rest of the world. GNP, consumption, investment, and government spending in this identity are all measured in real terms as discussed in Chapter 2.

We also saw in Chapter 2 that after subtracting depreciation, indirect taxes, and certain other items from GNP we get income. This relationship between GNP and income is important for the theory of aggregate demand because spending is heavily influenced by disposable income. In order to keep the analysis as simple as possible, we consider an economy in which income and GNP are the same; this implies that there is no depreciation or indirect taxation. Then the variable Y on the left-hand side of Equation 4–1 is income as well as GNP. The identity says that income equals the sum of consumption, investment, and government spending. For this reason it is called the **income identity.**

Although Equation 4–1 looks very simple, it is a key part of the theory. It represents two important ideas. First, total aggregate spending determines GNP—for reasons discussed in the previous section. Second, GNP is equal to income. Because GNP is equal to income we will frequently use the words interchangeably in our discussions. To avoid confusion, keep in mind that GNP, or simply *output,* and *income* always take on the same value and are always represented by the same symbol Y.

We now consider the components of aggregate demand. We start with consumption.

THE CONSUMPTION FUNCTION

How do consumers make their spending decisions? The **consumption function** is a description of the total consumption demand of all families in the economy. It states that consumption depends on **disposable income.** Disposable income, as we saw in Chapter 2, is income less taxes. The consumption function is based on the simple idea that the larger a family's disposable income, the larger that family's consumption will be. Thus, total consumption for all families in the economy will be larger if disposable income in the economy is larger.

The consumption function should be viewed as a simple approximation of actual consumption demand. Clearly consumption depends on other things besides current income: wealth, expected future income, and the price of goods today compared to tomorrow. We will discuss these and other factors that affect consumption in Chapter 8. The more elementary consumption function used in this chapter was first introduced to the study of macroeconomics by Keynes. Despite its simplicity, it has proved remarkably versatile as a macroeconomic tool.

The consumption function can be written algebraically as

$$C = a + bY_d. \qquad \text{The Consumption Function} \qquad (4\text{--}2)$$

Specifically, this algebraic formula says that consumption C is equal to some constant a plus another constant b times disposable income Y_d. Both constants $(a$ and $b)$ are positive. The constant a describes an element of consumption that is independent of disposable income. Less formally, Equation 4–2 simply says that consumption depends positively on disposable income.

When studying algebraic relationships like the consumption function in macroeconomics, it is very important to distinguish between the constants and the variables. Sometimes the constants are called **coefficients.** In this consumption function the variables are C and Y_d. The constants, or coefficients, are a and b. Variables move around; constants stay fixed. To highlight this important distinction we use lowercase letters for constants and uppercase letters for variables. This convention is used throughout this book.

Example. If the coefficient $a = 80$ and the coefficient $b = .9$, then the consumption function looks like this:

$$C = 80 + .9Y_d.$$

If disposable income is \$3,000 billion, then consumption will be 80 + .9 × 3,000, or \$2,780 billion. If disposable income rises to \$4,000 billion,

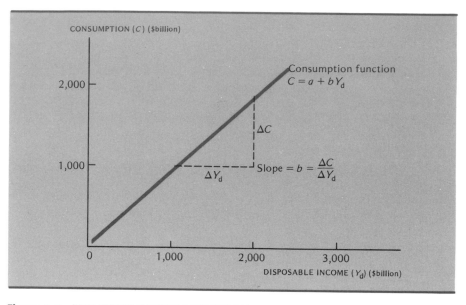

Figure 4-1. THE CONSUMPTION FUNCTION.
Consumption depends on income. The upward-sloping line shows that higher levels of disposable income correspond to higher levels of consumption. The slope of the line tells us how much consumption changes when disposable income changes. The slope of the line equals the marginal propensity to consume.

then consumption will rise to $80 + .9 \times 4,000$, or \$3,680 billion. If disposable income increases by \$1,000 billion, consumption changes by \$900 billion. Note how the variables, consumption and disposable income, change in this calculation but the coefficients stay fixed.

The coefficient b is called the **marginal propensity to consume.** It measures how much of an *additional* dollar of disposable income is spent on consumption. For the numerical values stated in the last paragraph, 90 percent of each additional dollar of income is spent on consumption.

We can also represent the consumption function graphically, as in Figure 4-1. The vertical axis measures consumption. The horizontal axis measures disposable income. The consumption function is shown as a straight, upward-sloping line. It indicates that as disposable income increases so does consumption.

The Consumption Function

1. Disposable income is the amount of income that people have available to spend after taxes.

2. The consumption function says that there is a predictable relationship between disposable income and consumption. The higher disposable income, the higher consumption.

3. The marginal propensity to consume is the fraction of an increase in disposable income that is consumed.

We can also write the consumption function in terms of income rather than disposable income. Disposable income is obtained by subtracting income taxes from income. If the tax *rate* is given by the constant t, then total tax payments are tY. Disposable income Y_d equals income Y minus taxes tY. Thus, we can write disposable income as $Y_d = (1 - t)Y$. For example, if the tax rate t is .3 and income Y is \$4,000 billion, then taxes are \$1,200 billion and disposable income is \$2,800 billion. By replacing disposable income Y_d with $(1 - t)Y$, the consumption function can be written

$$C = a + b(1 - t)Y. \qquad (4\text{–}3)$$

This says that consumption depends positively on income. For example, if the marginal propensity to consume b is .9 and the tax rate t is .3, then $b(1 - t) = .63$. An increase in income of \$100 billion will increase consumption by \$63 billion. This alternative way to write the consumption function is useful because it has the same income variable Y that appears in the income identity.

Graphs, Slopes, and Intercepts versus Algebra and Coefficients

Figure 4–1 and Equation 4–2 express exactly the same idea—that consumption depends positively on disposable income—in two different ways: graphically and algebraically. A third way is *verbal* presentation and analysis, which, although sometimes less precise, is necessary if you want to explain your economic ideas to those without economic training.

In general a graph is a diagram with a line or lines showing the relationship between two variables. The lines can be straight, as with the consumption line, or they can be bending, as with the aggregate demand curve studied in the next chapter (Figure 5–10). Relationships that are shown by straight lines are called *linear* relationships to distinguish them from bending lines. Sometimes lines are called **schedules,** a term that derives from the presentation of the relationship numerically as two columns of numbers that look like a train schedule. Graphs provide a more intuitive understanding, and, because visual images are sometimes easier to recall, graphs are good memory aids.

Algebra frequently provides more accurate and direct answers, and is needed in more complex problems. Frequently only a rough sketch is needed for a graphical analysis, but it is important to know that there is a precise connection between a graphical and an algebraic representation of an economic relationship. The variable on the vertical axis of a graph is usually the one on the left-hand side of the equal sign in the algebraic expression. For the consumption function, the variable on the left-hand side is consumption. The variable on the horizontal axis is usually the one on the right-hand side of the equal sign in the algebraic expression. For the consumption function, the variable on the right-hand side is disposable income. The place where the vertical axis and horizontal axis cross sometimes represents the zero value for both variables, but this is not necessary. It is important to look carefully at the scale on a diagram. For diagrams that are simply rough illustrations, no numerical scale will appear.

The place where the consumption line crosses the vertical axis in Figure 4–1 is called the **intercept.** It equals the coefficient a in the algebraic expression. It gives the value of consumption when disposable income is zero. More generally, the intercept of any line is the place where the line crosses the vertical axis.

The steepness of the consumption line is measured by its **slope.** The slope tells us how much consumption increases when income increases by one unit. The slope of the line is the coefficient b in the algebraic expression. Thus, if disposable income increases by an amount ΔY_d, then consumption increases by an amount ΔC given by b times ΔY_d. On the graph we move to the right by ΔY_d and up by b times ΔY_d. In general, a perfectly flat horizontal line has a slope of zero, and a perfectly vertical line has a slope of infinity. If the slope is positive then we say that the line slopes *upward* as we move from left to right; if the slope is negative then the line slopes *downward* as we move from left to right. The slope of the consumption function is positive (b is greater than zero), and clearly the consumption line slopes upward.

4.3 The Point of Balance of Income and Spending

So far we have discussed the determinants of only one of the components of spending—consumption—but we already have the ingredients of an elementary theory of income or GNP determination. Before considering the determinants of the other components of spending—investment I, and government G—we illustrate how this theory works. To do this, values for investment and government spending must be taken from *outside* the model. Variables determined outside a model are called **exogenous variables.** Of the four variables that we discussed so far (income Y, consumption C, investment I, and government spending G), this leaves two, consumption C and income Y, to be determined *inside* the model. Variables that are determined inside a model are called **endogenous variables.**

This basic idea that the endogenous variables must simultaneously satisfy a number of relationships is central to macroeconomic analysis. In the chapters that follow we will elaborate on this simple theory by adding more endogenous variables and more relationships that they must satisfy.

The elementary model consists of two basic relationships: the income identity, summarized algebraically in Equation 4–1, and the consumption function, summarized algebraically in Equation 4–3. These two relationships can be used to determine values for the two endogenous variables of the model: consumption C and income Y. *The values for C and Y are determined by requiring that both the consumption function and the income identity are satisfied simultaneously.*

Once we determine income and consumption in this way, we will have also determined GNP, of course, because income equals GNP. We illustrate the determination of income and consumption first using graphs and then using algebra.

GRAPHICAL ANALYSIS OF SPENDING BALANCE

In Figure 4–2 spending is measured on the vertical axis and income on the horizontal axis. Two intersecting straight lines are shown, a **spending line** and a **45-degree line.**

The spending line (the flatter of the two) shows how total spending depends on income. Total spending is the sum of consumption, investment, and government spending. In this model only consumption depends on income, through the consumption function. Investment and government spending are exogenous. The spending line is obtained by adding the consumption function in Equation 4–3 to investment and government spending. The equation corresponding to the spending line is

$$\text{Spending} = \underbrace{a + b(1 - t)Y}_{\substack{\text{Consumption from} \\ \text{Equation 4–3}}} + \underbrace{I}_{\substack{\text{Exogenous} \\ \text{investment}}} + \underbrace{G}_{\substack{\text{Exogenous} \\ \text{government spending}}}.$$

The spending line thus incorporates the consumption function.

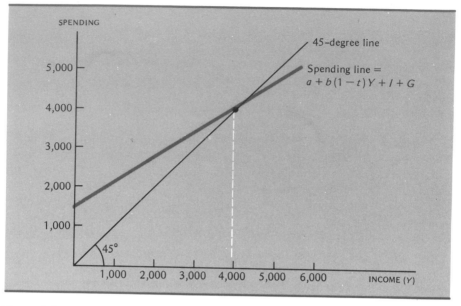

Figure 4-2.   SPENDING BALANCE.
The intersection of the two lines shows where consumption and income satisfy both the consumption function and the income identity. The point of intersection is the solution to the model consisting of Equations 4-1 and 4-3.

The 45-degree line is drawn halfway between the vertical spending axis and the horizontal income axis. For any point on the 45-degree line, income equals spending. This line thus represents the income identity. The line makes a 45-degree angle with the horizontal axis; hence its name. Sometimes Figure 4-2 is called a "Keynesian 45-degree" diagram, or a "Keynesian cross" diagram, because of its early use to illustrate this simple model with a Keynesian consumption function.

The point of intersection of the spending line and the 45-degree line is the point where consumption and income satisfy both relationships of the model. On the 45-degree line, the income identity is satisfied. On the spending line, the consumption function is satisfied. The intersection of the two lines thus gives the value of income that we are looking for. At this point total spending in the economy equals total income, and consumption spending satisfies the consumption function. Income and spending are in balance.

The 45-degree line is steeper than the spending line. The 45-degree line has a slope of 1. The consumption function has a slope $b(1 - t)$, which is less than 1. For example, if $b = .9$ and $t = .3$, then $b(1 - t) = .63$. Because the lines have different slopes, they will always intersect.[1]

---

[1] See the box on pp. 75-76 for a review of the concept of slope.

Spending Balance

1. The simple model of income determination consists of two relationships, the consumption function and the income identity. The model determines two endogenous variables: consumption and income. Two exogenous variables, investment and government spending, are determined outside the model.

2. Spending balance occurs when consumers are choosing their consumption levels, C, on the basis of a level of income that is the same as the level $Y = C + I + G$.

3. In terms of the equations, spending balance occurs at levels of consumption C and income Y that obey both the consumption function and the income identity.

ALGEBRAIC SOLUTION

The levels of consumption and income can also be found algebraically. Substitute the consumption equation, 4–3, into Equation 4–1. The result is

$$Y = \underbrace{a + b(1 - t)Y}_{C} + I + G. \tag{4–4}$$

The bracket below Equation 4–4 shows where C in the income identity has been replaced by the consumption function. Equation 4–4 has one endogenous variable: Y. Recall that I and G are exogenous variables. The variable Y appears on both sides of equation 4–4. To solve the equation for Y we gather together both terms involving Y on the left-hand side of the equation. Doing so we see that the value of Y that solves Equation 4–4 is given by

$$Y = \frac{a + I + G}{1 - b(1 - t)}. \tag{4–5}$$

This is the solution of the model and corresponds exactly to the value of Y, which is at the point of intersection in Figure 4–2. The solution value for consumption can then be obtained by plugging this value into the consumption function (4–3). That is,

$$C = a + b(1 - t)Y, \tag{4–6}$$

where Y comes from Equation 4–5.

Example. Suppose that investment equals $650 billion, and government spending equals $750 billion. Suppose, as in the previous examples, that the marginal propensity to consume, *b*, equals .9, the constant *a* equals 80, and the tax rate, *t*, equals .3. Then, according to the formula in Equation 4–5, income equals

$$\frac{80 + 650 + 750}{1 - .9(1 - .3)} = \frac{1,480}{.37},$$

or $4,000 billion. GNP is also equal to $4,000 billion. Using the consumption function (Equation 4–6) we get that consumption equals

$$80 + .9(1 - .3)(4,000),$$

or $2,600 billion.

Does a Tax Cut Pay for Itself?

When the government cuts the tax rate, it stimulates the economy. At the same time, the stimulus increases the government's tax revenue, because the amount of income being taxed increases. A tax cut pays for itself, to some extent. When the Reagan administration sponsored a large tax cut in 1981, this issue got a lot of attention.

The effect of a tax cut is to increase the fraction of GNP that flows to families as disposable income. In 1981, that fraction was 2128/3153, or 69.7 percent. By 1983, the fraction had risen to 71.3 percent. The tax rate, *t*, fell by 1.6 percentage points.

Equation 4–5 is the easiest way to figure out how a cut in the tax rate raises GNP. The actual values of investment, *I*, and government purchases, *G*, for 1981 were 546 and 630 billion 1982 dollars. We will assume that the intercept in the consumption function, *a*, is 80, and the marginal propensity to consume, *b*, is 0.9. Then the base level for real GNP in 1981, according to Equation 4–5, should have been 3370 billion 1982 dollars. Had the new tax rate gone into effect in 1981, real GNP would have been 3505 billion, again according to Equation 4–5, with the lower tax rate. Real GNP would have increased by 184 billion on account of the tax cut, had the cut gone into full effect in 1981.

Government revenue without the tax cut would been 30.3% × 3370 = 1021 billion 1982 dollars. Revenue with the lower tax rate but higher level of GNP would be 28.7% × 3505 = 1006 billion. The tax cut would lower revenue by 15 billion. That is, the higher level of GNP would not be enough to offset the lower tax rate.

The tax rate reduction does pay for a good deal of itself, however. Suppose someone had tried to compute the lost revenue without taking account of the stimulus of GNP. It might be calculated as the cut in the tax rate, 1.6 percent, times the level of GNP before the tax cut, 3370 billion, or 54 billion. But counting the favorable effect of the resulting economic expansion means that revenue only fell by 15 billion. The difference of 39 billion is the amount of the possible revenue loss that was paid back by the expansion, according to these calculations.

In later chapters, we will give some reasons why expansion resulting from a tax cut might not be as vigorous as the one considered here. In particular, we will stress the importance of the response of monetary policy. Still, it will remain true that a tax cut pays for some part of itself.

HOW SPENDING BALANCE IS MAINTAINED

It is important to understand the logic of finding the values of consumption and income that satisfy both the consumption function and the income identity. When people consume more in stores, firms will produce more. As we discussed in the microeconomic example, the firms will then employ more workers, or have their existing workers spend more time on the job. Their added production increases the wage incomes of their existing and new workers and adds to the profits of the owners of the firms. This added income in turn stimulates more consumption. When spending is in balance, the income that consumers are receiving is the same as the income generated by their spending.

What happens if spending is not in balance? Suppose that consumers are spending too much relative to their incomes. The economy would then be in an untenable situation. Consumers would notice that they were spending too much and would contract their consumption. But then firms would produce less and workers' incomes would fall. The process of contraction would continue until consumption fell to a point of balance with income.

How do we know that contraction of income and consumption will ultimately reach a point of balance rather than continuing to a complete collapse of the economy? When families contract their consumption because their income falls, the contraction in consumption is less than the fall in income. Some of the fall in income results in reduced taxes, so that disposable income does not fall as much as national income. Moreover, the marginal propensity to consume is less than 1, so that the fall in disposable income results in a smaller reduction in consumption. The smaller reduction in consumption thus generates a smaller drop in income on the second round. So the process of consumption and income contraction converges to a new lower point of balance. A numerical example of this type of convergence is presented in Table 4–1, page 85.

We do not present a formal model of the detailed process by which the economy reaches spending balance. The reason is that the process seems to operate quickly—more quickly than the business cycle or price adjustment. Our model assumes that the economy has already reached spending balance over each period of observation. Balance is not achieved by magic. But it is a useful simplification to talk about the economy after it has gone through the process.[2]

THE MULTIPLIER

In order to show how the elementary model can be used to analyze the short-run fluctuations in the economy, we consider what happens to income when there is a change in one of the exogenous variables. Suppose, for example, that there is a *decrease* in investment *I*. The exact reasons for the decrease are not important at this time, but for concreteness you may think of a sudden decline in expected profitability which reduces firms' desire to invest. What are the implications of this decline in investment demand?

We first consider the situation graphically using the spending line and 45° line in Figure 4–2, reproduced in Figure 4–3. The new diagram shows the impact of a decline in exogenous investment. It *shifts* the spending line downward by the amount of the decline in investment. If investment falls by $1 billion then the spending line shifts down by $1 billion. To see this, note that the intercept of the spending line is $a + I + G$. Hence, the change in the intercept is the same as the change in investment; government spending is not changing and a is constant. Figure 4–3 shows that income is lower as a result of the downward shift in the spending line.

Note that the decline in income is larger than the shift in the spending line, because the slope of the spending line is greater than zero. The economy thus "multiplies" the decline in investment into an even larger decline in income and GNP. This mechanism is called the **multiplier**. The steeper the spending line, the larger the decline in income.

The effect of the decline in investment on income can be calculated algebraically. Looking back to Equation 4–5, if we change investment by an

---

[2] Some elementary texts describe the adjustment process by focusing on inventories: If output is greater than spending, inventories begin to rise and this leads firms to cut back on output. Output and spending are thus brought into equality. As we stated above, we prefer not to introduce inventories at this stage of the analysis. We feel that the description in the text is a close approximation to reality. Many types of businesses—medical services, education—do not hold inventories of finished products yet their production responds to changes in demand.

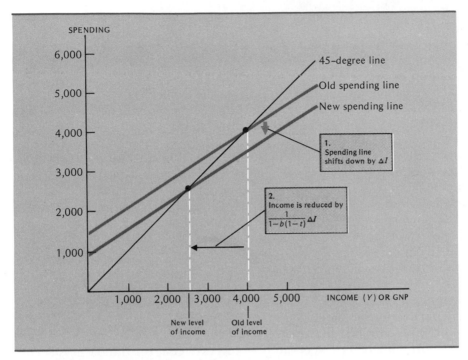

Figure 4–3. THE MULTIPLIER.
A decrease in investment demand shifts the spending line down. The new point of inter-section is at a lower level of GNP. The decline in GNP is larger than the decline in invest-ment, illustrating the multiplier mechanism. (Note that the drop in investment shown in the diagram is much larger than would be possible in the U.S. economy. The drop is exag-gerated here so that it can be easily seen in the diagram.)

amount ΔI then the change in income will be given by

$$\Delta Y = \underbrace{\frac{1}{1 - b(1 - t)}}_{\text{The Multiplier}} \Delta I. \qquad (4\text{–}7)$$

This is obtained by writing Equation 4–5 in terms of the changes in the vari-ables, and noting that neither government spending nor the constant coeffi-cient changes. All that is left is the change in investment.

The term $1/[1 - b(1 - t)]$, which multiplies the change in investment in Equation 4–7, is the multiplier. It is a general expression for the change in income associated with a change in investment. Since $b(1 - t)$ is less than 1, the value of expression 4–7 is greater than 1. Hence, the change in GNP is greater than the change in investment, just as we found using the graphical analysis. Note that the larger the marginal propensity to consume, b, the larger the multiplier.

Example. If the marginal propensity to consume, *b*, is equal to .9 and the tax rate, *t*, is .3, then the multiplier is equal to 1/.37 or about 2.7. A $10 billion decrease in investment results in a $27 billion decrease in income or GNP. Similarly, a $10 billion *increase* in investment results in a $27 billion increase in income or GNP.

This example can be used to illustrate the explicit actions of consumers and firms that result in the multiplier process. Suppose that a $10 billion decrease in investment occurs because Hertz, Avis, and several other large car rental companies in the United States suddenly get pessimistic about future profitability and stop buying new cars from General Motors, Ford, and Chrysler. Initially, the decreased purchases of new cars decrease income and GNP by $10 billion. But the reduced automobile production means that the incomes of workers in those companies will be reduced as they work fewer hours or are laid off. The income of shareholders of GM, Ford, and Chrysler will also be reduced, because of the decline in profits. In this example, the income of workers and shareholders falls by the full $10 billion. If the workers and shareholders have a marginal propensity to consume of .9 and pay taxes equal to 30 percent of their income, then they will reduce their consumption by $6.3 billion. Hence, GNP is cut by another $6.3 billion. The total reduction in GNP is now $16.3 billion.

But this is not the end. There is a third round. The workers and owners of the firms where the owners and employees of GM, Ford, and Chrysler cut their purchases by $6.3 billion will have a reduction in their income of this same amount. With the same taxes and marginal propensity to consume, they will thus cut their consumption by .63 times $6.3 billion, or by $3.969 billion. The total reduction in GNP is now $20.269 billion. The process will continue for a fourth and fifth round and so on, but by this time the reduction in income will be diversified across many different firms in the economy. Some of the reduced consumption demand will certainly get back to GM, Ford, and Chrysler.

If we keep summing the reduction in GNP at all these rounds we will eventually get a $27 billion reduction in GNP—the same as the direct computation using the multiplier. As we mentioned above, the total effect of these spending reductions on GNP would usually occur in a fairly short period, certainly less than a year. The different rounds of production are summarized in Table 4–1. Note how the eventual $27 billion reduction of GNP that we calculated directly through the multiplier is almost reached after just a few rounds. Note also how convenient it is to use the multiplier rather than go through all these tedious calculations.[3]

---

[3] The formulas for the calculations in the far right column of Table 4–1 add up to the for-

Table 4–1.   EXAMPLE OF THE MULTIPLIER PROCESS (billions of dollars)

| | Reduction in GNP | | |
	This Round	Sum to Date	Calculation
Round 1	10.000	10.000	Exogenous drop in investment
Round 2	6.300	16.300	$b(1-t)(10) = (.6300)(10)$
Round 3	3.969	20.269	$[b(1-t)]^2(10) = (.3969)(10)$
Round 4	2.500	22.769	$[b(1-t)]^3(10) = (.2500)(10)$
Round 5	1.575	24.344	$[b(1-t)]^4(10) = (.1575)(10)$
Round 6	.992	25.336	$[b(1-t)]^5(10) = (.0992)(10)$

Fluctuations in investment have always been associated with cyclical fluctuations in GNP. Such fluctuations in investment were emphasized by Keynes as an essential source of business cycle fluctuations. One of Keynes's main contributions was to show that relatively small fluctuations in investment could lead to large fluctuations in GNP. The mechanism underlying Keynes's theory was the multiplier; our example of a decline in investment leading to a large decline in GNP provides a simple illustration of Keynes's theory.

Changes in the other exogenous variable—government spending—also result in changes in income. The analysis is exactly the same as investment. An increase in government spending will raise income and GNP by a greater amount. The same multiplier process is at work. In fact, the formula for the government spending multiplier—the amount that income increases when government spending increases—is exactly the same as the investment multiplier.

The government spending multiplier can be derived in the same way that the investment multiplier was derived. To show this we have again reproduced the 45-degree line and spending line from Figure 4–2 in Figure 4–4. An increase in government spending will *raise* the spending line in Figure 4–4. This has an even larger effect on income, because of the multiplier process. Knowing the size of the government spending multiplier is important for assessing the impact of a change in government policy on the economy.

mula for the multiplier: that is,

$$\frac{1}{1 - b(1-t)} = 1 + b(1-t) + [b(1-t)]^2 + [b(1-t)]^3 + \dots$$

This result can be shown using the formula for a geometric series. A formal algebraic model of the adjustment process could come from putting *past* income rather than current income in the consumption function. This leads to a dynamic model—called the dynamic multiplier—that describes how consumption adjusts over time after a sudden change in investment.

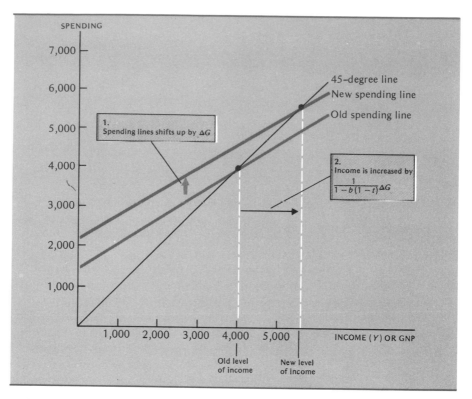

Figure 4–4. THE GOVERNMENT SPENDING MULTIPLIER.
An increase in government spending shifts the spending line up. Income or GNP expands
by the multiplier times the increase in government spending.

The Multiplier

1. When investment rises, GNP rises; investment is part of total GNP.

2. As GNP rises, disposable income also rises, so consumption rises.

3. The increase in GNP is larger than the increase in investment, because of the increase in consumption. The multiplier measures the amount of GNP stimulated by an increase in investment.

4. The formula for the multiplier is $\dfrac{1}{1 - b(1 - t)}$.

5. The government spending multiplier is exactly the same as the investment multiplier. When government spending increases, GNP increases by a larger amount.

4.4   Spending Balance with Foreign Trade

So far in this chapter we have assumed that the United States is a *closed* economy that does not trade with the rest of the world. We have ignored the influence of foreign trade and the value of the dollar on the macroeconomy. It is time to bring these crucial variables into the model—to consider the subject of **open-economy macroeconomics.**

EXPORTS AND IMPORTS

As we saw in Chapter 2, foreign trade is divided into exports, sales of goods and services to the rest of the world, and imports, purchases of goods and services from the rest of the world. **Net exports** are simply exports less imports. When exports are greater than imports, there is a **trade surplus;** conversely, when exports are less than imports, there is a **trade deficit.**

The first step in incorporating foreign trade into our macroeconomic theory is to add exports to, and subtract imports from, the income identity. Since exports minus imports is defined as net exports, this is equivalent to simply adding net exports to the identity. The income identity for an open economy then becomes

$$\underbrace{Y = C + I + G}_{\substack{\text{Income identity} \\ \text{for closed economy}}} + \underbrace{X}_{\substack{\text{Net exports} = \\ \text{Exports} - \text{Imports}}}. \qquad (4\text{--}8)$$

Recall that this income identity tells us two things: (1) Income and GNP are the same thing, and (2) aggregate demand—as measured by total spending—determines GNP. In thinking about how imports and exports affect aggregate demand for goods produced in the United States, keep in mind that consumption C, investment I, and government spending G by Americans all include some purchases of goods and services abroad. In order to get a measure of how much of American demand is for U.S.-produced goods, we need to subtract imports. For example, if Americans buy 1 million more cars, then consumption rises by 1 million cars. But if all these cars are imported from abroad then imports increase by 1 million cars and aggregate demand for U.S. goods (Y) does not change. The reason we add exports to the identity is straightforward: When foreigners increase their purchases of U.S.-produced goods, aggregate demand increases.

We will develop a relation between net exports and the level of U.S. income. The relation is negative. There is no reason to think that U.S. exports are much affected by U.S. income; they are affected instead by incomes in the countries purchasing the imports. But imports are affected by U.S. income. When U.S. income rises, consumers increase their spending on imported as well as domestic goods. Part of investment is also imported; when the total rises, the imported part rises.

We can summarize the relation between income and net exports in a **net export function:**

$$X = g - mY. \tag{4-9}$$

Here g is a constant and m is a coefficient. For each dollar that GNP rises, imports rise by m dollars. Exports remain unchanged, so net exports fall by the same m dollars.

Compare the net export function with the consumption function, which we discussed earlier in this chapter. Net exports, like consumption, depend on income. But net exports *decline* by m dollars for each dollar increase in income, whereas consumption *rises* by b dollars for each dollar increase in income (b is the marginal propensity to consume). The reason that net exports decline with income is that imports rise by m dollars for each dollar increase in income. For this reason the coefficient m is sometimes called the **marginal propensity to import.** The dependence of net exports on income means that we need to take account of the response of net exports to income when we calculate the effects of monetary and fiscal policy, much as we took account of the response of consumption earlier in this chapter.

Now we can proceed exactly as we did before, developing an equation for spending balance by putting the net export function and the consumption function into the income identity. We did that before to get Equation 4–4, which did not have net exports. The corresponding equation is

$$Y = a + b(1 - t)Y + I + G + g - mY. \tag{4-10}$$

Again, we can solve for the value of Y at the point of spending balance. Previously, we got Equation 4–5. Now we get

$$Y = \frac{a + I + G + g}{1 - b(1 - t) + m}. \tag{4-11}$$

Note how the impact of a change in government spending on output is

$$\frac{1}{1 - b(1 - t) + m}.$$

This is the **open-economy multiplier.** Note that the multiplier is smaller when the marginal propensity to import is larger. By setting m equal to zero the multiplier is the same as the multiplier for a closed economy. For example, if the marginal propensity to consume b is .9, the tax rate t is .3, and the marginal propensity to import m is .1, then the multiplier is $1/.47 = 2.1$, compared with a multiplier of $1/.37 = 2.7$ for the closed economy.

The Decline of the Multiplier

At your first exposure to the multiplier, you may be very impressed. If the marginal propensity to spend, b, is 0.9 and there are no taxes, then the multiplier is 10! But then when you consider the role of taxes in draining off income, you get the multiplier in Equation 4–7, which we said might be about 2.7. Then when we considered the fact that some of the purchasing power stimulated by growth in demand would go into imports rather than domestic spending, the multiplier dropped some more, to perhaps 2.1.

Other factors, which we will study in later chapters, will further reduce the multiplier. In the next chapter, we will consider the fact that higher demand raises interest rates, and these in turn discourage investment and net exports. Then the multiplier in our standard example will be only 1.1.

The analysis of the multiplier we present in this book is close to the New Keynesian school. Some of the other schools of thought we mentioned in Chapter 1 are skeptical about the multiplier. Some monetarists think that the multiplier is virtually zero. The new classical and real business cycle schools assert that the multiplier is low; moreover, to the extent that they believe that government spending stimulates output, it is through a different mechanism than the one we developed in this chapter. Briefly, in the real business cycle model, higher government spending raises the interest rate, and a higher interest rate stimulates more work effort.

At this point, we can begin to analyze how policy or other economic forces affect the trade deficit. Recall from Chapter 2 that the trade deficit, as measured in the national income accounts, is just the negative of net exports. Anything that lowers net exports will raise the deficit. Looking at the net export function, Equation 4–9, we can see that net exports, in turn, respond negatively to the level of GNP. Combining the two, we can say that forces that raise GNP will also raise the trade deficit. In particular, an increase in government spending, G, will raise GNP according to the multiplier derived in Equation 4–11. Thus, increases in G raise the trade deficit. Since increases in G also raise the fiscal deficit, we can see that the two deficits are related—when the government takes an action that raises its own deficit, it causes the trade deficit to rise as well.

In Chapter 2, we noted that the trade deficit is also the total amount that Americans are borrowing from overseas. An increase in the trade deficit means an increase in borrowing. Thus, we can express the relation between fiscal and trade deficits in the following way: When some force such as higher government spending raises government borrowing, part of the borrowing is done overseas. Instead of obtaining all of the resources to be devoted to government spending from the domestic economy, some of them come from foreign economies.

In the rest of the book, the models we develop will all take account of trade and the open economy.

Spending Balance in an Open Economy

1. Net exports appear in the income identity for an open economy.

2. The net export function describes the negative relation between income and net exports. It arises because higher U.S. income causes higher U.S. imports from other countries.

3. The multiplier in an open economy is smaller than in a closed economy.

4. Events that raise GNP, such as higher government spending, cause net exports to fall and the trade deficit to rise. Part of an increase in the fiscal deficit is financed overseas through a higher trade deficit.

Review and Practice

MAJOR POINTS

1. It is reasonable to set up a model for the short run in which firms respond to an increase in demand by producing more output rather than by raising prices.

2. Spending balance occurs when the public is making its spending plans on the basis of a level of income that is consistent with the GNP that is the sum of their spending.

3. The consumption function expresses the positive relation between income and consumption.

4. Spending balance occurs when consumption plus investment plus government purchases add up to the level of GNP upon which the consumers made their consumption plan.

5. The investment multiplier expresses the relation between investment and GNP. When investment rises by $1 billion, GNP rises by more than $1 billion because consumption rises as GNP rises.

6. Spending balance for an open economy occurs when the sum of all spending, including net exports, equals GNP.

7. The multiplier for an open economy is less than the multiplier for a closed economy.

8. An increase in government spending increases both the fiscal deficit and the trade deficit.

KEY TERMS AND CONCEPTS

Spending balance

Aggregate demand

Income identity

Consumption function

Disposable income

Marginal propensity to consume

Exogenous variable

Endogenous variable

Multiplier

Investment multiplier

Government spending multiplier

Marginal propensity to import

Net exports

Net export function

Trade deficit

QUESTIONS FOR DISCUSSION AND REVIEW

1. How do firms typically respond to an increase in demand in the short run?

2. What happens to consumption if income rises? If taxes are cut?

3. What is true at the point of spending balance? What happens if the economy is not at a point of spending balance?

4. What happens to GNP if consumers change their behavior and the coefficient a in the consumption function increases?

5. Why does an increase in investment or government purchases bring about a large increase in GNP?

6. Explain why the open-economy multiplier is smaller than the closed-economy multiplier.

7. How does an increase in government spending affect the trade deficit?

PROBLEMS

Numerical
1. Suppose that the model of the economy is given by

$$Y = C + I + G + X$$
$$C = a + bY_d$$
$$Y_d = (1 - t)Y$$
$$X = g - mY$$

where $I = \$650$ billion, $G = \$750$ billion, and the constants take the following values: $a = 80$, $b = .9$, $t = .3$, $g = 400$, $m = .1$.
   a. Show that the value of GNP at the point of spending balance is $4000 billion. Note that this is the same value found for the closed economy in the example on page 80. Compared to that model, is spending higher or lower? Is the multiplier higher or lower?
   b. What proportion of investment is private saving? Government saving? Saving by the rest of the world?
   c. Now suppose that I increases by $100 billion. By what proportion of the increase in investment do each of the three categories of saving increase?

Analytical

1. Imagine that you operate an economic forecasting firm. Your stock in trade is that you know the true model of the U.S. economy. It is given by

$$Y = C + I + G + X$$
$$C = a + bY_d$$
$$Y_d = (1 - t)Y$$
$$X = g - mY$$

   where *I* and *G* are exogenous, and it is assumed that you have numerical values for all of the constants in the model.
   a. Of the four spending components, which must you forecast before arriving at a forecast for the U.S. GNP? Explain.
   b. Now suppose that you are trying to forecast GNP for a centrally planned economy in which the production schedule for all goods are determined a year in advance. Would forecasting *C*, *I*, *G*, and *X* be a very good way of forecasting GNP?

2. For the model given in Problem 1, explain why private saving, government saving, and saving by the rest of the world are all endogenous variables.

3. Suppose the economy is described by the following simple model:

$$Y = C + G$$
$$C = a + bY_d$$
$$Y_d = (1 - t)Y$$

   a. Give an expression that relates private saving, S_p, to disposable income. This is called the saving function.
   b. What must the relationship be between private saving and the government budget deficit? (Hint: Refer back to the discussion in Chapter 2 concerning the relationship between saving and investment.)
   c. Solve for the values of S_p and the budget deficit; that is, derive an expression for each that is a function only of the exogenous variable *G*, and the constants in the model. Are your expressions consistent with your answer to Part b?

4. Balanced budget multiplier: Consider the following simple model with investment and government spending exogenous.

$$Y = C + I + G$$
$$C = a + bY_d$$

   Disposable income Y_d is given by $Y - T$, where *T* is total taxes. Suppose that taxes are not directly related to income so that *T* can be increased or decreased independently of income.
   a. Derive the change in *Y* associated with an increase in taxes *T*. Show the results graphically and algebraically. What is the tax multiplier? That is, what is $\Delta Y/\Delta T$?
   b. Compare the tax multiplier with the government spending multiplier derived in the text. Aside from the difference in signs, which is larger? Why?
   c. Now increase government spending *G* and taxes *T* by the same amount. For this change the government budget deficit $G - T$ does not change. If the budget was balanced before it will still be balanced. What happens to income *Y* in this case? Perhaps surprisingly it increases. Calculate by how much. That is, using algebra calculate $\Delta Y/\Delta G$, setting $\Delta G = \Delta T$. The result is called the balanced budget multiplier.

5. For the model given in Problem 1, which of the following statements are true?
   a. An exogenous increase in net exports (i.e., an increase in g) lowers the trade deficit and the government budget deficit.
   b. An increase in investment lowers the government budget deficit but raises the trade deficit.
   c. An increase in government spending and taxes of the same amount leaves both the government budget deficit and the trade deficit unchanged.

6. Imagine an economy in which the government spent all of its tax revenues, but was prevented (by a balanced budget amendment) from spending any more; thus $G=tY$, where t is the tax rate.
   a. Explain why government spending is endogenous in the model.
   b. Is the multiplier larger or smaller than the case in which government spending is exogenous?
   c. When t increases, does Y increase, decrease, or stay the same?

5

Financial Markets and
Aggregate Demand

IN THIS CHAPTER we move from spending balance to demand analysis by considering the roles of financial markets, interest rates, and investment. We develop three crucial pieces of macroeconomic analysis —the IS curve, which summarizes ideas about spending balance, the LM curve, which describes equilibrium in the money market, and the aggregate demand curve.

5.1 Investment and the Interest Rate

In the aggregate demand system we developed in Chapter 4, there were two exogenous forces that potentially can affect aggregate demand—investment and government spending. In this section we present an extension of that aggregate demand model. The extension has two important features: First, **financial variables**—interest rates and the supply of money—are shown to play an important role in the determination of aggregate demand, and, second, investment depends on these financial variables. Investment is no longer determined outside the model. Investment now becomes an endogenous variable.

The addition of financial variables to the model means that we will be concerned with the effects of changes in the money supply and interest rates, as well as with government spending. In the United States the money supply is controlled by the **Federal Reserve System**—the country's central bank, created by Congress in 1913. Changes in the money supply are referred to as **monetary policy.** The money supply can have powerful effects on the economy and the chairman of the Federal Reserve is regularly voted the second most powerful person in the country, after the president. **Fiscal policy,** on the other hand, involves changes in government spending, taxes, and transfers. Fiscal policy is determined by the president and Congress. Hence, the extended model will permit us to examine important public policy questions concerning the president, Congress, and the Federal Reserve. Such questions involve the relative importance of monetary versus fiscal policy and the appropriate mix of these policies.

In the basic model, you may have noticed that aggregate demand was independent of the price level. We talked about the possibility of firms adjusting their individual prices, but the general or average level of prices had no direct effect on demand. As soon as we add financial variables, we will find that aggregate demand depends on the price level: As the price level increases, aggregate demand decreases. Aggregate demand, and hence real GNP will also change if there is a shock to the price level—such as when the price of oil jumped upward in 1973 and 1979 and collapsed in 1986. Such shocks can affect the overall price level significantly. Unless monetary or fiscal policy offsets the shock, there will be a recession or a boom. The issue of how policy should respond to price shocks is one of the most important macroeconomic problems facing policy makers today.

THE INVESTMENT DEMAND FUNCTION

When we change investment from an exogenous variable to an endogenous variable, we need to specify a behavioral relationship to explain how investment is determined within the model. The relationship we use to describe investment is a simple but fundamental one. It states that investment depends negatively on the interest rate. This means that the demand for investment goods—the new factories, offices, and equipment used by business firms, as well as the new houses built for residential use—is low when interest rates are high, and vice versa.

The major reason for this negative relationship is that business firms and consumers finance much of their investment purchases by borrowing. When borrowing costs are high because of high interest rates, firms and consumers will tend to make fewer investment purchases. High borrowing costs effectively make investment goods more costly. Note that even if borrowings are not the source of funds for investment—such as when the funds come from selling financial securities—the interest rate should matter. If interest rates are high, then not holding those securities will represent a larger loss of income on those securities than if interest rates were low.

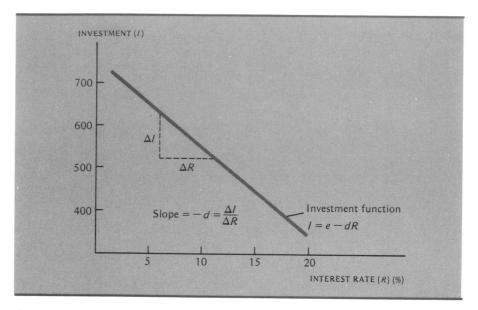

Figure 5–1.   THE INVESTMENT FUNCTION.
When the interest rate rises, the demand for investment falls. A higher interest rate means that the cost of funds required for investment is higher; only those investment projects that are particularly profitable will be undertaken.

Hence, people will be reluctant to sell those securities in order to purchase physical investment goods.

In algebraic terms the relationship for investment demand, called the **investment function,** can be represented as

$$I - e - dR. \tag{5–1}$$

As before, I is investment, R is the interest rate, and e and d are constant coefficients. Investment is measured in billions of dollars, and the interest rate is measured in percentage points. Equation 5–1 says that investment demand is equal to a constant e minus another constant d times the interest rate. The coefficient d measures how much investment falls when the interest rate increases by 1 percentage point. Note that we have kept the convention that lowercase letters represent constant coefficients, while uppercase letters represent variables. The investment function is shown graphically in Figure 5–1. It is a downward-sloping line.

Example. Suppose e equals 750 and d equals 2,000; then Equation 5–1 looks like

$$I = 750 - 2,000R.$$

When the interest rate is 5 percent, investment I is $750 - 2,000(.05)$, or $650 billion. An increase in the interest rate of 1 percent reduces investment by $20 billion. Note that we speak about the interest rate R as a percent, but use decimals in algebraic formulas: "The interest rate is 5 percent" means $R = .05$. This convention is used throughout the book.

THE MEANING AND INTERPRETATION OF *R*

Note that, in changing investment from an exogenous variable to an endogenous variable, we have introduced a new endogenous variable into the model: the interest rate R. There are, of course, many different interest rates in a modern economy: rates on *long*-term securities, rates on *short*-term securities, rates on *risky* securities, and rates on *safe* securities. When we use the term "*the* interest rate," we are therefore simplifying the financial structure of the economy. In thinking about this simplification—that is, in trying to relate R to something you can read about or look up in a newspaper—it is useful to imagine an average or representative interest rate that represents the behavior of all the different types of rates. For many purposes this abstraction is not too bad; interest rates on different types of securities—while not equal—tend to move in the same direction. That is, when interest rates on risk-free Treasury bills are abnormally high, so are interest rates on more risky corporate bonds. Of course, there are sometimes differences between short- and long-term interest rate behavior—known as term structure variations—which can be relevant for investment. These will be taken up in more detail in Chapter 12; for now, we will focus on the average representative interest rate R.

It is also important to distinguish between the **real interest rate** and the **nominal interest rate.** The nominal interest rate is simply the rate that you read about in the newspaper or that banks place in their windows to indicate what they will pay for different types of deposits. The real interest rate corrects the nominal rate for expected changes in the price level. Specifically, the real interest rate is the nominal interest rate minus the expected rate of inflation. For example, if your bank is paying 10 percent on deposits for a year, and you expect inflation to be 6 percent for the year, then the real rate of interest for you is 4 percent. The real rate of interest measures how much you will earn on your deposit after taking account of the fact that inflation will have increased the price of goods that you might purchase in a year. We usually mean the real interest rate when we use the symbol R in this book, but we do not generally add the adjective "real," unless the meaning is ambiguous, or we want to point out a particular reason to distinguish between the real and the nominal rates. Of course, for low rates of inflation the real rate and the nominal rate are very close.

The Investment Function

1. Investment demand is negatively related to the interest rate. When funds are more expensive, less investment takes place. The investment function describes this negative relationship.

2. The interest rate R that is in the investment function is an average of the many interest rates that we observe at banks and in the financial markets.

Portfolio Investment and Macro Investment

The difference between the macroeconomist's use of the term "investment" and its use in casual conversation may be a stumbling block. Macroeconomic investment, I, is limited to purchases of newly built houses, plant, equipment, and inventories. When a business or a family buys stocks, bonds, existing real estate, or other portfolio items, they also think of them as investments because these assets (should) provide a financial return. Such investments are not counted as macroeconomic investment, however, because they are just movements of existing assets from one person to another. They do not create any new productive facilities. When one person buys stock, somebody else sells that stock; one person's investment is another's disinvestment.

But portfolio opportunities still matter, because they always loom as an alternative to macroeconomic investment. A business can invest in plant, equipment, and inventories, and presumably it will enjoy a high return, or else why would it stay in that industry? But if its corporate treasurer recommended investing in a new plant predicted to provide a 5 percent return at a time when government securities were paying 6 percent, he would soon enjoy the status of ex-corporate treasurer.

What kind of competition is macroeconomic investment up against? In 1986, portfolio investments scored the following returns:

Stock market dividend rate	3.5%
6-month Treasury bills	6.0
Aaa corporate bonds	9.0
Baa corporation bonds	10.4
Tax-free municipal bonds	7.4

The returns to bonds generally grow higher as they get riskier, but in the case of tax-free municipals they can pay less and make their owners just as happy as corporate bond owners because no taxes are paid on the proceeds. Interestingly, the best investment historically has been the stock market, where capital gains have more than made up for the lower dividend rates.

If a business concludes that the likely return to a new plant is better than any of these other returns, taking into consideration taxes, capital gains, future inflation, and so on, then it will decide to build the plant. Hence the returns on alternatives, such as bonds, are an important determinant of the level of investment.

5.2 Net Exports and the Interest Rate

Another factor that we want to consider in building a complete model of aggregate demand is that net exports depend negatively on the interest rate. In Chapter 10, we will consider the reasons for this important relation in more detail. For now, we will look at the relation in the following way: When the U.S. interest rate is higher than interest rates in other countries, it becomes attractive for people in those countries to put their funds in *dollars*—that is, to lend funds to businesses in the United States and to the U.S. government. By the same token, it is less attractive for people in the United States to put their funds in other currencies—that is, to lend overseas, where returns are lower. This means that dollars become more attractive, and this drives up the price of dollars—that is, the exchange rate rises. But a higher exchange rate makes U.S. goods more expensive to foreigners and it also makes foreign goods less expensive to U.S. residents. Less expensive foreign goods will make U.S. imports rise. Similarly, more expensive U.S. goods will make U.S. exports fall. On both accounts *net exports—exports minus imports—fall when the U.S. interest rate rises* because the exchange rate rises.

How do we incorporate this negative relationship between net exports and the interest rate into our complete model of aggregate demand? We must add another term to the net export function of Equation 4–9 to incorporate the negative effect of the interest rate R on net exports:

$$X = g - mY - nR. \qquad (5-2)$$

The new coefficient, n, measures the decrease in net exports that occurs when the interest rate rises by one percentage point.

Example. Suppose g is 425, m is 0.1, and n is 500. Then the net export function is

$$X = 425 - .1Y - 500R.$$

> **The Net Export Function**
>
> 1. In addition to being negatively related to income, net exports are negatively related to the interest rate.
>
> 2. The negative relation to the interest rate occurs because higher U.S. interest rates raise the exchange rate. The higher exchange rate decreases exports and increases imports, thereby decreasing net exports.

5.3 The Money Market and the Interest Rate

Our next step is to explain how the interest rate is determined. The explanation relies on the theory of the demand for money.

THE DEMAND FOR MONEY

When we speak of **money** we have a rather special meaning in mind. Money is the currency issued by the Federal Reserve—for example, coin and dollar bills—together with the checking account balances held by the public in banks. Money is used to facilitate the purchase and sale of goods. When we buy goods we usually pay with currency, or with a check. Money does not include the much larger amounts of wealth held in mutual funds, bonds, corporate stock, and other forms, even though these forms of wealth are measured in dollars, because they are not usually used to pay for goods.

Three basic propositions about the demand for money are important for macroeconomics.

1. *People will want to hold less money when the interest rate is high and, conversely, will want to hold more money when the interest rate is low.*

This means that there is a negative relation between the demand for money and the interest rate R. People hold money for transactions purposes, to pay daily expenses and monthly bills. But they could obtain higher earnings by keeping their wealth in other forms, such as savings accounts or bonds. Currency pays no interest. And even though many checking deposits now pay interest, the rate is less than on other forms of wealth. Because of this, people tend to economize on the use of money for transactions purposes. A common way to do this is to go to the bank more often to withdraw money from a high-interest savings account to obtain currency, or simply to transfer funds to a lower-interest checking account. With more frequent trips to the bank, a smaller amount can be withdrawn each time from savings accounts. This means that, on average, a smaller amount of currency or checking balances will be held by the individual. For example, you could go to the bank every week, rather than every month, to obtain currency and thereby hold a smaller amount of currency on average.

How much economizing will occur will depend on the interest rate. The interest rate R represents how much a consumer or firm could earn by holding more in forms that pay full interest instead of in currency, which pays no interest, or checking deposits, which pay less than full interest. Clearly the more that can be earned by holding those other forms—the higher is R—the less money an individual will want to hold.

2. *People want to hold more money when income is higher and, conversely, less money when income is lower.*

The more a family receives as income, the more the family will normally be spending, and the more money the family will need for transactions purposes. When income increases, the transactions demand for money increases. More money will be needed to buy and sell goods.

This means that there is a positive relationship between income Y and the demand for money. As income in the economy increases, on average each family's income increases and the demand for money in the entire economy increases.

3. *People want to hold more money when the price level is higher and, conversely, less money when the price level is lower.*

If the price level rises people will need more dollars to carry out their transactions, even if their real income does not increase. At a higher price level, goods and services will be more expensive; more currency will be needed to pay for them and checks will be written for larger amounts.

This means that the demand for money is an increasing function of the price level. The positive relation between money demand and the price level is critical for macroeconomics. This is how the price level affects aggregate demand, as we indicate below.

To summarize these three basic ideas, the demand for money depends negatively on the interest rate R, positively on income Y, and positively on the price level P. An algebraic relationship that summarizes the effect of these three variables on the demand for money is presented in the following equation:

$$M = (kY - hR)P. \qquad (5\text{--}3)$$

Here M represents the amount of money demanded by firms and consumers. The other variables in Equation 5–3 have been defined already: P is the price level, R is the interest rate, and Y is income or GNP.[1] The lowercase

---

[1] Note that the appropriate interest rate for the money demand function is the nominal rate. Most alternatives to holding currency such as bonds pay a nominal interest rate. In order to keep our analysis simple we place the real interest rate, R, in the money demand function. If inflation is low this is a very good approximation.

symbols k and h are constant positive coefficients. The coefficient k measures how much money demand increases when income increases. The coefficient h measures how much money demand declines when the interest rate increases. Equation 5–3 is called the **money demand function.** It is a more complicated algebraic expression than the equation we used previously for consumption and investment demand. The money demand function shows that money demand depends on three variables (the interest rate R, income Y, and the price level P), whereas consumption demand and investment demand each depend on only one variable.

Example. If k equals .1625 and h equals 1,000, then Equation 5–3 looks like

$$M = (.1625Y - 1,000R)P.$$

If income Y is $4,000 billion, the interest rate is 5 percent ($R = .05$), and the price level P is 1, then the demand for money is equal to $600 billion. An increase in income of $10 billion will increase the demand for money by $1.625 billion. An increase in the interest rate of 1 percentage point will decrease the demand for money by $10 billion.

THE MONEY SUPPLY

The Federal Reserve System (or the "Fed" for short) determines the level of the **money supply.** In Chapter 7 we will study the interesting question of how the Fed goes about setting the money supply. For now, we will assume that the Fed has picked a certain level for the money supply.

We will also assume that the demand for money and the supply of money are equal. For this reason we do not introduce a new symbol to represent the money supply. The variable M means both money supply and money demand. Since these are always equal, this should cause little confusion. (Recall that the symbol Y also refers to two variables: income and GNP.)

How does the demand for money become equal to the supply of money? Suppose that the demand is greater than the supply. Since the supply of money is fixed by the Fed, the demand for money must fall if the two are to be equal. The demand for money can adjust down by an increase in the interest rate, a decline in the level of income, or a decline in the price level. For example, an increase in the interest rate will cause people to demand less money. In principle, all three variables could move, but in practice income and especially interest rates adjust more quickly, and do most of the job of bringing demand into equality with supply.

Money and the Interest Rate

1. Money is currency plus the balances in checking accounts.

2. The demand for money falls if the interest rate rises, if income falls, or if the price level falls.

3. The Federal Reserve determines the money supply.

4. The demand for money equals the supply of money. The interest rate and income move as necessary in any year so that money demand equals money supply.

5.4 The IS-LM Model

Our objective is to use the economic relationships introduced in the previous sections to determine GNP, investment, consumption, net exports, the interest rate, and the price level. These relationships represent the theory of how people behave. There are five economic relationships: the income identity, the consumption function, the investment demand function, the net export function, and the money demand function. The theory implies that all five relationships must hold at the same time.

The method of analysis proceeds as follows. We take as given the values for the variables determined outside our model in any year, for example, 1989. These are the exogenous variables: the money supply M and government spending G. They are determined by the Fed, the president, and Congress. We want to find values for income, consumption, investment, net exports, the interest rate, and the price level that are implied by the model and by the values of the money supply and government spending for that year. We also want to find out what happens if the money supply or government spending changes. Will interest rates and output rise or fall, and by how much? We proceed in two stages:

First, we put the price level on the back burner, and focus our efforts on finding GNP, the interest rate, consumption, investment, and net exports for the year. We can put the price level aside because it doesn't move very much in any one year. Recall that prices are sticky and adjust only gradually. It is very convenient for us to be able to look away from the price level and focus on the other variables; fortunately this is in tune with how the economy actually works.

Second, we find how much the price level is adjusted by firms, based on the demand for their products that we have calculated for the year.

Note that this method treats the price level a little differently from the other economic variables determined by the theory. Because the price level adjusts only after a period of time, its value this year is essentially predetermined by conditions in previous years. Since the price level is predetermined, we call it a **predetermined variable,** to distinguish it from the endogenous variables that are determined within the model during the year. The endogenous variables are GNP, consumption, investment, net exports, and the interest rate. The economic relationships and the key macroeconomic variables are summarized in the box below.

Key Macro Relationships (The Theory) and the Major Variables

Macro Variables

The *Endogenous* Variables: The *Exogenous* Variables:

Name	Symbol		Name	Symbol
Income	Y		Government purchases	G
Consumption	C		Money supply	M
Investment	I			
Net exports	X			
Interest rate	R			

The *Predetermined* Variable:

Name	Symbol
Price level	P

Five Relationships (How the Variables Interact with Each Other)

Algebra	Name	Numerical Example
$Y = C + I + G + X$ (4–8)	Income identity	
$C = a + b(1 - t)Y$ (4–3)	Consumption function	$C = 80 + .63Y$
$I = e - dR$ (5–1)	Investment function	$I = 750 - 2,000R$
$X = g - mY - nR$ (5–2)	Net export function	$X = 425 - .1Y - 500R$
$M = (kY - hR)P$ (5–3)	Money demand	$M = (.1625Y - 1,000R)P$

Suppose that the price level is given. For example, suppose that $P = 1$. Then the five macro relationships will determine values for the five remaining endogenous variables. The situation is analogous to that in Chapter 4 where we had to find values for two variables to satisfy two relationships. We first use graphs and then algebra.

Because graphs only allow for two variables, we need to reduce the five relationships to two relationships. A way to do this was originally proposed in 1937 by J. R. Hicks, the British economist who won the Nobel Prize in 1972. Hicks's graphical approach, called the IS-LM approach, is still used widely today because of its great intuitive appeal.[2]

THE IS CURVE

The **IS curve** is shown in Figure 5–2. *The IS curve shows all the combinations of the interest rate R and income Y that satisfy the income identity, the consumption function, the investment function, and the net export function.* In other words, it is the set of points for which spending balance occurs. The left-hand panel of Figure 5–2 shows how higher levels of the interest rate are associated with lower levels of GNP along the IS curve.

Slope. The first thing to remember about the IS curve is that it is downward sloping. Understanding the intuitive economic reason for this downward slope is very important. *The IS curve is downward sloping because a*

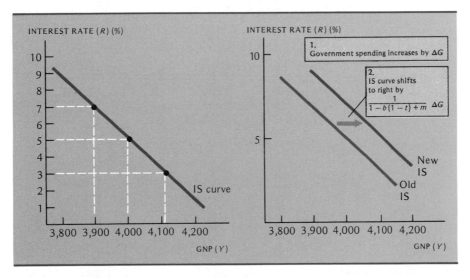

Figure 5–2.   THE IS CURVE.
The IS curve shows all the combinations of the interest rate *R* and income *Y* that satisfy the consumption, investment, and net exports functions, and the income identity. As shown in the left-hand panel, it is downward sloping; an increase in the interest rate reduces investment and net exports. Through the multiplier, GNP falls. The right-hand panel illustrates how the IS curve shifts to the right when government spending increases.

[2] See J. R. Hicks, "Mr. Keynes and the Classics: A Suggested Interpretation," *Econometrica*, Vol. 6, pp. 147–159, 1937. The IS–LM curve gets its name because, when all three relationships were satisfied, investment demand, "I," must equal income less consumption demand, or saving, "S." The "M" in the LM curve stands for the money supply and the "L" stands for liquidity preference, which is a synonym for money demand. (Money is more liquid —easier to exchange for goods and other items—than bonds or corporate stock.)

higher interest rate reduces investment and net exports, and thereby reduces GNP through the multiplier process. To find a specific point on the IS curve, choose an interest rate and calculate how much investment will result using the in-

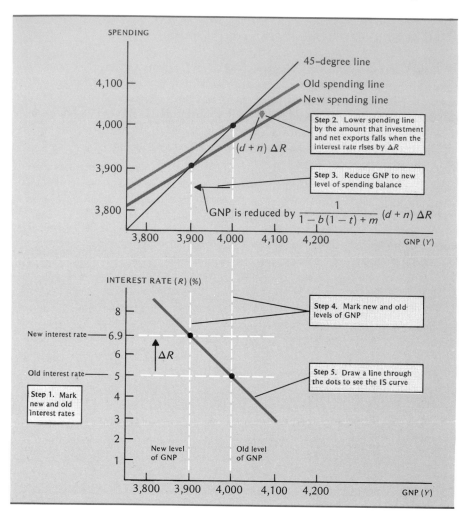

Figure 5–3.   GRAPHICAL DERIVATION OF THE IS CURVE.
The upper part of the diagram shows the 45-degree line and spending line. The lower part of the diagram is the graph where the IS curve is to be drawn. The lower diagram has the interest rate on the vertical axis, and GNP on the horizontal axis. Points on the graph are obtained as described in the instructions placed in boxes on the diagram. Start with an interest rate and find the position of the spending line for that interest rate. (Higher interest rates will lower the spending line because they reduce investment and net exports.) Then find the resulting level of GNP that satisfies the requirements of spending balance. Note how the slope of the IS curve will depend on the marginal propensity to consume *b*, the tax rate *t*, and the marginal propensity to import *m*, because these affect the multiplier. Note also that the slope depends on the sensitivity of investment and net exports to changes in the interest rates, controlled by the coefficients *d* and *n*.

vestment function. Subtract nR from the export function. The higher the rate of interest, the lower the level of investment and net exports. Pass this level of spending through the multiplier process to find out how much GNP will result. The more of both, the more GNP. The interest rate and this level of GNP are a point on the IS curve. A self-contained explicit graphical derivation of the IS curve is shown in Figure 5–3.

Shifts. The second thing to remember about the IS curve is that *an increase in government spending shifts the IS curve to the right.* An increase in government spending increases GNP through the multiplier; as GNP increases we move the IS curve to the right. Note that, conversely, a decrease in government spending pushes the IS curve to the left.

To find how much the IS curve shifts, pick an interest rate R and calculate a corresponding level of investment and net exports. Now increase government spending. Through the multiplier process, output will increase by the multiplier times the increase in government spending. Holding the interest rate constant, the IS curve shifts to the right along the horizontal GNP axis by the amount of the multiplier times the increase in government spending. This is shown in the right-hand panel of Figure 5–2.

THE LM CURVE

The **LM curve** is shown in Figure 5–4. *The LM curve shows all combinations of the interest rate* R *and income* Y *that satisfy the money demand relation-*

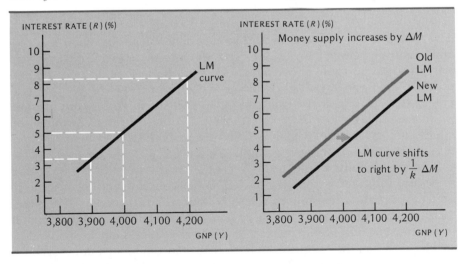

Figure 5–4.   THE LM CURVE.
The LM curve shows the values for the interest rate and income such that the supply of money is equal to the demand for money. As shown in the left-hand panel the LM curve is upward sloping. The right-hand panel shows how an increase in the money supply shifts the LM curve to the right.

ship for a fixed level of the money supply and for a predetermined value of the price level. The left-hand panel of Figure 5–4 shows that higher levels of the interest rate are associated with higher levels of GNP along the LM curve.

Slope. The first thing to remember about the LM curve is that it slopes upward. The reason for this is somewhat involved, but important to keep in mind: Imagine that the interest rate increases. What must happen to income if money demand is to remain equal to money supply? An increase in the interest rate R reduces the demand for money. But the money supply is fixed. Hence, income must adjust to bring money demand back up. A rise in income is what is required. A rise in income will increase the demand for money, and offset the decline in money demand brought about by the rise in the interest rate. In sum, the increase in the interest rate is associated with an increase in income. Thus the LM curve is upward sloping.

To understand better the derivation of the LM curve, it is helpful to introduce the concept of **real money.** Real money is defined as money M divided by the price level P. Because the term "real money" is used so much in macroeconomics we sometimes use the term **nominal money** when we mean just plain money M. Real money M/P is a convenient measure of money that corrects for changes in the price level. For example, if money increases by 10 percent and the price level increases by 10 percent, then real money does not change. The money demand function back in Equation 5–3 can be written in terms of real money if we simply divide both sides by the price level. That is,

$$M/P = kY - hR. \tag{5–4}$$

This says that the demand for *real* money depends positively on real GNP and negatively on the interest rate. The real money demand equation is an attractive way to think about money demand because it depends on two rather than three variables. Looking at Equation 5–4 we see that real money demand consists of two parts: One part, kY, increases with income, while the other part, $-hR$, decreases with the interest rate. Of course the same economic principles apply whether we write the money demand function in terms of real money or nominal money.

Looking carefully at Equation 5–4 it seems pretty clear why the LM curve slopes up. If the Fed is holding nominal money constant, and the price level isn't moving, then real money is also constant. If real money is constant, then an increase in the interest rate R, which reduces money demand by hR, must be offset by an increase in Y, which increases money demand by kY. Hence, when the interest rate R increases, income Y increases.

A self-contained graphical derivation of the LM curve, based on this line of reasoning, is shown in Figure 5–5. The left-hand panel of Figure 5–5 is a graph of the demand for real money as a function of the interest rate. Real money demand decreases with the interest rate. But note that an increase in

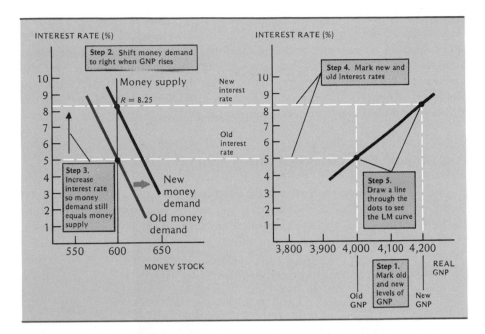

Figure 5–5.   GRAPHICAL DERIVATION OF THE LM CURVE.
The left-hand panel shows the demand for real money as a function of the interest rate. The demand schedule slopes downward because higher interest rates make the public conserve on money holdings. Money demand shifts to the right if real GNP rises. Higher GNP causes the public to hold more real money at a given interest rate. The LM curve is constructed in the right-hand panel. The instructions show how to get points on the curve. Start with a level of GNP and find the money demand suitable for that level. Then find the interest rate that equates money demand and money supply. The LM curve traces out the market-clearing interest rate for different levels of GNP.

GNP increases money demand and this shifts the money demand line to the right. If money demand is to stay equal to money supply, then the interest rate must increase, as shown in the diagram.

Shifts. The second thing to remember about the LM curve is that *an increase in the money supply shifts the LM curve to the right.* Conversely, a decrease in the money supply shifts the LM curve to the left. Looking again at Equation 5–4, we can get an economic understanding for this. An increase in the money supply increases the variable on the left-hand side, M/P. If money demand is to remain equal to money supply, then either output Y must rise or the interest rate R must fall. If we hold the interest on the LM diagram at a particular value, then output Y must increase, and the LM curve shifts to the right.

Changes in the price level also shift the LM curve. Again, look at the symbols in Equation 5–4 to keep track of what is going on. An increase in the price level reduces real balances. Hence, an increase in the price level does exactly the same thing to the LM curve as a decrease in the money supply. *An increase in the price level shifts the LM curve to the left.* The rationale: An increase in the price level means that less real money is available for transactions purposes. This means that either the interest rate must rise or real income must fall to reduce money demand. Either way the LM curve shifts to the left. Conversely, a decrease in the price level shifts the LM curve to the right, just like an increase in the money supply.

ALGEBRAIC DERIVATION OF THE IS AND LM CURVES

The algebraic statement that defines the IS curve is the expression of spending balance; that is, the GNP, Y, generated as total spending is equal to the level of income, Y, that consumers and importers assumed in making their spending decisions:

$$Y = a + e + g + [b(1 - t) - m]Y - (d + n)R + G. \qquad (5\text{--}5)$$

Note that the right-hand side is just the consumption function plus the investment function plus the net export function plus government spending. We want to express the IS curve as an equation giving the value of R that gives spending balance at a specified level of Y. We solve Equation 5–5 for R by moving the R term to the left-hand side and dividing by $d+n$:

$$R = \frac{a + e + g}{d + n} - \frac{1 - b(1 - t) + m}{d + n}Y + \frac{1}{d + n}\,G. \qquad \text{IS Curve} \qquad (5\text{--}6)$$

Government spending, G, increases the interest rate for a given level of income. Graphically, this looks like a shift of the IS curve to the right, a result that we saw in Figure 5–2. A higher value of G raises the IS curve or, equivalently, shifts the IS curve to the right.

The coefficient

$$\frac{1 - b(1 - t) + m}{d + n}$$

that multiplies Y in Equation 5–6 is the slope of the IS curve. Note that the slope of the IS curve depends on the sensitivity of investment to the interest rate, represented by the coefficient d. The algebraic formula shows that the slope of the IS curve is small—which means that the IS curve is fairly flat—if investment is very responsive to the interest rate. Then, small changes in the interest rate result in large changes in investment, and hence large fluctuations in GNP. Similarly, the IS curve will be flat if net exports are highly sensitive to the interest rate, that is, if the coefficient n is large. What matters is the sum of the two interest-rate coefficients, $d+n$. Note also that the

IS curve will be flat if the marginal propensity to consume b is large, if the tax rate t is small, or if the marginal propensity to import, m, is small. In these cases, the multiplier is large and changes in the interest rate have large effects on GNP.

An Example of an IS Curve. With the numerical values summarized in the box on page 104, the IS curve is

$$R = \frac{1255}{2500} - \frac{1 - .53}{2500} Y + \frac{1}{2500} G$$

or

$$R = .502 - .000188Y + .0004G. \qquad \substack{\text{Numerical Example} \\ \text{of IS Curve}} \qquad (5\text{--}7)$$

The slope of the IS curve is $-.000188$: Along the IS curve, when GNP rises by \$100 billion the interest rate falls by 1.88 percentage points. The IS curve that appears in Figure 5–2 is drawn accurately to scale for this numerical example. The IS curve on the left is drawn for government spending G equal to \$750 billion. The shift in the IS curve to the right in Figure 5–2 is due to an increase in government spending of \$40 billion.

The algebraic expression for the LM curve is obtained simply by moving R to the left-hand side of the money demand equation (5–4) and dividing by the coefficient h. That is,

$$R = \frac{k}{h}Y - \frac{1}{h}\frac{M}{P}. \qquad \text{LM Curve} \qquad (5\text{--}8)$$

Equation 5–8 says that an increase in real money balances M/P lowers the interest rate for a given level of income. This means that the LM curve shifts to the right, a result that corresponds to the graph in Figure 5–4. The slope of the LM curve is k/h. Note that the slope of the LM curve k/h is small—meaning that the LM curve is fairly flat—if the sensitivity of money demand to the interest rate is large, that is, if the coefficient h is large. Then, a small decline in the interest rate raises the demand for money by a large amount and requires a large offsetting decrease in income. The small change in the interest rate combined with the large change in income trace out a flat LM curve. Note also that the LM curve is flat if the sensitivity of money demand to income, k, is small.

An Example of an LM Curve. With the numerical values summarized in the box on page 104, the LM curve is

$$R = \frac{.1625}{1,000}Y - \frac{1}{1,000}\frac{M}{P}$$

or

$$R = .0001625Y - .001\frac{M}{P}.$$

Numerical Example
of LM Curve

(5–9)

This LM curve is drawn to scale in Figure 5–4. The shift of the LM curve in the right-hand side of Figure 5–4 corresponds to an increase in the money supply of $40 billion.

FINDING INCOME Y AND THE INTEREST RATE R

Finally we are ready to find the values of the interest rate and income that are predicted by the theory. We first proceed graphically. To satisfy all five relationships of the model, the values of R and Y must be on both the LM curve and the IS curve—that is, at the intersection of the LM curve and the IS curve. The IS curve takes care that the theory of consumption, investment, and net exports and the income identity are satisfied, while the LM curve takes care that the theory of money demand and money supply is satisfied. The values of the interest rate and income that we are looking for are thus at the intersection of the LM curve and the IS curve. The intersection is shown graphically in Figure 5–6.

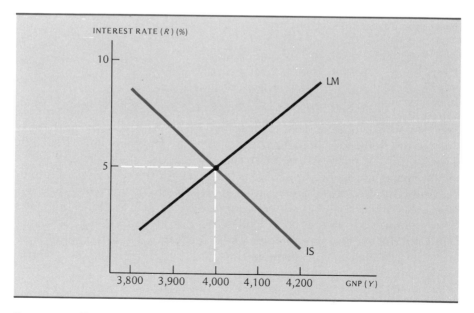

Figure 5–6.   THE INTERSECTION OF THE IS CURVE AND THE LM CURVE.
The values of the interest rate and income predicted by the macro model occur at the intersection of the IS curve and the LM curve. For these values, all five relationships of the model are satisfied. Along the IS curve consumption demand, investment demand, net export demand, and the income identity are satisfied. Along the LM curve money demand equals money supply.

Once we have determined the levels of income Y and the interest rate R we can determine consumption C, investment I, and net exports X. Consumption is obtained by putting the value of income into the consumption function, investment is obtained by putting the value of the interest rate into the investment function, and net exports are obtained by putting income and the interest rate into the net export function.

Recall that all these predictions of the model are made with the price level fixed, on the "back burner." This is fine for the short run—for about a year or so—but for no longer. We look at what happens to the price level in the next chapter.

5.5 Policy in the IS-LM Model

MONETARY POLICY

We are now ready to make the IS-LM approach go to work. Consider monetary policy. What happens if the Fed increases the money supply? We now know that an increase in the money supply shifts the LM curve to the right. The effect of such a change on the interest rate and income is shown in Figure 5–7. As the left-hand panel indicates, the theory predicts that

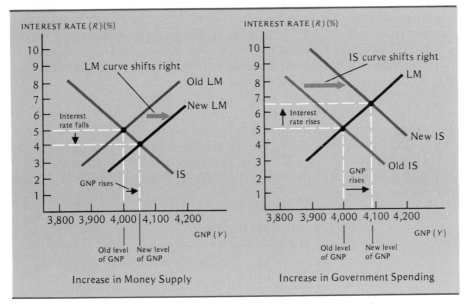

Figure 5–7. EFFECTS OF MONETARY AND FISCAL POLICY.
In the left-hand panel, an increase in the money supply shifts the LM curve to the right, thus raising GNP and lowering the interest rate. In the right-hand panel, an increase in government spending shifts the IS curve to the right, thus raising GNP and raising the interest rate. A comparison of the two panels illustrates a fundamental difference between monetary policy and fiscal policy: an expansionary monetary policy lowers interest rates and an expansionary fiscal policy raises interest rates.

when the money supply increases the interest rate falls and GNP rises. This increase in GNP will probably put upward pressure on prices, but we are saving the details for the next chapter.

What is actually happening in the economy when the Fed increases the money supply? Immediately after the increase there is more money in the economy than people demand. This tends to make the interest rate fall, so the demand for money increases. The lower interest rate then stimulates investment and net exports, which raises GNP through the multiplier process. In sum, GNP rises and the interest rate falls.

FISCAL POLICY

Suppose that Congress passes a bill that increases defense spending. We now know that an increase in government spending pushes the IS curve to the right. Figure 5–7 shows what happens to interest rates and GNP. In the right-hand panel *an increase in government spending increases the interest rate and increases income.*

What is going on in the economy when the government purchases more goods? First, the increase in government demand increases GNP through the multiplier. But the increase in GNP will increase the demand for money: More money is needed for transactions purposes. Since the Fed does not change the money supply, we know that interest rates must rise to offset the increase in money demand that came from the increase in GNP. This increase in the interest rate will reduce investment demand and net exports and thus offset some of the stimulus to GNP caused by government spending. The offsetting negative effect is called **crowding out.**

Numerical Example. Explicit numerical values for the effect of changes in the money supply and government spending can be obtained from the numerical IS and LM curves given in Equations 5–7 and 5–9. First set R in the IS curve equal to R in the LM curve. This is the algebraic equivalent of the graphical intersection of the LM and IS curves. Setting Equation 5–7 equal to Equation 5–9 means

$$\underbrace{.502 - .000188Y + .0004G}_{\text{IS curve}} = \underbrace{.0001625Y - .001\frac{M}{P}}_{\text{LM curve}}.$$

Isolating Y on the left-hand side of this equation gives the simpler form

$$Y = 1432 + 1.14G + 2.85\frac{M}{P}. \tag{5-10}$$

Suppose that the money supply M is \$600 billion, that government spending

G is $750 billion, and that the price level is 1. Then Equation 5–10 says that GNP is equal to $4,000 billion. Plugging this value for Y into either the equation for the IS curve or the equation for the LM curve, we find that the interest rate is 5 percent. Figure 5–6 is drawn accurately to scale for these values. Equation 5–10 says that an increase in government spending of $1 billion increases real GNP by $1.14 billion, for a ratio of 1.14. Compare this effect with the government spending multiplier of 2.1 that we found in the model where investment is exogenous and net exports depend only on income. The effect is smaller when we take account of the financial system, because interest rates rise and crowd out investment spending. As for monetary policy, if the price level is 1, then an increase in the money supply of $1 billion increases GNP by $2.85 billion.

IS-LM in the Business Pages

Not many reporters are versed in the IS-LM model. It's not surprising to find statements like this one in the financial pages:

A new recession is feared because higher Pentagon spending is raising interest rates. Those higher rates are discouraging housing purchases and plant and equipment investment.

More military spending shifts the IS curve outward. The economy moves up and to the right along the LM curve. It is true that interest rates are higher, but this is a symptom of higher GNP, not something that will cause a decline in GNP.

How about

There is concern about declining sales and employment because of the collapse of the dollar. That collapse will be accompanied by higher interest rates, which will lead to lower investment and total spending.

Same error. The lower dollar will lead to a diversion of demand to domestic products, which will shift the IS curve outward. GNP and the interest rate rise as the economy moves up the LM curve.

And

The only way to head off the impending recession is to bring the government's deficit under control. Otherwise, high interest rates will choke off economic activity.

It is true that an anti-deficit move (lower spending or higher taxes) will lower interest rates by moving the IS curve inward, but the result will be to worsen, not head off, an incipient recession.

THE PRESIDENT AND THE FED

In his Economic Report sent to Congress in February 1985, President Reagan made the following comment about the Fed: "The sharp reduction in money growth through mid-1982 . . . undoubtedly added to the length and severity of the 1981–82 recession." Is the president's comment on monetary policy correct in light of the macro theory described here? A reduction in money growth corresponds to a leftward shift in the LM curve. According to the IS-LM apparatus this should raise interest rates, lower GNP, and cause the economy to go into a recession. The sharper the reduction in money, the larger the reduction in GNP and the more severe the recession. Hence, the president's comment seems correct. But as we will see in the next two chapters, the Fed probably had to reduce money growth in order to reduce inflation, which was very high prior to 1981. Assuming that the president also wanted to reduce inflation, criticism of the Fed must be based on the fact that the reduction in money growth was too sharp, or not gradual enough.

THE RELATIVE EFFECTIVENESS OF MONETARY AND FISCAL POLICY

Monetary and fiscal policy differ in how effective they are in shifting aggregate demand. Two important issues must be faced in determining the relative effectiveness of monetary and fiscal policy:

1. The sensitivity of **investment demand** and **net exports** to interest rates
2. The sensitivity of **money demand** to interest rates

The issues can be given graphical interpretations in terms of the *slopes* of the IS curve and the LM curve. First, think about it intuitively.

When Is Fiscal Policy Relatively Weak? An expansionary fiscal policy will have a relatively *weak* effect on aggregate demand if interest rates rise a lot and have a large negative effect on investment and net exports. The fall in investment and net exports will offset the positive effect that government spending has on aggregate demand. The fall in investment and net exports will be large under two circumstances, corresponding to the two issues listed above.

1. If the sensitivity of investment demand and net exports to the interest rate is *very large.* Then a rise in interest rates will reduce investment and net exports by a considerable amount.
2. If the sensitivity of money demand to the interest rate is *very small.* Then the increase in money demand that arises as a result of the increased government expenditures will cause a big rise in the interest

rate. (The small interest rate sensitivity means that the interest rate has to move a lot.)

Another property of the economy that affects the strength of fiscal policy is the spending multiplier (see p. 83). A high spending multiplier means more effective fiscal policy. However, if the economy has high interest sensitivity of investment and net exports and low interest sensitivity of money demand, even a very large multiplier will not result in strong effects of fiscal policy.

When Is Fiscal Policy Relatively Strong? An expansionary fiscal policy will have a relatively *strong* effect on aggregate demand if interest rates don't rise by much or have a small effect on investment and net exports. This occurs under circumstances opposite to those listed under weak fiscal policy.

When Is Monetary Policy Relatively Weak? An expansionary monetary policy will have a relatively *weak* effect on aggregate demand if the drop in interest rates that occurs when the money supply is increased is small or has little influence on investment and net exports. This occurs under two circumstances.

1. If the sensitivity of investment demand and net exports to interest rates is *very small.* Then investment is not stimulated much by the decline in interest rates.
2. If the sensitivity of money demand to interest rates is *very large.* Then the increase in the money supply doesn't cause much of a drop in interest rates. (A small drop in interest rates is sufficient to bring money demand up to the higher money supply.)

When Is Monetary Policy Relatively Strong? An expansionary monetary policy will have a big effect if interest rates fall by a large amount and stimulate investment and net exports in a big way. This occurs under circumstances opposite to those listed under weak monetary policy.

THE IS-LM INTERPRETATION

The IS curve is relatively flat if investment demand and net exports are very sensitive to interest rates, because small changes in interest rates are associated with big changes in demand. Conversely, the IS curve is relatively steep if investment and net exports are very insensitive to interest rates.

The LM curve is relatively flat if money demand is very sensitive to interest rates, because small changes in interest rates are sufficient to reduce money demand when it increases with a change in income. Conversely, the LM curve is relatively steep if money demand is very insensitive to interest rates.

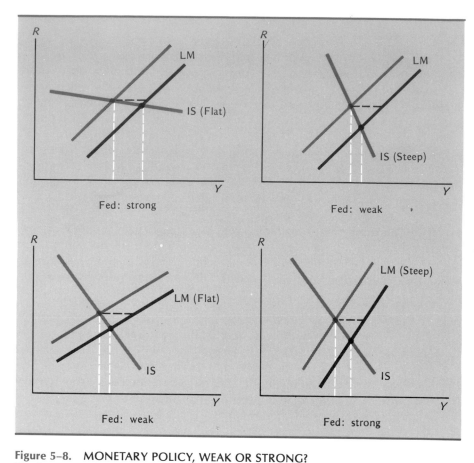

Figure 5–8.   MONETARY POLICY, WEAK OR STRONG?
The four IS-LM diagrams illustrate all the possibilities that have bearing on the strength of
monetary policy. In some cases the IS curve is flat; in other cases the LM curve is flat. In
every case the LM curve is shifted outward by the same amount. At the bottom of each
diagram the answer to "Weak or strong?" is given.

With these IS slope and LM slope interpretations of the interest rate sen-
sitivities, we now can review the previous discussion using the IS-LM diagrams. Eight cases exhaust the possibilities, and are shown in Figures 5–8
and 5–9.

Weak and Strong Policy

1. Monetary policy is strong if the IS curve is flat or the LM curve is
   steep. Monetary policy is weak if the IS curve is steep or the LM
   curve is flat.

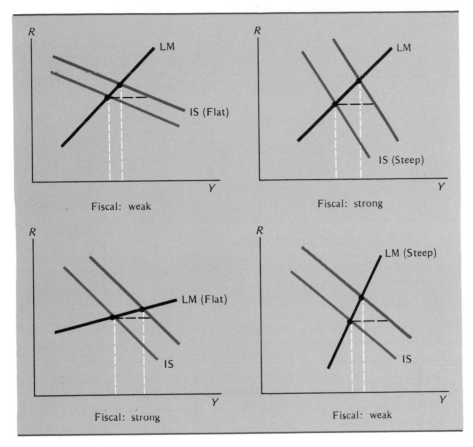

Figure 5–9.   FISCAL POLICY: WEAK OR STRONG?
The four IS-LM diagrams illustrate all the possibilities that have bearing on the strength of fiscal policy. In some cases the IS curve is flat; in other cases the LM curve is flat. At the bottom of each diagram the answer to "Weak or strong?" is given.

2. Fiscal policy is strong if the IS curve is steep or the LM curve is flat. Fiscal policy is weak if the IS curve is flat or the LM curve is steep.

3. For given slopes of the IS and LM curves, fiscal policy is more effective if the spending multiplier is large.

5.6 The Aggregate Demand Curve

In preparation for our analysis of price change and inflation in the next chapter, we now derive the **aggregate demand curve.** The aggregate de-

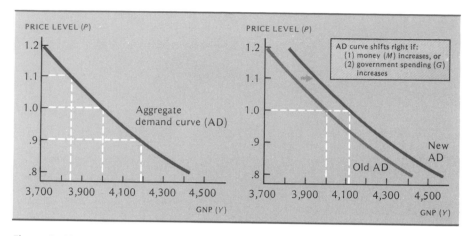

Figure 5–10.   THE AGGREGATE DEMAND CURVE.
On the left is the aggregate demand curve (AD). It shows that aggregate demand is a declining function of the price level. On the right, the aggregate demand curve shifts to the
right if either monetary or fiscal policy is expansionary.

mand curve is shown in Figure 5–10. The aggregate demand curve tells
how much people will demand at a given level of prices. The higher the
price level, the less aggregate demand. Hence, as with most demand curves
in microeconomics, the aggregate demand curve is downward sloping.

Except as a mnemonic device to remember which way the aggregate demand curve is sloped, the analogy between the standard microeconomic demand curve and the aggregate demand curve of macroeconomics is a weak
one, and should not be emphasized. The ideas behind the aggregate demand curve are much different from those that underlie the typical demand
curve of microeconomics. In particular, it is important to keep in mind that
the financial system—the demand and supply for money—lies behind the
aggregate demand curve.

Figure 5–11 is a graphical derivation of the aggregate demand curve. In
the top part of Figure 5–11 is an IS-LM diagram. Recall that changes in the
price level shift the LM curve. Higher prices shift the LM curve to the left,
and lower prices shift the LM curve to the right.

Now suppose that the price level rises. The LM curve shifts to the left,
raising the interest rate, lowering investment and net exports, and ultimately lowering GNP. Thus, a higher price level reduces GNP because it increases the demand for money. The increase in demand causes interest rates
to rise and causes GNP to fall. The different values for the price level and
GNP constitute the aggregate demand curve.

The IS, LM, and Aggregate Demand Curves

1. The aggregate demand curve shows what level of GNP will be demanded given a particular price level.

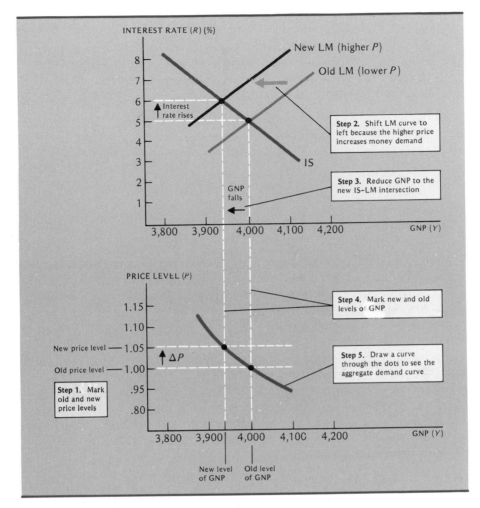

Figure 5–11. DERIVATION OF THE AGGREGATE DEMAND CURVE.
An increase in the price level shifts the LM curve to the left. This raises interest rates and reduces output. The resulting negative relationship between the price level and GNP is summarized in the aggregate demand curve.

2. The two economic principles governing the aggregate demand curve are spending balance and the equality of the demand and supply of money.

3. Spending balance is summarized by the IS curve. The IS curve is downward sloping because higher interest rates reduce investment and net exports and therefore reduce GNP. An increase in government spending pushes the IS curve to the right.

4. The condition that the supply and the demand for money are equal is summarized by the LM curve. The LM curve is upward sloping.

An increase in the money supply pushes the LM curve to the right.

5. The aggregate demand curve slopes downward. A higher price level means that real money balances are lower and therefore that the interest rate is higher. This means that investment, net exports, and GNP are lower.

6. An increase in government spending or an increase in the money supply shifts the aggregate demand curve to the right.

MONETARY AND FISCAL POLICY

Changes in the money supply and in government spending both shift the aggregate demand curve. This is shown in the right-hand panel of Figure 5–10. Suppose that the money supply increases. At a given price level, aggregate demand rises. More money means that a lower interest rate equates money demand with money supply. A lower interest rate stimulates more investment and net exports, which in turn requires a higher level of GNP for spending balance. In sum, the aggregate demand curve shifts to the right when the money supply increases.

Fiscal policy also shifts the aggregate demand curve. An increase in government spending shifts the aggregate demand curve to the right. At a given price level more government spending means more aggregate demand. Conversely, a decrease in government spending shifts the aggregate demand curve to the left.

Numerical Example. How do we get the aggregate demand curve using algebra? We have already got it. On page 114 Equation 5–10 represents the intersection of the IS and LM curves. It shows how GNP falls when the price level rises: The price level appears in the denominator on the right-hand side of Equation 5–10. Equation 5–10 is the aggregate demand curve. For the numerical example that we have been considering throughout this chapter, it shows how much GNP falls when the price level rises.

Note that the aggregate demand equation 5–10 also depends on the money supply M and government spending G. Changing M and G in this equation corresponds to the shifts in the aggregate demand diagram shown in Figure 5–10.

Review and Practice

MAJOR POINTS

1. Investment depends on the interest rate. A higher interest rate discourages some investment projects and lowers total investment.

2. Net exports also depend negatively on the interest rate. A higher interest rate attracts capital from other countries; this drives up the exchange rate and lowers net exports.

3. The demand for money also depends negatively on the interest rate.

4. When the Federal Reserve is holding the money stock constant, the interest rate has to move as necessary to equate the demand for money with the given money supply.

5. At a higher price level and the same money stock, a higher interest rate is needed to equate money demand with supply.

6. At a higher price level and the same money stock, a lower income level is needed to equate money demand with supply.

7. The IS curve shows the level of GNP that brings spending balance for each interest rate. It slopes downward.

8. The LM curve shows the interest rate that brings equality of supply and demand in the money market for each level of GNP. It slopes upward.

9. The IS-LM model answers questions about the effect of policy over the period when it is reasonable to consider prices fixed. Monetary expansion raises output and lowers the interest rate. Fiscal expansion raises output and raises the interest rate.

10. The intersection of the IS and LM curves tells the levels of GNP and the interest rate for a given price level and fiscal-monetary policy. It corresponds to a point on the aggregate demand schedule.

KEY TERMS AND CONCEPTS

Interest rate	Money supply
Real interest rate	Federal Reserve System
Nominal interest rate	Monetary policy
Investment function	Fiscal policy
Net export function	IS curve
Crowding out	LM curve
Money	Aggregate demand curve
Money demand function	

QUESTIONS FOR DISCUSSION AND REVIEW

1. What are the important determinants of aggregate demand? For each one, trace out what happens if it changes.

2. Why does a higher price level raise the interest rate? What could the Fed do to prevent the increase in the interest rate?

3. Explain why the IS curve slopes downward.

4. Explain why the LM curve slopes upward.

5. Explain why the aggregate demand curve slopes downward.

6. Why does a decrease in government spending reduce interest rates?

7. Why does an increase in the money supply reduce interest rates?

PROBLEMS

Numerical

1. This problem pertains to the numerical example listed in the box on page 104. Set the price level equal to 1.
   a. Use the algebraic form of the aggregate demand curve to find the level of GNP that occurs when the money supply is $600 billion and government spending is $750 billion.
   b. Use the IS curve and the LM curve to find the interest rate that occurs in this same situation. Explain why you get the same answer in each case.
   c. Use the consumption function to find the level of consumption, the investment function to find the level of investment, and the net export function to find the level of net exports for this same situation.
   d. Show that the sum of your answers for consumption, investment, government spending, and net exports equals GNP.
   e. Repeat all the previous calculations if government spending increased to $850 billion. How much investment is "crowded out" as a result of the increase in government spending? How much are net exports crowded out?

2. Savings and budget deficits: This problem pertains to the numerical example in the text and makes use of the answers to Problem 1.
   a. Set government spending at $750 billion and the money supply at $600 billion. Calculate government saving (the budget surplus). Calculate the level of private saving, and show that private saving plus government saving equal investment.
   b. Now repeat your calculations for a level of government spending equal to $850 billion. Does private saving plus government saving still equal investment? Why not?
   c. Explain why private saving increases as a result of government spending. In light of your calculations evaluate the statement: "Government budget deficits absorb private saving that would otherwise be used for investment purposes."

3. Compare the IS curve in the numerical example on page 111 with the IS curve that you get by increasing the coefficient d to 4,000.
   a. What is the slope of each IS curve? Explain in words why the second IS curve is flatter.
   b. For which value of d does an increase in the money supply have a larger effect on output? Why?
   c. Derive the aggregate demand curve in each case. Which has a larger coefficient for M/P? Is this consistent with your answer to Part b?

4. Compare the LM curve in the numerical example on pages 112–13 with the LM curve that you get by increasing the coefficient h to 2,000.
   a. What is the slope of each LM curve? Explain why the slopes are different.

b. For which value of h is monetary policy more powerful? Explain.
c. Derive the aggregate demand curve in each case. Which has a larger coefficient for M/P? Is this consistent with your answer to Part b?

5. Using the numerical example of the chapter, calculate values for the money supply and government spending that will increase GNP from $4,000 billion to $4,100 billion *without changing the interest rate at all*.

6. The following relationships describe the imaginary economy of Nineland:

$$Y = C + I \qquad \text{(Income identity)}$$
$$C = 90 + .9Y \qquad \text{(Consumption)}$$
$$I = 900 - 900R \qquad \text{(Investment)}$$
$$M = (.9Y - 900R)P \qquad \text{(Money demand)}$$

Y is output, C is consumption, I is investment, R is the interest rate, M is the money supply, and P is the price level. There are no taxes, government spending, or foreign trade in Nineland.

The year is 1999 in Nineland. The price level is 1. The money supply is 900 in 1999.

a. Sketch the IS curve and the LM curve for the year 1999 on a diagram and show the point where interest rate and output are determined. Show what happens in the diagram if the money supply is *increased* above 900 in 1999.
b. Sketch the aggregate demand curve. Show what happens in the diagram if the money supply is *decreased* below 900 in 1999.
c. Derive an algebraic expression for the aggregate demand curve in which P is on the left-hand side and Y is on the right-hand side.
d. What is the value of output and the interest rate in 1999 when the money supply is 900?

Analytical

1. Higher interest rates reduce investment and increase foreign saving. What then must happen to the combination of private and government saving after a rise in interest rates? If neither private nor government saving depends directly on the interest rate, how can this change come about?

2. Graphically derive the LM curve, as in Figure 5–5, using instead a graph that relates money demand to income. (Hint: Put the stock of money on the vertical axis and income on the horizontal axis, and set this diagram above the LM diagram.)

3. Consider the following statements: (i) The IS curve is steep when investment is insensitive to the interest rate. (ii) The LM curve is flat when money demand is insensitive to income. (iii) The LM curve is flat when money demand is sensitive to the interest rate. (iv) The IS curve is flat when the marginal propensity to consume is high.
a. Explain in words why each of these statements is true.
b. Confirm algebraically that each statement is true. (Hint: Begin by deciding which coefficient in the model changes. Then show how a change in that coefficient affects the expression for the slope of the IS or LM curve.)

4. Suppose that money demand depended only on income and not on interest rates.
a. What does the LM curve look like in this case?
b. Show graphically that G has no effect on the level of output, Y. What does G affect?
c. Show the same thing algebraically. Explain why the LM equation becomes the aggregate demand equation.

5. Show how the IS curve and the LM curve can be shifted to get a decline in output without a change in interest rates. What kind of mix of monetary and fiscal policy is needed to do this?

6. Suppose that two administrations, one Democratic and the other Republican, both use fiscal and monetary policy to keep output at its potential level, but that the Democratic administration raises more in taxes and maintains a larger money supply than the Republican administration.
   a. On a single graph, show how the IS and LM curves of these two administrations differ.
   b. Indicate whether the following variables will be higher under the Democratic or Republican administrations, or whether they'll be unchanged: consumption; investment; net exports; government saving; private saving.
   c. Under which administration will foreign holdings of U.S. financial assets grow more slowly?

6

Aggregate Supply and Price Adjustment

As WE saw in Chapter 5, aggregate demand determines output in the short run. A reduction in aggregate demand, for example, reduces GNP and throws the economy into a recession. But this is just the first stage. As prices begin to adjust, the economy will be able to recover and return to its potential output. In the long run, the aggregate supply of basic resources in the economy will determine output.

In this chapter, we will look first at the determinants of **aggregate supply** —the labor force, the stock of productive capital, and technology. Aggregate supply defines the economy's potential GNP. We then study the price-adjustment process, and the movement of the economy from situations where aggregate demand is above or below potential to situations where aggregate demand equals potential.

6.1 Aggregate Supply

The supply side of the macroeconomic model describes the economy's capabilities for producing output. The important determinants of aggregate supply are:

1. The number of people available for work and their productivity
2. The amount of equipment, structures, land, and other types of capital
3. The technology

LABOR

Not everybody in the population is in the labor force. It is against the law for children to work; many adults are in school, working at home, or in retirement; quite a few others are unable to work because they are disabled or sick. Some people are committed to working full time no matter what the incentives; others will choose the level of their work effort depending on the incentives provided by the labor market.

We define **potential employment** (N^*) as the volume of employment that the entire population would choose given existing incentives. It is the total amount of work that would be done if everybody could find a job and earn as much as people like themselves are already earning. Notice that potential employment is not the absolute maximum amount of work that the population is capable of doing. It is the amount they would want to do given the existing real wage, which, as we saw in Chapter 3, measures the purchasing power of wages. The real wage is the actual wage paid, W, divided by the price level, P. Potential employment might rise if the real wage increased.

In our analysis potential employment does not depend on any of the major macro variables: output, consumption, investment, the interest rate, or the price level. It is exogenous. Though potential employment depends on the real wage W/P, it does not depend on the price level P. The reason is that actual wages are assumed to vary in proportion to the price level, so that a change in the price level does not affect the real wage. This is a fairly realistic assumption for short-run macroeconomic fluctuations. Potential employment is not fixed, however. It grows steadily as the population grows.

The unemployment rate is not zero when employment is equal to potential employment. It is equal to about 6 percent. As we saw in Chapter 3, this level of unemployment is called the natural rate of unemployment, and is greater than zero partially because of transitional periods of unemployment when workers change jobs or are looking for new jobs. The unemployment rate is above the natural rate when employment is below potential employment; conversely, the unemployment rate is below the natural rate when employment is above potential employment.

CAPITAL

In any given year, the volume of physical capital—factories and equipment—is determined by investment in previous years. The capital stock increases from one year to the next as long as gross investment is greater than the depreciation of the capital stock. As long as net investment is positive, the capital stock is growing. However, any investment project undertaken this year to increase the capital stock won't add to the stock until the project is complete, which usually takes at least a year. In any case, the capital stock is so large that the flow of new investment can have little effect on it in a short span of time.[1] Chapter 13 will provide more detail on this point. For now all that matters is that capital, like potential employment, is independent of the other macro variables in any one year. Hence, we will treat the capital stock as if it were exogenous. We use the symbol K for the existing capital stock.

TECHNOLOGY

The technology tells us how much output can be produced from the amount of labor and capital used in production. A simple way to describe the technology is in terms of a **production function,** which shows how much output can be made from given amounts of labor and capital. The production function can be represented using symbols as follows:

$$Y = F(N,K). \tag{6-1}$$

This is simply shorthand notation for saying that the output Y that is produced in the economy depends on employment N and capital K. (Reading out loud we say: "Y is a function F of N and K.") The notation F with parentheses after it means a general function of the variables listed in parentheses. With such a notation we are not specific about what the function actually looks like, whether it is linear or the square root of N, or whatever.

The production function relates output to employment and capital whatever their levels, even if employment is below potential. It would tell us how much real GNP would be produced, for example, if there were a very severe depression and only half the normal number of people were at work.

POTENTIAL GNP

To determine the aggregate supply capabilities of the economy, we ask: How much output could be produced if employment were at its potential level and all the existing capital were in use? The answer is

$$Y^* = F(N^*,K). \tag{6-2}$$

---

[1] Technically, the capital stock is a predetermined variable, like the price level in our analysis. Its current value is determined by events in the past. But the capital stock is even "stickier" than the price level, and for this reason we ignore the fact that it depends on investment in our analysis of macroeconomic fluctuations. It could not be ignored in a study of long-term growth.

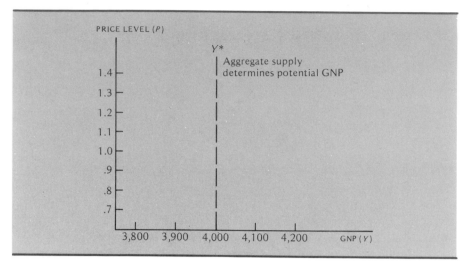

Figure 6–1.   AGGREGATE SUPPLY AND POTENTIAL GNP.
Potential GNP does not depend on the price level. It is marked on the price-GNP diagram as a vertical line. Potential GNP would be affected by changes in the incentives to work, the volume of capital, and technology.

The level of output, Y^*, is called **potential GNP.** It is the amount of output that would be produced if everybody who wanted to work could find a job. For this reason, Y^* is also frequently called the **full-employment level of output.** Recall that in Chapter 1 we compared actual GNP with estimates of potential GNP. Relative to actual GNP, potential GNP appears to grow steadily.

Potential GNP is not influenced by the price level or the other macro variables because potential employment is not influenced by these variables. In the price-GNP diagram that we used in Chapter 5 to draw the aggregate demand curve (Figure 5–10), potential output would be marked as a vertical line.[2] This is shown in Figure 6–1. Actual GNP fluctuates around potential GNP. In any year actual GNP can be either above or below potential GNP.

Do not be confused because potential GNP does not move in Figure 6–1, even though we have seen that potential GNP is steadily growing. Figure 6–1 shows the situation in a single year. If we wanted to show how potential GNP grows, we could move the potential GNP line to the right. In Figure 6–2, we show the upward-sloping trend line of potential GNP and look at the fluctuations of actual GNP around potential GNP.

---

[2] Some economists talk about the vertical aggregate supply schedule as the *long-run* aggregate supply schedule. They then use the term "short-run aggregate supply" for what we call the price-adjustment process. We believe that these are two very different concepts, so we reserve aggregate supply for issues genuinely concerned with the supply side of the economy. Price adjustment has to do with the interaction of demand and supply, so it is confusing to call it aggregate supply.

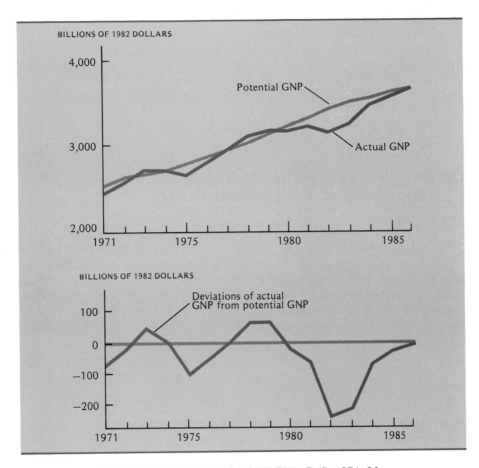

Figure 6–2. ACTUAL GNP RELATIVE TO POTENTIAL GNP, 1971–86.
The top chart shows how potential GNP grew and how actual GNP fluctuated around it.
The deviations of actual GNP from potential GNP are shown in the lower panel.

Aggregate Supply

1. Aggregate supply describes the amount of output that the basic resources of the economy are capable of producing.

2. Potential employment is the volume of employment that would occur if everybody was working who wanted to at prevailing incentives.

3. Potential output is the amount of output that can be produced, as shown by the production function, from potential employment and the existing capital stock.

4. Aggregate supply is the same as potential GNP. On a price-GNP diagram, it is marked by a vertical line at a level of output equal to potential output. Aggregate supply, or potential GNP, does not depend on the price level.

6.2 Price Stickiness and the Determination of Output and Unemployment in the Short Run

Recall that prices are sticky in the sense that they are not adjusted quickly by firms in response to demand conditions. Firms wait a while before adjusting their prices. For some period of time, therefore, the price level is stuck at a predetermined level. It is during this time that sellers are waiting to see how demand conditions change before they adjust their prices again. Prices eventually adjust, of course, but not until the next time period—a year or quarter later, for example. For the time being the price level is predetermined.

DETERMINATION OF OUTPUT

Figure 6–3 shows how aggregate demand determines output at some predetermined price. The aggregate demand curve is the same one derived in the previous chapter. The predetermined price is shown by the horizontal line drawn at P_0. GNP is determined by the point of intersection of the aggregate demand curve and the flat predetermined price line.

Shifts in the aggregate demand curve—caused perhaps by changes in the money supply or government spending—will result in increases or decreases in output. A rightward shift in the aggregate demand curve results in an expansion of output; a leftward shift in the aggregate demand curve results in a contraction of output.

The price level inherited from last year, when combined with the aggregate demand curve, determines the level of output. Output can be below potential output. Then we will observe unemployment and other unused resources. Or output can exceed potential output. These two possibilities are shown in Figure 6–4, where we have superimposed the vertical potential GNP line to indicate potential. In the left-hand panel of Figure 6–4, output is below potential. In the right-hand panel output is above potential.

Although the price level doesn't change immediately when firms find themselves producing above or below their potential, there is pressure for a price adjustment. When demand is below potential output there is pressure toward a downward move in prices; conversely, when demand is above potential there is pressure for an increase in prices.

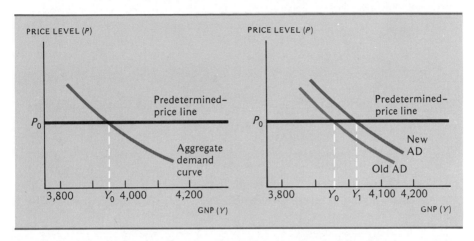

Figure 6–3. DETERMINATION OF OUTPUT WITH PREDETERMINED PRICE.
The horizontal line shows the price level predetermined for this year at level P_0. This year's output is at the intersection of the aggregate demand schedule and the horizontal line. In the left-hand panel the intersection occurs at the level of output marked Y_0. In the right-hand panel the aggregate demand curve shifts right, and output expands from Y_0 to Y_1.

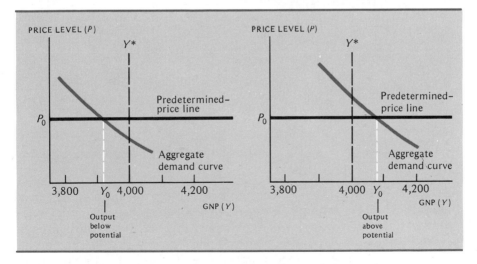

Figure 6–4. GNP CAN BE ABOVE OR BELOW POTENTIAL GNP.
On the left, the level of output is below potential. On the right, the level of output is above potential. Both of these positions will exert pressure on firms to change prices. On the left there is pressure to lower prices. On the right there is pressure to raise prices.

How the Real Business Cycle School Views Economic Fluctuations

The real business cycle school, led by Edward Prescott of the University of Minnesota, Charles Plosser of the University of Rochester, and others, believes that monetary forces have little or no effect on employment and output. Only non-monetary or "real" factors such as technical change affect output.

Members of the school disagree strongly with the ideas of Figure 6–4. They argue that the economy is always at the intersection of aggregate supply and aggregate demand (see, for example, Edward Prescott, "Theory Ahead of Business Cycle Measurement," *Federal Reserve Bank of Minneapolis Quarterly Review*, Fall 1986, pp. 9–23). They see no reason to develop a monetary or aggregate demand theory to explain fluctuations in total output because they feel that these fluctuations are due to technological factors.

Because it is an observed fact that output and employment go through recessions and booms, real business cycle theorists have to interpret those fluctuations as movements along an elastic supply curve or as shifts of the supply curve. They posit random shifts up and down in the production function. In years of high productivity, people work harder and output and employment are both high. Recessions are times when technology has regressed and people want to work less. The properties of the aggregate supply curve that we have described in this chapter are inconsistent with the real business cycle view. The aggregate supply curve in Figure 6–1 doesn't shift left or right from year to year the way GNP does.

Real business cycle theory, which is discussed in more detail in Chapter 14, Section 1, is highly controversial and is accepted by only a minority of macroeconomists. But it is a stimulating and important debate which may influence the way many macroeconomists think.

This adjustment leads to a changed price level for the *next year*, or period —not this year. For example, if aggregate demand is above potential in the year 2001, then the price level will be higher in 2002. When the aggregate demand curve is drawn to determine output for the year 2002, the predetermined price will be drawn at a higher level. If the intersection of the aggregate demand curve for the year 2002 and this new price line is still not at an output level equal to potential, then there will be a further adjustment in prices, but this will not occur until the year 2003. The process continues this way until aggregate demand equals potential output, at which point the desire for firms to adjust their prices will no longer be present. Whether or not

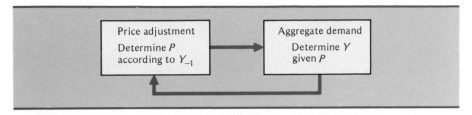

Figure 6–5.   DYNAMIC ANALYSIS AND PREDETERMINED VARIABLES.
The price-adjustment process is shown on the left. It determines the current price level based on the recent past level of output. Then the aggregate demand schedule, shown on the right, determines the level of output given the price level.

the process converges depends on the explicit price-adjustment process, which we consider in the next section.

The process by which the price level changes from one year to the next is *dynamic* in the sense that the variables are changing from one period to the next. The impact of a change in the money supply, for example, has effects on the price level that take place over a number of years. The model that we use to describe this dynamic process is an example of a **dynamic model.** The dynamic model is illustrated in Figure 6–5.

Determination of Output in the Short Run

1. In the short run, the price level is predetermined. It can change over time but, in a given year, the events of that year have almost no impact on the price level.

2. The level of output is determined by the point on the aggregate demand schedule corresponding to the price level.

3. In the short run, output can be below or above its potential level.

DETERMINATION OF UNEMPLOYMENT

We noted in Chapter 3 that Okun's law establishes a close relation between real GNP and unemployment. When an adverse shock shifts the aggregate demand curve inward, real GNP falls, as shown in Figure 6–3. Figure 6–6 starts with that shift and shows how it generates an increase in unemployment as well. From the decline in real GNP, the lower left-hand diagram converts it into a change in the percentage deviation of GNP from potential, $(Y - Y^*)/Y^*$. Then the right-hand part of the diagram computes the resulting increase in unemployment by applying Okun's law.

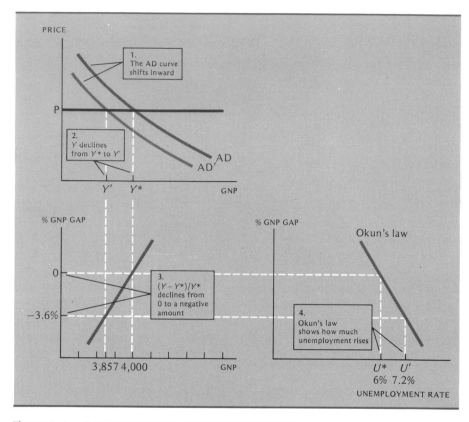

Figure 6–6. DETERMINATION OF UNEMPLOYMENT.
The upper left-hand diagram shows the aggregate demand curve in its original position
and after it shifts inward. Output declines from Y^* to Y'. The lower left-hand diagram
translates the GNP decline into percentage terms. The right-hand diagram uses Okun's
law to show the amount of increase in unemployment that occurs as a result of the decline in GNP.

A number of important mechanisms are at work in the process described
in Figure 6–6. If GNP declines, employers need a smaller amount of labor
input. They cut the length of the work week, they reduce the intensity of
work, and they cut the size of the work force. Most of the workers who are
laid off become unemployed. In addition, people who are looking for work
find it harder to locate jobs. Because of the importance of hours reductions
and the common pattern of retaining workers during temporary declines in
demand (called labor hoarding), a 3 percent decline in GNP is associated with
only a 1 percentage point increase in unemployment. This close negative
relation is one of the most reliable generalizations that macroeconomists
have found. Whenever some force causes GNP to decline, you can be confi-
dent that unemployment will rise.

6.3 Price Adjustment

Decisions about prices are made by individual firms. But, moving from the level of the firm to the macro level is tricky. Finding a good way to model aggregate price adjustment has occupied much of the research time of macroeconomics during the last 20 years. Mistakes in understanding price adjustment have generated some of the most glaring errors in the field of macroeconomics.

Firms adjust their prices in response to conditions in their markets. If demand has been strong and they are producing more than they think is appropriate given their current prices, they will raise their prices. If demand has been weak and they are producing less than is appropriate, they will lower their prices. When we look at the process in terms of aggregate variables—GNP and the price level—prices will tend to rise whenever GNP has been above potential and will tend to fall when it has been below potential. We have already mentioned this aspect of price adjustment in illustrating the dynamic analysis in the previous section.

Specifically, if demand in the previous period Y_{-1} is greater than Y^*, then the price level P this period will be raised (the subscript "-1" indicates the previous period). Conversely, if demand in the previous period Y_{-1} is below Y^*, then the price level P will be bid down. The difference $Y_{-1} - Y^*$ measures the pressure on prices to change. Note that, because P depends on Y_{-1}, it is *predetermined*, or set, according to demand conditions prevailing in the recent past.

Firms make their price decisions with the prices of their inputs in mind. The most important input is labor. Hence, the behavior of the wage rate is a major determinant of price adjustment. Wages tend to rise when conditions in the labor market are strong. Remember that, when real GNP is high relative to potential, unemployment is low and employment is high. These are conditions that are likely to lead to rising wages. Wage pressure comes at the same time as the direct pressure on prices and the two combine to give a relation between the deviation of GNP from potential and inflation.

Economic intuition and historical experience both support the notion that market pressure, as measured by $(Y_{-1} - Y^*)/Y^*$, and inflation should be related. Recently, economists have developed microeconomically based theories of price adjustment, and Chapter 15 will go into the details of some of these theories. What follows is a first look at the way price decisions by firms become magnified into an aggregate price-adjustment equation.

RELATIVE PRICE SETTING AND IMPERFECT INFORMATION

The price adjustment made by one firm will be *relative* to what that firm feels is the prevailing level of prices for its product. The reason for making a price adjustment is to change the price relative to other prices in the economy. When General Motors sets the suggested retail price for Chevrolets for the upcoming year, it is important that the company take account of what price Ford is likely to set. If GM comes out with a Chevrolet price that is way above the Ford price it will suffer a loss of sales, which it might have avoided had it known what Ford was up to. The prevailing level of prices—that is, the level of prices for closely related products during the price-setting period—is an integral part of the information a firm requires to make a good pricing decision.

Firms do not know with certainty the relevant prevailing level of prices. Moreover, because the firm is likely to keep its price at the new level for some time into the future, knowing the appropriate prevailing price will require estimating the future pricing decisions of other firms that will be setting their prices in the upcoming months. The firm must therefore form an estimate or expectation of the prevailing price level in the economy. If GM expects the price of Fords to hold steady, then it is more likely to hold its Chevrolet price steady. If GM expects Ford to increase its prices by 10 percent, then it will be more willing to raise its Chevrolet price by that amount, give or take the desired relative price adjustment it desires.

Suppose that firms try to raise their own prices above the prevailing price when demand conditions are strong and real GNP is above potential. Specifically, suppose that the typical firm raises its own price f percentage points above its forecast of the prevailing price for every percent by which GNP exceeds potential. In other words,

$$\frac{\text{Firm's price}}{\text{Forecasted prevailing price}} = 1 + f \frac{Y_{-1} - Y^*}{Y^*}.$$

For example, if the coefficient f equals .3 and the proportional deviation of GNP from potential, $(Y_{-1} - Y^*)/Y^*$, is .1, then the firm's price divided by its forecasted prevailing price will be 1.03. In other words, the firm's price will be 3 percent higher than the forecasted prevailing price.

Now suppose that the typical firm forecasts the prevailing price to be the same as last year's price; that is, the forecasted prevailing price equals P_{-1}. Then we can write the resulting price adjustment equation as

$$\frac{P}{P_{-1}} = 1 + f \frac{Y_{-1} - Y^*}{Y^*}. \tag{6-3}$$

Now, if we replace the 1 in Equation 6–3 by P_{-1}/P_{-1} and move it to the left-hand side, we get

$$\pi = f \frac{Y_{-1} - Y^*}{Y^*}, \tag{6-4}$$

where the Greek letter π stands for the **rate of inflation** $(P - P_{-1})/P_{-1}$. It says that the rate of inflation is positively related to the deviation of real GNP from potential. Such a relationship is called a **Phillips curve** after A. W. Phillips who first studied it.[3]

Forecasting this year's prevailing price to be the same as last year's price would not be a good assumption for price adjustment if prices were expected to rise in the future. Suppose that firms expect inflation. They must forecast the growth of the prevailing price and, if a relative price increase is called for, increase their own prices faster than the prevailing price is increasing. If GM, for example, forecast the price of Fords to increase by 10 percent, and desired a 2 percent cut in the relative price of Chevrolets to stimulate sales, it would increase its Chevrolet price by 8 percent. The implication of this type of behavior is to add a term π^e to the Phillips curve:

$$\pi = \pi^e + f \frac{Y_{-1} - Y^*}{Y^*}. \tag{6-5}$$

Note that this equation is the same as Equation 6-4 with expected inflation π^e added to the right-hand side. The curve is illustrated in Figure 6-7.

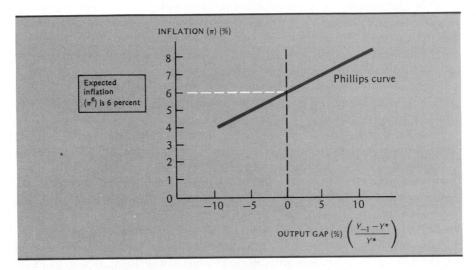

Figure 6-7. THE PHILLIPS CURVE.
The higher GNP is relative to potential, the higher will be the rate of inflation. When GNP is below potential, the Phillips curve predicts that inflation will be below the expected rate of inflation. In booms, when GNP is above potential, actual inflation will exceed expected inflation. The higher the expected rate of inflation, the higher is actual inflation. The expectational shift is important in explaining persistent inflationary periods, like the 1970s, in the United States.

[3] A. W. Phillips fit this type of relationship to data for the United Kingdom from 1861 to 1957. The fit was very good. Phillips actually related percentage changes in wages to the unemployment rate. See "The Relationship between the Unemployment Rate and the Rate of Change in Money Wage Rates in the United Kingdom, 1861–1957," *Economica*, November 1957, pp. 283–299.

When inflation becomes expected at the rate π^e, it shifts the Phillips curve upward.

The Phillips curve with the expectation term has an important property: If real GNP is above potential GNP on a permanent basis, then the rate of inflation will never stop increasing. As actual inflation rises, expected inflation, π^e, will also begin to rise: as firms see actual inflation increasing they will begin to expect higher inflation. But then actual inflation will have to be even higher, because GNP can exceed potential only if actual inflation exceeds expected inflation. This property of the price-adjustment equation has been called the **accelerationist** or, equivalently, the **natural rate property.** The terminology comes from the property that if real GNP is brought above its potential level, Y^*, then the inflation rate will rise and the price level will accelerate. There is no way for real GNP to be held constantly above its natural level without inflation constantly rising limitlessly. In an economy with reasonably stable prices, the level of real GNP will tend to be near potential, on the average.

This relationship between expectations and price adjustment was developed in the late 1960s by Edmund Phelps of Columbia University, and independently by Milton Friedman. At the time that they developed the relationship most economists had not considered the role of expectations in the Phillips curve. Friedman presented his controversial theory at a large convention of economists in his presidential address to the American Economic Association in 1967.[4] At that time inflation in the U.S. was still pretty low and many economists were skeptical of the Friedman-Phelps theory. As it turned out, data that became available in the 1970s showed that Friedman and Phelps were right.

Figure 6–8 shows that there has been a stable Phillips curve price-adjustment relationship of the type proposed by Phelps and Friedman for the period since 1951. The vertical axis measures the amount by which inflation exceeds expectations and the horizontal axis measures the gap between actual and potential GNP. According to the theory, this relationship should be stable over time, and upward-sloping. Except for the inflationary recessions of 1974–75 and 1981, and an episode related to the Korean War in 1952, the predicted relationship has existed in the United States. In Chapter 16, we will add another term to the equation that will help explain the 1974–75 and 1981 experiences as the result of sharp increases in oil prices.

WHAT DETERMINES EXPECTED INFLATION?

So far we have said nothing about what determines the expected inflation term π^e in the price-adjustment equation. The simplest idea is that π^e de-

---

[4] Friedman's presidential address is found in Milton Friedman, "The Role of Monetary Policy," *American Economic Review,* March 1968, pp. 1–17. Phelps first published his results in Edmund S. Phelps, "Money Wage Dynamics and Labor Market Equilibrium," *Journal of Political Economy,* July–August 1967, pp. 678–711.

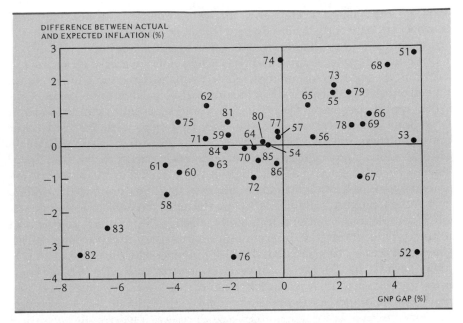

Figure 6-8. PRICE ADJUSTMENT IN THE UNITED STATES SINCE 1951.
The horizontal axis shows the percentage departure of GNP from potential. The vertical axis shows the amount of inflation relative to the expected amount. Years in the upper right are ones when output was above potential and inflation exceeded expectations. Years in the lower left are recession years when output was low and inflation subsided. Most years fit into the general pattern predicted by the price-adjustment relationship. A few, including 1974–75 and 1981, are departures; they are inflationary recessions. In this diagram, the expected inflation rate is measured as the inflation rate in the year before.

pends on past inflation. Suppose, for example, that GM thinks that the price of Fords will increase at 60 percent of last year's inflation rate. Suppose that all firms forecast inflation in the same way. Then the expectation π^e would be set to $.6\,\pi_{-1}$. Equation 6–5 would then become

$$\pi = .6\,\pi_{-1} + f\,\frac{Y_{-1} - Y^*}{Y^*}. \tag{6-6}$$

This Phillips curve is based on a particularly simple model of expected inflation. It is a rational way for firms to forecast in an economy where abnormally high inflation does not persist year after year but eventually returns to lower inflation, so that the best guess of inflation would be simply a fraction (like .6) of past inflation. On the other hand if high inflation tended to last a long time, then people would expect inflation to come down only a little, if at all. They might simply extrapolate from the past and set $\pi^e = \pi_{-1}$. In more complex inflationary environments, expected inflation would probably be more complex, perhaps depending on inflation in the previous two years. Or firms might attempt to guess where inflation was heading based on what they expect the Fed to do with the money supply: If they expect the Fed to start fighting inflation, they might forecast less inflation.

But even if firms attempted to bring future policy changes into their calculations, the past rate of inflation would probably have some influence on expected inflation. Firms know that some prices will continue to rise for a while, even if they suspect that the Fed would start fighting inflation right away. Some price increases would already have been announced by other firms, and these will take place in any case. Wage setting is also a factor in price decisions, and wage increases negotiated in earlier years would continue. The relative price-setting idea in the price-adjustment theory described above is also important for wage setting. For unionized workers, such as the United Automobile Workers, the contractual nature of wage setting is conspicuous. Contracts frequently set wages for as much as 3 years in advance. The contracts of different unions are set at different times. When wage contracts are renegotiated, they are influenced by the wages currently being paid to workers under contracts settled in previous years, and by what other workers are likely to get in upcoming years. The expected rate of increase in prevailing wages is thus influenced by past wage decisions, as well as by upcoming wage decisions. Overlapping contracts mean that expected inflation will be related to past inflation even if forecasters are perfectly rational and forward-looking.

We will come back to alternative ideas about expected inflation in Chapter 15. For now we will use Equation 6–6 as our Phillips curve.

Note that the larger the difference between real GNP and potential GNP, the faster will be the reduction in inflation. Suppose, for example, that the coefficient f in the price-adjustment equation is equal to .2. This value implies that a 5 percent fall of real GNP below potential GNP, which lasts for one year, will reduce the rate of inflation by 1 percent. When output is 10 percent below normal for one period the rate of inflation will be reduced by 2 percent. Of course, the price-adjustment equation works the other way around as well. If real GNP rises above potential GNP, then there will be an increase in inflation.

Price Adjustment

1. The process of price adjustment moves the economy toward potential GNP. When the price level is too high, GNP is less than potential, prices fall, demand rises, and eventually full employment is restored.

2. If no inflation is expected, the price-adjustment equation relates the rate of inflation to the deviation of GNP from potential.

3. Under conditions of expected inflation, the price-adjustment relation is shifted upward by the amount of the expected inflation.

4. A simple model of expected inflation is that expected inflation is given by a fraction of last year's inflation.

6.4 Combining Aggregate Demand and Price Adjustment

The aggregate demand curve, in combination with price adjustment, governs the dynamic response of the economy to a change in economic conditions. As an example, we will look at what happens to the economy when the money supply is increased. We assume the economy starts out with zero inflation and GNP equals potential GNP. The increase in money initially pushes the aggregate demand curve to the right and increases output. Gradually prices rise to bring the economy back into equilibrium at potential GNP. We now trace out the path of GNP as it returns to potential.

On the left in Figure 6–9 we show the aggregate demand curve intersecting the predetermined-price line. The intersection occurs where output is equal to potential GNP. Suppose that this is the situation in the year 2000 but that starting in 2001 the Fed increases the money supply. The aggregate demand shifts to the right, and GNP expands. The economy goes into a boom during 2001, and GNP is above potential GNP. Since the stimulus to aggregate demand comes from monetary policy we know from the IS-LM method of the last chapter that the interest rate falls, stimulating investment spending. Then the multiplier expands GNP. All this occurs during the year that the money supply increased.

With firms now operating above potential, they will adjust their prices upward. The price line will shift up. We can easily calculate the exact size of the price adjustment in 2002 using the price-adjustment equation (6–6): Calculate the inflation rate $(P - P_{-1})/P_{-1}$ associated with the level of GNP for 2001. Multiply this inflation rate by the previous price level P_{-1} to get the absolute change in the price level, $P - P_{-1}$, and hence the price level P for 2002. We shift the price line in Figure 6–9 upward by the amount of this price increase. Assuming that the Fed does not increase the money supply again, the same aggregate demand curve continues to apply in 2002. Thus, the new point of intersection of aggregate demand and the price line occurs at a lower level of output compared with 2001. The economy moves up and to the left along the aggregate demand curve.

What is happening in the economy? At a higher price level more money is demanded by people for transactions purposes. But since the Fed doesn't increase the money supply again, this puts upward pressure on the interest rate. The higher interest rate reduces investment below what it was in 2001,

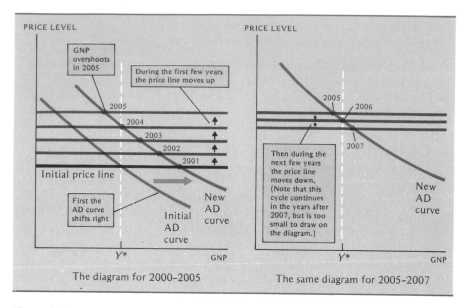

Figure 6–9.   AGGREGATE DEMAND AND PRICE ADJUSTMENT.
The diagram on the left shows the aggregate demand curve intersecting the predetermined-price line at potential GNP (Y*). After an increase in the money supply the aggregate demand curve shifts to the right. Then the price line begins to shift up and output declines. GNP falls below potential GNP, but then there is downward pressure on prices and the price line begins to fall. This is shown in the diagram on the right, where we see the same aggregate demand curve during the years after 2005.

and this reduction has multiplier effects throughout the economy. GNP falls.

According to Figure 6–9, GNP is still above potential in 2002. Thus there will be another upward adjustment in the price level. This time the price adjustment will be the sum of two effects. The two effects correspond to the two terms on the right-hand side of the price-adjustment equation (6–6). Because there was inflation the year before, there will be expectations of continuing inflation in 2002. This factor will add to inflation. On the other hand, output is no longer so far above potential. The contribution from that term in the Phillips curve will be smaller. In the scenario in Figure 6–9, the price rises even more in 2003 than it did in 2002. Again the aggregate demand curve doesn't move, so output falls again in 2003. As before, the interest rate rises because of the increased demand for money, and this reduces investment.

If output is still above potential or if inflation is still above where it started in 2000, there will be another price adjustment. Hence, GNP will continue to fall. Note that GNP will fall below—overshoot—potential because expected inflation keeps the price line moving up.

This overshooting is shown in Figure 6–9 where GNP falls below potential GNP in the year 2005. But this overshooting creates forces that reverse the decline in GNP and bring it back to potential GNP. When actual GNP is below potential GNP, the depressed economic conditions place downward pressure on prices. As firms bid down their prices the price line begins to shift down as shown in the right-hand panel of Figure 6–9. As the price line reverses its previous movement and begins to shift down, GNP will start to rise. The process continues period after period until GNP eventually returns to potential. In Figure 6–9 we show GNP getting very close to potential in the year 2007, though there are tiny movements (too small to see on the diagram) after that. By 2007 inflation has returned to zero, where it began in 2000, though the price level has permanently increased. The price level has increased by the same amount that the money supply increased.

Note how the graphical analysis in Figure 6–9 is divided into different phases. In the first phase (on the left), the price line is moving up. In the second phase (on the right), the price line is moving down. The graphs are divided into phases because it is confusing to draw in the new price lines in 2006–2007 on top of the previous ones for 2000–2005. Rather, the new diagram on the right has simply omitted the previous price lines. The important thing to imagine visually is that the price line moves up and then reverses direction, moving down. Getting out a pencil and paper and shifting the price lines yourself will convince you of the dynamic nature of this adjustment process. Alternatively this movement can be shown very nicely with computer graphics in which you can see the price line moving gradually over time (see the box on p. 146).

The fact that the economy returns to potential GNP, as shown in Figure 6–9, is a key result of macroeconomic theory. In the long run, an increase in money does not increase GNP. The increase in money eventually leads to an increase in the price level of the same magnitude. This raises interest rates back to where they were before the monetary expansion, and eventually reduces investment back to its original level. Note that all other variables—except the price level—are also back to where they were before the increase in the money supply. In the long run the increase in money had no effect on real variables. For this reason we say that money is *neutral* in the long run. But money is not neutral in the short run. It has a powerful effect on output in the short run before prices have had a chance to adjust. The same analysis holds in reverse for a decline in the money supply.

High Tech Macro Graphics

As is clear from the discussion in this chapter the adjustment of the economy to a change in the money supply or government spending is a dynamic process that takes place over a number of years. To illustrate this process with graphs it is necessary to keep the curves in the diagrams shifting year after year. These shifting curves trace out the movement of the economy as in Figure 6–9.

But just as one or two snapshots in the sports pages or even a chalk talk after the game cannot capture all the action of a football game, neither can the printed page or a blackboard completely capture the action of the economy as it responds to changes in government policy. Fortunately, recent advances in computer technology now permit a more comprehensive picture of the action in macroeconomics.

MACROSOLVE, a computer program written by Stephen King and

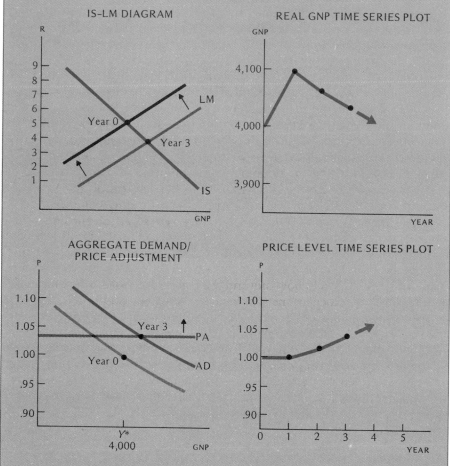

A MACROSOLVE COMPUTER SCREEN.
This is what the computer screen looks like after 3 periods. The arrows indicate the direction of movement. Note that the upper left-hand panel is the standard IS-LM diagram discussed in Chapter 5, the lower left-hand panel is Figure 6–9, and the right-hand panels are those shown in Figure 6–10.

Rick McConnell to go along with this text, provides state of the art computer graphics that show how the curves of macroeconomics shift over time. On an IBM-PC or compatible computer or an Apple Macintosh the program simultaneously shows not only the AD curve and price adjustment diagram in Figure 6–9, but also the IS-LM diagram, and even the time series charts for output and prices in Figure 6–10. Just as video replay helps both players and coaches (not to mention the fans) in football, MACROSOLVE is a great boon to students and teachers in macroeconomics.

As an illustration of how MACROSOLVE works, the sketch above shows what the computer screen looks like three periods after an increase in the money supply (the same case considered in the text).

There are four charts on the screen. In the upper left-hand area is the standard IS-LM diagram. The increase in the money supply has shifted the LM curve to the right from its initial position in period 0. By period 3, however, the LM curve is shifting back to the left as prices are rising. The arrows in the sketch illustrate the movement of the LM curve that you would see on the computer screen.

In the lower left-hand area is the same aggregate demand price adjustment diagram shown in Figure 6–9, but only with the price line that applies in period 3. Note how the aggregate demand curve has shifted to the right, and that the price line is shifting up.

Finally, on the right are the two time series charts that appear in Figure 6–10, now with only the first three periods shown and with arrows indicating how the lines would be extending themselves on the computer screen.

Figure 6–10 summarizes how GNP and the price level move over time according to the above calculations. The upper panel shows GNP and the lower panel shows the price level. Note how GNP returns to potential after overshooting and the price level permanently rises to a new level.

Fiscal policy works a little differently from monetary policy. Suppose that in the same circumstances government spending, rather than the money supply, is increased in 2001. Again the aggregate demand curve shifts to the right just as in Figure 6–9, and GNP rises. But now, from IS-LM results of the previous chapter, we know that interest rates rise during the first year, crowding out investment and net exports and partly offsetting the stimulus to demand from government spending. As the price level begins to rise, interest rates rise further, and more investment and exports are crowded out.

In the long run GNP returns to potential GNP even though government spending has been increased. As a result we know that in the long run investment spending and net exports must have been reduced by exactly the same amount that government spending was raised. Otherwise, the income identity would be violated. In the long run fiscal policy completely crowds

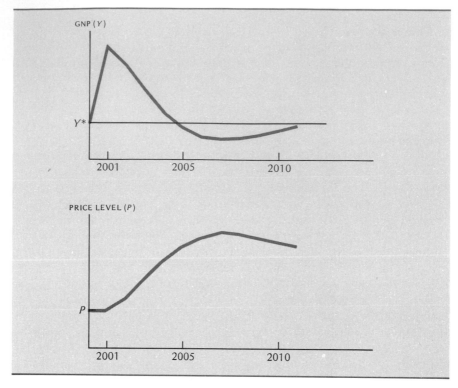

Figure 6-10.   GNP AND THE PRICE LEVEL AFTER AN INCREASE IN MONEY.
The top panel shows GNP and the bottom panel shows the price level. Time (years) is measured on the horizontal axis of both diagrams. The money supply is increased in the year 2001, which is marked on both graphs. At first, GNP increases and the price level does not move. In 2002 the level of GNP begins to fall, and the price level begins to rise. The movements continue in 2003 and so on until GNP returns to potential GNP, and the price level rises by the full amount that the money supply increases.

out investment spending and net exports. The rise in the price level increases the demand for money, leading to higher interest rates and less investment spending and net exports.

ALGEBRAIC DERIVATION

The response of the economy to a change in the money supply can also be analyzed with algebra. Suppose the aggregate demand curve is the one considered in the examples in Chapter 5. That is,

$$Y = 2,287 + 2.855\frac{M}{P}, \tag{6-7}$$

where we have set government spending to $750 billion. Combining this aggregate demand curve with one of the price-adjustment equations, 6–6, describes the evolution of the economy. We then use Equation 6–6 along with Equation 6–7. The algebraic calculations proceed in flip-flop fashion, just like the graphical analysis: Take the price level as given, use Equation 6–7 to find output Y, and plug the value of output into Equation 6–6. Calculate the inflation rate π and the price level P for the next year. Then go back to Equation 6–7 with the new price level, determine a new output level, and so on. The answers you get at each stage are the same as the ones that can be read off the numerical scales in Figure 6–9.

We have now completed our first description of the complete macroeconomic model. In the short run, the price level inherited from the previous year together with the current aggregate demand schedule determine the level of output. In the medium run, the process of price adjustment moves the economy closer to potential GNP. Eventually, the economy will reach potential GNP. Our next step is to use this complete model to examine the important issues of monetary and fiscal policy.

The Movement to Potential GNP

1. The aggregate demand curve and the price-adjustment line govern the movement to potential GNP. After being pushed away from potential GNP by monetary policy or fiscal policy—whether toward slack or overfull employment—the economy will eventually reach potential GNP.

2. Because expected inflation responds to past inflation, the economy overshoots potential GNP. However, it will still eventually reach potential GNP.

3. An increase in the money supply increases GNP in the short run, but eventually this effect wears off as the price level rises. In the long run an increase in the money supply has no effect on GNP.

4. An increase in government spending also increases GNP in the short run, though there is some reduction in investment and net exports. In the long run, the stimulus to GNP is completely offset by a decline in investment and net exports as interest rates rise. In the long run fiscal policy completely crowds out investment spending and net exports.

Review and Practice

MAJOR POINTS

1. Potential GNP is the level of real GNP that would be produced if everybody was working who wanted a job given existing incentives.

2. The aggregate supply schedule is a vertical line; supply equals potential GNP no matter what the price level.

3. In the long run, the economy moves to potential GNP.

4. In the short run, the price level is predetermined. GNP is determined by aggregate demand at the predetermined price level.

5. The process of price adjustment takes the economy to potential GNP over time. When output exceeds potential, prices rise; when output is below potential, prices fall.

6. If inflation becomes expected by the public, the price-adjustment schedule is shifted upward by the amount of the expected inflation.

7. The economy reaches potential GNP through the repetition of price adjustment year after year. Each year, conditions in the previous year determine the price level coming into the year. Then the aggregate demand curve determines GNP.

8. Because expected inflation fluctuates according to recent actual inflation, the economy overshoots its potential on the way to its final resting point at potential.

KEY TERMS AND CONCEPTS

Aggregate supply	Predetermined-price level
Potential employment	Dynamic model
Production function	Price adjustment
Potential output	Phillips curve
Full employment level of output	Expected inflation
Aggregate supply schedule	Accelerationist property

QUESTIONS FOR DISCUSSION AND REVIEW

1. What determines potential employment? Why doesn't potential employment depend on the price level?

2. What is the justification for taking the capital stock as given?

3. Explain how the Phillips curve is derived from a model of relative price setting. What happens to the Phillips curve if firms expect inflation?

4. Explain why money is neutral in the long run but not in the short run.

5. Does government spending completely crowd out private investment and net exports in the long run? What about the short run? Why?

6. Why does the economy overshoot potential GNP when expectations of inflation depend on last year's inflation?

7. What is the accelerationist hypothesis? What would happen to inflation if policy makers attempted to hold unemployment below the natural rate year after year?

8. If firms expect the Fed to start fighting inflation with an aim to bringing it to zero, will their expectations of inflation suddenly drop to zezo? Why?

PROBLEMS

Numerical

1. Suppose the economy has the aggregate demand curve derived in the examples of Chapter 5. That is,

$$Y = 2{,}287 + 2.855\frac{M}{P}$$

and the price-adjustment schedule

$$\pi = 1.2 \left(\frac{Y_{-1} - 4{,}000}{4{,}000}\right).$$

The money supply is $600 billion.

a. Plot the aggregate demand curve and the potential GNP line. Explain why the *aggregate demand curve is not a straight line.*

b. If $P_0 = .5$ what will Y_0 be? Will this place upward or downward pressure on prices?

c. Compute the path of the economy—that is, calculate GNP, the price level, and inflation—for each year until GNP is within 1 percent of potential.

d. Diagram the economy's path on the demand curve plotted in Part a. Then, draw your own version of Figures 6–9 and 6–10. (You may assume that inflation was initially zero.) From these graphs, does the economy overshoot or converge directly to equilibrium?

e. Assume now that inflation is given by $\pi = .6\pi_{-1} + 1.2\ [(Y_{-1}-4{,}000)/4{,}000]$. Compute the path of the economy for the first five years, and diagram the economy's path as in Part d. Now is there overshooting?

f. In Part e, what does the $.6\pi_{-1}$ term in the price-adjustment equation represent? Explain the relationship between this term and overshooting.

2. Again, suppose that the model of the economy is given by

$$Y = 2{,}287 + 2.855M/P$$
$$\pi = .6\pi_{-1} + 1.2[(Y_{-1}-4{,}000)/4{,}000]$$

a. For what value of M will GNP equal potential? Assuming that $M = \$550$ billion, calculate output, inflation, and the price level for years 0 through 5.

b. Using the numerical IS-LM equations given in Chapter 5, find out what happens to the interest rate, consumption, investment, and net exports in each of these years. What is the long-run equilibrium value for each of these variables?

c. Note that income, consumption, and investment tend to overshoot and undershoot at the same time. Using the IS-LM diagram, explain why this is necessarily so. Why isn't the same true of net exports?

Analytical

1. In view of Okun's law, is it possible for both output and the unemployment rate to increase from one year to the next? Explain.

2. According to the price-adjustment equation 6–6, is inflation a predetermined variable? Explain.

3. Using the expectations-augmented Phillips curve, explain what happens when the unemployment rate decreases for one year and then returns to the natural rate. Then describe what happens when the unemployment rate stays below the natural rate year after year.

4. From a position of potential GNP and zero inflation the government increases defense spending. Describe qualitatively, using words and graphs but no algebra, what happens to GNP, the price level, interest rates, consumption, investment, and net exports. Assume at first that expectations of inflation remain at zero. Then describe how your answers change if expectations of inflation depend on last year's inflation.

5. Suppose that there is a sudden and permanent decline in potential GNP. Describe the behavior of prices, output, interest rates, consumption, investment, and net exports.

6. Suppose that output is below potential output in year 0. Prices that year are given by P_0. In year 1 (with the level of potential output unchanged) the Fed stimulates the economy by shifting the aggregate demand curve until it intersects the point $(P_0, Y*)$.
   a. Sketch the aggregate demand curve for years 0 and 1. Describe the action taken by the Fed.
   b. Assume that the price adjustment process is given by Equation 6–6. If inflation in year 0 was zero, how will prices behave in year 1? Sketch the price-adjustment curve for year 1.
   c. Explain why output in year 1 will be above potential.
   d. In which direction should the Fed have shifted the aggregate demand curve in order to set $Y_1=Y*$? Is it possible to say?
   e. Given the Fed's action, is it possible to say whether prices will increase or decrease in year 2? Why or why not?

7. The Phillips curve originally described a relationship between inflation and unemployment. In this problem we look at some of the properties of the Phillips curve.
   a. Use Okun's law and the price-adjustment equation given in 6–5 to derive a relationship between inflation and unemployment. Is inflation related to current or past values of unemployment? Sketch a graph of this relationship, with inflation on the vertical axis and unemployment on the horizontal axis.
   b. How would a change in $Y*$ shift the curve? How about a change in $U*$?
   c. How would a change in π^e shift the curve?
   d. In view of your answers to Parts b and c, how might the Phillips curve have actually shifted in the 1970s? Explain.

8. When thinking about the adjustment process, remember that underlying the aggregate demand curve are the IS and LM curves.
   a. During the adjustment process, is it the IS or LM curve that moves? Why does it move?
   b. Assume that the economy is initially in equilibrium and then the IS curve is shifted out. Using the IS and LM graphs, show the adjustment process (i) for the case when the economy returns directly to equilibrium, and (ii) for the overshooting case.
   c. Repeat Part b for the case where the LM curve is initially shifted out.

9. Suppose that at the end of 1988 Y is equal to potential, $P=1.2$, and $M=\$720$ billion. Assume that prices in 1988 have risen by 5 percent. The aggregate demand and price-adjustment equations for the economy are given by:

$$Y = Y_0 + 2.855\, M/P$$
$$\pi = \pi^e + f[(Y_{-1} - Y^*)/Y^*]$$

a. What is the real money supply? What is the nominal money supply?
b. Suppose the Fed wishes to maintain output at potential for each of the years 1989 through 1992. If $\pi^e = \pi_{-1}$, what are the required increases in the real and nominal money stocks for each of the four years? Repeat your calculations for $\pi^e = .6\pi_{-1}$.
c. Qualitatively, how would your answers to Part b differ if the Fed expected government spending to increase in each of these years?

7

Macroeconomic Policy:
A First Look

MONETARY AND fiscal policy have powerful effects on the economy. Changes in the money supply or in government spending have an immediate impact on real GNP and a delayed impact on the price level. An increase in the money supply, for example, will stimulate output and employment in the short run, with inflation rising later, and real GNP eventually returning to normal.

Because monetary and fiscal policies have such powerful effects on the economy they are constantly being discussed and debated. When the chairman of the Federal Reserve Board testifies in Congress, hoards of news reporters crowd the room. Each sentence is dissected for clues about whether the Fed might increase or decrease money growth. FED CHAIRMAN HINTS TIGHTER MONEY POLICY might be the headline in the next morning's *Wall Street Journal*. Guessing right means big profits to those involved with financial markets, but the news also has an impact on all of us, as for instance on those of us buying or selling a home and concerned about what happens to mortgage interest rates.

Discussions about fiscal policy usually focus on the deficit. In the 1980s the deficit has been probably the most talked about economic statistic in the United States. Concerns about interest rates and investment were part of the reason. An increase in government spending will obviously increase the deficit if not matched by an increase in taxes. Our analysis shows that an increase in the deficit will increase interest rates, and crowd out some investment even as it stimulates the economy in the short run.

In this chapter we take a systematic look at the formulation and evaluation of macroeconomic policy, that is, monetary and fiscal policy. The fact that monetary and fiscal policy have the potential to affect the economy suggests that these policies might be used to improve macroeconomic performance. We will want to investigate whether this is the case.

Sometimes there are economic **shocks** or **disturbances** to the economy that might call for policy intervention. We distinguish between two types of disturbances in this chapter: **aggregate demand disturbances** and **price disturbances.** An aggregate demand disturbance is some event other than a change in policy that shifts the aggregate demand curve. A price disturbance is some event that shifts the price-adjustment relationship. The immediate effect of a price disturbance is to change the price level, unless policy acts to offset the disturbance. Another important policy problem is disinflation—getting the inflation rate down after it has been built into the economy. This chapter considers the appropriate policy responses.

We will also consider the issue of how to choose between monetary and fiscal policy. Both types of policies can shift aggregate demand, but they have different effects on investment and net exports.

7.1 Shocks and Disturbances to the Economy

Unforeseen or unpredictable events are commonplace in the economy. At the most basic level, many of the relationships we use to describe the economy depend on human behavior, which is frequently erratic. Keynes used the term "animal spirits" to characterize the moods of business people. Other economic relationships depend on technology—the money demand relationship, for example, depends on how technically advanced the financial system is. It seems that, no matter how successful we are in describing the systematic parts of economic behavior, there will always be some room for uncertainty, and thus for shocks and disturbances to our economic relationships. The model we developed in Chapters 4 through 6 would certainly be affected by such shocks.

SHOCKS TO AGGREGATE DEMAND

Consider some examples of shocks to the behavioral relationships of the extended model of aggregate demand:

1. Foreign demand suddenly shifts away from U.S. goods. Net export demand falls.

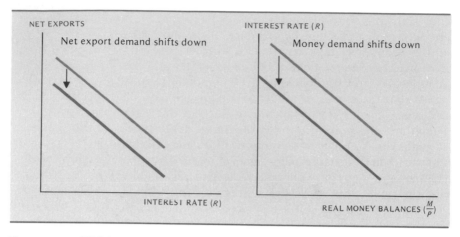

Figure 7–1.   SHOCKS: DOWNWARD SHIFTS IN NET EXPORTS AND MONEY DEMAND.
On the left, a shift in foreign demand away from U.S. goods shifts the net export schedule downward. On the right, deregulation reduces money demand. The money demand function shifts inward.

    2. A new type of credit card makes it easier to get by with less cash. The money demand schedule shifts inward.

These two examples are illustrated graphically in Figure 7–1. The reduction in the demand for exports shifts net exports downward for each interest rate. The decline in money demand shifts the demand for money inward for each interest rate.

Disturbances can be distinguished according to whether they are temporary or permanent. This distinction is important for policy makers: A temporary disturbance might be ignored because its effects will disappear soon anyway. In practice it is difficult to distinguish between temporary and permanent shocks when they occur.

ANALYZING THE EFFECTS OF AGGREGATE DEMAND SHOCKS

Disturbances both to spending and to money demand, the two major components of our model of aggregate demand, shift the aggregate demand curve: The downward shift in net export demand pushes the aggregate demand curve to the left. The downward shift in money demand has the same effect as an increase in the money supply, which we know shifts the aggregate demand curve to the right.

These shifts in the aggregate demand curve have immediate impacts on real GNP, as shown in Figure 7–2.

From the analysis used in Chapter 6 we can trace out the full dynamic movement of the economy in response to the aggregate demand shocks:

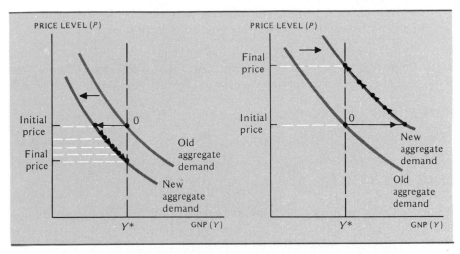

Figure 7-2.   DISTURBANCES SHIFT THE AGGREGATE DEMAND SCHEDULE.
On the left, aggregate demand has shifted inward because of the decline in the net export schedule. On the right, aggregate demand has shifted outward because of the decline in money demand. On the left, GNP falls at first. Then the economy moves down
and to the right along the AD schedule until it finally reaches equilibrium again at a lower
price. On the right, GNP rises at first. Then the economy moves up and to the left along
the AD schedule until it reaches equilibrium again at a higher price.

1. With real GNP below potential GNP after the drop in net exports, the
   price level will begin to fall. Firms have found that the demand for
   their products has fallen off and they will start to cut their prices. This
   drop in the price level is shown in Figure 7-2 as a movement down and
   to the right along the aggregate demand (AD) schedule. The lower
   price level causes the interest rate to fall. With a lower interest rate, investment spending and net exports will increase. The increase in investment and net exports will tend to offset the original decline in net
   exports. This process of gradual price adjustment will continue as long
   as real GNP is below potential GNP. By the time that real GNP has again
   recovered and returned to potential GNP, investment and net exports
   will have increased by just the amount that net exports fell in the first
   place. The interest rate will be lower by enough to stimulate this much
   investment and net exports. In the long run, real GNP will be back to
   normal, but during the period of gradual price adjustment the economy will have gone through a recession with an increase in unemployment.
2. When the demand for money drops, the aggregate demand curve will
   shift outward. The interest rate drops; investment, net exports, and
   consumption rise. But higher GNP will cause prices to rise, tending to
   raise the interest rate. Through this process of gradual price adjust-

ment the economy will eventually return to normal. In the meantime, however, the economy has experienced a period of inflation and a boom in economic activity.

To summarize the examples, in both cases there is a shock to aggregate demand that temporarily moves the economy away from potential GNP and sends the economy into either a boom or a recession. Through gradual adjustment of the price level the economy eventually returns to normal.

SHOCKS TO THE PRICE LEVEL

The shocks considered so far had the effect of shifting the aggregate demand curve. Another type of shock occurs when the price level shifts. There are several reasons why this might occur:

1. The price of an input to the economy might suddenly rise; the best example is an increase in the price of oil, such as occurred in the 1970s. Suppose that the members of the Organization of Petroleum Exporting Countries (QPEC) increase the price of crude oil; the aim is to increase the relative price of crude. But other price setters in petroleum-related industries—gasoline, heating oil, plastics, etc.—will at first increase their own price not knowing whether a change in profit margins is necessary. This will tend to increase the price of all petroleum-related products. Moreover, prices in other energy industries will also tend to increase. Unless there is a fall in the price of other goods, when the producing countries increase the price of crude oil there will be an increase in the overall price level.
2. A large group of workers—perhaps during a union negotiation—may get a wage increase that is abnormally high. When firms pass on the wage increase in the form of higher prices, there will be an upward shift in the price—a price shock.
3. Firms might simply make a mistake and increase their prices, perhaps because they mistakenly expected an increase in inflation.

A price shock is shown in Figure 7–3. If monetary and fiscal policies do not change, then real GNP will fall below potential GNP. After the initial price shock the economy will be operating below its full-employment level at Y_1. With no increase in the money supply, this will in turn cause prices to fall as firms try to cut prices to increase sales. The fall in prices corresponds to a downward movement in the price-adjustment curve, which will continue until real GNP is equal to potential GNP. Eventually, therefore, the economy returns to normal operating levels. In the meantime the price shock has caused a recession. The period of recession puts downward pressure on prices and offsets the original price shock.

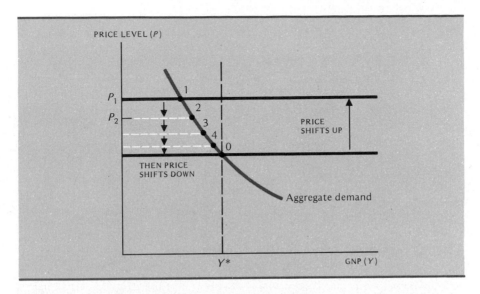

Figure 7–3. AN UPWARD SHOCK IN THE PRICE LEVEL.
Real GNP is reduced when the price level jumps up—the economy moves to point 1, up
and to the left along the aggregate demand curve. Then the process of price adjustment
causes the economy to return gradually to its original equilibrium as the price level falls.

Economic Shocks

1. There can be unexpected shifts in spending—for example, the
   amount of investment undertaken by businesses at any given interest rate might rise or fall.

2. There can be unexpected shifts in the money market—for example, the amount of money demanded by the public at any given interest rate might rise or fall.

3. Spending or money market shifts will in turn shift the aggregate
   demand curve. At first, real GNP will rise or fall. Later, as price adjustment occurs, real GNP will return to equilibrium and the price
   level will move to a permanently different level.

4. Prices may shift unexpectedly as well. When that occurs, real GNP
   will change at first. Then price adjustment will return the economy
   to its original equilibrium. Neither the price level nor GNP will
   change in the long run.

Three Oil Price Shocks

The U.S. economy was buffeted by three major oil price shocks between 1973 and 1986. In 1973, the Arab oil embargo ushered in a huge increase in the price of crude oil and oil products. In 1978, the Iranian revolution and the Iran-Iraq war set off another large increase. Then at the beginning of 1986, the oil market collapsed.

To measure the size of the shocks themselves, we can look at the retail price of gasoline, as reported in the consumer price index. The percentage changes in gas prices in the three shocks were:

	Embargo	Revolution (percentage change)	Collapse
First year	35	35	−22
First and second years	45	88	−30

Counting two years, the second shock was the biggest and the third shock was the smallest.

Oil price shocks are clearly passed along into total inflation. The increases in the rate of inflation as measured by the GNP implicit price deflator were:

	Embargo	Revolution (percentage change)	Collapse
First year	2.6	1.6	−.6
First and second years	3.3	1.7	000

Moreover, as the aggregate demand analysis suggests, the economy moves along the AD schedule when a price shock occurs. The changes in GNP relative to its normal growth path of 2 percent per year were:

	Embargo	Revolution (percentage change)	Collapse
First year	−2.5	0.5	0.5
First and second years	−5.8	−1.7	000

The effects on the first year were relatively weak except in the embargo in 1973–74; in the case of the revolution, GNP grew more than normal by 0.5 percentage points in 1979. The effects counting the second year are much more pronounced.

All of the predictions of our model are fulfilled by these data.

7.2 Responding to Aggregate Demand Shocks: Stabilization Policy

In considering appropriate responses to aggregate demand shocks, let us first consider the case of an inward shift in the aggregate demand curve caused by an increase in the demand for money. That is, a shock to money demand occurs because people want to hold more money at every interest rate and income level than they did before. This increased demand could be caused by an increase in uncertainty about the future, creating the need for very liquid assets such as cash and demand deposits. In the early 1980s many economists argued that such a shift was occurring because of the increased uncertainty about interest rate behavior. Interest rates certainly became much more volatile at the time. The interest rate on U.S. Treasury bills, for example, fell from 13 percent in February 1980 to 7 percent in June and climbed to 16 percent by December before dipping again in early 1981. These fluctuations could have been due to fluctuations in the demand for money.

Unless the Federal Reserve takes action to offset changes in money demand, interest rates will rise and the aggregate demand curve will shift to the left. What action would be appropriate for the Fed? An increase in the money supply to match the increase in money demand would exactly offset any leftward movement in the aggregate demand schedule. This is shown in Figure 7–4.

Other types of aggregate demand shocks raise many of the same issues for aggregate demand policy. Suppose, for example, that there is an investment

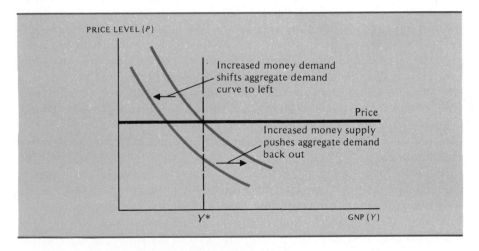

Figure 7–4.   INCREASE IN MONEY DEMAND.
An increase in money demand shifts the aggregate demand schedule to the left, raising interest rates and reducing real GNP. Timely action by the Fed to increase the money supply could prevent it.

boom caused by business optimism that pushes the aggregate demand schedule to the right. Without any policy response we know from the discussion above that this will result in a temporary increase in GNP followed by a period of increase in the rate of inflation. Policy makers could avoid this instability by taking some action to reduce aggregate demand: The money supply or government spending could be reduced or, alternatively, taxes could be raised. Any of these actions would have the effect of bringing the aggregate demand schedule back to the left.

The type of aggregate demand policy outlined in these two examples is called **countercyclical stabilization policy,** because it attempts to counter those disturbances to the economy that otherwise would cause cyclical fluctuations in real GNP and the price level. Such a policy is also sometimes called *activist,* because the policy makers are actively manipulating the instruments of monetary and fiscal policy.

WHEN DO MACROECONOMISTS DISAGREE ABOUT STABILIZATION POLICY?

The underlying objective of policy in the above examples is to maintain a steady or stable level of aggregate demand. The importance of a stable aggregate demand is one that has been recognized by most economists since the 1930s. Even economists who normally differ on other issues agree on the principle that it is desirable to maintain a stable growth of aggregate demand. Keynesians such as the late Walter Heller of the University of Minnesota, who was President Kennedy's chief economic adviser, and James Tobin of Yale University agree with monetarists such as Milton Friedman on this point. As we showed in Chapter 2, the U.S. economy has been much more stable in the period following World War II—even if one includes the turbulent 1970s and early 1980s. Many economists feel that this improvement in macroeconomic performance is related to the recognition of the importance of stable aggregate demand growth. The late Arthur Burns, a conservative non-Keynesian economist who was President Eisenhower's chief economic adviser and later chairman of the Federal Reserve Board, argued persuasively that changes in economic policy that stabilized aggregate demand were responsible for the improvement in performance after World War II.[1]

If macroeconomists agree on such a basic issue as the goal of stable aggregate demand growth, then what is all the highly publicized controversy and disagreement about? Primarily, it is about the means of achieving this goal. Monetarists—including Milton Friedman, Allan Meltzer of Carnegie-Mellon University, and Karl Brunner of the University of Rochester—argue

[1] See Arthur Burns, "Progress toward Economic Stability," in his *The Business Cycle in a Changing World,* Columbia University Press, 1979.

that the most effective way to maintain a steady growth of aggregate demand is to keep the rate of money growth constant. But how does such a view make sense in light of our previous arguments that timely changes in the money supply can be used to offset disturbances to the economy?

Monetarists have no disagreement about the powerful effects that changes in the money supply can have on real GNP in the short run—for example, Milton Friedman has said, "Because prices are sticky, faster or slower monetary growth initially affects output. . . . But these effects wear off. After about two years the main effect is on inflation."[2] However, for a number of reasons, monetarists feel that it is not possible to use monetary policy in the way that we illustrated. Their criticism of activist policy is that the impact of monetary policy occurs with a lag and the length of this lag is uncertain. Because of the lag, monetary stimulus or restraint may come too late. In an attempt to offset a decline in investment, the policy response may come after the recession is over, when the economy is recovering back to potential GNP. This might add to the expansion in economic activity and exacerbate the economic fluctuation. Figure 7–5 illustrates this possibility. Because of the practical difficulties of conducting monetary policy in an uncertain world, monetarists argue that attempts to manipulate monetary policy to offset disturbances to the economy could result in more rather than fewer fluctuations in economic activity.

A second argument of the monetarists against activist countercyclical policy is that the instruments of policy might be used to overstimulate the economy and bring about higher and higher rates of inflation. In our examples

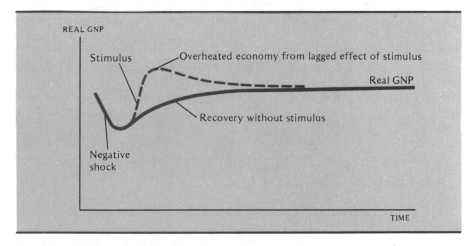

Figure 7–5.   LAGS IN POLICY.
A change in the policy instrument that arrives too late might exacerbate the fluctuations in the economy.

[2] See *Newsweek,* July 12, 1982, p. 64.

of countercyclical policy we never considered the possibility that policy makers might try to push the economy beyond its potential output, Y^*. But clearly this is feasible. With prices temporarily sticky, real GNP can be raised above potential output Y^*. The long-run consequence of such a policy will be a higher price level, but, in the short run, real GNP growth could appear quite attractive. The danger of such an inflationary policy becomes quite serious when policy decisions are made in a political environment, as usually happens in the United States. The long-run disadvantages of such a policy may be overlooked in favor of short-run advantages when election day nears.

Other arguments against the use of countercyclical policy have come from the new classical macroeconomists, such as Thomas Sargent of Stanford University and Neil Wallace of the University of Minnesota. The argument here is quite different from that of the monetarists; it questions whether systematic changes in the instruments of aggregate demand policy can have any effect at all on real GNP and employment. The new classical school focuses directly on the issue of price stickiness, which we have taken for granted in most of our discussion. If prices are not sticky—that is, if they are adjusted instantaneously without a lag—then any systematic attempt to use policy to affect real GNP will be offset by changes in the price level. In such a world aggregate demand policy has no role at all except to control prices.

A second related point of the new classical view is that the need for policy intervention is not adequately justified. For example, in the case where an increase in investment brings about a boom in the economy, the appropriate aggregate demand policy is to offset this boom by a contractionary monetary policy. The justification for such a policy is that it reduces the fluctuations in real GNP and the price level. However, the behavior of investment is altered as a result of the policy. The objection raised by the new classical school is that it might be more harmful to cut the investment demand than it would be to have the fluctuations in real GNP and the price level.

Policy Response to Demand Shocks

1. When an aggregate demand shock occurs, monetary or fiscal policy can offset the shock. Whatever inward or outward shift of the aggregate demand curve has taken place can be reversed through a policy move in the opposite direction.

2. Though almost all economists agree on the desirability of stable aggregate demand, many believe that active policy might add to the instability rather than offset it. Monetarists generally oppose enacting policy that attempts to act against aggregate demand shifts.

3. Another argument against active policy comes from the new classical school. They argue that a systematic policy of offsetting demand disturbances won't have any effect on GNP.

7.3 Responding to Price Shocks

The response to a price shock raises some more difficult issues than does the response to a demand shock. Even under the best of circumstances—no lags or uncertainty in the conduct of policy—such a shock will inevitably affect either the price level or real GNP.

Suppose, for example, that there is a price shock of the type illustrated in Figure 7–6. As we discussed above, with no policy response, such a price shock tends to reduce real GNP and raise the price level. This is shown in the left-hand panel of Figure 7–6.

Now, suppose that the monetary authorities increase the money supply in response to the price shock. As shown in Figure 7–6, this shifts the aggregate demand curve outward and tends to mitigate the downward fluctuation in real GNP. However, the increase in the money supply will exacerbate

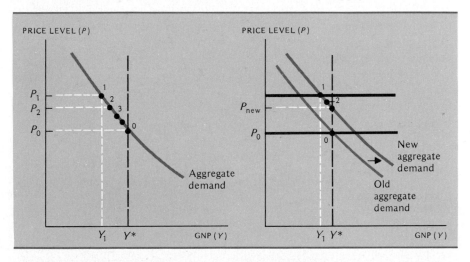

Figure 7–6. MONETARY RESPONSE TO A PRICE SHOCK.
On the left, monetary policy does not respond to the price shock. The shock raises the price level from P_0 to P_1. Output falls from Y^* to Y_1. Then the price-adjustment process starts. In the next year the price level drops to P_2. Eventually prices fall back to normal and output returns to potential output. On the right, monetary policy responds to the price shock. The money supply is increased and the aggregate demand curve moves outward. At the new intersection of the price line (point 1), there is less downward pressure on the price level because output at Y_1 is closer to potential than in the panel on the left. Assuming that the new aggregate demand curve is maintained, eventually the price level falls to the level marked P_{new}.

the fluctuation in the price level. If output does not fall much below potential there will be little downward pressure on the price level. The price level will stay high for a longer time and never return to normal if the money supply is not reduced again. As shown in the right-hand panel of Figure 7–6, the price line will remain at a higher level if the aggregate demand curve remains at its new higher position. In the sense that there is less downward pressure on the price level so that it never returns to normal, there is thus less price stability with the policy that tries to offset the fluctuation in real GNP. In other words, with a supply shock there is a trade-off between the stability of real GNP and the stability of the price level.

Policies that increase the money supply in response to positive price shocks are called **accommodative policies.** A policy that holds the money supply constant is called **nonaccommodative.** Figure 7–7 summarizes, for the two policies, the behavior of GNP and the price level after a price shock. The plots show the results of the calculations of GNP and the price level from Figure 7–6. Clearly the accommodative policy is better in terms of the performance of GNP, but is worse in terms of the performance of the price level.

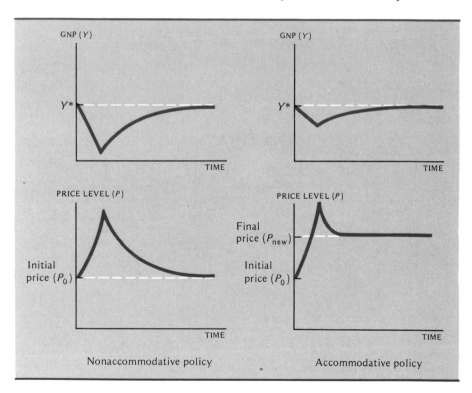

Figure 7–7.   THE RESPONSE OF THE PRICE LEVEL AND GNP TO PRICE SHOCKS FOR ACCOMMODATIVE AND NONACCOMMODATIVE POLICIES.
These charts summarize the calculations from Figure 7–6. The nonaccommodative policy is shown on the left and the accommodative policy is shown on the right. Output is more stable with the accommodative policy, but the price level is less stable.

Policy Response to Price Shocks

1. In the absence of a policy response (that is, with a nonaccommodative monetary policy), a positive price shock causes a rise in the price level and a sustained period of economic slack.

2. Price shocks create a serious problem for policy. If policy tries to limit the decline in GNP from a positive price shock, it will make the price level less stable. If it tries to head off the inflation, it will deepen the recession.

7.4 Macroeconomic Policy as a Rule

Our discussion of the appropriate response of monetary policy to price shocks naturally gives rise to the question of whether the money supply is an exogenous variable, as we have been assuming all along. If the money supply responds to the price level, then it no longer can be exogenous for it is determined in the model.

Treating policy variables as exogenous has long been a tradition in macroeconomics. But more recently an alternative view, that they should be treated as endogenous, is becoming more attractive. Endogenous policy is determined according to some behavioral relationship, or what is frequently called a **policy rule.** The most frequently discussed policy rule in macroeconomics is the fixed growth rate rule for the money supply that Milton Friedman and other monetarists have advocated. A fixed growth rate rule is simply to keep the growth rate of the money supply constant. But this is a very special rule in that it involves no response of the money supply to economic events. A more general rule would call for some response.

Even if policy makers do not determine policy according to a mechanical formula, they do respond to economic events much like the firms and consumers in the economy. Their behavior and its impact on the economy are therefore probably more accurately described by a systematic behavioral relationship. If so, we can think of the behavioral relationship as a policy rule.

We saw in Section 7.3 that an accommodative monetary policy was one that reacted to a positive price shock with an increase in the money supply. We showed the effect of this type of policy on the fluctuations of real GNP and the price level, by treating the money supply as exogenous. If the Fed regularly, or systematically, reacted to price disturbances in this way, then we would say that the Fed was following an accommodative policy rule. The money supply would not be an exogenous variable. It would join the list of endogenous variables to be determined in the basic macroeconomic model. As with the other endogenous variables, a behavioral relationship would de-

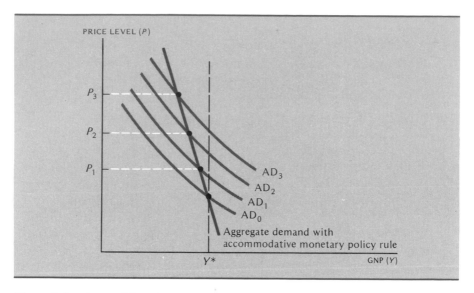

Figure 7–8.   THE AGGREGATE DEMAND SCHEDULE WITH AN ACCOMMODATIVE POLICY RULE.

If the price shock is small, so that the price level is P_1, the Fed sets the money supply so that the AD schedule is AD_1. For larger shocks that raise the price level to P_2 or P_3, the Fed raises the money stock more, so that the corresponding AD schedule is AD_2 or AD_3. The set of intersections traces out a steeper aggregate demand schedule. This schedule includes the monetary response.

scribe how the monetary authorities determined the money supply. In fact, the policy rule *is* that behavioral relationship.

The derivation of the policy rule and its effects on the economy can be shown graphically. In Figure 7–8 we show how the monetary authorities react to price shocks. There are several different price lines drawn. Each line represents a price shock of different magnitude. For each price shock, we show how the Fed reacts by shifting the aggregate demand schedule outward. This accommodative reaction leads to intersections of the aggregate demand curve and the price line at higher levels of real GNP than would otherwise occur, shown by the dark line. This line represents the combined effect of the accommodative policy and the price shocks. Note that it is downward sloping—like an aggregate demand curve—but it is steeper than the aggregate demand curve without the influence of policy. In effect, the policy of responding *as a rule* to price shocks leads to a steeper aggregate demand curve. An accommodative monetary policy rule twists the aggregate demand curve clockwise, making it steeper. The more accommodative the policy, the steeper the aggregate demand curve.

In Figure 7–9 we have drawn two aggregate demand curves that represent alternatives to the policy rule shown in Figure 7–8. One of the sched-

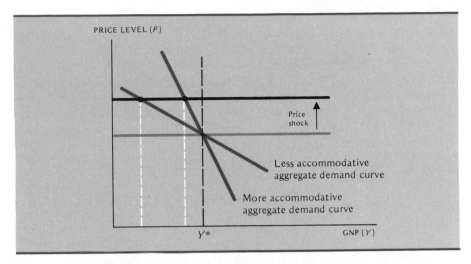

Figure 7–9. AGGREGATE DEMAND SCHEDULES WITH ALTERNATIVE MONETARY POLICY RULES.
More accommodative policy makes the aggregate demand schedule steeper. As a result, the downward shift in output after a price shock is smaller the more accommodative the policy.

ules is simply the aggregate demand schedule with a fixed money supply. Note that when there is a price shock the more accommodative rules translate into a smaller decline in real GNP. However, this also leads to less downward pressure on prices, and thereby less price stability. What is crucial is the slope of the aggregate demand schedule. The more accommodative policies result in more real GNP stability and less price stability. Less accommodative policies tend to increase price stability at the cost of less real GNP stability.

WHY FOCUS ON POLICY RULES?

Aside from the desire to model the economy and the effect of policy as accurately as possible, there are two important reasons why policy analysis in recent years has concentrated on rules rather than on exogenous changes in the policy instruments. These reasons will come up naturally in our later discussions of policy rules, but are worth mentioning briefly now. One reason is the recognition that expectations of policy can influence how policy affects the economy. If people anticipate a certain policy, then they will act differently than if that policy were unanticipated. By stipulating policy as a rule, policy makers are implicitly stating how policy will react to future contingencies. That the money supply will increase if there is a positive price shock is an example of such a rule.

A second reason for the emphasis on rules is the problem of time inconsistency. Unless there is a systematic way for policy makers to commit themselves to operating in a particular way in the future, there will be a temptation to change their plans from what they announce. That is, policy makers will be tempted—in order to stimulate the economy—to do things differently from what they had promised. The advantage of policy rules in such situations is that rules commit policy makers to behaving in a certain predictable way—as long as they do not break the rule! We will come back to the problem of time inconsistency[3] in Chapter 17.

Policy Rules

1. When macro policy is conducted according to a rule, it means that the policy instruments become endogenous variables—they respond in a known way to changes that occur in the economy.

2. One important example of a rule is the way the Fed responds to a price shock. The Fed can emphasize price stability by not adjusting money growth after a shock, which will worsen unemployment. Or, it can limit unemployment by adding to inflation through monetary expansion.

3. Many economists favor policy rules because their use may have favorable effects on the economy through expectations and because a binding rule may prevent shortsighted attempts to overstimulate the economy.

7.5 Disinflation

The problem of maintaining price stability in the face of price shocks is closely related to another type of price stabilization problem: that of bringing down the rate of inflation when it has become too high and has become incorporated into people's expectations and price-setting behavior. This latter problem is called the problem of **disinflation:** that is, reducing the rate of inflation. This problem requires us to pay close attention to the role of expectations in the Phillips curve.

---

[3] The importance of time inconsistency for macroeconomics was first pointed out in Guillermo Calvo, "On the Time Inconsistency of Optimal Policy in a Monetary Economy," *Econometrica,* Vol. 46, pp. 1141–1428, 1978, and in Finn Kydland and Edward Prescott, "Rules Rather than Discretion: The Inconsistency of Optimal Plans," *Journal of Political Economy,* Vol. 85, pp. 473–491, 1977.

The Phillips relationship, as we saw in Chapter 6, can be written

$$\pi = \pi^e + f\frac{Y_{-1} - Y^*}{Y^*}. \tag{7-1}$$

The most challenging problem of disinflation occurs when the expected rate of inflation equals last period's inflation rate; $\pi^e = \pi_{-1}$. With this expectation of inflation the only way that inflation can be reduced is by letting actual output Y drop below potential output Y^*. Equation 7–1 states that the *change* in the rate of inflation over its previous level π_{-1} depends on the percentage deviation of GNP from potential GNP.

The Phillips curve tells us that if the inflation rate is viewed by the policy makers as being too high and in need of reduction, then some type of a recession is inevitable. The essential policy questions related to disinflation are how long and how deep the recession should be. In other words, how sharply should the policy makers reduce the policy instruments to bring about a path for real GNP that is consistent with the desired reduction in inflation?

SETTING POLICY TO HIT A TARGET LEVEL OF GNP

To answer this question, we first need to show how the policy instruments, such as the money supply or government spending, can be manipulated to get a desired path for real GNP. Recall that, with the price-adjustment equation, the price level is predetermined during the course of any particular year. Recall also that monetary and fiscal policies shift the aggregate demand curve to the right or left. The intersection of the aggregate demand curve with the price line gives the current value of real GNP. Hence, by changing monetary policy the Fed can achieve just about any value of real GNP that it wants. Note that this ability of the monetary authorities to pinpoint real GNP perfectly needs to be qualified by the inherent uncertainty and lags in the effect of monetary policy that we discussed above. In addition, we know that aiming for a value of real GNP above potential GNP will soon result in an inflationary spiral. But in the policy problem considered here, this latter possibility is not an issue because the aim of policy is to set real GNP below potential GNP in order to put downward pressure on prices and reduce the rate of inflation.

So far we have used the aggregate demand method to find a level of GNP for a given level of the money supply or government spending. Now we must work the method in *reverse*. We want to find a level for the money supply for a given target level of GNP. The idea is illustrated in Figure 7–10. The economy is shown to be operating at potential output, Y^*. Suppose that the Fed wants to set the money supply to push the economy to a lower target level, Y_1. What level of the money supply should it choose? The answer, as shown in the right-hand panel of Figure 7–10, is to reduce the money sup-

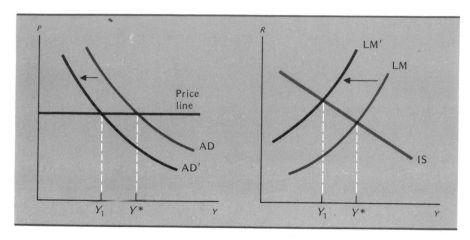

Figure 7–10.   AGGREGATE DEMAND IN REVERSE: THE MONEY SUPPLY IS SET TO HIT A GNP TARGET.

The left-hand panel shows the situation in the economy. Output is equal to potential output, Y^*. The Fed wants to set the money supply so that the output is reduced to the level Y_1. To do this it must shift the aggregate demand curve inward from AD to AD'. As shown in the right-hand panel, the Fed thus reduces the money supply by an amount that makes the LM curve shift in and intersect the IS curve at a level of output equal to Y_1.

ply to the level that sets the aggregate demand curve at a point of intersection with the predetermined price line at the target level of output Y_1.

Numerical Example. Suppose that the aggregate demand curve is the one that we studied in Chapter 5, Equation 5–10, namely,

$$Y = 1,432 + 1.14\,G + 2.855\frac{M}{P}. \tag{7-2}$$

Suppose that Congress has set government spending G at \$750 billion and that the predetermined-price level P equals 1. Potential GNP is \$4,000 billion. The Fed now wants to choose a money supply M to bring actual GNP below potential to \$3,900. For $G = 750$ and $P = 1$, the aggregate demand curve looks like

$$Y = 2,287 + 2.855M. \tag{7-3}$$

The level of the money supply is found by setting output Y in Equation 7–3 equal to 3,900 and finding M. The answer is

$$M = \frac{3,900 - 2,287}{2.855} = \frac{1,613}{2.855}, \tag{7-4}$$

or 566. Note how this calculation is just the reverse of setting M to a value and finding Y, as we did in the numerical example in Chapter 5.

Table 7-1.   THREE PATHS FOR INFLATION AND THE GNP GAP

Year	Path 1		Path 2		Path 3	
	GNP Gap	Inflation	GNP Gap	Inflation	GNP Gap	Inflation
0	0	10	0	10	0	10
1	0	10	−5	10	−10	10
2	0	10	−5	9	−10	8
3	0	10	−5	8	−10	6
4	0	10	−5	7	−10	4
5	0	10	−5	6	0	2
6	0	10	−5	5	0	2
7	0	10	−5	4	0	2
8	0	10	−5	3	0	2
9	0	10	0	2	0	2
10	0	10	0	2	0	2

Note: The GNP gap is the deviation of GNP from potential measured in percent; that is, gap = $(Y − Y^*)/Y^*$ times 100. Inflation is the percentage change in the price level. Each path shows the GNP gap and inflation over a 10-year period. The calculations are made with the Phillips curve of Equation 7-1 with f equal to .2. In the first path, policy holds real GNP at its potential level. Inflation stays at 10 percent. In the second path, real GNP is depressed below potential. Inflation drops steadily to 2 percent. When it reaches 2 percent, policy eases and GNP pulls back up to potential. In the third path, policy is even more contractionary at first; GNP is 10 percent below normal. Inflation drops to 2 percent sooner than in the second path.

ALTERNATIVE DISINFLATION PATHS

Suppose that the rate of inflation has risen to 10 percent, and that the Fed wants to disinflate. Table 7–1 shows three alternative paths for the deviation of GNP from potential GNP, $(Y − Y^*)/Y^*$, and corresponding paths for the inflation rate. Year zero shows the starting point, with inflation at 10 percent and GNP equal to potential GNP. The Fed begins to take actions to reduce inflation in Year 1. The values in Table 7–1 are obtained directly from the Phillips curve in Equation 7–1. For these calculations, we assume that the coefficient f in Equation 7–1 is .2. Recall also that we assume that the public believes that inflation will persist unless the Fed contracts the economy. The simple model of expected inflation with this property that we use is $\pi^e = \pi_{-1}$. Inflation expected this year is last year's actual inflation.

The three alternatives given in Table 7–1 are all feasible for the Fed to undertake. Clearly, if the Fed can pick any value of output Y it wants in the short run, it can also pick any value for the deviation of output from potential output, $(Y - Y*)/Y*$, since potential GNP ($Y*$) is exogenous. By setting the money supply so that the aggregate demand curve is in the appropriate place, the Fed can set output and hence the deviations of output from potential output to the desired level.

The three alternatives were selected to indicate the kind of choice that the monetary authorities have to make when faced with excess inflation. Perhaps the most important thing to note about the choices is that none of them is a good one. The latter two involve a recession, as the inflation rate is decreased. The first avoids a recession, but gets no reduction in inflation.

The second two paths are both successful in getting the inflation rate down from 10 to 2 percent. But there are important differences between the two paths. Path 2 involves a longer, but shallower recession. GNP is just 5 percent below potential for the entire period of the disinflation. However, it takes 8 years to get the inflation rate down to 2 percent. Path 3 involves a shorter recession, but it is quite deep. GNP is 10 percent below potential. In this case the inflation rate is reduced more quickly, reaching 2 percent in 4 years. Clearly, more extreme possibilities are open to policy makers. Or a compromise between Path 2 and Path 3 is another possibility. The paths we have presented in Table 7–1 are meant to be representative of the choices facing policy makers. We illustrate in Figure 7–11A how Paths 2 and 3 differ.

In comparing these paths it is important to note their implications for unemployment. Suppose that the natural rate of unemployment that corresponds to potential GNP is 6 percent. Recall from Chapter 3 that Okun's law translates a GNP gap of 1 percent into .3 percentage point of unemployment. Thus, for Path 2 the unemployment rate rises to 7.5 percent for 8 years, and for Path 3 the unemployment rate rises to 9 percent for 4 years. Of course the unemployment rate stays at 6 percent, the natural rate, for all years in Path 1.

Assuming that some reduction in inflation is desired, we must rule out Path 1. The choice is between Path 2 and Path 3. If very high unemployment is to be avoided, then a more gradual approach is appropriate. Moreover, the more gradual approach is better because it gives people more time to adjust their plans.

An illuminating way to compare the two disinflation paths is shown in Figure 7–11B. The rate of inflation is on the vertical axis and the GNP gap is on the horizontal axis. At the start of the disinflation, the inflation rate of 10 percent and the GNP gap of zero are shown by the point labeled "0" in the diagram. The alternative possibilities for inflation and the GNP gap are then shown as two big **C**s emanating from this initial point and ending up at the final point. The **C** for Path 3 is much more elongated than the **C** for Path 2. This illustrates how Path 3 pushes the economy into a deeper recession than does Path 2.

The alternative possibilities in Figure 7–11B are very similar to the choices faced by policy makers in the late 1970s and early 1980s when the

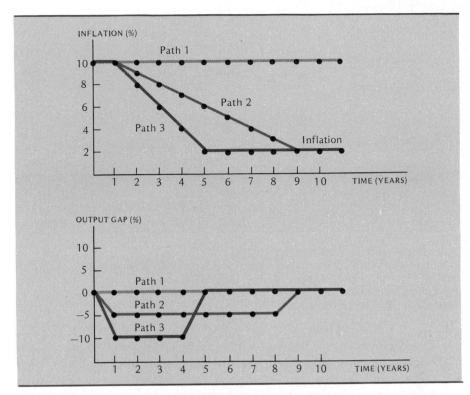

Figure 7–11A. A COMPARISON OF TWO DISINFLATIONS.
Path 2 shows a long, shallow recession (lower panel) and a slow decline in inflation (upper panel). Path 3 shows a short, deep recession and a speedy decline in inflation. Path 1 has no recession and no disinflation.

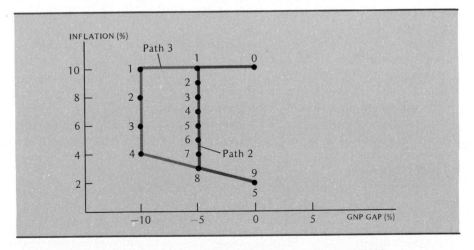

Figure 7–11B. INFLATION AND GNP DURING TWO DISINFLATIONS.
The inflation rate is on the vertical axis; the GNP gap is on the horizontal axis. Both disinflation paths start at "0" and end at the same point. Path 3 shows a much deeper recession than does Path 2.

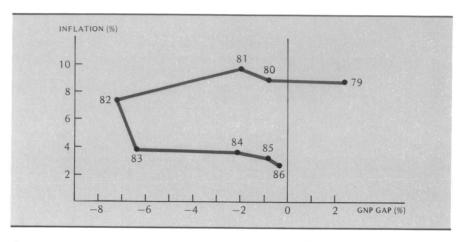

Figure 7–12. THE 1979–86 DISINFLATION.
As money growth was reduced, GNP fell below potential. For a while there was little effect on inflation. The tight monetary policy was continued and eventually inflation came down. Compared to our Paths 2 and 3 in Figures 7–11A and 7–11B, the actual path looks more like the deeper recession path.

rate of inflation in the United States had reached levels near 10 percent. In 1979 President Carter appointed Paul Volcker chairman of the Federal Reserve Board with a clear "go ahead" to reduce inflation. When President Reagan came into office in 1981 he gave the Fed further encouragement to reduce inflation. In President Reagan's report to Congress in February 1981, he listed as a key element of his plan to reduce inflation a "new commitment to a monetary policy that will restore a stable currency and healthy financial markets," and assumed as part of his plan that the growth rate of money would be "steadily reduced from the 1980 levels to one-half those levels by 1986."[4]

Figure 7–12 shows the actual rates of inflation and the GNP gap that occurred starting from 1979. Inflation was very high in 1979 when the GNP gap was close to zero. As the Fed tightened its policy the economy began to slow and GNP fell below potential GNP. Because of the slow reaction of prices to the depressed demand conditions, inflation did not slow for a while (in fact it increased slightly). The Fed continued with a tight policy and the GNP gap got larger, until inflation finally began to give way. There was an enormous reduction in inflation in 1982 and by 1986 inflation had come down to under 3 percent.

Comparing the actual 1979–86 experience with the two alternative paths, Paths 2 and 3, it looks as if Path 3 was chosen by the Fed. The GNP fell to about 7 percent below potential in 1982 and the inflation rate came down

---

[4] *A Program for Economic Recovery*, The White House, February 18, 1981.

much more quickly than in the gradual path. This disinflation was brought about mainly by monetary policy. Fiscal policy was in fact stimulative during that period. The beginning of the more contractionary monetary policies began in late 1979, and coincides fairly closely with the beginning of Paul Volcker's term as chairman of the Federal Reserve Board.

It is likely that a more gradual path was actually attempted by the Fed, but that mistakes led to the deeper recession. In retrospect there appears to

Other Schools of Thought on Disinflation

Figure 7–12 seems to give strong support to the general view we have expressed in this book: It takes time for prices to adjust, and during that time, there can be large departures of GNP from potential. A negative shock to aggregate demand, such as one chosen by the Fed to bring inflation to an end, sends the economy into recession.

Other schools of thought do not agree that recession is inevitably the result of a policy to bring down inflation. One of the most influential critics of the view expressed in this book is Thomas Sargent of Stanford University. Sargent has written,

. . . Inflation only *seems* to have a momentum of its own; it is actually the long-term government policy of persistently running large deficits and creating money at high rates which imparts the momentum to the inflation rate. An implication of this view is that inflation can be stopped much more quickly than advocates of the "momentum" view have indicated and that their estimates of the length of time and the costs of stopping inflation in terms of foregone output ($220 billion of GNP for one percentage point in the inflation rate) are erroneous. This is not to say that it would be easy to eradicate inflation. On the contrary, it would require far more than a few temporary restrictive fiscal and monetary actions. It would require a change in the policy regime; there must be an abrupt change in the continuing government policy, or strategy, for setting deficits now and in the future that is sufficiently binding as to be widely believed. [emphasis added]*

Sargent examines the experiences of four countries—Austria, Hungary, Germany, and Poland—in the aftermath of World War I to test his theory. In his view, the magnitude of the recession that accompanied huge decreases in the inflation rate in these countries was small in those instances where there was a complete change in government policy and the public believed that highly expansionary fiscal and monetary policy had ended.

* "The Ends of Four Big Inflations," in Robert E. Hall, ed., *Inflation: Causes and Effects*, a National Bureau of Economic Research Project Report, University of Chicago Presss, 1982, pp. 41–97.

have been an upward shift in the demand for money, which reduced aggregate demand for the reasons discussed in Section 7.1. But in 1982 it was difficult to tell that money demand was shifting. Because of this uncertainty and because the Fed was concerned about inflation, it was reluctant to offset the money demand shift by increasing money.

Disinflation

1. The price-adjustment equation is the key to understanding the problem of disinflation. Unemployment must rise above its natural rate to reduce inflation.

2. Monetary policy can be set to aim for a target for GNP. Policy makers have a choice of disinflationary paths—the more unemployment they choose, the faster disinflation will occur.

3. From 1979 through 1986, rapid disinflation occurred in the United States, with GNP well below potential and high rates of unemployment.

7.6 Monetary versus Fiscal Policy

In our discussion of policy in this chapter we did not emphasize the different qualities of monetary and fiscal policy. Either policy can shift the aggregate demand curve and thus affect output and prices. Here we discuss some of the issues that arise in the choice between monetary and fiscal policy.

Recall that *fiscal* policy is a change in government purchases of goods and services (G), a change in transfer payments (F), or a change in taxes (T). Each of these changes affects aggregate demand. Purchases directly add to demand, and transfers and taxes change income, which changes demand indirectly through the consumption function. A more **expansionary** (or a **looser**) **fiscal policy** is an increase in government purchases, an increase in transfers, or a decrease in taxes. A **contractionary** (or **tighter**) **fiscal policy** is the reverse.

Recall also that *monetary* policy is a change in the money supply (M). A more **expansionary,** or looser, **monetary policy** is an increase in the money supply. A **contractionary,** or tighter, **monetary policy** is a decrease in the money supply.

Note that we frequently measure changes in monetary and fiscal policy relative to growing trends in the variables. Thus, a contractionary fiscal policy frequently means a reduction in the growth *rate* of government expenditures (rather than an absolute decline) or an increase in the growth *rate* of

taxes (rather than an absolute increase). Similarly, a contractionary monetary policy frequently means a reduction in the growth rate of money.

Recall from our discussion in Chapter 5 that both fiscal and monetary policy are capable of shifting the aggregate demand schedule. A fiscal expansion stimulates spending directly. It causes the interest rate to rise. If the
fiscal expansion raises government purchases or stimulates consumption by
raising disposable income, then the higher interest rates tend to depress investment and net exports. By contrast, a monetary expansion lowers the interest rate. Investment and net exports grow and consumption responds to
that growth through the multiplier.

Even though both policies affect the basic variables of our analysis—output and the price level—in the same way by shifting the aggregate demand
schedule, there are important differences in their other effects. These differences are mediated by the interest rate. Monetary expansion favors investment and net exports, whereas fiscal expansion through higher
government purchases or tax cuts discourages investment and net exports.

Review and Practice

MAJOR POINTS

1. One important type of macroeconomic shock shifts the aggregate demand curve.
   Such a shock can originate anywhere in the spending and financial parts of the
   economy.

2. The other important type of shock shifts the price level.

3. In principle, monetary and fiscal policy can be used to offset shifts in aggregate
   demand, so that the shifts have little effect on GNP or the price level. But some
   economists question the feasibility or the wisdom of trying to counteract every
   demand shift.

4. Price shocks create a much more serious problem for policy. Without a policy response, shocks bring lower GNP and higher inflation. Policy can limit the GNP decline only by adding to the inflation.

5. It is advantageous to adopt a policy rule and to follow the rule each time a macro
   shock occurs. Some rules limit variations in unemployment at the cost of high
   variability in inflation. Other rules stabilize prices at the cost of variable unemployment. No rule achieves the ideal of low variation in both unemployment and
   inflation.

6. Another policy issue is how to phase out inflation once it is established. Policy can
   choose between ending inflation rapidly, with high unemployment, or disinflating gradually, with unemployment closer to the natural rate.

7. The government can put its aggregate demand policy into effect with either
   monetary or fiscal policy.

KEY TERMS AND CONCEPTS

Aggregate demand disturbance

Price disturbance

Accommodative policy

Countercyclical stabilization policy

Activist policy

New classical view on policy

Accommodation of price shock

Policy rule

Disinflation

QUESTIONS FOR DISCUSSION AND REVIEW

1. What are some of the possible reactions of the economy in the short run to an event that causes an aggregate demand shift? A price shock? What about in the long run? What if both types of shocks occur at the same time?

2. Explain how the economy would respond to a negative price shock if there were no policy response.

3. What are the dangers of a vigorous response to a demand shock? What are the benefits?

4. Explain how the Fed can choose the slope of the aggregate demand curve.

5. Explain why an extended period of excess unemployment is needed to bring about disinflation. Do you find your explanation completely convincing?

6. What factors should policy makers consider in deciding whether to use fiscal or monetary policy to shift the aggregate demand curve?

PROBLEMS

Numerical

1. Suppose the economy is initially described by the following equations:

$$Y = C + I + G$$
$$C = 80 + .63Y$$
$$I = 750 - 2,000R$$
$$M = .1625Y - 1000R$$
$$\pi = 1.2 \ [(Y_{-1} - 4,000)/4,000]$$

The money supply is equal to $600 billion, government spending is $750 billion, and output is at its potential level of $4,000 billion with a price level of 1. Then there is a money demand shock. The new money demand equation is given by:

$$M = .1625Y - 2,000R.$$

a. In the year of the shock, compute the value of GNP, the price level, interest rates, and the real money supply.

b. Using aggregate demand curves, illustrate the economy's path in the year of the shock, and in subsequent years.

c. Calculate the new long-run equilibrium values for income, prices, interest rates, and the real money supply.

d. Could the Fed have done something to avert the adjustment process? If no, why not? If yes, describe exactly what they could have done.

2. Repeat Exercise 1, assuming now that the shock is to investment. The new investment equation is given by:

$$I = 800 - 2{,}000R$$

What change in fiscal policy, if any, would have offset the shock?

3. Suppose the economy has the aggregate demand schedule

$$Y = 2{,}287 + 2.855 \frac{M}{P}$$

and a price-adjustment schedule

$$\pi = .6\pi_{-1} + 1.2[(Y_{-1} - Y^*)/Y]^* + Z,$$

where Z is an exogenous price shock; potential GNP is $Y^* = 4{,}000$.

a. Graph the aggregate demand schedule for $M = 600$. Graph the price-adjustment schedule. Find the price level for $Z = 0$.
b. Suppose the economy starts with a price level of 1.0 and zero expected inflation. A price shock of 5 percent occurs in the first year ($Z = .05$). No further price shocks occur ($Z = 0$ in all future years). Trace the path of the economy back to potential by computing the values of the price level, GNP, unemployment, and expected inflation in each year for 5 years.
c. Repeat the calculations for the following monetary accommodation: The money supply is 5 percent higher starting in the second year. Compare this new path for inflation and unemployment to the original path.
d. Suppose, instead, that monetary policy tries to limit inflation by contracting the money stock by 5 percent starting in the second year. Repeat the calculations and compare to the original path.
e. Now suppose that there is no price shock ($Z = 0$ in all years), but that the economy starts with expected inflation of 3 percent. Compute the path to potential. How much excess unemployment (over the natural rate of 6 percent) occurs in the process of returning to potential? Use Okun's law.

4. Consider the following model of aggregate demand:

$$
\begin{aligned}
C &= 835 + .56Y_d & &\text{(Consumption)} \\
I &= 640 - 2{,}000R & &\text{(Investment)} \\
M &= 139.5P/(R + .66) & &\text{(Money demand)}
\end{aligned}
$$

Government taxes (T) equal tY where the tax rate t is .29. Government purchases G are constant at 690. Each time period represents one year. In addition, prices adjust according to

$$\pi = \pi_{-1} + .3[(Y_{-1} - Y^*)/Y^*] \quad \text{(Price adjustment)}$$

Suppose that it is January 1991 and that you have just been hired as an adviser to the chairman of the Fed. Because the Fed is trying to put on a low-budget image, the chairman asks you to bring a hand calculator to your new job. History has repeated itself and the rate of inflation in 1990 was 10 percent. That is, the price level increased from .909 in 1989 to 1.0 in 1990. The Fed set the money supply for 1990 at 186, and the real output in the economy in 1990 was equal to potential. What was potential output in 1990?

Assume that potential output remains constant at its 1990 value for the rest of the 1990s. What follows pertains to your new Fed job.

a. The chairman asks you what actual output will have to be in 1991, 1992, and 1993 in order for inflation to be reduced to 7 percent in 1992, to 4 percent in 1993, and then held constant at 4 percent for 1994. What is your answer based on the above model?

b. The chairman decides to disinflate the economy according to the path that you calculated in Part a, and asks you to give a recommendation to the Federal Open Market Committee (FOMC) about where to aim the money supply in 1991, 1992, and 1993 to achieve this path. What do you say?

c. Suppose the FOMC ignores your recommendation and increases the money supply by 20 percent to 223 in 1991. What will happen to output in 1991 and inflation in 1992?

Analytical

1. Suppose that the economy is initially in equilibrium and that there is a permanent increase in money demand. The following year the money supply is increased so that at the old equilibrium level of prices, income, and interest rates, money supply equals money demand.

a. Illustrate the shock and the Fed's reaction to it with an aggregate demand graph. Using arrows, like in Figure 7–2, sketch the economy's path.

b. What happens to prices, income, and interest rates in the year of the shock, the year immediately following the shock, and all subsequent years?

c. Whose views of countercyclical stabilization policy does this example illustrate?

2. Evaluate the following statement: It is price changes, not higher prices, that bother people so much. Therefore, the best response to a price shock is full accommodation. This will prevent output from falling below potential, as well as avoiding any additional price changes.

3. Explain the following statement: The reason that price shocks pose a dilemma for policy makers is that they cannot directly control the price level. Contrast this situation to the case of aggregate demand shocks.

4. Suppose that the Fed fully accommodates a price shock, shifting out the aggregate demand curve until aggregate demand equals Y^* at the higher price level. The behavior income and the price level are given by the following graphs:

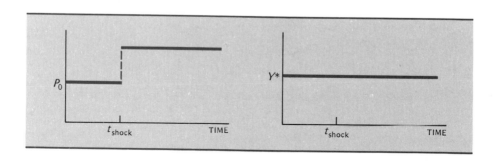

a. Assuming that aggregate demand is given by the usual relationship, which of the following equations must describe the adjustment of prices?

$$\pi = f[(Y_{-1}-Y^*)/Y^*] \qquad \pi = .6\pi_{-1} + f[(Y_{-1}-Y^*)/Y^*]$$

b. Assume now the same policy response, but that prices are governed by the other equation. Describe the path followed by output and prices.

5. Suppose the Fed used monetary policy to keep the interest rate at 7 percent no matter what else happened in the economy.
   a. When would such a policy be inflationary? How would the nominal money stock and output behave in this instance?
   b. When would such a policy be deflationary? How would the nominal money stock and output behave in this instance?
   c. What other policy is available for targeting the interest rate? What are its advantages?

6. "Stagflation" was a term coined in the 1970s to describe a sustained period of high inflation and unemployment. Using graphs, describe how stagflation may come about in the wake of a price shock.

7. The "political business cycle" is said to occur because the administration expands policy in the election year in order to get reelected. How could this be prevented?

8. One example of a monetary policy rule is $Y=Y^*$.
   a. What does the aggregate demand curve look like for such a policy rule?
   b. Explain why the money stock is an endogenous variable under such a rule. How is the money stock affected by price shocks? By aggregate demand shocks?
   c. Explain why $P=P_0$ is not a feasible policy rule.

9. When the Reagan administration came into power in 1981, three of its primary objectives were to reduce inflation, lower taxes, and increase defense spending.
   a. Explain why the achievement of all three goals required an extremely restrictive monetary policy.
   b. Could the same rate of disinflation have been achieved with a less restrictive monetary policy and a more restrictive fiscal policy? If not, why not? If so, explain how the following variables would have been affected during the 1981–84 period: output, inflation, interest rates, consumption, investment, the trade deficit, and the government budget deficit.

PART II

The Micro Foundations of Aggregate Demand

8

Consumption Demand

THE STUDY of consumer behavior—what, how much, and when individuals consume—has been a lifetime occupation of thousands of economists. This is not surprising for the consumer occupies center stage in economics. A first principle of microeconomics is that consumers choose their consumption plans in order to maximize their satisfaction or utility. And ever since Adam Smith the performance of an economic system has been judged by how efficiently it allocates scarce resources to satisfy the wants of consumers. It is natural, therefore, to start with consumers in our examination of the micro foundations of macroeconomics.

Traditionally, macroeconomists have been concerned with consumption because consumption is such a large and important component of aggregate demand. In Part I we saw that consumption is about two-thirds of all spending and that the response of consumption to changes in income—the consumption function—is a crucial ingredient in macroeconomic analysis. In the first section of this chapter we look at the empirical evidence on consumption. We show that this evidence raises questions about the simple consumption function and then we show how consumption theory has been reconstructed in light of this empirical evidence. We also examine the response of consumption to interest rates.

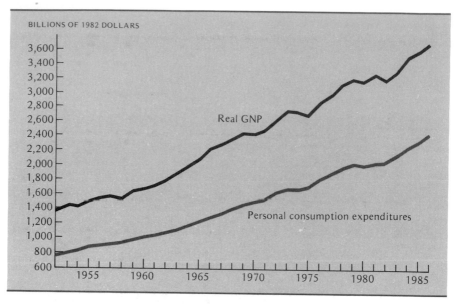

Figure 8–1.   CONSUMPTION EXPENDITURES AND GNP.
Real GNP and real personal consumption expenditures grow at about the same rate over long periods of time so that, on average, consumption expenditures maintain roughly a two-thirds share of GNP. However, over the business cycle, consumption expenditures fluctuate much less than GNP. Consumption expenditure is less volatile than the other components of GNP. Source: *Economic Report of the President,* 1987, Table B–2.

8.1 Fluctuations in GNP, Consumption, and Income

As the overall economy grows and fluctuates, so does consumption. Figure 8–1 shows how real GNP and personal consumption expenditures have grown and passed through cycles together during the last three decades. Note that, *over the long run, consumption expenditures and GNP grow at about the same rate, but, over short-run business cycles, consumption expenditures fluctuate less than GNP.*[1] The smoother path for consumption expenditures is particularly evident during the 1980–84 period when real GNP fell and rose sharply, while consumption expenditures slowed down only slightly before returning to a more normal pace. This relatively smooth behavior of consumption expenditures compared to GNP is one of the most important facts of the business cycle.

The smoothness of consumption differs greatly by type of consumption. Figure 8–2 shows the breakdown of personal consumption expenditures

[1] Note that the increasing gap between real GNP and real consumption in Figure 8–1 is not inconsistent with the fact that the *ratio* of real consumption to real GNP remains constant. The gap gets larger as the level of the two series increases.

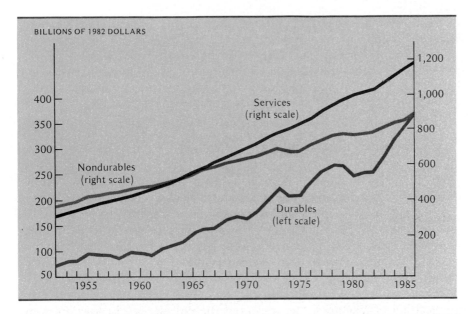

Figure 8–2. FLUCTUATIONS IN THE COMPONENTS OF REAL PERSONAL CON-
SUMPTION EXPENDITURES.
Expenditures on services grow smoothly with little cyclical fluctuation. Expenditures on
durables are the most volatile component of consumption. Source: *Economic Report of
the President,* 1987, Table B–2.

into its three components: durables, nondurables, and services. Note that
the relatively smooth behavior of consumption expenditures is most striking
for services, which grow steadily regardless of the fluctuations in the economy. Nondurables fluctuate a bit more, but most of the business cycle fluctuations in consumption expenditures are due to durables. When recessions
occur people reduce their purchases of durable items such as furniture and
automobiles much more than nondurable items such as food; service items
such as medical care hardly fluctuate at all. Note, too, that services now represent the largest and fastest growing component of consumption. As services become more important we might expect overall consumption
expenditures to become less volatile.

Overall consumption behavior would show even smaller fluctuations if we
looked at the true economic measure of **consumption** rather than at **consumption expenditures**. The distinction between consumption and consumption expenditures is a subtle one, but takes on special importance in
the case of durables. Consider a car, for example. Expenditure on a car
occurs at the time that we buy the car and bring it home from the car dealer,
even if we finance it by borrowing. Consumption of the car is then spread
out over several years as we drive the car and it gradually deteriorates
through normal wear and tear. Expenditure occurs when the car is ac-
quired; consumption occurs as the car is used up. Consumption of durables

is spread out more over time and is smoother than expenditure on them. For services and nondurable items there is no meaningful distinction between consumption and expenditure: When we purchase a haircut we consume it at the same time. Because consumption of durables fluctuates less than expenditures on durables, it is clear that total consumption has smaller fluctuations than total consumption expenditures.

GNP AND PERSONAL DISPOSABLE INCOME

Why does consumption fluctuate less than GNP? Part of the answer can be found in the behavior of disposable personal income. As we saw in Chapter 4, according to the simplest theory, consumption depends on personal disposable income: When fluctuations in disposable income are small, fluctuations in consumption will be small as well. We stressed in Chapter 2 that GNP is very different from the personal disposable income that is available to consumers for spending. GNP is about 40 percent greater than personal disposable income. Part of GNP is not really income at all because it includes the depreciation of machines, factories, and the housing stock. An important part of GNP is unavailable to consumers because it is paid to the various levels of government in the form of taxes. Still another part is plowed back into corporations in the form of retained earnings rather than being paid out to consumers. On the other hand, some people receive transfers from the government—such as unemployment compensation or social security—that are not related to current production.

Although the difference between GNP and disposable income is large on average, what is more important for our purposes is that the difference shrinks during recessions and expands during booms. Taxes fall during recessions, and transfers increase because more people collect unemployment insurance and social security. Therefore disposable income does not fall as much as GNP. These changes in taxes and transfers are sometimes called **automatic stabilizers** because of their stabilizing effect on disposable income; we will be studying them in more detail in Chapter 11. Retained earnings also fall during recessions, because corporations don't cut their dividends very much, further mitigating the effect on disposable income. The sum of these effects is shown in Figure 8–3, where real GNP and real disposable income are plotted for the years 1952–86.

Figure 8–3 shows that personal disposable income fluctuates less than GNP. On average, when GNP falls during a recession disposable income does not fall as much. There are exceptions to this general rule, but, again, on average, over this period a fall in real GNP of $10 billion reduced real disposable income by only $4 billion.[2]

---

[2] This relationship was estimated by comparing real disposable income and real GNP in the United States each year during the 1952–86 period. The least-squares relation between the *change* in real disposable income and the *change* in real GNP has a slope coefficient of .4. The

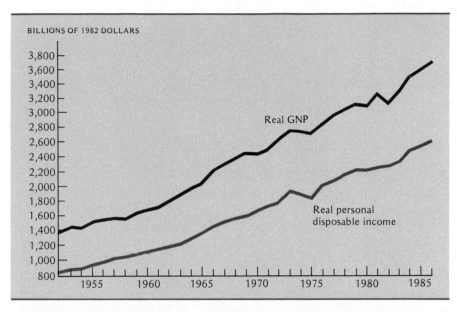

Figure 8–3. REAL GNP AND REAL PERSONAL DISPOSABLE INCOME.
Disposable income fluctuates much less than real GNP. The automatic stabilizers—taxes and transfers—as well as the dividend policies of corporations prevent disposable income from falling as far as GNP during recessions. Source: *Economic Report of the President,* 1987, Tables B–2 and B–26.

THE RELATION BETWEEN REAL DISPOSABLE INCOME AND CONSUMPTION

As we have just seen, part of the reason that consumption fluctuates less than real GNP is that disposable income fluctuates less than GNP. But can all of consumption behavior be explained by current personal disposable income as the simplest consumption function would suggest? In Figure 8–4 we examine the relationship between personal consumption expenditures and personal disposable income for the period from 1952 through 1986. Each dot in Figure 8–4 represents real consumption and real disposable income in the United States for one year. We can summarize the relationship by drawing a straight line through the dots.[3] The straight line gives the relationship

$$C = .91Y_d, \tag{8–1}$$

least squares line is the straight line that minimizes the sum of squared vertical distances between the dots and the line.
    [3] We estimated this relationship by finding the straight line that minimizes the sum of the squared vertical distances between the dots and the line (that is, the least-squares line) for the years from 1952 through 1986. This line has a negligible intercept or constant term, which is therefore omitted from Equation 8–1.

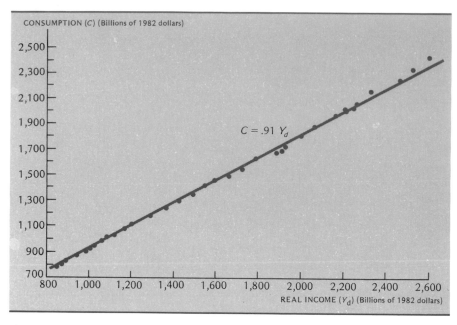

Figure 8–4.   **THE RELATION BETWEEN REAL DISPOSABLE INCOME AND REAL CON-SUMPTION EXPENDITURES.**
The horizontal position of each dot shows real disposable income in that year and the vertical position shows real consumption in that year. The straight line is a simple consumption function that is fit through the scatter of dots. The vertical distances between the line and the dots measure the error in the consumption function. Source: *Economic Report of the President,* 1987, Tables B–2 and B–26.

which is in the form of the simple consumption function; the **marginal propensity to consume** (MPC) is .91. On average, the U.S. public spends about 91 percent of its disposable income on consumption goods, and saves 9 percent. Figure 8–4 indicates that consumption is sometimes less and sometimes greater than predicted by the simple consumption function. The errors are given by

$$\text{Error} = C - .91Y_d \qquad (8\text{–}2)$$

and are measured by the vertical distances between the line and the dots in Figure 8–4. The errors appear to be small. The simple consumption function seems to give a surprisingly good description of consumption.

8.2 Defects in the Simple Keynesian Consumption Function

Unfortunately, Figure 8–4 paints too rosy a picture about the reliability of the simple consumption function. Although the errors in Figure 8–4 appear

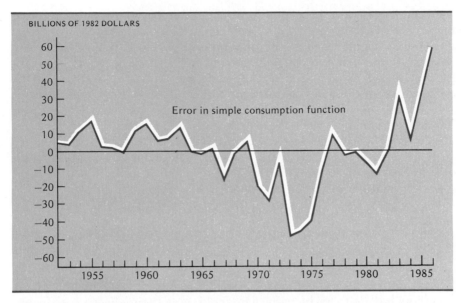

BILLIONS OF 1982 DOLLARS

Error in simple consumption function

Figure 8–5.   ERROR ANALYSIS IN THE SIMPLE CONSUMPTION FUNCTION.
This diagram gives a microscopic view of the errors in the simple consumption function
that are barely visible in Figure 8–4. It blows up the distance between the actual consumption-income dots and the simple consumption-income line in Figure 8–4. The distances are then plotted each year from 1952 through 1986. Big negative errors are
evident in 1973 through 1975, and big positive errors are evident in 1986. Source: The
errors are computed from Equation 8–2 with consumption and income data from Figure
8–4.

small to the naked eye, for some purposes—such as forecasting or policy
analysis—they are actually quite large. A more revealing picture of the
errors is found in Figure 8–5, where the error in the simple consumption
function (as calculated in Equation 8–2) is plotted for each year. The vertical scale in Figure 8–5 is much larger than the vertical scale in Figure 8–4.
This magnifies the errors much as does an enlargement of a photograph
and makes them easier to analyze.

Very large negative errors occurred in 1973 through 1975. People consumed much less than normal given their disposable incomes; they acted as
if they distrusted their income figures in those years. Why? Perhaps they
were becoming pessimistic about their incomes in the future; the stock market had recently fallen and the price of oil rose dramatically starting in
1973. These uncertainties about the future could have led to caution and
increased saving.

At the other extreme an enormously large positive error occurred in
1986. People consumed much more than normal of their disposable income. Perhaps they were then more optimistic about the future: The boom
in the stock market continued and inflation remained low. Future real in-

come prospects were becoming more favorable because the 1986 tax reform was expected to reduce personal income taxes in the future. An earlier
and famous episode of high consumption occurred just after World War II,
when consumers went on a buying binge. As in 1986, optimism about the
future as much as pent-up demand during the war might account for this
earlier error in the simple Keynesian model.

Note that these informal but plausible explanations of the errors in the
simple theory imply a much more sophisticated consumer than the one that
simply looks at current income, as the Keynesian model postulates. Expected future income enters the decision. The main contribution of the
newer theories of consumption described in the next section is to bring
these expectations of the future explicitly into account.

THE EFFECT OF CONSUMPTION ERRORS ON FORECASTING AND POLICY

Some perspective on the practical importance of these errors in the consumption function can be gained by looking at their effect on economic
forecasting and policy. These errors can have significant effects on economic forecasts. For example, the error in the consumption function in
1986 was $58 billion. From 1985 to 1986 real GNP increased by $91 billion.
A forecaster who missed the error in the consumption function in 1986
would have underpredicted real GNP growth by more than 100 percent—
predicting GNP growth of about 1 percent rather than the 2.5 percent that
actually occurred. By ignoring the negative consumption errors in 1974
and 1975, forecasters would have completely missed the declines in real GNP
in those years.

These large forecasting errors can obviously lead to economic policy
errors. More fiscal stimulus might have been called for in 1974 and 1975 if
the unusually low consumption demand had been correctly forecast in advance. Moreover, if consumers don't automatically spend 91 cents of every
dollar of additional disposable income—as the simple model predicts—then
a reduction in taxes aimed at stimulating demand might not work as
planned; it might generate too little or too much stimulus. More complicated consumer behavior makes policy-making difficult, especially if policy
makers don't understand the more complicated behavior.

SHORT-RUN VERSUS LONG-RUN MARGINAL PROPENSITY TO CONSUME

There is one systematic feature of the errors in the simple consumption
function that is difficult to see in the charts with a naked eye, but which
nonetheless has provided a crucial insight and stimulus to advanced re-

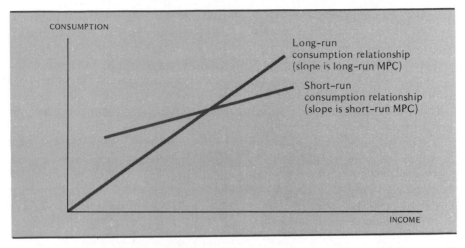

CONSUMPTION

Long-run
consumption relationship
(slope is long-run MPC)

Short-run
consumption relationship
(slope is short-run MPC)

INCOME

Figure 8–6. THE MARGINAL PROPENSITY TO CONSUME IN THE SHORT RUN AND IN THE LONG RUN.
The steeper line shows how consumption rises with income in the long run. Its slope is the long-run marginal propensity to consume (MPC). The flatter line shows how consumption rises with income in the short run. Its slope is the short-run MPC.

search on consumption: *On average, consumption is smoothed out compared to disposable income; consumption fluctuates less than disposable income.* This phenomenon can be detected and illustrated by using the concept of the long-run and short-run marginal propensity to consume. Figure 8–6 shows how the long-run and the short-run marginal propensities to consume differ for total consumption. The **long-run marginal propensity to consume** tells us how much consumption will increase over the long haul when personal disposable income rises. For total consumption the long-run marginal propensity to consume is .91, as we have already seen in Equation 8–1.

The **short-run marginal propensity to consume** tells us how much consumption will rise over the short run—during one year or during one business cycle—when disposable income rises. As Figure 8–6 illustrates, the short-run marginal propensity to consume is less than the long-run marginal propensity to consume.

Table 8–1 shows the actual difference between the short-run and the

Table 8–1. SHORT-RUN AND LONG-RUN MARGINAL PROPENSITY TO CONSUME, 1953–86

	Total Consumption	Nondurables Plus Services	Durables
Long-run MPC	.91	.76	.15
Short-run MPC	.76	.46	.30

Note: The long-run MPCs are based on the least-squares fit of the annual *levels* of real consumption and real disposable income. The short-run MPCs are based on the fit of the year-to-year *changes* in the same two variables.

long-run marginal propensity to consume in the United States from 1953 to 1986 for total consumption and two of its components. The short-run marginal propensity to consume can be calculated statistically by noting how much consumption changes from one year to the next when disposable income changes. For total consumption the short-run MPC is .76, compared with .91 for the long-run MPC. The difference is even more pronounced for consumption of nondurables plus services: Nondurable and services consumption falls by 46 cents in the short run for each dollar decrease in disposable income, but the fall is 76 cents over the long run if that dollar shortfall in income persists. Note that the difference between the long-run and the short-run MPC is reversed for durable expenditures; unlike the other components of consumption, durables are more sensitive to income in the short run than in the long run. A complete theory of consumption has to come to grips with these empirical observations.

GNP, Consumption, and Income

1. Consumption fluctuates much less than GNP. The least stable component of consumption expenditures is durable consumption. Services and nondurable consumption grow more smoothly.

2. The main reason that consumption fluctuates less than GNP is that disposable income fluctuates less than GNP. Consumption is financed out of disposable income.

3. Over the past few decades in the United States consumption has more or less tracked income according to a simple Keynesian consumption function with a marginal propensity to consume of .91. Of each incremental dollar of disposable income, 91 cents has been spent on consumption goods and 9 cents has been saved.

4. There have been significant deviations from the simple consumption function. Just after World War II, consumers spent more than the simple function predicted. In the mid-1970s, they spent quite a bit less. And in 1986 they again consumed much more than the simple function predicted.

5. A systematic feature of consumption behavior is that the short-run marginal propensity to consume is less than the long-run marginal propensity to consume. Over short periods consumption falls less than the amount by which income falls; over longer periods of time, a decrease in consumption begins to catch up to a decrease in income.

8.3 The Forward-Looking Theory of Consumption

A number of different theories of consumption have been developed in response to the deficiencies in the simple consumption function. The most durable and widely accepted today are the **permanent-income theory** developed in the 1950s by Milton Friedman and the **life-cycle theory** developed independently at about the same time by Franco Modigliani of the Massachusetts Institute of Technology.[4] The two theories are closely related, and together they have served as a foundation for most of the rational expectations research on consumption in macroeconomics in the 1970s and 1980s. We will refer to them jointly as the **forward-looking theory of consumption.** The theory embodies the basic idea that individual consumers are forward-looking decision makers. The life-cycle theory gets its name from its emphasis on a family looking ahead over its entire lifetime. The permanent-income theory is named for its distinction between permanent income, which a family expects to be long-lasting, and transitory income, which a family expects to disappear shortly. In practice the theories differ primarily in the types of equations used to express the basic idea of forward-looking consumers and to implement this idea empirically.

Like the simple consumption function, the forward-looking theory of consumption assumes that families or individuals base their consumption decisions on their disposable incomes. To simplify matters we will begin by ignoring factors other than disposable income that might also influence consumption, such as interest rates. The forward-looking theories break ranks with the simple consumption function by saying that consumers do not concentrate exclusively on this year's disposable income. Instead, they also look ahead to their likely future disposable income, which will depend on their future earnings from working, on their future income from wealth they have accumulated, and on how high taxes will be in the future. Based on their current income and expected future disposable income they decide how much to consume this year after taking account of their likely consumption in future years as well.

The consumption decision is thus much like a plan; this year's consumption is the first year of a plan that covers perhaps the next 50 years. Next year, the plan will have to be adjusted to take account of all the new information that has become available, but if everything works out as expected the plan will be followed. Although few consumers actually sit down and work out formal forward-looking plans in great detail, it is likely that a sig-

---

[4] Friedman published his findings in 1957 in a famous book *A Theory of the Consumption Function* (Princeton University Press); the findings on the life-cycle theory were published in a series of papers, the most important of which are F. Modigliani and R. E. Brumberg, "Utility Analysis and the Consumption Function: An Interpretation of Cross-Section Data," in K. K. Kurihara (ed.), *Post-Keynesian Economics,* Rutgers University Press, pp. 388–436, and A. Ando and F. Modigliani, "The 'Life-Cycle' Hypothesis of Saving: Aggregate Implication and Tests," *American Economic Review,* Vol. 53 (March 1963), pp. 55–84.

nificant fraction do some informal planning when they borrow to buy now, planning to pay off the loan later with future anticipated earnings, or when they save for retirement. We will talk about a very self-conscious plan, of the sort that an economist might make, but we recognize that most families are much more informal in their planning.

THE INTERTEMPORAL BUDGET CONSTRAINT

To describe how such a planning process results in a consumption decision, we will focus on a single family. The family could consist of a single individual, but would more typically be a family with parents and children. The first aspect we will look at is the budget constraint the family faces. The budget constraint applies not to one single year, but to many future years taken together. The constraint is more flexible in any one year than it is over time; in any one year a family can consume more than its disposable income by borrowing or by drawing down some of its financial assets. But a family can't go on forever consuming more than its disposable income—eventually it will run out of assets or places to borrow. The family faces an **intertemporal budget constraint** that limits its consumption over the years. In some years, a family will consume less than its income; the excess of income over consumption—saving—is then added to the family's financial assets and can be used for consumption in later years. Consumption this year is thus reduced so that consumption in later years can be increased. The budget constraint incorporates the accumulation of assets that results from savings.

The intertemporal budget constraint can be described in words as follows:

$$
\begin{array}{ll}
& \text{Assets at the beginning of next year} \\
= & \text{Assets at the beginning of this year} \\
+ & \text{Income on assets this year} \\
+ & \text{Income from work this year} \\
- & \text{Taxes paid this year} \\
- & \text{Consumption this year}
\end{array}
\left.\begin{array}{l} \\ \text{Disposable} \\ \text{income} \\ \end{array}\right\} \text{Saving}
$$

Assets include items such as bank deposits, bonds, corporate stock, and pension funds. There are two types of income: (1) income on assets, such as interest payments from the bank where the family holds its deposits, and (2) income from work. If a family adds to its assets then it also adds to its future income on those assets. Hence it is important to distinguish between the two types of income.

Disposable income is, of course, income on assets plus income from work minus taxes. Note that the budget constraint simply states that each year's savings—disposable income less consumption—is added to assets.

To give a clearer picture of the intertemporal budget we introduce the following symbols:

A_t = Assets at the beginning of year t
R = Interest rate on assets
E_t = Income from work during year t
T_t = Taxes during year t
C_t = Consumption during year t

The small subscript indicates the year. The interest rate (R) tells us how much income a given amount of assets will earn. For example, if the interest rate is 5 percent and assets A_t equal \$1,000 in year t then income on assets is \$50 in year t. (The interest rate R is the *real* interest rate, that is, the nominal interest rate less the expected rate of inflation.)

Using these symbols the intertemporal budget constraint can be written as

$$A_{t+1} = A_t + RA_t + E_t - T_t - C_t. \tag{8-3}$$

The six algebraic terms in Equation 8–3 correspond one-for-one with the six items listed in the budget constraint that we wrote in words above. The subscript $t + 1$ indicates assets at the beginning of year $t + 1$. (For example, if year t is 1988 then year $t + 1$ is 1989.) The budget constraint, Equation 8–3, applies to all years of the family's future—working years and retirement years. By applying this equation year after year, the family can figure out what its asset position will be many years in the future, given expectations about the interest rate, income from work, and taxes. By reducing consumption this year the family can increase its assets in future years. The increased assets—plus the interest earned on these assets—could be used for consumption on timely items such as the children's education, for retirement, or as a bequest. (The interest rate R is measured in fractions in this formula: If the interest rate is 5 percent then set R equal to .05 in Equation 8–3. Then R times A, for example, equals \$50 if A equals \$1,000.)

A consumption plan is feasible if it does not involve an impractical asset position at any time in the future. Any positive amount of assets is practical, since it means the family is lending to others, rather than borrowing. For most people, it is impractical to have their assets drop significantly below zero. Our concept of assets is *net* across all borrowing and ownership of the family—if a family buys a house with a 20 percent down payment and takes on a mortgage for the remaining 80 percent, its net asset position is positive. The value of the house as an asset exceeds the liability of the mortgage. Borrowing from a positive net asset position is perfectly practical—almost everybody does it. But it is difficult to borrow when there is a negative net asset position. An exception might be medical or business school students who can borrow because their expected future incomes are so favorable.

PREFERENCES: STEADY RATHER THAN ERRATIC CONSUMPTION

Many different consumption plans are feasible. As long as the family is careful not to consume too much, it has a wide choice about when to schedule its consumption. It could consume very little in the early years and build up significant assets by middle age. Or it could consume as much as possible and keep its assets only barely positive. Which of the feasible plans will the family choose? The forward-looking theory of consumption assumes that *most people prefer to keep their consumption fairly steady from year to year.* Given the choice between consuming $10,000 this year and $10,000 next year, as against $5,000 this year and $15,000 next year, people generally choose the even split. There are exceptions but it seems reasonable that most people prefer not to have ups and downs in their standard of living.

Figure 8–7 shows a typical path for income for a family with a steady consumption plan. Income from employment is low in the early years and gradually rises until retirement as job experience and seniority increase. During retirement income from work is zero. Note how consumption is relatively large compared to income in the early years of work; young families tend to borrow when they can in anticipation of greater future income in later years. During the years immediately before retirement, consumption is relatively low as the family saves more in anticipation of retirement. Finally,

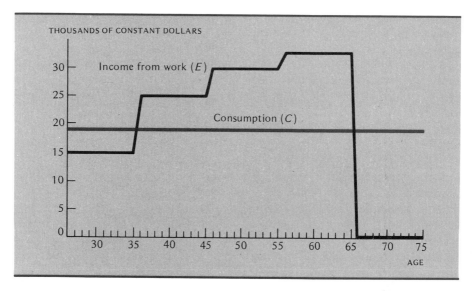

Figure 8–7.   ILLUSTRATION OF STEADY CONSUMPTION COMPARED TO INCOME GROWTH AND DECLINE.
Income from work is assumed to grow as experience and seniority increase and then drop to zero during retirement. Thoughtful forward-looking consumers who prefer a smooth consumption path will tend to borrow during their early years, save in their middle-age years, and draw down their assets during retirement.

during retirement consumption is much greater than income as the family draws down its assets.

PREFERENCES: HOW LARGE AN INHERITANCE FOR THE NEXT GENERATION?

Figure 8–7 illustrates the important features of the typical smooth consumption path. But the assumption that families prefer a smooth consumption path is still not sufficient to pin down one consumption path among those that are feasible. The family can choose a high smooth consumption plan or a low smooth consumption plan. Different smooth paths of consumption will leave the family with different levels of assets at the end of the parents' lifetimes. Figure 8–8 shows the path of assets for the smooth consumption path already shown in Figure 8–7 (Path 2) along with asset paths for higher (Path 1) and lower (Path 3) consumption paths.

A higher consumption path leaves fewer assets at the end of the lifetime. To pin down the consumption path completely we need to make an assumption about what the parents' preferences are for assets at the end of their lifetimes. How much will they want to leave to the next generation as inheritance? If parents are convinced that their children can make it on their own, they may prefer to consume most of their assets during retirement. Or they

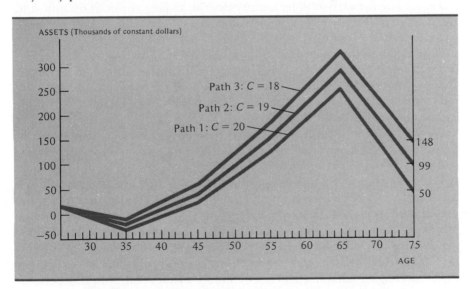

Figure 8–8. ASSETS AND BEQUESTS UNDER SMOOTH CONSUMPTION PATHS, STARTING WITH $15,000.
If consumption follows Path 1 over the family's lifetime, assets will follow the path marked 1, with little left for the next generation. If consumption follows Path 2, sufficiently more assets are accumulated to leave more for the next generation. Along Path 3, consumption is even lower and assets left for inheritance are even higher.

might want to reward their children for doing well by giving a large bequest. There is little agreement among economists on what motivates bequests.[5] Fortunately, however, many of the important empirical predictions of the life-cycle and the permanent-income hypotheses hold regardless of what assumption we make about inheritance. We will discuss the effect of alternative assumptions below, where the assumption about inheritance does matter.

THE MARGINAL PROPENSITY TO CONSUME OUT OF TEMPORARY VERSUS PERMANENT CHANGES IN INCOME

It should already be apparent from Figure 8–7 that there is a relation between the family's current assets plus its expectations about future earnings from work and its consumption decision. If news comes along that the family is better off, either because it has higher assets today or because it expects higher earnings in the future, the family will adjust its consumption upward. Moreover, it will adjust its future consumption plans upward by about the same amount. If the family reacted to good news by changing only current consumption and not future planned consumption, it would be planning a consumption path that was not smooth.

By how much does consumption change when disposable income changes? For forward-looking consumers the answer depends on how long the change in income will last—in particular, whether the change is viewed as *temporary* or *permanent*.

Consider first the case where income increases permanently. An interesting and important example is a permanent cut in taxes, though any other change such as the winning of a state lottery that pays the family a yearly payment for life would serve just as well. Suppose that the family learns that its taxes will be lower by a certain amount, say $1,000, this year, next year, and every year in the future. Disposable income increases in the first year by $1,000, and the increase is viewed as permanent. Assume that the tax cut was unexpected so that the family could not have planned for it in advance. If the family didn't change its consumption plans, future assets would pile up quickly. Next year, assets would be higher by $1,000. In later years, this would grow as interest compounded. But next year, there would be another increment to assets in the amount of $1,000, and in later years this too would earn compound interest. Moreover, if the family raised its consumption, assets would still pile up unless the increase in consumption were equal to the decrease in taxes, $1,000. The family's exact plan would depend on how much of the income improvement it wanted to pass on to the next gen-

---

[5] Douglas Bernheim, Andrei Shleifer, and Lawrence Summers argue that parents use bequests to influence their childrens' actions in "The Strategic Bequest Motive," *Journal of Political Economy*, Vol. 93 (December 1985), pp. 1045–1076.

eration. Assuming that the amount of the improvement passed on is zero we get a simple conclusion: *The marginal propensity to consume from the increase in disposable income is 1. Consumption rises by the full amount of the increase in income when the increase is viewed as permanent.* If the family wanted to pass on some of the increased income as a bequest then the marginal propensity to consume would be smaller.

Now consider a temporary tax cut of $1,000 that will last only one year; taxes are then expected to return to their normal level in the remaining years. Again assume that the tax cut was unexpected so that the family could not have adjusted its plans in advance. If the family raises its consumption by $1,000 in the year of the tax cut then it will finish the year with nothing extra saved. At the end of the year it will have to reduce its consumption to the level previously planned, which would go against the rule that consumption should be smooth. The family can achieve a better consumption plan by raising consumption less than the tax cut and accumulating some assets. Hence, the marginal propensity to consume will be less than 1. But how much less?

We can determine the amount by using the forward-looking model. If the family didn't change its consumption plans at all, the $1,000 would be added to the family's assets and start earning interest at rate R. Suppose that the interest rate is 5 percent. As the years passed, the increment to assets, including compound interest, would become quite large. After 50 years, $1,000 left to compound at 5 percent interest becomes $12,000. But rather than leave this much more for the next generation, the typical family will probably raise its planned consumption. If it raises planned consumption by the amount of the interest, $50 per year, then after 50 years the family will have just the additional $1,000, not the extra $11,000 in compound interest. Thus, one option for the family is to plan to consume an extra $50 per year and leave an extra $1,000 to the next generation. Or, the family could consume just a bit more and leave nothing extra to the next generation. The intertemporal budget constraint, Equation 8–3, can be used to figure out how much more than $50 the increase in consumption would have to be to exhaust the $1,000 windfall after 50 years.

The forward-looking theory predicts the following consumption rule from this planning process: *If a family receives an unexpected temporary increment to its disposable income, it will raise its consumption by the interest earned by the increment, plus a bit more if it does not want to pass the full amount on to the next generation.* If the tax cut is $1,000 then the rise in consumption is $50, or a little more if not all of the $1,000 is passed on. The marginal propensity to consume from the one-year temporary tax cut, or any other temporary increase in income, is a little greater than the interest rate, or about .05 in this example. It is far, far less than the marginal propensity to consume arising from a permanent increase in income, which is closer to 1. It is also much less than that suggested by the simple consumption function we looked at earlier in the chapter. The difference between the marginal propensity to consume out of a temporary change in income and the marginal propensity to consume out of a permanent change in income is the single most important feature of the newer theories of consumption based on a forward-looking consumer.

ANTICIPATED VERSUS UNANTICIPATED CHANGES IN INCOME

In each of the above examples we assumed that the change in income was unanticipated. If the change was anticipated then the family would adjust its plans in advance. How? Suppose, for example, that the family learns about the temporary tax cut of $1,000 one year in advance. Then it would increase its consumption before the tax cut actually took place. Postponing the increase in consumption to the year of the tax cut would mean that the planned consumption path would not be smooth and this would violate the steady consumption rule. The increase in the consumption path would be slightly less than in the case where the tax cut was unanticipated simply because there is one more year of consumption to spread the improved income over. If the family wanted to leave the full $1,000 to the next generation then the increase in consumption would be slightly less than the interest rate times the tax cut. If the tax cut occurred with 50 years on the planning horizon then consumption would be spread over 51 years. The increase in consumption would thus be about $48.

Note that the marginal propensity to consume in the year that the tax cut is anticipated is astronomical. The change in income is zero in that year and consumption increases by about $48. The marginal propensity to consume is literally infinite! But the important point is that with forward-looking consumers the marginal propensity to consume depends not only on whether the change in income is temporary or permanent, but also on whether it is anticipated or unanticipated.

8.4 How Well Does the Forward-Looking Theory Work?

The key point of the forward-looking theory of consumption is that the marginal propensity to consume from new funds depends on whether the new funds are a one-time increment or will recur in future years. The marginal propensity to consume from temporary increases is low—only a little above the interest rate. The marginal propensity to consume from permanent increases in earnings is high—close to 1.

Consumption in the economy as a whole is the aggregation of the consumption decisions of millions of families. Most tests of the forward-looking model focus on aggregate consumption. Many of the events that matter a great deal for an individual family—births and deaths, promotions, winning big at the racetrack—don't matter at all in the aggregate. The "law of large numbers" guarantees that purely random individual experiences do not influence the total. But some of the influences affecting individual families are common across all families, as, for example, when the economy goes into recession.

THE SHORT-RUN AND LONG-RUN MPC: A ROUGH CHECK OF THE THEORY

Before looking at the particular methods that Friedman, Modigliani, and other economic researchers have used to test this theory formally, let's see how well it explains the facts of aggregate consumption that we presented in the previous section. The most important statistical regularity that the simple consumption function misses is that the short-run marginal propensity to consume is less than the long-run marginal propensity to consume; that is, consumption does not increase as much with income over short-run business cycle periods as it does over long-run growth periods. If consumers usually expect short-run business cycle fluctuations in their income to be temporary, then forward-looking consumption theory provides an explanation for this finding. If they expect the drop in income that they experience during a recession to be temporary, then they will not cut their consumption as much as if they thought the drop was more lasting. Similarly, they will not increase their consumption so much during the boom stage of a cycle. Is it plausible that many consumers tend to view recessions and booms as temporary? The experience of much of the last 30 years is that business cycle recessions and booms have in fact been temporary. If consumers can remember this experience then an expectation that recessions are temporary seems reasonable. Moreover, economic forecasters usually predict a return to a steady growth path following a recession—they at least remember what happened in the last cycle—and their forecasts are covered on television, in newspapers, and in magazines.

There is even an important exception that seems to prove the rule. In the recession that followed 1973 the dramatic increase in the price of oil and other energy sources probably made many consumers feel that the drop in real income they were experiencing was unlike a typical recession and was likely to be more permanent. According to the forward-looking consumption model, consumers therefore would have cut their expenditures by more than the decreased consumption of a typical recession. This is just what happened in 1973 through 1975. (See Figure 8–5, which shows that consumption was well below normal during that period.) Overall the forward-looking theory of consumption seems to pass this rough check pretty well.

Why Is the Saving Rate Higher in Japan than in the United States?

Personal saving is the difference between consumption and personal disposable income. The *personal saving rate* is personal saving as a percent of personal disposable income. For example, in 1986 consumption in the United States was $2,762 billion, personal disposable income $2,879 billion, so saving was $117 billion and the saving rate was 4.1 percent (the calculation is $(117/2879) \times 100 = 4.1$). The 4.1 percent personal saving rate was the lowest in the United States since the post–World War II consumption binge of 1947. This low saving rate is just another way to think about the huge error in the consumption function in 1986 shown in Figure 8–5 and discussed in the text (consuming an abnormally high fraction of disposable income is the same thing as saving an abnormally low fraction of disposable income).

A 4.1 percent saving rate is low even by U.S. standards, but saving rates in the United States are always low by Japanese standards. For most of the post–World War II period the personal saving rate in Japan was almost double that in the United States. In a detailed study of savings behavior in Japan and the United States, Fumio Hayashi of Osaka University showed that Japanese saving rates are higher than U.S. saving rates, even for alternative saving definitions that include business and government saving and after adjustments for several different measurement concepts.

Why is the saving rate higher in Japan? The forward-looking theory of consumption may provide part of the answer. In countries with high growth rates, the young tend to have higher incomes than the old people did when they were young. Since young people tend to save and old people tend to dissave according to forward-looking models, the young people with higher incomes will tend to raise the overall saving rate.

Because Japan has a higher growth rate than the United States, the Japanese saving rate will be higher according to the forward-looking model. Simulations of detailed life cycle models suggest, however, that the growth differential between Japan and the United States is not the entire explanation of the saving rate differential.

There are other possible explanations. Land and housing prices are very high in Japan. Hence, families need to save more for a down payment to buy a house. Further there is not as extensive a social security system in Japan; families may feel they have to save more for old age. The tax system in Japan is also thought to favor saving.

There are also some noneconomic explanations. As stated by Hayashi, "If all else fails, there is a cultural explanation. The Japanese are simply different. They are more risk-averse and more patient. If this is true, the long-run implication is that Japan will absorb all the wealth in the world. I refuse to comment on this explanation."*

* Fumio Hayashi, "Why Is Japan's Saving Rate So Apparently High?" in S. Fischer (ed.), *Macroeconomics Annual,* Vol. 1, National Bureau of Economic Research, 1986.

ANDO AND MODIGLIANI: DO ASSETS MATTER FOR CONSUMPTION?

One of the earliest formal statistical tests of the forward-looking theory was done by Albert Ando of the University of Pennsylvania in collaboration with Modigliani. Ando and Modigliani formulated consumption as depending on two factors: (1) current income from work and (2) total assets. In their formulation a change in income, given the value of assets, is assumed to be indicative of a permanent change in income (the current level of income would be representative of all future income). Hence, the marginal propensity to consume from a change in income from work—holding constant the level of assets—would be close to 1. The equation would have to be made more complicated if current income is known to be different from likely future income. On the other hand, their formulation assumes that a change in the value of total assets, given the level of income, would tend to be a temporary change—an example would be a one-time increase in the value of corporate stock. Hence, the marginal propensity to consume from a change in the value of total assets would be close to the interest rate. Algebraically, the Ando-Modigliani consumption function thus takes the form

$$C = b_1 Y_d + b_2 A, \qquad (8\text{--}4)$$

where Y_d is disposable income, A is assets, and b_1 and b_2 are coefficients. Note that Equation 8–4 is a modification of the simple Keynesian consumption function: assets have been added as a second factor to income. When Ando and Modigliani fit this simple equation to data in the United States during the period after World War II they found that b_1 was close to .7 and that b_2 was close to .06, thereby providing striking confirmation for their ideas about consumption. Moreover, the addition of total assets to the equation could eliminate some of the errors in the simple Keynesian consumption function that we noted earlier. For example, the bulge of consumption relative to income in the years just after World War II could be explained by the high level of consumer assets in those years. The decline in consumption starting in 1973 could be explained by the drop in the stock market and other asset valuations.

FRIEDMAN: DOES PAST INCOME MATTER FOR CONSUMPTION?

Friedman expressed the ideas about forward-looking consumers in a slightly different way. He simply defined permanent income as a fixed long-run level of income that has a present value equivalent to the family's assets and expected future income. All other changes in income are then viewed as transitory. Friedman then argued that the marginal propensity to con-

sume from permanent income should be close to 1, and the marginal propensity to consume from transitory income should be closer to zero.
Algebraically, he formulated the consumption function as

$$C = b_p Y_p, \qquad (8-5)$$

where Y_p is permanent disposable income and b_p is a coefficient. According
to Friedman's formulation b_p should be close to 1.

An important part of Friedman's formulation was his assumption that
permanent income is an average of income over the last several years. Thus,
if current income suddenly increased there would be only a small increase in
permanent income; income would have to increase for several years in a row
before people would expect that permanent income had increased. To test
the theory he thus substituted an average of current income and previous
income over the past several years for permanent income in Equation 8–5.
Effectively, therefore, consumption should depend on past income as well as
on current income. Past income should matter for consumption because it
helps people to forecast future income. Although it is an admittedly simple
model of people's expectations, Friedman found that his formulation of the
consumption function fit the facts better than the simple Keynesian function with current income.

WHERE DO WE STAND NOW?

The empirical work of Ando, Modigliani, and Friedman is now more
than 30 years old. Economic research in the 1970s and 1980s has led to
more revealing tests of the forward-looking theory and has raised puzzling
new questions. Three strands of the new research are particularly important: the use of rational expectations to measure future income prospects,
the analysis of data on the histories of thousands of individual families, and
case studies of particular economic policy "experiments."

Rational Expectations. The hypothesis of consumers as forward-looking
decision makers already postulates a considerable degree of rationality to
consumers. The hypothesis of rational expectations postulates more, but
not necessarily less plausible, rationality. Recall that Ando, Modigliani, and
Friedman postulated rather naive assumptions about what people expected
about their future income: It would tend to stay where it was recently. The
rational expectations approach attempts to look at the actual historical behavior of income and use this to describe statistically how people expect income to behave in the future.

The approach is a statistical formalization and a much finer version of the
rough check on the theory that we described at the start of this section.
Rather than just saying that people expect business cycles to be temporary,

the approach assumes that people act as if they have a little algebraic model of the behavior of income over the business cycle in their heads, and that they use this model when guessing their future income. Of course, nobody except perhaps an economist would actually use such a model in their personal family planning: The idea is that by watching television, reading the newspaper, or just talking with friends people get a view of future economic developments that is not much different from that of the average professional economist who actually uses such a model.

The rational expectations approach is used by many economists engaged in macroeconomic research.[6] The most straightforward version of this approach is to substitute the forecasts of income from such a model into the permanent-income equation, 8–5, for consumption. More technical versions substitute forecasts of future income into the intertemporal budget constraint, Equation 8–3, and calculate the optimal plan for consumption directly without the intermediate step of Friedman's permanent-income equation. Using rational expectations this way clearly requires advanced mathematical skills and understandably the approach has attracted economists who specialize in such skills.

Does Consumption Take a Random Walk?

One of the more fascinating findings of rational expectations research on the forward-looking consumption theory is that consumption should follow a *random walk*. A random walk is a technical term that connotes the image of a drunken sailor walking around changing directions every few seconds in a completely unpredictable manner. The best forecast of which direction that sailor will be walking in the next few minutes is the direction he is now walking, regardless of where that direction is taking him. Similarly, in economics a variable follows a random walk if the best guess of the variable next period is the same as the variable this period. Many economists feel that common stock prices follow a random walk.

A family's consumption takes a random walk if the best forecast of that family's consumption next year is the family's consumption this year. Why should the consumption of a forward-looking family who

---

[6] The research referred to is found in a series of papers published in the *Journal of Political Economy:* Robert Hall, "Stochastic Implications of the Life Cycle–Permanent Income Hypothesis: Theory and Evidence," *Journal of Political Economy,* Vol. 86 (December 1978), pp. 971–988, and Marjorie Flavin, "The Adjustment of Consumption to Changing Expectations about Future Income," *Journal of Political Economy,* Vol. 5 (October 1981), pp. 974–1009. Lars Peter Hansen and Kenneth Singleton have incorporated rational expectations into the budget constraint in a formal intertemporal planning process in their "Stochastic Consumption, Risk Aversion, and the Temporal Behavior of Asset Returns," *Journal of Political Economy,* Vol. 91 (April 1983), pp. 249–265. All these papers are technically demanding. They are listed here as sources; we suggest them as reading only for the more mathematically inclined students.

has rational expectations follow a random walk? The only reason a forward-looking family would change its level of consumption would be if its income changed in a way that could not be predicted. Recall that consumption smoothing implies that the family will try to consume the same amount every year: Consumption next year should be the same as consumption this year, so should consumption the year after that, and so on. Hence, the best predictor of what a family will consume next year is what the family is consuming this year! This year's consumption reflects all the available information on the family's future income expectations.

Because the future is not certain, consumption next year will of course be different than the family planned. If there is a surprise increase in income because the family won the lottery, then consumption next year will be greater than planned. But with rational expectations any such changes that have not already been incorporated into the consumption plans are unpredictable. Hence, the best guess of consumption next period is consumption this period.

Many economists have tested the random walk theory of consumption for the United States and other countries. Although the theory is approximately correct there are some discrepancies. In particular, changes in consumption seem to be positively related to past income. This indicates that consumption is more sensitive to income than would be predicted by the simple forward-looking model with rational expectations. Some of the reasons for this excess sensitivity are described in the text.

Although much of this research is new, it is already clear that the forward-looking consumption theory does not fare as well when people are assumed to forecast rationally. One problem is that consumption is a bit too responsive to temporary changes in income, although clearly not as responsive as in the simple Keynesian consumption theory. In other words, the forward-looking theory with rational expectations suggests that the short-run marginal propensity to consume should be even smaller than is observed in the United States data summarized in Table 8–1.

Individual Family Histories. One of the most important improvements in our knowledge of the economy in recent years is the availability of data on the economic histories of individuals and families over a span of several years. At the University of Michigan, for example, a survey called the Panel Study on Income Dynamics has kept tabs on the major economic and personal events of thousands of families since 1969. Such surveys that collect information on individuals over a number of years are typically called **panel** or **longitudinal surveys.** They are useful to macroeconomists because they tell how families experience recessions and booms individually. Aggregate.

data tell us only about all families in the economy added together. One study has looked at how well the forward-looking consumption model performs in describing the consumption behavior of about 2,000 families in the Michigan panel data set.[7] The results show an excess sensitivity of consumption to temporary changes in disposable income. The marginal propensity to consume from temporary income was about 30 percent of the marginal propensity to consume from permanent income. This seems a bit higher than the 10 percent ratio that the pure forward-looking model suggests. The results seem to say that about 80 percent of the families behaved according to the forward-looking model, while about 20 percent behaved according to a simple model in which consumption is proportional to disposable income.

Policy Experiments. In 1968 during President Johnson's administration, Congress passed a temporary surcharge on the personal income tax; the surcharge raised taxes by 10 percent. The purpose was to restrict consumption temporarily and thereby reduce aggregate demand in an economy overheated by Vietnam War expenditures. A similar temporary tax change occurred during President Ford's administration, but in the reverse direction. When the economy was in the trough of the 1974–75 recession, a tax rebate and social security bonus of $9.4 billion was paid out in the second quarter of 1975. The hope was to stimulate the economy by increasing aggregate demand. According to the forward-looking theory of consumption, families who realized that these tax changes were temporary would adjust their consumer expenditures by only a small amount; if so, the policy changes would not have their desired effect of restricting demand in 1968 or stimulating demand in 1975. On the other hand, according to the simple consumption function, these tax changes would be translated into large changes in consumption and thereby in aggregate demand.

Although clearly not conceived as experiments, these two changes in policy gave economists a rare opportunity to test the predictions of the forward-looking theory of consumption. It is probably as close as macroeconomists will ever get to a laboratory experiment. As it turned out, the response of consumption to the change in disposable income seemed to be small in both cases. After the increase in taxes in 1968 consumers simply saved less of their reduced income and thereby reduced their spending only slightly. In the second quarter of 1975 the rate of saving as a fraction of disposable income rose to almost 10 percent from about 6 percent in the first quarter. Almost all of the increase in disposable income was saved, evidently because people knew the temporary nature of the income changes. In addition to providing evidence in favor of the forward-looking theory of consumption, the lesson from these two policy experiments has been to

[7] Robert Hall and Fredric Mishkin, "The Sensitivity of Consumption to Transitory Income: Estimates from Panel Data on Households," *Econometrica*, Vol. 50 (March 1982), pp. 461–481.

make policy makers much more reluctant to use such temporary tax changes to affect aggregate demand. Economists in the Ford administration wrote in the 1977 *Economic Report of the President:* "Consumers normally adjust expenditures to their 'permanent' or long-run income." In 1977 President Carter came into office proposing another rebate to stimulate the economy out of an apparent slowdown in the recovery, but the proposal was criticized by many economists and was not passed by Congress.

Alan Blinder of Princeton University has systematically studied the response of consumer spending to temporary changes in consumer income using a rational expectations approach similar to that described above.[8] His overall finding was that the marginal propensity to consume from a temporary tax change is about half of the marginal propensity to consume from a permanent tax change. This ratio is a bit above that found in the Michigan panel data (.3). Blinder's data suggest that the world is split about 50–50 between forward-looking consumers and those who consume a constant proportion of their current disposable income. But Blinder emphasizes that these estimates are not precise. Perhaps the most important lesson from these experiments is that the response of the economy to a temporary income tax change is not the sure, predictable stimulus predicted by the simple consumption function.

DEFECTS IN THE FORWARD-LOOKING MODEL

Overall the empirical research discussed above indicates that the forward-looking model works fairly well: The marginal propensity to consume from temporary income is always less than the marginal propensity to consume from permanent income, as the theory predicts. But why doesn't it work better? Why does consumption respond as much as it does to temporary income? One reason is that the tests might be incorrectly estimating expectations of future income. In the case of temporary tax changes, for example, families may not be so aware of the machinations of the government. Perhaps they pay no attention to the news about tax changes. If they, like most people, see the benefits of a tax cut in the form of reduced withholding deductions from their paychecks, they may mistakenly assume that this cut in deductions is permanent. Then they will apply their regular marginal propensity to consume from income, which will be, say, .9. Moreover, when they find their deductions back up to the old level, they will reduce consumption accordingly.

Or suppose the family pays close attention to the economic news and believes that a temporary tax cut will accomplish its purpose of stimulating the

---

[8] Alan Blinder, "Temporary Income Taxes and Consumer Spending," *Journal of Political Economy,* Vol. 89 (February 1981), pp. 26–53. The figures on tax rebates and saving mentioned in the previous paragraph are tabulated in Blinder's paper.

economy. The family will benefit in the next year or two from the more favorable performance of the economy. According to the life-cycle and permanent-income hypotheses, the family should immediately increase its
consumption because of its expected increase in economic well-being. Even
though such a family would spend only a little of its tax rebate, it might raise
its total consumption level because of the improved national economy.

Another possibility is that consumers cannot borrow as easily as the forward-looking model suggests and that especially during recessions they cannot obtain the funds to maintain their consumption. Economists call such
consumers **liquidity constrained.**[9] Such consumers might be described very
well by the simple Keynesian model; they would increase their expenditures
as they receive more income regardless of whether it is permanent or temporary.

In concluding our discussion of the forward-looking model of consumption, it is important not to lose sight of the central ideas by focusing too
much on the particular equations or tests that express the ideas. The basic
point is that families are thoughtful about consumption decisions. The way
they react to a change in economic circumstances depends on the context of
the change. If the change is transitory—if it involves a windfall gain or loss
—consumption is likely to respond relatively little. If the change in income
will sustain itself for the foreseeable future, consumption will change almost
by the full amount of the change in income.

The Forward-Looking Model of Consumption

1. The forward-looking model of consumption tries to improve the
   simple consumption function by relating consumption to expected
   future income rather than just to current income. It pictures families as making a consumption plan well into the future.

2. The theory says that the marginal propensity to consume from
   one-time, transitory income is low, perhaps as low as .05. The marginal propensity to consume from permanent increases in income is
   close to 1.

3. When the government tries to influence consumption spending
   through tax policy, the effects are sensitive to the permanence of
   the policy change. A one-time tax rebate, as in 1975, probably has
   little effect on consumption spending. A permanent tax cut probably has a much larger influence.

---

[9] Walter Dolde has studied the problem of liquidity-constrained consumers in "Capital
Markets and the Short Run and Behavior of Life Cycle Savers," *Journal of Finance*, Vol. 33
(May 1978), pp. 413–428.

8.5 Real Interest Rates, Consumption, and Saving

Thus far we have assumed that consumers want a steady consumption path. They would like to consume about the same amount this year as next year and every year thereafter. This is a reasonable assumption if the price of future consumption goods is not too low or too high relative to present consumption goods. But suppose that the price of future consumption goods is suddenly expected to fall—suppose, for example, that sales taxes will be repealed starting next year! Clearly people would postpone their consumption expenditures until next year to take advantage of the lower price. They would do this as long as they were not so impatient that they couldn't get along without the goods this year. Consumption today would fall and consumption next year would rise.

The interest rate becomes a factor in consumption because it affects the price of future consumption relative to current consumption. In fact, the *real* interest rate is the relative price between present consumption and future consumption. It thus directly affects the choice of whether to consume more today or more tomorrow. Recall that the interest rate quoted in the newspaper, the *nominal* interest rate, does not correct for changes in purchasing power. The real interest rate R equals the nominal interest rate minus the expected rate of inflation π^e. For example, if the nominal interest rate is 11 percent, but prices are expected to rise at 4 percent per year, then the real interest rate is 7 percent. If you postpone one unit of consumption this year, you can consume 1.07 units next year by investing at an 11 percent nominal rate and losing 4 percent to inflation.

If the real interest rate is positive, as it generally is, people face an incentive to defer spending. A dollar saved today will buy more than a dollar of goods tomorrow. Hence people will tend to defer consumption unless they are too impatient. Economists have a measure of impatience called the **rate of time preference.** If the real interest rate is higher than the rate of time preference, then people will tend to shift their consumption a bit toward the next year. If the real rate of interest is high, today's consumption will tend to be low. This factor makes consumption negatively related to the real rate of interest. Saving, which is simply the difference between disposable income and consumption, is therefore positively related to the real rate of interest.

Changes in the interest rate do something else in addition to changing the price of tomorrow's goods relative to today's. They change income. If interest rates rise, for example, a family can earn a higher real return from its accumulated assets. This makes the family better off. On this account, planned consumption is higher. This increase in consumption might offset the reduced consumption that comes from the incentive to defer consumption from today to tomorrow. Hence, we can't say unambiguously whether consumption in the first year falls or rises—the *income* effect makes it rise while the incentive to make a *substitution* of future consumption for present consumption makes it fall. Similarly, the effect of change in the real interest rate on saving is also ambiguous.[10] Of course, this offsetting tendency of the income effect and the substitution effect is common to many relative price changes in economics—not only the interest rate.

It is a controversial matter whether or not consumption is negatively related to the interest rate in the U.S. economy.[11] The most difficult problem in interpreting the data is that consumption depends on disposable income as well as on the interest rate, and during the business cycle income and the interest rate tend to move together. It is difficult to separate out the effect of one variable on the other.

Another complication in examining the relation between real interest and consumption is that the real interest rate is not observed directly. What we observe is the nominal interest rate. To convert it to a real rate, we must subtract the expected rate of inflation. Measuring the expected rate of inflation is difficult.

EFFECT OF REAL INTEREST RATES ON WORK

There is one last complication in our analysis of consumption. For this whole chapter we have assumed that individuals do not or cannot change how much they work. Income from work was taken as exogenous. But some people are free to vary how much they work. In particular, if real interest rates rise the value of income from working today relative to tomorrow rises. People could gain from working harder and longer hours now and taking time off to spend the earnings later. Hence, in principle, income from work is a positive function of the real interest rate. Because saving is the difference between disposable income and consumption, this positive effect of real interest rates on income from working reinforces the negative effect of real interest rates on consumption to make saving positively related to income.

Detecting empirically the effect of real interest rates on work effort has proved even more elusive than detecting the effect of real interest rates on consumption. It appears that most people cannot or do not adjust their work effort very much in response to interest rate changes. This corresponds with casual observation.

---

[10] The income and substitution effects are shown graphically in the appendix to this chapter.

[11] Michael J. Boskin, "Taxation, Saving, and the Rate of Interest," *Journal of Political Economy*, Vol. 86 (April 1978, pt. 2), pp. 53–527, and E. P. Howrey and S. H. Hymans, "The Measurement and Determination of Loanable-Funds Saving," *Brookings Papers on Economic Activity*, Vol. 3, 1978, pp. 655–705, are two widely cited recent empirical studies of the effect of interest rates on consumption and saving in the United States.

Consumption, Saving, and the Interest Rate

1. The consumption planning process should take the interest rate into account. The real interest rate—the nominal interest rate less the expected rate of inflation—is the trade-off facing the consumer between current and future consumption. When real interest rates are high, future consumption becomes cheaper relative to consumption this year.

2. It is difficult to isolate the effect of interest rates on consumption in actual data. There is no strong empirical confirmation of the theoretical possibility that saving responds positively to real interest rates, at least for the variation in real interest rates observed in the United States.

8.6 Consumption and the IS Curve

In Chapter 5 we introduced the IS curve. It shows all the combinations of real GNP and interest rates where spending balance occurs. To find a point on the IS curve, we consider a particular interest rate. Then we find the level of GNP that gives spending balance at the interest rate. The IS curve is downward sloping in the IS-LM diagram with the interest rate R on the vertical axis and output Y on the horizontal axis. The slope of the IS curve and how much it is shifted by fiscal policy are crucial for evaluating the effects of monetary and fiscal policy.

Recall that the simple Keynesian consumption function was used in the derivation of the IS curve in Chapter 5. How is the IS curve affected by the factors considered in this chapter?

THE SLOPE OF THE IS CURVE

Consider first the slope of the IS curve. The smaller the marginal propensity to consume (MPC), the steeper the slope of the IS curve. A small MPC means that the multiplier is small and changes in interest rates thereby have a small effect on output. The results considered in this chapter make us scale down the MPC. We saw that consumers have a lower MPC out of disposable income because the cyclical fluctuations in disposable income are viewed as temporary. On this account the IS curve is steeper than it seemed in Chapter 5, because output is less sensitive to the interest rate.

However, the interest rate effects on consumption considered towards the end of this chapter have an opposite effect on the IS curve. If consumption depends negatively on the interest rate, then a higher interest rate will shift the consumption function down, in which case the level of GNP corresponding to spending balance will be lower. On that account the IS curve is flatter than it seemed in Chapter 5, because output is more sensitive to the interest rate.

On balance it is a empirical question whether the true IS curve that incorporates the issues raised in this chapter is flatter or steeper than the IS curve derived in Chapter 5.

SHIFTS IN THE CURVE DUE TO TAX CHANGES

The IS curve in Chapter 5 did not distinguish between temporary and permanent changes in taxes. A cut in tax payments of any kind would shift the IS curve to the right by the same amount and thereby stimulate output by the same amount. The forward-looking theory of consumption says that the shift in the IS curve should be much larger if the tax cut is permanent rather than temporary. A purely temporary tax cut—such as the 1975 tax rebate—would have a very small effect on the IS curve.

Because it is sometimes difficult to tell whether people think a tax cut is permanent or temporary, the forward-looking theory points to an element of uncertainty in our ability to determine how much the IS curve will shift in response to tax changes.

Finally, the forward-looking theory says that the IS curve will shift to the right in response to an *expectation* of future tax cuts. Future tax cuts will stimulate consumption today because lifetime disposable income has increased. The strong growth of consumption in 1986, for example, may have been due to the expectation of future tax cuts in 1987 and 1988 that were enacted in 1986.

Review and Practice

MAJOR POINTS

1. Consumers finance their consumption from their incomes, and consumption has tracked income reasonably closely in U.S. history.

2. However, there have been significant deviations from a simple consumption function.

3. The forward-looking consumption theory relates consumption to current and expected future income rather than to just current income.

4. In this view, the marginal propensity to consume from transitory income is much lower than that from permanent changes in income.

5. Tax policy does not operate in a mechanical way through disposable income.

Families raise their consumption only if a tax cut makes them feel better off, which may not happen with some types of cuts.

6. Though higher real interest rates ought to stimulate saving by making consumers defer consumption, this hypothesis has not been firmly established by the data.

7. The marginal propensity to consume is one of the determinants of the slope of the IS curve. Because of automatic stabilizers and the low short-run marginal propensity to consume of forward-looking consumers, the IS curve may be steep.

KEY TERMS AND CONCEPTS

Consumption

Disposable income

Keynesian consumption function

Marginal propensity to consume (MPC)

Long-run marginal propensity to consume

Short-run marginal propensity to consume

Forward-looking theory of consumption

Intertemporal budget constraint

Smooth consumption path

Friedman permanent-income model

Ando-Modigliani life-cycle model

Marginal propensity to consume out of temporary income

Marginal propensity to consume out of permanent income

Rational expectations tests

Panel data tests

Real interest rate

Rate of time preference

Income effect

Substitution effect

Automatic stabilizers

QUESTIONS FOR DISCUSSION AND REVIEW

1. List some of the reasons that disposable income is less than GNP. What factors tend to raise disposable income even though they are not part of GNP?

2. How can you tell if a simple consumption function governs the relation of consumption and income?

3. What is an estimate of the marginal propensity to consume from the historical relation of consumption to income? Why is this estimate probably an overstatement of the reaction of consumption to a temporary tax cut? What is an estimate of the short-run marginal propensity to consume?

4. Outline the way that a family might plan its consumption. How would it react to learning that tax rates are going to rise in the future?

5. Why is the marginal propensity to consume out of temporary income a bit above the real interest rate?

6. List some of the reasons that a tax cut has an uncertain effect on consumption.

7. Review all the steps involved in constructing the IS curve, including the possibility that consumption responds to the interest rate.

PROBLEMS

Numerical

1. Use the intertemporal budget constraint for this problem. To make calculations easy assume that a family lives for 5 years with 4 years of work and 1 year of retirement. (A more realistic assumption would be a 50-year horizon with 40 years of work and 10 years of retirement.) Consider a family that wishes to consume the same amount each year. Assume earnings of $25,000 per year and an interest rate of 5 percent. Assume initial assets of zero.

   a. Find the level of consumption such that the assets at the end of 5 years are roughly zero, say within $100. What is the level of assets at the beginning of retirement?

   b. Repeat the calculation of consumption, but with initial assets of $1,000. By how much does consumption rise? Compare this to the interest earnings on $1,000 at 5 percent, namely, $50 per year. Would the increase be closer to $50 if the family lived for 50 years?

   c. Repeat the calculation of consumption, with initial assets of zero, but with earnings of $26,000 per year. By how much does consumption rise? Explain why the increase in consumption is larger than in Part b.

2. Suppose that we have a consumption function of the form

$$C = 80 + .9Y_p,$$

where Y_p is permanent disposable income. Suppose that consumers estimate their permanent disposable income by a simple average of disposable income in the present and previous years:

$$Y_p = .5(Y_d + Y_{d,-1}),$$

where Y_d is actual disposable income.

   a. Suppose that disposable income Y_d is equal to $3,000 in Year 1 and is also equal to $3,000 in Year 2. What is consumption in Year 2?

   b. Suppose that disposable income increases to $4,000 in Year 3 and then remains at $4,000 in all future years. What is consumption in Years 3 and 4 and all remaining years? Explain why consumption responds the way it does to an increase in income.

   c. What is the short-run marginal propensity to consume? What is the long-run marginal propensity to consume?

   d. Explain why this formulation of consumption may provide a more accurate description of consumption than the simple consumption function that depends only on current income.

3. Suppose that consumption is given by the same equation as in Problem 2, but that consumers set their permanent income Y_p equal to the average of their expected income in all future years.

   a. Suppose that, as in the previous problem, disposable income was $3,000 in Years 1 and 2, but suppose also that in Year 2 consumers expect that disposable income will be $3,000 in all future years. What is consumption in Year 2?

   b. Suppose that in Year 3 disposable income rises to $4,000, and that consumers expect the $4,000 level to remain in all future years. What is consumption in Year 3?

   c. Explain why consumption in Year 3 is different from that in Problem 2 even though the disposable income is the same.

4. Suppose again that consumption is given by the same equation as in Problem 2 and that permanent income is estimated in the same way as in Problem 2. Place this consumption function into a simple macro model like the one in Chapter 4. That is, disposable income Y_d is equal to income Y less taxes T, where taxes equal .3Y, and the income identity is $Y = C + I + G$.

   a. Suppose that in Year 2 investment I is $650 and government spending G is $750. Suppose that disposable income Y_d in Year 1 was $2,800. What are consumption, income, and disposable income in Year 2?

   b. Suppose that in Year 3 government spending increases to $800 and then remains at $800 for all future years. What are consumption, income, and disposable income in Year 3? (Make sure to use your calculation from Part a of disposable income in Year 2 when you calculate consumption in Year 3.)

   c. Calculate income and consumption for years 4, 5, and 6. Do you see a pattern developing?

   d. Where do you think income will end up after it stops changing? Compare your answer to the simple case where consumption depends on current disposable income only, so that the multiplier formulas of Chapter 5 apply.

5. Suppose that the consumption function is given by

$$C = 130 + .63Y - 1,000R$$

   rather than by the consumption function in Chapter 5. Add this consumption function to the other four equations of the macro model:

$$Y = C + I + G + X$$
$$M = (.1625Y - 1,000R)P$$
$$I = 750 - 2,000R$$
$$X = 425 - .1Y - 500R$$

   Treat the price level as predetermined at 1.0, and let government spending be $750 and the money supply be $600.

   a. Derive an algebraic expression for the IS curve for this model and plot it to scale. Compare it with the IS curve in the examples of Chapter 5. Which is steeper? Why?

   b. Derive the aggregate demand curve and plot it to scale. How does it compare with the aggregate demand curve in the example of Chapter 5?

   c. Calculate the effect of an increase in government spending on GNP. Is the effect larger or smaller than in the case where consumption does not depend on the interest rate? Describe the process of crowding out in this case.

   d. Calculate the effect of an increase in the money supply on GNP. Is the impact larger or smaller than in the case where consumption does not depend on the interest rate? Explain.

6. The problem of the family choosing a consumption plan can be analyzed using utility functions from intermediate microeconomics. In fact, this is how the forward-looking theory has been tested in recent research. Consider a very simple 2-year horizon for a family planning consumption. The family wants to determine how much to consume in Year 1 and in Year 2. Let consumption in Year 1 be C_1, and let consumption in Year 2 be C_2. Suppose that the family's satisfaction, or utility, from consuming C_1 and C_2 is given by the function

$$\text{Utility} = \sqrt{C_1} + \frac{1}{(1 + RT)} \sqrt{C_2},$$

where RT is the rate of time preference. Start with the rate of time preference equal to zero.

a. Show that this utility function means that the family prefers smooth consumption to erratic consumption. Which plan for consumption gives the family the greater utility: $3,600 in the first year and $4,900 in the next, or $4,250 in both years?

b. Show that when the rate of time preference is high the family will prefer to consume more in the first period. Do the following comparison: First set RT equal to zero and evaluate the utility of $3,600 in the first year and $3,000 in the second year versus $3,300 in both years; then raise RT to .25 and make the comparison again.

Analytical

1. Which of the following stylized facts are consistent with forward-looking theories of consumption? Which are not? Justify your answer in each case. Where the facts are not consistent with the theory, can you suggest some alternative explanations?

   a. The *marginal* propensity to consume out of current income is less for old people than for middle-aged people.

   b. The *marginal* propensity to consume out of current income is less for farmers than for most other occupations.

   c. Most European countries have both more extensive social welfare systems for older people and higher saving rates than does the United States.

   d. The saving rate for the United States fell in the early 1980s.

   e. The marginal propensity to consume out of temporary tax cuts is around .3 to .5.

   f. Across the population as a whole, people with lower incomes have lower saving rates than people with higher incomes.

   g. The amount of wealth in the economy is far greater than what current wage earners will consume in their retirement.

2. Suppose that actual GNP is below potential GNP, that inflation is low, and that the president and Congress want to cut taxes in order to increase aggregate demand and bring the economy back to potential.

   a. Describe the situation using an IS-LM diagram. Show where you want the IS curve to move in order to reach potential.

   b. In light of the forward-looking theory of consumption, describe some of problems that might arise with the tax cut plan.

3. Draw a sketch of an IS-LM diagram. Compare two cases, one where the consumption function depends on the interest rate, the other where the consumption function does not depend on the interest rate. Compare the relative effectiveness of monetary and fiscal policy in the two different situations.

4. Explain the following puzzle: Saving depends positively on the interest rate, investment depends negatively on the interest rate, and saving equals investment. How does an increase in the money supply that lowers the interest rate and thereby increases investment also increase saving? It would seem that with the lower interest rate saving would be lower. What's going on?

5. An important implication of the permanent income hypothesis is that fiscal policy operates with a lag.

   a. Explain why a permanent increase in government spending may cause the IS curve to shift out slowly over time, rather than shift out all at once.

   b. If permanent income is a weighted average of last period's and this period's income, what determines the speed at which the IS curve shifts out over time?

Appendix: A Graphical Approach to Consumption Planning

In this appendix we show how a two-period consumption planning problem can be represented graphically. Suppose that the representative family must choose how much to consume this year and next year. Figure 8–9 shows how the family's preferences for consumption in the two periods might look; the vertical axis is consumption next year (Year 2) and the horizontal axis is consumption this year (Year 1). The curved lines are **indifference curves**; they give the alternative values for consumption in the two years between which the family is indifferent. The slope of the line measures how many dollars of consumption next year must be given up when consumption this year rises by one dollar for the family to maintain the same level of satisfaction, or utility. This is sometimes called the **marginal rate of substitution** between consumption this year and consumption next year. The family is better off when the indifference curves are farther out and up.

The straight line in Figure 8–9 is simply the intertemporal budget constraint for the two periods. The slope of the line is $-(1 + R)$ because the family will have an additional $(1 + R)$ dollars of consumption next year for each dollar of consumption that is reduced (and thus saved) this year. (The equation for the budget line comes directly from Equation 8–3 with no taxes, no initial assets, and no bequest and is applied for two periods. Then Equation 8–3 is $A_2 = E_1 - C_1$ in Year 1, and $0 = (1 + R) A_2 + E_2 - C_2$ in Year 2. Putting A_2 into the equation for Year 1 gives the equation for the budget line.) The point on the line marked $*$ represents the amount of income from work this year and next year. Moving up the line from $*$ means that the family

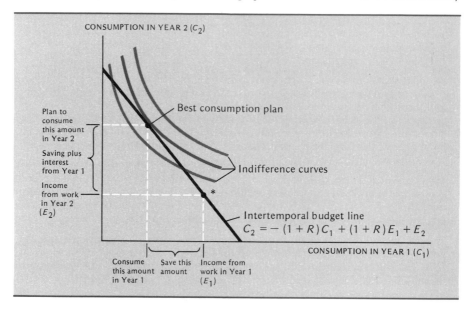

Figure 8–9. INDIFFERENCE CURVE AND INTERTEMPORAL BUDGET LINE FOR CONSUMPTION PLANNING.
The indifference curve is the combination of consumption in the two years that gives the same level of satisfaction to the family. The straight line is the budget constraint. The family tries to get to the highest indifference curve. This occurs where the indifference curve and the budget line just meet at a point of tangency.

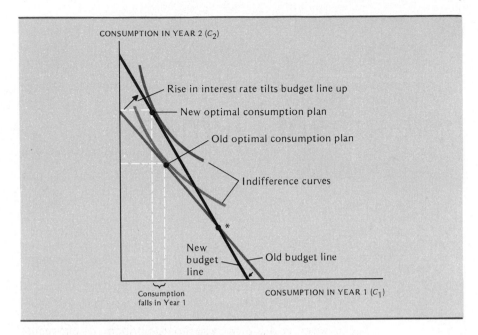

Figure 8–10.   INCREASE IN THE INTEREST RATE.
As the interest rate increases, the budget line gets steeper. This leads to a higher level of utility. As drawn, the family consumes less this period. But it is uncertain whether the family will consume less if other indifference curves are drawn.

is saving this year, because income is greater than consumption. Moving down on the line means that the family borrows this year.

The family tries to maximize utility or, in terms of the graph, to get to the highest indifference curve. This occurs at a point of tangency between the budget line and the indifference curve, as shown in the diagram. At this point the slopes are equal so we know that the marginal rate of substitution between consumption next year and consumption this year is equal to 1 plus the interest rate.

Now, suppose that the interest rate increases. This is shown in Figure 8–10. The budget line will then tilt in a steeper direction, pivoting around the point *. A higher level of utility is thereby achieved. As the graph is drawn, less is consumed this year. But note that this depends very much on how the indifference curves are drawn. (Try to draw another for which the reverse occurs.) The tilting of the curve represents the substitution effect, which certainly causes consumption this year to fall. But the budget line has also moved out to the right from where it was before on the indifference curve. This is the income effect. It certainly leads to more consumption today.

9

Investment Demand

INVESTMENT IS the most volatile component of aggregate demand. While smaller in magnitude than consumption, it fluctuates more. And through the multiplier process its fluctuations lead to fluctuations in total output and income. Keynes argued that investment was the primary driving force in the economy, fluctuating erratically because of capricious shifts in business expectations, with consumption responding passively according to the simple consumption function.

In looking at the microeconomic underpinnings of investment we will see that Keynes's distinction between investment and consumption is not so pronounced. For one thing, investment, much as consumption, responds to income and output in a systematic way. When investment rises, it may be the result, not the cause, of an increase in spending elsewhere in the economy. Moreover, while investment decisions do depend on business expectations, these expectations are based on calculated estimates of future changes in demand and prices that businesses are likely to face. In making their investment decisions, business firms are at least as forward-looking as the consumers that we described in Chapter 8.

9.1 Fluctuations in Investment Spending

We saw in Chapter 2 that investment spending is divided into three categories:

1. Nonresidential fixed investment—business purchases of new plants and equipment

2. Residential fixed investment—construction of new houses and apartments
3. Inventory investment—increases in stocks of goods produced but not yet sold

Nonresidential fixed investment was 10.9 percent of GNP in 1986. Residential investment was 5.1 percent of GNP in the same year. But the shares of the different types of investment in GNP are not a good measure of their importance in economic fluctuations. Although plant and equipment investment is the dominant component of total investment, it is the most stable over time. Since inventory investment is negative as stocks of unsold goods fall and positive when stocks of goods rise, its share of GNP is not a very meaningful statistic. Yet, inventory investment is particularly volatile and has a major role in recessions. Finally, residential investment is important because housing construction drops when mortgage interest rates go up.

Figure 9–1 shows how tightly fixed investment is linked to overall economic activity. When investment falls like it did in the mid-1970s and early 1980s, the economy goes into a recession. The fluctuations of investment are larger in percentage terms than the fluctuations in real GNP. Unlike consumption, investment contributes more than its share to the fluctuations in real GNP. Note that investment slowed down in 1986, although there was no

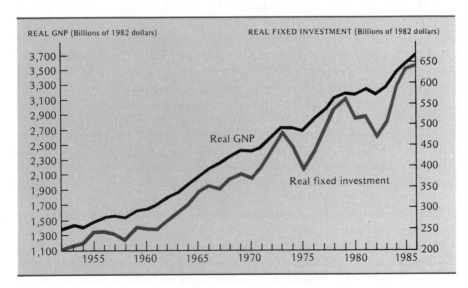

Figure 9–1. FIXED INVESTMENT AND GNP.
Real fixed investment and real GNP fluctuate together. Investment and GNP rose together in the great expansion of the 1960s, fell together in the recession beginning in 1974, rose again in the late 1970s, and fell together in the early 1980s. However, the fluctuations in fixed investment are larger than the fluctuations in total GNP. Source: *Economic Report of the President*, 1987, Table B–2.

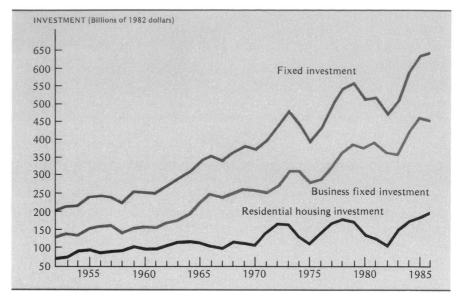

Figure 9–2. HOUSING VERSUS FACTORIES AND EQUIPMENT.
Separating housing investment from business investment reveals some important timing differences. Both business investment and housing investment fluctuate widely during recessions and booms. But housing investment leads real GNP while business investment moves together with real GNP. Source: *Economic Report of the President,* 1987, Table B–2.

slowdown in real GNP growth in 1986. Sometimes fluctuations in investment occur without fluctuations in GNP, assuming, of course, that consumption, government spending, or net exports move in the opposite direction.

The behavior of the two components of fixed investment—business (nonresidential) and residential—is shown in Figure 9–2. In most recessions, residential investment turns down before business investment turns down. We will show later that rising interest rates have large negative effects on residential investment and that the start of most recessions is accompanied by rising interest rates. Note that in 1986 business fixed investment declined even though residential investment continued to grow. As we will see this decline may have been due to the increase in taxes on business capital that was passed into law in 1986.

Real GNP and *business* fixed investment move together almost in tandem. We cannot tell from the data whether movements in GNP are inducing movements in business investment or movements in business investment are inducing movements in GNP. A third mechanism to be considered is that both GNP and business investment are responding to the same underlying stimulus, which is causing both to move together.

In the economy as a whole, the volume of investment observed is the joint outcome of three factors: (1) **investment demand,** decisions made by businesses about the amount of investment to undertake; (2) **saving supply,** decisions made by consumers about the amount to save; and (3) **investment supply,** decisions made by producers of investment goods about how much to supply.

This chapter focuses on investment dei̲ ̲nd. A complete model of the economy that combines saving behavior as described in Chapter 8 and the supply side of the economy is necessary to give a complete picture of investment. But we have already had a preview of the demand and supply process in Chapters 4 through 6. The economy reconciles the decisions of the various groups with the interest rate and the price of capital goods. If businesses want to invest more than consumers are willing to lend, the interest rate rises enough to depress investment and stimulate savings to the point of equality. If businesses want to invest more than the producers of investment goods want to produce, the price of capital goods rises. Then investment demand falls and the supply of capital goods rises, again to the point of equality.

Investment Analysis

1. Investment is the flow of newly produced capital goods. It consists of plant and equipment investment, residential investment, and inventory investment.

2. Investment is much more volatile than consumption. Declines in business fixed investment are closely timed with declines in the overall economy. Declines in housing investment lead the declines in the overall economy.

3. The overall level of investment depends on three elements: the investment demand of firms and households, the funds available for investment, and the amount of investment goods produced. Interest rates and the prices of investment goods move to equate the three elements. In this chapter we focus on the demand side.

9.2 How a Business Looks at the Investment Decision

In examining the micro foundations of investment demand we will start with business fixed investment and look at the decision process of a typical business firm. From a firm's perspective there are really two decisions that can be distinguished. The first thing for the managers to decide is how many factories and machines they want. That is, what is the firm's desired

capital stock? The second question is how fast to build the factories and when to order the machines that they want. That is, what is the **flow of investment**? The simple investment function that we introduced in Chapter 5 focuses on the flow of investment while ignoring the desired capital stock. Here we start with the question of the desired capital stock, and derive the flow demand subsequently.

It is helpful to pose the typical firm's problem in the following rather abstract way: Suppose a firm has already figured out how much output it plans to produce during the upcoming period, say a year. Further, suppose that, whatever capital it will use, it will *rent* from another firm in the equipment rental business. For example, a firm in the business of offering typing services to its customers would rent word-processing equipment from a computer-leasing firm. (Many firms own most of their capital, but we will look at that case a little later.) The idea of thinking about a firm's investment decision as a choice about how much capital to rent was developed by Dale Jorgenson of Harvard University. He developed such models of investment starting in the early 1960s.[1] It is a useful abstraction because it makes the capital decision much like the decision to employ other factors used in production, such as labor and raw materials.

How much capital will the firm choose to rent? Microeconomics tells us the answer: the amount that equates the marginal benefit to the marginal cost. The **marginal benefit** is the amount of dollars saved by using fewer of the other factors of production when more capital is employed. A firm with more capital will need fewer workers, less energy, or fewer materials to produce the same amount of output. For example, with a word processor, a firm offering typing services might require fewer hours from proofreaders and typists, and perhaps fewer correction materials (like Liquid Paper). Note that the firm must look ahead to determine the marginal benefit of employing more capital during the period that it will rent the capital. Firms are thus assumed to be *forward-looking* in this theory of investment.

The **marginal cost** of capital is just the rental cost charged by the renting firm. For example, it is the amount that the computer-leasing firm charges each year for word-processing equipment.

The firm's decision can be illustrated graphically. The most important input to production is labor, so consider the case where the input displaced by capital is labor. The production function relating labor input to output produced is shown in Figure 9–3. When there is more labor input, there is more output. For example, for the typing services firm, when typists and proofreaders work more hours, more typed pages are produced. When there is more capital in the firm, the production function relating labor input to output produced is shifted upward, as shown in Figure 9–3. In this

---

[1] The basic framework described here is due to the work of Dale Jorgenson, in particular, his "Capital Theory and Investment Behavior," *American Economic Review,* Vol. 53 (May 1963), pp. 247–259.

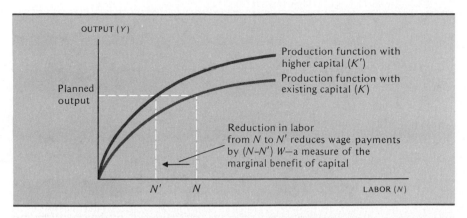

Figure 9–3. THE PRODUCTION FUNCTION AND THE MARGINAL BENEFIT OF CAPITAL.
The production function shows the amount of output produced from different amounts of labor. The lower production function describes the situation with the existing capital of the firm. In order to produce the planned output, the firm will have to employ N workers. The upper production function applies if the firm decides to rent some extra capital. In that case, to produce the planned output, only N' workers need to be employed. The marginal benefit of capital is the reduced wage payments, $(N - N')W$.

case fewer hours given by typists and proofreaders result in the same number of typed pages. In Figure 9–3, N is the level of employment needed to produce planned output with the existing capital stock, and N' is the reduced level of employment needed to produce planned output if extra capital is rented. If the wage per worker is W, the marginal benefit of the extra capital is $(N - N')W$.

We assume that capital has a **diminishing marginal product,** which means that the amount of the upward shift in the production function and corresponding decrease in labor requirements decline as the amount of capital grows. For example, if the typing services firm began with one full-time typist and one half-time proofreader, the first word processor would result in more labor saved than a second word processor. The third and fourth word processors would displace essentially no labor. We can describe the relationship between capital and the marginal benefit of additional capital in a **marginal benefit of capital** schedule, as shown in Figure 9–4.

The marginal benefit of capital schedule is the firm's **demand curve for rented capital** as well. To choose its level of capital, the firm simply finds the amount of capital that equates the marginal benefit of capital to the marginal cost, which is the rental price. We call the rental price of capital R^K. The superscript K is a mnemonic for capital. Figure 9–5 illustrates the process.

What happens if the firm decides to produce more output? Looking back at Figure 9–3, you can see that producing more output with the same capital

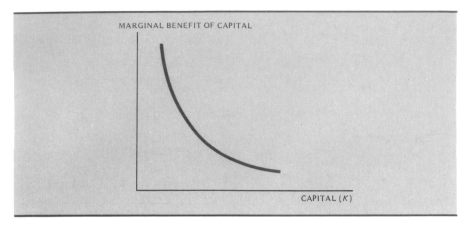

Figure 9–4. THE MARGINAL BENEFIT OF CAPITAL SCHEDULE.
The marginal benefit of capital is a declining function of the amount of capital, because of the diminishing marginal product of capital. The position of the schedule depends on the level of planned output and on the wage rate.

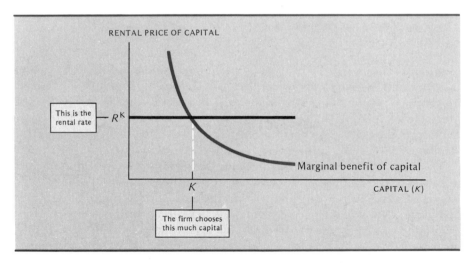

Figure 9–5. CHOOSING THE CAPITAL STOCK.
The marginal benefit of capital schedule is the firm's demand function for rented capital. The firm chooses its capital stock by equating the marginal benefit of capital to its rental price. With planned output and the wage rate held constant, the firm will choose to rent more capital and employ less labor if the rental price falls.

stock will require more labor. That, in turn, raises the marginal benefit of capital. To equate the marginal benefit to an unchanged rental price of capital, the firm will have to rent more capital. Figure 9–6 shows how the firm responds to an increase in output.

We have not said anything yet about investment, only about the firm's de-

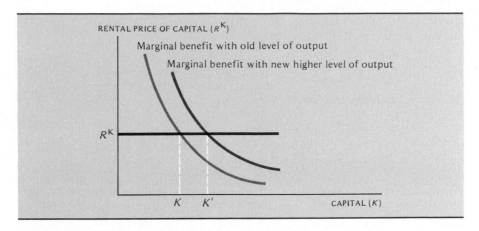

RENTAL PRICE OF CAPITAL (R^K)

Marginal benefit with old level of output

Marginal benefit with new higher level of output

R^K

K K' CAPITAL (K)

Figure 9–6. EFFECT OF HIGHER OUTPUT.
When planned output rises and the rental price of capital and the wage remain the same,
the firm's demand for capital rises. Higher planned output shifts the marginal benefit for
capital schedule to the right. The firm's demand for rented capital rises from K to K'.

cision to rent capital. A firm could rent more capital without bringing about
any investment in the economy as a whole. The firm might just rent some
existing capital that another firm had decided not to rent anymore. The relation between the decisions of individual firms and total investment in new
capital goods is the subject of Section 9.3.

DETERMINATION OF THE RENTAL PRICE OF CAPITAL

How would the market set the rental price of capital? We can answer this
by looking at the costs faced by a rental firm—like a computer-leasing firm
—that is in the business of owning machines and renting them out. We will
make use of the following terms and assumptions:

P^K is the price for purchasing a new machine from a producer of machines. The price is assumed to be unchanging for now. The price is measured in "real" terms, that is, relative to the price of other noncapital goods,
like haircuts or typing services.

R is the real interest rate.

d is the rate of depreciation. At the end of each year, the rental firm has
to spend an amount d times the original amount spent on the machine P^K in
order to make up for wear and tear on the machine.

R^K is the rental price of the equipment. This is the amount received by the
rental firm for renting out the machine for one year.

First, consider the cost side of the rental operation. Suppose the rental
firm decides to sell the machine after one year in the rental market. At the
beginning of the year it borrows P^K to buy the machine at an interest rate of

R and incurs an interest cost of RP^K. It has to pay dP^K to make up for depreciation. Total rental costs are therefore

$$(R + d)P^K. \tag{9-1}$$

In words, Equation 9–1 states:

> The cost of renting out one machine for one year =
> (The rate of interest + The rate of depreciation)
> × The price of a new machine.

For example, if the price of a word processor is \$10,000, the interest rate R = .05, and the depreciation rate d = .15, then the rental price is \$2,000 per year.

What will be the market rental price? If the renter does not have a monopoly in the rental market, the market rental price will exactly equal the cost of renting. If it were any higher, new firms would enter the rental business and bid down the rent. If the rent were below cost, some rental firms would go out of business and rents would rise. Thus, the rental price of a machine for a year is just as spelled out above—the interest rate plus the rate of depreciation times the price of a new machine. Algebraically, we have

$$R^K = (R + d)P^K. \tag{9-2}$$

Now we can go back to Figure 9–5 and relate the demand for capital by the firm that uses capital to the underlying determinants of the rental price of capital. Remember that the firm's demand for capital is a declining function of the rental price, so that the demand for capital is a declining function of the price of new equipment and a declining function of the real interest rate.

Demand for Capital and Rental Price

1. The demand for capital declines if the rental price of capital rises. The rental price will rise if the price of new equipment rises or if the interest rate rises.

2. The demand for capital rises if planned output rises.

3. The demand for capital rises if the wage rises.

THE RENTAL PRICE AND THE DECISION TO BUY NEW CAPITAL GOODS

A good deal of the capital equipment in U.S. industry is in fact rented, so the analysis we have just presented is more than an abstraction. But the bulk of capital is owned by the firm that uses it in production. Moreover, the one-year perspective we used to solve for the rental price of capital is not representative. Most firms purchase capital for the long run. Their concern is not just with the payoff in the first year, but with the financial success of the project over a decade or more. They must look ahead and estimate the benefits of a new capital project under the assumption that it will operate for quite a number of years.

The attraction of Jorgenson's rental price approach is that it gives the same answer to the question of what should be the desired capital stock as the more realistic approach in which the firm buys the capital and uses it for a number of years. Firms are constantly formulating and evaluating investment projects. An investment project that consistently earns more than the rental price of capital is worth undertaking. The project is a winner because the firm earns more than it would have to pay to borrow money to finance the project plus pay to cover the depreciation of the capital required for the project. Similarly, an investment project that consistently earns less than the rental price of capital is not worth undertaking. It is a loser.

Because of the diminishing marginal product of capital, as the winning projects are put into effect they will depress the earnings of future projects. Eventually, the last winning project will earn just the borderline revenue, namely, the rental price of the capital. On the margin, the firm taking a long-term view and purchasing its own capital will reach just the same point it would if it chose to rent capital and made a year-by-year decision about the amount of capital to use. Both the capital budgeting approach and the rental approach arrive at the same conclusion: *The firm makes use of capital up to the point where the marginal benefit of capital equals the rental price of capital.*

Not all investment decisions fit neatly into this analysis. If the firm's technology requires that investment take place in large lumps—like building blast furnaces or power plants—it may not be able to find a combination of projects with the property that the marginal benefit of investment in each year is just equal to the rental price of capital. It may have to settle for a situation where the marginal benefit is higher in some years and lower in others. The basic criterion for selecting winning investment projects remains the same for these lumpy investments. On the average, the marginal benefit of capital will be equated to the rental price even in those cases. An investment theory based on the equality of marginal benefit and rental price seems a reasonable approximation of dealing with the aggregate economy, even when some of the thousands of firms in the aggregate are making decisions about lumpy investments.

EXPECTED CHANGES IN THE FUTURE PRICE OF CAPITAL

So far we have assumed that the relative price of capital, P^K, does not change, and is therefore not expected to change. What happens if the relative price of capital goods is expected to change? The forward-looking aspects of the firm's investment decision now become important. Consider first the rental firm. Suppose that the price of capital is *expected* to *decrease* during that period that the capital equipment is rented out. On this account the rental firm stands to take a loss. It purchased the capital for P^K, and the capital will be worth less than that, say P^K_1, next year when the equipment is returned. The rental firm expects to lose $P^K - P^K_1$. In order to cover this expected loss, the rental firm will increase the rental price that it charges by the exact amount of the expected loss. For example, if the price is expected to fall from $P^K = \$1,000$ to $P^K_1 = \$950$ next year, then it would increase the rental price by $50. Conversely, if the rental firm expected an increase in the price of capital, it would stand to gain. It could cover its costs by charging a lower rental price. In general the rental price is decreased by the amount of the *expected* increase in price of capital, ΔP^K.

With capital goods prices expected to change, the formula for the rental price becomes the old formula in Equation 9–1 less the expected change in the price of capital equipment:

$$R^K = (R + d)P^K - \Delta P^K.$$

The same thing can be written a bit more compactly as

$$R^K = (R - \pi^K + d)P^K,$$

where the π^K is the expected percentage change in the relative price of capital equipment. Thus: $\Delta P^K / P^K$.

This modification of the earlier rental price formula becomes very important when the price of capital is expected to change by a large amount relative to the price of other goods. As we will see below, for example, changes in taxes can alter the effective price of capital. If these changes in taxes are *anticipated* by firms, then the rental price of capital will change. Since firms increase their desired capital stock when the rental rate falls, a decline in the rental rate due to an expected change in taxes will increase capital spending.

9.3 The Investment Function

To keep things simple in our derivation of the investment function, we will assume that firms purchase all of their capital. As we have just seen, the rental price of capital is the central economic variable for investment decisions.

The firm's **investment demand function** tells how much capital equipment the firm will purchase given its planned level of output and the rental price of capital. If the firm has been in business for a while, it will have an existing stock of capital at the beginning of the year. After examining the planned level of output and the rental price of capital, it will decide upon a level of capital to use during the year. Finally, it will purchase enough new capital to make up the difference. In a nutshell, this is the theory of investment.

Earlier, we showed that the firm chooses the amount of capital it uses by equating the marginal benefit of capital to the rental price of capital. When the amount of capital is high, the marginal benefit of further capital is low. By adjusting the amount of capital, the marginal benefit can be brought into equality with the rental price. The result of this process is the firm's **desired capital stock,** which we call K^*.

An example of an algebraic formula describing the desired capital is

$$K^* = .5(W/R^K)Y. \tag{9-3}$$

In this formula, W is the wage rate, Y is the firm's level of output, and R^K is the rental price of capital. The formula says that the desired capital stock equals .5 times the ratio of the wage to the rental price of capital, times the level of output. Hence, the firm will want to increase its use of capital whenever the wage to rental price ratio rises. When labor becomes more expensive relative to capital, the firm substitutes toward capital. Whenever planned output Y rises the firm will also want to use more capital.

Now consider how the **actual capital stock** changes. Suppose that the firm finishes the last year with a capital stock of K_{-1} (the subscript "-1" means last year) that is not equal to the desired capital stock for this year, K^*. If there is no depreciation then the level of investment will increase the capital stock by the amount of the investment. That is, investment equals the change in the capital stock:

$$I = K - K_{-1}. \tag{9-4}$$

If the firm wants its capital stock K to equal the desired capital stock K^*, then its investment demand I during the year is obtained by substituting $K = K^*$ into Equation 9–4. That is,

$$I = K^* - K_{-1}. \tag{9-5}$$

This much investment added to its existing capital will give the firm its desired level of capital for this year. This formula is the firm's **investment**

function. The investment function for the example formula for the desired capital stock $K*$ in Equation 9–3 can be written out as

$$I = .5(W/R^K)Y - K_{-1}. \tag{9–6}$$

Then it is apparent that *investment depends positively on the wage rate, negatively on the rental price of capital, and positively on output.*

The effect of output on investment is called the **accelerator.** To simplify the notation, set $.5(W/R^K)$ equal to the simple expression v. Then, Equation 9–3 states that $K* = vY$. If the firm always adjusts its capital stock each year so that it is equal to the desired stock, then

$$\underbrace{K = vY}_{\text{This year}} \quad \text{and} \quad \underbrace{K_{-1} = vY_{-1}}_{\text{Last year}} . \tag{9–7}$$

Investment, which is the change in the capital stock, must therefore be given by the difference between the two expressions in Equation 9–7. That is,

$$I = vY - vY_{-1} = v\Delta Y. \tag{9–8}$$

In words, the *level* of investment I depends on the *change* of output ΔY. When output accelerates, that is, when its change gets bigger, investment is stimulated. A rise in output from one level to another causes a burst of investment, but if output remains at its higher level, investment subsides. This accelerator process seems to explain a large fraction of the movements in investment.[2] It certainly is part of the reason for the close association between investment and GNP that we noted at the beginning of the chapter.

DEPRECIATION AND GROSS INVESTMENT

If the capital stock depreciates, as of course it does in reality, then the investment equations we have derived so far are only for net investment; recall that net investment is the change in the capital stock. A gross investment equation can be easily derived by adding a term to Equation 9–6 that measures the part of investment that goes for replacing worn-out capital. One assumption is that a constant fraction d of the existing capital stock wears out each period.[3] Then d times K_{-1} is added to Equation 9–6 and to all the re-

[2] See Peter K. Clark, "Investment in the 1970s: Theory, Performance and Prediction," *Brookings Papers on Economic Activity,* Vol. 1, pp. 73–113, 1979.

[3] There has been relatively little research on replacement investment. A good but somewhat mathematical discussion is in Martin S. Feldstein and Michael Rothschild, "Towards an Economic Theory of Replacement Investment," *Econometrica,* Vol. 42, pp. 393–423.

lated forms of the investment demand function in this chapter. Depreciation accounts for a very large part of gross investment. In 1986, for example, gross private domestic investment was $686 billion, while depreciation was $455 billion. Net investment was therefore $231 billion.

Properties of the Investment Function

1. When the growth of output Y is high, investment is high.

2. When the rental price of capital (R^K) is high, investment is low. In particular:
   a. When the real interest rate is high, investment is low.
   b. When the price of new capital goods is high, investment is low.

3. When wages are high, investment is high.

LAGS IN THE INVESTMENT PROCESS

A somewhat unrealistic element in the investment function we just derived is that the capital stock is adjusted to its desired level immediately. The investment function in Equation 9–6 assumes that the firm puts new capital in place as soon as it becomes aware that the level of output, the rental price of capital, and the wage warrant the new capital. For some kinds of equipment, this assumption is reasonable. But for many projects, there is a **lag** of several years between the firm's realization that new capital is needed and the completion of the capital installation. To put it another way, much of the investment occurring this year is the result of decisions made last year, the year before, and even the year before that. The decisions were governed by the expectations prevailing in those years about economic conditions this year. New information about this year's conditions that became available after the launching of the projects cannot affect this year's investment in those projects. Much of this year's investment was predetermined by earlier decisions.

To set down an algebraic expression of lags in the investment process, we will assume that firms invest so that their capital stock is adjusted *slowly* toward the desired capital stock. Suppose that firms change their capital stock by a fraction s of the difference between the desired capital stock and the capital stock at the end of the last year. That is,

$$I = s(K^* - K_{-1}). \tag{9–9}$$

Comparing this equation with Equation 9–5 we see how the investment function is modified to take account of lags in the investment process. The investment demand function in Equation 9–5 has all the properties of the original investment demand function plus one more: The more slowly that the capital stock is adjusted (the smaller is s), the weaker will be the reaction of investment demand to any of its determinants—planned output, the rental price of capital, or the wage rate.

Economic researchers have reached the conclusion that the responsiveness of investment to its determinants is very much attenuated by lags.[4] No more than a third of investment can take place in the year that economic changes make it apparent to firms that more capital is needed. Investment in this category includes tools, trucks, office equipment, and other portable items that are not produced to order. Major investments like whole plants or new custom-made equipment take one or more years to put in place.

THE AGGREGATE INVESTMENT DEMAND FUNCTION

Our discussion has looked at investment in the firm. We need to go from the firm to the economy as a whole. We will assume that total investment in plants and equipment is governed by Equation 9–9, with the wage to rental ratio taken as an economy-wide average and output taken as total real GNP. Of course, going from the firm to the total economy involves an element of approximation, because the firms we are adding together do not all have the same investment functions. Still, an aggregate investment demand function is a reasonable approximation. Even if firms are diverse, the basic properties of the investment process still hold: Investment responds positively to planned output and negatively to the rental price of capital. The strength of the response depends on how quickly investment plans can be carried out.

The Investment Function

1. The firm's investment demand function tells how much investment it needs to make this year in order to raise its capital stock to the desired level. Investment demand depends negatively on the rental price of capital and positively on the planned level of output and on the wage.

---

[4] See Peter K. Clark, "Investment in the 1970s: Theory, Performance and Prediction," *Brookings Papers on Economic Activity,* Vol. 1, pp. 73–113, 1979.

2. Lags in putting new investment in place limit the response of investment to changes in its determinants. Between one-tenth and one-third of the ultimate amount of investment occurs in the first year.

9.4 Taxes and Investment

Taxation of capital tends to discourage investment by reducing the earnings the firm receives from its investment. This effect of taxation can readily be incorporated into the rental price formula.[5] We first consider the effect of permanent tax changes.

PERMANENT TAX CHANGES

Consider again our derivation of the rental price of capital. Suppose the rental firm has to pay a tax rate of u on rental income. In addition, suppose the rental firm receives a payment of z dollars as an investment incentive from the government for each dollar of capital purchased. We derived the formula for the rental price by equating the rental income of the rental firm to the costs of renting. We can modify that analysis to take account of taxes by equating the after-tax rental income to the after-tax costs of renting. After-tax rental income is $(1 - u)R^K$. The effect of the investment incentives is to make the cost of purchasing a machine equal to $(1 - z)P^K$. Equating after-tax rental income to after-tax costs gives

$$(1 - u)R^K = (R + d)(1 - z)P^K. \tag{9-10}$$

Dividing by $1 - u$ gives

$$R^K = \frac{(R + d)(1 - z)P^K}{1 - u}. \tag{9-11}$$

The net effect of taxation and investment incentives is to multiply the rental cost by $(1 - z)/(1 - u)$.

For example, suppose the marginal tax rate applied to the revenue from capital is 50 percent. That is, $u = .5$. This by itself would double the rental price of capital—if rental firms lose half their revenue to taxation, they have to double their earnings to cover the costs of holding capital.

---

[5] This method of incorporating taxes into the rental price of capital is based on the work of Robert E. Hall and Dale W. Jorgenson, "Tax Policy and Investment Behavior," *American Economic Review*, Vol. 57 (June 1967), pp. 391–414.

Suppose further that there is an investment incentive of 10 percent, and that tax deductions for depreciation on investment are worth 30 cents of current benefits for each dollar of investment. The combined effect of the two make z equal .4. In this example, the tax multiplier in the rental price of capital, $(1 - z)/(1 - u)$, is .6/.5, or 1.2. The tax system adds 20 percent to the rental price of capital.

For investments that are financed by issuing debt or taking on mortgages, the tax system gives further incentives to invest because firms can deduct their interest costs as well. Suppose that borrowing adds another 20 cents in current tax benefits for each dollar of investment. In that case, z would be .6 and the tax multiplier would be .4/.5, or .8. Tax incentives then outweigh the direct effect of taxes, and the net effect of the tax system is to subsidize investment.

Changes in taxes and tax incentives for investment are powerful tools for changing investment spending. As shown in the box below, the Tax Reform Act of 1986 raised the rental price of capital by as much as *10 percent.* A reduction in the corporate tax rate from 46 to 34 percent tended to lower the rental price, but an elimination of the investment tax credit, a lower depreciation allowance, and a reduction in the value of deductions for interest payments (due to the lower tax), tended to raise it by a larger amount.

Suppose the desired capital stock falls by .75 percent for each percentage point that the rental price of capital is increased (that is the elasticity is −.75). Then the desired capital stock would fall by 7.5 percent as a result of this legislation. If the capital stock of plants and equipment in the United States is about $4,000 billion, then this reduction would amount to a fall in investment of $300 billion. Even if it were spread over 10 years, the effect on aggregate demand in each year could be substantial.

The Effect of the Tax Reform Act of 1986 on the Rental Price of Capital

The Tax Reform Act passed by Congress and signed into law in 1986 by President Reagan had a large effect on the rental price of capital. The Tax Reform Act lowered the tax rate on corporations from 46 to 34 percent, eliminated the 10 percent investment tax credit, and allowed less depreciation of capital for tax purposes. Overall these changes raised the rental price of capital and thereby reduced incentives for firms to invest. While the cut in the corporate tax rate lowered the rental price of capital, the other changes raised the rental price by a larger amount. The effect of the Tax Reform Act on the tax parameters are approximately as follows:

Source of Change in Tax Parameters (u, z)	Values of Tax Parameters	
	Old Tax Law	New Tax Law
Effects on tax rate (u) Corporate tax rate cut from .46 to .34	$u = .46$	$u = .34$
Effects on investment incentives (z) 1. Investment tax credit repealed	.10	.00
2. Less accelerated depreciation	.25	.22
3. Smaller deduction of interest costs because of lower tax rate	.20	.18
Total: (1) plus (2) plus (3)	$z = .55$	$z = .40$
Tax Multiplier: $(1 - z)/(1 - u)$	$.45/.54 = .83$	$.60/.66 = .91$

Hence, the Tax Reform Act raised the rental price of capital by about 10 percent. This could represent a substantial drop in investment demand. Perhaps this is why business investment fell in 1986 as we discussed in Section 9.1.

The Tax Reform Act of 1986 has another more positive effect on business investment, however. It "leveled the playing field" in the jargon of tax reformers. Investment incentives such as investment tax credits and accelerated depreciation tend to favor certain industries at the expense of others. By eliminating these incentives, tax rates will be more equal across industries. Investment will thereby be allocated more efficiently.

ANTICIPATED TAX CHANGES

The above calculations assume that the tax rates are always in effect and that tax changes are not anticipated by firms. If firms are forward-looking, as we have argued they are, then anticipations of future tax changes can also affect investment. The effects are tricky to calculate, and can go in a direction opposite from unanticipated changes.

Suppose, for example, that U.S. firms anticipated in 1985 that the 10 percent investment tax credit would be repealed starting in 1986. In fact, this is a very realistic example, because such a repeal was proposed by the Reagan administration and widely discussed in 1985. The repeal occurred as part of the Tax Reform Act of 1986. And the repeal was made effective on January 1, 1986.

Firms that anticipated such a change would realize that they would have to pay 10 percent more for capital goods starting in January 1986 than in 1985. Accordingly they would want to buy capital in 1985 before the effective price rise. If possible they would shift their purchases of equipment from 1986 to 1985.

Rental firms would also cut their rental price in 1985 in anticipation of the repeal of the investment tax credit. With the effective price of capital goods expected to increase, rental firms could charge less for rent because of the expected capital gain on the capital that they owned. With a decrease in the rental price there would be more investment in 1985. Hence, an *anticipated* elimination of the investment tax credit would increase investment in the year that the elimination was anticipated.

The behavior of investment in the United States in 1985 and 1986 provides dramatic confirmation of this forward-looking anticipatory behavior of firms. Investment in business equipment grew by 19 percent at an annual rate in the last quarter of 1985 and then fell by about the same amount in the first quarter of 1986. Evidently firms bunched their capital purchases in the last months of 1985 right before the effective date of the repeal. Investment remained rather low throughout 1986 as we have discussed previously.

These same anticipatory effects can work in the opposite direction. If firms anticipated a re-enactment of the investment tax credit, perhaps because of a prolonged economic slump, then the rental price of capital would increase at the time of anticipation, and investment would actually fall.[6]

Tax Incentives

1. The government can influence the level of investment through tax policy. Heavier taxation raises the rental price of capital and discourages investment.

2. Tax incentives such as investment tax credits and depreciation deductions lower the rental price of capital and stimulate investment.

3. Anticipated increases in tax incentives can reduce investment today, because firms will postpone their capital purchases until they can take advantage of the credit.

---

[6] For rational expectations approaches to consequences of anticipated changes in investment incentives, see Lawrence H. Summers, "Taxation and Corporate Investment: A q-theory Approach," *Brookings Papers on Economic Activity,* Vol. 1, pp. 67–140, 1981, and John B. Taylor, "The Swedish Investment System as a Stabilization Policy Rule," *Brookings Papers on Economic Activity,* Vol. 1, pp. 57–97, 1982.

9.5 Residential Investment

The economic theory of residential investment can be approached in much the same way as the theory of business investment. We can start again with the concept of the *rental price*. Because a significant amount of housing of all kinds is rented in the open market, there is nothing unfamiliar about the idea of a rental price of housing. Even though many American families own their houses rather than rent them, we can examine their decision about how large a house to own by looking at the rental price they pay implicitly when they own. Let R^H represent the rental price for houses. As before, the rental price is the interest rate plus a rate of depreciation times the price of houses (P^H):

$$R^H = (R + d)P^H. \tag{9-12}$$

An important quantitative difference is in the rate of depreciation, d. The equipment that makes up the bulk of business investment depreciates at around 10 percent per year, so d is .10 in the formula for R^K. Houses hardly depreciate at all. A reasonable value for d in the formula for R^H is .02. Consequently, the real interest rate is a much larger fraction of the rental cost of housing than it is of the rental cost of business investment. As we will see, residential investment is much more sensitive to interest rates than is business investment.

The public has a demand function for housing just as it has a demand function for any good. When the rental price of housing is high, the public demands less rental housing. We can find the public's **desired stock of housing** by finding where the rental price of housing intersects the demand curve, as in Figure 9–7.

Lags in housing construction are not nearly as long as in business investment. It is reasonable to suppose that the bulk of housing can be put in place within a year after a change in demand. The investment demand function for housing is just

$$I = H^* - H_{-1}, \tag{9-13}$$

where H is the stock of houses and H^* is the desired stock of houses.

The accelerator principle operates for housing investment as well as for business investment. The stock of housing is related to the level of real income. Thus investment, which is the change in the stock, is related to the change in real income.

HOUSING INVESTMENT AND MONETARY POLICY

Of all the components of aggregate demand, housing investment is the most sensitive to real interest rates. We have already noted one reason for

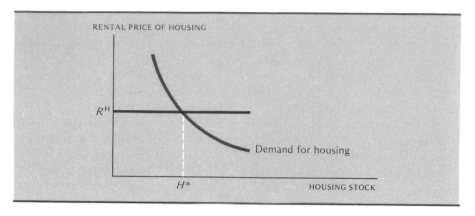

Figure 9–7. DETERMINATION OF THE DESIRED HOUSING STOCK.
The desired stock of housing, $H*$, is found at the point on the demand curve for housing where the rental price of housing, R^H, has the value determined by the real interest rate and the price of houses.

the sensitivity: Because housing depreciates at a low rate, the real interest rate is the dominant element in the rental price of housing. Most of what you pay your landlord is compensation for the capital tied up in your apartment. If you own a house, most of your annual cost is mortgage interest. Therefore, when monetary contraction or other influences raise interest rates, housing investment declines the most. The substantial drop in housing construction from 1979 to 1982 seems clearly attributable to the high interest rates prevailing during those years. Mortgage interest rates in 1982 were over 15 percent. On the other hand, housing construction was increasing in 1986 as mortgage interest rates dropped below 10 percent, even though nonresidential investment was falling.

Housing Investment

1. Housing investment is negatively related to the interest rate R. A higher interest rate makes housing more expensive by raising the rental price. A higher rental price depresses investment demand.

2. Housing investment is positively related to real GNP. Higher incomes raise the demand for housing and so raise investment demand.

3. Housing is the component of investment most sensitive to monetary and fiscal policies through interest rates. Because housing depreciates so slowly, its rental price is dominated by interest cost.

9.6 Inventory Investment

Inventories are stocks of goods in the process of production and also finished goods waiting to be sold. In 1986, total inventories in manufacturing and trade were about $600 billion. Gross national product originating in those sectors was about $1,500 billion, so about 40 cents' worth of inventories were held for each dollar in annual GNP. To put it another way, inventories were about 5 months of GNP. A significant amount of capital is tied up in inventories in the U.S. economy.

Inventories fit into the general framework for analyzing investment set up at the beginning of this chapter. Inventories have a rental price, equal to the real interest rate times the price of goods held in inventory.

Firms choose a desired level of inventories by equating the marginal benefit of inventories to the rental price. What benefits do inventories provide the firm? We can distinguish two basic functions. First, and quantitatively most important, inventories are an intrinsic part of the physical production process. We will call this the **pipeline function** of inventories. In the oil industry, large amounts of oil are unavoidably in transit in pipelines at any moment. The pipeline function also includes goods in process. Inside an auto plant, you will always find stocks of parts ready to be made into cars together with a large number of cars partway through the assembly process. It would be costly to the auto manufacturer to coordinate the flow of parts and speed up the assembly process in order to cut down on the volume of inventories. The manufacturer has made a basic decision about the design of the production process that balances the advantages of inventories against their holding cost. About two-thirds of all inventories seem to be held because of the pipeline function.

The other third of inventories are finished goods. Auto plants have cars sitting in parking lots ready for shipment to dealers. The dealers themselves also keep quite a number of cars in their lots and showrooms. As a general matter, substantial inventories of finished goods ready for sale are held at the wholesale and retail level. One of the reasons for holding these inventories is to maintain a **buffer stock** to accommodate unexpected changes in demand. The buffer stock is the second major function of inventories. The grocery store keeps dozens of bottles of ketchup on the shelves because there is always a chance that an unusual number of people will buy ketchup on any given day.

Buffer-stock inventories are held at a certain average level that equates the marginal benefit to the rental cost. When sales surge, the inventories decline to below the desired stock. The firm then adjusts its purchases to replenish the stock. When sales fall short of expectations, inventories build up. The firm then decreases its purchases to run inventories down to their desired level.

Occasionally, unintended disinvestment and investment in buffer-stock inventories show up in the aggregate amount of inventory investment throughout the economy. For example, in the first quarter of 1986, aggregate final sales of goods in the U.S. economy declined in real terms. The production of goods continued to rise rapidly despite the drop in sales. As a result, inventory investment bulged. At annual rates inventory investment was $40 billion 1982 dollars in the first quarter of 1986. By the fall, production was brought down below the level of sales, and inventory investment was negative $12 billion in the fourth quarter of 1986.

We can get an idea of the relative importance of the pipeline and buffer-stock influences on inventory investment by looking at the relationship between the *change* in real GNP and the *level* of inventory investment in the U.S. economy. Figure 9–8 shows this relationship for the years 1953–86.

We can draw two important conclusions about inventory investment from Figure 9–8. First, inventory investment tends to be closely related to

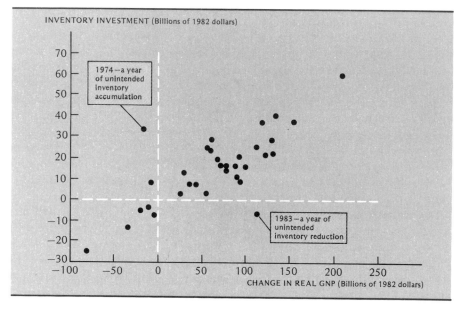

Figure 9–8. INVENTORY INVESTMENT AND THE CHANGE IN GNP.
The amount of inventory investment tends to be closely related to the change in real GNP. Each dot corresponds to a year in the period from 1953 through 1986. The horizontal axis shows the change in real GNP and the vertical axis shows the real amount of inventory investment. As a rule, inventory investment is high when real GNP is growing and low when it is contracting. There are two large exceptions—1974 and 1983—that prove the rule. The dot in the upper left is for 1974, when real GNP fell but inventory investment was high. In 1974, there was probably substantial unwanted inventory accumulation. The dot to the right and below the general trend is for 1983, when real GNP grew rapidly but inventory investment was negative. In 1983, there was probably unintended reduction of buffer stocks because sales were unexpectedly high. As a general matter, intended changes in inventory stocks dominate unintended changes. Years of high GNP growth are years of high inventory investment and vice versa.

changes in production. When higher levels of output are being produced, there are more goods in the pipeline. Filling up the pipeline to the higher level requires more inventory investment. Consequently, years of rapid GNP growth tend to be years of high inventory investment. This is the third important place were the accelerator principle is in operation. The accelerator effect is particularly strong for inventory investment, because lags are less important for inventories than for any other component of investment.

Second, there are occasional episodes when businesses are caught by surprise and inventories pile up or are depleted unintentionally. In these episodes, inventory investment departs from its usual relation to the change in real GNP. In Figure 9–8, the small number of dots away from the prevailing upward-sloping line are years when unintended accumulation or depletion of inventories occurred. There is no systematic tendency for buffer stocks to absorb every change in real GNP. Instead, big movements of buffer stocks are a rare surprise. Research on inventory behavior has confirmed the general proposition that relatively few important movements of inventories can be traced to surprises in sales.[7]

Inventory Investment

1. Inventories provide two benefits to firms. The production process involves a pipeline of partly produced goods. When the level of output is high the stock of goods in the pipeline is high. Inventories of finished goods also function as a buffer stock against unexpected changes in sales.

2. The pipeline function of inventories dominates inventory investment in most years, but occasionally economy-wide surprises in sales are large enough for changes in buffer stocks to contribute an important component to inventory investment.

3. The increase in pipeline inventories when output rises is a major part of the accelerator in the short run.

9.7 The Investment Function and the IS Curve

Total investment is the sum of investment in plants and equipment, residential housing, and inventory. We can summarize the ideas of this chapter in an overall investment function. Investment depends positively on real GNP Y and negatively on the interest rate R.

[7] See Albert A. Hirsch and Michael Lovell, *Sales Anticipations and Inventory Behavior,* John Wiley & Sons, New York, 1969.

The accelerator principle is important in investment. Higher output requires firms to invest in new plants and equipment, it causes families to want to increase their stock of housing, and it calls for higher pipeline stocks of inventories. For all three reasons, an increase in GNP stimulates added investment. However, the stimulus is stronger in the short run than in the long run. If the economy moves once and for all to a higher level of GNP, there will be a bulge of investment as the economy moves to the new, higher stock of plants, equipment, housing, and inventories desired at the new level of GNP. Once the new stock is reached, investment will subside to normal levels.

Investment depends negatively on the real interest rate. When the real rental cost of plants and equipment rises, firms substitute toward other inputs, especially labor. When the real rental price of housing rises, families substitute toward other forms of consumption. When the real cost of holding inventories rises, firms reduce their stocks of inventories, though this effect appears to be small. But the influence of higher real interest rates in depressing total investment is unmistakable.

Investment is central to the IS curve—in fact, as we mentioned in Chapter 5, the "I" in IS stands for investment. The IS curve can be defined as the set of combinations of real GNP and the interest rate where investment and saving are equal.

As a general matter, the IS curve slopes downward because it takes a lower interest rate to stimulate spending enough to achieve spending balance at a higher level of GNP. The investment function is a key part of that process. Lower interest rates stimulate investment—the effect is most important for housing and least important for inventories. The interest sensitivity of investment is an important determinant of the slope of the IS curve. If investment is highly responsive to the interest rate, the IS curve is flat—small changes in the interest rate cause large changes in investment and thus large changes in the level of GNP. If investment is not very responsive to interest rates, and other components are also unresponsive, the IS curve will be steep. Because investment and other categories of spending are unable to respond in the very short run (say one month) to changes in interest rates, the IS curve is close to vertical in the short run.

Example. An investment equation with an accelerator effect might be

$$I = 350 + .1Y - 2{,}000R.$$

When combined with the consumption function and net export equation of Chapter 5, the IS curve is

$$R = .342 - .000148Y + .0004G.$$

Review and Practice

MAJOR POINTS

1. There are three types of investment: business purchases of new plants and equipment, construction of new housing, and addition to inventories.

2. A business determines its desired capital stock by equating the marginal benefit of capital to the rental price of capital. A household determines its desired stock of housing in the same way.

3. The desired capital stock falls if the rental price of capital rises. It rises if output or income rises. A business's desired capital stock rises if the wage rises, because it will substitute away from labor and toward capital.

4. The rental price depends on the real interest rate and the price of capital goods.

5. The investment function tells how much investment will occur in a given year depending on conditions in that year. Although firms would like to invest up to the point where actual capital equals desired capital, they generally cannot do so. Only a fraction of the move to the new level can occur in the first year.

6. Because of the lag in investment, a large fraction of the investment that occurs in one year is actually the result of investment projects initiated in earlier years. This part of investment is predetermined in the current year and does not respond to current economic conditions.

7. For plants and equipment, it is a good approximation to say that suppliers will supply whatever amount of new investment goods that businesses demand.

8. Tax incentives, including the depreciation deductions and interest deductions, have an important influence on investment. A higher investment credit lowers the rental price of capital and stimulates investment.

9. Inventory investment contributes an important part of the fluctuations in total investment. The stock of inventories tends to be proportional to real GNP, so an increase in GNP is accompanied by a period of inventory investment.

10. Overall, investment responds positively to real GNP; this response is called the accelerator. Investment responds negatively to the real interest rate.

11. The interest sensitivity of investment is a major determinant of the slope of the IS curve. If investment responds strongly negatively to interest rates, the IS curve is flat.

KEY TERMS AND CONCEPTS

Investment

Nonresidential fixed investment

Plant and equipment investment

Residential investment

Inventory investment

Investment demand

Marginal benefit of capital

Rental price of capital

Demand for capital

Rate of depreciation

Desired capital stock

Investment demand function

Accelerator

Tax incentives

Depreciation deductions

Desired stock of housing

Final goods inventories

Pipeline function of inventories

QUESTIONS FOR DISCUSSION AND REVIEW

1. What variables adjust so that the level of investment chosen by firms and households is equal to the amount of funds available for investment?

2. Why do investment and GNP move so closely together?

3. Suppose that a firm can reduce its energy bill by adding some capital. How does this enter the marginal benefit of capital schedule?

4. Why does the marginal benefit of capital schedule shift upward when output rises?

5. Explain the various predetermined elements in the investment function.

6. What are the effects of tax policy on investment in the long run?

7. Why is housing especially important in the economy's response to a high interest rate policy?

8. Explain exactly what happens to the three categories of investment as you move down the IS curve.

PROBLEMS

Numerical

1. Suppose that the demand for investment is given by the model

$$I = s(K^* - K_{-1}),$$

where K^* is the desired stock of capital given by

$$K^* = .1Y/R,$$

where Y is output and R is the interest rate. Assume that there is no depreciation and that $R = .05$. Let $s = .25$ to start.
   a. Calculate the desired capital stock in Year 1 if output is 200. Calculate the level of investment in the first year if the capital stock was 400 at the beginning of the first year.
   b. Suppose now that output rises from 200 to 250 in Year 2, and then remains at this new level forever. Calculate the level of investment and the capital stock in Years 2, 3, and 4. What are the new long-run levels of investment and capital? Explain why investment reacts with a lag to the increase in output.
   c. Repeat the calculations in Parts a and b for $s = 1$ and comment on the difference between your answers.

2. Repeat Problem 1 for the case where investment is given by

$$I = s(K^* - K_{-1}) + .1K_{-1}.$$

The last term on the right is replacement investment. Explain the reason for the differences between the answers to Questions 1 and 2.

3. Suppose that the investment function is given by

$$I = 350 - 2,000R + .1Y$$

rather than by the investment function given in Chapter 5. Add this investment function to the other four equations of the IS-LM model:

$$Y = C + I + G + X$$
$$C = 80 + .63Y$$
$$X = 425 - .1Y - 500R$$
$$M = (.1625Y - 1,000R)P$$

Treat the price level as predetermined at 1.0, and let government spending be 750 and the money supply be 600.

a. Derive an algebraic expression for the IS curve for this model and plot it to scale. Compare it with the IS curve in the examples of Chapter 5. Which is steeper? Why?

b. Derive the aggregate demand curve and plot it to scale. How does it compare with the aggregate demand curve in the example of Chapter 5?

c. Calculate the effect of an increase in government spending on GNP. Is the effect larger or smaller than in the case where investment does not depend on output Y? Describe what is going on.

d. Calculate the effect of an increase in the money supply on GNP. How does the impact compare with the situation where investment does not depend on output?

4. Multiplier-accelerator interaction: Consider a macro model that has both a consumption function that depends on lagged income (like Friedman's permanent-income equation) and an investment equation that depends, with a lag, on changes in income. Ignore interest rate effects. In particular assume that the following equations describe the economy:

$$Y = C + I + G$$
$$C = 80 + .63Y_p, \text{ with } Y_p = .5(Y + Y_{-1})$$
$$I = 650 + .2(Y_{-1} - Y_{-2})$$
$$G = 750$$

a. By algebraic substitution of C and I into the income identity, obtain a single expression for output Y in terms of output in the previous years (Y_{-1} and Y_{-2}).

b. Calculate the constant level of output Y that satisfies all the relationships in the model. (Hint: Set $Y_{-1} = Y$ and $Y_{-2} = Y$ in the equation from Part a and solve for Y using algebra.)

c. Suppose that Y has been equal to the value that you calculated in Part b for the past 2 years (Years 1 and 2). But now suppose that government spending increases by $50 billion (in Year 3). Calculate the effect on output in Year 3. Calculate the effect on output in Years 4 through 10. Be sure to use the relationship that you derived in Part a, substituting the values for Y_{-1} and Y_{-2} that you calculated in the previous two steps.

d. Plot the values of Y on a diagram with the years on the horizontal axis. Do you notice any "cyclical" behavior in Y? Explain what is going on. (This algebraic model was originally developed by Paul Samuelson of M.I.T. while he was a student at Harvard in the 1930s.)

5. (This problem refers to the material in Appendix A.) Consider the case where the price of capital goods, P^K, and the revenues from investment, J, are the same each year. Work with the equation for the financial position V:

$$V_t = (1 + R)V_{t-1} - dP^K + J.$$

Always start with $V_0 = -P^K$. In the last period of the project the firm sells the capital good for P^K.

a. Show that, regardless of the length of the project, V is zero if the revenues from investment $J = (R + d)P^K$.

b. Calculate the financial position for each year of a 10-year project that costs $100,000 and earns a revenue of $16,000 per year. Use an interest rate of 5 percent and a depreciation rate of 10 percent. Is the project a winner or a loser?

c. Repeat the above calculation for an interest rate of 10 percent. Is the project a winner or a loser? Explain the difference between this answer and the answer to Part b.

Analytical

1. What theory of inventory investment predicts that inventory investment is negative when GNP suddenly rises? What theory predicts the opposite? For both theories explain what happens at firms during a sudden *decline* in GNP.

2. Consider a firm whose capital stock is initially equal to its desired capital stock, where $R=.05$, $d=.1$, $P_k=100$, and P_k is initially not expected to change in the future.

a. Suppose P_k suddenly rises to 110. Ignoring taxes, what must the firm expect P_k to be next year in order for its desired capital stock to remain unchanged?

b. Suppose now that P_k is expected to return to 100 the following year and to remain at 100 in all future years. Assume that this is in fact what happens. Describe the behavior of investment in the year of the price increase and in all future years. Consider both the case where the capital stock adjusts immediately to its desired level, and the case where it adjusts with a lag.

3. In this problem we consider an economy in which the price of *new* capital goods never changes. It is always equal to 100.

a. Assuming $R=.05$, $d=.1$, and a corporate income tax of 50 percent, what is the rental cost of capital?

b. The government is considering an investment tax credit (ITC) where 10 percent of the purchase price of a new capital good can be subtracted from a firm's taxes. Under such a proposal, what will the rental cost of capital be? Assuming that the ITC is unanticipated, describe the behavior of I and K^* in the year that it is implemented.

c. Assuming that the old capital goods are perfect substitutes in production for new capital goods, what will the price of old capital goods be under the ITC? If the value of a firm's capital stock changes in the year the ITC is implemented, will this change directly affect the firm's investment decision?

d. Assume now that such a proposal is announced a year ahead of time. What will the rental cost of capital be in the year in which firms learn about the ITC? Compare your answer to the rental cost calculated in Parts a and b. Explain any differences.

e. Compare the level of investment in the year in which the ITC is announced to what it would be without the ITC. Compare the level of investment in the following year when the ITC is implemented to what it would be if the ITC was implemented *unannounced* that year.

4. How sensitive would you expect automobile production to be to the interest rate? In answering this question, consider (i) the sensitivity of the desired stock of automobiles to the interest rate, (ii) the lags in the adjustment of the automobile stock to its desired level, and (iii) the impact of changes in final automobile sales on inventory investment in automobile manufacturing.

5. Paradox of thrift: Suppose that investment demand depends on the level of income but not on the interest rate, according to the formula

$$I = e + dY$$

and that consumption also depends on income according to the consumption function

$$C = a + b(1 - t)Y.$$

a. Sketch the spending line for the economy that shows how total spending increases with income Y. (Put spending on the vertical axis and income on the horizontal axis, like Figure 4–3 of Chapter 4.) Draw a 45-degree line and indicate where spending balance is.
b. Suppose that consumers decide to be more "thrifty," to save more. They do this by reducing "a" once and for all. Show the new point of balance in the diagram.
c. What happens to investment as a result of consumers' attempts to save more? Explain.
d. Explain the "paradox of thrift" that the attempt to save more may result in a reduction in private saving. What happens to total saving?
e. Explain why the paradox of thrift is a short-run phenomenon. Introduce interest rates into the investment function, and add a money demand function and price-adjustment equation to the model. If the economy is operating at potential GNP before the reduction in a, will it eventually return to potential after the reduction in a? What happens to saving and investment when prices have fully adjusted?

6. Suppose the desired capital stock is given by the expression

$$K^* = vY/R^k$$

where v is a constant and R^k is the rental cost of capital.
a. Assuming that output in the economy is fixed at Y^*, will a permanent increase in the interest rate have a permanent or temporary effect on the level of investment?
b. Is your answer to Part a consistent with the investment function incorporated in the IS curve?
c. Suppose now that output in the economy is growing each period so that $\Delta Y = g$. Assuming that the actual capital stock adjusts immediately to its desired level, answer Part a.

7. Sketch an IS-LM diagram. Compare two cases: one in which the investment demand function depends on income, the other where it is independent of income. In which case are both monetary and fiscal policy more effective? Explain.

8. Suppose that GNP is below potential GNP, and that inflation is low. The president and Congress are talking about reducing taxes on investment in order to get the economy back to potential.
a. Sketch the situation on an IS-LM diagram. Show where you want to move the IS curve to get back to potential.
b. In light of lags in the investment process and the forward-looking nature of firms' investment decisions, describe some of the problems that the policy makers need to worry about in enacting the tax legislation.

9. The 1986 Tax Reform Act called for an increase in taxes on businesses and a decrease in taxes on consumers, with total revenue remaining about the same. Describe the effects of tax on *investment demand*. Be explicit: Are these effects likely to occur immediately, or will they occur with a lag? Distinguish between the effects that work through the rental rate on capital and effects that work through the accelerator. Which of these two effects is likely to be larger in the long run?

Appendix A: Capital Budgeting and the Rental Price of Capital

In this appendix we show that Jorgenson's rental price approach gives the correct answer to the question of what should be the desired capital stock for a firm that *buys* capital. As discussed in the text the key result is that investment projects that earn more than the rental price will be undertaken, and those that earn less than the rental price will not be undertaken. We use a capital budgeting formulation of the firm's investment decision.

Suppose that a firm is considering buying some capital equipment that will contribute an amount J_t to revenue in each future year t. The year of the decision is $t = 0$. The equipment costs P^K.

The firm keeps track of its financial position—benefits less costs—for this capital project using an intertemporal budgeting process in the following way. Let V_t be the financial position in year t. The firm starts in the hole by the cost of the capital equipment, P^K. That is, the financial position in Year 0,

$$V_0 = -\text{The price of the capital equipment} = -P^K. \qquad (9\text{--}14)$$

For example, if the capital equipment cost $1,000, then $V_0 = -\$1,000$. In the next year, the firm may be even deeper in the hole because it pays interest at rate R on the funds it used to pay for the project last year plus the additional spending it made at the end of last year to make up for wear and tear, or depreciation. For example, for the $1,000 equipment, if the interest rate is 5 percent ($R = .05$), and 10 percent of the equipment needed to be replaced because of wear and tear ($d = .10$), then the financial position would be reduced by another $50 + \$100 = \$150$. On the other hand, the project contributed an amount J_0 to revenue in its first year. For example, if the revenue is $200, the position in the project at the beginning of the second year is

$$V_1 = -\$1,000 - \$50 - \$100 + \$200 = -\$950. \qquad (9\text{--}15)$$

The same process repeats each year. In words:

> Position at the beginning of next year
> = Position at the beginning of this year
> + Interest at that position this year
> − Depreciation this year
> + Revenue from the project this year

The general algebraic form is

$$V_t = V_{t-1} + RV_{t-1} - dP^K + J_{t-1}. \tag{9-16}$$

Note that this equation is like the intertemporal budget constraint from the forward-looking consumers in Chapter 8. It is essentially the firm's intertemporal budget for the project in question. At the end of the project, the firm will be able to sell the capital equipment. If the firm has been paying for all the wear and tear each year, so that the equipment is "like new," then the firm will be able to sell the equipment for what it paid for it. The firm will sell the equipment for P^K and the firm's financial position will be increased by P^K at the end of the project. (Recall that we assume that the price of new equipment is unchanging.)

With the repeated application of Equation 9–16, the firm can figure out its financial position in the project as long as the project is still in existence. The firm's projects will fall into two categories: **winners,** for whom the position becomes positive (the initial investment pays itself back) and then becomes more and more positive, and **losers,** for whom the position is always negative and the project never pays for itself. A reasonable theory of investment is that the firm goes with the winners and rejects the losers. This is equivalent to the capital budgeting recommendation, which says that projects that have a positive present discounted value should be undertaken, and those with a negative present discounted value should be rejected. The present discounted value of a project is simply the financial position V_t as we have defined it divided by $(1 + R)^t$. When the financial position is positive, so is the present discounted value. When the financial position is negative, so is the present discounted value.

Now, to prove that the rental approach gives the same answer as the capital budgeting approach we need to show than *an investment project that consistently earns more than the rental price is a winner; a project that consistently earns less than the rental price is a loser.*

Suppose a project earns exactly the rental price each year, that is,

$$J_t = (R + d)P^K. \tag{9-17}$$

As we noted, the financial position at the start is

$$V_0 = -P^K. \tag{9-18}$$

In the next period the financial position is

$$V_1 = -(1 + R)P^K - dP^K + J_0, \tag{9-19}$$

where we have used the budget equation, 9–16. Substituting $J_0 = (R + d)P^K$ into Equation 9–19, we get

$$V_1 = -(1 + R)P^K - dP^K + (R + d)P^K, \tag{9-20}$$

which, after canceling out terms on the right-hand side, simply equals $-P^K$. If you repeat this procedure to obtain the financial position after two years, V_2, three years, V_3, and so forth, you will find that the firm's financial position is always equal to minus *the current price of a machine.* At the end of the project the firm sells the machine. Because the firm receives the current price of the machine, P^K, the financial position at the end of the project is exactly zero. That is, the investment is just on the borderline between being a loser and being a winner.

If the investment earned a little more than the rental price each year, the firm's financial position would end up positive. The investment would be a clear winner. If the investment earned a little less than the rental price each year, the financial position would turn out negative. The firm would reject it. Hence, the rental price is the key factor in the investment decision, even though the firm is buying the capital.

Appendix B: Tobin's *q* and the Rental Price of Capital

We saw in Section 9.3 that investment takes place with a lag. This lag has implications for the observed relationship between investment, the rental price of capital, and a related variable called Tobin's *q*. To understand this relationship, suppose that the rental price R^K suddenly falls below the marginal benefit J of capital. The situation is illustrated in Figure 9–9, which is a replica of Figure 9–5. The firm will want to raise its capital stock until the marginal benefit of new capital is reduced to the new rental price. But if the firm must adjust its capital slowly, the marginal benefit of capital will remain above the rental price during the adjustment period when the firm is investing in new capital. Only when the adjustment is complete and the actual capital stock equals the new desired level will the marginal benefit of capital equal the rental price. In the meantime, the greater is the difference between desired capital stock and the actual capital stock, the greater is the

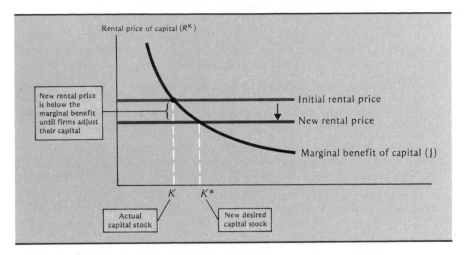

Figure 9–9.   DESIRED CAPITAL GREATER THAN ACTUAL CAPITAL.
When the rental rate on capital falls, firms do not immediately adjust their capital to the new desired level. The adjustment takes place with a lag. Until the capital stock is adjusted the rental price of capital R^k is below the marginal benefit of capital J.

difference between the rental price and the marginal revenue of capital. Investment is positively related to this difference between J and R^K.

Alternatively stated, investment will be a positive function of the ratio of the marginal benefit of new capital J to the rental price of capital R^K. When this ratio (J/R^K) is greater than 1, the rental price is below marginal benefit of capital and the firm is investing in new capital. When the ratio is less than 1, the firm wants to reduce its capital stock and is thus not investing at all.

The ratio J/R^K of the marginal benefit of capital to the rental price of capital has an interesting interpretation. Suppose that the firm issues shares that can be bought or sold on a stock market, such as the New York Stock Exchange. If the interest rate on bonds is R, then the market value (MV) of the firm's shares should be such that the return on the shares, J/MV—the ratio of the marginal benefit of capital (J) to the value of the shares (MV) that represent ownership of that capital—is equal to the interest rate R. Then the return on holding the firm's shares is the same as the return on bonds. In other words, the market value MV of the firm's shares is directly related to the marginal benefit J of capital by the formula $MV \times R = J$. For example, if $J = \$10$ per share, and $R = .05$, then the market value MV of shares should equal $\$200$.

There is a similar relation between the price of capital at the firm, P^K, and the rental rate, R^K. Ignoring depreciation, the formula for the rental price of capital says that $P^K \times R = R^K$. Combining these two formulas we get

$$\frac{J}{R^K} = \frac{MV \times R}{P^K \times R} = \frac{MV}{P^K} = q.$$

The ratio on the far right (MV/P^K), the market value of the firm divided by the price of the firm's capital, is called Tobin's "q," after James Tobin of Yale University who emphasized the importance of the ratio for invest-ment.[8] It is clear from our discussion thus far that investment should be pos-itively related to q.

Tobin's q provides a very useful way to formulate investment functions because it is relatively easy to measure. Data on a firm's share price can usually be obtained from a stock exchange, and the price indexes for capital are tabulated as part of the national income and product accounts (NIPA). For this reason, Tobin's q is a useful gauge of the climate for investment. For example, in 1983 when investment was booming in the United States, Tobin's q was quite large, even though the measured real interest rate and the rental price of capital suggested an unfavorable climate for investment. The microeconomics of investment that underlie Tobin's q approach to in-vestment are really no different from the rental price approach that we focus on in this chapter.

[8] See James Tobin and William Brainard, "Asset Markets and the Cost of Capital," in Bela Balassa and Richard Nelson (eds.), *Economic Progress, Private Values and Public Policy: Essays in Honor of William Fellner,* North-Holland, 1977, for more details about q.

10

The Foreign Trade Balance and the Exchange Rate

FOREIGN TRADE exerts a powerful influence on aggregate demand. For example, when consumers decide to purchase Japanese or German cars rather than American cars, aggregate demand for U.S. goods declines. The immediate short-run impact is a decline in GNP and employment in the United States.

The mid-1980s saw a remarkable and unprecedented development in the foreign trade of the United States. A huge trade deficit was the result. Between 1980 and 1986, U.S. production of goods, as measured by real GNP, rose by 15.4 percent. On the other hand, the total use of goods by Americans—consumption, investment, and government purchases—grew by 22.2 percent. The gap between production and use of goods was met by imports of goods. Had the United States produced the same volume of goods it used, it would have been well above full employment in 1986 instead of just below full employment.

The international value of the dollar affects foreign trade and thereby influences aggregate demand, GNP, and employment. Fluctuations in the dollar have become even more important since the 1970s when the United States and other countries stopped trying to fix the dollar's value. The fluctuations are now sometimes so large—as when the dollar rose rapidly in 1984 and fell equally rapidly in 1987—that they overwhelm longer-run competitive factors that determine trade between countries. The huge

259

trade deficit with Japan from 1984 to 1987, for example, was largely caused by macroeconomic factors, but it brought forth demands for tariffs and restrictions against Japanese products.

10.1 Foreign Trade and Aggregate Demand

Figure 10–1 shows what happened to the flows of goods and services into and out of the United States over a 30-year span. Generally, imports and exports have been about equal, but in some years, especially most recently, there have been important swings. The huge excess of imports over exports in the mid-1980s will be a particularly important subject of this chapter.

The quantity of goods and services flowing into and out of the United States is not the only important dimension of trade. It matters how much we have to pay for imports and how much we can get for our exports. In this respect, the nominal or dollar flows are important in foreign trade, whereas it is the real flows that concern us in considering domestic production. If imports become more expensive, it is costly to the United States even if net exports in real terms do not change. The **terms of trade** are the ratio of the price of exports to the price of imports. When the prices of imports rise, we say there has been an adverse shift in the terms of trade.

When the value of American imports exceeds the value of exports, either because of a high quantity of imports or because of the high price of imports, the United States must borrow enough from foreigners to pay for the difference. As we saw in Chapter 2, U.S. borrowing from abroad is called a capital inflow. For example, in 1986, net exports were –106 billion dollars; the United States had to borrow $106 billion in order to finance the excess of imports over exports. Actually, total borrowing was even larger because the United States also paid transfers to people outside the country of about $15 billion.

A capital inflow of $121 billion is very large by historical standards. Capital inflows of this magnitude in the 1980s brought the United States from a net creditor position with the rest of the world to a net debtor position. In other words, by 1986 Americans owed more to foreigners than foreigners owed to Americans.

Foreign Trade and Aggregate Demand

1. Foreign trade influences United States aggregate demand in two ways. First, Americans can purchase their goods from abroad instead of from United States producers. When they do, their imports contribute to aggregate demand in the rest of the world instead of to United States aggregate demand. Second, foreigners can purchase goods produced in the United States. These exports enter U.S. aggregate demand.

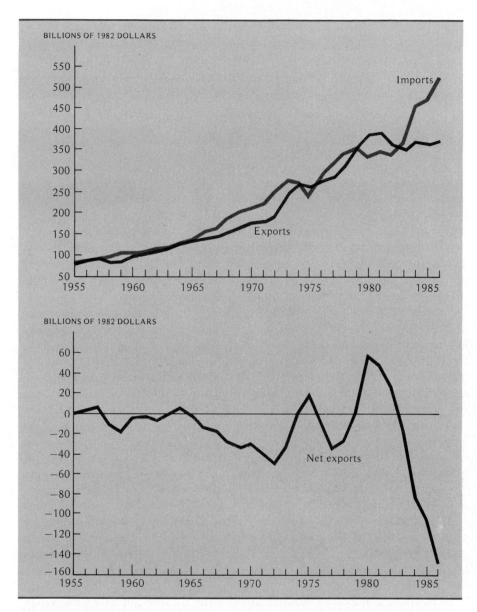

Figure 10–1.   EXPORTS, IMPORTS, AND NET EXPORTS IN 1982 DOLLARS.
The top panel shows the quantities of goods exported out of and imported into the
United States in constant 1982 dollars. The difference between the two is net exports,
shown separately in the bottom panel. Imports grew very rapidly in the mid-1980s while
exports were roughly constant. Net exports turned sharply negative.

2. When exports are less than imports, Americans must finance the difference plus any other expenditures abroad by borrowing. This borrowing—or equivalently investment by foreigners in the United States—is called capital inflow from abroad.

10.2 The Exchange Rate

The **exchange rate** is the amount of foreign currency that can be bought with one dollar. For example, on February 28, 1985, the exchange rate between the West German mark and the dollar was 3.1 marks per dollar. If you went to a bank with $100 on that day you could have obtained 310 marks. Like other prices the exchange rate can change: On October 26, 1987, the exchange rate between the mark and the dollar had fallen to 1.8 marks per dollar. The exchange rate between the dollar and foreign currencies is listed in the financial pages of most newspapers.

The exchange rate is determined in the **foreign exchange market** where dollars and other currencies are traded freely. The foreign exchange market is not in one location; it is a global market. Banks all over the world actively buy and sell dollars and other foreign currencies for their customers. The banks are linked by a network of telecommunications that allows instantaneous contact around the globe. Because of different time zones, the foreign exchange market is open 24 hours a day.

In today's monetary system the dollar exchange rate is allowed to **float** against the currencies of other large countries. For this reason the system is called a floating or **flexible exchange rate system.** The United States and other major Western countries permit a free market in foreign exchange. Neither the United States nor other major countries try to fix the exchange rate with the dollar within narrow bands as they did prior to the early 1970s. This does not mean that the United States is powerless to affect the exchange rate or must ignore the exchange rate when it sets macro policy. As we will see, changes in monetary and fiscal policy have strong influences on the exchange rate, and these influences must be considered when setting macro policy.

Since there are many countries in the world, there are many exchange rates for the dollar. A convenient single measure of the dollar exchange rate is the **trade-weighted exchange rate**, which we will denote by the symbol E. This is an average of several different exchange rates, each one weighted according to the amount of trade with the United States. Figure 10–2 shows the trade-weighted exchange rate E for the United States for the years 1967 to 1986. The dollar fluctuated widely during this period. **Depreciation** of the dollar occurs when the exchange rate E falls. **Appreciation** of the dollar occurs when the exchange rate E rises. The dollar depreciated steadily by

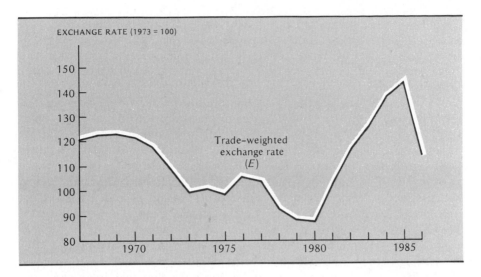

Figure 10–2. THE EXCHANGE RATE.
The trade-weighted exchange rate is the best overall measure of the dollar exchange rate. It is an average of exchange rates with many different currencies including the Canadian dollar, the French franc, and the West German mark, the Japanese yen, and the British pound. The exchange rate fluctuates by large amounts. It was very high in the early 1970s and in the early 1980s. The dollar was low in the late 1970s. Source: *Economic Report of the President*, 1987, Table B–105.

17 percent from 1976 to 1980. The dollar then turned around and appreciated by over 60 percent through 1985. During 1986 it again depreciated.

THE EXCHANGE RATE AND RELATIVE PRICES

In our discussion of the role of the exchange rate in foreign trade, we will speak of the rest of the world (ROW) as if it were a single country with a single monetary unit, a single price level P_w, and a single level of GNP. Then, the trade-weighted exchange rate E is simply the exchange rate between the dollar and the foreign monetary unit. Like the exchange rate, the price level in the rest of the world P_w is measured by taking an average of the price levels in the countries that trade with the United States.

The **real exchange rate** is a measure of the exchange rate that is adjusted for changes in purchasing power between the United States and the ROW. It is a measure of the relative price of goods produced in the United States compared with goods produced in the ROW. The real exchange rate can be written in symbols as

$$\text{Real exchange rate} = \frac{\text{foreign price of U.S. goods}}{\text{foreign price of ROW goods}} = \frac{E \times P}{P_w}.$$

When the real exchange rate is high foreigners have to pay more for goods produced in the United States compared to the price of goods produced in the rest of the world. For example, when the mark-dollar exchange rate rises from 1.8 to 2.0 marks per dollar, the price of a $1000 Apple computer produced in the United States rises from 1,800 marks to 2,000 marks in West Germany. Note that the exchange rate for the individual item is multiplied by its price in the United States to get the price outside the United States; similarly, we multiply E times P in the numerator of the real exchange rate to get a measure of the average price of U.S. goods in the ROW.

Recall our basic assumption that prices set by United States producers are fixed in the short run. Aggregate demand in this period, domestic or foreign, will not influence the dollar price level P in this period. We make the same assumption about the ROW. The price level P_w set by ROW producers is fixed in the short run.

The exchange rate E, on the other hand, varies minute by minute. Thus the real exchange rate (EP/P_w) varies minute by minute. The price of United States products in the ROW is flexible in the short run because the exchange rate is flexible. By the same token, the dollar price of ROW products is flexible in the short run.

When the dollar appreciates, ROW products become cheaper to Americans. At the same time, United States products become more expensive in the ROW. If the United States and the ROW produced identical, readily transportable products, the exchange rate would not fluctuate in the short run. We would always buy from the cheapest producer. The exchange rate would always have the single value that equated the dollar prices of United States and ROW products. The real exchange rate would never change. If the United States and the ROW produced all the same products, the exchange rate could not fluctuate in the short run and would change in the longer run only by as much as prices in the ROW rose by more than prices in the United States. This theory of exchange rate fluctuations is called **purchasing power parity.** The theory does not work for short-run fluctuations. Exchange rates fluctuate far more than the theory predicts. We can see this easily. According to the theory, the *real* exchange rate ought to be constant over time. The real exchange rate between the dollar and the rest of the world is shown in Figure 10–3. The real exchange rate is not at all constant.

Clearly, purchasing power parity is not a good theory of the determination of the exchange rate in the short run. On the other hand, the theory has a powerful economic logic. How can we reconcile the fact of wide variations in the real exchange rate with the principle that people buy at the lowest possible price?

One answer is that different countries produce different products. Japanese cars are not identical to American cars, for example. When the dollar appreciates, Japanese cars become cheaper, but the United States public does not stop buying American cars altogether. Instead, the new price advantage of Japanese cars raises Japanese sales in the United States somewhat

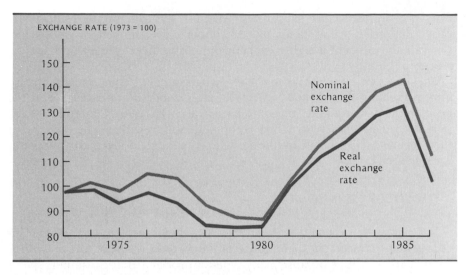

EXCHANGE RATE (1973 = 100)

Figure 10–3. THE REAL EXCHANGE RATE.
The real exchange rate between the United States and the ROW is the nominal exchange rate adjusted for changes in the domestic purchasing power of the dollar and the currencies of the ROW. When the real exchange rate falls, it means that Americans find foreign goods more expensive. Through much of the 1970s, the real exchange rate fell. The price of American goods relative to foreign goods fell from .99 in 1974 to .83 in 1979. In the early 1980s, the relative price of American goods rose dramatically; then it fell sharply in 1986. Source: *Economic Report of the President,* 1987, Table B–105.

and depresses sales of American cars somewhat. The same thing occurs in hundreds of other markets. Appreciation of the dollar makes it more difficult for United States producers to sell their output, but it does not wipe them out. The exchange rate has room to vary. It is not locked in place by purchasing power parity.

10.3 The Determinants of Net Exports

THE EFFECT OF THE EXCHANGE RATE

As we have just seen, fluctuations in the exchange rate change the relative price of United States and ROW goods, and thereby affect the demand for imports and exports. Imports depend positively on the exchange rate. If the dollar is strong, it buys a lot of foreign currency, and the goods sold by the ROW are correspondingly cheaper. When the dollar appreciated in the early 1980s, many United States industries, especially autos and steel, suffered from the reduced price of their foreign competitors. The same thing is true in all sectors, though the effect is less severe for products where the ROW does not produce close substitutes. And for services, utilities, and many other important components of GNP, imports are difficult or impossible. Overall, the effect of a higher exchange rate is to divert some aggregate demand to the ROW.

Exports, too, are sensitive to the exchange rate. A strong dollar—that is, a high exchange rate—makes United States goods more expensive in the ROW. In the period of the strong dollar in the early 1980s, United States export industries like construction equipment suffered from the increase in their prices as perceived by the ROW, even though dollar price increases were moderate.

THE EFFECT OF INCOME

In Chapter 4, we noted that net exports depend on U.S. GNP. Higher incomes make consumers spend more on imported products; this relation is particularly sensitive because many types of products that consumers spend extra income on, such as electronics and cars, are frequently imported. In addition, some investment goods are imported, such as machine tools from Germany. When GNP rises and investment strengthens, part of the increased investment goods come from overseas. Thus, in general, imports respond positively to GNP. On the other hand, there is little connection between U.S. exports and U.S. GNP. Hence net exports depend negatively on GNP.

THE NET EXPORT FUNCTION

As we have seen, we can combine imports and exports into a single measure, net exports X, defined as exports less imports. Our conclusions about the determinants of net exports are:

1. Net exports depend negatively on the real exchange rate. When the dollar is strong, exports are lower and imports are higher. Net exports are lower on both counts.
2. Net exports depend negatively on real income in the United States. This dependence comes from subtracting imports, which depend positively on real income.

We can summarize these ideas in a simple algebraic formula:

$$X = g - mY - n\frac{EP}{P_w}. \qquad \text{Net Export Function} \qquad (10\text{--}1)$$

Equation 10–1 is the net export function. It says that net exports equal a constant g minus a coefficient m times income Y, minus a coefficient n times the real exchange rate. The net export function summarizes how net exports depend negatively on both income Y and the real exchange rate (EP/P_w).

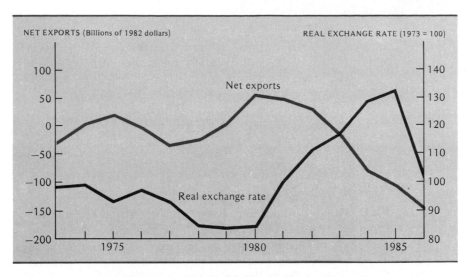

Figure 10–4. NET EXPORTS AND THE REAL EXCHANGE RATE.
The real exchange rate and net exports move at the same time, but in opposite directions. When the real exchange rate rises, net exports fall; conversely, when the real exchange rate falls, net exports rise. Source: *Economic Report of the President*, 1987, Tables B–2 and B–105.

How well does the net export function work? Figure 10–4 shows how closely net exports and the exchange rate were related during the 1970s and the early 1980s when the dollar was floating. The negative relation is quite evident; note especially that the increase in the dollar exchange rate in the 1980s was accompanied by a decline in net exports. The effect of the other determinant of net exports—real income in the United States—is not so evident in Figure 10–4 because exports rose as income in the ROW increased in this period. However, in the early 1980s the economy of the United States grew more rapidly than those of many European countries and this added to the trade deficit.

Example. A numerical example of the net export function can be written

$$X = 500 - .1Y - 100\frac{EP}{P_w}. \qquad \text{\small Numerical Example of} \atop \text{\small Net Export Function} \qquad (10\text{--}2)$$

Suppose that the price level in the United States and the price level in the ROW are both predetermined at the value of 1.0. If output Y is $4,000 billion and the exchange rate E is 1.0 then net exports X equal zero. If output Y rises by $100 billion, then net exports fall by $10 billion because imports rise by this amount. If the exchange rate rises from 1.0 to 1.3, about as much as it did from 1980 to 1984, then net exports would fall by $30 billion.

Net exports is an endogenous variable that depends on the exchange rate. To complete our theory we therefore need to explain what determines the exchange rate. As we have just seen, purchasing power parity doesn't work very well. We now go on to develop a theory that relates the exchange rate to the interest rate.

Net Exports, Income, and the Exchange Rate

1. The exchange rate is the amount of foreign currency that can be exchanged for one dollar.

2. The real exchange rate is the exchange rate corrected for changes in the price level in the United States and in the rest of the world. Purchasing power parity says that the real exchange rate should be constant. Increases in the price level in the United States would be offset by declines in the dollar exchange rate, leaving the real exchange rate unchanged. Purchasing power parity does not hold in the short run, but it does hold in the long run.

3. Net exports are negatively related to the real exchange rate and to real income.

10.4 The Exchange Rate and the Interest Rate

Fluctuations in the exchange rate are closely related to interest rates in the United States and the ROW. In particular, policies in the United States that raise interest rates tend to cause the dollar to appreciate. The appreciation of the dollar in the early 1980s, for example, was related to the monetary fiscal policies that brought extraordinarily high interest rates. Why are interest rates and the exchange rate positively related?

The financial markets of the major developed countries are closely linked. Investors are constantly comparing the returns they make by investing in Germany (in stocks and bonds that pay in marks), in Japan, in Britain, and in many other countries. There are billions of dollars and marks and trillions of yen of "hot money" that will migrate almost instantly to the place where it will earn the highest return.

As we stressed in Chapter 2, when the dust settles, trade flows and capital flows have to equal each other, except for measurement error. The net exports of the United States must be equal to the amount of U.S. capital flowing to the rest of the world less the amount of foreign capital coming into the United States. It is not possible for there to be a large U.S. trade deficit at the same time that large amounts of capital are flowing out of the United

States to seek a higher return in other countries. The exchange rate and interest rates fluctuate minute by minute to keep trade flows and capital flows equal to each other.

When the U.S. interest rate is high in comparison to foreign interest rates, capital will be attracted to the United States. Even a fraction of a percentage point of extra return could bring hundreds of billions of dollars of wealth to be invested in the United States. In order to prevent such a large flow, something else must happen at the same time that the U.S. interest rate rises in order to deter the huge capital flow. What happens is an appreciation of the dollar. When foreign investors see the combination of attractive U.S. interest rates and a strong dollar, they reason in the following way: On the one hand, I like the high return I can earn in dollars. But, on the other hand, I am not so sure that the return I will earn in my own currency is any better than at home. The dollar is strong today, but it is likely to come back to normal over the next year or two, as it always has in the past. As the dollar depreciates, I will lose some of my capital when I convert it back to my own currency.

The more the dollar rises when the U.S. interest rate rises, the more powerful will be the second part of that logic. Hence, there is some degree of appreciation of the dollar that will block the huge capital inflow that would otherwise accompany a higher U.S. interest rate. Figure 10–5 shows the relation between the U.S. interest rate and the exchange rate that is needed to stave off the capital inflow.

In algebra, we can express the positive relation between the real exchange

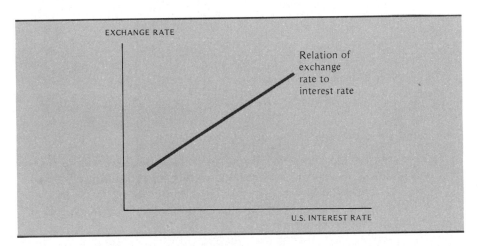

Figure 10–5. RELATION BETWEEN THE U.S. INTEREST RATE AND THE EXCHANGE RATE.
A higher U.S. interest rate requires a stronger dollar. If not, huge capital inflows would occur, which would be inconsistent with trade flows. The stronger dollar discourages the capital inflow that would otherwise occur by creating expectations of a subsequent depreciation of the dollar, which would offset the advantage of the higher U.S. interest rate.

rate and the U.S. interest rate as

$$\frac{EP}{P_w} = q + vR. \tag{10-3}$$

where R is the U.S. interest rate and q and v are constants. Recall that it is the rise in the U.S. interest rate relative to foreign interest rates that brings about the rise in the exchange rate. In Equation 10–3 we suppress the foreign interest under the assumption that it does not move as much as the U.S. interest rate. More details on the relation between the exchange rate and the U.S. interest rate appear in the appendix to this chapter.

Example. If prices are measured in a way so that the real exchange rate EP/P_w is equal to one when purchasing power parity holds, then the relation between the U.S. interest rate and the real exchange rate might be

$$\frac{EP}{P_w} = .75 + 5R. \quad \text{\small Numerical Example of Exchange Rate—Interest Rate Relation} \tag{10-4}$$

When the net export function, Equation 10–2, is combined with this relation, we get the numerical example of the net export relation we used in Chapter 5:

$$X = 425 - .1Y - 500R.$$

The Interest Rate and the Exchange Rate

1. The exchange rate and the interest rate are positively related. When the interest rate rises, say because of an increase in government spending, the exchange rate also rises.

2. The relationship between the interest rate and the exchange rate comes about as investors shift their funds between different countries to obtain the best return. When the interest rate rises in the United States, investors buy dollar-denominated bonds and this drives up the exchange rate.

3. The exchange rate remains high as long as interest rates are high. A high exchange rate implies that the dollar is expected to depreciate and this makes investors indifferent between high-interest dollar assets and lower-interest foreign assets.

10.5 The IS Curve and Economic Policy in an Open Economy

Recall that the IS curve describes the combinations of interest rates R and incomes Y that satisfy the income identity and the equations for spending: consumption, investment, and net exports. *Without* net exports in the income identity, the IS curve is downward sloping because higher interest rates reduce investment and, through the multiplier, reduce GNP. *With* net exports, more things happen to spending when the interest rate rises. An increase in the interest rate raises the exchange rate and thereby reduces net exports; this tends to augment the effect of the interest rate on investment and makes the IS curve flatter than it would be in a closed economy. Not only do high interest rates cause firms to invest less, they also cause Americans to meet their needs with imported goods and foreigners to divert their demand away from United States products.

But the presence of net exports also reduces the size of the multiplier, and this tends to make the IS curve steeper. Net exports depend negatively on GNP. As GNP rises, part of the increase in spending goes overseas and does not enter domestic aggregate demand. This spillover abroad is sometimes called **leakage** and it reduces the size of the multiplier.

In Chapter 5, we derived the open-economy IS curve graphically. The next section adds some more details in the process of deriving it algebraically.

ALGEBRAIC DERIVATION OF THE OPEN-ECONOMY IS CURVE

The IS curve is derived algebraically by substituting the functions for consumption C, investment I, and net exports X into the income identity. That is,

$$Y = \underbrace{a + b(1 - t)Y}_{C} + \underbrace{e - dR}_{I} + \underbrace{G + g - mY - n(EP/P_w)}_{X}. \tag{10-5}$$

Putting the interest rate on the left-hand side gives

$$R = \frac{a + e + g}{d} - \frac{1 - b(1 - t) + m}{d} Y - \frac{n}{d} \frac{EP}{P_w} + \frac{1}{d} G. \tag{10-6}$$

This equation relates the interest rate R to output Y, the real exchange rate EP/P_w, and government spending G. It shows that the interest rate is negatively related to the real exchange rate. Appreciation of the dollar shifts the IS curve downward; depreciation raises the curve. To get the IS curve, substitute Equation 10–3 into Equation 10–6 in order to eliminate the real exchange rate:

$$R = \frac{a + e + g - ng}{d + nv} - \frac{1 - b(1 - t) + m}{d + nv} Y + \frac{1}{d + nv} G. \tag{10-7}$$

The coefficient on Y shows that the IS curve slopes downward for two reasons: the negative response of investment to the interest rate, described by d, and the negative response of net exports, described by nv.

The IS curve of Equation 10–7 is conceptually the same as the one we discussed in Chapter 5.

EFFECTS OF MONETARY AND FISCAL POLICY

Monetary and fiscal policy have important effects on trade and the exchange rate. Suppose that the Fed increases the money supply. This shifts the LM curve to the right, lowering interest rates and stimulating investment. The decline in interest rates depreciates the exchange rate; net exports rise. Because of the rise in investment and net exports, GNP rises. However, the increase in GNP tends to decrease net exports because imports rise. There are thus two offsetting effects of an increase in the money supply on net exports. Exports definitely rise, but imports might rise by a greater amount. In any case, interest rates fall, the dollar depreciates, and GNP rises. Conversely, when the money supply is decreased, interest rates rise, the dollar appreciates, and GNP falls.

Now suppose that government spending is increased. The IS curve is pushed to the right, and interest rates rise. The rise in interest rates reduces investment spending, but also causes the exchange rate to appreciate. The higher exchange rate reduces exports as U.S. goods become relatively expensive compared with foreign goods. Hence, the increase in government spending crowds out export industries as well as investment. Imports also rise because of the increase in the dollar and because GNP has increased. Thus an increase in government spending increases the trade deficit or reduces the trade surplus, as it stimulates the economy.

The Budget Deficit and the Trade Deficit

What happens to the trade deficit when the government runs a fiscal budget deficit? Suppose the budget deficit comes from a large tax cut that puts much more disposable income in the hands of consumers. There is no corresponding reduction in government spending, and consumers choose to spend most of the increase in disposable income. Then the IS curve shifts outward. The interest rate rises. The dollar appreciates and net exports decline. Thus a budget deficit causes a trade deficit.

The accounting identity we studied in Chapter 2 suggests that there should be a relation between budget and trade deficits. Funds available for investment in the United States are private saving less the government deficit plus the capital inflow from abroad (the trade deficit). Unless an increase in the budget deficit depresses investment significantly, it will have to cause a capital inflow.

U.S. experience in the 1980s demonstrated this principle on a grand scale. The following chart shows how the tax cut of 1981, with large spending cuts, brought about a gigantic budget deficit. From trade surpluses at the beginning of the decade, very large trade deficits emerged in 1984, 1985, and 1986.

DEFICIT, BILLIONS OF DOLLARS

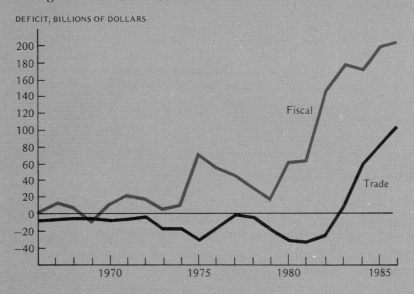

The budget deficit causes an accumulation of government debt. In a closed economy, the nation owes the debt to itself. But when the budget deficit is financed through a capital inflow, the borrowing is from the rest of the world. In effect, the United States owes the part of the national debt accumulated since 1981 to Japan and the other countries that have financed the U.S. trade deficit by running trade surpluses.

Trade deficits are not the inevitable result of budget deficits. In the mid-1980s, Japan had a budget deficit even larger than the one in the United States, but Japan had a trade surplus. The explanation is the remarkably high rate of saving of the Japanese. Private saving in Japan is enough to finance a large volume of investment, a huge government deficit, and leave enough left over to make large investments in U.S. government debt and other forms of lending to the United States.

PRICE ADJUSTMENT

What happens in these alternative policy scenarios after the short run when firms begin to adjust their prices? If output was equal to potential output in the case of the increase in the money supply, the price level would begin to rise because output increases above potential. The increase in prices will lower real money balances and the interest rate will begin to rise. As it does the real exchange rate will begin to rise. These adjustments will continue until the economy has returned to potential. Eventually the price level will have increased by the amount of the original increase in the money supply. The real exchange rate will have returned to normal so that the nominal exchange rate E will have depreciated by the amount of the increase in the price level. In the long run money is neutral.

An increase in government spending will also eventually bring about an upward adjustment in prices. The reduction in real balances will raise interest rates, further reducing investment and net exports. Eventually, output will return to potential output, and the sum of investment and net exports will have declined by exactly the amount of the increase in government spending. The real exchange rate and the interest rate will be permanently higher after the process is complete.

Open-Economy IS Curve and Policy

1. The downward slope of the IS curve in an open economy comes in part from the positive relation between the interest rate and the exchange rate. Net exports decline when the interest rate rises.

2. The offset to fiscal expansion through crowding out is stronger in an open economy. Fiscal expansion raises the interest rate and depresses net exports.

3. Monetary policy has an enhanced effect through the interest rate in an open economy. A monetary expansion lowers the interest rate and stimulates net exports as well as investment.

10.6 The Exchange Rate and the Price Level

One of the macroeconomic principles we have stressed in this book is that the price level is very unresponsive to most economic events in the short run. For example, a sudden contraction in monetary policy does not seem to have any measurable impact on the price level within the first year, even though its eventual effect is to lower prices considerably. One important exception is that prices respond quickly to changes in costs of imports such as oil. The dramatic price rises of 1974–75 and 1979–80 and the sudden slowing of inflation in 1986 can be linked directly to events in the world oil market. To a certain extent, fluctuations in the exchange rate can influence the price level in a similar way. A rise in the dollar is like a decline in world oil prices; it makes imports cheaper. A collapse of the dollar, as in 1986–87, is an adverse price shock.

In a small economy, the domestic price level is closely tied to the exchange rate. Many consumption and investment goods are imported; those that are not compete with imports. A small country's exports trade in large world markets and are usually constrained to sell at home for essentially the world price. Hence, changes in a small country's exchange rate bring immediate and important changes in that country's price level.

In the large U.S. economy, the situation is quite the reverse. For Japanese cars, for example, the U.S. market is over half the total market worldwide. The setting of the U.S. dollar price for foreign products is a major business decision for the makers of those products. Frequently, the outcome of that decision is to keep the dollar price of foreign products unchanged in the United States, even though the exchange rate has risen or fallen sharply. As a result, profit margins on foreign products sold in the United States can vary enormously as the exchange rate fluctuates. During the period of the strong dollar in the early 1980s, the U.S. prices did not fall nearly as much as the exchange rate rose. Consequently, importation of many products became highly profitable. In the auto market, many individuals got into the importation business by purchasing cars in Europe and shipping them to the United States. When the dollar declined in 1986 and 1987, prices did not rise very much. Profit margins shrank abruptly.

From its peak in early 1985 until late 1986, the real exchange rate declined by over 15 percent. The real price of imports to the United States rose by only about 1 percent over the same period. All of the rest of the change in the exchange rate was absorbed by a decline in profit margins by importers. For Japan, the numbers are particularly striking: Stated in yen, the cost of producing products in Japan rose by about 6 percent from the beginning of 1985 to the middle of 1986. But the number of yen received by the Japanese for their typical exported product declined by 23 percent over the same period.[1]

Because importers tend not to adjust their U.S. prices quickly in response to changes in the exchange rate, large movements in the exchange rate do not create price shocks in the U.S. economy. The price-adjustment process we described in Chapter 6 and will discuss more extensively in Chapter 16

---

[1] The data are from Paul Krugman and Richard Baldwin, "The Persistence of the U.S. Trade Deficit," *Brookings Papers on Economic Activity*, 1:1987, pp. 1–43.

applies reasonably well to the prices of imported goods as well as those made in the United States. We will not stress the immediate impact of the exchange rate on the U.S. price level. That impact would be large in a small, highly open economy, but appears to be quite small in the U.S. economy.

10.7 Protectionism versus Free Trade

All industries in the United States that produce products that can be shipped from one country to another face foreign competition. These industries make up the tradables sector. Only industries like services, communications, and utilities are insulated from that competition. If foreign competition could be eliminated or discouraged, domestic producers would enjoy increased profits. The losers would be U.S. consumers, who would pay higher prices as a result of lessened competition.

Industries in the tradables sector push constantly in favor of protectionist measures. These measures include:

1. Tariffs, which are a tax on imports
2. Quotas, which limit the quantity of imports
3. Outright bans of certain imports

The incentive to seek protection exists all the time. However, the likelihood of convincing Congress to enact protectionist legislation rises dramatically when imports are high and domestic industries are suffering from diminished sales and high unemployment.

The history of protection in the United States can be characterized in the following way. In normal times, under the leadership of the president, trade barriers are gradually reduced. Consumer interests predominate in the long run; purchasers in the United States are generally free to take advantage of bargains that foreigners make available. But in times of recession or large trade deficits, Congress forces the president to sign protectionist measures. Tariffs and quotas are tightened in those times. When the emergency is over, protectionism lingers for some years, but eventually is eliminated.

In 1987, even after a number of years of intensive pressure for protection, tariffs were still generally only a few percent on the great majority of imports. Some special protectionist steps were in effect, including

1. Voluntary quotas enforced by Japan on its exports of cars to the United States. Robert Crandall of the Brookings Institution has estimated that these quotas raised the price of the typical Japanese car to a U.S. purchaser by between $2000 and $3000.[2]

---

[2] Robert Crandall, "The Effects of U.S. Trade Protection for Autos and Steel," *Brookings Papers on Economic Activity,* 1:1987, pp. 271–288.

2. Voluntary restrictions on steel exports to the United States by a number of steel makers. Crandall finds that these restrictions have had relatively little effect on the U.S. price of steel.
3. The Multifiber Agreement, which restricts international trade in a number of fibers used in making textiles.
4. The Semiconductor Suspension Agreement, which requires Japanese computer chip makers to adhere to prices set by the U.S. government. These prices are well above the market prices that would prevail under free trade.
5. Special duties on rubber shoes.

An independent government agency, the International Trade Commission (ITC), has the power to impose protectionist measures even without special congressional action. The president has to approve each measure recommended by the ITC, and this has substantially limited the scope of ITC action. Both the voluntary restraints in steel and the semiconductor agreement were the results of requests from domestic industries for ITC action. If those agreements were to fail, the ITC could use its power to impose special tariffs on imports.

MACROECONOMIC EFFECTS OF PROTECTIONISM

A tariff or quota has the effect of shifting the net exports schedule in the direction of higher net exports given the exchange rate. That shift enters the spending process just as any other shift in a spending schedule or an increase in government purchases. The IS curve shifts to the right. The interest rate and GNP increase along the LM curve, which remains unchanged. All the usual accompaniments to a spending stimulus occur. In particular, the higher interest rate makes the dollar appreciate.

Because protectionism makes the dollar appreciate, the actual effect on prices and trade is smaller than it might appear at first. Although a tariff makes imports more expensive, a stronger dollar offsets this to some extent. In other words, the exporting country pays part of the tariff, rather than the U.S. consumer. Moreover, to the extent that the exporter tends to stabilize its dollar price in the United States, as we discussed in the previous section, it is even more true that the exporter, not the consumer, pays the tariff. At the same time, the macroeconomic stimulus becomes smaller, because if U.S. consumers see no price change, they will not cut their imports. Note that this effect cannot apply to quotas. If a quota forces the quantity of imports to decline, it must cause an increase in the prices paid by U.S. purchasers.

Protectionism

1. Protectionist policies lessen foreign competition facing domestic producers. They generally help domestic producers and hurt domestic consumers. They include tariffs on imports, quotas on the quantities of imports, and bans on some imports.

2. Protectionist measures stimulate net exports. They shift the IS curve outward, raise the interest rate, and raise GNP.

3. Protectionism raises the exchange rate, which discourages net exports and offsets some of the effects of protection.

U.S. Competitiveness

Reading the financial pages, you would guess that the main reason for the huge U.S. trade deficit in the mid-1980s was a dramatic loss of competitiveness. That is, the United States could not produce goods cheaply enough to compete with low-cost foreign producers. Some commentators saw this as the result of low wages paid in the Far East and Latin America; others saw it as the result of low productivity and high costs in the United States.

It is an interesting fact that trade theory, as developed in this chapter and in the thinking of the great majority of economists, finds no reason to think that a country with a high standard of living (and thus high wages and costs) will have a trade deficit.

One of the best ways to see this is to look at the situation of the United States just after World War II. At that time, wages of American workers were far higher, in purchasing power, than wages in any other major country. Yet the United States had large trade surpluses, in relation to GNP, in every year from 1946 through 1952. The reason for the surpluses was simple. Postwar reconstruction created investment opportunities abroad for U.S. investors. The resulting capital outflow was a trade surplus.

Purchasing power parity, which we stressed as the principle underlying trade theory, shows why a high-income country can export in competition with low-income countries. The exchange rate will fluctuate so that, on the average, U.S.-made goods sell at the same price in world markets as those made in Singapore, South Korea, and Taiwan.

Of course, the exchange rate can only equalize selling prices on the average across all goods. For any particular product, a high-wage country may not be able to compete. For example, the United States does not seem to be able to produce VCRs that can compete with those made in Japan. But there are other products where the United States is dominant. Almost all the computer software used anywhere in the world was developed in the United States, for example. And most of the Pacific basin countries that are highly competitive in manufactured products buy large amounts of United States lumber as a result of a cost advantage to the United States in that industry.

Purchasing power parity guarantees that any seller, no matter how high its costs, will be competitive in some markets. In addition, fluctuations in the exchange rate bring temporary departures from purchasing power parity, as we noted earlier in this chapter. During a temporary period of a strong currency, a country will have a trade deficit because all of its products have become less competitive.

Every industry in the United States should strive to become more competitive all the time. It should aim for the maximum level of profits by lowering its costs as much as possible. The payoff is higher real incomes for Americans, not necessarily an improved trade account.

10.8 Stabilizing the Exchange Rate

The wild swings in the exchange rate shown in Figure 10–2 have been upsetting to both Americans and foreigners. When the dollar was strong, U.S. producers of tradables suffered, while U.S. purchasers of imports had the advantage of bargains. The collapse of the dollar in the mid-1980s reversed the situation. Many observers have suggested that the world would have been better off with more stable exchange rates, though there is not detailed analysis that has tried to add up the benefits and costs of both consumers and producers. Most discussions consider only the interests of producers and fail to give weight to the benefits that consumers receive when the rest of the world is making bargains available to the United States.

How might U.S. policy be changed to stabilize the exchange rate? Recall that there is a simple relation between the exchange rate and the U.S. interest rate, holding constant economic conditions in the rest of the world. When the rest of the world is quiescent, the United States would have to hold its own interest rate constant in order to keep the exchange rate constant. Figure 10–6A illustrates the necessary policy in terms of the LM curve. A commitment on the part of the Fed to keep the interest rate constant means that the LM curve is perfectly flat. A shock in spending—say unexpectedly strong investment—would shift the IS curve to the right, as shown in the figure. GNP would rise by the full amount of the spending shift together with the resulting multiplier effects. The normal offset from higher interest rates would not occur. Thus GNP would be highly vulnerable

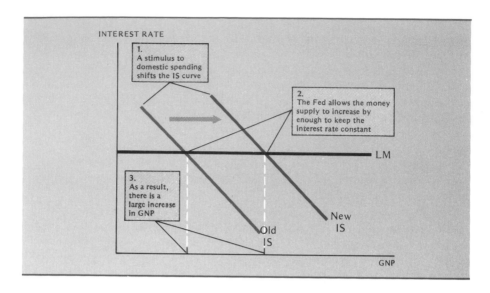

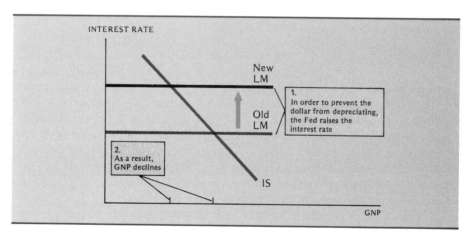

Figure 10–6. EFFECT OF A SPENDING SHOCK AND A FOREIGN SHOCK UNDER EX-
CHANGE RATE STABILIZATION.
(A) When the Fed is operating monetary policy under the principle of keeping the exchange rate stable, it must keep the interest rate constant. That is, the LM curve is a horizontal line. When the IS curve shifts, it causes large changes in output. (B) When a
change occurs in the rest of the world, such as a monetary contraction in a major foreign
country, the Fed must raise the interest rate to prevent depreciation of the dollar, if it has
a policy of stabilizing the exchange rate. Such a move contracts output in the United
States.

to spending disturbances under a policy that kept the exchange rate constant.

Note that the flat LM curve also indicates that fiscal policy is more powerful when the central bank stabilizes the exchange rate. An increase in government spending pushes the IS curve to the right. With floating exchange rates, we saw that the increase in government spending partially crowds out private investment *and* net exports because interest rates rise and the exchange rate appreciates. With the exchange rate stabilized there is no appreciation of the currency and the interest rate does not rise. Hence, there is no crowding out. Production increases by the full amount of the shift in the IS curve. This is illustrated in Figure 10–6A.

Figure 10–6B shows what would happen if there were a shock in the rest of the world that would normally have made the dollar depreciate (such as an increase in interest rates in other countries). The Fed has to shift the LM curve upward by enough to prevent the depreciation. As a result of the higher interest rate, the level of GNP would fall, as the economy moved up and to the left along the IS curve. When the Fed takes an action like this—deliberately contracting the economy to raise the dollar—it is called "defending the dollar." It sacrifices stability of employment and output in the United States in order to stabilize the exchange rate.

The important point is that making monetary policy responsible for stabilizing the exchange rate prevents monetary policy from achieving other goals, such as stability of employment or prices. We cannot ask the Fed to prevent fluctuations in the purchasing power of the dollar without recognizing that it must sacrifice the stability of other variables, which may be more important.

Stabilizing the Exchange Rate

1. To stabilize the exchange rate, the Fed would have to set a horizontal LM curve.

2. With a stable exchange rate, a domestic spending shock would have a large effect on GNP. The normal cushioning through interest-rate fluctuations would not occur, because it would cause exchange-rate fluctuations.

3. With a stable exchange rate, the Fed would have to change the U.S. interest rate in response to each foreign shock. It could not insulate GNP and employment from those shocks as it can with a floating rate.

Review and Practice

MAJOR POINTS

1. The long-run value of the exchange rate is determined by purchasing power parity. In the short run, expectations and conditions in financial markets create large deviations from purchasing power parity.

2. The interest rate differential between two countries is equal to the expected rate of depreciation.

3. Rational expectations suggests that when the real exchange rate is above purchasing power parity it is expected to decline to parity slowly.

4. There is a close relationship between the exchange rate and the interest rate. When interest rates are high the exchange rate also tends to be high.

5. The net export function depends negatively on income and on the real exchange rate.

6. The multiplier is smaller in an open economy than in a closed economy. This makes the IS curve steeper.

7. In an open economy an increase in the interest rate has a larger first-round effect on spending because it reduces net exports as well as investment. This makes the IS curve flatter.

8. An expansionary monetary policy lowers the interest rate and the exchange rate. Investment and exports are stimulated.

9. An expansionary fiscal policy raises the interest rate and the exchange rate. The policy crowds out the investment industries and the export industries.

10. Changes in the exchange rate do not have large immediate effects on the price level. The U.S. price of imported products is sticky.

11. Protectionist policies such as tariffs and quotas will reduce the trade deficit and stimulate GNP in the short run. They also tend to make the dollar appreciate, which offsets some of their effects. Protectionism is harmful to consumers because it raises prices of foreign products.

12. If the Fed sets a policy of stabilizing the exchange rate, it must give up other goals, such as employment stability. When the exchange rate is being held constant, domestic spending shocks have large effects on GNP. In addition, the policy makes GNP vulnerable to shocks occurring in foreign countries.

KEY TERMS AND CONCEPTS

Purchasing power parity	Flexible exchange rate
Interest rate parity	Marginal propensity to import
Interest rate differential	Tariffs
Exchange rate	Quotas
Real exchange rate	Protectionism
Net export function	Exchange rate stabilization

QUESTIONS FOR DISCUSSION AND REVIEW

1. Explain how you would compare the return on a Japanese bond with the return on a U.S. bond.

2. What happens to the exchange rate between the dollar and the Italian lira when chronic inflation in Italy is well above inflation in the United States?

3. Why is it rational for investors to expect that the exchange rate will depreciate when it is above normal? Under what circumstances would it not be rational to expect this?

4. Summarize the steps and assumptions that link the exchange rate and the interest rate. What would happen to the relationship if the ROW decided to use a more expansionary policy?

5. Describe what happens to consumption, investment, and net exports when you move down the IS curve.

6. What happens to net exports, investment, and consumption when government spending is decreased? Distinguish the long run from the short run.

7. What happens to net exports, investment, and consumption when the money supply is decreased? Why is monetary policy neutral in the long run, but not in the short run?

8. Describe the changes to the U.S. price of Japanese cars when the yen appreciates, in the short and medium runs.

9. What would happen to the interest rate, GNP, exchange rate, and trade deficit if a uniform 10 percent tariff were placed on all imports?

10. What must the Fed do to keep the exchange rate constant if interest rates in Europe rise because of monetary contraction there?

PROBLEMS

Numerical

1. Consider a macro model consisting of the following relationships:

$$Y = C + I + G + X$$
$$C = 80 + .63Y$$
$$I = 350 - 2,000R + .1Y$$
$$M = (.1625Y - 1,000R)P$$
$$X = 500 - .1Y - 100(EP/P_w)$$
$$EP/P_w = .75 + 5R$$

where government spending G equals 750 and the money supply M equals 600. Suppose that the ROW price level P_w is always equal to 1.0, and that the U.S. price level is predetermined at 1.0.

a. Which are the endogenous variables and which are the exogenous variables in this relationship?

b. Find the values of Y, R, C, I, X, and E that are predicted by the model.

c. Derive an algebraic expression for the aggregate demand curve in which the money supply M, government spending G, and the price level P explicitly appear. For $M = 600$ and $G = 750$ draw the aggregate demand curve accurately to scale.

d. Keeping the price level P at 1.0, calculate the effect a decrease in government spending of $10 billion will have on output, the interest rate, consumption, investment, net exports, and the exchange rate. Do the same thing for an increase in the money supply of $20 billion.

2. Using the same numerical example in Problem 1, calculate private saving, the government budget surplus, and the capital inflow from abroad for the case where $G = 750$ and $M = 600$. Show that the sum of these three equals investment. Repeat your calculation for $G = 740$ and for $M = 620$. Comment on what happens to the three components of saving.

3. For the same numerical example as in Problem 1 calculate a change in the mix of monetary and fiscal policy that will leave output equal to the level it is when $M = 600$ and $G = 750$, but in which the interest rate is 3 percent rather than 5 percent. Describe what happens to the value of the dollar, net exports, the government budget deficit, and investment for this change in policy.

4. Now assume that prices adjust according to the price-adjustment equation

$$\pi = 1.2(Y_{-1} - Y^*)/Y^*,$$

where π is the rate of inflation and Y^*, potential output, is equal to $4,000 billion. Continuing where you left off in Problem 1d, calculate the effect on the endogenous variables in the second, third, and fourth years after the increase in the money supply of $20 billion. Do the same for the decline in government spending of $10 billion. Describe the economy after prices have fully adjusted.

5. Consider a small economy that is much more open than the one in the previous examples. Its net export function is

$$X = 800 - .1Y - 400(EP/P_w)$$

and the relationship between the interest rate and the exchange rate is

$$EP/P_w = 10R + .5.$$

The other equations are the same.

a. Explain why this economy is more open.

b. Calculate what happens in the first year and in the long run when the money supply increases by $10 billion. Calculate what happens when government spending increases by $10 billion.

Analytical

1. Suppose it was agreed that the United States would spend less on defense and that Japan would spend more.

a. How would a reduction in defense spending affect the U.S. trade balance?

b. How would an increase in Japan's defense spending affect the U.S. trade balance?

c. To the extent that the United States and Japan purchase defense goods from each other, how will this affect your answer?

2. Purchasing power parity (PPP) is a theory of exchange rate behavior as described in Section 10.2.

a. Explain why the real exchange rate never changes under the theory of purchasing power parity.

b. What governs the behavior of nominal exchange rates under PPP? Under what conditions are nominal exchange rates sticky?

c. Suppose that inflation in the United States is 4 percent while in the rest of the world it is 7 percent. Under PPP, how does E change over time?

d. PPP clearly doesn't hold up in the short run; see Figure 10–3, where the real exchange rate is calculated using the GNP deflators for the United States and the ROW. If the real exchange rate were instead calculated using price indices for manufactured goods, would you expect it to vary by more or less than it does in Figure 10–3?

3. On any given day, interest rates will differ from country to country. For example, U.S. government securities may pay 10 percent interest while comparable Japanese securities are paying 5 percent interest.

a. Assume Japanese investors have access to U.S. securities. Why would any of them invest in Japanese securities when they could earn a higher interest rate on U.S. securities? Be specific.

b. Is it likely that any American investors would want to hold the Japanese securities?

c. Suppose that PPP (see Question 2) holds exactly, that interest rates in the United States and Japan are 10 percent and 5 percent respectively, and that the U.S. inflation rate is 5 percent. If international investors are to be indifferent between holding U.S. and Japanese securities, what must the Japanese inflation rate be?

4. Given the net export function developed in this chapter, explain why the effect of fiscal policy on the trade balance is unambiguous, whereas the effect of monetary policy is ambiguous.

5. The topic box in Section 10.5 summarizes the relationship between trade deficits and budget deficits.

a. Are *increases* in the trade deficit an inevitable result of *increases* in the budget deficit?

b. Consider the cases where investment is very sensitive to the interest rate and where it is very insensitive. Compare the effect that an increase in the budget deficit will have on the interest rate, the exchange rate, investment, and the trade deficit for each case.

6. In Chapter 5 we developed a model in which net exports were a function of the interest rate. In this chapter we have described in more detail why net exports depend on the interest rate.

a. What factors determine the sensitivity of net exports to the interest rate?

b. Consider the cases where net exports are very sensitive to the interest rate and where they are very insensitive. Compare the effect that an increase in the money supply will have on output, the interest rate, investment, and the trade balance for each case.

c. Suppose foreign manufacturers maintain a fixed dollar price for their goods regardless of the exchange rate. Will this result in net exports being more or less sensitive to the interest rate?

d. Given this behavior, explain why the only way the monetary authorities could act to reduce the trade deficit is by inducing a recession.

7. Suppose that the economy is at potential, but that the trade deficit is thought to be too large and the dollar is overvalued. Describe a change in monetary and fiscal policy that will keep the economy at potential, but will lower both the dollar and the trade deficit. Explain intuitively how the change in policy will bring about the desired results. Illustrate your answer using an IS-LM diagram.

8. Suppose that the economy is operating at potential but that inflation is thought to be too high. Macro policy will therefore have to turn contractionary, in order to reduce inflation. Describe the pros and cons of using monetary policy or fiscal policy to bring about the contraction, paying attention to the international factors.

Appendix: The Interest Rate and the Exchange Rate under Rational Expectations

The purpose of this appendix is to derive the relationship between the real exchange rate and the real interest rate—Equation 10–3 and the example in Equation 10–4. The derivation requires that we consider expectations of exchange rate movements, and for this purpose we use the rational expectations assumption.

INTEREST RATE PARITY

The bond markets of the United States and the ROW are closely linked. Investors are constantly comparing the returns they can make from holding their funds in the United States in dollar-denominated form to the returns they can make in the ROW in German marks, Japanese yen, British pounds, etc. A key consideration is the comparison of returns they can earn in these markets.

Suppose that an investor is comparing the return for holding a dollar-denominated bond in the United States to the return for holding a mark-denominated bond in Germany. An investor comparing a U.S. bond with a German bond has to do more than compare the interest rate paid on the two bonds. The dollar earnings of the mark bond could be different from the interest rate because the dollar might appreciate or depreciate. Suppose that the German bond pays 10 percent interest, and that the exchange rate is 2.0 marks per dollar. Then a United States investor with 100 dollars could obtain 200 marks, buy a mark bond, and get back 220 marks at the end of the year (interest plus principal). But suppose that the dollar depreciated by 2 percent over the year so that the exchange rate is 1.96 marks per dollar at the end of the year. Then the 220 marks could be exchanged back into about 112 dollars (220/1.96 = 112.2). The net return on the German bond, measured in dollars, is 12 percent, more than the stated interest of 10 percent on the bond in Germany. The depreciation of the dollar makes the difference.

Investors will compare the dollar interest rate to the mark interest rate plus the expected rate of depreciation of the dollar. Suppose the dollar interest rate is 10 percent, the mark interest rate is 5 percent, and the expected rate of depreciation of the dollar is zero. Then the comparison made by investors will strongly favor U.S. bonds. No investor would want to hold the mark-denominated bonds in this situation.

What conditions would make investors willing to hold the mark-denominated bonds? One answer, obviously, would be for the United States interest rate to fall to 5 percent, or the German interest rate to rise to 10 percent. But even if interest rates

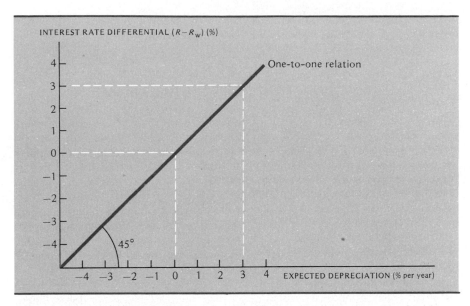

Figure 10-7. EXPECTED DEPRECIATION AND THE INTEREST RATE DIFFERENTIAL.
There is a one-to-one relationship between the interest rate differential and the expected
depreciation of the dollar. If dollar bonds are yielding a higher interest rate compared to
foreign bonds, investors must be expecting that the dollar will depreciate in the future. As
the dollar depreciates, it will reward the holders of foreign bonds by enough to make up
for the lower interest rate paid on the bonds.

remain different, the expected appreciation or depreciation of the dollar can bring
the expected return on the two bonds into equality. When we observe that the dollar
interest rate is 10 percent and the German interest rate is 5 percent, we can reasonably guess that markets are expecting around a 5 percent annual depreciation of the
dollar.

Of course the same relationship holds for bonds denominated in any foreign monetary unit. In general, *the interest rate differential between dollar bonds and bonds denominated in the foreign monetary unit is equal to the expected rate of depreciation of the
dollar in terms of the foreign monetary unit.* More formally,

$$R - R_w = \text{Expected rate of depreciation of the dollar,} \qquad (10\text{--}8)$$

where R is the dollar interest rate and R_w is the interest rate in the rest of the world.
For example, if $R = .05$ and $R_w = .10$, the expected rate of depreciation of the dollar
is $-.05$. In other words, the dollar is expected to appreciate by 5 percent. This relationship between the interest rate differential and the expected depreciation is
called **interest rate parity.** The relationship is shown graphically in Figure 10-7.
The expected depreciation of the dollar is shown on the horizontal axis and the interest rate differential is shown on the vertical axis. The slope of the line is equal to

1. When the interest rate differential increases by 1 percentage point, the expected depreciation of the dollar increases by 1 percentage point.[3]

TESTING INTEREST RATE PARITY USING FUTURES MARKETS

We saw that purchasing power parity does not work in the short run. How well does interest rate parity work? To test the relationship we need a measure of investors' *expected* rate of depreciation of the currency. An easy way to find out what people expect about future exchange rate movements is to look at the **forward** or **futures markets** for foreign exchange. In a futures market for marks, for example, one can buy marks for delivery in the future, say a year from now. Futures markets reveal at what prices investors are willing to buy and sell foreign exchange in the future. The prices on forward or futures markets are found in the financial pages of most newspapers. Prices on forward markets are found along with other exchange rate quotes. Futures markets for foreign exchange are usually listed with wheat or soybean futures.

Suppose that the exchange rate for marks for delivery one year from now is 2.1 marks per dollar. Suppose that today's exchange rate is 2.0 marks per dollar. Then, according to the futures market, investors expect the dollar to appreciate against the mark by 5 percent. If interest rate parity holds then the dollar interest should be 5 percent below the German interest rate. In practice, the percentage difference between the futures exchange rate and the current exchange rate—the measure of expected depreciation—is almost exactly equal to the interest rate differential for any currency that can be freely traded. Interest rate parity seems to work fairly well.

This is not a complete test of interest rate parity, however. By using the futures market an investor covers the risk associated with changes in the exchange rate. A futures market locks in the yield by guaranteeing the exchange rate in the future. For this reason equality of the percentage difference between the future and current exchange rate, and the interest rate differential, is called **covered interest rate parity.** Without using the futures market the investor takes a chance that the exchange rate will be different from what was expected. The investor is exposed to the risk of a currency change.

An alternative test of (uncovered) interest rate parity that takes risk into account is based on the rational expectations method of estimating the expected future exchange rate. This approach supposes that investors predict the exchange rate based on how it has behaved in the past. Essentially investors are assumed to have a model of the exchange rate. By guessing what this model is, and by using it to project the size of appreciations and depreciations, the economists can see if interest rate parity holds. Such tests indicate that interest rate parity is a good approximation. Takatoshi Ito of the University of Minnesota, for example, has found that uncovered interest rate parity holds for the dollar-yen exchange rate. Most of the discrepancies can be

---

[3] If the interest rates in the interest rate parity condition are *real* rates, then the exchange rate should be the real exchange rate. If the interest rates are nominal then the exchange rate should be the nominal exchange rate. In this book we generally interpret the interest rates as real interest rates, and we do so here.

attributed to restrictions on the purchase and sale of foreign bonds. Other discrepancies have been noted by other researchers.[4]

THE EXCHANGE RATE AND ITS EXPECTED DEPRECIATION

Thus far we have related the interest rate differential to the expected rate of depreciation of the dollar. Our next step is to discuss how markets form expectations of the rate of depreciation of the dollar. We base our analysis on the idea of rational expectations.

Although not accurate in the short run, purchasing power parity is a reasonable guide for the tendency of the exchange rate in the long run. It appears that the exchange rate has generally fluctuated around purchasing power parity, sometimes above and sometimes below. For example, when the dollar exchange rate rose high above purchasing power parity in the late 1960s, it eventually fell back toward purchasing power parity. When the dollar was very low in the late seventies, it eventually rose again. Similarly, in 1984 when the dollar zoomed above purchasing power parity, it eventually began to fall again. Historical experience suggests that the movements of the dollar back toward purchasing power parity are larger when the dollar is far away from purchasing power parity than when it is close to parity.

Investors are likely to be aware of these general movements of the dollar. They therefore expect that when the dollar is high, the exchange rate will ultimately depreciate down to its normal level as set by purchasing power parity. Similarly, when the dollar plunges below the level of parity, investors expect the dollar to appreciate over the future, to restore parity in the long run. In general, there is a relationship between the expected rate of depreciation and the level of the exchange rate: *The higher the exchange rate, the larger the expected depreciation of the exchange rate; conversely, the lower the exchange rate, the larger the expected appreciation of the exchange rate.*

If the exchange rate returns to normal at a speed of 10 percent per year, then the relationship says

Expected depreciation of the dollar = .10 (Exchange rate − Parity),   (10–9)

where "parity" stands for the level of purchasing power parity. For example, if the exchange rate is 1.3 and purchasing power parity is 1.0 then expected depreciation is .03, or 3 percent per year. A graphical representation of the relation between the expected rate of depreciation and the level of the exchange rate is shown in Figure 10–8.

It is important to distinguish between the rational, expected future behavior of

---

[4] Takatoshi Ito shows how the interest rate parity between the dollar and the yen became more and more accurate as restrictions on Japanese investments were relaxed. The results are reported by Takatoshi Ito, "The Use of Vector Autoregressions to Test Uncovered Interest Parity," National Bureau of Economic Research, Working Paper 1493. Discrepancies have been detected by Lars P. Hansen and Robert Hodrick, "Forward Exchange Rates as Optimal Predictors of Future Spot Prices: An Econometric Analysis," *Journal of Political Economy,* Vol. 88 (Oct. 1980), pp. 829–853.

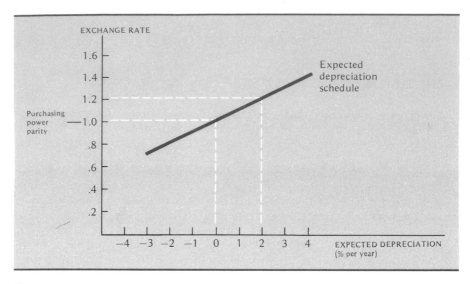

Figure 10–8.   EXPECTED DEPRECIATION AND THE LEVEL OF THE EXCHANGE RATE.
Based on past experience, investors expect the exchange rate to return to the level of
purchasing power parity at a fairly slow rate. If the exchange rate is above the parity level,
investors expect depreciation. If it is below, investors expect appreciation. There is an
upward-sloping relation between the level of the exchange rate and the expected depreciation of the dollar.

the exchange rate as given by Equation 10–9 or Figure 10–8, on the one hand, and
the actual behavior of the exchange rate, on the other. The expected behavior is
smooth and slow, moving back to parity at a rate of at most 10 percent per year.[5]
The actual behavior is jerky, with possible movements of 10 percent in a single week.
The foreign exchange market is like the stock market. It undergoes large, completely unexpected movements in response to surprising economic news. According
to the rational expectations view, participants in the market have expectations of
small movements in the exchange rate—sometimes up, sometimes down—even
though large movements are the rule. The small movements give the best forecast
on the average, given the information available to investors. Even the most informed expert cannot guess in advance all the movements that will occur.

   Recall that we are deriving a relation between the dollar interest rate and the exchange rate. So far, we have two separate relations, summarized in Equations 10–8
and 10–9. One is between the interest rate differential and expected depreciation
(Equation 10–8). The other is between the level of the exchange rate and expected
depreciation (Equation 10–9). We can combine the two to get a relation between the
interest rate differential and the level of the exchange rate:

---

[5] This is a very rough estimate and is meant to suggest the slow expected movement.

$$R - R_w = .10 \text{ (Exchange rate} - \text{Parity)}. \qquad (10-10)$$

Equals expected
depreciation
from Equation 10–8

Equals expected
depreciation
from Equation 10–9

That is, when the dollar interest rate is high relative to the foreign interest rate, the exchange rate is high relative to parity. But this is not exactly what we are looking for. We want to say something about the dollar interest rate itself, not the interest rate differential.

THE INTEREST RATE DIFFERENTIAL AND THE U.S. INTEREST RATE

Interest rates in the United States are determined by the various ingredients that we discussed in Chapters 4 through 7, including monetary and fiscal policy. Interest rates in the ROW are determined in the same way, again with ROW monetary and fiscal policy. If conditions and policies in the ROW are opposite to those in the United States, the interest rate differential is large. If they are similar, the differential is small.

The United States is a major force in the world economy. When its conditions and policies change, it exerts a significant influence on interest rates in the ROW. For example, when the United States adopted a policy of monetary contraction starting in late 1979, not only did the dollar interest rate rise, but so did interest rates in most other countries.

In order to create a complete model of foreign interest rates, we would need to build a complete macro model of the ROW. Instead, we will make use of a simple summary of what such a model would tell us about the relation between the interest rates in the United States and in the ROW. United States interest rates influence ROW rates, but by less than point for point. When monetary contraction in the United States raises dollar interest rates by one point, the ROW interest rate rises by a fraction of a point. For example, suppose that the fraction is .5. Then, algebraically our model of foreign interest rates might be

$$R_w = .025 + .5R. \qquad (10-11)$$

In this example, when the United States interest rate is 5 percent ($R = .05$), the ROW interest rate is also 5 percent ($R_w = .05$). When the dollar interest rate rises to 10 percent ($R = .10$), the ROW interest rate rises to 7.5 percent ($R_w = .075$). This relationship can be written in terms of the interest rate differential by subtracting both sides of Equation 10–11 from the interest rate R. That is,

$$R - R_w = .5R - .025. \qquad (10-12)$$

In words, when the United States interest rate is high, the interest rate differential is high. The relationship between the interest rate differential and U.S. interest rate is shown in Figure 10–9.

Now we have everything we need to derive the relation between the United States

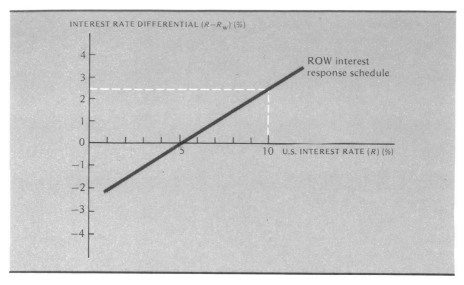

Figure 10-9. THE RELATIONSHIP BETWEEN THE U.S. INTEREST RATE AND THE INTEREST RATE DIFFERENTIAL.

The interest rate in the ROW will react to the interest rate in the United States. A policy generating higher interest rates in the United States will generally be partly matched in the ROW. As a result, there is an upward-sloping relation between the dollar interest rate and the differential between the U.S. interest rate and the ROW interest rate. The relation slopes upward. On the average, the interest rate differential rises when the dollar interest rate rises by one point.

interest rate and the exchange rate. We first proceed using the algebraic examples. The interest rate differential is related to the United States interest rate in Equation 10–12. The interest rate differential is also related to the exchange rate in Equation 10–10. By substituting the interest rate differential in Equation 10–12 for the interest rate differential in Equation 10–10 we get

$$\text{Exchange rate} = \text{Parity} + 5R - .25. \qquad (10\text{–}13)$$

In this example, if the United States interest rate is 5 percent ($R = .05$) then the exchange rate equals purchasing power parity. If purchasing power parity is 1.0, an increase in the United States interest rate from 5 to 6 percent will appreciate the dollar from 1 to 1.05, or by 5 percent. Note that if purchasing power parity is 1.0, Equation 10–13 is identical to Equation 10–4 in the main text of this chapter.

Figure 10–10 shows how all the relationships fit together graphically. It puts the three graphs in Figures 10–7, 10–8, and 10–9 together. Starting from an arbitrary interest rate, the interest rate differential is calculated on the lower left. The expected depreciation must match this differential, as shown on the lower right. The expected depreciation relation tells what the exchange rate must be, as shown on the upper right. The result is one point on the exchange rate–interest rate curve, shown on the upper left. This curve appeared earlier in the chapter as Figure 10–5.

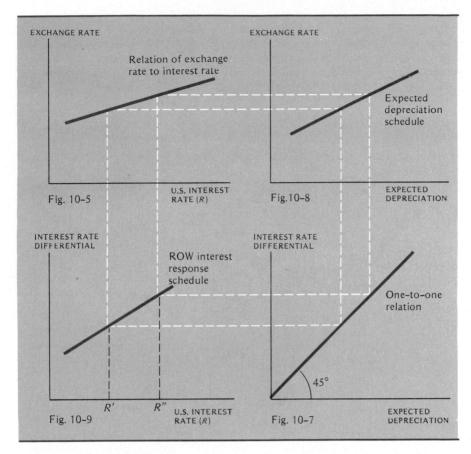

Figure 10–10. DERIVATION OF THE INTEREST RATE–EXCHANGE RATE RELATION.
Pick an interest rate, say R'. From Figure 10–9, reproduced at the lower left, the interest rate differential can be found. Then from Figure 10–7, reproduced at the lower right, the expected rate of depreciation can be found. From Figure 10–8, reproduced at the upper right, the exchange rate can be found. Now pick a higher interest rate, say R'', and you will get another point on the relation with a higher exchange rate.

You may find the story behind the interest rate–exchange rate relationship a little indirect. It says that the dollar appreciates when dollar interest rates rise because higher interest rates fit into the world economy only if the dollar is expected to depreciate, and, in order to depreciate, the dollar must appreciate first.

What is going on in the economy to bring about these changes in the exchange rate? Suppose that the U.S. interest rate rises, both absolutely and relative to the ROW interest rate. United States and ROW investors will now find dollar securities more attractive. They will try to sell their foreign-denominated bonds and buy dollar-denominated bonds. At some point in this process, they will be trying to buy dollars and sell foreign exchange. Consequently, the price of dollars relative to foreign exchange—the exchange rate—must rise to clear the market. Thus the higher interest rate brings about an increase in the exchange rate. As the process proceeds, the higher exchange rate brings expectations of greater depreciation, until investors no longer find dollar bonds more attractive, even though dollar interest rates are still higher.

11

The Government's Budget Deficit and Aggregate Demand

In 1986 the U.S. government budget deficit was $204 billion, or about 5 percent of GNP. In the previous year Congress passed the Gramm-Rudman-Hollings bill, which required that Congress itself should gradually shrink this deficit to zero by 1991. If Congress could not meet the deficit reduction targets then the law called for automatic across-the-board cuts in all programs. Although this law has been challenged in the courts, it underscores the seriousness of the budget deficit in the United States.

How does the budget deficit affect the economy? First, government purchases contribute directly to demand. Second, transfer payments such as social security or unemployment compensation augment income. Third, personal and business income taxes reduce income. In the latter two cases demand is indirectly influenced because incomes change. The effect of the budget deficit is best analyzed in terms of these three components of the deficit: *purchases* plus *transfers* plus *interest on the national debt* less *taxes*. In this chapter we will examine in detail the effects of these three components on the economy.

Traditionally in macroeconomics government purchases have been considered exogenous—not explained in the model. This was so, for example, in the basic model of Part I where government purchases G were taken as an exogenous variable. Empirically speaking, however, the government sector reacts to the state of the economy—partly because of conscious attempts to affect the economy. Transfers and taxes react to the state of the economy even more than purchases do.

One of the most significant recent developments in macroeconomics is the effort to describe the government's reaction to economic fluctuations and to build this behavior into the model. The equation describing government behavior is typically called a **reaction function.** Sometimes it is called a **policy rule** because, as we saw in Chapter 7, government actions are policy in one way or another, and if the behavior is systematic it is like a rule. For example, generally, government taxes decline in recessions.

There are two ways to look at economic policy—from the **normative** perspective and from the **positive** perspective. Normative policy analysis asks what is the best policy and how one policy is better than another. For instance, normative analysis might study what policy can give the lowest rate of unemployment consistent with a prescribed rate of inflation. Positive analysis tries to describe policy actions without inquiring whether or not they are good for the country. In Chapter 7 we took the normative perspective and will do the same in Chapter 17. In this chapter, on the other hand, most of our discussion will be positive and descriptive.

11.1 Government Budgets

Because the United States has a federal system of government we need to distinguish between the different types of government: federal, state, and local. In 1986 federal government purchases were 42 percent of total purchases, and state and local purchases were 58 percent.

THE FEDERAL GOVERNMENT BUDGET AND DEFICIT

The best place to start looking at the budget deficit's effect on the economy is with the federal **budget.** The federal government budget summarizes all three of the types of effects on aggregate demand: purchases, transfers, and taxes. The overall budget totals do not distinguish between purchases and transfers. Rather, purchases of goods and services and transfers are lumped together as government **outlays.** The federal government's budget for 1986 is shown in Table 11–1.

Government outlays consist of purchases and transfers. Purchases involve the use of goods and services by the government, while transfers move funds to people outside the government. Less than a third of federal outlays take the form of purchases of goods and services. National defense accounts for about three-quarters of federal purchases. Federal purchases in 1986 were $367 billion, out of which $278 billion went for defense. Clearly, a major direct contribution of the government to aggregate demand is military spending. Purchases for other purposes were less than 10 percent of

Table 11–1.   THE 1986 BUDGET OF THE UNITED STATES GOVERNMENT (billions of dollars during the calendar year)

RECEIPTS	826
Individual income taxes	362
Corporate income taxes	83
Social security taxes	329
Other taxes and receipts	52
OUTLAYS	1030
Purchases	
National defense	278
Other purchases	89
Transfer payments	398
Grants to local governments	104
Interest on the debt	136
Subsidiaries less enterprise profits	25
DEFICIT	204

Source: *Economic Report of the President*, 1987, Table B–78.

the budget. In 1986 total federal purchases of goods and services were about 9 percent of GNP.

Note that a substantial part of the government's expenditures is interest on the debt. As the debt has risen with high deficits in recent years, these interest payments have also risen. In 1986 interest payments on the debt represented about $1,133 for each person in the labor force on average. There is little that the government can do to change interest payments in a given year. The payments depend on past deficits and on the interest rate on past borrowing.

Aside from national defense the major role of the federal government is to take in funds through taxes and pay them out as transfers. Most of the transfer takes the form of taxing families through the personal income tax and the social security tax and then paying out the proceeds as family benefits. The great bulk of these benefits are social security payments for retirement, disability, and medical needs.

The $204 billion deficit at the bottom of Table 11–1 is simply expenditures less tax receipts. The deficit in 1985 was about the same: $198 billion.

STATE AND LOCAL GOVERNMENT BUDGETS

One of the major developments in government policy during the Reagan administration was to shift responsibility away from the federal government to the local level, especially state governments. If this decentralization process continues, the state and local governments will play an increasingly important role in the economy in the future.

Table 11–2 shows the receipts and outlay figures in 1986 for all state and local governments combined in the United States. Compared with the federal government, a much larger percentage of state and local government

Table 11–2. THE 1986 COMBINED BUDGETS OF STATE AND LOCAL GOVERN-
MENTS (billions of dollars)

RECEIPTS	619
Personal tax	152
Corporate tax	20
Sales and property taxes	296
Payroll tax	47
Grants from federal government	104
EXPENDITURES	558
Purchases (goods and services)	498
Transfer payments	107
Net interest paid	−33
Subsidies less enterprise profits	−14
SURPLUS	61

Source: *Economic Report of the President,* 1987, Table B–79.

outlays are purchases of goods and services that add directly to demand.
Transfers are about 20 percent of total outlays. The largest single purchase
item for state and local governments is education—about one-third of total
purchases. Much as defense dominates federal government purchases, education dominates state and local government purchases.

In marked contrast to the federal government, the state and local governments ran a combined budget surplus in 1986. A combined budget surplus
at the state and local level has been typical in recent years. This state and
local surplus tends to offset the federal government deficit. Many municipal
governments have laws that prevent their operating budgets from going
into large deficits. In recent years balanced budget laws have been enacted
in many states. Of course, some local governments do run serious deficits
even though there is a general surplus. In 1975, for example, when the city
of New York ran such a large deficit that it essentially went bankrupt, all
state and local governments combined ran a surplus of $5.5 billion. Another
example is the deficit run by many school districts in California in 1986
when the combined state and local surplus was $61 billion.

A large percentage of state and local government receipts—about 40
percent—comes from property taxes and sales taxes. The federal government raises only a negligible part of its revenues from these sources. This
means that the economy will have different effects on state and local governments' budgets than it has on the federal government's budget.

11.2 Fluctuations in the Deficit: Purchases, Transfers, and Taxes

From the point of view of macroeconomic **fluctuations,** what matters most
about the government budget deficit is not its average level, but the way the
budget responds to conditions in the economy. How large is this response?
How do the fluctuations in the government deficit compare with the fluctu-

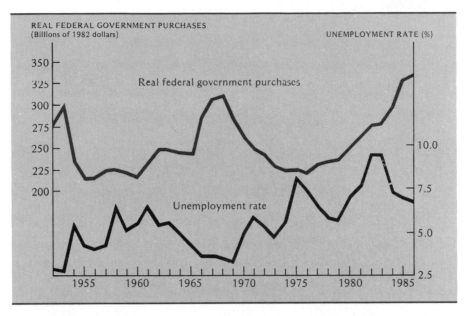

Figure 11–1. REAL FEDERAL GOVERNMENT PURCHASES AND UNEMPLOYMENT.
Federal purchases of goods and services have not responded in any systematic way to
the state of the economy, as measured by the unemployment rate. There was a big increase in federal spending during the Vietnam War in the late 1960s, and again in the
early 1980s. Except possibly for the 1980s, the government has not chosen to try to crank
up the economy during recessions by raising its direct contribution to aggregate demand.
Source: *Economic Report of the President,* 1987, Tables B–2 and B–33.

ations in the economy as a whole? We will try to answer these questions separately for the three components of the deficit.

First, federal purchases of goods and services do not seem to change
much as real activity in the private economy fluctuates. This is shown in Figure 11–1. During the post–World War II period, federal spending has fluctuated mostly because of defense spending. Federal spending rose during
the Vietnam War when unemployment was low, and during the defense
buildup of the early 1980s. Except possibly for the early 1980s when defense spending increased as the Fed tightened monetary policy and there
was a recession, federal spending has not increased during recessions.

Every recession brings programs to raise spending and provide added
government employment. In fact, however, spending programs have been
small and have taken several years to get into gear. Programs launched in
the depths of a recession frequently do not generate a significant contribution to aggregate demand until several years later. By then, the economy
might be approaching boom conditions. This is another example of the lags
in the effect of policy that we mentioned in Chapter 7.

On the other hand, the federal government's transfers usually do fluctuate in the right direction, offsetting other movements in the economy. Gov-

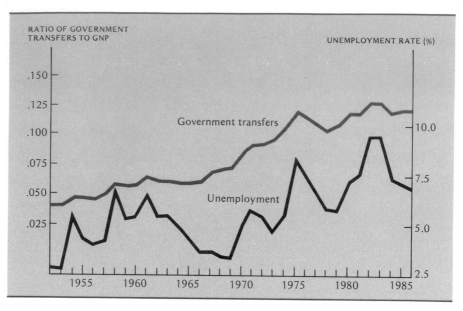

Figure 11–2. GOVERNMENT TRANSFERS AND UNEMPLOYMENT.
Government transfer payments tend to rise in years of high unemployment and fall in years of low unemployment. This has been especially true during the last 15 years. The synchronization has been achieved mainly through unemployment insurance and other programs that make the rise in transfers during recessions automatic. Source: *Economic Report of the President,* 1987, Tables B–1, B–33, and B–77.

ernment transfers rise when unemployment rises, as can be seen clearly in Figure 11–2.

Government transfers rise in recessions and fall in booms largely through the normal operation of benefit programs. No discretionary intervention on the part of government officials is required. When unemployment rises and incomes fall, a number of government programs automatically increase their income transfers to families. For this reason they sometimes are called **automatic stabilizers.** These programs are listed in Table 11–3.

Taxes also rise and fall with the level of economic activity. The data are summarized in Figure 11–3. In each recession since 1952 federal government tax receipts dropped sharply. This behavior is particularly dramatic in the 1969–70, the 1974–75, and the 1981–82 recessions. The drop in tax receipts in these periods is larger in percentage terms than the drop in real GNP. During the last 20 years when real GNP fell or rose by 1 percent, real federal tax receipts fell or rose by 1.86 percent. That is, the **elasticity** of year-to-year changes in real tax receipts with respect to changes in real GNP was 1.86 (an elasticity is the percentage change in one variable induced by a 1 percent change in another variable).[1]

---

[1] The elasticity is the slope of the linear relationship between the percentage change in real federal tax receipts and the percentage change in real GNP. The slope was estimated by fitting a line through observations made during a 1969–86 sample period.

Table 11–3. AUTOMATIC STABILIZERS: GOVERNMENT TRANSFER PROGRAMS THAT RESPOND TO THE STATE OF THE ECONOMY

Program	Description
Unemployment insurance	A combined federal-state program that pays benefits to workers who have lost their jobs
Food stamps	A federal program that pays benefits to any family with an income below a certain threshold; in recessions, additional families become eligible
Welfare programs	A combined federal-state program that pays benefits to poor families with dependent children; as incomes fall during recessions, payments increase
Medicaid	A combined federal-state program that assists poor families with medical benefits; the number drawing these benefits rises during recessions
Social security	A federal program that supports older people in retirement; some people who are eligible for retirement or other benefits choose to work instead, and their number declines in a recession and the volume of benefits rises

One reason that tax receipts fall by more than real GNP—why the elasticity is greater than 1—is that the items that are not taxed do not fluctuate much compared with the items that are taxed. Depreciation, which is not taxed, hardly fluctuates at all. Corporate profits, on the other hand, fluctu-

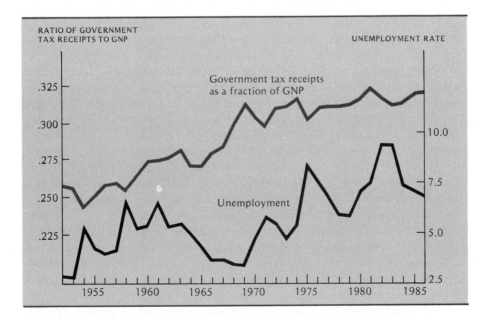

Figure 11–3. GOVERNMENT TAX RECEIPTS AND UNEMPLOYMENT.
As the economy fluctuates in and out of recessions and booms, government tax receipts also fluctuate. Tax receipts tend to fall in years of high unemployment and rise in years of low unemployment. The decline in tax receipts mitigates the drop in demand and helps stabilize the economy. Source: *Economic Report of the President,* 1987, Tables B–1, B–33, and B–76.

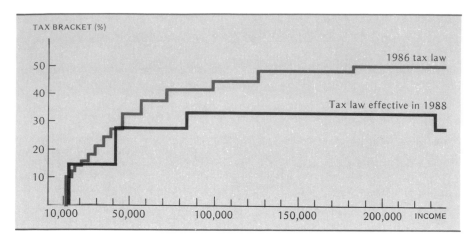

Figure 11–4.   THE OLD AND NEW TAX STRUCTURES.
The two lines show the tax rate paid on additional income in each range. The colored line shows the tax law before the 1986 tax reform. The black line shows the new tax law passed in 1986 and effective in 1988. The tax is for a family of four.

ate widely. Another reason that the elasticity is greater than 1 is that average tax *rates* rise and fall with income. Part of the fluctuations in tax rates occur automatically because of the progressive tax system in the United States. Figure 11–4 shows how the tax rate increases with income for a typical family for both the new tax system to take effect in 1988 and the previous tax system in the United States. As incomes fall in a recession some people fall into lower tax brackets, or even fall into the region where no taxes are paid. Hence, the proportion of their income that is paid in taxes goes down as income falls. Conversely, the proportion goes up as income rises. (With the new tax system there is a small drop in tax rate for high income earners, but the effect on total tax revenue of this drop is very small.)

Some of the reductions in tax rates in recessions have occurred because the tax law was changed by Congress in order to mitigate the drop in aggregate demand. These are **discretionary changes** rather than automatic changes, but they have been fairly regular and should be included as part of our behavioral description of the reaction of government to the economy. Proposals to cut the taxes to stimulate the economy out of a recession in the early 1960s were made by President Kennedy, and most of these changes were enacted into law by Congress. Proposals to cut taxes were made by President Reagan during the depressed economic conditions of the early 1980s. Although the rationale for these tax cuts was not the conventional countercyclical one—some in the Reagan administration argued that the tax cuts would greatly increase supply, others argued that they were necessary to offset the effect that inflation had on tax rates—in retrospect they fit right in to the general story that tax rates are usually cut during periods of high unemployment. Other examples are the temporary tax surcharge of 1968 and the tax rebate of 1975 that we discussed in Chapter 8.

Indexing the Tax Brackets

It is important to realize how inflation can change tax rates in a progressive tax system. Suppose that there is an inflation that raises nominal incomes, but leaves real income the same. Even though their real income is constant people will move into higher tax brackets, or at least have more of their income taxed in the higher brackets. This means that their tax payments will go up even though they aren't making more income. One way to avoid this problem is to **index** the tax system: When the tax system is indexed an increase in inflation raises the tax brackets by the same amount. For example, a 10 percent inflation will raise the $30,000 bracket to $33,000. Under indexing, taxes do not increase because of inflation. For example, a person who made $29,000 before the 10 percent inflation and $31,900 afterward is still in the same tax bracket.

In Chapter 4 we wrote tax receipts T as a constant proportion of income Y:

$$T = tY, \tag{11-1}$$

where t is the constant tax rate. The discussion of the previous two paragraphs means that it is incorrect to treat the tax rate t as a constant. The tax rate t actually falls when income Y falls, and rises when income rises.

Much of the overall impact of the government's influence through taxes and transfers eventually shows up in personal disposable income. Recall that in Chapter 8 we looked at the relation between disposable income and GNP and found that the fluctuations in disposable income were much smaller (look back to Figure 8–3 for a review). Disposable income changes by only about 40 percent as much as total income. Consumers see only about 40 percent of the total loss in the economy's income when a recession hits. Automatic stabilizers and discretionary changes in taxes and transfers soak up much of the other 60 percent. (Recall that a bit of the 60 percent is due to the fact that corporations try to maintain their dividend payouts when corporate profits fall during recessions.)

Note that the effect of such countercyclical movements in taxes and transfers is to reduce the multiplier of the IS-LM model. When there is an increase in investment spending, for example, the increase in GNP leads to a smaller increase in disposable income and hence a smaller effect on consumption. The multiplier effect is smaller due to the automatic stabilizers.

11.3 The Effects of the Government Deficit

The budget deficit of the federal government is constantly in the limelight and is frequently a political issue. Consider, for example, the presidential election of 1984. Republicans, including President Reagan, had warned about the dangers of deficits for years; yet one of the records of Reagan's first term was huge deficits with projections for even larger deficits in the future. So far those projections have proved correct.

Walter Mondale chose the record-setting deficit as the primary issue in the campaign, telling potential voters that Reagan paid for the economic recovery by mortgaging the future. He even gambled by proposing in advance to raise taxes to close the deficit. In the television debates Reagan defended himself by saying that deficits have nothing to do with high interest rates, that the deficit was largely due to an unexpectedly deep recession, and that the economy would grow out of the deficit on its own without tax increases. Both Reagan and Mondale had economists to back them up in their opposing views. Concern with the deficit has continued. The Gramm-Rudman-Hollings legislation passed in 1986 is an expression of that concern. Yet debate continues about the seriousness of the deficit and its effect on the economy.

Why is the government deficit so controversial and mysterious? Part of the reason is that the deficit is just a summary statistic that reflects the behavior of many other variables. It is really just the tip of an iceberg. We emphasized that the budget deficit is simply the difference between government *expenditures* (purchases and transfer) and *receipts*. Moreover, from the government accounting identity discussed in Chapter 2, we know that deficits must be financed by issuing *bonds* or *money* to the public. The overall impact of the budget on the economy can thus be pieced together by looking at the effects of receipts, expenditures, bonds, and money.

In this section we address some of the questions raised about the deficit in the 1980s by examining the cyclical behavior of the deficit, the empirical relation between deficits and interest rates, and the implications of the simple fact that the government must borrow to finance its deficits.

CYCLICAL VERSUS STRUCTURAL DEFICITS

The government budget deficit always goes deep in the red during recessions. We know the reasons for this from the last section: Expenditures rise and receipts fall during recessions. The automatic stabilizers exacerbate the swing of the deficit during a recession.

Figure 11–5 shows the relationship between the deficit and the cyclical fluctuations in unemployment for the years 1952 to 1986. When the econ-

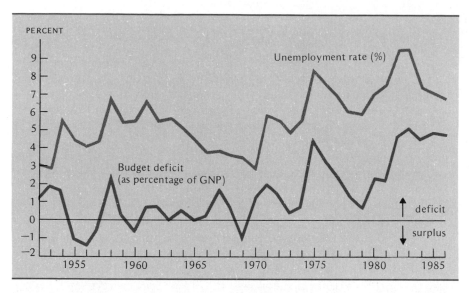

Figure 11–5.   THE CYCLICAL BEHAVIOR OF THE DEFICIT.
The chart shows the budget deficit, as a percentage of GNP, and the unemployment rate. The latter is a measure of the state of the economic cycle. Over the years 1952–86 the federal budget was in deficit when the economy was in a slump. The deficit is strongly cyclical. Source: *Economic Report of the President,* 1987, Tables B–33 and B–76.

omy is below potential the budget deficit is large. When the economy is above potential the budget is in surplus, or at least less in the red. President Reagan's claim that the economy would automatically grow out of the deficit as it recovered from the recession thus seems to have had some empirical validity. This happened, after all, in the other recessions over the last 33 years.

But in order to evaluate President Reagan's claim it is necessary to ask what the deficit would look like if the economy were back to normal. Is it reasonable to claim that the deficit would disappear as the economy approached full employment? Economists have developed the concept of the **full-employment deficit** to answer questions like this.[2] The full-employment deficit is the deficit that would occur if the economy were at full employment. The full-employment deficit takes out the cyclical effects on the deficit. This is done by estimating reaction functions for expenditures and receipts and calculating what expenditures and receipts would occur at potential GNP and full employment.

[2] The idea of the full-employment deficit was used by E. Cary Brown, "Fiscal Policy in the Thirties: A Reappraisal," *American Economic Review,* Vol. 46 (December 1956), pp. 857–879. He showed that the actual deficits observed in the early 1930s were large surpluses in the full-employment deficit.

How the Economy Destroys Budget Projections

A good way to get a feel for the influence of the economy on the government budget is to look at the difference between projected and actual budget totals. Each year the president submits a budget proposal to Congress to take effect starting the following fiscal year. For example, in January 1982 President Reagan submitted a budget proposal for fiscal year 1983 to start on October 1, 1982. The proposed budget for fiscal year 1983 had *outlays* of $757 billion, *receipts* of $666 billion, and therefore a budget *deficit* of $91 billion. But as usual the actual budget in 1983 turned out to be much different from the proposal: Outlays were greater at $796 billion, receipts were less at $601, and the deficit thus turned out to be $195 billion. What happened?

Two important things. First, the economy turned out to be in worse shape than the Reagan economists had forecast; they thought real GNP would grow by 3 percent throughout 1982, but it actually *fell* by 2 percent.* This disappointment meant that tax receipts were much less than in President Reagan's original budget proposal simply because income was much less than his economists thought it would be. With less income people would pay less taxes. The 1983 tax shortfall is an excellent illustration of the impact that the economy has on the budget. Moreover, with a sagging economy unemployment was worse than the economists had thought and this raised transfers for unemployment and welfare.

The other thing that happened was that Congress did not enact all the spending cuts that Reagan had proposed. This was partly because the economy turned out to be in such bad shape that nobody wanted to cut outlays, risk reducing demand, and possibly make the recession worse; this is a further example of the effect of the economy on the decisions of government. Another reason that outlays were greater than Reagan originally proposed was that many did not want his cuts in any case.

The strong impact of economic conditions on the budget is more than just a good illustration; it creates serious problems for budget planners. Imagine the frustration of a member of Congress who has just begun to feel relieved about having struck a bargain for a cut of $10 million rather than $15 million in a favorite transfer program, only to wake up and read in the morning paper that a wiggle in the economy has raised the cost of the program by $3 billion!

* The real GNP projection is from the *Economic Report of the President,* 1982, p. 210. The budget projections are from Table B–72 of the same report and the actual budget figures are from Table B–72 of the 1984 report.

In more recent years the concept of the full-employment deficit has usually been discussed by distinguishing between the structural and cyclical parts of the deficit. The **structural deficit** is the same thing as the full-employment deficit, and the **cyclical deficit** is the difference between the actual deficit and the structural deficit.

HAVE DEFICITS BEEN RELATED TO INTEREST RATES IN RECENT U.S. HISTORY?

The relation between the deficit and interest rates is one of the most important issues with respect to the government's role in aggregate demand. In Chapters 4 and 5 we showed that an increase in the government's budget deficit, brought about by either an increase in expenditures or a cut in taxes, would raise interest rates and expand output by shifting the IS curve to the right. How does that theory fit the facts? Here we look at some of the relevant facts. Figure 11–6 shows the historical relation between a measure of the real interest rate and the budget deficit. Two things are important from the chart.

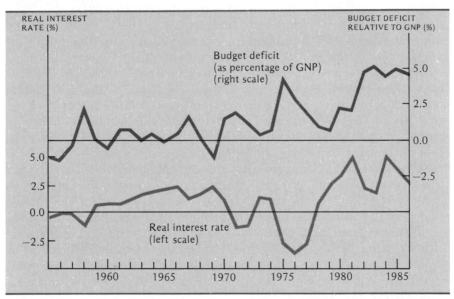

Figure 11–6. BUDGET DEFICITS AND REAL INTEREST RATES.
During much of the past 30 years interest rates have fallen during periods when the federal government was running a deficit. However, this does not mean that deficits cause lower interest rates. Falling interest rates and deficits are both largely the result of recessions. The mid-1980s was one of the few periods where high budget deficits and high interest rates occurred at the same time. Note: The real interest rate is the 3-month Treasury bill less the average of the rate of change in the GNP deflator during the previous 3 years.

First, over short-run periods and for much of the last 30 years, it appears that the real interest rate falls when the deficit goes into the red. Deficits do not appear to cause high real interest rates. Before you jump to any conclusions recall the previous discussion that pointed to the cyclical behavior of the deficit. Deficits occur when the economy is in a slump. Now, there are many reasons for interest rates to be low during a slump; the demand for money is low and investment demand is low. It is thus likely that much of the relation between interest rates and the deficit during the last 30 years is due to other factors in the economy.

Second, there seems to be evidence of a positive relation between the budget deficit and interest rates during the 1982–86 period. Real interest rates were higher than normal rates during this period and the budget deficit reached a high-water mark as well. Perhaps the very large deficits—and prospects for future deficits—raised interest rates as Walter Mondale claimed. This would be the prediction of the IS-LM model.

THE DEFICIT AND THE EXPLOSION OF GOVERNMENT DEBT

When the government runs a deficit it must borrow from the public. The top panel of Figure 11–7 shows how budget deficits have led to an explosion of outstanding national debt in recent years, especially since the start of the Reagan administration in 1981. Most of the debt consists of interest-bearing bonds, but part is non-interest-bearing money. As we will see in the next chapter, the Federal Reserve System **monetizes** part of the government debt when it purchases it and issues currency and non-interest-bearing deposits. In the United States the Fed has monetized only a small amount of the debt. It monetizes the debt primarily to provide sufficient money for the economy to work efficiently, rather than to raise revenues.

During World War II the government also ran a large deficit as is typical of most wars. Government expenditures were, of course, abnormally high in the war years; rather than raise taxes temporarily to pay for the war the government borrowed the money. This shifted some of the burden of the war to future generations who would have to pay the interest on the borrowings. After the war years the federal government ran a surplus in its budget with some exceptions during recessions. The debt fell slightly during the surplus years, but was relatively unchanged compared to the increase during World War II.

Scaling the debt by nominal GNP gives a better perspective of the importance of the debt for the whole economy. At the end of World War II the government debt relative to GNP reached an all-time high of a bit over 100 percent. Since World War II the public debt divided by GNP fell steadily until the mid-1970s. Since then the stock of outstanding debt has again begun to grow relative to GNP as we had a big deficit in the recession of 1974–75 and even bigger deficits in the 1980s. The ratio of the debt to GNP

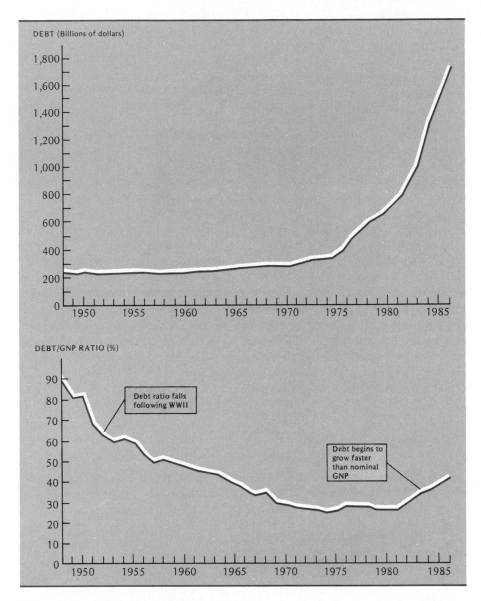

Figure 11–7.   THE NATIONAL DEBT.
The national debt has had two big periods of rapid growth: during the war years in the 1940s and during the early 1980s. In between the debt stayed fairly constant. It dropped as a ratio of GNP during this middle period. Source: *Economic Report of the President,* 1987, Tables B–1 and B–73.

is still below the levels reached at the end of World War II, but the ratio is growing rapidly, and continued large deficits will raise the public debt to levels about which we know relatively little empirically.

We can express the relation between the deficit and the accumulation of debt formally as

Debt at the start of next year
= Debt at the start of this year
+ Purchases this year
+ Transfers this year $\Big\}$ Deficit
+ Interest on the debt this year
− Receipts this year.

Using the notation D for debt, G for purchases, F for transfers, T for receipts, and R for the interest rate, we can write this as

$$D_{t+1} = D_t + G_t + F_t + RD_t - T_t. \tag{11-2}$$

Each of the terms in Equation 11–2 corresponds with the verbal description of the relation between the deficit and debt accumulation. Note that Equation 11–2 is nothing more than an **intertemporal government budget constraint** faced by government officials. It corresponds exactly to the intertemporal budget constraint for the households in our analysis of forward-looking consumption (Chapter 8). The only difference is that the government is usually a net debtor; hence we call its outstanding financial stock D. The household's asset stock was simply called A; we assumed that the household was usually a net lender.[3]

RICARDIAN EQUIVALENCE

The intertemporal budget constraint emphasizes the important fact that when the government reduces taxes in an attempt to increase disposable income, it must borrow. This borrowing, along with interest, must be paid back eventually. If so, it is a possibility that the forward-looking consumption theory of Chapter 8 might have overstated the effect of tax cuts on consumption. Consider what happens when we combine the government's budget constraint with the family's budget constraint. Suppose that the rational forward-looking family reasoned as follows:

Ultimately, the government has to finance its expenditures. If it grants a tax cut this year, it will have to make up for it in future years with higher taxes to pay off the debt. We aren't any better off because of the tax cut; it is no more than a rearrangement of taxes, not truly a cut at all. We should not

---

[3] Note that the government budget is balanced when the stock of government debt is not growing. The stock of government debt is usually stated in nominal terms. A reasonable alternative is to measure the stock in real terms. If there is inflation then the nominal budget is in deficit when the *real deficit* is balanced. The real deficit is simply the change in the real debt.

change our consumption. Moreover, all other families will see the situation the same way, so total consumption will not rise.

The possibility that tax cuts would be discounted against future tax increases was first pointed out by the British economist David Ricardo. Although he ultimately rejected the possibility, the proposition is still usually referred to as the **Ricardian equivalence.** The idea has been reviewed and elaborated on by Robert Barro of Harvard University.[4] Ricardian equivalence says that the large budget deficits in the 1980s in the United States had no effect on interest rates because they were due to tax cuts. According to the Ricardian equivalence proposition these tax cuts would not stimulate consumption because consumers would realize that future tax increases would be necessary to pay interest on the government debt. The experience of the 1980s may prove to be the crucial test of the Ricardian equivalence proposition. Thus far the evidence tends to be contrary to Ricardian equivalence. Interest rates have not skyrocketed as a result of the budget deficits of the 1980s, but as Figure 11–6 shows, real interest rates do seem relatively high. Consumption expenditures also seem higher than normal. As we noted in Chapter 8 the saving rate was very low in 1986 and consumption was greater than a simple Keynesian consumption function would predict for all years from 1983 through 1986.

One potentially important criticism of the Ricardian equivalence proposition is that people do not live forever. What if the government doesn't plan to repay the taxes until this generation is gone and the next generation has to pay the bills? The typical family still might not adjust its consumption if it cares about the next generation; it will want to make sure that the next generation does not have to restrict its consumption in order to pay off the government's tax liability. Robert Barro has argued that the family should be viewed as a dynasty in which future generations are as important as the current generation. If so, tax cuts that are expected to result in future tax increases will not affect consumption even though individual generations do not live forever.

Deficit Control: The Gramm-Rudman-Hollings Approach

On December 12, 1985, the U.S. Congress enacted the Balanced Budget and Emergency Control Act of 1985, commonly known as Gramm-Rudman-Hollings (GRH). The intent of this legislation was to set a fixed schedule for reducing the federal budget deficit and eventually eliminating it. Although this legislation was challenged by the courts, it illustrates what draconian measures appear necessary to

[4] See Robert Barro, "Are Government Bonds Net Wealth?" *Journal of Political Economy,* Vol. 82 (November–December 1974), pp. 1095–1117.

bring the budget deficit under control in the U.S. In his 1987 Economic Report, President Reagan confirmed his agreement with the intent of the legislation: "My budget for 1988 continues this process [of budget reduction] by meeting the Gramm-Rudman-Hollings deficit target of $108 billion." But this is a projection. What does it take to actually hit targets like these?

The Gramm-Rudman-Hollings targets called for a balanced budget by fiscal year 1991. The intermediate targets for deficit reduction between 1986 and 1991 were stipulated in GRH as follows (in billions of dollars):

Fiscal Year	Deficit Target
1986	171.9
1987	144.0
1988	108.0
1989	72.0
1990	36.0
1991	0.0

How was GRH supposed to work? The president's budget, submitted in January or early February of each year, was required to be consistent with the targets. President Reagan's proposed budget for the fiscal year 1988 (from October 1, 1987, through September 30, 1988), for example, proposed outlays of $1024.3 billion and estimated receipts of $916.6 billion, giving an implied deficit of $107.8 billion, just under the target. Of course proposing a particular budget deficit doesn't guarantee that the deficit will be reached. The essential part of GRH was that automatic budget-cutting procedures would be activated if the president and Congress failed to agree.

The directors of the Congressional Budget Office (CBO) and the Office of Management and Budget (OMB) were required by GRH to prepare a joint report by August 20 of each year estimating whether the deficit for the upcoming year will meet the target. If the estimated deficit exceeded the target (there is a $10 billion tolerance range), then an *automatic sequestration* process would be triggered.

Automatic sequestration would work as follows. The joint OMB-CBO report would stipulate across-the-board reductions for each account. The comptroller general would then review the OMB-CBO report and issue a report to the president stating where the budget is to be reduced. The president would then have until September 1 to issue an order that eliminated the budget excess. The order would take effect on October 1, although action would not actually take place until a final order was issued on October 15. The president's order would modify or suspend each provision of the law that would automatically require a spending increase, and also would eliminate new programs so as to meet the deficit target.

The first year of GRH (1986) was special because start-up provisions were put in for the first year, but, in fact, the 1986 budget deficit of $220.7 billion turned out to be way above the $171.9 billion target, and even higher than 1985! The legislation was challenged in the courts, but the targets continued to be taken seriously by the president and many members of Congress.

President Reagan indicated that he would veto any legislation that increases taxes. If this threat of veto prevents any increased tax legislation, then it is clear that very deep budget cuts must occur in 1988 and 1989 if the targets are to be met. As a matter of accounting these cuts must almost certainly come either from the defense budget or from transfer programs such as social security. These items represent by far the largest part of the budget, and they are items that were not affected much by budget cutting in the 1980s.

11.4 The Government and the IS Curve

Fiscal policy can shift the IS curve in two ways. First, government purchases of goods and services G enters spending directly. In Chapter 5 we looked at how changes in G shift the IS curve through the multiplier process. We noted in this chapter that over the last 30 years the federal government rarely offsets the fluctuations in aggregate demand by altering its purchases of goods and services. Historically government purchases do not appear to be an effective instrument to control aggregate demand but rather another shock or disturbance to aggregate demand. Recent experience with large deficits do not indicate that this situation is likely to change soon.

Second, policies on taxes and transfers can influence consumption. A tax cut increases income and stimulates consumption and so shifts the IS curve to the right. However, the magnitude of this shift is highly uncertain because of people's uncertainty about how permanent the tax cut will be. Moreover, there is a possibility that some people may increase their saving because they figure that taxes will rise in the future in order to pay the interest on the increased government debt.

Fiscal policy also influences the *slope* of the IS curve. We noted in this chapter that the automatic stabilizers operating through taxes and transfers reduce the multiplier. Because of the automatic stabilizers an increase in interest rates along the IS curve brings about a smaller decline in consumption and GNP. Therefore the IS curve is steeper as a result of the automatic stabilizers.

Review and Practice

MAJOR POINTS

1. Government purchases, transfers, and receipts are not exogenous. They respond to the state of the economy.

2. Expenditures rise and receipts are reduced by recessions. Real tax receipts fall by a greater percentage than real GNP during recessions. This is mainly because of the progressive tax system.

3. The deficit fluctuates cyclically in time with the overall economy.

4. The structural or full-employment deficit has had these cyclical effects removed.

5. The government budget constraint relates the deficit to the public debt.

6. The debt has declined relative to GNP for most of the period since World War II. In recent years it has begun to increase again.

7. Higher government purchases of goods and services shift the IS curve to the right, though the federal government has not used this policy instrument to try to stabilize the economy in the past few decades.

8. Taxes influence both the position and the slope of the IS curve. A tax cut shifts the IS curve to the right, though the magnitude of the shift is uncertain. Automatic stabilizers make the IS curve steeper.

KEY TERMS AND CONCEPTS

Outlays	Progressive taxes
Purchases	Automatic stabilizers
Policy rule	Government budget constraint
Reaction function	Government debt
Full-employment deficit	Defense expenditures
Indexing	Ricardian equivalence
Elasticity of tax revenues	

QUESTIONS FOR DISCUSSION AND REVIEW

1. Explain the differences between government purchases and government transfers. Which is larger for the federal government? For state and local governments? Which fluctuates more with the business cycle? In which direction?

2. What are the major automatic stabilizers? What is their significance for economic fluctuations?

3. Why is the budget typically in deficit during periods when the unemployment rate is high? What is the full-employment budget deficit? Does the full-employment deficit fluctuate with the state of the economy?

4. Explain why a progressive tax structure leads to an increase in taxes in proportion to income when the economy is growing rapidly in a boom.

5. Why has the deficit usually been large when interest rates have been low? Does this mean that the deficit does not cause interest rates to rise as predicted by the IS-LM model?

6. Describe the behavior of the government debt since World War II. Why has the debt declined as a fraction of GNP until recently?

PROBLEMS

Numerical

1. Use the following example of a progressive tax schedule to compute what happens to average tax rates in the economy during a typical recession.

Income Bracket	Marginal Tax Rate
0–9,999	0
10,000–29,999	.2
30,000–49,999	.4
50,000 and above	.6

To make it easy suppose that there are just three income groups of taxpayers. Just before the recession there are 200,000 taxpayers making $20,000, 700,000 making $40,000, and 100,000 making $60,000.

   a. Compute the average tax rate for the whole economy before and just after the recession if everybody's income drops by $10,000 during the recession. Has anyone moved to a different tax bracket?

   b. What happens to the average tax rate if everybody's income is reduced by $20,000?

   c. Suppose that the government introduces a "flat tax" whereby everyone making equal to or more than $10,000 pays the same proportional tax of 25 percent. For this new tax system recalculate your answers to Parts a and b.

   d. Comment on the effect on stabilization policy of a move from a progressive tax rate system to a flat tax rate system.

2. Suppose that federal tax receipts, transfers, and purchases are given by $T = .25YP$, $F = .15YP$, and $G = 400$, all in billions of *current* dollars. Suppose that at the start of 1984 the federal debt D was $800 billion, the interest rate R was 9.5 percent, real GNP was $3,500 billion, and the price level P was 1.08.

   a. Calculate the actual and full-employment budget deficit for 1984 in current dollars assuming that real potential output is $3,700 billion. Include interest payments in your calculation of the deficit using Equation 11–2.

   b. Two forecasts made in early 1985 (the Reagan administration's and an average of three private forecasters: DRI, Chase Econometrics, and Wharton) for real GNP growth, the rate of inflation $(P - P_{-1})/P_{-1}$, and the interest rate for 1985 through 1988 are given below:

	Real GNP Growth		Inflation		Interest Rate	
	Admin.	Priv.	Admin.	Priv.	Admin.	Priv.
1985	3.9	3.6	3.8	3.6	8.1	8.2
1986	4.0	2.8	4.4	3.9	7.9	8.9
1987	4.0	3.4	4.2	4.4	7.2	9.4
1988	4.0	3.6	3.9	4.8	5.9	8.4

Assuming that G increases at 5 percent per year calculate the deficit for 1985 through 1988 for the two sets of forecasts. Start with the 1984 figures in Part a. Be sure to use Equation 11–2 to calculate the change in federal debt.

3. Assume that government outlays and taxes are initially zero, as is the stock of government debt. In year 1 the government begins to spend $50 billion per year, in real terms, on environmental protection. Each year the government issues enough debt to finance this program, as well as to repay the interest on the previous stock of debt. The stock of government debt and the deficit, measured in current dollars, obey the equations

$$D_t = (D_{t-1} + G_{t-1})(1+R)$$
$$DEF_{t-1} = D_t - D_{t-1}$$

where G is measured in current dollars. The initial price level is 1.

a. For an interest rate of 5 percent and an inflation rate of zero, calculate the real and nominal values of government debt and the deficit for each of the first five years.
b. Now suppose prices rise at an annual rate of 5 percent. Assuming that the interest rate remains at 5 percent, repeat your calculations for Part a.
c. Finally, assume an inflation rate of 5 percent and an interest rate of 10.25 percent. Again, repeat your calculations for Part a.
d. Compare the path of real debt under parts a, b, and c. Explain any differences.
e. Comparing Parts a and c, you should find that the real debt stock is the same for Part c, but that the real deficit each year is higher. Why doesn't a higher deficit lead to a higher stock of debt?
f. In which case was inflation anticipated by financial markets? Explain your answer.

4. Suppose that instead of G being exogenous it is given by the formula

$$G = 750 - .1(Y - Y^*)$$

where Y^* is potential GNP and is equal to $4,000 billion. Suppose that the other relationships in the economy are given by the example considered in Chapter 5:

$$C = 80 + .63Y$$
$$I = 750 - 2,000R$$
$$M = (.1625Y - 1,000R)P$$
$$X = 425 - .1Y - 500R$$

where the price level is predetermined at $P = 1$ and the money supply is 600.

a. Derive an algebraic expression for the IS curve for this model. Plot it to scale. Compare it with the IS curve of Chapter 5 in which government purchases are exogenous. Which is steeper? Why?
b. Derive the aggregate demand curve and plot it to scale. How does it compare with the aggregate demand curve when government spending is exogenous?
c. Calculate the effect on GNP of an increase in the money supply of $10 billion. Is the effect larger or smaller than the case where the government spending is exogenous? Explain in words what is going on.
d. Is this equation an accurate description of government purchases in the United States? If not, what other components of the government budget act as automatic stabilizers? How are the impact of aggregate demand and price shocks affected by such stabilizers?

5. (Simple proof of the Ricardian equivalence) Consider the intertemporal budget constraint for families that we introduced in Chapter 8 and the intertemporal budget constraint for the government that we introduced in this chapter. Suppose that taxes are cut by $1,000 in Year 1 and the government debt increases.

   a. If the interest rate is 5 percent, by how much will taxes have to increase next year if the government debt is to come back to normal by the end of next year?
   b. What is the effect of this decrease and subsequent increase in taxes on the intertemporal budget constraint for consumers? How would you expect this change to affect consumption?

Analytical
1. The president is required by law to submit each year projections of budget deficits for the next 5 years. In discussing this law about budget projections, President Reagan said in 1985, "Frankly, I pay no attention to [the budget projections]. . . . There isn't any economist in the world who can do that and accurately tell you what you're going to need down the road." He then proposed that the law be abolished (*New York Times,* January 12, 1985).

   a. Obtain a copy of a recent Economic Report of the President and evaluate whose forecasts in Numerical Problem 2 have proven more accurate: the Reagan administrations or the private forecasters.
   b. In light of the relation between the economy and the budget (again, see Numerical Problem 2), comment on President Reagan's proposal.

2. Suppose our model of the economy is the simple spending balance model of Chapter 4. The equations of the model are

$$Y = C+I+G$$
$$C = 100+.9Y_d$$
$$Y_d = Y+F$$

where $I=750$ and F stands for government transfer payments.

   a. You are told that government outlays equal 500, and there are no taxes. With this information can you calculate the point of spending balance?
   b. What is the maximum value of income for which there could be spending balance? What is the minimum value?
   c. Explain why government transfers and spending affect aggregate demand differently. Be specific.

3. Explain why imports act as automatic stabilizers. Compare the case where imports consist mainly of necessities to the case where they consist mainly of luxury goods.

4. Suppose it is 1993, and the newly elected president, in order to win, has promised (i) not to raise taxes, (ii) not to tamper with social security and other transfer programs, and (iii) not to cut defense. At 6 percent unemployment, output is very close to potential. There still, however, are the nagging two problems of the government budget deficit and the trade deficit.

   a. In the short run, how can the administration reduce the budget deficit without breaking any of its campaign promises? Be specific about the policy. What effect will the policy have on output and interest rates? How will this policy reduce the budget deficit? Describe the effect of this policy on the trade deficit. Is it unambiguous?
   b. Will this policy reduce the budget deficit in the long run? Again, be specific. What are its long-run effects on the trade deficit?

   c. What will the effects of such a policy be, in the short run and in the long run, on the real value of government debt outstanding?

   d. Recall the relationship between nominal interest rates and expected inflation discussed in Chapter 5. How might the expectations of such a policy affect long-term nominal interest rates in the 1980s?

   e. By comparing nominal interest rates with the actual rate of inflation, it has been suggested that real interest rates in the mid-1980s were at nearly an all-time high. How would the preceding analysis affect such a judgment?

5. Suppose that government spending is increased when the economy is below potential GNP. Why doesn't the decrease in government saving lead to a decline in total saving and to a drop in investment?

6. Sketch an IS-LM diagram. Compare two cases, one in which government spending is exogenous, the other where government spending declines when the economy rises above potential GNP and increases when the economy is below potential GNP. Which curve is steeper? For which curve is monetary policy most powerful?

7. Suppose that President Reagan finally agreed to raise personal income taxes by $100 billion per year starting in 1989 in an attempt to reach the Gramm-Rudman-Hollings deficit targets by 1991. However, the legislation he signed actually increased taxes only until 1991—starting in 1992 taxes would automatically be lowered back down by $100 billion. What would be the effect of this tax increase on *consumption demand*? Use the forward-looking theory of consumption to explain what the impact of the tax increase would be.

8. Consider once again the simple spending balance model of Chapter 4. Suppose now that the model is

$$Y = C+I+G$$
$$C = 100+.9Y_d$$
$$Y_d = Y+F-T$$

where $I=750$ and G, T, and F are initially zero.

   a. Calculate the initial point of spending balance.

   b. Suppose the country goes to war for a year, requiring government expenditures of 100, and that taxes are temporarily raised to 100 in that same year. Calculate consumption and the point of spending balance in the war year and in all future years.

   c. Now suppose that the government issues war bonds instead of raising taxes. The war bonds are 5 percent consoles. Consoles are bonds on which interest is paid forever and the principal is never repaid. Again, calculate consumption and the point of spending balance in the war year and in all future years.

   d. What is the net effect of the government running a deficit in the war year instead of raising taxes? Is your result consistent with the idea of Ricardian equivalence? If not, how can you explain the difference?

12

The Monetary System

A MONETARY system is an arrangement through which people express economic values and carry out transactions with each other. A well-developed monetary system is essential to a smoothly operating economy. History has shown that poorly developed monetary systems have been responsible for severe recessions and inflations. But even normal, everyday economic life is greatly facilitated by an efficient monetary system.

The monetary system is just one of many social arrangements that exist in any civilization. Language is another. Weights and measures are a third. Some of these arrangements have evolved without formal or conscious social agreements; others have been the result of organized planning and formal agreement. Although monetary systems originally evolved informally in primitive cultures, in modern times most countries have enacted laws and institutions that define their monetary systems. One of the concerns of macroeconomics is whether certain revisions to these laws and institutions might improve macroeconomic performance.

The monetary system takes on a central role in aggregate demand because prices and wages do not move quickly enough to offset shifts in money supply or money demand. As we saw in Chapter 5, shifts in the LM curve—the curve for which money supply equals money demand—first result in changes in GNP, and later in changes in inflation. In this chapter we look at the microeconomic foundations of *money supply* and *money demand*. In doing so we will see that the monetary system is an intrinsically interesting part of the economy, and would be a subject worthy of study even without its role in macroeconomics.

12.1 The Elements of a Monetary System

A monetary system must specify two things: first, the way that payments are to be made; second, the meaning of the numbers that merchants put on goods and the numbers that appear in contracts. The first is called the **means of payment,** and the second the **unit of account.**

In most monetary systems one item is designated as a universally acceptable means of payment. Traditionally, it was a precious metal, gold or silver. With gold or silver serving as the means of payment, it was natural for merchants to price their goods with numbers that corresponded to units of these precious metals; horse traders would find it natural to charge a certain number of gold pieces for a horse. Hence, designated amounts of precious metals became units of account as well as a means of payment. For example, in England at the time of William the Conqueror, silver was the universally accepted means of payment and the pound of silver became the unit of account. Ever since, the English unit of account has been called the pound, though its purchasing power has become much less than the value of a pound of silver.

As financial systems developed, means of payment came into use that were different from the underlying unit of account. For example, in the United States before the Civil War, the unit of account was .04838 of an ounce of gold, but the most common means of payment was paper money issued by private banks. A dollar bill from a bank carried a promise that it could be redeemed for gold at any time.

In the twentieth century, governments became more involved in the monetary system. In the United States, banks are not allowed to issue dollar bills; only the Federal Reserve has that power. Moreover, the unit of account no longer has anything to do with gold. Instead, it is the government's dollar bill. Though dollar bills are widely used as means of payment, other means of payment are even more important, such as checks and credit cards.

Although there is no law in the United States that requires prices to be quoted in dollars, nobody would choose to quote prices in another unit, such as French francs. The public is familiar with dollar prices and reluctant to think in any other terms. Even if you are good at doing arithmetic in your head, it is a lot more convenient to do all of your financial thinking in one set of units.

Together, the government's paper money and coins are called **currency.** Until the nineteenth century, currency was virtually the only means of payment. As monetary systems evolved during the nineteenth and twentieth centuries, currency began to be replaced by other means of payment in the great majority of transactions. Nevertheless, all transactions continued to be denominated in the units of the government's currency. By law, if you owe somebody a dollar debt, that person can require you to pay in currency. For larger debts, this right is rarely exercised. Instead, the person's right to receive currency sets up a situation where the two of you agree on some alternative, more convenient way to settle the debt. The other person may agree to accept a personal check from you. A check is an instruction to the banking system to make accounting entries to transfer wealth from you to the other person.

A great many customs exist about what means of payment are acceptable besides currency. In prisoner-of-war camps during the Second World War, prisoners used cigarettes as a means of payment. In modern times, credit cards are frequently an acceptable means of payment. Stores that accept credit cards let you know with a little sign in the window. Credit cards are another way to issue instructions to the banking system to transfer funds from one person to another. Like accepting checks, the acceptance of a credit card in place of currency is voluntary. When you buy a house, neither a personal check nor a credit card is likely to be accepted. You will be expected to present a bank check, which is a promise by the bank itself to pay from its own funds and a guarantee that the funds actually exist. Customs differ by country as well. In Greece today, for example, currency rather than a personal check is a much more common means of payment than it is in the United States.

Monetary economists have attempted to pin down exactly what things should be counted as the means of payment.[1] Unfortunately, this is a very difficult task. Many techniques are available for conveying purchasing power. Currency and checking accounts certainly should be counted as a means of payment. But what about the funds in savings accounts that can be electronically transferred in an instant to checking whenever a payment is desired? Some means of payment, like credit cards, do not involve an asset at all. Despite these problems, the fact that there are means of payment other than currency is crucially important for monetary economics.

As discussed in Chapter 5, we use the term **money** to mean currency plus the deposits in checking accounts. Checking accounts are usually held at banks, but sometimes at other financial institutions, such as savings and loan associations. Some checking accounts pay interest, but usually at rates below market interest rates. The Federal Reserve monitors the sum of currency and checking accounts in the United States, which they call M_1. In 1986, M_1 was \$730 billion, of which \$184 billion, or 25 percent, was currency. M_1 is one of three major monetary aggregates that are tabulated and regularly published by the Fed; the other two are M_2 and M_3. The items included in M_1 most certainly can serve as a means of payment in transactions. But as we mentioned above, there are many other means of payment. Other types of

---

[1] The research discussed in D. Patinkin, *Money, Interest, and Prices,* covers much of the work on the various definitions of money.

deposits, such as savings deposits or small-time deposits against which checks cannot be directly written, are not included in the M_1 definition of money; these are included in M_2 (M_2 includes everything that is in M_1 as well). Money market mutual funds and money market deposit accounts at banks that can be used for checking are also included in M_2. In 1986 M_2 was $2,805 billion. Items that are even less likely to be used for transactions purposes—such as time deposits over $100,000—are included in M_3, which was $3,488 billion in 1986 ($M_3$ includes everything in M_2 as well).

The difficulty in determining exactly what should be counted as the means of payment indicates the difficulty in deciding which of the definitions of money one should look at. Currency and checking deposits are not quantitatively the most important part of transactions. Far more dollars' worth of transactions are made by credit card than with currency. Nevertheless, M_1 and M_2 are significant primarily because currency and deposits are closely related to the operations of the Federal Reserve. But because there are other means of payment besides currency and deposits, a careful examination of changes in the monetary system is a necessary part of interpreting the behavior of M_1 and M_2.

12.2 Money Supply: How the Fed Controls It

We now consider how the Fed controls the money supply. The money supply consists of currency (CU) and checking deposits (D) that individuals and firms hold at banks. We will not distinguish at this point between M_1 and M_2 by distinguishing between different types of deposits. Rather we let the symbol D represent all deposits at banks (or private financial institutions more generally) and let M be the resulting money supply. The money supply M is thus defined as

$$M = CU + D. \tag{12-1}$$

Because deposits at banks are part of the money supply, we must consider how the Fed's actions affect these deposits. Table 12–1 shows a set of balance sheets for four sectors of the economy: the private nonfinancial sector (consumers and businesses), the banks, the Federal Reserve, and the government. This balance sheet shows how the sectors are related financially.

In the balance sheet assets are shown on the left and liabilities on the right. Assets are the things owned by the individual or organization and liabilities are the amounts owed to others. For example, loans are assets for banks and liabilities for borrowers. Note that all of the things listed in these accounts appear at least twice—once in somebody's assets and again in somebody else's liabilities.

The "banks" column of the balance sheet includes all depository institutions that accept checking deposits and that hold reserves at the Fed. Thus

Table 12–1.   FINANCIAL RELATIONSHIPS (BALANCE SHEETS) BETWEEN THE BANKS, THE FED, THE GOVERNMENT, AND THE PRIVATE SECTOR

Private Nonfinancial		Banks		Fed		Government	
Assets	Liabilities	Assets	Liabilities	Assets	Liabilities	Assets	Liabilities
Currency (CU)					Currency (CU)		
Deposits (D)			Deposits (D)				
Bonds (B)		Bonds (B)		Bonds (B)			Bonds (B)
		Reserves (RE)			Reserves (RE)		
	Loans	Loans					

"banks" include not only commercial banks, but also those savings and loan associations and mutual savings banks that provide checking services to their customers. The "Fed" column of the balance sheet includes the assets and liabilities of all twelve district banks of the Federal Reserve System.[2]

Note where the major assets and liabilities appear on the balance sheets of each sector:

Currency (CU) and Deposits (D). The private sector holds currency that is issued by the Fed.[3] As we discuss below, it is the Fed's job to supply the currency that the private sector demands even though the government prints and mints currency at the Treasury Department. The private sector also holds deposits at the banks. These are assets of the account holders and liabilities of the banks.

Government Bonds (B). Government bonds are shown as a liability of the government. The private sector, the banks, and the Fed hold bonds as assets.

Reserves (RE) are what the banks hold on deposit at the Fed. The Fed acts as a banker's bank. It accepts deposits from banks. These reserves must be held by law at a fixed fraction of the private nonfinancial sector deposits that the banks have as liabilities.

Loans (L). The last line in the balance sheet shows the loans of the banks to the private sector. One of the main reasons that banks are in business is to

[2] The twelve District Federal Reserve Banks are in Atlanta, Boston, Chicago, Cleveland, Dallas, Kansas City, Minneapolis, New York, Philadelphia, Richmond, St. Louis, and San Francisco. The San Francisco Fed has the largest amount of reserve assets. Open-market operations take place at the New York Fed.

[3] Part of the reserves held by the banks is in the form of paper money in the vaults of the bank. The term currency in the text always means paper money and coin *outside* banks. Vault cash is essentially equivalent to bank reserves held on deposit at the Fed.

issue loans to their customers. They take deposits from some individuals and make loans to others. This is the **intermediation role** of the banks. They intermediate between individuals. But banks are important in macro-economics because their liabilities (deposits) are part of the money supply.

The Fed controls the money supply by selling bonds to, or by purchasing bonds from, the banks and the public. These purchases or sales of government bonds by the Fed are called **open-market operations.** To see how these open-market operations affect the money supply, we first define the **monetary base** (M_B). The monetary base is defined as currency plus reserves.[4] That is,

$$M_B = CU + RE. \tag{12-2}$$

The Fed does not try to exercise separate control of reserves and currency. Instead the Fed controls only the total of the two. The Fed lets the banks and the private sector decide how much of the monetary base is currency and how much is reserves. Any bank can withdraw currency from its reserve account whenever it wants, and any bank can put currency into its reserve account and receive credit dollar for dollar. For example, when legalized gambling started in Atlantic City, the banks in the Philadelphia Federal Reserve District found that their customers were using a lot more cash. The banks therefore withdrew currency from their reserve accounts and made it available to their customers.

Using open-market operations the Fed can add to or subtract from the total amount of bank reserves plus currency whenever it chooses. An open-market operation to expand the monetary base involves a purchase by the Fed of government bonds from the banks. Look again at the balance sheet in Table 12-1. When a bank sells a bond to the Fed, the bank receives a credit in its reserve account that adds to the total amount of reserves. The simple fact that assets must equal liabilities in the Fed's balance sheet indicates that any purchase of bonds must lead to an increase in the sum of currency and reserves—that is, in the monetary base. Whenever a bank transfers funds to another bank, nothing happens to total reserves—one bank's reserves rise by the exact amount that the other bank's fall. But a purchase of bonds by the Fed must raise the monetary base. Similarly, a sale of bonds by the Fed must reduce the monetary base.

The effects of the Fed's open-market operation on the monetary base over the last 20 years are shown in Table 12-2. The monetary base increased fourfold during this period. Note that the amount of currency is much larger than the amount of reserves. About three-quarters of the monetary base is currency.

There is a direct relationship between the monetary base and the money

[4] Phillip Cagan of Columbia University has done much of the research on the determination of the monetary base and its relation to the money supply in the United States. See his *The Determinants and Effects of Changes in the Stock of Money, 1875–1960,* Columbia University Press, 1965. Cagan refers to the monetary base as high-powered money.

Table 12–2.   CURRENCY, RESERVES, AND THE MONETARY BASE (billions of dollars)

	Dec. 1966	*Dec. 1976*	*Dec. 1986*
Currency	39	82	183
Reserves	16	26	56
Monetary base	55	108	239

Source: *Economic Report of the President,* 1987, Table B–66.

supply, and this is how the Fed achieves its control of the money supply. The relationship between the monetary base and the money supply is due to two factors:

1. Reserve requirements: Banks are required to hold a certain ratio of their checking deposits on reserve at the Fed. This ratio is called the **reserve ratio** (r). For example, r might equal .1 (or 10 percent). Reserves (RE) are then given by the formula

$$RE = rD. \tag{12–3}$$

2. Currency demand: Most people want to hold some of their money in the form of currency. We will discuss the determinants of currency demand in Section 12.3. For now we can describe this demand in terms of a simple ratio. The **currency deposit ratio** (c) measures how much currency people want to hold as a ratio of their deposits. For example, the currency deposit ratio c might equal .2. Currency demand is thus given by

$$CU = cD. \tag{12–4}$$

Now we can derive the relationship between the monetary base and the money supply. From the definition of the money supply,

$$M = CU + D = cD + D = (1 + c)D,$$
$$M_B = CU + RE = cD + rD = (c + r)D.$$

Dividing M by M_B, we get

$$M = \frac{1 + c}{r + c} M_B. \tag{12–5}$$

The coefficient that multiplies M_B is called the **monetary base multiplier,** which we will call m. If $r = .1$ and $c = .2$, then the monetary base multiplier is 4. Open-market operations that increase the monetary base by $1 billion would then increase M by $4 billion. Because of this multiplier, the monetary base is sometimes called **high-powered money.** Here the reserve ratio and the currency ratio are assumed to be fixed, so the Fed can control the money supply as accurately as it wants by controlling the monetary base. In reality, as we show in Section 12.3, the currency ratio can vary, so control of the money supply is not so simple.

REQUIRED RESERVES AND EXCESS RESERVES

In the United States, the reserve requirement for banks is now 12 percent. Banks are penalized if they fall below their requirements, and for this reason they always keep some **excess reserves** over and above their **required reserves.** This is illustrated in Table 12–3, which is a more detailed

Table 12–3. RESERVES: REQUIRED, BORROWED, AND EXCESS

Banks		Fed	
Assets	Liabilities	Assets	Liabilities
			Currency
	Deposits		
Bonds		Bonds	
Loans			
Required reserves			Required reserves
Excess reserves			Excess reserves
	Borrowed reserves	Borrowed reserves	

version of Table 12–1, focusing only on the banks and the Fed. The amount of excess reserves is small because banks do not receive any interest on their reserve balances at the Fed. They prefer to keep reserves close to the minimum required amount and invest the rest of their funds in loans or bonds. Excess reserves were only 1.5 percent of total reserves in 1984. Excess reserves rose to 2.3 percent of total reserves by 1985 as interest rates fell, but the amount was still small. In the mid-1960s, when interest rates were very low, excess reserves were higher but still fairly small, ranging up to 4 percent of total reserves. In recent years it is a good approximation to say that all bank reserves are required reserves.

Would banks hold reserves if they were not required to hold them? Reserve requirements were initially enacted into law in order to make sure that banks would have enough funds on hand if their depositors wanted to cash in their deposits. Even without reserve requirements, banks would hold some reserves for this purpose, but probably much less than 12 percent. Holding assets in interest-bearing short-term government securities is almost as safe as holding assets in reserves. Government securities can be readily sold if there is a need for cash. But reserves are also used to carry out the instructions of a bank's depositors to transfer reserves from one account to another and from one bank to another. A large bank executes several million transfer instructions from checks, credit cards, and electronic requests every day. In the process, it will be holding positive amounts of reserves as a normal part of its business. Someone in the melon business always owns a certain amount of melons at any one time even though they turn over constantly. Similarly, someone in the reserve business is likely to own reserves. Again, however, the amount of reserves necessary to carry out the business of a bank is probably much less than 12 percent.

BORROWED RESERVES AND THE DISCOUNT RATE

An important addition to this simple story of how the Fed and the banking system determine the money supply is that reserves at the banks can increase even if there is no open-market operation. One of the traditional functions of the Fed has been to provide loans to troubled banks. This tradition developed because of the frequent bank failures and bank panics in the late nineteenth and early twentieth centuries. The Fed was created to serve as "lender of last resort" to the banks. In recent years this role of the Fed has become apparent again. When several large loans at Continental Illinois Bank in Chicago went bad in the early 1980s, there were not enough funds to pay off the depositors. The small depositors were insured by the Federal Deposit Insurance Corporation (FDIC), a federal agency set up in the 1930s to insure bank deposits. But the many depositors holding amounts well over $100,000 were not insured. In this case the bank received loans so that even the large depositors obtained their funds.

The Fed usually makes loans to banks at the borrowing "window" of one of the twelve District Federal Reserve Banks. As shown in Table 12–3, the bank borrowings are a liability of the banks and an asset of the Fed. The interest rate on the borrowings is called the **discount rate.** In the past changes in the discount rate have signaled movements in the Fed's monetary policy. In recent years the discount rate has been adjusted to follow market interest rates, though usually with a time lag. When market interest rates are above the discount rate, the banks prefer to borrow at the discount window and make profits by lending out at a higher rate. Hence borrowings increase with market interest rates. There is a limit on this, however, because the Fed refuses to lend very much to banks without good reason.

What happens when a bank borrows reserves from the Fed? Looking at Table 12–3, you can see that the bank's assets will rise by the amount of the borrowed reserves. A new item will appear in the bank's liabilities, borrowings from the Fed. And the Fed's liabilities will rise by the amount of the reserves it has issued to the bank. Finally, the Fed's assets will contain a new item, a loan to the bank.

Thus *an increase in borrowed reserves increases the monetary base just as an open-market operation does.* However, if the Fed wants to insulate the monetary base from changes due to an increase in borrowings then all it needs to do is make an offsetting open-market sale. Even when banks are borrowing heavily at the discount window, the Fed can set the monetary base at any level it chooses. Hence, the existence of borrowed reserves does not change the basic principle of money supply analysis that the Fed can control the monetary base. In discussing monetary policy, money market economists and financial columnists sometimes find it convenient to refer to reserves or the monetary base net of borrowings. Total reserves less borrowed reserves are called **nonborrowed reserves.** The monetary base less borrowings is called the **net base.**

THE FEDERAL OPEN-MARKET COMMITTEE

Decisions about monetary policy in the United States are made by the Federal Open-Market Committee (FOMC). Its voting members consist of those on the Federal Reserve Board and some of the presidents of the District Federal Reserve Banks. The FOMC meets about eight to ten times each year. Two basic types of decisions are made by the FOMC at its meetings. First, it sets **target ranges** for the money supply. Target ranges state the maximum and minimum growth rates for the money supply over the upcoming year. The Fed typically sets growth ranges for each of the monetary aggregates, M_1, M_2, and M_3, but because of uncertainties about the demand for M_1 which made hitting the target very difficult the Fed omitted targets for M_1 when it stated targets in February 1987. The target ranges are usually first set in July for the following year and then revised if necessary the following February. The target range for M_1 growth was 3 to 8 percent for 1986, but actual M_1 growth was 15 percent, far in excess of the target. The target range for M_2 growth was 6 to 9 percent for 1986, and actual M_2 growth was just at the upper bound of 9 percent. When money growth falls outside of the target range the Fed must justify the discrepancy to Congress.

A second decision of the FOMC is what to tell the New York trading desk, which actually carries out the open-market operations, to do from week to week during the year. The details of how the FOMC communicates its decisions to the trading desk change quite frequently. Through much of the 1970s the FOMC told the trading desk to buy and sell government securities to keep the interest rate at values roughly consistent with the money supply targets. To do this they used a money demand function like that in Equation 5–5 (p. 101). If M_1 seemed to be growing above its target the FOMC would instruct the trading desk to raise the interest rate. The higher interest rate would then reduce the demand for money and bring M_1 back within the target range. This interest rate procedure was changed abruptly in October 1979 soon after Paul Volcker became chairman of the Fed. After 1979, the Fed told the trading desk to buy and sell government bonds in order to bring the monetary base to levels consistent with the targets for the monetary aggregates. One reason for the change in operating procedures was that the FOMC wanted to raise interest rates, by large amounts if necessary, to reduce economic growth and reduce inflation. But Congress and many others would tend to criticize the Fed if it chose to raise interest rates. Rather than look as if it was deciding to raise interest rates, the FOMC decided to communicate with the trading desk using the monetary base. If interest rates rose the chairman of the Fed could then tell Congress "the FOMC doesn't decide on interest rates." In fact, interest rates did rise to historically high levels after 1979. In recent years (starting in mid-1982) the FOMC has returned to an operating procedure that essentially uses interest rates rather than the monetary base.

Money Announcements, Expectations, and Interest Rates

As Fed monetary targeting came to be understood in financial markets in the 1970s and early 1980s it gave rise to a whole industry of money and Fed watchers in financial markets. Each Thursday the Fed announces the money supply for the most recent week for which data are available. The results are always published in the *Wall Street Journal* and other financial newspapers. During the 1970s and early 1980s if the money supply announcement was greater than market participants forecasted, the interest rate would usually rise.* Hence, making a good forecast of the money supply was a good way to make a lot of money speculating on the bond markets.

Why would interest rates increase when the money supply turned out to be unexpectedly high? There are two possible explanations, both based on the theory of rational expectations. According to one explanation, an unexpected increase in the money supply indicates that the Fed is likely to raise interest rates in the future in order to bring money growth back within its range. The expectations of high interest rates in the future raise interest rates today. The second explanation is that higher money growth indicates more inflation down the road. More inflation will eventually raise nominal interest rates, and this will tend to raise interest rates today. Statistical tests seem to indicate that the former explanation is more accurate.+ These tests are confirmed by the fact that money supply surprises now have less effect on interest rates because the Fed is paying less attention to money growth.

* This interest rate effect has been documented by Brad Cornell, "Do Money Supply Announcements Affect Short-Term Interest Rates?" *Journal of Money, Credit, and Banking*, Vol. 11 (February 1979), pp. 80–86.
+ Charles Engel and Jeffrey Frankel have examined this question using data on interest rates and exchange rates. See their paper, "Why Interest Rates React to Money Announcements: An Explanation from the Foreign Exchange Market," *Journal of Monetary Economics*, Vol. 13, pp. 31–39, 1984.

DISTINGUISHING BETWEEN MONETARY AND FISCAL POLICY

Our analysis of the money supply and the monetary base raises some definitional questions about monetary and fiscal policy. The government budget identity implies a relationship between the monetary base, government bonds, and government expenditures that must be kept in mind when distinguishing between monetary and fiscal policy. The monetary base, government bonds, and the deficit are related to each other by the following government budget identity:

$$G + F + RD - T = \Delta M_B + \Delta B, \tag{12-6}$$

where ΔM_B is the change in monetary base and ΔB is the change in government bonds. It says that the government budget deficit is financed by increasing either the monetary base or government bonds. Note that the base as well as government expenditure and taxes appear in this expression, so that there is a link between monetary policy and fiscal policy.

To separate monetary policy changes from fiscal policy changes, we therefore need to specify what is happening to budget financing.

Fiscal policy is defined as **bond-financed changes** in government expenditures and taxes. That is, the monetary base and the money supply remain unchanged, and bonds are issued if government spending increases or taxes are reduced.

Monetary policy is defined as an increase in the monetary base matched by a reduction in government bonds. This exchange of money for bonds is an open-market operation. Note that open-market operations do not affect government purchases (G), transfers (F), or taxes (T). Thus open-market operations do not affect fiscal policy.

The Monetary System and the Fed

1. The monetary system in the United States is based on the dollar, which is the unit of account and a means of payment.

2. The institutions most prominent in providing the means of payment are the Federal Reserve System and banks. The liabilities of the Fed—currency and reserves—make up the monetary base.

3. The money supply consists of currency and deposits at banks and other financial intermediaries. The supply of money is directly related to the monetary base.

4. The Fed controls the monetary base by buying and selling bonds. In doing so it controls the supply of money.

Financing Government through the "Printing Press"

How much does the United States resort to the printing press to raise revenues to pay for government expenditures? The monetary base gives a good measure of this. Suppose, for example, that Congress passes a bill authorizing the navy to build new ships for an amount of $2 billion. But Congress does not raise taxes to pay for the ships. In order to pay for the ship construction, the government issues bonds. But rather than selling the bonds to the public, it sells the bonds to the Fed in exchange for currency which it then pays out to the workers and firms that build the ships. In effect, the increase in government expenditures was financed by the printing of more currency. Note that the monetary base increased by $2 billion.

Just as in this example, the increase in the monetary base is a measure of the amount of government revenue that is raised each year through the printing press rather than through taxes or borrowing. In 1986 the monetary base increased by about $22 billion dollars. Compared to the $1,030 billion of government expenditures during 1986 this is a trivial amount: Only 2 percent of government expenditures were financed by the printing press in 1986. This small percentage is typical in recent U.S. history. Hence, the printing presses are not a very important source of revenue for the United States in modern times. But this was not always true. About 80 percent of American Revolutionary War expenditures were financed by printing paper money called "continentals." So much money was printed that a serious inflation occurred: Prices rose by over 300 percent from 1776 to 1778, and by 1,000 percent from 1778 to 1780. Hence the phrase, "not worth a continental." The printing press set off even worse inflations in Germany and several other European countries in the 1920s, and in Argentina, Brazil, and other South American countries in the 1970s and 1980s.

12.3 The Demand for Money: Currency and Checking Deposits

The alternative operating procedures for the Fed, outlined in Section 12.2, have significant macroeconomic implications. But before we can discuss them, we must examine the determinants of the demand for money.

Families and businesses constantly face decisions about how to conduct their financial affairs. They face big issues, such as how to finance the purchase of a house or a major capital investment, or how to hold wealth for retirement. They also face much smaller issues, such as whether to buy things with currency, checks, or credit cards or by special credit arrangements or electronic transfers of funds. Their choices depend on their incomes, wealth, volume of transactions, and the relative prices of all the different financial services available in the market. There is no clean separation between specifically monetary decisions and more general economic decisions. The blurring of choices about transactions and about bigger financial issues has increased in the past decade as deregulation of financial institutions has proceeded.

At the most general level, we could look at the demands for currency and checking deposits—or what we call money—as just parts of a large set of demand functions for financial instruments and services. Modern finance theory has tackled the question of how to set up these demand functions, taking into account the central role of economic uncertainty. Our approach is less general. Among the many demand functions, the demand for currency and checking deposits is particularly important for macro issues.

James Tobin of Yale University, who was awarded the Nobel Prize in economics for developing modern portfolio theory, first applied his portfolio ideas to the same money demand functions that we consider here.[5] Tobin was interested in developing a microeconomic foundation for the demand for money that Keynes had originally introduced in *The General Theory*. Keynes referred to the demand for money as **liquidity preference,** a term which is still used quite frequently, and which has permanently left the "L" in the LM curve (the "M" refers to the money stock). The term **liquid,** when applied to a financial instrument, means that it can be sold readily; money is the most liquid of all assets. The originator of many ideas about money demand, Keynes was responsible for stressing the importance of money demand in macroeconomic fluctuations.

Keynes distinguished among three motives in people's demands for money: a **transactions** motive, a **precautionary** motive, and a **speculative** motive. More recent research—such as Tobin's—has refined these categories, and Keynes's classification scheme has been revised somewhat. However, our discussion of money demand will touch on all three of these elements.

WHAT ARE THE OPPORTUNITY COSTS OF HOLDING FUNDS AS MONEY?

When you put funds in a checking account, you are giving the bank the use of the funds. The bank earns the interest you would have earned if you had invested it. In exchange, the bank may pay you some interest, but less

---

[5] See James Tobin, "Liquidity Preference as Behavior Toward Risk," *Review of Economic Studies,* Vol. 25 (February 1958), pp. 65–86.

than what the bank is earning. In addition, if you have a sufficiently high balance, the bank may excuse you from service charges you would otherwise have to pay. Your opportunity cost per dollar in your checking account is the interest you forego (the rate you might have received elsewhere less the amount you receive from the bank) less the avoided service charges. As usual in microeconomics, what matters precisely is the *marginal* opportunity cost—the interest foregone on the last amount added to your balance less the reduction in service charges if you took it out. For example, suppose you would earn 9 percent elsewhere and your bank pays 5 percent interest on checking accounts. Suppose that, over the year, it will excuse you from $2 in service charges if you raise your average balance by $100, so you earn 2 percent on the $100. Then your opportunity cost for the $100 of funds placed in your checking account is

$$9\% - 5\% - 2\% = 2\%.$$

We call the opportunity cost of holding money R_o, the subscript "o" standing for "opportunity." When you think about the added convenience of having another $100 in your account on the average over the year, you will keep in mind that you are sacrificing 2 percentage points of annual return on the funds.

Whatever complicated system the bank has for paying you interest on the one hand and charging you for services on the other, you can boil it down to an annual net opportunity cost of the account. This is the price we have in mind for checking deposits as one of the many financial services available to you.

For currency, the computation of the opportunity cost is easy. There are no service charges at all. Currency pays no interest. Therefore, the cost of holding currency is just the foregone interest. If you are contemplating meeting your needs by holding an average amount of currency of $500, and you could earn 9 percent on the funds elsewhere, then the cost is just 9 percent of $500, or $45 per year.

Another hypothetical way of handling your finances might avoid money altogether. You could open a special savings account and obtain a credit card. The savings account would allow you to write three checks a month, one of which could pay for your credit card charges. You would pay for everything with the credit card. Suppose the special savings account pays you 8 percent interest (1 percent less than the 9 percent that you could get outside the bank) and the credit card has no finance charges if you pay the bill on time. If you keep an average balance of $2,500 in the account, your only cost would be the opportunity cost of 1 percent of $2,500, or $25 per year.

By now it should be clear that each type of financial service has its own opportunity cost. But consumers do not simply pick the cheapest service on the market. Different services have different characteristics. Choosing among them is like choosing laundry detergent at the grocery store.

THE TRANSACTIONS DEMAND FOR MONEY: AN INVENTORY THEORY

One of the reasons that families and businesses hold currency and keep funds in their checking accounts is the same as the reason stores keep inventories of goods for sale. Because income is received periodically (say once every month) and expenditures occur every day, it is necessary to hold a stock of currency and checking deposits. This inventory theory of the demand for money falls into Keynes's category of **transactions motive.**[6]

We first illustrate the inventory theory of money demand with a simple case. Suppose a family earns an amount W every month. The family consumes W over the month, in equal amounts each day. If the family draws down its money to zero just before being paid, then its money balance starts at W and declines smoothly to zero over the month. Figure 12–1A illustrates how the family's money holdings decline smoothly each day during the month. Its average level of money balances M is $W/2$. This family has a demand for money ($W/2$) that is proportional to its income W and does not respond to the prices of financial services. For one reason or another, the family has rejected ways other than money to hold its funds.

Next, take the same family with one additional financial option. It can have its paychecks deposited for free in a savings account. It can transfer any amount of funds to its checking account. The cost of each transfer is k. The cost k includes the value of the time of the family members who make the transfer—it might involve a trip to the bank. The checking account has an opportunity cost R_o. The family chooses an average balance to hold in its checking account. The higher the average balance, the fewer transfers have to be made from the savings account. But the higher the average balance, the larger is the opportunity cost. The family wants to balance one cost against the other. For example, if the family makes one transfer at the beginning of the month its money balance is the same as in Figure 12–1A. If the family makes two transfers to checking, one at the start of the month and one halfway through the month, as in Figure 12–1B, the average money balance is half as much as when the family makes one transfer. If three transfers are made, as in Figure 12–1C, the average money holdings are lower still.

In general, the average money balance, M, is half the amount transferred from savings to checking on each transfer. The total number of transfers is the size of each transfer, 2 times M, divided into the total amount of consumption planned over the month, W. That is, the family will make $W/2M$

---

[6] The inventory theory of the demand for money was first worked out by William Baumol, "The Transactions Demand for Cash: An Inventory Theoretic Approach," *Quarterly Journal of Economics,* Vol. 56 (November 1952), pp. 545–556, and James Tobin, "The Interest Rate Elasticity of the Transactions Demand for Cash," *Review of Economics and Statistics,* Vol. 38 (September 1956), pp. 241–247.

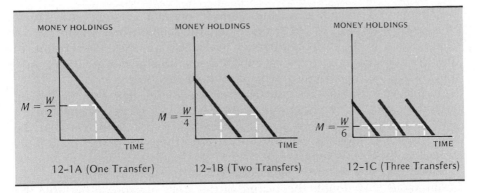

Figures 12–1A, B, and C.   THREE ALTERNATIVE MONEY MANAGEMENT STRATEGIES.
In A, the family puts all its money in checking at the start of the month. Average money holdings are large. In B, the family leaves half its income in a savings account at the start of the month and withdraws the rest at the middle of the month. Average money holdings are less than in A. In C, the family makes three withdrawals and money holdings are even lower. Hence, when there are more withdrawals, the money balance is lower.

transfers during the month. The total cost of the transfers is k times $W/2M$ (remember that k is the cost of one transfer). The opportunity cost over the month is just R_o times the average balance, that is, R_oM. The family wants to choose its average balance to minimize the sum of the two costs. Algebraically it wants to find M to minimize total cost:

$$\frac{kW}{2M} + R_oM. \tag{12–7}$$

A famous theorem from management theory is the **square-root rule** for inventories. The square-root rule says that stores should hold inventories proportional to the square root of sales. The same square-root rule applies to the demand for money. Specifically, the theorem says that the value of the average checking balance M that minimizes total cost is given by[7]

$$M = \sqrt{\frac{kW}{2R_o}}. \tag{12–8}$$

[7] Calculus is not necessary to derive the square root rule. Rather one can use a "complete the square" approach as follows. The total cost is

$$kW/2M + R_oM = \sqrt{(kW/2M + R_oM)^2}$$
$$= \sqrt{(kW/2M)^2 + kWR_o + (R_oM)^2}$$
$$= \sqrt{(kW/2M)^2 - kWR_o + (R_oM)^2 + 2kWR_o}$$
$$= \sqrt{(kW/2M - R_oM)^2 + 2kWR_o}.$$

The second term under the last square-root sign does not depend on M. Thus costs are minimized when the first term under the square-root sign is at its smallest value, which is zero. This

The square-root rule gives the family's transactions demand for cash. Note that the formula would be the same if they chose to keep their transactions balance in the form of currency instead of in a checking account. In that case, because currency earns no interest, the opportunity cost of currency would be the interest rate paid on their savings account.

According to the square-root rule, the family holds less money if the opportunity cost R_o of holding money increases. The services of money are just like anything else the family consumes; they make do with less when the price rises. The square-root rule also says something about the relation between total spending and income W and the family's demand for money: Demand depends on the square root of total income. In comparing two families, one with double the income of the other, we should find that the second family has a transactions balance only 41 percent higher (the square root of 2 is 1.41).

MONEY AS A STORE OF WEALTH

Some families hold their wealth in the form of money—if they completely distrust all financial institutions they might accumulate dollar bills under a mattress. Criminal activities generate wealth that is held as currency to avoid detection. People who are not thinking very hard about their affairs sometimes leave large amounts idle in their checking accounts at zero or low interest rates.

Hoards of inactive large-denomination paper money are apparently a large fraction of the total demand for currency. Almost half of the total value of currency outstanding is in the form of $100 bills. The records of the Fed show that $100 bills last for quite a number of years, whereas the usual life of a $1 bill is only about 18 months. Apparently, the large bills do not change hands very often. The sheer volume of currency is surprising: There are about 100 million families in the United States; if the $184 billion in currency were distributed evenly among them, each would have $1,840 in currency at any one time. Very few families hold anything like this much. It is unlikely that businesses, which try to get their currency into the bank as quickly as possible, can account for much of the extra currency outstanding. Therefore, a few people must have extremely large hoards. Many of them are probably outside the country. In politically unstable nations, U.S. currency is one of the safer ways to hold wealth.

Keynes's notions of precautionary and speculative demand for money fit

---

term is equal to zero when

$$M = \sqrt{kW/2R_o},$$

which is the square-root rule. Alternatively, if you have had calculus you can differentiate (12–7) with respect to M.

into this store-of-wealth category. Under the precautionary motive individuals save some wealth in the form of money in case of an emergency need for funds. Since currency and checking deposits are the easiest funds to obtain, it might seem natural to hold money for this purpose. However, in the United States, other interest-bearing assets serve the precautionary demand perfectly well. In politically unstable countries or in countries without a well-developed financial system, this motive for holding money would be more important.

Keynes's speculative motive captures the idea that changes in market interest rates will change the value of bonds. For individuals, bonds paying fixed interest rates are one of the main alternatives to holding the money in financial institutions. But, when interest rates rise, the price of these bonds falls.[8] Keynes argued that when interest rates were high more people would expect them to fall or, equivalently, would expect bond prices to rise, and would therefore want to hold bonds and less money. Thus, the demand for money declines as interest rates rise. Changes in bond prices also add risk to holding bonds. It was this risk that James Tobin formalized in his portfolio theory. People are assumed to be averse to risk; hence, they do not put all their wealth in a risky asset. Some of their wealth will be held as relatively riskless money. Unless they are unwilling to take on any risk, they will balance their wealth between money and bonds. This balancing gives rise to a demand for money as an aversion to risk.

THE DEMAND FOR CHECKING DEPOSITS TO PAY FOR BANKING SERVICES

An important motive for holding checking account balances is to pay the bank for the services it provides. With most checking accounts, you can eliminate service charges by keeping a high enough balance. Instead of paying you interest and then charging you for the services you use, the bank offsets one against the other. In effect, you are earning a reasonable return on your wealth, but the return is paid in banking services rather than in cash.

The custom of offsetting interest and service charges had its origin in restrictions on the amount of interest banks could pay on checking accounts. Starting in the 1930s, the federal government prohibited the payment of interest on checking accounts. Only since 1980 have these limitations been lifted. However, the practice of encouraging depositors to keep larger balances by foregoing their service charges will continue. If interest is paid explicitly, it is taxable; if it is paid as banking services, it is not taxed. As long as

---

[8] Interest rates and prices of existing bonds have an inverse relation. When the interest rate falls, the market price of a bond issued earlier rises. The bond continues to pay its interest payments, but new bonds have smaller payments. Hence, the old bond has a higher market price.

this feature of the tax system continues, there is an incentive to conceal interest by paying it as services.

For business customers, banks have traditionally linked loans and deposits. A business is more likely to get a loan if it has kept large deposits with a bank. Some loans require explicitly that part of the proceeds be kept as "compensating balances," which are inactive, non-interest-bearing balances in checking accounts. Again, the bank is charging for its services by paying its depositors less than market interest rates on their deposits.

As deregulation of financial markets proceeds, banks will probably shift in the direction of paying closer to market interest on deposits and charging more explicitly for their services. We will have more to say about the implications of this shift later in the chapter.

DEMAND FUNCTIONS FOR MONEY

We do not have any firm basis for dividing up the total demand for checking account balances or currency into the categories just listed—transactions demand, store of wealth, and payment for banking services. We can offer a few rough guesses. First, the transactions demand for both forms of money appear to be a fairly small fraction of total demand. An upper-bound estimate of the amount of money the typical family should hold, on the average, for transactions purposes is $1,000. Then total transactions demand should not exceed $1,000 times 100 million, or $100 billion. In 1986, currency alone was $184 billion and checking accounts were about twice as much.

Nobody holds currency to compensate a bank for services. Hence, the rest of the demand for currency presumably comes from people who want the anonymity it provides. For checking accounts, probably much of the demand comes from the motive of compensating banks for services.

Because the transactions demand is a small fraction of total demand, the square-root rule cannot be sufficient to explain the total demand for money. Empirical studies of the demand for money indicate that money holdings have not grown quite as fast as income, but they have grown much more than the square root of income.[9]

The response of the demand for money to the price of holding money—the opportunity cost—is much more uncertain. For checking accounts, it is hard to measure the price in the first place, because it involves both foregone interest and foregone service charges. We do not have any systematic information about the reduction in service charges that the typical bank customer can obtain by holding a larger checking balance, but we can look at the relation between interest rates and cash holdings.

---

[9] See Stephen Goldfeld, "The Demand for Money Revisited," *Brookings Papers on Economic Activity,* Number 3, pp. 577–683, 1973.

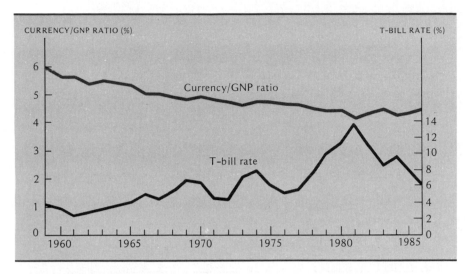

Figure 12-2. CURRENCY DIVIDED BY GNP.
Holdings of currency have declined slowly in recent decades. The upper line is the total amount of currency in circulation, divided by nominal GNP—a measure of nominal demand. The interest rate is also shown in the diagram. Higher interest rates are associated with less currency as a percentage of GNP. Source: *Economic Report of the President, 1987,* Tables B-1, B-65, and B-68.

Currency holdings have declined gradually relative to GNP since 1959. This is shown in Figure 12-2. The most interesting finding about currency in circulation is the weakness of its downward trend. Even though credit cards are much more widely used today and checking accounts have more favorable terms than they used to, the public has decreased only slightly the amount of currency it holds per dollar of production. Some economists have inferred that the "underground economy"—activities not reported to the Internal Revenue Service and not part of GNP, such as "under-the-table" wages or illicit drug sales—is growing rapidly in order to explain the sustained level of demand for currency. But many other forces could be at work as well.

We would expect that periods of low income and high interest rates would be periods of low holdings of currency, but the evidence suggests that this tendency is weak. Currency holdings (in real terms) do drop a little during recessions, but not so much during periods of high interest rates. With the extreme interest rates of 1981, however, currency fell quite a bit.

The behavior of checking deposits is shown in Figure 12-3. There is a long-standing trend away from checking deposits, presumably related to the growth of credit cards and other means of payment, as well as growth of new types of accounts in banks and elsewhere offering convenient transfer and bill-paying arrangements. Checking balances tend to rise when real GNP rises. Also, they tend to fall when the interest rate rises. The negative re-

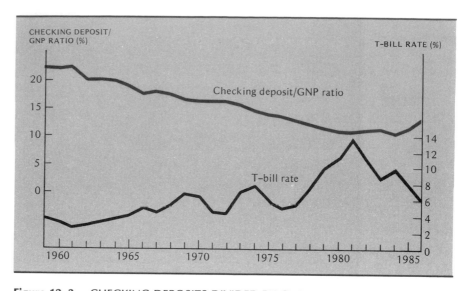

Figure 12–3. CHECKING DEPOSITS DIVIDED BY GNP.
Checking deposits have declined steadily when divided by nominal GNP, a measure of nominal demand. The interest rate is also shown in the diagram. Higher interest rates are associated with lower checking deposits. Source: *Economic Report of the President*, 1987, Tables B-1, B-65, and B-68.

sponse to the interest rate is not absolutely obvious to the naked eye but is revealed in Figure 12–3 by the increase in deposits as a fraction of GNP as interest rates fell in 1985 and 1986. The negative relationship is confirmed with statistical methods.[10]

We can summarize the previous discussion about the demand for currency and checking deposits in two demand functions,

$$CU = CU(R,PY) \tag{12–9}$$

$$D = D(R_o,PY), \tag{12–10}$$

where CU is currency and D is checking deposits. The first equation shows that the demand of currency is a function of the market interest rate R and nominal income PY (the price level P times real income Y). The second equation shows that the demand for checking deposits is a function of the opportunity cost of checking deposits R_0 and nominal income. Total money demand is the sum of these two demands. Our discussion implies the following characteristics for total money demand:

1. Demand depends negatively on the costs of holding currency and checking balances. In the case of currency, the cost is just the interest

[10] See Stephen Goldfeld, "The Demand for Money Revisited," *Brookings Papers on Economic Activity*, Number 3, pp. 577–683, 1973.

rate, R. In the case of checking deposits, the cost is the difference between the market interest rate and the rate on checking deposits, less the reduction in service charges obtained by having a larger balance. We have called this cost R_o.

2. Demand is positively related to the price level P.
3. Demand is positively related to real income or output Y.

Note that in our discussion of money supply in the previous section, we defined $c = CU/D$, the ratio of currency to deposits. Our discussion in this section shows that this ratio is not a simple constant. Rather it depends on movements in R and R_o.

We can also summarize our discussion about the determinants of the opportunity cost of checking deposits R_o with a simple algebraic formula. Before 1980 when little interest was paid on checking deposits, it was a reasonable approximation, at least for the short run, that R_o and R moved together. When the market interest rate rose a percentage point, the cost of checking balances also rose a point. In the longer run, this was probably not true, because banks could decrease their service charges when the interest rate rose. But service charges did not respond immediately to changes in economic conditions. Hence, the cost of checking deposits moved with the interest rate.

Since 1980, banks have been free to pay interest on checking deposits, and since 1982, there have been no limits on the interest provided the balance was over \$2,500. As deregulation of banking proceeds, all legal restrictions on the terms of checking accounts will probably be lifted. As a result, the opportunity cost of checking balances R_o will probably be less closely associated with the market interest rate. Checking accounts will not automatically become more expensive when interest rates rise, because banks will pay variable interest rates on checking balances. This change in banking institutions may have important macroeconomic consequences, as we will see later in this chapter.

We will write the cost R_o of checking deposits as depending on two coefficients that reflect these changes in the banking institutions:

$$R_o = q_1 R - q_0, \tag{12-11}$$

where q_1 and q_0 are the coefficients. In this formula, q_1 gives the dependence on the market interest rate and q_0 is the marginal reduction in service charges. Before 1980, when accounts could not pay interest, q_1 was 1 and q_0 was large. In the new system, q_1 is close to zero, because the bank offers interest at close to the market rate. But q_0 is also now close to zero—accounts paying close to market rates don't provide free services.

Velocity and Money Demand

Velocity is an old and controversial concept in monetary economics. The term is still used quite frequently when discussing Fed policy. The term is meant to convey the speed at which the money stock is turned over from one individual to another during a period of time such as a year. In practice velocity is usually calculated by dividing the money stock—in the case of M_1, currency plus checking deposits—into nominal GNP. That is,

$$\text{velocity} = \frac{\text{nominal GNP}}{M_1}.$$

If the value of this velocity ratio is 6, for example, then one might be tempted to say that the money stock has turned over six times in spending on a year's GNP. However, since total GNP is only a small fraction of the total number of transactions in the economy—all transactions in intermediate goods and all financial transactions are excluded—money really turns over much more frequently than six times in a year.

Velocity is best thought of in terms of the demand for money. When the demand for money as a function of nominal income shifts up, because of a fall in interest rates, for example, velocity shifts down. Conversely, when the demand for money as a function of nominal income shifts down, velocity moves up. The value of velocity is shown in the figure below for the 27-year period from 1959 to 1986. The growth of velocity increased dramatically in the early 1970s, and then collapsed in 1982.

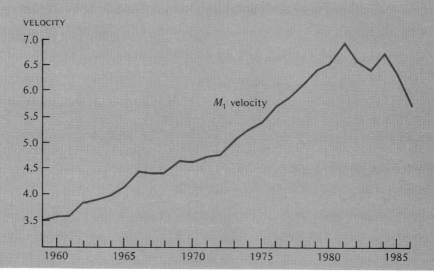

The inverse relationship between velocity and money demand is most easily seen by comparing this figure with Figures 12–2 and 12–3, which show the ratio of currency to GNP and checking deposits to GNP, respectively. The sum of these two ratios is simply the ratio of M_1 to GNP, which is precisely the inverse of velocity. When the sum of the currency and checking deposit ratios declines—as it has through much of this period—velocity must increase. As an exercise, explain the movements in velocity in the figure above using what you know about changes in the demand for currency and checking deposits during this period.

The Demand for Money

1. The demand for currency depends negatively on the interest rate and positively on income and the price level.

2. The demand for checking deposits depends negatively on the difference between the market interest rate and the rate on checking deposits, and positively on income and the price level.

12.4 The LM Curve and the Fed's Policy Rule for the Monetary Base

We saw in Section 12.2 how the Fed can use open-market operations to change the monetary base and thereby change the money supply. The central question of monetary policy is how the Fed decides upon the level of the monetary base. Consider three alternative instructions for open-market operations that the FOMC can give bond traders at the open-market desk in New York:

1. *Target the Level of* M_1. The bond traders are to keep the total amount of checking balances and currency (M_1) at a prescribed target level. If M_1 goes above target, they are to sell bonds, which reduces the monetary base and so reduces M_1. If M_1 goes below target, the traders are to buy bonds, raise the monetary base, and thus stimulate the level of M_1.

2. *Target the Interest Rate.* The bond traders are to keep an eye on the short-term interest rate and to keep it at a prescribed target level. If the rate goes over the target, they are to buy more bonds. This lowers the interest rate. If the rate goes below the target, they are to sell bonds, reduce the monetary base, and raise the rate back to the target.

3. *Target the Level of* GNP. The bond traders are to keep GNP at a pre-scribed target level. If GNP goes above target, they are to sell bonds, which will raise interest rates, contract the economy in general, and lower GNP. If GNP goes below target, they are to buy bonds and expand the economy.

We will look at each of these three policies in turn, to see what are the implications of the policy for the relations between the interest rate and the level of output.

MONEY SUPPLY (M_1) TARGET

The first policy for setting the monetary base is to adjust it as necessary to keep the sum of checking balances and currency—the money supply M_1—at a prescribed level. What kind of adjustments of the monetary base are likely to be required? Recall that the relationship between M_1 and the monetary base M_B can be written

$$M_1 = mM_B, \qquad (12\text{–}12)$$

where m is the money multiplier. The money multiplier depends on the ratios of reserves to deposits (r) and on the ratio of currency to demand deposits (c)—the **currency deposit ratio.** Recall that the exact formula is $m = (1 + c)/(r + c)$. When the reserve ratio (r) is high, the base multiplier is low. When the currency deposit ratio (c) is high, the base multiplier is low. (For example, suppose that r is .12. Then when $c = .2$ the money multiplier is about 3.8, and when $c = .4$ the money multiplier is about 2.3.) The reserve ratio and the currency deposit ratio will depend on the interest rate and consumer preferences.

As a close approximation, the ratio of reserves to deposits is equal to the *required* reserve ratio .12 and will therefore not change by much as long as reserve requirements are not changed. Suppose also that the currency deposit ratio is constant, independent of the interest rate. In that case, the relation between the monetary base and M_1 is one of strict proportionality. The multiplier m is constant. To hold M_1 at a prescribed level, all the Fed has to do is keep the base at the corresponding level. The money stock cannot shift when the base is held constant.

For two reasons, however, the money multiplier is not constant and is likely to be affected by interest rates.

First, recall that some reserves are held in excess of required reserves. These excess reserves decline when interest rates rise because reserves do not pay interest. Hence, r declines when interest rates rise. On this account, the money multiplier m increases when interest rates rise. Conversely, the money multiplier will decline when interest rates fall. Although this effect is

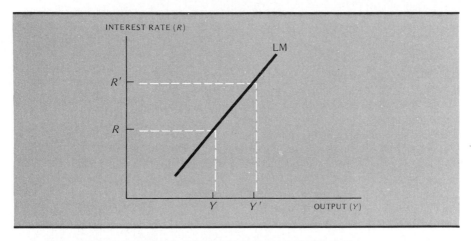

Figure 12–4. LM CURVE WITH A MONEY SUPPLY (M_1) TARGET.
This LM curve is identical to the one derived in Chapter 5. The LM curve shows all the possible combinations of GNP and the interest rate when the price level is held constant. Because the Fed is holding the money supply constant, a higher level of GNP requires a higher interest rate. When GNP rises from Y to Y', the interest rate rises from R to R'. The LM curve could look very different if the Fed were using a different policy rule.

probably small, it means that the Fed will have to decrease the base when interest rates rise in order to keep M_1 on a fixed target.

Second, the currency deposit ratio will also depend on the interest rate. The demand for checking balances is probably more sensitive to interest rates than is the demand for currency. High interest rates make the public economize on checking balances relative to paper money. Thus, when interest rates rise the multiplier goes down. The Fed has to raise the base in order to keep M_1 at its prescribed level.

The LM curve for a money supply target is simply an upward sloping line shown in Figure 12–4, the same line we derived in Chapter 5. We will want to compare the slope of this line with the other two policies: the interest rate target and the monetary base target.

INTEREST RATE TARGET

Under the second policy the Fed is to keep the interest rate at a prescribed level. This is a very different policy. Under this policy, the base would change every day as necessary to keep interest rates at the target. If the demand schedule shifted upward because of a higher level of GNP, the supply of the monetary base would rise by enough to intersect the monetary base demand curve at the same interest rate. Thus, the LM curve is a horizontal line at the prescribed interest rate, as shown in Figure 12–5.

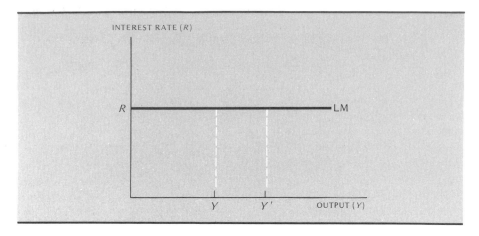

Figure 12–5. THE LM CURVE WITH AN INTEREST RATE TARGET.
When the Fed is keeping the interest rate at the prescribed level R the LM curve is a horizontal line at that interest rate. When GNP rises from Y to Y′, the interest rate does not change.

GNP TARGET

The third policy is for the Fed to keep GNP at a prescribed level. The Fed's operating policy rule is to expand and contract the base as necessary to keep GNP on target. Under this policy, the LM curve is simply a *vertical* line. If an event elsewhere in the economy causes interest rates to rise, the Fed's operating rule would call for it to lower the base as needed to keep real GNP on target. The event would stimulate GNP if the Fed were pegging the money supply, but, instead, the Fed is "leaning against the wind" to keep GNP constant. Note that targeting GNP may be more difficult for the trading desk than targeting interest rates because GNP is observed with a lag.

12.5 How the Fed's Rule Determines the Effect of Fiscal Policy

Suppose that the Fed holds the money supply constant, so that the LM curve is upward sloping—neither perfectly vertical nor perfectly horizontal. Now consider a fiscal stimulus which increases aggregate demand and GNP rises. At a higher level of GNP, with no change in interest rates, consumption and investment will be higher. This increase will be partly offset by higher imports. But if GNP rises and interest rates remain the same, the money market will be out of balance. Higher interest rates are needed to offset the higher money demand that goes with higher GNP. Higher interest rates depress investment and possibly consumption. They also cause the dollar to appreciate and so depress net exports. Consequently, the rise in GNP is dampened. The IS-LM analysis sorts out all of these considerations and finds the point where both GNP and the interest rate have risen by just the right amount to restore expenditure balance and equality of demand and supply for the monetary base.

Diminished private spending in response to higher government spending is called **crowding out.** Since the Fed can control the slope of the LM curve it can control crowding out. But crowding out also depends on the interest rate sensitivity of the demand for money. If account-holders can benefit from higher interest rates by leaving funds in their checking accounts rather than shifting to other investments, the LM curve will be steeper.

Consider how the other two policy rules for the Fed can influence the effect of fiscal policy. Suppose that the Fed tries to keep the interest rate constant. Under this policy, the Fed eliminates the feedback effects of interest rates that normally limit the ramifications of fiscal policy. Investment, consumption, and net exports are not held back by a rise in the interest rate. GNP rises by the full amount of the rightward shift in the IS curve. A monetary policy that keeps interest rates constant when fiscal policy changes is said to **accommodate** the fiscal policy. This is illustrated in Figure 12–6.

At the other extreme, suppose the Fed adjusts the monetary base as necessary to keep GNP constant. In this case, the negative feedback effect through the interest rate is complete. Fiscal policy raises the interest rate without altering GNP. However, the composition of GNP may well be changed. If the fiscal stimulus takes the form of higher government purchases of goods and services, consumption, investment, and net exports must fall if GNP is to remain the same. The interest rate rises by enough to depress these categories

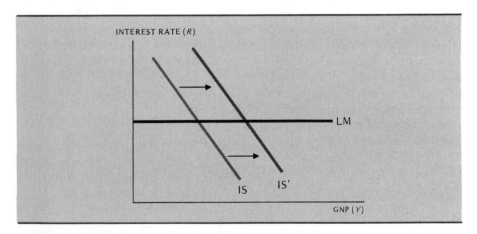

Figure 12–6. FISCAL EXPANSION WITH A HORIZONTAL LM CURVE.
When the Fed conducts monetary policy by holding the interest rate at a prescribed level, the LM curve is a horizontal line. When the IS curve shifts to the right on account of a fiscal stimulus, the result is a large increase in GNP and no change in the interest rate.

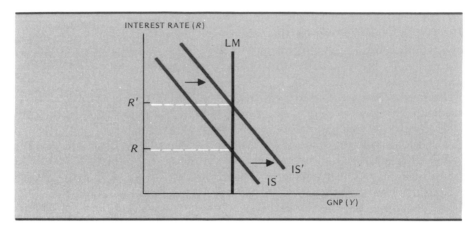

Figure 12–7. FISCAL EXPANSION WITH A VERTICAL LM CURVE.
When the Fed conducts monetary policy so as to keep GNP constant, the LM curve is vertical. A shift in the IS curve has no effect on GNP—it only raises the interest rate.

of spending just enough to offset the increase in government purchases. Similarly, if the fiscal stimulus comes from higher transfers and lower taxes, higher interest rates depress investment and net exports by enough to offset the increase in consumption. Then the LM curve is a vertical line and fiscal policy does not affect GNP at all, as shown in Figure 12–7.

12.6 Unavoidable Shocks to the IS Curve and LM Curve

One of the factors that enter into the choice of policy rule for the Fed—that is, how steep an LM curve should it establish—is the likelihood of unanticipated and unavoidable shifts in these curves. Suppose, for example, that the IS curve shifts around a lot because of erratic investment demand. The situation is illustrated in Figure 12–8. Then the best thing for the Fed to do is maintain a steep LM curve. Any drop in investment thereby brings a drop in interest rates, which mitigates the decline in investment.

But suppose that the LM curve shifts repeatedly, perhaps because of changes in financial technology or changes in the public's desire to hold currency. Then the steep LM curve is not a good idea. A flat LM curve would result in fewer of these financial shocks affecting aggregate demand. This is shown in Figure 12–9.[11]

As we mentioned earlier in this chapter, the Fed has placed less emphasis on the money supply and more emphasis on interest rates in recent years. In

[11] The idea that random shocks are important for deciding how steep the LM curve should be was first shown by William Poole, "The Optimal Choice of Monetary Policy in a Simple Stochastic Macro Model," *Quarterly Journal of Economics,* Vol. 84 (May 1970), pp. 197–216.

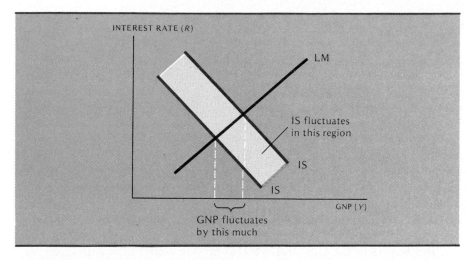

Figure 12–8.   RANDOM SHIFTS IN THE IS CURVE.
The band around the IS curve illustrates the random shifts. A steep LM curve insulates real GNP from such shifts.

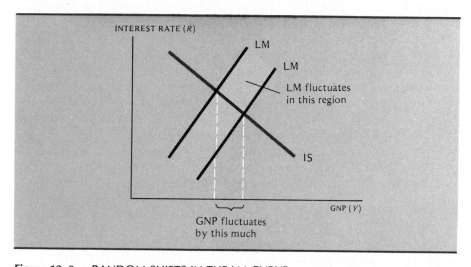

Figure 12–9.   RANDOM SHIFTS IN THE LM CURVE.
Now it is better for the Fed to maintain a flat LM curve. Interest rate pegging would be a good idea.

fact, it apparently abandoned M_1 targets in early 1987. One of the rationales for this shift is given by the analysis of this section: Shocks to the LM curve have become more serious in the last few years (see, for example, the huge downward shift in velocity in the figure in the box on page 342). With more uncertainty about the LM curve, interest-rate rather than money targeting is the appropriate policy rule for the Fed.

12.7 Lags in the Effect of Monetary Policy

Monetary policy does not control the demand for goods and services directly. There is usually a lag in its effect. There are two principal channels of monetary policy and both act through interest rates: the response of investment and the response of net exports through the depreciation of the dollar.

In Chapter 9, we stressed the lags in the investment process. Businesses take months to get almost any investment plan into effect; those involving the construction of new plants or the ordering of special equipment can take years. Housing investment takes six months or a year to respond strongly to a change in the interest rate.

Less is known about the lags in the response of net exports to dollar depreciation. Exchange rates respond immediately to changes in the interest rate. But buyers in the U.S. and overseas do not switch their purchases immediately when U.S. goods become cheaper. Americans who have learned that Japanese cars offer good value do not immediately reconsider U.S.-produced alternatives when the value of the dollar declines causing the dollar price of Japanese cars to rise. It takes time for foreigners to discover the advantage of American products as well.

The peak effect of monetary expansion on GNP probably occurs between one and two years after the expansion. At first, a monetary expansion drives down the interest rate without much effect on GNP. The money market handles the monetary expansion through lower interest rates instead of higher GNP. After a year or so, the response of spending to the interest rate is stronger and GNP expands.

The lag in the economy's response to monetary expansion greatly complicates the conduct of monetary policy. As we have mentioned before, recessions generally hit the economy by surprise. The Fed learns that the economy is headed for trouble only a few months before the trouble is at its worst. It can step on the gas to try to head off the recession, but the peak effect of the stimulus will occur well after the worst part of the recession. In fact, if the recession is brief and is followed by a brisk recovery, the monetary stimulus may hit hardest when it is least needed; in the worst case, it can worsen the boom that follows the recession.

Because the main effect of monetary expansion occurs in the year after the expansion is launched, when formulating monetary policy the Fed must always think about the likely conditions in the economy a year in the future. Even if the economy is in bad shape this year, the Fed will not expand if it anticipates that the economy will recover on its own by next year. There is little the Fed can do to help the economy this year; any stimulus it adds now will only create problems next year.

The Fed never knows with any confidence what will happen in the future. Even if it does not know confidently that the economy will be in good shape on its own next year, the Fed will not take vigorous action this year. If it is 50 percent likely that the economy will be below potential next year and 50 percent likely that it will be above potential, the best action for the Fed is to do nothing. As a general matter, the more uncertain the Fed is about conditions next year, the more cautious it will be about policy actions this year.

Lags in Monetary Policy

1. Monetary policy operates through interest rates. Consequently, there is a lag before the policy influences GNP.

2. The evidence suggests that the peak effect of monetary policy on GNP occurs after a lag of between one and two years.

3. Today's monetary policy has to be formulated with the state of the economy a year from now in mind. Even if GNP is well below potential, it may not be desirable to launch a monetary expansion.

4. Uncertainty about the future state of the economy adds to the caution of monetary policy-makers.

5. The net effect is to limit the monetary policy to much smaller adjustments than would be used if the effect of the policy occurred instantly.

12.8 Coordinated Fiscal and Monetary Policy

Fiscal expansion raises GNP and raises the interest rate. Monetary expansion raises GNP and lowers the interest rate. Therefore, mixes of fiscal and monetary policies can bring any desired combination of changes in GNP and the interest rate. For example, to raise GNP and keep the interest rate constant, an expansionary monetary and expansionary fiscal policy could be combined. To raise the interest rate and keep GNP constant, a combination of expansionary fiscal policy and contractionary monetary policy could be used.

Frequently the actual mix of monetary and fiscal policy comes under heavy criticism because it leaves the interest rate too high. In 1981, for example, when President Reagan came into office, monetary and fiscal policies were combined to give high interest rates for the level of GNP. An expansionary fiscal policy was launched. It granted large tax cuts to consumers and significant investment incentives to businesses. A contractionary monetary policy to reduce inflation begun a little over a year earlier was endorsed by the Reagan administration and continued at the Fed under the direction of chairman Paul Volcker. The result was just as suggested by the IS-LM analysis—interest rates rose.

The mix of policies pursued early in the Reagan administration is one that would be expected to bring a large federal deficit. The tax cut contributed directly to the deficit by reducing federal revenue. Monetary contraction added to the deficit by keeping GNP at low levels, limiting revenue and increasing transfer payments. Another contributor to the deficit was the very high level of interest rates. Higher rates added to the federal government's interest bill. The deficit was $146 billion in 1982, $176 billion in 1983, $170 billion in 1984, $198 billion in 1985, and $204 billion in 1986.

The choice between monetary and fiscal policy is also influenced by international considerations. A monetary expansion lowers the exchange rate. A fiscal contraction lowers the exchange rate. To keep GNP constant and lower the exchange rate a combination of monetary expansion and fiscal contraction would be appropriate.

Because U.S. policy influences the international value of the dollar and the current account, policy-makers who are concerned about those two indicators lose some of their freedom of action. To take an extreme case, suppose U.S. policy were dedicated to keeping the value of the dollar at a constant level relative to the average of the Deutschemark, the British pound, and the yen. In effect, U.S. interest rates would have to be kept at the same level as average rates in Germany, Britain, and Japan. Any fiscal expansion would have to be countered with a monetary expansion. Normally, a fiscal expansion would raise U.S. interest rates and cause the dollar to appreciate. The parallel monetary expansion would keep interest rates at their original level and prevent the appreciation.

A policy-maker who is concerned about the current-account deficit will be constrained in a different way. If the deficit is to be kept small, expansionary fiscal policy must be ruled out. A large government deficit is likely to bring a large current-account deficit, as we indicated earlier.

Review and Practice

MAJOR POINTS

1. A monetary system is an agreement on the way to quote prices and convey purchasing power.

2. In the United States the Fed issues currency and also reserves. Reserves are accounts at the Fed equivalent to currency. The sum of currency and reserves is the monetary base.

3. Through open-market operations, the Fed can set the monetary base to whatever level it chooses. To increase the base, the Fed purchases government bonds and issues new reserves to pay for the purchase. To decrease the base, the Fed sells government bonds.

4. The three major motives for holding money are as follows: the transactions demand; as a way to store wealth; and to pay the bank for the services it provides.

5. The Fed's policy rule determines the LM curve. A policy of targeting M_1 gives a steep but not vertical LM curve. A policy of targeting the interest rate gives a horizontal LM curve. A policy of targeting GNP gives a vertical LM curve.

6. The effects of a fiscal stimulus depend on the Fed's policy rule. If the Fed chooses a horizontal LM curve by targeting the interest rate, fiscal stimulus raises GNP strongly. If the Fed chooses a vertical or near-vertical LM curve by targeting GNP, then fiscal stimulus raises interest rates but has little or no effect on GNP.

7. Monetary policy influences GNP with a lag. The immediate effect of monetary stimulus is to lower interest rates. After the lags in investment and foreign trade work themselves out, the stimulus raises GNP. Because of the lag and because of the Fed's uncertainty about the future, monetary policy needs to be used with caution.

8. Fiscal and monetary policy can be used in tandem to achieve any desired combination of GNP and the interest rate. Fiscal and monetary expansion together can raise GNP without changing the interest rate. Fiscal expansion and monetary contraction can raise the interest rate without changing GNP. Monetary expansion and fiscal contraction can lower the interest rate without changing GNP.

9. Monetary policy influences the exchange rate and net exports. Monetary expansion makes the dollar depreciate but has an ambiguous effect on the trade deficit.

KEY TERMS AND CONCEPTS

Means of payment	Monetary base	Compensating balances
Unit of account	Reserve requirements	Open-market operation
Currency	Transactions motive	Discount rate
Reserves	Precautionary motive	Interest rate target
Checking deposits	Speculative motive	M_1 target
Money supply	Store of wealth	GNP target
Financial intermediaries		

QUESTIONS FOR DISCUSSION AND REVIEW

1. Why is the dollar the unit of account and the medium of exchange in the United States?

2. In what sense do commercial banks play a role as financial intermediaries? What other role do they play in determining the nation's money supply?

3. Why doesn't the Fed have separate control over both the quantities of reserves and currency?

4. Why do some banks borrow reserves from the Fed? How does the Fed decide on the discount rate on these borrowings?

5. How does the Fed control the monetary base? What types of open-market operations increase the monetary base?

6. Why do banks require businesses to maintain compensating balances on deposits at the banks rather than simply charging them a service charge?

7. Does the demand for currency depend on the real rate of interest or on the nominal rate of interest?

8. How does the Fed choose the slope of the LM curve?

9. Why might the Fed choose a vertical LM curve? A horizontal one?

10. What happens when monetary policy is contractionary and fiscal policy is expansionary?

PROBLEMS

Numerical

1. Suppose that money demand is given by the expression in Equation 12–8,

$$M = \sqrt{\frac{kY}{2R_o}}$$

where the opportunity cost of holding money is given by the expression in Equation 12–11,

$$R_o = q_1 R - q_0$$

and the transaction cost k is equal to 2.

a. Assuming $q_1=1$ and $q_0=.06$, what is the level of money demand at $Y=2,500$ and $R=.08$? Suppose the money supply is set equal to this value. Find the interest rate at which money supply equals money demand for $Y=1,000$ and $Y=4,000$. Plot the points to scale on a graph.

b. Now let $q_1=.25$ and $q_0=0$. Find the level of money demand at $Y=2,500$ and $R=.08$. Again, supposing that the money supply is set equal to this value, find the interest rate at which money supply equals money demand for the values of Y given in Part a. Plot these points on the same graph.

c. Suppose the Fed's policy rule is to target M. For which values of q_0 and q_1 given above will the LM curve be steeper? Give a brief economic interpretation of your result.

d. How does the change in the parameters given in this problem parallel recent economic history? What events have triggered this change? Given this change, are spending shocks more or less destabilizing to output than they were before?

2. In this problem we consider the relationship between monetary policy and the financing of the deficit.

a. Suppose that the reserve ratio, r, is equal to .1, and the currency ratio, c, is equal to .2. Assume that $G-T+F=\$200$ billion. By how much would the money supply, the monetary base, currency, and bank reserves have to change if the Fed were to finance the entire budget deficit?

b. Suppose now that the money supply is initially equal to $600 billion with output equal to potential. Suppose further that potential output is increasing by 2 percent per year, prices are expected to grow by 3 percent, and monetary velocity is expected to remain constant. If the Fed wishes to keep output at potential, what percentage of the deficit will it finance?

3. Suppose that the required reserve ratio is .12 for deposits and that there are no

excess reserves. Suppose also that the total demand for currency is equal to .3 times deposits.

a. If total reserves are $40 billion, what is the level of the money supply?

b. By how much does the money supply change if the Fed increases the required reserve ratio to .20? Assume that total reserves are unchanged at $40 billion.

c. By how much does the money supply change if the Fed purchases $1 billion of government bonds in the open market? (Keep the required reserve ratio at .12.)

Analytical

1. Suppose that as a result of recent tax cuts, the amount of activity in the underground economy was significantly reduced.

   a. What effect would this have on the demand for currency?

   b. Explain why such a change would have an expansionary effect on the economy (holding the Fed's open-market operations fixed).

   c. Describe the Fed's response to such a change under each of the three policy rules discussed in Section 12.4.

2. Use Equation 12–8 to write an expression for real money demand as a function of real income and real transactions costs. Assuming that nominal income and nominal transactions costs increase proportionately with changes in the price level, describe how real money demand is affected by a change in prices. How is the nominal demand for money affected?

3. Consider the following cash management problem. An undergraduate student earns $400 a month which she uses to meet personal expenses. All expenses are paid for in cash. She maintains a savings account at a local bank which pays 1 percent per month (12 percent annually) in interest. At the beginning of each month she deposits her $400 paycheck in her savings account, and makes periodic cash withdrawals throughout the month. Cash withdrawals are made through an automatic teller at a service charge of 25 cents each.

   a. Calculate the student's average currency holdings and the number of withdrawals made each month.

   b. Suppose it's observed that the student always withdraws $40. There are several possible explanations. Perhaps she doesn't wish to risk losing larger amounts of cash. Protection against such loss is one of the benefits of a savings account. In addition, she may wish to avoid the temptation of spending more money than she can really afford. Call this the "piggy bank" value of savings accounts. What must the value of such benefits be, expressed as a rate of return, in order for her withdrawals of $40 to be optimal?

4. Suppose that competition in the credit card industry drives down the cost of using credit cards.

   a. How is that likely to affect money demand? Illustrate the macroeconomic impact using an IS-LM diagram.

   b. If the Fed is aware of such a trend, but cannot be certain of its timing, what kind of policy rule should it use?

5. Explain the effect that a lowering of the discount rate has on the money supply. In particular, consider the effect of such a change on the money multiplier and the monetary base.

6. Suppose that banks began both to pay market rates of interest on all checking accounts and to charge the full costs of providing such accounts. These costs would not be waived, regardless of one's average balance. Describe the possible effects of such a change on money demand?

7. The velocity of money, V, is defined by the expression

$$V = PY/M.$$

A policy rule frequently used by the Fed can be described as follows. First, it is assumed that the velocity of money remains roughly constant from year to year. Next, the Fed forecasts this year's rate of inflation (which is viewed as being predetermined, and thus beyond their control). Finally, the Fed chooses its target rate of growth for real output. This results in a target rate of growth for the money stock.
   a. Suppose that inflation for the current year is forecasted to be 5 percent and that the Fed's target rate of growth for output is 2 percent. By how much should it increase the money stock this year?
   b. Suppose now that money demand is given by the expression

$$M/P = kY - hR.$$

   Derive an expression for the velocity of money, V. On what does V depend?
   c. What kinds of changes in the economy could affect V? Consider both the cases where $h>0$ and $h=0$.
   d. Explain why the policy rule described above is only useful when money demand is not very sensitive to interest rates.

8. Suppose that the U.S. government budget deficit is reduced through a cut in government purchases.
   a. First assume that the Fed targets the *money supply* and does not change the target when the budget deficit is reduced. What happens to the exchange rate, net exports, and private saving? Use an IS-LM diagram and an aggregate demand curve with a price line to illustrate your answer. Be sure to distinguish between the short-run and the long-run effects, and describe in words how the economy adjusts over time as prices adjust.
   b. Now assume that the Fed targets the *interest rate* and does not change the target when the budget deficit is reduced. Answer the questions in Part a for this alternative Fed policy. Explain your answer using diagrams.

9. Monetary policy is one of the most hotly debated issues in macroeconomics. Yet, the policy implications of the IS-LM model would seem to be rather clear: As suming that the Fed wishes to maintain output at potential, simply set the LM curve to intersect the IS curve at Y^*. Provide a brief explanation of why monetary policy isn't so simple a matter.

PART III

The Micro
Foundations of
Aggregate
Supply and Price
Adjustment

13

Aggregate Supply and Economic Growth

An economy in which prices and wages are perfectly flexible is always exactly in full employment because wages and prices can adjust instantaneously to offset the effect of disturbances. The full-employment economy is an abstraction, but it provides a useful framework that economists employ when they want to focus on the problems of long-term growth of potential output, rather than on short-run economic fluctuations. In the longer run, the U.S. economy behaves in the way described in the flexible-price economy.

The **aggregate supply** of productive factors—labor and capital—is the driving force determining total output in the full-employment economy. Monetary policy determines the price level and the inflation rate, but the money supply has no effect on total output. Fiscal policy determines the division of output among consumption, investment, net exports, and government purchases. Because fiscal policy influences investment, it affects the growth of physical capital and thereby the long-run growth of aggregate supply. We will also see that fiscal policy—in particular tax policy—can influence the growth of potential output by altering the supply of labor.

Macroeconomic models that assume flexible prices and wages bear the name **classical,** because it was this assumption that was used by the classical economists of the early twentieth century—for example, Alfred Marshall and A. C. Pigou of Cambridge University. In the 1930s, John Maynard Keynes began to emphasize the importance of wage and price rigidities.

The classical models still play an important role in economic analysis. The term **neoclassical growth model** is sometimes used to refer to the classical model because it was revived in the 1950s to study the problem of long-term growth.

13.1 The Microeconomics of the Labor and Capital Markets

We have already shown that a firm's production can be represented by a **production function** that governs how much output can be obtained from a specified amount of labor and capital. As we showed in Chapter 6, aggregate supply, or potential output, in the economy can be similarly described by an aggregate production function that relates total output to total labor and capital inputs:

$$Y = F(N,K), \tag{13-1}$$

where Y is output, N is employment, and K is the stock of capital. Because aggregate supply depends on labor and capital, the microeconomics of aggregate supply can be approached through the microeconomics of the capital and labor markets.

In Chapter 9 we discussed the microeconomics of the capital market: the demand and supply for capital. The *demand* for capital K depends negatively on the rental price of capital. The *supply* of capital depends on the amount of saving that has occurred in the past. As an accounting identity, saving equals investment, and the capital stock is the accumulated investment of the past. The stock of capital is a predetermined variable set by past investment and saving decisions. Time must pass for investment to occur and for the capital stock to change.

As for the microeconomics of the labor market, Figure 13–1 shows how

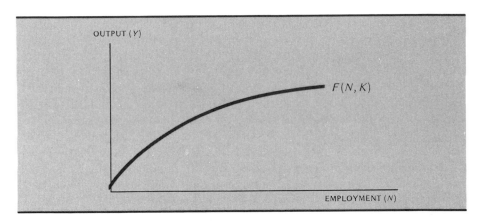

Figure 13-1.   THE PRODUCTION FUNCTION IN TERMS OF LABOR INPUT.
With a given capital stock, the volume of output Y produced from various levels of employment N shows diminishing marginal product.

production depends on labor for a given capital stock. The production function curves toward the horizontal axis. The **marginal product of labor** declines as the amount of employment increases. Recall that the marginal product of labor is the additional output that is produced by one additional unit of work. The marginal product of labor is the slope of the production function in Figure 13–1. Note how the production function gets less steep as more labor is employed.

THE DEMAND FOR LABOR

If the labor market is competitive and firms take the market wage and the market price of their product as given, then they will choose the level of employment so that the marginal product of labor equals the real wage. The real wage is the dollar wage W divided by the price level P; that is, W/P. This demand for employment is implied by profit maximization. If firms had employment below this level, the marginal product of labor would exceed the real wage and an opportunity for improved profit would exist. A firm could hire a worker for the wage W, produce more output in the amount given by the marginal product of labor, sell that output at price P, and make a profit on the deal. Firms will pursue this opportunity for profit until their additional hiring pushes the marginal product of labor down to the real wage. The point of maximum profit is shown in Figure 13–2.

The demand function for labor is a negative function of the real wage because the marginal product of labor declines with increased labor input, as shown in Figure 13–3.

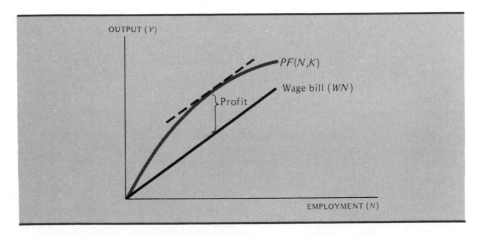

Figure 13–2. PROFIT MAXIMIZATION.
Profit is the difference between the value of output, P times $F(N,K)$, and the wage bill, W times N. It reaches a maximum when the slope of P times $F(N,K)$ equals the slope of W times N; that is, the value of the marginal product of labor equals the wage.

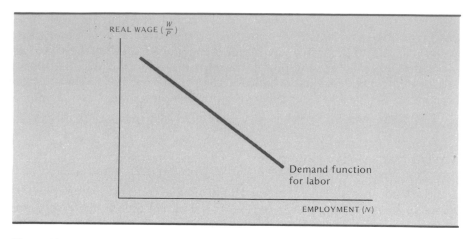

Figure 13–3. THE DEMAND FUNCTION FOR LABOR.
The demand function for labor is a downward-sloping relation between the real wage,
W/P, and the level of employment, N. For each real wage, it gives the level of employment that firms will choose by equating the marginal product of labor to the real wage.

THE SUPPLY OF LABOR

The supply of labor is determined by the decisions of individual workers about how much of their time to spend working. Some people have the alternative of spending time away from work. The real wage determines the incentive to work. At higher real wages, the incentive to enter the labor market is stronger and, on that account, people will want to work more. However, for most people, wages are the dominant source of income. At higher wages, they are better off. People who are better off choose to spend more time at home and away from the job. On this account, higher real wages bring lower labor supply. Microeconomic theory labels these two contrasting influences the substitution effect and the income effect.

Microeconomic Estimates of Income and Substitution Effects in Labor Supply

Many labor economists have attempted to measure the size of the income and substitution effects in labor supply by looking at individual behavior. The earliest studies were based on samples of individuals for a single year. More recently researchers have used *panel* data sets in which the hours of work and the wage rate of thousands of individuals are observed for a number of years. Panel data sets were discussed in Chapter 8 on consumption. Other recent studies are based on negative income tax *experiments* in the 1960s and 1970s. In these experiments, groups of individuals were given a cash grant and then taxed at a higher rate on additional income. Other groups—the control groups —were not given a cash grant and faced the normal tax rates. By comparing the experimental groups with the control groups the size of the income effect and the substitution effect could be directly estimated.

The table below summarizes the findings of several researchers who have used panel and experimental data on employment behavior in the United States. In all cases total labor supply elasticity is small and sometimes negative, indicating a steep or even backward-sloping labor supply curve. Hence, there is much empirical support for the steep labor supply curve.

However, the estimates of the substitution and income effects have a wider variation. In some studies the substitution effects are quite large, but in others they are small, sometimes even negative. Unfortunately, this wide variation in estimates of substitution effects makes it difficult to calculate with much certainty the impact on labor supply of tax rate changes that hold income constant.

Researchers	Labor Supply Elasticity	=	Substitution Effect	+	Income Effect
Panel Data					
Orley Ashenfelter, James Heckman	−.15		.12		−.27
Farrel Bloch	.06		.12		−.06
Michael Boskin	−.29		.12		−.41
John Ham	−.16		−.05		−.11
Jerry Hausman, Paul Ruud	−.08		.55		−.63
Marvin Kosters	−.10		.04		−.14
Terrence Wales, A.D. Woodland	.14		.84		−.70
Experimental Data					
Jerry Hausman and David Wise	.10		.11		−.01
Terry Johnson and John Pencavel	.02		.19		−.17
Michael Keely and Phillip Robins	−.09		.05		−.14

Source: John Pencavel, "Labor Supply of Men: A Survey," in O. Ashenfelter (ed.), *Handbook of Labor Economics*, Amsterdam, North-Holland, 1987.

Substitution Effect. As something becomes more expensive, people substitute away from it. In the case of labor supply, as time at home becomes more expensive (as its opportunity cost, the real wage, rises) people substitute away from time at home and toward time in the labor market. To put it another way, the real wage provides an incentive for work, and people substitute toward work when the real wage rises.

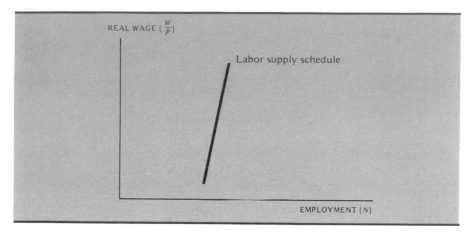

Figure 13–4. LABOR SUPPLY SCHEDULE.
The labor supply schedule gives the amount of labor offered in the labor market for various levels of the real wage. At higher real wages, the incentive to work is greater, but people have more income, and this tends to offset the incentive. The evidence suggests that the labor supply schedule is almost vertical.

Income Effect. As income rises, people tend to consume more of most things. In this case, they consume more of their own time at home and offer less of their time in the labor market. Higher real wages make people better off and they work less on that account.

The labor supply schedule, illustrated in Figure 13–4, shows the net effect of these two offsetting influences. Research by a number of economists has agreed rather closely that the net effect of the two influences of the real wage on labor supply is roughly zero.[1] However, it is important to keep in mind that the agreement is that the net effect is zero, not that each of its components is zero. The substitution effect, prompting people to work more when the real wage rises, has been shown to be strong in some studies. In these studies the income effect happens to be equally strong in the opposite direction. If the substitution effect is large then an increase in work incentives without an increase in income could increase labor supply dramatically.

EMPLOYMENT WITH FLEXIBLE WAGES AND PRICES

If both the wage W and price P can adjust, then the real wage W/P can also adjust. Employment in the labor market occurs at the intersection of

---

[1] The most recent econometric studies have used experimental data or panel data of the type we described in Chapter 8 in our analysis of consumption (see page 363 for a summary). A useful survey of available results is found in John Pencavel, "Labor Supply of Men: A Survey," in Orley Ashenfelter (ed.), *Handbook of Labor Economics,* Amsterdam, North-Holland, 1987.

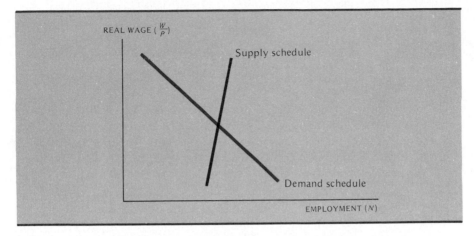

Figure 13–5.   LABOR MARKET EQUILIBRIUM.
In the model with perfectly flexible wages and prices, the real wage fluctuates to equate the supply and demand for labor. There is no unemployment.

the supply and demand schedules. This is shown in Figure 13–5. At the real wage W/P, the quantity of labor N chosen by firms equals the quantity supplied by the public. The labor market is in a standard microeconomic equilibrium. Unemployment cannot occur—if the real wage were too high to provide jobs for everyone interested, the real wage would fall, stimulating labor demand by firms and discouraging labor supply by workers. It would fall immediately to the point where supply and demand were equal and unemployment disappeared.

An interesting and important feature of the model with flexible wages and prices is that the level of output in any one year is determined solely by the labor market. We showed above how the level of employment and the real wage are determined at the intersection of the supply and demand schedules. At any point in time the stock of capital K is predetermined by past investment decisions. The level of output comes immediately from putting the level of employment N and the predetermined level of the capital stock K into the production function $Y = F(N,K)$. The labor market is dominant in this model because it determines aggregate supply, or potential output. And with perfectly flexible wages and prices, output is always equal to potential output.

Full Employment with Flexible Wages and Prices

1. The classical model assumes that wages and prices are completely flexible. It uses basic microeconomic principles to study the capital and labor markets and describe the equilibrium level of employment, capital, and output.

2. With flexible wages and prices, the real wage moves immediately to the level that equates the demand for labor to the supply.

3. The demand for labor is determined by employers. They choose the level of employment that equates the marginal product of labor to the real wage.

4. The supply of labor is determined by workers. The real wage has two roles in labor supply—it provides the incentive to work and it provides most families the bulk of their income. A higher real wage has substitution and income effects in the opposite directions. Consequently, labor supply is not very sensitive to the real wage.

13.2 The Natural Rate of Employment

When the labor market is in equilibrium, at full employment, not everyone who wants to work has a job. Unemployment is a feature of the economy even at full employment. In fact, there is unemployment even when the economy is in a boom. In 1969, for example, during the Vietnam War period when the economy was operating way above capacity, the unemployment rate was 3.4 percent. Although excess unemployment is a sign of excess supply of labor, there is a certain level of unemployment, which we saw in Chapter 3, called the natural rate of unemployment, which exists even without excess supply.

Part of the unemployment present in equilibrium is *frictional*. Every month, millions of people move from one activity to another. In the spring, for example, high school and college students finish the school year and move into the labor market, hoping for either summer work or permanent work. Even more important, people are constantly changing jobs, either because they feel they can find better jobs or because their earlier jobs have ended. Frictional unemployment occurs because it takes time for people to find jobs. During the period when they are looking, they count as unemployed.

Another reason that substantial unemployment exists even in equilibrium is that not every labor market is in equilibrium at the same time. Even when equilibrium prevails, roughly speaking, in the economy as a whole, some markets will have excess supply and some will have excess demand. In the 1980s, employers have had trouble finding software engineers at the same time that steel workers have been out of work in large numbers. The markets with excess supply contribute positive amounts of unemployment, but those with excess demand cannot have negative unemployment. The average unemployment rate must always be positive.

A third important reason for significant unemployment in equilibrium is the adverse experience suffered by certain groups in the labor market. Young people, members of racial minorities, and the unskilled contribute disproportionately to the unemployment that is found when the economy as a whole is at full employment. These people spend long periods between jobs because of their difficulty in finding work; to the extent that they meet the survey's requirement for having made some type of job-seeking effort in the four weeks before the survey, they are counted as unemployed. They tend to find jobs that last only a few months, so they are thrown back into the market fairly quickly. Of all the weeks of unemployment suffered in the economy, a large number is contributed by a fairly small fraction of the labor force who tend to spend many weeks each year looking for work and relatively few weeks working.[2]

We have been discussing unemployment in equilibrium. When the economy is out of equilibrium, unemployment can be above or below its natural rate. When it is above, all the types of unemployment we listed become more severe.

MEASURING THE NATURAL RATE OF UNEMPLOYMENT

Estimating the natural rate of unemployment is of course extremely important for policy-making. In 1987, for example, the unemployment rate dropped to just below 6 percent. If the natural rate of unemployment is 7 percent, then policy-makers should have become concerned that the economy was expanding at a dangerous pace. If the natural rate is 5.6 percent, then the economy could safely expand for a while longer.

Unfortunately, economists differ on how to measure the natural rate and on the numerical estimates they come up with. Some try to define the natural rate as the point of equilibrium where actual inflation equals expected inflation. That is, years when the rate of inflation turns out to be the same as the amount of expected inflation are years when the actual unemployment rate equals the natural rate. Such a measurement is dependent on a way of measuring expected inflation. Estimates of the natural rate from this approach vary from 5 to 7 percent. A consensus estimate might be 6 percent.

A more straightforward way to measure the natural rate is based on the idea that, over a sufficiently long span of years with about the same number of booms as slumps, the average unemployment rate should be equal to the natural rate. Sometimes the market is perturbed in one direction, sometimes in another. The average unemployment rate should be close to the natural rate.

[2] See Kim Clark and Lawrence Summers, "Labor Market Dynamics and Unemployment: A Reconsideration," *Brookings Papers on Economic Activity*, Vol. 1, 1979, pp. 13–61.

The average unemployment rate for all workers (including military personnel in the United States) from 1952 through 1986 was 5.6 percent. Based on the logic we just reviewed, this average can be considered an estimate of the natural rate of employment. But most economists would consider 5.6 percent an optimistic estimate of the natural rate in the 1980s.

One problem with this simple approach to measuring the natural rate is that the rate might be changing gradually over time, perhaps because of changes in the demographic composition of the labor force. For a number of reasons, the natural rate probably rose in the 1960s and 1970s. First, the fraction of the labor force that has particularly high turnover rates—teenagers and young adults—rose when the baby boomers left school and started work. The baby boom reached its peak birthrate in 1957, so the influx was most important in the mid- and late 1970s. The importance of this factor has declined in the 1980s. Second, the dispersion of disequilibrium across the sectors of the economy apparently rose in the 1970s and 1980s.[3] In particular, the steel and auto industries had substantial unemployment due first to the sharp increases in fuel prices and later to the strong dollar.

Average unemployment has been much higher since the early 1970s. The average unemployment rate rose from 4.7 percent for 1950–74 to 7.5 percent for 1975–86. This rise points in the direction of a higher natural rate but is not conclusive evidence. The later period saw three major events all pushing toward disequilibrium with unemployment above the natural rate. Two oil shocks raised unemployment, first in 1974 and again in 1979. An abrupt shift in monetary policy that successfully lowered inflation also pushed unemployment to extraordinary heights in 1982; the unemployment rate reached a peak of 10.6 percent in November 1982. It is possible that almost the entire period from 1975 through 1986 was one of unemployment above the natural rate. In other words, the single decade included in the computation of the recent average unemployment rate may not be long enough to average out disequilibrium to zero. It may take another decade of experience, we hope without so many adverse shocks, to reveal the current natural rate.

The Natural Rate of Unemployment

1. The natural rate is the amount of unemployment present when the overall economy is in equilibrium.

2. The natural rate is positive because people are continually entering the labor market to find work or moving from one job to another. Another reason is that some sectors may have excess supply even when the economy as a whole is at full employment. A third reason

---

[3] See David M. Lilien, "Sectoral Shifts and Cyclical Unemployment," *Journal of Political Economy,* Vol. 90 (August 1982), pp. 777–793.

is that some disadvantaged groups spend a large fraction of each year out of work.

3. The average amount of unemployment since 1950 has been 5.6 percent, and there is an argument that this is a good measure of the natural rate. However, there are reasons to believe that the natural rate rose in the 1970s and is still above 5.6 percent in the 1980s.

13.3 Long-Term Economic Growth

Compared to the fluctuations in actual output, potential output appears to grow rather steadily from year to year. The labor force increases, the capital stock usually rises, and productivity improves. We can study the process of growth with the production function. Because we are concerned about changes from one year to the next, we need to keep track of the dates of the variables involved. We do this with a subscript on the variable to indicate the year. Further, we need to set up the analysis so that the role of productivity improvement is made explicit.

We will define A_t as an index of *overall* productivity in year t. If A_t grows by 1 percent, it means that the economy can produce 1 percent more output from the same amount of labor and capital. A_t is a measure of **total factor productivity;** it incorporates the increased productivity of both labor and capital. Total productivity should be distinguished from labor productivity, which we discussed in Chapter 3. In terms of the production function, the productivity index fits into the analysis in the following way:

$$Y_t = A_t F(N_t, K_t). \tag{13-2}$$

The production function with the productivity index in front provides a way to determine the sources of growth of output. When output grows, it must be the result of some combination of growth in labor, in capital, and in productivity. In most years, all three forces are contributing.

There is a simple formula that growth specialists—economists such as Edward Denison of the Brookings Institution—use to assign credit for growth. The rate of growth of output equals the rate of growth of productivity plus the weighted rates of growth of labor and capital:

$$\Delta Y/Y = \Delta A/A + .7\Delta N/N + .3\Delta K/K. \tag{13-3}$$

The derivation of this formula is shown in Appendix A in this chapter. The growth formula shows how total growth relates to growth in the three determinants. In words the formula says that the rate of growth of output is equal to the rate of growth of productivity plus .7 times the rate of growth

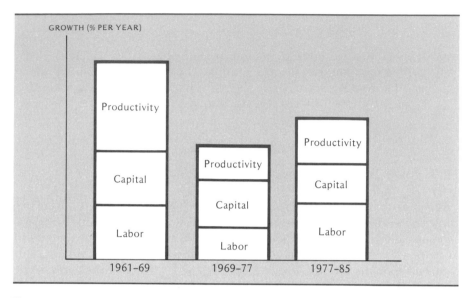

Figure 13–6. SOURCES OF GROWTH.
The height of each bar shows the actual annual growth rate of real GNP over 8-year intervals. Each bar is broken into blocks showing the contributions from labor growth, from capital growth, and from productivity growth. The contributions are calculated using Equation 13–3 in the text. Source: Data on real GNP growth and labor growth are from the *Economic Report of the President,* 1987, Tables B–2 and B–43. The capital stock data are calculated from investment data in the same source, Table B–2.

of labor input plus .3 times the rate of growth of capital input. What is interesting about the formula is its lack of dependence on the details of the production function. All that matters from the production function is the weight .3 and its complement .7. These can be derived from data on the relative shares of capital and labor in national income. In Chapter 2 we saw that these income shares are roughly .3 and .7.

The formula can be used to study the contributions of each factor to long-term growth in the United States over the last 30 years. In order to smooth out the business cycle fluctuations, it helps to look at average contributions over longer periods. The data are shown over 5-year intervals in Figure 13–6. Growth reached its peak in the mid-1960s. All three variables were at high levels at that time. Since then, productivity growth has fallen a lot, and capital growth has fallen. Only labor growth has remained at its earlier level.

13.4 Policies to Stimulate Growth

The government can influence all three of the determinants of growth—productivity, capital formation, and labor input. Disappointing rates of growth since the beginning of the 1970s have led to a number of federal policies to stimulate growth.

POLICIES TO IMPROVE PRODUCTIVITY

Of the three factors, productivity growth has fallen most significantly, and the idea of stimulating productivity has been attractive to policy-makers. But there have been few proposals for concrete action. Unfortunately, the process of improvement in productivity growth is not well understood by economists.

Perhaps the most important role that the government can play in improving productivity growth is in the area of education. In the United States, state and local governments provide most of the support for primary and secondary schools and universities. A highly skilled labor force is obviously a key ingredient to successful productivity growth.

The federal government also has played a role in sponsoring research in science and engineering. Many experts feel that the U.S. government could do more as have the governments of other countries such as Japan.

The tax legislation of 1981 provided tax incentives for research and development expenditures. Certain types of R&D became eligible for a special tax credit. If programs of R&D are an important source of productivity growth, then tax incentives like these should yield some further growth. The use of public funds for this purpose, through the tax system, is justified if the sponsors of R&D are unable to capture the full benefits themselves. R&D expenditures, which declined relative to GNP in the 1970s, have been increasing more rapidly in the 1980s. The increase apparently began before the tax incentives of 1981 so it may have been due to other factors.

POLICIES TO STIMULATE CAPITAL FORMATION

Until recently, government policy to stimulate growth concentrated almost entirely on capital formation. A rising capital stock will add to economic growth; our growth formula in the previous section made this clear. Numerically, an extra percentage point of capital growth will add about .3 percentage point to growth in output. To get an added 1 percent of growth in output, the capital stock would have to grow 3.3 percent per year.

Consider a numerical illustration. At the end of 1984, the capital stock was about $6,000 billion 1982 dollars, counting plants, equipment, housing, and inventories. The 3.3 percent growth in capital needed to add a point to growth of output would be

3.3 percent times $6,000 billion =

$198 billion in added investment (1982 dollars).

Total fixed investment in 1986 was $650 billion 1982 dollars. Investment would have to rise by $198/650 = 30$ percent to add just 1 percentage point to growth in output. Of course, 1 percent more growth would take us a long way to restoring the previous growth path that the United States experienced in the mid-1960s, and would compound itself to an impressive increase in living standards in 20 years. Moreover, it is possible that the increase in new plants and machines would bring forth additional technical innovations which could spur productivity growth.

Under the right combination of economic conditions, a large increase in investment is possible. For example, investment was at depressed levels in 1962 when President Kennedy sponsored the first investment tax credit. The new investment incentive plus generally expansive conditions caused investment to rise from $272 billion 1982 dollars in 1962 to $354 billion in 1966, an increase of 30 percent. If you look back at Figure 13–6, you will see that the contribution of capital to economic growth rose by over a percentage point in the mid-1960s.

Although an increase in investment of 30 percent is feasible, it does not appear to be sustainable. Output growth can be raised by a percentage point for a few years, but then investment tends to decline to more normal levels. For example, annual growth of the capital stock reached its peak from the Kennedy stimulus at 7 percent per year in 1966, but then subsided to about 5 percent through 1974. During most of this period, the investment tax credit was in effect. Between 1975 and 1982, the growth of the capital stock fluctuated between 1 and 4 percent per year. The investment credit was in effect at a higher rate throughout these disappointing years.

As we discussed in Chapter 9, the Tax Reform Act of 1986 repealed the investment tax credit and, although the corporate tax rate was also reduced, the overall effect is negative for the growth of total investment. On this account the recent tax reform is bad for economic growth. The discussion in Chapter 9 suggested that investment could drop by $60 billion as a result of tax reform. This would reduce real GNP by 1.5 percent. On the other hand, the tax reform eliminated some of the dispersion of tax rates in different industries and this should make the allocation of capital more efficient, thereby stimulating economic growth for a period of time.

Growth through Capital Formation

1. Because the coefficient of capital growth in the growth formula is about .3, it takes about 3.3 percent of growth in capital to add 1 percent to output growth.

2. In 1986, it would have taken a 30 percent increase in the amount of investment to raise the growth of the capital stock by 3.3 percent.

3. Increases of this magnitude in investment have occurred in the past, but only when special incentives were combined with other favorable conditions. Even then, the high levels of investment were sustained only for a few years.

POLICIES TO INCREASE LABOR SUPPLY

In the growth equation, employment growth has over twice the leverage of capital growth. Each percentage point of extra growth of employment adds .7 percent to output growth. To put it the other way around, it takes 1.4 percent of added employment growth to increase output growth by 1 percent per year. One of the main rationales for President Reagan's 1981 tax cuts was the improvement of work incentives—a "supply-side" rationale advocated strongly by supply-siders such as economist Arthur Laffer and Congressman Jack Kemp. The Tax Reform Act of 1986, which lowered tax rates further, has a similar rationale.

The income tax depresses the incentive to work by reducing the wage that workers receive for their work. On this account, one might expect that a cut in income taxes would stimulate work by improving incentives. A prime selling point of the supply-side policies put into place in 1981 was precisely this incentive argument. But a cut in income taxes also makes people better off, which depresses labor supply. The net effect of a simple tax cut could therefore be quite small. This is illustrated in Figure 13–7. If the labor supply curve is steep, as statistical evidence seems to suggest, the intersection of supply and demand occurs at almost the same level of employment. A prediction of large stimulus to employment and output from tax cuts would be contrary to the evidence.

Supply-side policies need not take the exclusive form of tax cuts. In fact, the federal government's need for revenue makes it impossible to improve work incentives dramatically by cutting taxes. Another type of supply-side policy is tax reform. A tax reform could be revenue-neutral—it could keep revenue the same although tax rates are cut. This could be done by eliminating deductions and lowering tax rates on earned income. Because revenue is the same, the typical taxpayer pays the same amount of tax and there is no income effect. The cut in taxes due to the lower tax rate is offset by the increase in taxes due to the elimination of deductions. This type of reform necessarily involves a reduction in the progressivity of the income tax. What matters for work incentives is the *marginal* tax rate, the rate applied to the last dollar of earnings. A flat tax system that puts roughly the same tax rate on all dollars of earnings above the first few thousand dollars of income could raise the same amount of revenue with lower marginal rates. The Tax Reform Act of 1986 significantly flattened the income tax (look back at Fig-

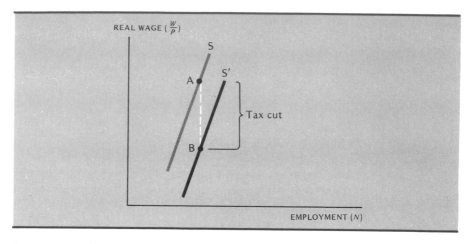

Figure 13–7.   SHIFT IN LABOR SUPPLY FROM A TAX CUT.
A tax cut shifts the labor supply function downward in proportion to the cut. *S* is the labor supply schedule before the tax rate cut; *A* is an arbitrary point on it. *S'* is the supply schedule after the cut. *B* is a point on *S'* where the real wage after tax is the same as the real wage after tax on *S*. *B* is below *A* by the amount of the tax cut. The amount of labor supplied at *B* is the same as at *A* because the real wage received by workers is the same at *B* as at *A*. A downward shift in a schedule that is nearly vertical has almost no substantive effect.

ure 11–4 to compare the tax reform with pre-reform tax laws). With this reform the personal income tax will raise about the same amount as before the reform. Hence, the reform will have no income effect to depress work. The labor supply schedule should shift by the full amount of the substitution effect. The 1987 *Economic Report of the President* estimated that labor supply will increase by 3.1 percent as a result of the tax reform. Real GNP will therefore increase by about 2.2 percent. These are one-time permanent effects on the level of the labor supply and output, of course, not on their respective growth rates. Nonetheless, the impact is significant and more than offsets the negative effects on capital growth of the tax reform.

Growth through Increased Work Effort

1. The classical model provides a good way to analyze programs to stimulate growth through improved work incentives. However, the analysis applies only in the long run.

2. Because the labor supply schedule is nearly vertical, even a large tax cut has only a small effect on employment. The incentive effect of lower tax rates raises incentives to work, but the higher level of income depresses work.

3. If the tax change is a tax *reform,* which keeps tax receipts constant, rather than a tax *cut,* it improves incentives without changing average income. Then the incentive effects are not offset by income effects.

13.5 Monetary and Fiscal Policy in a Full-Employment Economy

The aggregate demand side of the economy, as expressed in the IS-LM model, is relevant for an economy with perfectly flexible prices and wages, but the implications of the analysis are much different from a model with price rigidities. With price rigidities, aggregate demand—the consumption, investment, net export, and money demand relations—determines the level of output in the short run. With perfect price flexibility, output is determined purely by aggregate supply; aggregate demand determines the price level, the interest rate, the exchange rate, and the allocation of output between consumption, investment, government, and net exports.

We first touched on this result in Chapter 6, when we introduced gradual price adjustment. When prices adjust, actual GNP eventually moves toward potential GNP. After an increase in the money supply, the price level eventually increases by the same proportion. After an increase in government spending, the price level eventually rises by enough to completely crowd out investment. With perfectly flexible prices, all these adjustments take place *instantaneously.* The long-run results also apply in the short run. With perfectly flexible prices, output is always equal to its potential.

FISCAL POLICY IN THE CLASSICAL MODEL

An expansionary fiscal policy is one that stimulates spending. Because total spending always equals potential, an expansionary fiscal policy only drives up the interest rate; it has no effect on output. The only exception to this rule is a fiscal policy change that alters incentives in such a way as to change full-employment output. An example is the tax reform discussed in the previous section.

These effects are shown in Figure 13–8. Fiscal expansion moves the IS curve to the right. The price level rises, pushing the LM curve to the left and increasing the interest rate. We have already described how and to what extent the interest rate rises—by enough to depress total spending by the same amount that fiscal policy raised spending. This is what keeps output equal to potential. The amount of the increase in the price level depends on

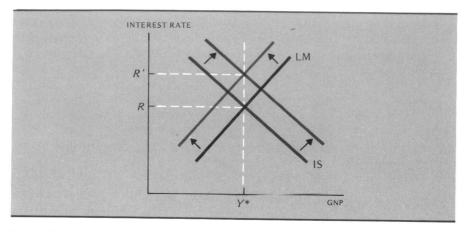

Figure 13–8. FISCAL EXPANSION IN THE CLASSICAL MODEL.
An expansionary move, such as an increase in government purchases, shifts the IS curve upward. But prices rise immediately, pushing up the LM curve. The interest rate rises so as to depress spending by the same amount that the fiscal stimulus raised it. Real output does not change. The intersection with the LM curve occurs at the higher interest rate (R') and at a higher price level. The price level rises because the higher interest rate depressed money demand; that is, the price level rises to offset the effect of the interest rate.

the *slope* of the LM curve. If the LM curve is vertical, the price level does not increase at all. A vertical LM curve results from an absence of sensitivity of money demand to the interest rate, or from a deliberate policy on the part of the Fed to keep the price level constant.

Even though fiscal policy does not influence the level of real output on the demand side in the classical analysis, it has substantive economic effects on the interest rate, on the composition of output, and on the price level.

Because the classical model views the economy as always at full employment, fiscal policy would be unnecessary for stabilization purposes. The motivation for a change in fiscal policy would always be to alter the composition of output, not to stabilize the total level of output.

Effects of Fiscal Policies with Flexible Prices

1. Increased government purchases of goods and services raise the interest rate and depress consumption, investment, and net exports. Private spending falls by exactly the amount that government purchases rise.

2. Income tax cuts raise consumption. The interest rate rises by enough to depress investment and net exports by the amount of the increase in consumption.

3. Investment incentives raise investment. The interest rate rises by enough to keep the sum of investment and net exports at its previous level.

Unless the LM curve is vertical, each of these three policies raises the price level as well.

MONETARY POLICY IN THE CLASSICAL MODEL

The analysis of monetary policy in the classical equilibrium model is particularly simple. Monetary policy cannot influence total output or the composition of output. Only the price level is affected by a change in monetary policy. The IS-LM analysis of a change in monetary policy is shown in Figure 13–9.

The monetary expansion has only one effect—to raise the price level. Nothing else in the economy changes. Because monetary policy does not influence output or employment, none of the agonizing choices facing monetary policy-makers in the real world exists in the classical model. Monetary policy can be given the simple task of keeping the price level at a certain prescribed level. As it does so, it will never interfere with the goal of full employment. Monetary policy is *neutral*.

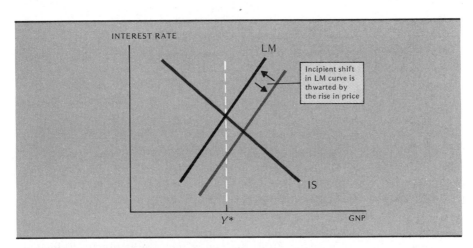

Figure 13–9. MONETARY EXPANSION IN THE CLASSICAL MODEL.
A monetary expansion shifts the LM curve to the right. But prices rise immediately and push it back to the left. The net effect is zero. Not only is the total amount of output unaffected by the monetary expansion, but the composition of output among consumption, investment, government, and net exports is unaffected by the move. The price level rises by the full amount of the increase in money.

13.6 Long-Run Output Growth and Inflation

We have just seen that increases in money raise the price level with no effect on output or the interest rate in the classical model. Does it follow that continual increases in the money supply—say 5 percent per year, year after year—will continually increase the price level, year after year, without affecting output? In other words, does a higher rate of growth of the money supply merely lead to a higher inflation rate without affecting the growth of output? For the IS-LM model with perfectly flexible prices, the answer is clearly yes. A succession of years can be analyzed simply by piecing together the results from each year.

Recall the algebraic form of the money demand function from Chapter 5:

$$\frac{M}{P} = kY - hR, \tag{13-4}$$

where k and h are constant coefficients. With flexible prices, the two variables on the right-hand side of the money demand function are determined outside the money market: The interest rate, R, is set by spending balance, and the level of real GNP, Y, is set by aggregate supply. Moreover, the money stock, M, is set by the Fed. We can insert the three given variables into the money demand equation and solve for the price level:

$$P = \frac{M}{kY - hR}. \tag{13-5}$$

Thus, the price level is proportional to the money stock. In an economy where R and Y do not change over time, the rate of inflation will equal the rate of growth of the money stock:

$$\Delta P / P = \Delta M / M. \tag{13-6}$$

The result that output is unaffected by the *growth rate* of money is sometimes referred to as the **superneutrality of money,** to distinguish it from the notion of neutrality that we discussed in Section 13.5. It is a property of the classical model, but, to the extent that the classical model represents the real world in the long run, it is a result that should apply in reality in the long run.

There are several reasons why superneutrality may not hold in the real world—even in the long run. First, the tax system might not be superneutral. For example, firms can deduct interest payments from their taxes. But nominal interest rates and therefore interest payments rise with inflation, giving firms a tax break. This lowers the rental price of capital.

Second, a higher rate of inflation makes it more attractive for people to

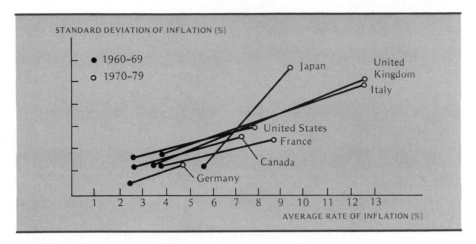

Figure 13–10.   INFLATION AND FLUCTUATIONS IN INFLATION FOR SEVEN COUNTRIES.
The chart shows the year-to-year variability of inflation on the vertical axis and the average rate of inflation on the horizontal axis. As inflation increased in all seven countries the variability also increased. The standard deviation is a measure of variability with the property that about two-thirds of the observations are within a band of plus or minus one standard deviation.

hold real capital—factories, houses, trucks—compared to currency or non-interest-bearing deposits. This tends to increase the amount of real capital in the economy, and thereby increase aggregate supply. James Tobin of Yale University and Robert Mundell of Columbia University have emphasized this departure from superneutrality.

Third, in practice, high inflation rates are usually accompanied by *fluctuations* in inflation from year to year, and in fluctuations in relative prices. The relationship between the level and the variability of inflation is illustrated in Figure 13–10. These fluctuations in inflation make business planning difficult and could lead to inefficiencies in the production process. If so, then aggregate supply will be reduced. This negative effect of inflation on real output was emphasized by Milton Friedman in the address he gave when accepting the Nobel Prize in 1976.

A final reason that inflation might reduce real output is that it makes holding currency and reserves very costly. This creates inefficiencies in the monetary system and could reduce productive efficiency. Because currency and reserves do not pay interest, people will try to economize on them when inflation and interest rates rise. Economizing on currency and reserves requires using time (trips to the bank) or resources (computers that automatically transfer funds from checking to savings accounts) that could be put to more productive or enjoyable use. In countries with extremely high inflation rates people spend much time just completing transactions. In extreme cases people begin to use foreign currencies—as in Israel in the inflation of the early 1980s. If they can't use alternative means of payment, then the monetary system may break down as in the hyperinflations in Eastern Europe in the 1920s.

Review and Practice

MAJOR POINTS

1. The classical model is one in which prices and wages are perfectly flexible. The economy is always operating at full employment in the classical model.

2. Even when the economy is operating at potential, there is some unemployment. This level of unemployment is called the natural rate.

3. The natural rate of unemployment has probably increased during the last 25 years, but may now be declining again as the labor force grows older.

4. Monetary policy only affects the price level in the classical model. Money is neutral. The levels of employment and real output are determined by aggregate supply.

5. At any one time, when the capital stock is predetermined, aggregate supply is determined in the labor market. Employment is given by the equality of labor demand and labor supply.

6. Over the longer run the capital stock grows as investment accumulates and this further increases aggregate supply.

7. During the last 25 years the decline in the rate of total factor productivity growth has been largely responsible for the decline in real output growth.

8. In the classical model, increases in the rate of money growth increase the rate of inflation, but do not affect output growth. Money is superneutral.

9. In the real world there are a number of reasons to expect that money growth is not superneutral, even in the long run. Taxation distortions and increases in inflation variability are two factors that might cause higher inflation to reduce output.

KEY TERMS AND CONCEPTS

Classical model

Perfectly flexible prices and wages

Demand for labor

Substitution effect in labor supply

Income effect in labor supply

Labor market equilibrium

Natural rate of unemployment

Sources of economic growth

Labor and capital share

Tax rate cut

Tax reform

Neutrality

Superneutrality

Velocity

Quantity equation

Inflation variability

Tax distortions from inflation

Total factor productivity

QUESTIONS FOR DISCUSSION AND REVIEW

1. Why is the demand for labor a negative function of the real wage?

2. Explain why microeconomic theory predicts that for labor supply the income effect is negative and the substitution effect is positive. What do empirical studies indicate about the sum of these two effects?

3. Explain why the classical model predicts that the level of real GNP in any one year is determined solely in the labor market. What would happen to the real wage, the price level, and the nominal wage if the money supply was increased?

4. Describe how economists measure the natural rate of unemployment. Did the natural rate of unemployment increase or decrease from the early 1960s through the early 1980s? Why?

5. Explain the difference between labor productivity and total factor productivity.

6. Does an increase in the rate of growth of labor add more or less to the growth rate of output than the same size increase in the rate of growth of capital? Explain why.

7. Describe three different policies that could be used to increase the growth rate of potential GNP. Identify whether the policy is aimed at productivity, capital formation, or labor supply.

8. Does fiscal policy completely crowd out private spending in the classical model? Explain.

9. Give three reasons why a change in the growth rate of money might affect potential GNP.

PROBLEMS

Numerical

1. Consider the following two tax schedules (the same schedules used in Problem 11–1):

Income Bracket	Marginal Tax Rate	
	Progressive	*Flat*
$0–$9,999	0	0
$10,000–$29,999	.2	.25
$30,000–$49,999	.4	.25
$50,000 and above	.6	.25

a. Calculate the taxes paid by someone earning $20,000, $30,000, and $40,000 under each schedule. For each salary level, indicate whether the income effect of changing to a flat tax will increase or decrease labor supply.

b. Describe the effect that the flat tax will have on the marginal tax rate for each salary level in Part a. Again, indicate for each salary level whether the labor supply will increase or decrease due to the substitution effect.

c. For each of these salary levels, indicate whether the supply of labor will increase, decrease, or whether it is ambiguous. Give the economic intuition behind your result in each case.

d. Explain why tax payments from workers currently earning $30,000 will unambiguously increase under the flat tax. Is the same true for workers earning $20,000 and $40,000? Why or why not?

2. Assume that over a 10-year period the growth rate of capital is 4 percent, the growth of employment is 2 percent, and the growth rate of real output is 5 percent. Calculate the growth rate of total factor productivity. Suppose that a permanent cut in the budget deficit increases investment, and the growth rate of capital rises by 1 percent. How much does the growth rate of output increase? Suppose that a tax reduction increases the supply of labor by 1 percent in 1 year. What happens to the growth rate of real output?

3. Suppose that the production function takes the special form $Y = AN^{.7}K^{.3}$. By taking logarithms and first differences of this production function show that the growth formula is satisfied. (If you have had calculus, calculate the marginal products of labor and capital. Derive the labor demand function. Calculate the labor share and the capital share.)

Analytical

1. In a model with perfectly flexible prices, explain why inflation depends only on current spending shocks and not on past spending shocks. Is the same true of the models of sticky prices developed in Part I? Compare the predictions of the model of flexible prices and the model of sticky prices with respect to the persistence of inflation. In which model does inflation tend to change slowly over time? In which model can inflation jump from low to high or positive to negative from one period to the next?

2. In the text it was suggested that the Tax Reform Act of 1986 had approximately no income effect. What effect, then, did the act probably have on the total amount of income taxes paid?

3. Consider a tax reform package like the Tax Reform Act of 1986 that contains positive incentives for labor supply and negative incentives for investment. Assume that prices are perfectly flexible.
   a. Suppose that such reform is unanticipated. How do output, prices, and the interest rate in the first year of the tax reform compare with what they would have been without tax reform? Is investment unambiguously reduced?
   b. Suppose such legislation was announced a year in advance. Describe its impact on output, the interest rate, and investment in the year of the announcement and in the implementation year.
   c. Suppose that $K^* = vWY/R^*$ as in Chapter 9, where W is the real wage and v is some constant. Describe the factors that determine investment in the long run and how such reform affects these factors.

4. Suppose that there is a reduction in investment incentives in an economy with perfectly flexible prices.
   a. Show what happens to the aggregate demand curve.
   b. Show what happens to the IS and LM curves.
   c. Assume that neither consumption or net exports varies with the interest rate. Does investment fall? Why or why not?
   d. Now assume that net exports vary negatively with the interest rate. What happens to investment?

5. Consider a model with perfectly flexible wages and prices. Suppose that the real wage W/P is fixed because labor contracts are perfectly tied to the price level. In other words, whenever the price level P rises by 1 percent the nominal wage W rises by 1 percent as well, so that the real wage W/P stays fixed. Labor contracts of this type are called "indexed" contracts. Draw a labor supply-demand diagram in which the fixed real wage is greater than the point of interaction of the labor supply and labor demand curves.

a. Indicate the amount of excess supply of labor on the diagram. Does this excess supply measure the total amount of unemployment in the economy?

b. Explain what happens in this setup if the central bank increases the growth rate of money supply. What happens to the excess supply of labor? What happens to inflation?

6. Using an IS-LM diagram, illustrate how a change in the mix of monetary and fiscal policy can be used to lower the interest rate without affecting the price level. Why would policy-makers be interested in changing the mix in this way?

7. In Chapter 12 we discussed different policy rules for the Fed. There we used a model with sticky prices. Here we want to consider the effect of such rules in an economy with flexible prices.

a. Compare the effects of IS and LM shocks in an economy with sticky prices with the effects of such shocks in an economy with flexible prices, assuming that the Fed targets the money supply.

b. Explain why an interest rate target is, in general, infeasible in an economy with flexible prices. Is the same thing true in the long run in an economy with sticky prices?

c. Discuss the use of an output target in an economy with flexible prices.

8. Here we examine another of the Fed's policy options in an economy with flexible prices: targeting the price level.

a. Diagram what happens to the IS and LM curves in the event of an IS shock, assuming the Fed does nothing.

b. Now suppose the Fed wants to reestablish the initial price level. Show how it should move the LM curve.

c. Diagram the IS shock and the Fed's response on an aggregate demand graph.

d. Does the Fed's policy of targeting the price level affect C, X, or I? If so, explain why. If not, can you relate this result to the neutrality of money in an economy with flexible prices?

9. Suppose that there is a sudden reduction in total factor productivity.

a. Describe what happens to output, the marginal product of capital, the optimal capital stock, and investment demand in the year of the productivity shock.

b. Is the shock inflationary, deflationary, or is it not possible to tell?

Appendix A: Deriving the Growth Formula

Suppose that A, N, and K grow by rates $\Delta A/A$, $\Delta N/N$, and $\Delta K/K$. We will derive a formula for the growth rate of output, $\Delta Y/Y$. First, we approximate the growth rate of output using the production function of Equation 13–2:

$$\Delta Y/Y = \Delta A/A + \Delta F(N, K)/F(N, K). \qquad (13–7)$$

In other words, the growth rate of the *product* of A and $F(N,K)$ is the *sum* of the growth rates of A and $F(N,K)$.

Second, the part of the change in output that comes from changes in employment and capital can be further broken down using the marginal products of the two. Let M_N be the marginal product of labor and M_K be the marginal product of capital. Then

$$\Delta F(N,K)/F(N,K) = M_N \Delta N/Y + M_K \Delta K/Y. \qquad (13–8)$$

In words this expression states that the proportional change in F can be divided up into two components that measure the contributions of the proportional changes in N and K. (If you have had calculus, this formula can be derived by taking the total derivative of F and dividing by Y.) Putting this into the formula for $\Delta Y/Y$ we get

$$\Delta Y/Y = \Delta A/A + M_N \Delta N/Y + M_K \Delta K/Y. \qquad (13-9)$$

If firms are using labor and capital up to the points where their marginal products are equal to the real wage and real rental prices, then

$$M_N = W/P \text{ and } M_K = R^K/P. \qquad (13-10)$$

Now the formula is

$$\Delta Y/Y = \Delta A/A + (W/P)\Delta N/Y + (R^K/P)\Delta K/Y. \qquad (13-11)$$

We can rewrite this as

$$\Delta Y/Y = \Delta A/A + (WN/PY)\Delta N/N + (R^K K/PY)\Delta K. \qquad (13-12)$$

WN/PY is the fraction of revenue, PY, paid out to labor in the form of compensation, WN. Similarly, $R^K K/PY$ is the fraction of revenue earned by capital. From the national income accounts, we find that these fractions are about .7 and .3. Thus,

$$\Delta Y/Y = \Delta A/A + .7\Delta N/N + .3\Delta K/K,$$

which is the growth formula (Equation 13–3).

Appendix B: The Algebra of Rational Expectations in the Classical IS-LM Model

The IS-LM model with perfectly flexible prices is a convenient framework for illustrating some of the techniques economists use for rational expectations analysis. It is convenient because the effects of changes in money are so simple—only the price level changes. In a more complete model the effects of changes in money on real output and the real interest rate have to be taken into account. Here we show algebraically how the classical model works when expectations are rational.

Where do expectations enter the IS-LM model with perfectly flexible prices? In the difference between the real and the nominal rates of interest. That is, in the **expected rate of inflation.** Suppose that the demand for money takes the form:

$$M_t = hY - k(R + P_{t+1} - P_t) + P_t, \qquad (13-13)$$

where the symbols are defined as usual. The term $R + P_{t+1} - P_t$, that is, the real rate of interest plus the expected rate of inflation, is the nominal rate of interest. (Note that inflation is usually defined as the *percentage* change in the price rather than the actual change; this is an approximation that works fairly well for low to moderate inflation rates.) Equation 13–13 is a standard money demand relationship, in which we have emphasized how the nominal interest rate depends on the expected inflation rate. During year t, people do not know what the value of the price level will be in the following year, P_{t+1}; they must therefore form expectations of P_{t+1}. The rational expectations approach is to assume that people have a fairly good idea about how the economy works when they form these expectations of the future.

The classical model works in such a way that M_t affects the price level P_t, but not output Y or the interest rate R. To emphasize this, rearrange the symbols in Equation 13–13 to get

$$P_t = nP_{t+1} + M_t/(k+1) - g, \tag{13–14}$$

where $g = (hY - kR)/(1+k)$ and $n = k/(1+k)$. The last term on the right of Equation 13–14—represented by the symbol g—depends only on the real interest rate and real output. It is therefore independent of monetary policy in the classical model; it can be treated as if it were a constant. For simplicity let's assume that this term is zero. That is set $g = 0$. This simplifying assumption makes no difference for the points illustrated here. The remaining terms contain the money supply, the price level, and the expected price level next year. The entire relationship between money and prices in the classical model is thus contained in this formula.

Note that if we knew the expectation of next year's price level it would be straightforward to determine the effect of the money supply on this year's price. For example, if P_{t+1} equals 1, then an increase in M_t of 1 unit would increase P_t by $1/(1+k)$ units. However, next period's price is not known and people must forecast it using the information that they have about how the classical model works. This information is reflected in Equation 13–14. People who literally understand Equation 13–14 will try to forecast P_{t+1} using Equation 13–14. They could do this by looking forward using the same equation but applying it to the next year. That is,

$$P_{t+1} = nP_{t+2} + M_{t+1}/(k+1) \tag{13–15}$$

where we have simply added 1 to each subscript to give the next year. Note that we have set $g = 0$. This equation could be used to forecast P_{t+1} except for the fact that it now depends on P_{t+2}, which is unknown. But this unknown could be handled by leading equation 13–15 one more period; that is,

$$P_{t+2} = nP_{t+3} + M_{t+2}/(k+1). \tag{13–16}$$

Clearly this same idea can be used again and again with forecasts of prices being pushed further and further into the future.

By successive substitution, the three previous equations can be combined to get

$$P_t = \underbrace{n^3 P_{t+3}}_{\substack{\text{future price} \\ \text{level}}} + [1/(1+k)] [\underbrace{M_t}_{\substack{\text{this year's} \\ \text{money}}} + \underbrace{nM_{t+1} + n^2 M_{t+2}}_{\substack{\text{money in two} \\ \text{future years}}}] \tag{13–17}$$

which shows how this year's price depends on the expectations of the money supply in future years plus an expectation of the price level in the future. This process of successive substitution can be continued for an arbitrary number of periods, but eventually the coefficient that multiplies the future price level will get very small and can be ignored.[4] This coefficient is $n = k/(k+1)$ multiplied by itself many times.

---

[4] There is a subtle issue here that macroeconomists have been hotly debating since rational expectations was introduced. The future price term can be ignored only if the price level is not exploding exponentially. But there is nothing in the model itself to rule out such a "speculative bubble." Some macroeconomists have attempted to test for the existence of such bubbles in price data. See Robert Flood and Peter Garber, "Market Fundamentals versus Price-Level

Since $k/(k+1)$ is less than 1, this coefficient will be small. Thus, eventually we will be left with an expression for the price level of the form

$$P_t = [1/(1+k)] [\underbrace{M_t}_{\substack{\text{this} \\ \text{year's} \\ \text{money}}} + \underbrace{nM_{t+1} + n^2M_{t+2} + n^3M_{t+3} + \ldots}_{\substack{\text{money in all} \\ \text{future years}}}]. \tag{13-18}$$

Equation 13–18 is a relationship that shows how the price level depends on the money supply. It looks messy, but its message is quite simple. It says that the price level depends on the money supply this year, *and* on the anticipated money supply many years in the future. Of course the importance of future money supplies diminishes as we go further into the future. This dependence of the price level on anticipated future values of the money supply is a fundamental feature of rational expectations.

What does Equation 13–18 tell us about the effect of changes in money on the price level? Two cases need to be distinguished: a temporary and a permanent increase in money. Suppose that the money supply increases by one unit. If the increase in money is permanent, then Equation 13–18 tells us that the price level will increase by the same amount as the increase in money. This is because the coefficients on the M terms in Equation 13–18 sum to 1. On the other hand, if the increase in money is temporary, for 1 year only, then the price level only increases by $1/(1+k)$—the coefficient of M_t in Equation 13–18. This increase may be substantially less than 1. For example, if $k = 4$, then the temporary increase in money increases the price level by only 20 percent of the amount that it increases when the money change is permanent. The rational expectations of future behavior of money growth can be quite important quantitatively.

What happens if the money supply is anticipated to increase temporarily 2 years from now? Then, according to Equation 13–18, the price level will increase by $[1/(1+k)] [k/(1+k)]^2$ today. The mere anticipation of a future money increase can have effects today.

While the classical model is a convenient framework for illustrating the algebra that lies behind rational expectations it also gives us a simple way to make some actual computations. Macroeconomists use these same algebraic techniques in more complete models with price and wage rigidities. Because output, prices, and real interest rates respond to changes in money in such models, the technical analysis is somewhat more involved.

Bubbles: First Test," *Journal of Political Economy*, Vol. 88 (October 1980), pp. 745–770. Others have focused on bubbles as potentially important parts of the workings of models. See Olivier Blanchard and Mark Watson, "Bubbles, Rational Expectations, and Financial Markets," NBER Working Paper No. 945, Cambridge, Mass., 1982.

14

New Classical Theory

THE WORLD appears to behave much differently from the predictions of the classical model with perfectly flexible wages and prices that we discussed in the previous chapter. GNP is not always equal to potential GNP. The evidence we examined in Chapter 1 indicates that actual GNP frequently departs from its normal level. In Figure 14–1 we review this evidence. There were seven recessions in the United States between 1950 and 1986 during which such departures have been most obvious. The Great Depression of the 1930s was deeper and more prolonged than any of these recessions. Recessions and booms were commonplace before the First World War as well. The departures do not last forever; eventually actual GNP returns to its potential. In the longer run, the classical model of Chapter 13 does appear to be a good description of how the economy works. But the classical model has problems explaining the short-run economic fluctuations that constitute the study of macroeconomics. The model lacks features that explain why output departs from potential for prolonged periods.

There is another important feature of economic fluctuations that is missing from the classical model: the behavior of prices. There is a general tendency for prices to gradually rise when GNP is above potential and to fall when GNP is below potential. This evidence is also reviewed in Figure 14–1. The movement of prices sometimes lags behind real GNP, and sometimes outside price shocks like higher oil prices mask the correlation. In times of significant inflation, the price-GNP correlation can be detected only by looking at the inflation rate—not at the price level. If inflation is high, a decline in real GNP will bring about a decline in the inflation rate—the rate of change in the price level. No absolute decline in the price level will be ob-

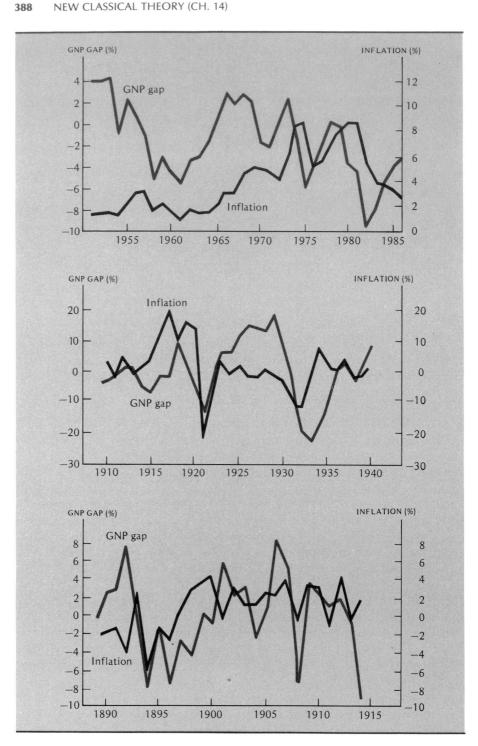

served. For example, during the decline in real GNP relative to potential GNP in the early 1980s, the price level—the GNP deflator—did not fall. However, the rate of inflation declined markedly. Before the 1950s, on the other hand, when inflation was low, actual declines in the price level were observed.

This chapter and the next take up theories of the persistent departures of GNP from potential and of the tendency for prices or inflation to rise in booms and fall in slumps. In this chapter we look at theories that maintain the flexible price-wage assumption of the classical model, but that differ from the classical model by incorporating *information problems* that may exist in the economy. These theories bear the name **new classical**, because they maintain the basic classical assumptions of flexible prices and wages. In the next chapter we look at theories based on price and wage rigidities—the explanation of macroeconomic fluctuations that underlies the basic model of this book.

14.1 Real Business-Cycle Theories

Before incorporating informational factors into the classical model, let's ask in what way the pure classical model does not appear to be capable of explaining economic fluctuations. In Chapter 13, we suggested that the classical model describes an economy that grows smoothly and never experiences recessions and booms. But the basic logic of the neoclassical model does not rule out short-run fluctuations in output. After all, potential GNP—or aggregate supply—could fluctuate. The prolonged deviations of unemployment from the natural rate might represent the optimal response of labor supply to such fluctuations in potential. Explanations of economic fluctuations that rely on fluctuations in aggregate supply are called **real business-cycle** theories, to distinguish them from other theories that emphasize monetary factors and shifts in aggregate demand. Finn Kydland of Carnegie-Mellon University and Edward Prescott of the University of Minnesota have argued that real business-cycle models provide a good explanation of economic fluctuations.[1] As we saw in Chapter 13, the level of employment

---

[1] See, for example, their paper: "A Competitive Theory of Fluctuations and the Feasibility and Desirability of Stabilization Policy," in Stanley Fischer (ed.), *Rational Expectations and Economic Policy,* University of Chicago Press for the National Bureau of Economic Research, 1980. Robert King and Charles Plosser have emphasized real theories in "Money, Credit and Prices in a Real Business Cycle," *American Economic Review,* Vol. 74 (June 1984), pp. 363–380.

◀ **Figure 14–1.** GNP AND INFLATION.
The charts show in more detail the historical relationship between GNP and inflation fluctuations described in Chapter 1. Each chart shows the deviation of GNP from potential GNP (colored line) during a particular historical period in the United States. The behavior of inflation (black line) is also shown. Departures of real GNP from potential GNP occur regularly. Inflation usually falls when GNP is below normal and rises when GNP is above normal.

in the classical model is determined in the labor market at the intersection of the supply and demand functions for labor (Figure 13–5). What might make the level of employment fall, as it does in every recession? There are only two answers: Either the *demand* schedule shifts downward or the *supply* schedule shifts downward.

SHIFTS IN LABOR DEMAND

The demand schedule for labor shows the marginal product of labor for each level of employment. If the schedule shifts downward, it means that the marginal product of labor is lower at a given level of employment. That is, for the demand function to shift downward, the productivity of labor has to fall. It is hard to think of recurrent events that make all workers throughout the economy less productive for prolonged periods of time and then gradually become productive again. For example, one is hard put to identify a technological reason for a downward shift in productivity in 1981 and 1982 when U.S. output and employment fell in that recession. Models that emphasize aggregate demand would point to the behavior of the Fed in fighting inflation. But some events do bring about shifts in productivity. For example, an increase in the price of oil will make firms use less oil and may therefore reduce the marginal productivity of labor. Most frequently, however, productivity shifts seem to influence only one sector—say the demand for U.S. auto workers drops because the Japanese have made sudden improvements in their cars. Or labor demand in oil-producing regions of the U.S. falls when the price of oil falls as in 1985–86. For events to influence all sectors, there must be some relationship between sectors. An example suggested by Edward Prescott is that business schools could start teaching a new productivity-increasing management technique that quickly becomes known throughout the economy.

Moreover, in order for a shift in labor demand to cause a noticeable change in employment in the classical model, it is necessary for the labor supply schedule to be reasonably sensitive to changes in the real wage. Recall that, as long as the labor supply schedule is not perfectly vertical, when labor demand shifts down employment falls. But employment wouldn't fall at all if the labor supply schedule were vertical, as in Figure 14–2. A good theory of recessions and booms within the neoclassical model has to show that labor supply is reasonably sensitive to the real wage. Some real business-cycle economists have suggested that labor supply is quite elastic in the short run, even though people will not raise or lower their volume of work very much in the long run in response to permanent changes in real wages.

Another way to explain the large labor supply responses is to assume, realistically, that households must supply labor in an "all-or-nothing" fashion (0 or 8 hours per day). Gary Hansen of the University of California, Santa Bar-

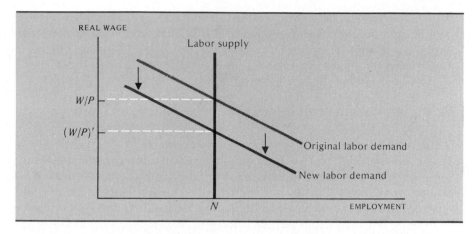

Figure 14–2.   DECLINE IN LABOR DEMAND WITH INELASTIC LABOR SUPPLY.
The labor demand schedule shifts downward. Because the labor supply schedule is vertical—insensitive to changes in the real wage—employment does not fall.

bara, and Richard Rogerson of the University of Rochester have shown that
such an assumption may help to explain high employment variability.[2]

SHIFTS IN LABOR SUPPLY

The second way that the classical model could explain fluctuations is
through shifts in labor supply. If some outside factor makes people want to
work more hours, then the economy will move down and to the right along
the labor demand schedule and employment will rise. One outside factor
identified by the economists favoring this interpretation of the business
cycle is the real interest rate. As we discussed in Chapter 8, when the real interest rate is high, people will seek to work more hours (at the same real
wage) than they would at a lower real interest rate. A high real rate makes it
attractive to work more now and consume later, because the saved earnings
will be augmented by the high real rate. Thus the labor supply curve—
drawn as a function of the real wage—shifts out.

Many macroeconomists are skeptical of both versions of the real business-
cycle model of recessions and booms. They question whether shifts in labor
demand are large and persistent enough to explain economic fluctuations

[2] See Gary Hansen, "Indivisible Labor and the Business Cycle," *Journal of Monetary Economics,* November 1985, pp. 309–328, and Richard Rogerson, "Indivisible Labor, Lotteries,
and the Business Cycle," Unpublished paper, 1985. For a recent survey of microeconomic empirical work on intertemporal substitution in labor supply see Orley Ashenfelter, "Macroeconomic Analysis and Microeconomic Analysis of Labor Supply, *Carnegie-Rochester Series on Public
Policy,* Vol. 21, pp. 117–156, 1985 (North Holland).

and whether the labor supply schedule is sufficiently sensitive to the real wage. They also question whether the shift in labor supply associated with changing real interest rates is big enough to explain the large movements in employment that occur over the business cycle.[3]

14.2 Imperfect Information: The New Classical Theory

An important modern view of fluctuations sees them as the outcome of people not being fully informed about what is happening in the economy. These **information-based models** attempt to explain the departures of actual GNP from potential GNP using the microeconomic theory of firm supply. Prices and wages are assumed to be flexible in these models. The positive relation between price and output is attributed to movements along firms' supply curves. The original research establishing the information-based model was done by Robert Lucas of the University of Chicago. The resulting positive relationship between prices and output is usually called the **Lucas supply curve.**[4]

The role of information is very important in these models. According to microeconomic theory, a firm produces up to the point where its *price equals marginal cost.* Marginal cost depends on the price of the firm's inputs to production. If the price of the firm's output rises *relative* to the price of other goods in the economy, including its inputs, then the firm will produce more. However, if all other prices rise by the same amount that the firm's output price rises, then there will be no incentive for the firm to produce more. In other words, the firm will produce more only if the price of its output rises relative to some other prices in the economy—in particular, its input prices. Yet when the *general* price level rises, as it does in booms, there is not necessarily any change in relative prices. Hence, the firm's output price will not rise relative to its input price. So how do we explain the boom that usually occurs when the general price level rises?

Something must be added to the model to generate the price-output relation that we know is an important characteristic of the departures of GNP from potential. The addition is an assumption about the information available to different firms. This information assumption is what provides a connection between general price movements and the supply decisions of firms. Lucas refers to the model as being "rigged" by these information assumptions.[5]

---

[3] See, for example, the comments of Martin Feldstein on Finn Kydland and Edward Prescott in Stanley Fischer (ed.), *Rational Expectations and Economic Policy,* University of Chicago Press for the National Bureau of Economic Research, 1980, pp. 187–189, or Lawrence H. Summers, "Some Skeptical Observations on Real Business Cycle Theory," *Federal Reserve Bank of Minneapolis Review,* Fall 1986 pp. 23–27.

[4] See Robert E. Lucas, Jr., "Some International Evidence on Output Inflation Trade-offs," *American Economic Review,* Vol. 63, pp. 326–334, 1973.

[5] See Robert E. Lucas, Jr., "Tobin and Monetarism: A Review Article," *Journal of Economic Literature,* Vol. 19, pp. 558–567, 1982.

THE FIRM'S INFORMATION ABOUT THE PRICE LEVEL

Firms are assumed to have difficulty getting information about prices in the economy other than their own output price. There are temporary information barriers through which firms cannot see what is going on in other markets. Put another way, firms specialize in monitoring conditions in their own market. They know very quickly when demand drops off, and prices begin to fall. On the other hand, they are relatively uninformed about developments in other markets and learn relatively slowly what is happening in these other markets.

Some algebra and graphs will help to explain how this works. We will use the subscript i to represent an individual firm. The representative firm's supply curve is given by

$$Y_i = h(P_i - P) + Y_i^*, \tag{14-1}$$

where Y_i is the firm's production, P_i is the firm's price, P is the aggregate price, and Y_i^* is the firm's potential or normal production. In words the equation says that the firm's output Y_i is greater than the normal Y_i^* by an amount equal to a constant h times the difference between the firm's price P_i and the general price level P. We enter the general price level into the supply curve as an indicator of the prices in all other markets. As we described above, the firm will supply more output only if its price rises relative to these other prices. The supply curve is upward sloping ($h > 0$) in terms of the difference between P_i and P, and is shown graphically in Figure 14–3.

Note that, if the price of the firm's product rises by the same amount as

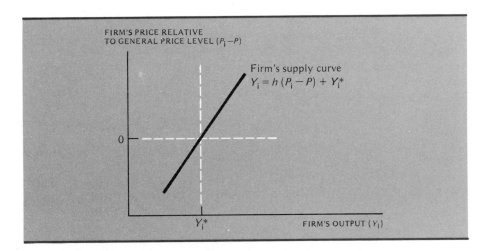

Figure 14–3. THE FIRM'S SUPPLY CURVE.
The firm's supply decision depends on its own price relative to the general level of prices in the economy. If P_i and P rise in the same proportion, then Y_i does not change.

the overall price level, there will be no change in the firm's supply, according to the supply equation. The firm will see that, although it can receive more for its output, the prices of all other items in the economy have increased by the same amount. Hence, in relative terms there has been no change.

Suppose, however, that the firm did not know what was going on in other markets in the economy. The information about the rest of the economy could arrive late, or the managers of the firm might not have the time to monitor economic conditions throughout the economy. Suppose, further, that each firm is on an island, so to speak, where instantaneous communication among islands is not possible.[6] When information is restricted in this way, firms will not know the prices of other commodities in the economy, even if they are perfectly rational in their forecasts. Hence, they do not know the aggregate price level; they have to guess it. We therefore rewrite Equation 14–1 to reflect this fact:

$$Y_i = h(P_i - P^e) + Y_i^*. \tag{14-2}$$

The superscript e on the P indicates the firm's *estimate* of the overall price level. We simply have replaced P by P^e in changing Equation 14–1 into Equation 14–2.

Now consider again the case where all prices in the economy rise by the same amount. Each firm will observe only the increase in price of its own product, and will have to make a guess about all the other prices as summarized in the index P. If the firm does not adjust its guess of P, then it will clearly produce more. The firm thinks that its own relative price has increased. If the other firms in the economy behave the same way, then they could all produce more as a result of the general increase in prices. In this way, all the firms in the economy would mistake the general price rise for an increase in their own price. With all firms producing more than their potential Y_i^*, output in the economy as a whole will surely be above potential. Hence, we have an explanation of a departure of real GNP from potential GNP, based on the confusion within individual firms about what is going on elsewhere in the economy.

THE FIRM'S INFORMATION ABOUT THE PRICE LEVEL: A MORE SOPHISTICATED VIEW

In the explanation given above, firms do not change their expectations of the aggregate price level when they observe the prices of their own prod-

[6] In describing one of the early information-based models, Edmund S. Phelps of Columbia University used the island analogy. The imaginary islands are sometimes called Phelpsian islands. See his edited volume *Microeconomic Foundations of Employment and Inflation*, W. W. Norton, New York, 1970, pp. 1–26.

ucts. In an economic environment where there is a close relationship between economic activity in different industries, a firm would be naive not to guess that other firms in the economy were having the same type of experience. In other words, the observation that the price is high in one firm's market is an indication to that firm that prices are likely to be high in other markets. This would be especially true in a highly inflationary economy, where an increase in the price of one commodity is usually only an indication that inflation is continuing: The price of everything is going up, too.

Consider, first, an extreme case where economic conditions are such that relative prices of different products never change; that is, all the fluctuations in prices are due to general inflation where all prices move together. If relative prices never change, then firms would realize that any change in their own price simply represents an equal change in all prices. The firms would instantaneously adjust their expectations of other prices by the same amount that their own price increased. In Equation 14–2, P^e would increase by exactly the amount that P_i increased. Hence, the firm's production would not change. In this example, the information-based explanation for the departure of real GNP from potential disappears. Although this example is extreme, even in a less extreme situation we would expect firms to make use of information available in their own market when guessing economic conditions elsewhere. More specifically, when a firm observes the price of its own product it will adjust its expectation of prices elsewhere. This adjustment will be based on the relationship between the firm's price and the general price level that the firm has experienced over time.

In the three panels of Figure 14–4, we illustrate three different price experiences of a representative firm. Each of the points in the diagrams represents a year's experience of two variables: the general price level P that prevailed in the economy, and the firm's own price P_i that it received for its product. On the vertical axis of each diagram we indicate the general price level P. We measure P compared to the firm's forecast, before each year begins, of the general price level P. This forecast is done without any knowledge of (or is not conditional on) events in its own market. This could be next year's forecast of the overall price level from an econometric consulting firm. We represent this forecast by $\hat{P}$. On the horizontal axis of each of the diagrams is the firm's own price. It also is measured relative to the unconditional forecast of the general price level at the start of each year.

A point toward the top of each diagram indicates a year with a high general price level, compared with what was forecast at the start of the year. Points at the bottom represent a surprisingly low price. Looking in the other two directions, points to the right indicate years when the firm experienced a relatively high price for its product. Points to the left show low prices at the firm. Each of the diagrams has many such points, indicating many years of experience for the representative firm.

Two positively sloped lines appear in each of the diagrams. One line is a 45-degree line with a slope of 1. This line shows the points where the firm's

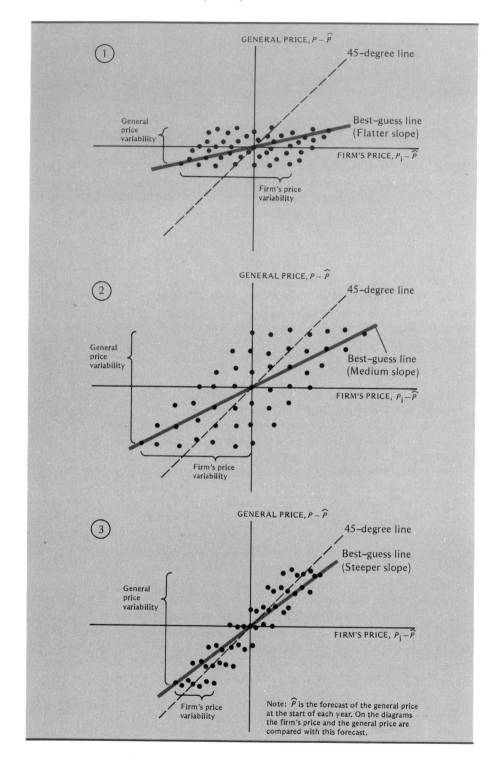

price is equal to the overall price level; there is no relative price advantage to the firm for movements along this line. As we move up the line, both the firm's price and the general price move up in the same proportion, leaving relative conditions for the firm unchanged. Points to the *right and left* of the 45-degree line represent relative price differences. For example, the farther a point is to the left of the 45-degree line, the more the firm's own price falls short of prices elsewhere. We have drawn the points to be evenly spaced about the 45-degree line. This means that the firm's experience is that its own price is just as likely to be above as below the general price level.

The difference between the diagrams is in how spread out the points are in the various directions. The top panel has a large spread in the horizontal direction. The middle panel has about equal spreads in both directions. The bottom panel has a small spread in the horizontal direction. These differences affect how informative the firm's own price is for making inferences about the general price level.

The second upward-sloping line in each of the diagrams reflects this difference. This line represents the best guess of the general price level given the firm's observation of its own price. We call it the **best-guess line**. It is the best guess because it is the line that makes the vertical distances between the points and the line as small as possible. If the manager of the firm observed these historical points and wanted to make a guess of the general price level given an observation of the firm's price, a common sense approach would be to find a line that makes the differences between the general price level and the firm's price as small as possible. In statistical terminology this is the least-squares line, because actually the sum of the squares of the vertical distances between the points and the line are being minimized.

We can represent the best-guess line with an algebraic formula:

$$P^e = \hat{P} + b(P_i - \hat{P}). \tag{14-3}$$

In words this means that the firm's guess P^e of the general price is greater than what was forecast $\hat{P}$ at the start of the year by an amount equal to a constant b times the difference between the firm's own price P_i and the forecast of the general price $\hat{P}$. The coefficient b is the slope of the best-guess

◀ **Figure 14-4.   THREE ALTERNATIVE PRICE EXPERIENCES OF A FIRM.**
(1) In the top panel there is a large relative price variability and a small general price variability. The firm's best-guess line is fairly flat. Its slope b is near zero. The firm's own price is not very informative in helping the firm guess the general price level. (2) In the middle panel the general and the relative price variabilities are the same. There is a large general price variability compared with the top panel. The best-guess line is now steeper than in the top panel. Its slope b is about halfway between zero and 1. (3) In the bottom panel there is a small relative price variability compared with the top panel. The best-guess line is much steeper than in the top panel. Together the three panels show that the smaller the relative price variability and the larger the general price variability, the steeper the best-guess line.

line. For example, if the coefficient b is .3, the forecast of the general price $\hat{P}$ is 1.0, and the firm observes a price P_i in its own market equal to 1.1, then the best guess of the general price is $1.0 + .3(1.1 - 1.0) = 1.03$. In the example, the firm observes a price 10 percent higher in its own market, and its guess is that the general price is 3 percent higher than originally forecast.

Note that if $b = 0$ then the firm's own price does not influence its estimate of the general price level. This is the least informative case, where there is much relative price variability and little general price variability. At the other extreme is the case where $b = 1$. Then the firm increases its estimate of the general price level by exactly the amount that its own price increases. This case corresponds to the extreme example we considered earlier, where there are never any changes in relative prices.

In general, however, the coefficient b is less than 1 and greater than zero. The size of b depends on whether the relative price variability is large compared with the general price variability. The larger the general price variability, the steeper the best-guess line and the more the firm changes its estimate of the general price level when it sees its own price increase. For example, in a typical high-inflation economy, the general price variability is high. Firms usually guess that their own price increase is a signal for another increase in inflation. The relation between price variability and the slope of the best-guess line is an important implication of the information-based theory, as we show below.

THE LUCAS SUPPLY CURVE

If we substitute the firm's best guess (Equation 14–3) into the firm's supply equation (14–1) we get

$$Y_i = h[P_i - \hat{P} - b(P_i - \hat{P})] + Y_i^* \tag{14-4}$$

or,

$$Y_i = h(1 - b)(P_i - \hat{P}) + Y_i^*. \tag{14-5}$$

Equation 14–5 shows how the representative firm produces more when its own price is greater than the unconditional forecast of the general price level. It has the same form as the firm's supply function except for the fact that the supply coefficient is related to the coefficient b. If b is near 1, then $h(1 - b)$ is near zero and the firm does not supply much additional output. At the other extreme, when b is near zero the supply coefficient is larger.

The aggregate supply curve for the entire economy is obtained by adding up all the representative firms' supply curves. Real GNP, which we continue to denote by Y, is the sum of all the individual firms' Y_i. The aggregate price

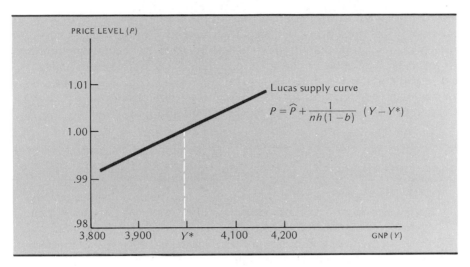

Figure 14–5.   THE LUCAS SUPPLY CURVE.
When aggregate price variability is large compared with relative price variability, the slope of the aggregate supply curve is steep. Firms do not respond by much to changes in their own prices because they suspect that such changes represent changes in the general price level. ($\hat{P} = 1.0$ in this diagram.)

level P is simply the sum of the individual firms' prices P_i divided by n, the number of firms.

If we use this notation, and add up Equation 14–5 for all the firms in the economy, we get

$$Y = nh(1 - b)(P - \hat{P}) + Y^*, \tag{14-6}$$

which is the Lucas supply curve for the entire economy. We illustrate the Lucas supply curve in Figure 14–5, where the price level is the vertical axis and output is the horizontal axis. Note that the slope of the Lucas aggregate supply curve depends on b, the slope of the best-guess line. Because the slope b in turn depends on the importance of general versus relative price variability, we now can see that the aggregate supply curve itself depends on these variabilities. When the variability of the general price level is greater, the slope of the Lucas supply curve is steeper.

It will be useful to compare the Lucas supply curve with the price-adjustment curve we introduced in Part I. To do this, we rewrite the Lucas supply curve with the price level on the left-hand side:

$$P = \hat{P} + \frac{1}{nh(1 - b)}(Y - Y^*). \tag{14-7}$$

The main difference between the Lucas supply curve (written in this way) and the price-adjustment curve is that, in the former, prices adjust without any lag. Prices must be viewed as perfectly flexible in the Lucas aggregate supply curve, rather than predetermined as in the price-adjustment curve. In terms of the algebra of the equation, one can see that there is no lag, because the current value of Y is on the right-hand side of Equation 14–7, rather than the lagged value of Y. By contrast, the price-adjustment equations in Chapter 6 had lagged Y on the right-hand side.

The Lucas Supply Curve

1. Because of imperfect information, firms cannot observe exactly what is going on in other markets. They make a best guess about what is going on by looking at their own market. In particular, if the prices of the goods they are selling are high, that is an imperfect signal that other prices are high.

2. Firms produce more when all prices rise more than the firms expected. Each firm in the economy sees a higher price but mistakenly thinks that it represents a relative price increase. Conversely, firms produce less when the price is unexpectedly low.

3. The positive relationship between GNP and unexpected price rises is called the Lucas supply curve.

14.3 Policy Implication of the Imperfect Information Model

In Figure 14–6 we combine the Lucas aggregate supply curve with the standard aggregate demand curve that we derived in Part I. To determine the impact of an increase in the money supply on real GNP and the price level, we want to shift the aggregate demand curve to the right. If the aggregate supply curve stays put, then the rightward movement of the aggregate demand curve will stimulate real GNP and raise prices.

Whether or not the aggregate supply curve stays put depends on whether people's expectations of the price level change. If these expectations adjust upward in response to the increase in the money supply, then the aggregate supply curve will shift up. As is shown in Figure 14–6, the expectations-induced shift in the aggregate supply curve will tend to reduce the impact of the increase in the money supply.

The case where expectations are rational is of particular interest because much of the policy effectiveness debates of the 1970s centered on it. Expectations are rational if people in the economy make the most of the information that is available when making forecasts. To make the concept

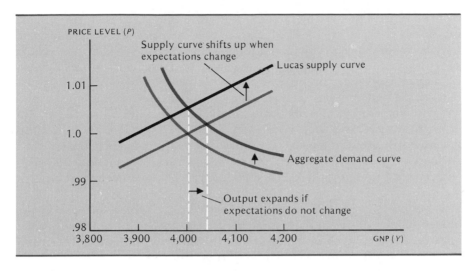

Figure 14-6. AGGREGATE DEMAND AND THE LUCAS SUPPLY CURVE.
A rightward shift of the aggregate demand curve causes the aggregate supply curve to shift as well, because expectations change. Output stays the same and the price level rises.

operational, economists have generally assumed that the information available to people includes a model of the economy—for example, the same model that we have been using—as well as complete knowledge of economic policy. No economist actually thinks that many people go through the formal process of solving a model. Rather, here, as in many other areas of economics, the model is a reasonable summary of a more informal thought process.

To derive the policy implications of the Lucas supply function with rational expectations, let us focus on a model with the aggregate demand curve:

$$Y = k_0 + k_1 (M/P). \qquad (14-8)$$

The coefficients k_0 and k_1 are the intercept and slope of the aggregate demand schedule. For example, if k_0 equals 2,287 and k_1 equals 2.855, the aggregate demand curve is the same as the one Chapter 5. (The coefficient k_0 incorporates government spending.) The rest of the model is given by the Lucas supply function, Equation 14-6, which we rewrite as

$$Y = c(P - \hat{P}) + Y^*, \qquad (14-9)$$

with c equal to $nh(1 - b)$.

Now suppose that the economy is operating at potential GNP ($Y = Y^*$), and that the Federal Reserve increases the money supply. That is, M rises. Looking closely at Equation 14–8, we can see that the price level P, or output Y, must increase. Since people are rational in forming their expectations of P, they also are looking at Equations 14–8 and 14–9 trying to figure out what is going to happen to Y and P when the money supply goes up. They also anticipate the money supply increase and therefore *expect* that the price level will rise. That is, their rational expectation of the price level $\hat{P}$ increases. But note from the Lucas supply function shown in Equation 14–9 that this means that Y does not rise at all: P and $\hat{P}$ rise in the same proportion when an increase in M is anticipated. Now looking back at Equation 14–8 it is clear that if Y does not change then P must rise by the same amount that M increases.

In summary, with rational expectations, an *anticipated* increase in the money supply will result in no increase in real GNP. It will result only in an increase in the price level that matches the increase in money. *Anticipated monetary policy is ineffective: It has no effect on real GNP.*[7]

Another important policy implication of the information-based model concerns the problem of disinflation. Recall that, in the model of Chapter 7, there was no painless way to bring down the rate of inflation. Some reduction of actual GNP below potential GNP was necessary if we were to get a reduction in the rate of inflation. The implications of the information-based model are quite different.

Suppose that we want to reduce the rate of inflation from 10 to 3 percent. Then if the Fed reduces the rate of money growth from 10 to 3 percent immediately—announcing that it will do so—the information-based model with rational expectations implies that the price level and the expected price level will immediately change their inflationary path from 10 to 3 percent. Prices can adjust instantaneously, and people know this. Since P and $\hat{P}$ never diverge, real GNP never departs from potential GNP. The disinflation is achieved without any recession! If true, this would be extremely important for policy-makers in an inflationary situation. In order to reduce inflation instantaneously and painlessly, they would merely have to announce a sharp decline in the growth rate of money. People would immediately reduce their expectations of inflation, and actual inflation would be reduced by exactly the same amount.[8]

The policy ineffectiveness results are illustrated in Figure 14–6 above. When expectations are rational the supply curve shifts up by the same amount as the aggregate demand curve. Compare this with the case where

[7] This implication of the Lucas supply function and rational expectations was first pointed out by Thomas Sargent and Neil Wallace in "Rational Expectations, the Optimal Monetary Instrument, and the Optimal Money Supply Rule," *Journal of Political Economy,* Vol. 83, pp. 241–254, 1975.

[8] See Thomas J. Sargent, "The Ends of Four Big Inflations," in Robert E. Hall (ed.), *Inflation: Causes and Effects,* University of Chicago Press for the National Bureau of Economic Research, 1982, pp. 41–97.

expectations are sluggish or otherwise dependent on the past. Then the aggregate supply curve does not shift up as much. Hence, anticipated changes in money do affect output.

There are two crucial assumptions behind the policy ineffectiveness and instantaneous disinflation results: (1) Prices are perfectly flexible, and (2) expectations are rational. We showed in Figure 14–6 that monetary policy can be effective if people's expectations adjust slowly. Alternatively, if the money supply is increased unexpectedly, so that people do not anticipate the increase, then their expectations will not adjust and monetary policy will have an effect.

The "new classical" policy results derived from the information-based model should be distinguished from those of the "classical" model of Chapter 13 and of Section 14.1. While both analyses assume that prices are perfectly flexible, the analysis using the Lucas supply function generates movements in real GNP that are consistent with departures of real GNP from potential. Recall that in the classical model there were no departures of real GNP from potential; monetary policy was always neutral. In the analysis presented in this section, anticipated increases in the money supply are neutral, but unanticipated or surprise increases are not.

New Classical Theory in Washington

The information-based models apparently had some influence on economic decisions in the early months of the Reagan administration's first term. Some of the early advisers to the administration argued that the rate of inflation could be brought down very quickly, with little or no recession, by announcing an immediate reduction in money growth. Their forecast was heavily influenced by the Claremont Economics Institute Econometric Model, which attempted to incorporate some of the rational expectations ideas; the Claremont modelers prepared such an optimistic inflation-output forecast for the administration. Furthermore, many of the ideas underlying the Lucas supply model with rational expectations were paraphrased by the director of the Office of Management and Budget, David Stockman, in order to deride the econometric models that were giving less optimistic forecasts of inflation and GNP growth—including that of the Congressional Budget Office. Before the House Committee on the Budget on March 26, 1981, Stockman said, "Standard econometric models fail to portray accurately the crucial influence of monetary policy . . . these models do not capture the effects of expectations. The defects . . . are so pervasive as to preclude their uses . . ."

While some of the ideas behind the Lucas supply curve and rational expectations were used in the political debates, such applications were not endorsed by Lucas or other developers of the theories. Lucas was quoted in *Business Week* at the time (March 2, 1981), stating that applications of rational expectations ideas to such new or unfamiliar policies were likely to be inaccurate: "For that purpose rational expectations doesn't have much to add." Nevertheless, the policy debate and the actual decision to have a contractionary monetary policy were probably influenced by these theories—however inappropriately or inaccurately. Perhaps a better understanding on the part of policymakers, or at least by their advisers, of the actual meaning and empirical validity of the information-based models might have prevented this.

14.4 Does the Imperfect Information Theory Explain the Departures?

Perhaps the most remarkable thing about the Lucas aggregate supply function is that in principle it can explain the major patterns of economic fluctuations without the use of sticky prices. This is in sharp contrast to the model developed in Part I, where we rely on sticky prices to explain the fluctuations. This fact perhaps more than anything else underlies the early enthusiasm for imperfect information models. As we have just seen, without sticky prices, economic policy works quite differently from the models we have focused on in this book. In fact, monetary policy can lose its effectiveness altogether when prices are not sticky.

Stating that a theory can explain the fluctuations *in principle* is much different from stating that it explains the actual fluctuations. In principle, the theory can explain the departures of real GNP from potential GNP as coming from price surprises, and it can explain the positive relation between output and prices from the basic theory of firm supply along with certain information barriers. To check whether the theory works *in practice,* however, we need to look at the magnitude and timing of the actual fluctuations, and compare these with the magnitude and timing of the price surprises. For this we can make use of the available empirical research.

There have been many empirical investigations designed to determine whether the theory does explain the facts of economic fluctuations. Some of these investigations compare price surprises—that is, the difference between P and $\hat{P}$—with the fluctuations in the economy. If positive price surprises usually occur when the economy goes into a boom, and if negative price surprises usually occur when the economy goes into a slump, then there would be good evidence for the theory. Note that even measuring price surprises is a difficult empirical undertaking, for it requires getting a measure for $\hat{P}$ to subtract from P. Most studies attempt to measure $\hat{P}$ by using statistical techniques to infer the public's forecasts. Others attempt to obtain direct measures of people's forecasts by using survey data. Because it is very difficult to get a good measure of $\hat{P}$, these empirical tests must be interpreted with some caution.

Nevertheless, based on research completed over the last 10 years, it does not appear that price surprises are of sufficient magnitude or are timed appropriately to explain the departures. Statistical studies have shown that there is a very weak relation between price surprises (that is, $P - \hat{P}$) and the departures of real GNP from potential GNP. Moreover, for recent years, the relation seems to go the wrong way![9]

Some researchers have attempted to test the information-based theory by looking for a relationship between money surprises and the departures of real GNP from potential GNP. For most theories of aggregate demand, there is a close relationship between price surprises and money surprises. When the Federal Reserve increases the money supply, there usually is a surprise increase in prices. This was illustrated in the previous section on policy. Robert Barro of Harvard University has been the champion of this approach.[10] Early research seemed to indicate that money surprises were important—even more important than actual or forecasted money. In Figure 14–7 we show some of the data used by Barro in his empirical work. As the figure shows, there clearly is a close relation between money surprises and the movements of the departures of actual GNP from potential GNP. However, except for the 1970s, there is also a fairly close relation between actual money and the departures, a result that supports the sticky-price models we have used in this book. Actual money does not fare very well in the 1970s, however. Apparently, the actual money supply is increasing more rapidly because of inflation, and this tends to blur the usual relation between actual money and the departures of actual GNP from potential GNP.

Figure 14–7 indicates that Barro's finding that money surprises are much more important than actual money might not stand up to attempts to deal with the longer-run movements in money in the 1970s. In fact, Barro's results have been brought into question by later researchers, and it now appears that actual money is also a factor in the departures of actual GNP from potential GNP.[11] This casts further doubt on the information-based model as an alternative to the sticky-price model.[12]

[9] See Thomas Sargent, "A Classical Macroeconometric Model of the United States," *Journal of Political Economy*, Vol. 84, pp. 207–238, 1976, and Ray Fair, "An Analysis of a Macroeconomic Model with Rational Expectations in the Stock and Bond Markets," *Journal of Political Economy*, Vol. 67, pp. 539–552, 1979.

[10] See Robert J. Barro, "Unanticipated Money, Output, and the Price Level in the United States," *Journal of Political Economy*, Vol. 86, pp. 549–580, 1977.

[11] See Frederic Mishkin, "Does Unanticipated Money Matter? An Econometric Investigation," *Journal of Political Economy*, Vol. 91, pp. 22–51, 1982.

[12] For a further discussion of the data presented in Figure 14–7 and more elaboration on this theoretical presentation of the information-based models, see John B. Taylor, "Rational Expectations Models in Macroeconomics," in K. Arrow and S. Honkapohja (eds.), *Frontiers of Economics*, Basil Blackwell, 1986.

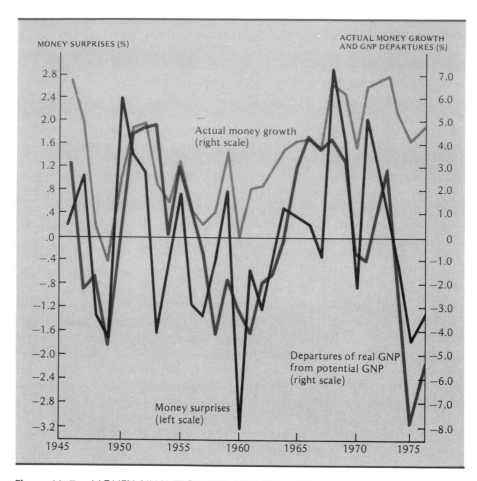

Figure 14–7.   MONEY, UNANTICIPATED MONEY, AND REAL ACTIVITY.
Plotted are Barro's data on actual money, money surprises, and the departures of real GNP from potential GNP, $(Y - Y^*)/Y^*$.

Finally, the information-based models—without some additional changes —are not capable of explaining the *persistence* of the departures of actual GNP from potential GNP. Recall that such persistence is an important feature of the fluctuations. The information-based models imply that real GNP always snaps right back to potential GNP. To explain the longer persistence, other things—like slow adjustment of employment to changes in demand— must be added to the model.

Two other problems with the theory should be mentioned. First, the in-formational restrictions placed on firms do not appear to be realistic in many situations. In particular, the assumption that firms know the price of the goods they are selling, but not the price of the goods they are buying, does not seem plausible for most firms. Second, the assumption of perfectly flexible prices does not appear to describe how most markets work. While it is true that some auction markets—such as the New York Stock Exchange —have rapid changes in prices, most markets have some rigidities in their prices. Many firms *set* their prices for a period of time. Rather than being price takers as in the information-based model, they are price setters. The price of labor—the wage rate—is particularly sticky. In labor markets the wage paid to workers is frequently set for a number of years.

If the new classical theory seems to have all these problems, what is the reason for spending so much time developing and studying it? The theory has had enormous impact on the way that all macroeconomists work. As James Tobin, the Keynesian macroeconomist from Yale University, has stated, "The ideas of the [new classical macroeconomics] are too distinctive and powerful to be lost in the shuffle. They are bound to shape whatever orthodoxy emerges."[13] Although rational expectations is an appropriate and useful assumption in models with sticky prices, the assumption was first introduced in new classical models. The use of rational expectations to analyze consumption, investment, and the exchange rate, as described in Part II, incorporates techniques developed in the new classical models. Moreover, the new classical theory illustrates in a very simple and elegant way the difference between anticipated and unanticipated macroeconomic policy. In the information-based model, there is an enormous difference between anticipated and unanticipated policy. Anticipated policy has no effect on real GNP, whereas unanticipated policy has a powerful effect. There is also a difference between the effects of anticipated and unanticipated policy in models based on sticky prices—as we will show in Chapter 15—but the difference is not as pronounced, or as easy to illustrate.

Anticipated and Unanticipated Money: Policy and Tests

POLICY

1. The Lucas supply function with rational expectations implies that only unanticipated changes in the money supply affect real output. Anticipated changes in the money supply affect only the price level, leaving real output equal to potential. This is the "policy ineffectiveness proposition."

2. Two crucial assumptions underlie the policy ineffectiveness result: Prices and wages are perfectly flexible, and expectations are rational. If prices are sticky, anticipated changes in the money supply have an effect on real output, even if expectations are rational.

---

[13] James Tobin, "The Monetarist Counterrevolution Today—An Appraisal," *Economic Journal*, Vol. 91, pp. 29–42, 1981.

TESTS

1. The new classical theory, in which the Lucas supply function is central, is an improvement over the pure classical model because it can explain in principle the departures of output from potential, and the positive price-output correlation.

2. In careful statistical tests the theory does not seem to stand up to the facts, however. Anticipated money as well as unanticipated money affect output, and price surprises have a small effect on output.

Review and Practice

MAJOR POINTS

1. The pure classical model does not explain the departures of output from potential. It can explain the fluctuations in the economy only by hypothesizing large and persistent fluctuations in potential output.

2. Real business-cycle theories are based on the pure classical model. In these theories fluctuations in potential output are due to changes in labor supply or labor demand. There is no role for monetary factors in economic fluctuations in these real models.

3. Another fact of the business cycle that is missed by the classical models is the positive correlation between prices and output.

4. The new classical theory was developed to explain the departures of real output from potential, while retaining the assumption that prices are flexible. In the new classical theory, output rises above potential because firms mistake general price increases for relative increases in their own prices. They are fooled into producing more than they would if they were perfectly informed. Imperfect information is crucial to the new classical models.

5. The relationship between prices and output in the new classical models is called the Lucas supply function. According to this function, GNP rises above potential when the price level is higher than was forecast at the start of the year. Conversely, GNP is below potential when the price level is lower than was forecast at the start of the year.

6. The slope of the Lucas supply curve depends on the variability of the general price level. The greater the variability of the price level, the steeper the Lucas supply curve, and the less firms increase their output when their own price rises above what was expected.

7. According to the Lucas supply function with rational expectations, only unanticipated changes in money affect output. An anticipated decrease in the money supply lowers the price level but does not reduce GNP. Unanticipated decreases in the money supply do decrease GNP, however.

8. Careful tests of the new classical theory indicate that it is not able to explain the actual fluctuations in the economy. Price surprises do not lead to large changes in output, and anticipated changes in money do seem to affect real output.

9. A crucial assumption behind the policy ineffectiveness result is that prices and wages are perfectly flexible.

KEY TERMS AND CONCEPTS

Price-output correlation

Real business-cycle theories

New classical theory

Imperfect information

Firm supply curve

Relative price

Local price

General price

Unconditional forecast of general
   price

Guess of general price given local price

Best-guess line

Price surprises

Relative and general price variability

Lucas supply curve

Slope of Lucas supply curve

Price-adjustment curve

Anticipated money

Unanticipated money

Policy ineffectiveness proposition

QUESTIONS FOR DISCUSSION AND REVIEW

1. What are the real theories of economic fluctuations? What do they assume about shifts in labor supply and labor demand? What do they assume about the slopes of labor supply and labor demand?

2. Why might the real interest rate increase labor supply?

3. What is the Lucas supply function? Why do the deviations of output from potential depend on price surprises?

4. Why does the Lucas supply curve require that firms are misinformed about what is happening in other markets?

5. Why is the Lucas supply curve steep if the variance of the general price level is high?

6. What is the policy ineffectiveness proposition? Explain what happens to the price level and output in the new classical model when the Fed increases the money supply and announces it in advance.

7. What two assumptions are crucial to the policy ineffectiveness proposition? If these two assumptions are dropped, explain what would happen when the money supply is increased.

8. Describe why prices and output are positively correlated during economic fluctuations according to the new classical theory. Compare this explanation to that using a slow price adjustment.

9. Describe how tests of the new classical theory have indicated that it cannot fully explain the facts of economic fluctuations.

PROBLEMS

Numerical

1. The labor supply schedule is $100 + 2W/P$. The labor demand schedule is $200 - 8W/P$. Find the levels of the real wage and employment in equilibrium. Now suppose that demand falls, so that the demand schedule is $190 - 8W/P$. By how much does the wage fall? By how much does employment fall? Explain why the wage falls by a larger percentage than does employment.

2. The aggregate demand schedule is $120 - 20P$. The Lucas supply curve governs the economy. There are 100 firms. Each one has the supply schedule $Y_i = 4(P_i - P^e) + 1$. Each one forms its forecast of the overall price level by using last year's price, P_{-1}, and its own price; $P^e = P_{-1} + .5 (P_i - P_{-1})$. Find the Lucas aggregate supply function by solving for P_i. Now assume that $P_{-1} = 1.00$. Find the levels of aggregate output and price at the intersection of the aggregate demand and Lucas aggregate supply curves. Suppose demand rises, so that the aggregate demand schedule is $131 - 20P$. Find output and price. Compute the price surprise and explain why output rises when the price surprise occurs.

3. Suppose that the Lucas supply curve is

$$Y = c(P - \hat{P}) + Y^*,$$

with $c = 20,000$ and $Y^* = 4,000$ (billions of dollars). For example, when the price level P is 1.01 and the expected price $\hat{P}$ is 1.0, output Y is 4,200, or 5 percent above potential output $Y^* = 4,000$. Suppose that the aggregate demand curve is

$$Y = 1,101 + 1.288 \, G + 3.221 \, M/P.$$

   a. Suppose that the economy has been at rest for some period with output at potential, and that no changes in policy are expected for the near future. The money supply M is 600 and government spending is 750. What is the price level? (Hint: If there are no surprises the actual and the expected price levels will be the same.)

   b. Now suppose that the Fed announces that it will increase the money supply from 600 to 620. What are the new levels of output and price level?

   c. Now suppose that the Fed announces that it will increase the money supply from 600 to 620 but actually increases it to 670. What are the new levels of output and price level?

4. Suppose that automatic stabilizers cause government purchases to rise when GNP is below potential and to fall when GNP is above potential. Algebraically we might represent this as

$$G = 750 - g(Y - Y^*),$$

where potential output Y^* is 4,000. The coefficient g measures the strength of the automatic stabilizer.

   a. Substitute this expression for G in the aggregate demand function in Problem 3, and solve for output Y in terms of P (M is held fixed at 600). This is the aggregate demand curve incorporating the automatic stabilizer. Describe how the slope of the aggregate demand curve depends on the coefficient g.

   b. For three different values of g (0, .01, and .1) describe the effect on output of an unanticipated increase in money like the one in Problem 3c. Assume that people know the value of g in each case. Do the effects on output depend on the value of the coefficient g? If so, then does it appear that even well-understood automatic stabilizers are effective in that they influence output? Explain your results intuitively. Why might automatic government spending stabilizers affect output while anticipated changes in money do not? (See B. T. McCallum and J. K. Whitaker, "The Effectiveness of Fiscal Feedback Rules and Automatic Stabilizers under Rational Expectation," *Journal of Monetary Economics*, Vol. 5, pp. 171–186, 1979, for a further discussion of this type of policy problem.)

Analytical

1. (Real Business Cycle Theory) Consider an economy in which prices are flexible, but in which aggregate supply varies positively with the interest rate. Recall that this may be the case if labor supply shifts to the right with increases in the interest rate. Aggregate demand continues to be described by spending balance and money market equilibrium conditions. The economy is described by the following three equations:

$$Y = a_0 - a_1 R \qquad \text{(IS curve)}$$
$$M/P = kY - hR \qquad \text{(LM curve)}$$
$$Y = c_0 + c_1 R \qquad \text{(Aggregate supply)}$$

   a. Describe how output, interest rates, and the price level are determined in this economy. Depict the situation graphically.
   b. Describe the effects of an increase in the money supply on output, interest rates, the price level, consumption, investment, and net exports. Does monetary neutrality hold in this model?
   c. Describe the effects of an increase in government spending on output, interest rates, the price level, consumption, investment, and net exports.
   d. From Part c, is an increase in government spending necessarily inflationary, deflationary, or ambiguous? If it is ambiguous, on what does it depend?

2. If the Lucas supply function is written with output on the right and price surprises on the left, it looks like a Phillips curve. Explain what happens to this Phillips curve when relative price variability increases and when general price variability increases. Explain how your results can give rise to a test of the new classical theory.

3. Assume that agents know the true model of the economy, which is given by an aggregate demand curve and a Lucas supply curve. They may or may not, however, know the true value of the money supply.
   a. On the same graph, draw two aggregate demand curves; one for $M=M_0$, and one for $M=M_1>M_0$.
   b. On the same graph, draw a Lucas supply curve assuming agents believe that $M=M_0$. Explain how you know where to position this graph.
   c. Assume now that M is actually equal to M_1. Depict the equilibrium price level, given the assumption of Part b.
   d. Now assume that agents know that M equals M_1. Again, depict the equilibrium price level. For which equilibrium is the price level higher? Explain your result.
   e. Compare the levels of Y, C, X, and I across the equilibrium of Parts c and d.

4. Suppose our model of the economy is given by an aggregate demand curve and a Lucas supply curve as in Equations 14–8 and 14–9. Assume further that agents have complete information about the model of the economy including the value

of the money supply. Potential output is equal to 4,000. The aggregate demand curve goes through the point (4,000, 1.5).

   a. Consider three possible Lucas supply curves going through the points (4,000,1), (4,000,1.5), and (4,000,2). What is the value of P for each of these curves?

   b. Which of the three curves in Part a is the rational expectations Lucas supply curve? In what sense would the other two curves not satisfy rational expectations?

5. In Chapters 6 and 7 we saw that output could deviate from potential in the short run, but that output would always return to potential in the long run after prices had time to adjust. In this chapter we also saw how output could deviate from potential. What defines the "long run" in this model? That is, what must happen in order for output to return to potential? Is this likely to take a very long time?

6. On a graph (3 to 4 inches square) sketch an aggregate demand curve and a Lucas supply curve. Label their intersection point as Y^* and P^*. Now draw two aggregate demand curves, one each a quarter inch to either side of your initial curve. Label the intersection points with the Lucas supply curve $Y+,P+$ and $Y-,P-$. Finally, draw two more aggregate demand curves, three quarters of an inch or so to either side of the original curve, and label the intersection points with $++$ and $--$ subscripts.

   a. What kinds of shocks can cause the aggregate demand curve to vary in the way shown on your graph? What is the relationship between the magnitude of those shocks and the variability in Y and P?

   b. Suppose initially that shocks to the money supply cause the aggregate demand curve to vary within the narrow region. Assume that the Lucas supply curve shown in your graph is the appropriate curve given the magnitude of these shocks. In what sense is the curve "appropriate"?

   c. Now suppose that shocks to the money supply cause the aggregate demand curve to vary within the wider region. How will the Lucas supply curve appropriate to these shocks compare with your initial Lucas supply curve? Sketch the new curve. How do the swings in output and the price level compare with $P--$, $P++$ and $Y--$, $Y++$?

   d. Use these results to explain why output may not deviate much from potential in periods of either highly stable or highly variable prices, but that it may deviate considerably from potential in the transition period from stable to variable prices. Relate your analysis to the experience of the U.S. economy in the late 1960s.

15

The Theory of Wage and
Price Rigidities

IN THIS chapter we take a detailed look at the microeconomics of wage and price rigidities. Although the new classical models and the real business-cycle models with perfectly flexible prices are in principle able to explain economic fluctuations, many economists do not feel these models explain the actual empirical regularities very well. We considered the empirical evidence in the last chapter. The evidence suggests that models based on wage and price rigidities deserve consideration as the explanation of why real GNP departs from potential GNP for prolonged periods.

One of the most important concepts concerning wage and price rigidities is that they are temporary. The word "sticky," rather than "fixed," connotes the tendency for wage or price rigidities to give way under market pressures. Eventually prices and wages adjust and play their well-known role in allocating goods and employment in an efficient manner. As they do, the economy gradually returns to full employment. Once prices have fully adjusted, the levels of employment and production are given by the long-run classical conditions discussed in Chapter 13.

15.1 Wage Determination

The most comprehensive information about wage determination in the United States pertains to the formal contracts of workers who are members of large labor unions. We will consider this group of workers first, and then go on to discuss the non-union sector.

WAGE DETERMINATION IN THE LARGE UNION SECTOR

Of the 20 percent of U.S. workers who are unionized, about half are involved in collective-bargaining situations that are regularly tracked by the Bureau of Labor Statistics. In total, this group consists of about 10 million workers. Although only 10 percent of the labor force, this group receives enormous attention in the media and in public policy discussions. The industries and unions that make up this group almost personify big business and big labor: It includes the steel, trucking, automobile, aerospace, airlines, tobacco, aluminum, coal, rubber, and electrical industries. Some economists, such as John Dunlop of Harvard and Lester Thurow of M.I.T., have argued that this group establishes wage patterns that other union and non-union workers imitate, although recent empirical studies on the subject indicate that the evidence is mixed.[1]

Government policies to influence wage inflation directly, in which corporate executives and union leaders are told or encouraged by government officials to moderate wage and price increases, almost invariably are aimed at this group. Such policies are called **incomes policies**. For example, in 1978 the Carter administration set forth a voluntary wage and price restraint program in which large firms were asked to submit data on pay to a government Council on Wage and Price Stability. As explained by President Carter's economic advisers, "Compliance was encouraged by appealing to firms and workers to restrain price and pay increases in the public interest."[2]

In most of these industries, contracts last 3 years. Unless there is an early reopening or a delay in negotiating a new contract, the workers signing 3-year contracts will do so every 3 years. For example, the electrical workers negotiated contracts in 1976, 1979, 1982, and so on. About 80 percent of the workers under major collective-bargaining agreements are under 3-year contracts, 15 percent are under 2-year contracts, and only 5 percent are under 1-year contracts. In Figure 15–1 we have plotted the number of workers involved in 3-year contracts each year since 1974.

The important fact that all workers do not sign contracts at the same time is evident in Figure 15–1. Contracts are unsynchronized. Wage negotiations are staggered over the 36 months of the basic contract cycle. At any one

[1] See Daniel J. B. Mitchell, *Union Wages and Inflation,* Brookings Institution, Washington, D.C., 1980, p. 171, or Richard B. Freeman and James L. Medoff, *What Do Unions Do?,* Basic Books, New York, 1984, Chapter 3.

[2] See *Economic Report of the President,* January 1981, p. 59.

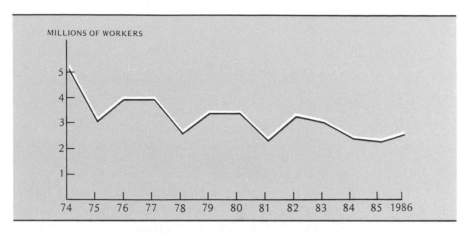

Figure 15–1. NUMBER OF UNION WORKERS IN COLLECTIVE BARGAINING SETTLEMENTS.
Each year only about one-third of the 7 or 8 million workers in major unions (1,000 or more workers) are involved in collective bargaining negotiations. Source: *Current Wage Developments,* Bureau of Labor Statistics, April or March issue, 1975–87.

time, only a small fraction of the workers are signing contracts; the remaining workers either have recently signed their contracts or will sign their contracts in the future. The period in which one contract is in force overlaps the period in which other contracts are in force.

An example will be helpful to illustrate the characteristics of a typical long-term contract. The United Mine Workers signed a contract with the bituminous coal operators in May 1981. The contract affected about 160,000 workers, lasted 40 months, and expired in September 1984. (A 40-month contract would be rounded to 3 years for the Bureau of Labor Statistics' calculations shown in Figure 15–1.) The contract stipulated wage increases that averaged 11 percent per year. The wage increases were $1.20 per hour in the first year, $1.10 in the second year, $1.00 in the third year, and $.30 in the last quarter. This pattern is illustrated in Figure 15–2. These contracted wage increases were made through September 1984. A new 3-year contract was negotiated and signed on October 1, 1984.

Part of the wage increase in the 1981–84 agreement was deferred to the second and third years of the contract. These deferred increases indicate that management and labor had expectations of continued high inflation. It would have been possible to **index** the contract to inflation. In an indexed contract wages automatically increase if there is inflation. But there were no indexing provisions in the coal contract; these increases would—and did— occur regardless of economic conditions and indicate the extent of the nominal rigidity that such contracts impose on the economy. The more recent contract signed in 1984 called for much smaller wage increases (about 3 percent per year), and it was not indexed either. The 1984 contract expires

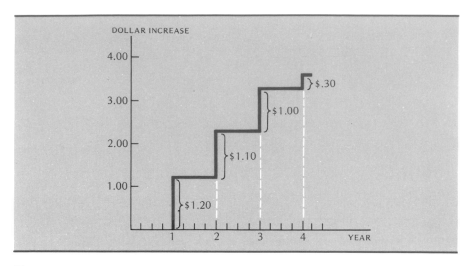

Figure 15–2.   CURRENT AND DEFERRED WAGE INCREASES IN THE 1981–84 COAL CONTRACT.

The largest percentage increase occurred in the first year, but a significant part of the increase was deferred to the second and third years. An inflation rate of about 11 percent was built in to the contract; there was no indexing. The 1984–87 coal contract that followed had a much smaller inflation rate built into the contract.

in January 1988 (another 40-month contract). During the 1984–87 period much smaller nominal wage increases were locked in by contracts like this.

The current and deferred wage and benefit increases in all of the major union contracts are shown in Figure 15–3 for the period from 1968 through 1986. The colored line indicates the change in the first year of the contract; the black line indicates the average yearly change over the life of the contract (3 years in the case of the coal contract). As with the coal contract, a significant amount of the wage increase occurs in the second and third years of the contract. There is some front-end loading, however, in that the largest increases occur in the first year of the contract period.

Part of this front-end loading occurs because—unlike the coal contract—some of the contracts included in Figure 15–3 have indexing clauses. To see the relationship between front-end loading and indexing, recall that indexing clauses stipulate that the wage increase in the later years will be based in part on changes in the consumer price index. For example, one contract would increase the wage rate by .5 percent if the consumer price index increases by 1 percent. This would be 50 percent indexing. Because some inflation was generally expected when these contracts were negotiated, both management and labor would expect that the wage would increase because of indexing. For this reason, when there is more indexing, the pre-set deferred increase for later years is smaller. About 50 percent of the major union workers have indexed contracts; most of these contracts have less than 100 percent indexing.

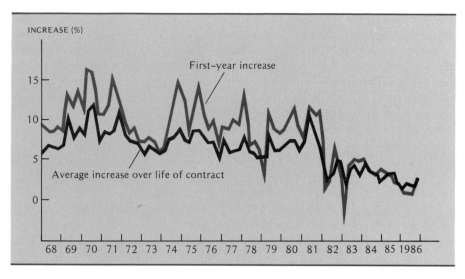

INCREASE (%)

First-year increase

Average increase over life of contract

68 69 70 71 72 73 74 75 76 77 78 79 80 81 82 83 84 85 1986

Figure 15–3. CURRENT AND DEFERRED WAGE INCREASES IN MAJOR UNION CONTRACTS.
Historically, the average increase over the life of the contracts is only slightly less than the increase in the first year. In recent years the two increases are almost the same. Hence, a substantial portion of compensation is deferred to the second and third years of the long-term contracts. Source: *Business Conditions Digest,* February 1987, p. 50.

The effect of the severe recession of the early 1980s is quite apparent in the contract negotiations shown in Figure 15–3. The unemployment rate increased dramatically from about 8 percent in mid-1981 to close to 11 percent by the end of 1982. It was during this period that the wage settlements dropped from nearly 10 percent to below 5 percent. Since 1982 the wage settlements have remained under 5 percent. The huge step downward in wage increases, of course, underlies the United States's success with inflation since 1982.

Thus far we have seen that most workers in large labor unions change their contracts about once every 3 years. What are the factors that determine the size of the wage adjustment when it does occur? Wage and salary decisions are made in collective-bargaining meetings for which both management and labor leaders spend extensive time preparing. While the outcome of any one bargaining situation cannot be predicted with much certainty, a number of factors clearly influence the outcome in particular directions.

The first and perhaps most important is the state of the labor market. If unemployment is high, then labor will be in a relatively weak bargaining position. Conversely, if unemployment is low, then workers will be able to bargain for larger wage increases. The threat of a strike is more credible in good times than in bad. Moreover, firms are likely to settle for larger wage increases in tight market conditions, because they will be better able to pass on their costs in the form of higher prices.

A second factor influencing wage bargaining is the wage paid to comparable workers in other industries. Because not all contract negotiations are synchronized, there are two components of this comparison wage: the wage settlements of workers who have recently signed contracts, and the expected wage settlements of workers who will be signing their contracts in the near future. Looking back at the wage settlements in recently signed contracts makes sense in a current negotiation because those settlements will be in force during part of the contract period under consideration. This backward-looking behavior tends to give some built-in inertia to the wage determination process. If one union group gets a big increase, then the next group of workers in the wage determination cycle will also tend to get a big increase. Lester Thurow describes the process as follows: "Suppose that this year the machinists' union is negotiating a new three year contract. Last year the auto workers negotiated a three year contract for a 10% rise per year. No leader of the machinists can settle for less than 10% and still remain in office. And in two years' time the auto leader will be similarly imprisoned by what the machinists negotiate today."[3] But looking forward to future settlements also makes sense, because the current contract will be in force when these changes take place. In other words, wage determination generally combines elements of forward-looking and backward-looking behavior.[4]

A third factor that will influence wage decisions is the expected rate of inflation. If inflation is expected to be high, then workers will ask for larger wage increases and management will be willing to pay them because their own prices are expected to rise. As with the effect of comparable wage increases, the effect of expected inflation will have both a backward-looking element and a forward-looking element.

WAGE DETERMINATION IN THE NON-UNION SECTOR

It is very common for workers who are not in unions to receive wage and salary adjustments once each year. Although there is no formal contract involved it is unlikely that this wage decision will be changed before the next scheduled adjustment period. Hence, the nominal wage rigidity is very similar to that in the union contracts. One difference is that the entire wage adjustment usually occurs at one time rather than part being deferred as in the

[3] Lester Thurow, "Thurow's Third Way," *The Economist,* January 23–29, 1982.
[4] The implication of staggered wage setting combined with rational expectations of future wage, price, and unemployment is discussed in more detail in John B. Taylor, "Staggered Wage Setting in a Macro Model," *American Economic Review,* Vol. 69 (May 1979), pp. 108–113.

second and third years of the large union contracts. This is probably due to the shorter time between wage adjustments.

For example, our university adjusts our salaries once each year. We get a letter from the dean in May or June giving our salary for the 12-month period beginning September 1. This nominal wage rate is rarely changed before the next salary adjustment period the following year. This type of annual wage setting is common in many sectors of the economy.

In preparation for a wage adjustment, the management of non-union firms must obtain information very similar to that obtained by management of unionized firms preparing for a collective-bargaining meeting. In a large non-union firm there are usually specialists called wage and salary administrators who must make a wage decision. They obtain information about the current labor market situation. They conduct wage surveys or subscribe to a wage survey performed by an outside group. They also attempt to forecast the rate of inflation.

Although the wage decision will usually be made under more competitive conditions than exist in a collective-bargaining situation, these factors—the state of the labor market and wage and price inflation—will influence the final outcome in similar directions. If unemployment is very low and is expected to remain low for the next year, then management will try to pay a relatively high wage compared to other firms employing similarly skilled workers. An attractive wage will prevent workers from quitting and help to lure workers from other firms if necessary for expansion. On the other hand, if unemployment is high, there will be less of a worry that workers will quit to look for jobs elsewhere. Moreover, if the year is expected to be bad for sales, an expansion of production requiring more workers would be unlikely.

If wages are expected to be relatively high at other firms—either because of recent wage decisions of these firms or because of expected wage increases at other firms—then the wage will necessarily be higher. Information about both recent wage decisions and intended wage decisions in the near future can be obtained from wage surveys.[5]

Although there is little direct evidence on when most non-union firms have their scheduled wage increases, it is unlikely that they all occur at the same time. Hence, there is a type of nonsynchronization that we observe for the union sector. Figure 15–4 illustrates the simple situation where there are four wage-adjustment periods through the year: January 1, April 1, July 1, and October 1. It is clear from this illustration that staggered wage setting gives rise to an overlapping of wage decisions.

---

[5] Recently some formal theories have been developed to explain this relative wage setting. See Janet Yellen, "Efficiency Wage Models of Unemployment," *American Economic Review*, Vol. 74 (May 1984), pp. 200–205. Or see Lawrence F. Katz, "Efficiency Wage Theories: A Partial Evaluation," in S. Fischer (ed.), *Macroeconomics Annual*, Vol. 1, National Bureau of Economic Research, 1986, pp. 235–289. The term "efficiency wage" theory is used for these explanations because paying a wage close to the going wage for similar work is usually supposed to increase efficiency by reducing turnover, or by making the workers feel better.

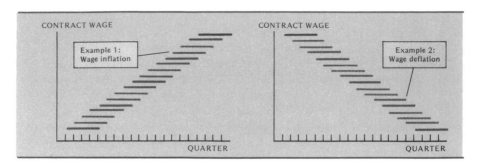

Figure 15–4. STAGGERED ANNUAL WAGE SETTING WITH FOUR WAGE-ADJUST-
MENT PERIODS THROUGHOUT THE YEAR.
There are four groups of workers in each example. The contract wage of each worker
group is denoted by a different color shade from very dark to very light. Because wages
are not all set at the same time (that is, they are not synchronized), the contract wage of
one group overlaps that of all the other groups. This is shown in the diagram with the flat
contract wage lines on top or below each other. In the left panel, there is a general inflation: Each group attempts to get ahead of the previous group. In the right panel, there is a
general deflation: Each group tries to get below the previous group.

WHY ARE WAGES SET FOR LONG PERIODS WITH FEW
CONTINGENCIES?

We have just seen that unionized workers generally have their wages predetermined in 3-year contracts. Only a fraction of these contracts are contingent on the cost of living, and none, to our knowledge, is contingent on
any other economic variable. Furthermore, wage setting in non-union firms
seems to operate in much the same way, though wages are reconsidered annually instead of every 3 years.

Adjustment Costs. The costs of adjusting wages and salaries may be high.
Consider the situation where wage rates are determined in collective-bargaining negotiations between large corporations and labor unions. In preparation for these negotiations management spends months surveying wages
in other industries, estimating changes in labor productivity, forecasting
changes in the firm's own profits, and obtaining estimates of the general inflation during the upcoming contract period. To be adequately informed
during the collective-bargaining sessions, labor leaders must be equally and
independently prepared; hence, they must also spend months preparing for
negotiations. Moreover, there is a threat of a strike in almost every collective-bargaining situation. An actual strike is obviously costly for both sides,
but the mere preparation for a possible strike is also costly. The firm must
accumulate and finance additional inventories to be used if a strike occurs.
Hence, production will be abnormally high before negotiations, and abnormally low after negotiations as firms draw down inventories when a strike

does not occur. These swings in production raise average costs to the firm. Given these high costs it is understandable that many collective-bargaining negotiations occur only once every 3 years.

Indexing. Why aren't the contracts that are negotiated contingent on events that may occur before the next renewal? We have noted that some of the contracts in recent years have included cost-of-living adjustments whereby the wage is indexed to the consumer price level. However, these clauses rarely involve 100 percent protection from cost-of-living changes, and many contracts (about half) do not have any such clauses. Moreover, cost-of-living clauses represent only one of many possible contingency clauses. For example, the contracts could be directly linked to the unemployment rate, GNP, or more local measures of the performance of the economy and the value of workers' time.

The primary reason that more contracts are not indexed to the cost of living is that such indexing can be harmful if prices are rising because of supply-side shocks. Suppose that the marginal productivity of labor is reduced because of a shift in the production function. Recalling the classical model of Chapter 13, we know that such a shift will eventually require a reduction of the real wage; that is, W/P must decline so that it is equal to the marginal productivity of labor. But a 100 percent indexed contract will prevent such a decline. The escalator clause will call for an increase in W in the same proportion as the increase in P. Hence, W/P remains constant and too high. It is understandable that many firms and workers are reluctant to institute an arrangement that rules out any adjustments in the real wage if prices should rise suddenly during the contract period. Of course, if the reason for the increase in prices is a general monetary-induced inflation, then there will be no need for a reduction in the real wage. Unfortunately there is usually no way to tell in advance whether the price rise is due to monetary effects or to shifts in the production process.

Why not index wages to unemployment, GNP, or other indexes that might indicate whether the shocks are to money or to productivity? Part of an answer is similar to the reason we gave for caution in indexing to the cost of living. For instance, some of the shifts in overall unemployment are not relevant for the productivity of a particular group of workers. When a special event, not a recession, makes unemployment zoom for auto workers, the unemployment rate may not reveal much about the jobs available to computer workers.

A final reason that contracts do not have many indexing clauses is that they add complexity. There are good reasons to have a straightforward contract that the rank and file can easily understand and vote on. Similarly, contingency clauses appear to add uncertainty about the wage that the workers will actually get. Many workers would object to this added uncertainty, even though the economic theorist may argue that the uncertainty makes the worker better off.

Although we have focused on labor union contracts, the same arguments pertain to the more informal wage-setting procedures used by firms employing non-union workers. A review of each worker's performance is costly, and obtaining survey information about wages paid elsewhere and forecasts of inflation requires time and expense. To make such an adjustment more than once a year is probably prohibitive for many firms. The arguments stated above against extensive contingency clauses also apply to this type of wage setting. Moreover, indexing would do little to improve the workings of annual wage-setting arrangements; waiting less than a year to make an adjustment after the fact is usually adequate.

WHY IS WAGE SETTING STAGGERED?

In a decentralized economy like that of the United States, firms and workers decide by themselves when their wages and salaries are adjusted. The fact that these decisions are not synchronized therefore seems natural; one would be surprised to see a coordinated wage (or price) adjustment without some centralized orchestration of such a move. Historical accident would be enough to explain why the auto workers always negotiate just before the machinists.

It is important to know, however, whether the lack of synchronization in the United States serves any microeconomic purpose. If it does not, then proposals for reforming the economic system to bring about more synchronization would be innocuous for microeconomic welfare but could have some macroeconomic advantages.

Imagine what would happen if all wages and prices were set at the same time, and without a central planner to tell workers and firms what to do. A firm that thought that a relative wage increase was appropriate for its workers would have a difficult time knowing what other wages would be in order to achieve that relative increase. A wage survey would tell only about current wages in other firms, not the direction in which they were heading.

Staggered wage setting provides information to firms and workers about wages and prices elsewhere. Even though other wages will be adjusted before the current contract expires, there will be some period of time when the desired relative wage is in force. Nonsynchronized wage and price setting thus seems desirable in a decentralized economy.[6]

Moreover, staggered wage setting adds some stability to wages. Without staggering all wages and prices would be up for grabs each period; there would be no base for setting each wage. Tremendous variability would be introduced to the price system.

The situation is different in some other countries, especially in those

---

[6] See Gary Fethke and Andrew Policano, "Will Wage Setters Ever Stagger Decisions," *Quarterly Journal of Economics,* November 1986, for further discussion of the rationale for nonsynchronized wage setting.

where the government plays an active role in wage setting. For instance, a significant number of wage decisions are synchronized in Japan, where each spring there is a *shunto* or simultaneous wage adjustment for the large companies. However, the government is actively involved in the *shunto*. Prior to the *shunto*, extensive deliberations take place to determine the appropriate wage adjustment for that year. Here, the government is a prime player. Some economists feel that such a system would be desirable for the United States.

15.2 Price Determination

Basic microeconomic theory gives a detailed account of how the prices of individual items are determined in auction markets. In an auction market, the price fluctuates day by day or even minute by minute to keep demand and supply equal. Imagine an auction market for plywood, for example. The demand for plywood is based on the market price and on the price of substitutes for plywood—aluminum, plastic, etc. The supply of plywood depends positively on the price. Plywood producers make plywood up to the point where marginal cost equals the market price. Their supply schedule slopes upward because marginal cost rises when output rises. When higher prices of plywood substitutes shift the demand function to the right, both plywood output and the plywood price rise, as shown in Figure 15–5.

One of the important conclusions of standard microeconomic analysis is the following: *When the demand schedule shifts to the right, the price rises by more than cost.* Firms earn extra profit, especially in the short run. The

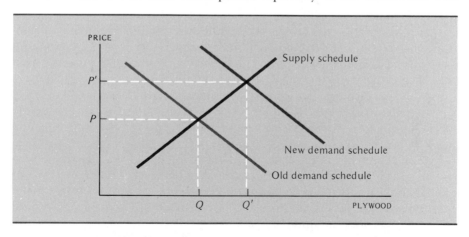

Figure 15–5.   EFFECTS OF AN INCREASE IN DEMAND IN AN AUCTION MARKET FOR PLYWOOD.
When the demand schedule for plywood shifts to the right, the price (P) and the quantity (Q) rise. A higher price is needed to induce the production of the higher quantity, because marginal cost rises with output.

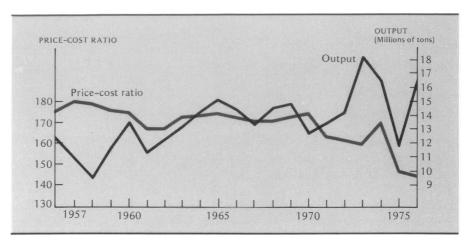

Figure 15–6. OUTPUT AND THE PRICE-COST RATIO IN THE STEEL INDUSTRY.
Steel is a cyclical industry and output has varied sharply, mainly due to shifts in the demand schedule for steel. The ratio of the price of steel to an index of costs of production
remained quite constant over the period. The price did not move up and down the marginal cost schedule of the steel industry. Source: Robert W. Crandall, *The U.S. Steel Industry in Recurrent Crisis: Policy Options in a Competitive World,* Washington, D.C., The
Brookings Institution, 1981, Appendix A.

profit arises because a higher price is needed to ration demand to the point
where it equals the added production that is feasible in the short run. In the
longer run, the price will fall to a point equal to long-run cost, as new firms
enter the market and existing firms raise their productive capacity by adding new factories.

Direct observation of many markets indicates that this prediction of standard micro theory of price fluctuations in response to demand fluctuations
does not hold. Demand can vary widely without appreciable movements in
the price. When prices change, it is usually because costs change, not because demand changes. For example, consider what happened to steel prices
and demand in the 1960s and 1970s. The steel market is not an auction
market. Figure 15–6 shows that steel demand seems to have little effect on
price compared to cost.

The steel industry is not exceptional in having prices that are stable relative to costs in the face of wide fluctuations in demand. The same is true of
most manufactured goods and services. On the other hand, many raw materials, especially agricultural products, have prices that fluctuate a great deal
in response to changes in demand.

Figure 15–7 shows the *ratio* of the average wage *W* to the price level *P* for
the United States economy over the last 25 years. Recall that this ratio is just
the real wage. If prices were determined just by costs for the economy as a
whole, then this ratio would be stable over business cycles. On the other
hand, if demand were important in pricing decisions, then the ratio would

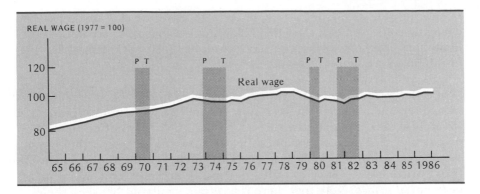

Figure 15–7. THE REAL WAGE DURING RECESSIONS AND BOOMS.
The diagram shows real wage—in particular, average hourly compensation for all private nonfarm employees in the United States—divided by the price level. Recessions are marked on the diagram. The real wage is very stable during recessions and booms. There is no tendency for the real wage to increase during recessions. If anything the real wage appears to fall slightly, but the fixed markup equation appears to be a good approximation. Source: *Business Conditions Digest,* February, 1987, p. 49.

fall when demand was strong as prices would be bid up relative to wage costs. As is evident in Figure 15–7, there is no tendency for the real wage to fall during booms or to rise during slumps. There is a general upward movement in the real wage due to increase in labor productivity, but there is no noticeable cyclical movement that might be related to demand. If anything, the real wage appeared to fall during the most recent recessions.

One of the important implications of the stable relationship between prices and costs is that a jump in costs very quickly results in a jump in prices. We can express this algebraically as

$$\pi = \text{wage cost contribution} + Z \qquad (15–1)$$

where π is the rate of inflation (rate of growth of prices from one year to the next) and Z is the change in an index of costs of production other than wage costs.

The idea that prices respond quickly and fully to costs is called the **markup hypothesis.** The markup is the gap between price and total cost of production. The markup hypothesis says that the gap is close to constant. Under the markup hypothesis, costs are the prime determinant of price and changes in demand have little effect on price.

WHY DO FIRMS SET PRICES AS A FIXED MARKUP OVER COSTS?

According to the markup equation, prices are rigid, but in a somewhat different way from wages. Like wages, prices respond relatively little to demand. But, unlike wages, prices do seem to move quickly in response to changing costs. Some of the explanations for this behavior are information limitations, long-term price contracts, customer relations, managerial rules of thumb, and oligopoly pricing.

Information Limitations. When the demand for a firm's product shifts, it is frequently unclear what the reason is. It could be a temporary change, in which case no change in price would be necessary. By waiting to see how persistent the change in demand is before changing the price, the firm obtains information about the nature of the shift. This strategy makes the firm's prices less sensitive to shifts in demand, and creates a lag in the adjustment of prices. Note that there is a certain similarity between these information limitations and those of the new classical models discussed in Chapter 14. Here, however, the prices are sticky rather than perfectly flexible.

There is also uncertainty about the effect of a change in a firm's costs. When there is an increase in the cost of fuel, for example, to run the firm's machines, it is not immediately clear to the firm what that change in cost will do to the economy in general. A reasonable strategy for the firm is to pass on the cost increase and see what happens to demand. If demand falls off then that is a sign that the cost increase is a genuine relative price increase, and the firm will eventually have to lower its price to maximize profits. In the case where the wages of the firm's workers increase, there is a similar tendency to pass on the costs, until it is clear that profits could be improved by doing otherwise.

Note that expectations of the future will affect these pricing strategies. If firms know that any increase in wages generally results in inflation, perhaps because the Fed accommodates the wage increases, then the tendency to pass on the wage increases in the form of higher prices will be even greater.

Contracts. Many firms have explicit contracts with the purchasers of their products. For example, steel companies make long-term agreements to supply steel to auto producers. In other cases, there is no formal contract, but there is a long-term understanding that continued purchasing will take place. The contracts provide that the purchaser can purchase however much it needs, at a price negotiated at the time the contract is signed. The contract lets the price rise in the future if costs rise, but does not make the price depend on the quantity sold by the producer to all of its customers.[7]

---

[7] The same type of nonsynchronized or staggered wage setting that we discussed in the previous section also occurs in price setting. That is, "price contracts" are usually staggered. Olivier Blanchard of M.I.T. has studied the implications of staggered price setting in an input-output framework in his "Price Asynchronization and Price Level Inertia," in R. Dornbusch and M. H. Simonsen (eds.), *Inflation Debt and Indexation*, Cambridge, Mass., M.I.T. Press, 1983, pp. 3–24.

Customer Relations. A firm has an incentive to develop a reputation for charging a price related to cost. If it changes prices for other reasons, customers will suspect they are being gouged. The customers will then have to spend resources verifying that the price increase is legitimate. It is in the mutual interest of the firm and the customer to develop a long-term relationship in which the customer does not have to worry about the firm making opportunistic price changes.

Managerial Rules of Thumb. Firms typically sell thousands of separate products. Setting prices is a critical management decision that cannot be delegated too far down in the company. Middle management usually does not have the discretion to set arbitrary prices for each product. Instead, top management formulates pricing rules that are handed down to middle managers. The typical pricing rule makes price depend on costs and not on the amount of the product being produced. To make the rule sensitive to the volume of production, top management must figure out the short-run marginal cost schedule for each product.

Oligopoly or Monopolistic Competition. In concentrated industries, firms may have an implicit agreement not to let prices drop to the competitive level. It is in their mutual interest to stabilize the price near the monopoly level. However, when the price is above long-run marginal cost, each firm has an incentive to cut the price a little and sell more output. A stable oligopoly needs a simple rule so that violations can be detected easily. The rule must allow firms to respond to costs, however. A simple agreement on a dollar price level could last only a year or so in an inflationary economy. The simplest viable rule in the longer run requires each firm to set a price based on costs, but prohibits price changes for any other reason.

The same type of pricing behavior can exist in less concentrated industries where there is some short-run monopoly power for each firm because the products are slightly differentiated from other products. These industries are characterized by monopolistic competition. An example is the magazine business. *Time* and *Newsweek* are slightly different products, but a large price difference would shift sales from one magazine to the other. Stephen Cecchetti of New York University has studied the behavior of American magazine prices and found striking evidence of sticky prices. He argues that this is consistent with a monopolistically competitive view of pricing.[8] He found that the average time between price changes in magazines was about *3 years* during the high inflation period of the 1970s when inflation averaged over 7 percent per year. Moreover, the average size of the price change—about 25 cents—was remarkably stable during the 1950s, 1960s,

---

[8] Stephen G. Cechetti, "The Frequency of Price Adjustment," *Journal of Econometrics,* April 1986, pp. 255–274.

and 1970s. According to Cecchetti, "It is very unlikely that the administrative costs of actually changing prices can explain this [infrequent price adjustment]. The obvious explanation is that each magazine fears that if it 'moves' first to adjust its price for inflation, it will raise its relative price above that of the competition, losing sales."

FACTUAL AND THEORETICAL RATIONALES FOR WAGE AND PRICE RIGIDITIES: AN ASSESSMENT

Though the theoretical explanations we have discussed for long-term wage contracts, staggered wage setting, and markup pricing are plausible, they are not based on the standard auction model of microeconomic theory. For this reason, some macroeconomists remain unconvinced or skeptical of the theories.[9] Modifications of standard micro theory designed to explain wage and price rigidities have only begun in recent years, and it appears that no one single modification is enough to explain all the aspects of the rigidities. It is not an easy job to modify or improve basic micro theory, but the facts indicate that some such modifications or improvements are necessary. Attempts to build formal theoretical models of wage and price rigidities are one of the most important elements of current research in macroeconomics.

One such attempt—called *contract theory*—is examined in some detail in the appendix to this chapter. Optimal contract theory endeavors to generalize the standard microeconomic model of auction markets to allow for longer-term relationships between individuals lasting a year or more. The idea is to include in contracts contingencies for unpredictable events during the life of the contract, such as inflation, productivity changes, or higher profits. Labor union contracts between a union and a firm are an example, but optimal contract theory also addresses more implicit contracts such as the unwritten contracts between any worker and her employer. Thus far optimal contract theory has not been entirely successful in explaining wage rigidity and deviations of unemployment from the natural rate. One reason is that the optimal contracts are contingent on all possible events. Since we know that real world contracts are contingent on many variables, the challenge of optimal contract theory is to show why such contingency clauses are missing in the real world. One possibility is that some variables—like a firm's profit—are not perfectly observable by both parties to the contract; in particular the firm may have an incentive to claim to workers that profits are low.[10]

---

[9] See, for example, Robert E. Lucas, Jr., "Methods and Problems in Business Cycle Research," in Robert E. Lucas, Jr. (ed.), *Studies in Business Cycle Theory,* Cambridge, Mass., MIT Press, 1981, pp. 271–296, or Robert E. Lucas and Thomas J. Sargent, "After Keynesian Economics," in Robert E. Lucas and Thomas J. Sargent (eds.), *Rational Expectations and Economics Practice,* Minneapolis, University of Minnesota Press, 1981, pp. 295–319.

[10] Another approach to the microeconomic underpinnings of sticky wages and prices is the "efficiency wage" model mentioned in footnote 5 on page 419. Still another approach models

Even as such research is proceeding, we find the evidence in favor of long-term contracts, staggered wage and price setting, and markup pricing sufficiently convincing that we think it would be a serious mistake to ignore them in macroeconomics and rely instead on the classical model with perfectly flexible wages and prices. There seem to be good rationales for these aspects of wage and price rigidities—no one has proved that they are inconsistent with the basic idea of rational decision-making on the part of firms and workers. They are certainly not inconsistent with rational expectations. But we recognize that the details of the case are far from being worked out.

What Does a Union Labor Contract Look Like?

Sometimes the best method of economic research is to simply go out and look carefully at how people do business. Consider, for example, the labor agreement between the United Mine Workers and the Bituminous Coal Operators discussed in the text. The entire National Bituminous Coal Contract of 1984 is printed in a compact booklet, small enough for a coal miner to carry in a shirt pocket or a lunch box. The contract is jam-packed with 267 pages of text describing worker-employer rights as well as wage payments through 1988 for all types of workers from rock drillers to bit sharpeners. The contract also specifies the extra payments for overtime—time-and-a-half beyond the 8-hour day and 40-hour week.

As with most labor contracts the firm is given a free hand in choosing employment as long as it pays according to the wage schedule. There is a layoff clause that ensures that the most senior workers are laid off last. The layoff clause guarantees that laid-off workers will be hired back in order of seniority and before new workers are hired.

The contract already tells us much about what happens when the demand for coal falls off. Suppose, for example, that Westmoreland Coal Company—one of the operators who signed the agreement—starts getting fewer orders from U.S. Steel and other steel companies that use bituminous coal. Clearly, the response of Westmoreland Coal is not to lower the wage and thereby prevent a drop in profits. The wage is fixed by the contract that Westmoreland and the other operators signed. Instead, when demand drops Westmoreland will start mining less coal and begin to lay off workers at its Virginia and West Virginia mines in order to reduce losses. The laid-off workers are then placed on a panel—as stipulated in the contract—from which they will

---

firms in monopolistic competition where small costs of adjusting prices at the firm level can lead to large social welfare costs. See N. Gregory Mankiw, "Small Menu Costs and Large Business Cycles: A Macroeconomic Model of Monopoly," *Quarterly Journal of Economics*, May 1985, pp. 529–539.

National Bituminous Coal Wage Agreement of 1984

From Article IA:
"... the right to hire and discharge are vested exclusively in the Employer."

From Article XVII:
"In all cases where the working force is to be reduced, Employees with the greatest seniority at the mine shall be retained ..."

* We thank Joseph Michael Queen of Birmingham, Alabama, for sending us this pocket-sized version of the 1984 agreement after reading about the 1981 agreement in the first edition of this text.

be returned to employment on the basis of seniority when demand picks up. The behavior of Westmoreland, as agreed to in this contract, is apparently just like what we assumed for the typical firm in this book.

Temporary Wage and Price Rigidities

WAGES

1. Union wage contracts in the United States last as long as 3 years. The contracts are not synchronized with one another. There is some indexing to inflation, but it is less than 100 percent and appears in only about half of the contracts.

2. Non-union workers typically have wage adjustments about once per year. These adjustments are staggered over time, much as the union contracts. Since the wage is rarely changed within the year, this wage-setting process creates rigidities much like formal contracts.

3. Wages are set for long periods because collective bargaining, threats of strikes, or simply careful reviews of worker performance make adjusting the wage costly. Wages are rarely indexed in the U.S. because supply shocks as well as demand shocks occur. With indexing, the real wage does not adjust enough after supply shocks. Moreover, extensive contingency clauses add complexity and apparent uncertainty to wage contracts.

PRICES

1. Prices are set according to a stable markup over costs. When demand falls, firms try to keep their profit margins constant, at least until they see if the change is permanent.

2. The real wage does not fluctuate much in the United States during business cycles. This stability is a reflection of the markup pricing strategies.

3. Firms use markup pricing because of information limitations, customer relations, simple rules of thumb, and oligopolistic strategy.

15.3 Policy Implications

Three important policy implications can be drawn from the theoretical and factual background of the previous section. The first concerns the problem of *disinflation;* that is, bringing the rate of inflation down from a level that is thought to be too high. The second concerns the *effectiveness of monetary policy when expectations are rational.* The third concerns the *long-run trade-off between inflation and unemployment.*

DISINFLATION AND THE REAL EFFECTS OF MONETARY POLICY

These issues are best understood by first considering an extreme case. In Section 15.1 we mentioned the May 1981 coal contract which called for annual wage increases of approximately 11 percent for 3 years. Suppose, for illustrative purposes, that *all* workers in the United States economy sign the same 11 percent 3-year wage contract, but starting May 1991. All wages in the economy would be locked into 11 percent increases for 3 years. According to Equation 15–1, the markup pricing equation, prices would also be locked into 11 percent increases for 3 years. General inflation would be 11 percent. If real GNP were at potential and growing at 3 percent per year, then we know from our study of long-run growth in the classical model in Chapter 13 that the money stock would be increasing by 14 percent per year. With no shifts in the demand for money, real GNP growth plus inflation equals money growth.

With this economic situation in mind, imagine now that in June 1991 the chairman of the Federal Reserve Board decides that this is too high, and at the June meeting of the Federal Open-Market Committee (FOMC) proposes to end inflation—to disinflate—by cutting money growth from 14 to 3 percent. The FOMC goes along and instructs the open-market desk in New York to sell government securities at a sufficient rate to reduce reserve growth and hence money growth from 14 to 3 percent *immediately.*

The results of this hypothetical policy action should now be clear. With an 11 percent inflation built in to the economy, the only possibility is that real GNP growth is reduced substantially, probably to a negative rate. (The amount of the reduction depends on the slope of the aggregate demand schedule.) The economy is thrown into a deep recession. As sales begin to fall, firms lay off workers and unemployment rises. Unless contracts are reopened, the recession will last 3 years—until the scheduled end of the labor contracts. Only then might we expect an end to the inflationary wage increases, a subsequent decline in inflation, and eventually an economic recovery as the 3 percent money growth permits 3 percent real GNP growth with zero inflation.

The fact that monetary policy can affect real output and employment, even if expectations are rational, is also demonstrated by this example. Everyone in the economy could be perfectly aware of the new policy action by the Fed. But as long as everyone is locked into contracts, the contractionary effect occurs. Note also that the Fed could have brought about a boom starting in June 1991 by increasing the rate of monetary expansion from 14 percent to some higher number. Policy that is anticipated in advance can have an effect with rational expectations, as long as knowledge of the policy change comes after the contracts are set.

In such a situation, a sharp decline in money growth is certainly costly. A far better approach would be for the Fed to *announce* its disinflation plans before the contracts are set. For example, in April 1991 the Fed could announce that it will reduce money growth from 14 to 3 percent in September 1994 when the labor contracts expire. This would give management and labor the chance to adjust their new contracts to incorporate the new anti-inflationary monetary policy; if the policy announcement were credible—this is a big if—then the recession could be entirely avoided. Disinflation without recession would be a reality.

Of course, we already know that the actual U.S. economy is not like the hypothetical economy in this extreme example. Contract signing is not synchronized in the major union sector and most non-union workers are employed under wage-setting arrangements in which the wage is set for 1 year. Hence, a sharp decline in money growth would begin to have some immediate effect on inflation as those workers signing new contracts see the rise in unemployment. Again, it would be better to announce the program in advance so that newly negotiated contracts could take account of the lower anticipated rate of inflation.

But the decline in inflation will be more gradual than the sharp 11 percent decline in money growth because only a small fraction of wages could be adjusted at first. A gradual decline in the rate of money growth would be better in that it would permit a gradual decline in inflation consistent with the configuration of contracts in the economy. An announced gradual reduction in money growth would be the least costly way to reduce inflation. Rather than an immediate reduction of 11 percent, recent studies suggest a reduction of about 1 percent in the first year, 2 percent in the second year, 6 percent in the third year, and 2 percent in the fourth year.[11] If such a policy could be announced in advance and be believed, it would minimize the harmful side effects of a monetary disinflation. The alternative paths for a monetary disinflation are illustrated in Figure 15–8 for the hypothetical 1991–95 example.

The important role of contracts during a disinflation is recognized by economists of differing persuasions. Arthur Okun, who was happy to be identified as a Keynesian, emphasized contracts in much of his writings.[12] In their best-selling book *Free to Choose*, Milton Friedman and Rose Friedman argued:

> The most important device for mitigating the side effects is to slow inflation *gradually but steadily* by a policy announced in advance and adhered to so it becomes credible. The reason for the gradualness and advance announcement is to give people time to readjust their arrangements—and to induce them to do so. Many people have entered into long-term contracts . . . on the basis of anticipations about the likely rate of inflation. These long-term contracts make it dif-

---

[11] See John B. Taylor, "Union Wage Settlements during a Disinflation," *American Economic Review*, Vol. 73 (December 1983), pp. 981–993.

[12] A comprehensive discussion of Okun's view is found in *Prices and Quantities: A Macroeconomic Analysis*, Washington, D.C., Brookings Institution, 1980.

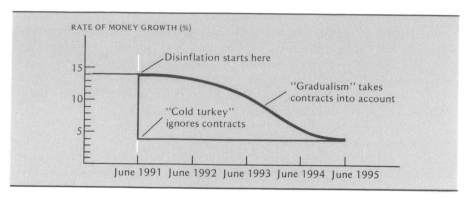

Figure 15–8. ALTERNATIVE DISINFLATION PATHS FOR THE MONEY SUPPLY.
The least costly policy is one that is gradual and announced. The largest deceleration
should occur near the third year because of the 3-year contracts that expire at that time.
Suppose that inflation has risen to 14 percent by mid 1991. The Fed wants to reduce it.
An immediate short reduction in money growth—"cold turkey"—would probably cause
a big recession like that in the early 1980s.

ficult to reduce inflation rapidly and mean that trying to do so will impose heavy
costs on many people. Given time these contracts will be completed or renewed
or renegotiated, and can then be adjusted to the new situation.[13]

What about reforming the wage determination process in the United
States so that contracts are shorter and more synchronized? If all contracts
were 1 year in length and synchronized, then the above example indicates
that it would be possible to have a sharper reduction in inflation in a shorter
period of time. But it would still be important to announce the policy in advance and to make it as credible as possible. The disadvantages of such a
change would be the increased negotiating costs and the likely increased
volatility of relative wages and prices—as we discussed above.

Another reform that has been suggested by Milton Friedman and others
would be to induce the private sector to use more wage indexing. This
would in effect make wages more flexible because they could adjust before
the contract expires. The problem with indexing—as we have already
pointed out—is that it prevents real wage adjustments when these are
needed because of changes in labor productivity.[14]

---

[13] Milton Friedman and Rose Friedman, *Free to Choose*, p. 273.
[14] Stanley Fischer, "Wage Indexation and Macroeconomic Stability," in Karl Brunner and
Alan Meltzer (eds.), *Stabilization of the Domestic and International Economy*, Carnegie-Rochester
Conference Series in Public Policy, New York, North-Holland, 1977, pp. 107–148, and Jo
Anna Gray, "Wage Indexation: A Macroeconomic Approach," *Journal of Monetary Economics*,
Vol. 2, pp. 221–36, 1976, have explored these effects of indexing on macroeconomic fluctua-
tion.

15.4 A Simple Model of Staggered Wage Setting

We have already seen that staggered wage setting models predict that changes in the money supply will affect real output even if expectations are rational. But what happens in a sustained inflation with wages, prices, and the money supply increasing at a constant rate? What do the theoretical models of staggered wage setting and markup pricing indicate will happen to output and unemployment? Will there be a way for wage setting to adjust to such a situation so that the unemployment rate is equal to the natural rate for any sustained rate of inflation?

A simple stylized algebraic model of staggered wage setting and price determination will be useful in addressing this and other questions. The model brings together most of the facts about wage and price setting discussed in this chapter, and illustrates their macroeconomic implications in a simple way. Wage setting is nonsynchronized, prices are given by a markup over costs, and expectations are rational.

Suppose that all wage contracts last 2 years, that all the wage adjustment occurs at the beginning of each year, and that there is no indexing. Half the workers sign contracts at the start of even-numbered years and half at the start of odd-numbered years. This configuration of assumptions is shown in Figure 15–9, where X represents the contract wage and W the average wage. Since we need to distinguish between past and future variables, let the subscript "−1" represent the *previous* year and let the subscript "+1" represent the *next* year. Of course, events in the next year are not known; people

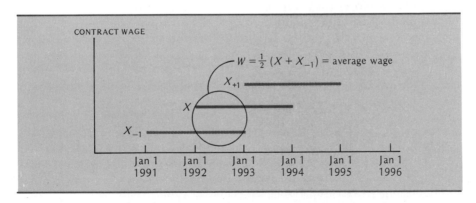

Figure 15–9. CONFIGURATION OF WAGE SETTING IN THE SIMPLE MODEL.
There are two groups of workers in the economy. One group has a wage adjustment January 1 of the even years and the other group has a wage adjustment January 1 of the odd years. The average wage W is shown to be equal to the average of this period's contract wage X and last period's contract wage X_{-1}. In the picture the average wage for 1992 is shown. It is the average of the contract wage set in 1991 and the contract wage set in 1992.

must form expectations of them. The average is given by

$$W = \frac{1}{2}(X + X_{-1}).\qquad(15\text{--}2)$$

In words, the wage W this year is the simple average of the contract wage signed last year, X_{-1}, which is still outstanding, and the contract wage signed this year, X. For example, suppose that the contract wage is 10 in 1991 and 8 in 1992. Then the average wage is 9 in 1992 (the wage of 8 set in 1991 is still outstanding in 1992).

An algebraic relationship that describes how the contract wage is set each period might be given by

$$X = \underbrace{\frac{1}{2}(W + W_{+1})}_{\substack{\text{Effect of expected} \\ \text{average wage}}} - \underbrace{\frac{c}{2}[U - U^*) + (U_{+1} - U^*)]}_{\substack{\text{Effect of current and future} \\ \text{unemployment}}},\qquad(15\text{--}3)$$

where U is the unemployment rate and U^* is the natural rate of unemployment; c is a coefficient describing the response of wages to unemployment.

Equation 15–3 leads to an interesting observation. Rewrite Equation 15–3 with W and W_{+1} replaced by the expressions in Equation 15–2. That is,

$$X = \frac{1}{2}[\underbrace{\frac{1}{2}(X + X_{-1})}_{\substack{W \text{ from Equation} \\ 15\text{--}2}} + \underbrace{\frac{1}{2}(X_{+1} + X)}_{\substack{W_{+1} \text{ from Equation} \\ 15\text{--}2}}] - \frac{c}{2}(U - U^* + U_{+1} - U^*). \quad(15\text{--}4)$$

Now gather together the X terms (without the subscripts) and put them on the left-hand side of the equation. After some cancellation (you can work it out in the margin), we get the simpler expression:

$$X = \frac{1}{2}(\underbrace{X_{-1}}_{\substack{\text{Backward-looking} \\ \text{component}}} + \underbrace{X_{+1}}_{\substack{\text{Forward-looking} \\ \text{component}}}) - c(U - U^* + \underbrace{U_{+1}}_{\substack{\text{Expected future unemployment} \\ \text{is also a factor}}} - U^*).\qquad(15\text{--}5)$$

Equation 15–5 shows how wage determination has a backward-looking component X_{-1} and a forward-looking component X_{+1}. The backward-looking component—which we discussed in words above—is what makes inflation persistent from year to year. Workers base their wage decisions partly on what previous wage decisions were. The forward-looking component—also discussed previously in words—is what makes expectations of the future so important. Expectations of moderate wage settlements next year will tend to moderate wage settlements this year. For example, if wage settlements next year are expected to be 10 percent lower, then, according to Equation 15–5, actual settlements this year will be 5 percent lower. The coefficient of X_{+1} is $1/2$.

Equation 15–5 also shows how expected future unemployment conditions next year can affect wage settlements this year. If the unemployment rate is expected to rise next year by 2 percent, then wage settlements this year will be 2 times c percent lower. For example, if c equals .5 then wage settlements this year will be 1 percent lower. The expectation of a slump in the future with its accompanying increase in unemployment has a simple effect: it decreases wage inflation today.

Because of the markup relationship all these effects on wages will be passed through to prices. The policy implications are therefore clear. Expectations of a monetary policy that is noninflationary in the future and that will let unemployment rise if necessary in the future, should inflation rise, will have favorable effects on inflation today. These favorable effects on inflation can actually work with little or no adverse effects on unemployment. The expectation of a credible stance against inflation in the future should therefore have a favorable effect on the trade-off between inflation and unemployment.

Consider, finally, the operations of the model in a steady inflation. Say the contract wage X increases by the same amount each year. For example, let the amount of increase be 10. In a steady inflation the *change* in the contract wage this year, $X - X_{-1}$, and the change in the contract wage next year, $X_{+1} - X$, will be the same, namely 10. Equation 15–5 can then be written as

$$\underbrace{\frac{1}{2}(X - X_{-1})}_{5} \underset{=}{} \underbrace{\frac{1}{2}(X_{+1} - X)}_{5} \underset{-}{} \underbrace{c(U - U^* + U_{+1} - U^*)}_{0}. \qquad (15\text{--}6)$$

Notice that there is a $10/2 = 5$ on the left-hand side and a $10/2 = 5$ on the right-hand side. The two cancel out. The term involving unemployment must equal zero. This implies that $U = U^*$ and that $U_{+1} = U^*$. In other words, the unemployment rate is always equal to the natural rate. The same result holds, of course, for any steady change in prices, not just 10. Regardless of the rate of inflation, as long as it is steady and anticipated, there is no trade-off between inflation and unemployment in the long run.

The simple model consisting of Equations 15–1, 15–2, and 15–3 can be viewed as an alternative, more microeconomic-based, representation of the price adjustment equation that we introduced in Chapter 6, Equation 6–6. As such it can be combined with a model of aggregate demand that tells how the money supply and government spending shifts demand when prices are predetermined. The "gradualism" versus "cold turkey" simulations described in Section 15.3 are based on such a model that combines staggered wage setting, markup pricing, and aggregate demand. Simulating such a model requires a large computer and sophisticated computer programs. Fortunately, most of the results can be conveyed in a more intuitive and less complex way by introducing some simple approximations to capture the essence of forward-looking and rational expectations behavior. We turn to this in the next chapter.

Policy with Wage Contracts and Rational Expectations

1. Long-term contracts make it difficult for the economy to adjust immediately to changes in monetary policy. Even if expectations are rational, a deceleration of money growth will reduce output and employment, because workers and firms are locked into their contracts.

2. Since *new* contracts are negotiated with an eye to the future, they will be influenced by expectations of future policy actions. Old contracts will remain in place, unless extreme hardship develops.

3. In the long run, wage contracts adjust to expectations of higher rates of inflation. Regardless of the rate of inflation, as long as it is steady, the unemployment rate will return to the natural rate.

Review and Practice

MAJOR POINTS

1. Most detailed information about wage setting in the United States comes from the large labor union sector. About 20 percent of all workers in the United States belong to labor unions. About 80 percent of the contracts signed by large unions last 3 years.

2. Workers who are not in a large labor union typically have their wages adjusted about once each year. The size of the wage adjustment is influenced by expectations of inflation, expectations of the wages paid to other workers, and the level of unemployment.

3. Wage setting is staggered. Not all workers obtain wage adjustments at the same time. This staggering adds to the inertia of wage rigidities.

4. Prices are set as stable markup over costs, including labor costs. Prices are not as responsive to demand as they would be in an auction market.

5. Wage and price rigidities arising from overlapping contracts and other sources make the process of disinflation slow and painful.

6. A specific model of wage adjustment with overlapping contracts confirms that the same unemployment rate is consistent with any chronic rate of inflation.

KEY TERMS AND CONCEPTS

Three-year contracts	Income policies
One-year wage adjustment	Front-end loading
Large union sector	Indexing
Staggered wage setting	Relative wage concerns

Collective bargaining

Markup pricing

Adjustment costs

Oligopoly

Productivity shocks

Implicit contracts

Disinflation

Policy effectiveness with rational
  expectations

Long-run trade-off between inflation
  and unemployment

Contract theory

Monopolistic competition

Forward-looking component of wages

Backward-looking component of wages

Credibility

Gradualism

QUESTIONS FOR DISCUSSION AND REVIEW

1. Describe the typical long-term union wage contract in the United States. What is indexing? Are many contracts indexed? Why?

2. What is staggered wage setting? Why does it occur?

3. Describe the typical wage adjustment for workers who are not in unions. Are these wage-setting dates staggered? Why aren't wages adjusted more frequently?

4. What is markup pricing? Is it a good description of most firms' pricing strategies in the United States?

5. Explain how markup pricing might be the result of information limitations at firms about what is going on in the economy.

6. Is monetary policy effective when expectations are rational? Why? Do any wages adjust when expectations of future monetary policy change?

7. In disinflating, is it better to be gradual or to be quick in reducing money growth?

8. What are the forward-looking and the backward-looking components of wage determination? What is their significance?

9. Why is there no long-run trade-off between inflation and unemployment, even though there is a short-run trade-off?

10. What good does it do for the Fed to maintain its own credibility about its promise not to tolerate inflation in the future?

PROBLEMS

Numerical

1. A worker has a contract with an employer. The worker will work as many hours as the employer chooses and will be paid $10 for each hour. The marginal product of the worker is $25 - .125H$ dollars per hour when the worker is working H hours. The marginal value of the worker's time is $.5H - 50$ dollars per hour when he is working H hours. How many hours will the employer ask the worker to work? Is this the efficient level? What if the marginal product schedule is $30 - .125H$? How can you measure the inefficiency of this amount of work?

2. Using tight monetary policy, the Fed is able to bring about a deceleration of prices, so that inflation falls from 10 percent to zero. The time path of the price level is as follows:

Year	Price Level
1	1.000
2	1.100
3	1.188
4	1.259
5	1.310
6 and later	1.336

There are two groups of workers, those whose wages are set in odd years and those whose wages are set in even years. When the wage is set, it is equal to 10 times the price level in the preceding year, raised by the amount of inflation that occurred in that year relative to the year before; that is, $W = 10P_{-1}(1 + \pi_{-1})$. In the second year of the contract, the wage is increased in proportion to the inflation that occurred in the first year relative to the year before; that is, $W = W_{-1}(1 + \pi_{-1})$. Compute the wages paid to the two groups and the average wage across the two groups starting in Year 2. Compute the rate of wage inflation and the real wage. Comment on the problems that disinflation creates when there are lags in wage setting, using the numbers from this example.

3. A firm enjoys a monopoly; its average revenue schedule is $15 - .25Y$ and its marginal revenue schedule is $15 - .5Y$ (Y is its amount of output). Its marginal cost schedule is $(Z + W)(.3 + .01Y)$. Z and W are the price of materials and the wage rate, respectively. For $Z = 2$ and $W = 8$, find the price and amount of output that maximize the monopolist's profit. Now suppose that the intercept in marginal and average revenues rises from 15 to 21 because demand rises. Find the price and level of output. Compare these to the case of markup pricing, where $P = Z + W$, and P does not change when demand rises. Now go back to the original average revenue and marginal revenue schedules and compute price and output when Z rises to 3. Again, compare these to the case of markup pricing. Conclude by comparing the general nature of markup and monopoly pricing, using your calculations as examples.

Analytical

1. Suppose initially that the economy is in equilibrium with unemployment equal to the natural rate and inflation equal to 10 percent. The Fed would like to reduce inflation down to 0. Listed below are several different descriptions of the way in which wages and prices are set. For each of them, indicate a desirable strategy for disinflating, and explain in each case the short-run consequences of such a strategy.
   a. Wages and prices are perfectly flexible, as in the classical model of Chapter 13.
   b. Wages are governed by 3-year contracts, while firms use markup pricing. All wage contracts in the economy are renegotiated at the same time.
   c. Wages and prices are set as in Part b except that wage contracts are staggered. One-third are renegotiated each year.
   d. Wages are set annually. They are a function of the prior year's wage, the prior year's inflation rate, and the prior year's unemployment rate. Prices are set as a markup over cost.

2. Suppose that the government encouraged unions to moderate their wage increases in exchange for a promise of tax cuts if inflation should exceed wage increases. Such a proposal was actually made by the Carter administration in the late 1970s. Explain why such a policy might be useful in an economy with staggered wage setting and markup pricing.

3. In what way does an economy in which prices are determined by the condition that marginal revenue equal marginal cost respond differently to an aggregate demand shock than an economy in which prices are set as a markup over cost? Does it matter how wages are set in the latter case? How does each type of economy respond to a price shock?

4. Suppose that wage contracts last for three years. Each year, one-third of the economy's wage contracts are renegotiated. Contract wages are set according to

$$X = 1/3(W+W_{+1} + W_{+2})-c/3 \{(U-U^*) + (U_{+1}-U^*) + (U_{+2}-U^*)\}.$$

   a. Provide an expression for the average wage rate, W.
   b. Derive an expression analagous to Equation 15–5. How far backward- and forward-looking is the wage determination process? What determines the responsiveness of contract wages to *current* labor market conditions?

5. In this chapter we developed a model in which contract wages change in response to *current and expected future* conditions in the labor market. How does such a model provide the underpinnings for our price adjustment equation of Chapter 6, where prices respond to output *with a lag*?

6. Evaluate the following statement: Synchronized wage contracts offer the best prospect for "cold turkey" disinflation. But they also provide the Fed with the greatest temptation to cheat. Moreover, if the Fed loses credibility, disinflation with synchronized contracts can be very painful. Therefore, it is probably better that contracts are staggered.

7. "If expectations are rational, monetary policy has no effect on output, and disinflation without recession is possible." Is this statement true or false? Explain your answer calling on both models with the Lucas supply function and models with wage contracts and sticky prices.

Appendix: Contract Theory: An Extension of Auction Market Theory

In this appendix we consider a very explicit and detailed theory that was developed by macroeconomists in the 1970s to explain wage rigidities in labor markets. The theory focuses on employment contracts between workers and firms—and for this reason it is called **contract theory.** Like the information-based new classical theory described in Chapter 14, it makes explicit use of the idea that both firms and consumers *optimize;* that is, they maximize profits or utility. Contract theory assumes that firms and workers enter into contracts that govern employment and wage payments for a number of years in advance. Because contracts predetermine the behavior of firms and workers, they may cause rigidity in that they rule out quick adjustments in response to changing conditions.

Contract theory can be viewed as an attempt to extend economic theory systematically beyond *auction* markets so that it can deal with markets in which there are contracts. As we have seen, an auction market is one like the grain or stock markets where thousands of bidders are constantly buying and selling units of a homogeneous commodity. The labor market is completely different from an auction market. Each person's services are unique. Employers have to investigate each potential worker's qualifications carefully and a worker has to check out each potential employer. Once a good match is found and a worker has been trained for a job, both worker and employer have an incentive to preserve the match. Hence, employment relations need to be governed by some type of contract, even if it is not written down in a formal way.

Standard microeconomic theory treats the labor market as an auction market. Since we know that labor markets—and many other markets, for that matter—are not auction markets, contract theory is potentially an important area of economic research. Like the information-based theory, it has been the focus of much research over the last 15 years.[15]

THE AUCTION MARKET MODEL: A REVIEW

In Figure 15–10 we review the classical model using a supply and demand diagram for the labor market. The vertical axis is the real wage; the horizontal axis is employment. The intersection of the supply curve and the demand curve determines the real wage and the amount of employment.

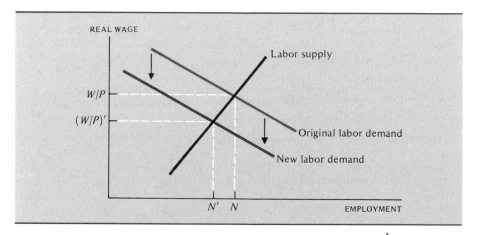

Figure 15–10.   AN AUCTION MARKET FOR LABOR.
A downward shift in the labor demand curve reduces the real wage and employment. The amount of employment at the intersection is efficient.

---

[15] The research began with papers by Costas Azariadis, "Implicit Contracts and Underemployment Equilibria," *Journal of Political Economy*, Vol. 83, pp. 1183–1202, 1975, and Martin N. Baily, "Wages and Employment under Uncertain Demand," *Review of Economic Studies*, Vol. 41, pp. 37–50, 1974.

Suppose that there is a disturbance that decreases the demand for labor. For example, suppose that labor becomes less productive because of a change in production technology. This shifts the labor demand curve to the left. The real wage immediately adjusts downward, as does employment.

The exact procedure through which the real wage instantaneously adjusts in the market is usually left unstated. In principle there must be some auctioneer calling out alternative real wages and obtaining information about demand and supply at those real wages. The fact that such auctioneers are not observed in labor markets is of course one of the reasons for developing an alternative to the auction market model.

An important property of the auction market model is that the amount of employment determined at the intersection of the demand and supply curves is **efficient.** That auction markets are efficient is a fundamental result of microeconomics. To understand the concept of efficiency, consider a furniture-manufacturing firm producing chairs and tables. The firm's managers hire carpenters (the workers) to make the chairs and tables. The number of hours that the carpenters actually work will depend on two things: (1) how valuable the carpenter's time is to the firm and (2) how valuable the carpenter's additional earnings are to the carpenter; less technically, (1) the firm's demand for labor, and (2) the worker's supply of labor.

We first consider the firm. In deciding how many hours to employ the carpenters on a given day, the firm maximizes profits by taking the real wage as given. (Think of the auctioneer calling out a real wage to the firm.) The basic result of the theory of the firm is that profit maximization occurs at the level of employment where the *marginal productivity of an additional hour of work equals the real wage.* In terms of the example, the firm will be maximizing its profits when the value of the chairs that a carpenter can make by working an additional hour equals the real cost of employing that carpenter for an additional hour. The reason for this result is fairly intuitive: If the marginal productivity of an additional hour of work were more than the real wage, then the firm could increase profits by having the carpenters work more hours. If the marginal productivity of an additional hour of work were less than the real wage, then the firm would want the carpenters to work fewer hours. The condition that the marginal product of labor equals the real wage is what generates the downward-sloping demand-for-labor curve: As the real wage falls, the firm increases employment, thereby reducing the marginal productivity of additional employment.

Now consider the work decision of the carpenters. They will want to work up to the point where the increased utility through the higher income from an additional hour of work is equal to the decrease in utility from the loss in leisure time due to the additional hour of work. In other words, they want to balance the loss in leisure time from more work with the gain in income through more work. The point of balance will depend on the real wage, because the real wage translates hours of work into income. The higher the real wage, the more the worker will want to work. A higher real wage increases the gain from working relative to the loss.

These ideas can be stated more formally using a basic result from microeconomics: The carpenters will want to work up to the point where the *ratio of the marginal utility of an additional hour of leisure to the marginal utility of additional income is equal to the real wage.* If this condition is not satisfied, then the carpenters will be able to increase their utility by working a different number of hours. For example, if the real wage is greater than the marginal rate of substitution, then the carpenters will increase utility by working more hours.

At all points along the labor demand curve in Figure 15–10 the marginal product of labor equals the real wage. At all points along the labor supply curve, the marginal rate of substitution equals the real wage. Hence, at the intersection of these two curves—that is, at the point of equilibrium in the auction market—both marginal conditions are satisfied. With both conditions satisfied we know that the marginal rate of substitution is equal to the marginal productivity of labor. This is the fundamental condition of efficiency. The auction market—with the real wage determined by the auctioneer so that demand is equal to supply—generates this condition.

THE OPTIMAL CONTRACT MODEL

Now consider how this auction market model would be modified to deal with contracts. A basic property of a contract is that it specifies actions to be taken in the future. For example, it spells out a wage to be paid next year. Hence, in order to build a model of contracts, it is necessary to consider a situation where some events explicitly take place in the future. At the time that the contract is written these events are unknown.

The economic events are assumed to be the same as those that affected the auction model of the labor market in Figure 15–10. It is of interest to see how the response of the contract market to these shocks differs from that of the auction market. In particular, we assume that the disturbance that shocks the market is a shift in the labor demand schedule, and that this shock comes from a reduction in labor productivity. Unlike the auction market model, however, the labor contract must be written in advance of the time when the disturbance occurs. The contract is written this year and the shock occurs next year.

Neither the firms nor the workers know in advance what type of a disturbance will in fact occur. They are likely to have some idea of the probability of the disturbance to occur, however, and we will assume that everyone thinks that the chances are 50–50 that a negative shock will occur, and 50–50 that a positive shock will occur. It is as if a coin is tossed: heads, labor productivity shifts up; tails, labor productivity shifts down. In terms of the labor demand curve, the two possibilities are illustrated in Figure 15–11.

The contract is 1 year in duration, and applies only to the next year, when the uncertain disturbance will occur. Both workers and firms have a view of the world as illustrated in Figure 15–11 and agree that the probability of a good year (high productivity) is the same as that of a bad year (low productivity). That is, the objective probabilities correspond to the subjective probabilities of the workers and the firms; this is the *rational expectations* assumption. Under these circumstances it is optimal for the contract to be written in the form of *contingency clauses* that stipulate what the level of employment and the wage rate will be in the case that the next period is a good year and in the case that it is a bad year. These contingencies will have the following form:

If productivity is *high*,
employ workers for L_1 hours,
pay real wage W_1/P_1.
If productivity is *low*,
employ workers for L_2 hours,
pay real wage W_2/P_2.

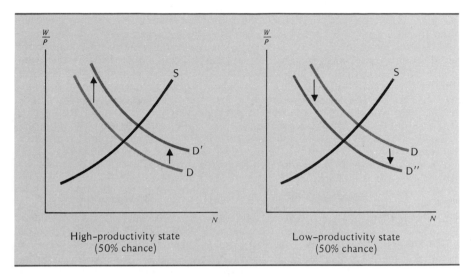

Figure 15–11.   UNCERTAINTY ABOUT LABOR DEMAND.
Which way the labor demand curve shifts in the next period is uncertain. Either it will shift up, as in the left panel, or it will shift down, as in the right panel. Both possibilities have an equal (50–50) chance of occurring.

Note that the optimal contract entails a wage rate and number of hours that can be different in the two possible states of productivity. Presumably, the contract would specify that there be more hours worked in the case where productivity is high than in the case where productivity is low. (An example of a contingency clause is arrangements for indexing or cost-of-living adjustments as discussed in Section 15.1, in which the nominal wage changes automatically when the price level changes.)

What do the contingency clauses say about the levels of employment in the two states of productivity? The amount of work in each state must be efficient. That is, the marginal product of labor in the state must be equal to the marginal rate of substitution between income and leisure. Suppose the contract set a lower level of work where the marginal product of labor exceeded the marginal rate of substitution. Then another contract would be available that was better in that state for both the firm and the workers. It would set a higher level of employment; the extra profit to the firm from the additional output would be worth more than the time given up by the workers.

As a separate matter, the contract sets the real wage in each state. Think first about the average level of wages in the two states. The firm cannot make the terms of the contract too much in its own favor relative to the workers. If it did so the workers would go to another firm to sign a contract. The firm must take as given the opportunity that the workers have to sign such a contract with another firm, and thereby increase their expected utility. In the contract model, therefore, the firm takes as given the level of utility that the workers can obtain elsewhere. This proposition is a generalization of the situation in the auction model where the firm takes the real wage as given, representing the opportunity that workers have if they go to another firm.

Now think about the levels of the wage in the two states. The workers' assessment of their utility in the next period will also involve an averaging of the two future possibilities. However, the uncertainty about the future productivity shock has a special additional effect on the preferences of workers. Optimal contract theory assumes that workers are *risk averse* when dealing with this uncertainty. If people are risk averse, they would prefer a certain outcome to an uncertain one. Risk-averse workers would prefer a contract that gave them equal real incomes in the high productivity case and in the low productivity case. Paying the same income whether the workers are more or less productive reduces the risk to the worker.

While it is assumed that workers are risk averse, no similar assumption is made for firms. Firms are assumed to be *risk neutral,* which simply means that they are indifferent between a certain outcome and an uncertain outcome provided the two give the same amount of profit, on the average. The rationale for treating firms as risk neutral (while workers are risk averse) is that firms are owned by thousands of people, most of whom have investments in many other firms as well. Because of their diversification, they have less at stake with respect to this one firm. The workers, on the other hand, work only at this one firm. (The managers of the firms should be distinguished from the owners. Profits of the firm are paid out to the owners; except for profit-sharing arrangements, the managers are paid wages and salaries just like any other worker.)

Because of these considerations, the optimal contract has the striking property that the real wage may be *lower* in high-productivity states than in low-productivity states. Workers will achieve the same level of overall satisfaction in both states, but they will be working more hours in the high-productivity state.

By contrast, in the auction market, the real wage would be *higher* in the high-productivity state. The crucial difference is the following: In the contract theory, efficiency is achieved by the workings of the contract. *Essentially, there is a market in labor contracts, rather than in labor itself.* The wage that is set in the contract does not guide the allocation of labor—the firm does not decide each year how much labor to use in a given state by equating the marginal product of labor to the real wage. Instead, the contract stipulates the amount of work. The only function of the wage is to compensate the worker for accepting the contract. In contrast, the auction market is a market for labor services. Firms in the market equate their marginal product to the real wage they find in the market.

Labor contract theory was originally developed to explain the departures of actual employment from its efficient level. Contracts seemed to be a potential explanation of the price and wage rigidities that we know can lead to such departures. However, the simplest contract theory turned out to show the contrary: Contracts *per se* do not lead to inefficiencies. They may alter the short-run distribution of income, if some parties to the contract are more risk averse than others, as with the workers versus the firm.

There are other ingredients that can be added to the contract model in order to generate the observed inefficiencies. A key assumption underlying optimal contract theory was that the firm and workers both can observe the fluctuations in productivity. Workers would not agree to the contract if they could not verify the state of productivity. If management could fool workers into accepting a false statement about productivity, they might claim that productivity was high and the workers should work hard. The additional work might cost the firm relatively little, because the firm might be committed to about the same amount of pay in high- as in low-productivity periods.

Contract theorists have examined this case; they call it "asymmetric information." Asymmetric information constrains the form of contracts so that they are "incentive compatible." That is, workers must be sure that the firm has no incentive to lie about productivity. The incentive compatibility constraints in effect limit the contingencies on which the contract can be based. It is not surprising that such limits can lead to inefficient contracts.[16]

[16] For more discussion of inefficient contracts see Guillermo Calvo and Edmund S. Phelps, "Employment-Contingent Wage Contracts," in Karl Brunner and Allan Meltzer (eds.), *Stabilization of the Domestic and International Economy,* Carnegie-Rochester Conference Series in Public Policy, 1977, pp. 160–168; Robert E. Hall, "Employment Fluctuations and Wage Rigidities," *Brookings Papers on Economic Activity,* Number 1, pp. 91–124, 1980; and Sanford Grossman and Oliver Hart, "Implicit Contracts, Moral Hazard, and Unemployment," *American Economic Review,* Vol. 71 (May 1981), pp. 301–307.

16

Aggregate Dynamics and Price Adjustment

IN THIS chapter we develop a model of price adjustment that brings together the theories of price-wage rigidities and rational expectations. It thus responds to the important issues raised in the previous chapter, yet it is simple enough that we can incorporate it in our full model of the economy. In fact, the algebra and graphs that we use to analyze the price-adjustment model are very similar to those that we used to study the price-adjustment relationships in Chapter 6. Here, however, we examine *changes in the coefficients* of the model of price adjustment and of expected inflation that occur when macro policy or the economic environment changes. We also examine with more practical examples the *dynamic response of inflation and output to disturbances* that was presented in Chapter 7. Finally, we study *empirical tests of the model* using the actual macroeconomic data of the United States, Germany, and the United Kingdom during the 1970s and 1980s.

16.1 The Wage-Price Process as a Whole

In Chapter 6 we introduced the *Phillips curve* as our basic model of price adjustment: According to the Phillips curve, inflation rises when demand conditions are tight, when expectations of inflation rise, or when there are price shocks. Using algebra the Phillips curve can be written:

$$\pi = \underbrace{f\left(\frac{Y_{-1} - Y^*}{Y^*}\right)}_{\substack{\text{Market conditions} \\ \text{(slack or tight)}}} + \underbrace{\pi^e}_{\substack{\text{Expectations} \\ \text{of inflation}}} + \underbrace{Z.}_{\text{Price shocks}} \qquad (16\text{--}1)$$

$$\underbrace{\hphantom{f\left(\frac{Y_{-1} - Y^*}{Y^*}\right) + \pi^e}}_{\text{Determinants of wage inflation}}$$

The last term *(Z)*, representing price shocks, was not made explicit in the discussion of Chapter 6; it represents the upward shift in the price-adjustment relationship that we discussed in Chapter 6 and again in Chapter 15.

One of the most important properties of Equation 16–1 is that there is no long-run trade-off between inflation and the level of GNP. A country with a high average inflation rate that is generally expected to continue will not have any higher output than a country with a low inflation rate that is generally expected to continue. This is easily seen from Equation 16–1: On average, the effect of supply shocks will be zero $(Z = 0)$, and expected inflation π^e will equal actual inflation π in the long run regardless of the level of actual inflation. Hence, according to Equation 16–1, the market conditions term $(Y_{-1} - Y^*)/Y^*$ equals zero, or, equivalently, actual output equals potential output. As we saw in Chapter 6, the proposition that there is no long-run trade-off between output and inflation is sometimes called the *natural rate property* because the unemployment rate is equal to the natural rate regardless of the rate of inflation; it is also sometimes called the *accelerationist property* because attempts to keep output above normal result in accelerating prices.

Three specific aspects of the theory of wage and price rigidities of Chapter 15 provide a simple interpretation of Equation 16–1:

1. *Prices are set as a markup over the costs of production,* including wage costs and the cost of materials, such as crude oil, iron ore, and timber. Because of markup pricing, if there are no changes in the price of crude materials then the rate of change in prices π will equal the rate of change in wages. The first two terms on the right-hand side of Equation 16–1 reflect influences on the rate of change in wages— market conditions and expectations of inflation—as we will see in the next two paragraphs. The last term Z reflects changes in the price of raw materials. According to this interpretation, the primary reason for the price shock Z is changes in the price of raw materials. A major example of this type of shock was the increase in the price of oil in 1973 and again in 1979 when a cartel of oil-producing countries increased the price of crude oil dramatically.

2. *Wages respond with a lag to unemployment.* When unemployment is high and the labor market is slack, currently negotiated wages fall, or rise

by less than they would under favorable conditions. The average wage thus moves in the direction needed to bring the labor market into balance, but it moves only a fraction of the way each period because only a fraction of the wages are changed each period. As we have seen, there is a close relationship—Okun's law—between the unemployment rate and the departures of GNP from potential: When the unemployment rate is above normal, GNP is below normal, and vice versa. Because Okun's law is so accurate, we can represent the pressure of labor market conditions on wage inflation by the output gap $(Y_{-1} - Y^*)/Y^*$. The subscript "-1" indicates that current wage change is related to market pressure in the previous period, reflecting the lags in wage adjustment.

3. *Wages respond to expected inflation.* When workers expect prices and other workers' wages to rise by 8 or 10 percent per year they will start off their negotiations asking for this much of an increase. One of the reasons that workers might expect inflation in the future is that other workers have recently signed 3-year contracts with 8 to 10 percent increases in the second and third years. This is the reason for the the expectations term π^e on the right-hand side of Equation 16–1. The price-adjustment equation says that the combined effect of a 1 percentage point increase in expected inflation is to raise wage inflation by 1 percentage point.

16.2 Changes in the Coefficients of the Price-Adjustment Model

The theory of wage and price rigidities underlying the price-adjustment relationship suggests that it would change if economic conditions or policy change. In particular, the sensitivity of inflation to recent market conditions (f) is likely to change when the economic environment changes. Here we consider two important examples of changes in the economic environment: an increase in the amount of indexing and a reduction in the size and length of business cycles.

THE EFFECT OF WAGE INDEXING

As we saw in Chapter 15, there is some indexing in the United States of union labor contracts (cost-of-living adjustment provisions). Indexing is more prevalent in other countries—a good example is Italy. With indexing, each time the price level rises by 1 percent, wages rise by a fraction of a percent a, automatically. How would indexing affect the price-adjustment relationship? Indexing means that the wage will respond to the *current* rate of inflation as well as to the lagged rate of inflation. The effect of this is to speed up the overall response (f) of inflation to changes in unemployment. To see this, suppose there is an increase in output that initially increases wage inflation by 1 percent. Through markup pricing, this will quickly have an upward influence of 1 percent on prices. But, if wages are indexed, the upward adjustment of price inflation will mean a further upward adjustment of wage inflation of the amount a. This in turn will increase price inflation by a, through the markup process. Again indexing will raise wage inflation, now by an amount a times a, or a^2. And the process will continue for a third round, where inflation will increase by another multiple of a (a^3). The whole process is called a **wage-price spiral**. As long as indexing is less than 100 percent, the process will eventually settle down, but the end result has been to make wages adjust more to the increase in output than if there had not been any indexing. The total effect is

$$1 + a + a^2 + a^3 + \ldots = \frac{1}{1-a},$$

using the formula for the geometric series. Note that the total effect is much like the formula for the multiplier. For example, if a equals .5 then the effect of market conditions on inflation is doubled: $1/(1 - .5) = 2$. In general, *indexing makes nominal wages more responsive to market conditions,* as represented by a higher value for the coefficient f in Equation 16–1.

For the same reasons, indexing also increases the response of inflation to price shocks Z. When the cost of materials rises, firms increase their price. But because of indexing, this price increase will raise wages. In turn, the increase in wages then increases prices again. The wage-price spiral thus multiplies the effect of a raw materials price on inflation. If there is no indexing, so that the wage does not respond at all to prices, other costs would go directly into prices with a coefficient of 1. But because wages rise when prices rise, there is a feedback effect—the wage-price spiral. The feedback effect more than doubles the impact of a price shock.

LENGTH AND SEVERITY OF BUSINESS CYCLES

In Chapter 15 we saw that long-term contracts are set in a forward-looking manner: Workers and firms look ahead to future labor market conditions, and to price and wage inflation. If workers expect a recession to be short then they will be more reluctant to accept lower wages than if they expect the recession to last for a number of years. In the price-adjustment equation, the market conditions term $(Y_{-1} - Y^*)/Y^*$ partially represents how recent excess supply or demand is indicative of future excess supply or demand. Usually business cycles last for a number of years, so, if output is below potential this year, that is an indication that output will probably be below normal for a few more years.

But suppose that departures of output from potential become less persistent; for example, suppose that the average length of business cycles is reduced from 4 years to 2 years. Then if GNP is below potential today there is no implication that GNP will be below potential 2 years from now. The best guess is that GNP will be back to potential 2 years from now. As a result inflation will be less responsive to recessions. Algebraically, the coefficient f in Equation 16–1 will be smaller when recessions are expected to be less prolonged.

Robert Solow of M.I.T. has argued that this type of coefficient change has occurred in the period since the Second World War in the United States.[1] Since business cycles have become shorter, the downward response of wages to high unemployment has been reduced. Phillip Cagan of Columbia University and Jeffrey Sachs of Harvard University have also found evidence of this.[2]

16.3 Models of the Expected Inflation Term

One of the most difficult issues in the price-adjustment equation is the measure of expected inflation, π^e. There are two important factors to consider:

1. *Forward-looking forecasts.* When wages are set, the fact that prices and other wages are expected to rise in the future influences the wage that emerges from whatever process the worker and the employer use to determine wages. For example, when a 3-year contract is negotiated, the built-in wage increases in the second and third years are larger if inflation is expected to continue during the contract. The amount of inflation that is forecast to occur in the future is therefore part of the expected inflation term. If workers and unions are informed about the economy, then these forward-looking forecasts will match rational expectations theory.

2. *Staggered contracts and backward-looking wage behavior.* The influence of today's expectations on the expected inflation term is only part of the story, however. Because of wage contracts and staggered wage setting, the expectations term involves inertia that cannot be changed overnight. Workers and firms must take account of the wages that will be paid to other workers in the economy. Since wage setting is staggered over time, some wages must be set looking back at the previous wage decisions of other workers; once these wages are set they are not changed during the contract period unless economic conditions change drastically. Wage inflation has a momentum due to contracts

---

[1] See Robert M. Solow, "The Intelligent Citizen's Guide to Inflation," *The Public Interest,* Vol. 38, pp. 30–66, 1975.

[2] Phillip Cagan, "Changes in the Cyclical Behavior of Prices," in his *The Persistence of Inflation,* New York, Columbia University Press, 1979, pp. 69–94, and Jeffrey Sachs, "The Changing Cyclical Behavior of Wages and Prices," *American Economic Review,* Vol. 70 (March 1980), pp. 78–90.

and relative wage setting. The expectations term must take account of this momentum as well as of the pure expectational influence.[3]

There is no reason to choose between these explanations. Both are part of the simple algebraic model of staggered contracts with rational expectations discussed in Chapter 15.

CHANGES IN THE MODEL OF EXPECTED INFLATION

For macroeconomic policy the particular model of the expected inflation term is crucial. Any reasonable model of expectations will give the long-run result that there is no long-run trade-off between the levels of inflation and output. But much of macroeconomic policy is concerned about the short run, and here different models of expected inflation make quite a difference.

Any *model* of expected inflation must be consistent with the *actual behavior* of inflation as observed over a number of years. If inflation typically tends to have momentum, then the public's model of expected inflation will also have momentum. But if inflation tends to be temporary, because of a policy to stabilize prices, for example, then people's view of expected inflation will incorporate the belief that a burst of inflation will probably not be followed by continuing inflation.

For the above reasons, any model of expected inflation is therefore itself endogenous to the type of economy or type of policy that is in operation. If policy changes, the model of expected inflation should change. Consider some examples:

1. *Changes in monetary policy.* When the Fed announces that it is switching to a new policy that puts more weight on controlling inflation, and the public believes it, the model of expected inflation will change.
2. *Introduction of specific policies for wage restraint.* The federal government has experimented with a variety of mandatory and voluntary programs for cutting wage inflation. Typically, these involve the announcement of a national wage norm and some method for punishing or exposing employers that exceed the norm. Economists have proposed alternative policies based on tax penalties for excessive wage increases. If the public believes that a policy of this type is working, the model of expected inflation will change.

If people are highly skeptical about promised changes in government programs, then they may well take the view that the only convincing evidence

---

[3] For more detail on this point and a contrast with other texts that emphasize only pure expectational effects, see John B. Taylor, "Staggered Wage Setting in a Macro Model," *American Economic Review*, Vol. 69 (May 1979), pp. 108–113.

that expected inflation has changed is for actual inflation to change. If so, a simple backward-looking model of the expected inflation term is closer to the truth—at least for the period of time that it takes the government to convince people that it means business.

In what follows we will work through some of the implications of a particular example of a model of expected inflation and examine how the process might change.

A simple model says that this year's expected inflation depends on actual inflation last year and the year before:

$$\pi^e = .4\pi_{-1} + .2\pi_{-2}. \tag{16-2}$$

This equation is more complicated than the model of the expectations term that we considered in Chapter 6, but conceptually the same ideas are at work. In Chapter 6 we assumed that expected inflation depended only on the rate of inflation last year π_{-1}. In Equation 16–2, expected inflation also depends on inflation two years ago.

To illustrate the implications of this model of the expected inflation term, we will look at four examples of how prices adjust to different disturbances.

EXAMPLE 1: EFFECT OF A ONE-YEAR STIMULUS

The economy starts with zero expected inflation. Policy-makers choose to push output above normal by 3 percentage points for one full year. From then on, output is kept at its normal level. Throughout the period, there is no contribution to inflation from materials prices (Z is zero). What happens to the price level?

In order to answer this question, we need to know the numerical value of the coefficient, f, that governs the unemployment effect in Equation 16–1. A reasonable value, inferred from the last few decades of experience, is $f = .25$. That is, if real GNP is 1 percent above potential in a particular year, inflation is .25 percentage point higher on that account.

In the first year, the output gap is above normal by 3 percent, which adds .75 percent to inflation in the second year through the first term in the price equation. Materials prices and expected inflation are both zero, so inflation π in Year 2 is .75. In the second year, output is back to normal, so there is no contribution from the first term. However, expected inflation is up because of the actual inflation the year before. Because last year has a coefficient of .4, expected inflation is .3. This is the only term affecting inflation, so inflation is .3 in Year 3. In the fourth year, again only expected inflation is contributing to actual inflation, so expected inflation is .4 times last year's inflation of .3 plus .2 times the .75 inflation of 2 years ago. The sum is .27. Thus, inflation in Year 4 is .27. In the fifth year, expected inflation is .4 times last year's rate of .27 plus .2 times the .3 inflation of the year before.

Table 16–1. INFLATION EFFECTS OF A ONE-TIME STIMULUS TO OUTPUT

Year	Inflation (%)	Output Gap (%)
1	.00	3
2	.75	0
3	.30	0
4	.27	0
5	.17	0
.	.	.
.	.	.
.	.	.
∞	.00	0

That is, inflation in Year 5 is .17. This process continues year after year. If you keep computing in this way, you will get results that gradually approach zero. But the measurable effects of the one year of stimulus continue for quite a few years. The results are summarized in Table 16–1.

This example illustrates the *dynamic* nature of the trade-off between output and inflation in an economy where expected inflation responds to actual inflation, on the one hand, and then gets built into actual inflation, on the other hand. A 1-year period of lower unemployment brings a sustained increase in the inflation rate. The effect is dynamic because an effect in one year has an effect that lasts for many years.

The intuitive reason that a temporary period of higher output prompts a sustained increase in inflation is that higher output raises actual inflation. In the next year, expected inflation must be higher. Once expected inflation is up, it tends to remain up, because expected inflation feeds point for point into actual inflation. In our simple model, expected inflation gradually dies out if there is no further inflationary stimulus from lower unemployment or higher materials prices.

EXAMPLE 2: EFFECT OF A MATERIALS PRICE SHOCK

The full story of the response of the economy to an increase in materials prices involves the aggregate demand side of the economy. But, even without the demand side, we can answer the question, what would happen to inflation if aggregate demand policy were manipulated in such a way that output remained at its normal level at the time of the materials price shock and during its aftermath?

Suppose that the rise in the price of materials is 1 percent for 1 year and then is zero in future years. Because of indexing, the contribution to the price-adjustment equation, Z, is 2.5 percent. Output is held at its normal level in every year. Expected inflation starts at zero. In the year of the shock, materials prices are the only contributor to inflation, so the immediate impact is to give 2.5 percentage points of inflation: Inflation π in Year 1

Table 16–2.   EFFECT ON INFLATION OF A MATERIALS PRICE SHOCK WHEN OUTPUT IS HELD AT POTENTIAL

Year	Inflation (%)	Output Gap (%)
1	2.50	0
2	1.00	0
3	.90	0
4	.56	0
.	.	.
.	.	.
.	.	.
∞	.00	0

is 2.5. In the year after the shock, neither output nor materials prices are contributing to inflation, but expected inflation is up because of the actual inflation in the previous year. It gets a weight of .4, so expected inflation in the second year is 1.0, and that is the actual inflation rate as well: Inflation is 1.0 in Year 2. In the second year after the shock, expected inflation is .2 times actual inflation in Year 1 plus .4 times actual inflation in Year 2, or .9 percent: Inflation in Year 3 is .9. This process continues until inflation gradually reaches zero. The results are summarized in Table 16–2.

EXAMPLE 3: EFFECT OF A ONE-YEAR INFLATION

Another question we can answer using just the price equation has the opposite flavor of the two earlier ones: Suppose monetary policy is conducted so that there is inflation in one year but no inflation in any later year. What happens to output in the inflationary year and in the subsequent years? In the first year, output will rise as the economy responds to the stimulus that brings on the inflation. But, in the second year, output must be below normal. By assumption, inflation is to be zero, but expected inflation is positive because actual inflation was positive the year before. Hence there must be a negative contribution from output.

If inflation in the second year is to be 1 percent, and the contributions from materials and expected inflation are zero, it must be that output is 4 percentage points above normal in the first year. That is, inflation in Year 2 is 1 percent, which equals $.25[(Y_{-1} - Y^*)/Y^*]$ so that $(Y_{-1} - Y^*)/Y^*$ equals .04. Going into the third year, expected inflation is .4 times actual inflation in the second year, 1 percent, or .4 percent of expected inflation. We want actual inflation to be zero, so

$$.25[(Y_{-1} - Y^*)/Y^*] + .004 = 0.$$

Thus, the output gap is −1.6 percent. In the third year, the history of inflation is 1 percent 2 years ago and zero last year. Expected inflation is .2 percent. To make actual inflation zero, output must again exceed the fall below its normal level:

$$.25[(Y_{-1} - Y^*)/Y^*] + .002 = 0,$$

so that the output gap is $-.8$ percent. From this point on, expected inflation is zero. The unemployment rate drops back to its normal level in the fourth year and remains there. These calculations are summarized in Table 16–3.

Table 16–3. OUTPUT GAPS ASSOCIATED WITH A SINGLE YEAR OF INFLATION

Year	Inflation (%)	Output Gap (%)
1	0	4.0
2	1	−1.6
3	0	− .8
4	0	.0
>4	0	.0

The net effect of the policy of one point of inflation for 1 year is to push output 4 percent above normal in the year before. But in the two subsequent years, output has to be below normal by 1.6 and .8 percentage points. If you add up the total output gain from this policy you will see that it is positive: 4.0 minus 1.6 minus .8 equals 1.6. The economy achieves 1.6 percent more output. The inflation output trade-off is sensitive to the way that expected inflation is related to actual inflation. The favorable trade-off in the example we just looked at arises because one point of actual inflation contributes less than one point of expected inflation. The one point of inflation in the first year generates .4 point of expected inflation in the second year and .2 point in the third year. If expected inflation is more sensitive to actual inflation, the trade-off would be less favorable. In particular, if one point of actual inflation ultimately contributed a whole point to expected inflation, the trade-off would be even—the total output loss associated with a rise and equal fall in inflation would be zero.

EXAMPLE 4: EFFECT OF EXTENDED HIGH OUTPUT

Finally, suppose that aggregate demand policy provides whatever stimulus is needed to keep output 3 percentage points above normal for every year starting with Year 1. What will happen to the rate of inflation?

We already know that an attempted policy of permanent stimulus will break down sooner or later, because expected inflation will respond to the policy and will move up to anticipate its effects. What happens in our simple model of expected inflation? It turns out that the simple model does not obey this accelerationist proposition. Even if the simple model worked fairly well in describing expected inflation over the last 30 years of U.S. experience, when inflation ebbed and flowed several times, it would clearly change under different conditions of extended periods of high inflation.

If we trace through the operation of the simple model under sustained stimulus, we get the following: The first year is exactly the same as the policy that kept output above normal just for the first year. Actual inflation is .75 percent in the second year. In the third year, expected inflation is .30 percent. In addition, because output is still 3 percentage points above normal, the first term of the price equation contributes another .75 percent. Actual inflation is 1.05 percent in Year 3. In the fourth year, expected inflation is $(.4)(1.05) + (.2)(.75) = .57$. Output remains 3 percentage points above normal and contributes its usual .75 percent. The sum is 1.32 percent: Inflation in Year 4 is 1.32. In the fifth year, expected inflation is .74 percent and actual inflation is 1.49. The process continues indefinitely, with actual inflation rising each year. Ultimately, inflation stabilizes at 1.88 percent per year.

The behavior we have just described is a complete violation of the natural rate–accelerationist proposition. The output gap is permanently 3 percentage points above normal, whereas the natural rate proposition says that output must be equal to potential, on the average. Inflation reaches a constant level of 1.88 percent per year, instead of rising to unlimited levels as predicted by the accelerationist proposition. The problem is that we are not allowing our simple model of expected inflation to adjust to a fundamental change in the economic environment. If policy-makers decide to introduce permanent inflation, then the simple model of expected inflation no longer makes sense.

To see the problem, note that, if inflation reaches the constant level of 1.88 percent, we can substitute 1.88 for π_{-1} and π_{-2} in Equation 16–2. Expected inflation is $\pi^e = 1.13$ percent per year. Expected inflation is chronically well below actual inflation. The government has tricked wage setters into thinking that inflation is less than it really is.

In the long run, people will not fall into this trap. They will revise expected inflation to the full level of actual inflation, and the natural rate–accelerationist proposition will hold. Our simple model of expected inflation will not work under sustained constant inflation. Instead, it is a model suited to a world where inflation is not sustained, but comes in occasional bursts that then subside.

It is likely that the model of expected inflation will change to something like

$$\pi^e = .5\pi_{-1} + .5\pi_{-2}.$$

This formula has the property that expected inflation becomes equal to actual inflation if the actual inflation is sustained for 2 years. If you go back

Table 16–4. INCREASE IN INFLATION WITH PERMANENT HIGH OUTPUT

Year	Inflation (%)	Output Gap (%)
1	.0	3
2	.750	3
3	1.125	3
4	1.688	3
5	2.156	3
6	2.672	3
.	.	.
.	.	.
.	.	.
∞	∞	3

Note: The expectations term is given by Equation 16–2 with a .5 coefficient on last year's inflation, and .5 on the previous year's inflation.

over our calculations of the effect of a policy of keeping output 3 percent above normal permanently, you will find that the alternative model predicts that inflation will rise each year and become greater without limit. The amount of the increase is shown in Table 16–4. Eventually, the process settles down to a constant amount of increase in inflation of .5 percentage point each year.

The last example seems to show the accelerationist proposition at work. When policy-makers hold output above normal year after year, inflation gets worse each year. If output is 3 percentage points above normal, inflation eventually worsens by .5 percentage point each year.

The alternative model of expected inflation is far from satisfactory, however. Although the *level* of expected inflation becomes equal to the level of actual inflation, the rate of increase of expected inflation constantly lags behind the rate of increase of actual inflation. Even though the game policy-makers are playing must eventually become evident to everybody in the economy, expected inflation constantly lags behind actual inflation. In reality, a policy that added .5 percentage point to inflation each year would probably not keep output above normal indefinitely.

We could look at more complicated models of expected inflation that try to keep up with the rate of change of inflation as well as its level, but the main ideas should already be clear. There is a very general point at work here: *No mechanical model of expected inflation is universally applicable.* If the public has a particular way of arriving at expected inflation, the government can design a policy that fools the public and makes actual inflation continually exceed expected inflation. But then the public will revise its method of calculating expected inflation so that it will no longer be fooled.

If the government uses a policy that does not attempt to fool the public by making actual inflation exceed expected inflation, then there can be a stable way that the public arrives at expected inflation. In particular, if the government aims at a non-inflationary economy and acts to offset occasional bursts of inflation from materials prices and elsewhere, then our simple model of expected inflation is a reasonable description of the process. Inflation does persist after it develops, but a point of past inflation does not contribute a full point to expected inflation.

A policy that attempts to keep output above normal permanently will fail. Eventually the public will catch on to the policy and revise expected inflation by a method that makes it keep up with actual inflation.

With any given method for determining expected inflation, the government can figure out an expansionary policy that keeps unemployment below normal permanently. For example, with our simple model of expected inflation, a policy of continued inflation will keep unemployment below normal. The model of expected inflation would not apply with such a policy.

16.4 The Combined Operation of Price Adjustment and Aggregate Demand

We now integrate the price formulations, Equations 16–1 and 16–2, into a model of aggregate demand, working in terms of a numerical example. A simple form of the aggregate demand function is

$$Y = 2,067 + 3.221\frac{M}{P}. \tag{16–3}$$

Note that monetary policy is more powerful in this example than in the aggregate demand function in Chapter 5, which did not include the effect of interest on consumption goods such as automobiles. Fiscal policy determines the level of the constant, 2,067. Government spending is assumed to be fixed at \$750 billion. The starting value for the money supply M is \$600 billion. Potential output is assumed to be \$4,000 billion.

Consider the case where the Fed targets M_1. Note that a higher price level means a lower level of aggregate demand. Recall the mechanism lying behind this conclusion:

1. If the price level is higher relative to the money stock, the LM curve is farther to the left in the IS-LM diagram.
2. The intersection with the IS curve occurs at a lower level of real GNP and a higher interest rate.
3. Investment is lower because the interest rate is higher and because output is lower.
4. Net exports are lower because the interest rate is higher and the exchange rate is higher.
5. Consumption is lower because real income is lower and because interest rates are higher.

The second major element of the complete model is the price-adjustment equation, Equation 16–1. The third is the model of expected inflation.

The Four Relationships of the Numerical Example

Aggregate demand	$Y = 2{,}067 + 3.221(M/P)$
Price adjustment	$\pi = .25[(Y_{-1} - Y^*)/Y^*] + \pi^e + Z$
Expected inflation	$\pi^e = .4\pi_{-1} + .2\pi_{-2}$
Price Level	$P = (1 + \pi_{-1})P_{-1}$

To analyze the three equations we can proceed graphically, as we did in Chapter 6, or algebraically. The graphical approach would use an aggregate demand diagram with price adjustment (see Figure 6–9). Each year we would treat the price level as predetermined and determine output at the intersection of aggregate demand and the flat price line; then calculate the price level for the next year using the price-adjustment diagram.

Here we proceed algebraically using the numerical example, but the analysis is equivalent: Take the price level as predetermined each year, and use the aggregate demand curve to determine output. Then use the model of the expectations term and the price-adjustment equation to determine the price level for the next year. At the new price level determine output in the next year and so on. We use this approach to look at the following four different examples: (1) recovery from a demand-deficient recession, (2) recovery from stagflation, (3) a boom, and (4) an oil price shock. In the first two examples we start the economy off from a position below full employment without asking how the economy got there. In the second two examples we start the economy at full employment and then push it away from full employment with a shock.

EXAMPLE 1: RECOVERY FROM A DEMAND-DEFICIENT RECESSION

Suppose the economy starts out at a position below full employment. Suppose, as well, that expected inflation at the outset is zero. How does the economy get back to equilibrium with full employment and stable prices?

In the first year, output is determined by the aggregate demand function given the initial price level and the money stock. This level of output is below potential. Consequently, the first term of the price-adjustment equation pushes the price level downward. Materials prices and expected inflation contribute nothing at this point. Inflation is negative. The price level falls slightly.

In the second year, the process continues. Output is still below potential, so the $(Y - Y*)/Y*$ term in the price-adjustment equation pushes the price level down some more. But actual deflation in the previous year makes expected inflation negative in the second year. The result is a larger decline in the price level in the second year than in the first year.

In the third year, there is even more deflation, because the negative contribution from expected inflation is even larger. In the fourth year, deflation is about the same as in the third year. Expected inflation is making a somewhat larger negative contribution. But output has been improving steadily. As the price level falls, output rises, according to the aggregate demand function. Consequently, the negative contribution from the $(Y - Y*)/Y*$ term is not as large as it was in earlier years.

In the fifth year, the price level falls some more, but not by as much as in the fourth year. The rate of inflation rises, in the sense that the rate of deflation is no longer as high. However, prices are still falling, and output rises some more.

Skipping to the ninth year, the price level has fallen far enough to restore full employment. However, the rate of inflation is still negative, because expected inflation is negative. The price level continues to fall and the economy enters a period that is slightly above full employment.

Some years later, the price level is again at equilibrium and output is at its potential level. But now expected inflation is very slightly positive. The economy overshoots a little and enters a period of less than full employment. By this time, the economy is so close to equilibrium that the rest of the process of cycling to equilibrium is almost invisible.

We now introduce a convenient diagram (Figure 16–1) to look at the movements of output and inflation. This diagram shows that the rate of inflation is the vertical axis and the level of output is the horizontal axis.

The basic mechanism of a recovery is simple. From a point of deficient aggregate demand, the economy gets back to full employment by moving to a lower price level. As the price level falls, the LM curve shifts to the right, the interest rate falls, investment and export demand rise, and output rises.

The complete model describes this process. The most critical feature of the model is the response of the price level to output. In our portrayal of the complete model, a 1-year period in which output is 1 percent below potential lowers the price level by .25 percent below what it would have been if output had been at potential. It takes 9 years to restore full employment from a starting point below potential, with zero initial expected inflation and no disturbances from materials prices throughout the recovery.

If the price level is significantly more sensitive to output, then the recovery would take place much faster. For example, if the coefficient in the price-adjustment equation is 1.00 point instead of .25 point of deflation per point of departure from potential, it takes only a little over 3 years to get back to full employment from a starting point below full employment.

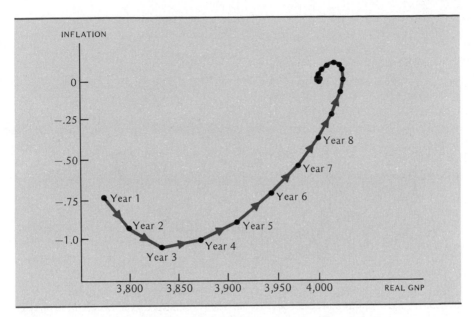

Figure 16-1.   ECONOMIC RECOVERY (EXAMPLE 1).
In the first year, real GNP is far below potential. In the next year inflation falls. In the year after that, inflation becomes even more negative because expected inflation becomes negative. Throughout the first nine years, the price level is falling, so aggregate demand rises and output approaches potential. Because of the momentum of deflation, the price level continues to fall after Year 7 and the economy enters a period with GNP above potential. The economy makes a spiral approach to equilibrium, where output equals potential and inflation is zero.

EXAMPLE 2: RECOVERY FROM STAGFLATION

The case we just studied started with deficient aggregate demand but zero expected inflation. An even unluckier economy might start with both deficient demand and positive expected inflation—the condition Nobel laureate Paul Samuelson of M.I.T. has called **stagflation.**[4] An economy recently hit by a serious materials price shock might be in this condition.

At the beginning of a recovery from stagflation, two terms in the price-adjustment equation are fighting against each other. Expected inflation is positive, but the $(Y - Y^*)/Y^*$ term is negative. Either one could win. In the case shown in Figure 16–2, expected inflation wins in the first year, and inflation is positive.

Because inflation won in the first year, the price level is a bit higher in the second year and the level of real GNP actually falls some more. Then ex-

[4] Paul Samuelson, "Worldwide Stagflation," in Hiroaki Nagatani and Kate Crowley (eds.), *The Collected Scientific Papers of Paul Samuelson,* Vol. 4, Cambridge, Mass., M.I.T. Press, 1975, pp. 801–807.

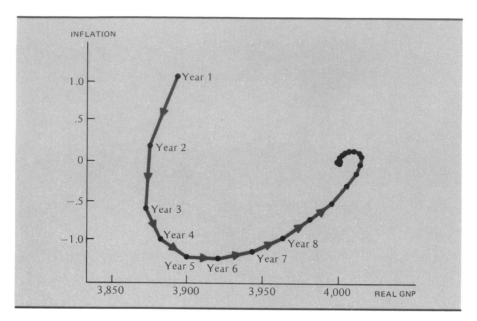

Figure 16–2.   RECOVERY FROM STAGFLATION (EXAMPLE 2).
In the first year, inflation remains positive because of expected inflation. In the second year, real GNP is even lower because the price level has risen. From then on, the recovery is similar to the one in Figure 16–1, which started from zero expected inflation. The economy approaches equilibrium in a spiral.

pected inflation declines and the $(Y - Y^*)/Y^*$ term dominates. The price level falls slightly going into Year 3 and output rises a bit. In Years 4 through 9, the price level falls some more and the recovery proceeds. By Year 9, output is back up to potential but, because expected inflation is negative in that year, the economy overshoots a little. Output remains slightly above potential for a number of years.

If you compare Figures 16–1 and 16–2, you will see that the main effect of starting from a point of positive expected inflation is to delay the recovery for about 2 years. During these two years, the economy of Figure 16–2 is working off expected inflation and suffering from little growth of real output, while the economy of Figure 16–1 is getting started on its recovery. Again, falling prices are the key to recovery. In the two years when expected inflation is working against falling prices, the stagflation economy of Figure 16–2 cannot expand.

EXAMPLE 3: A BOOM

What happens in the short, medium, and long runs when an outward shift in aggregate demand sets off a boom? At first, higher aggregate demand

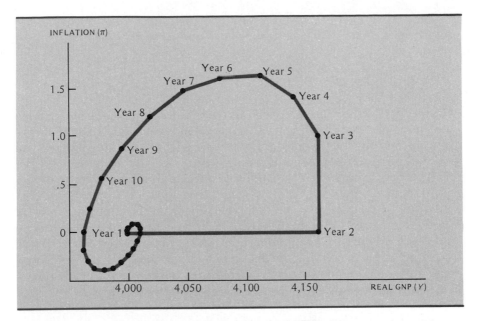

Figure 16–3. A BOOM (EXAMPLE 3).
The economy starts in equilibrium in Year 1, with output equal to potential and zero inflation. In Year 2 the aggregate demand curve shifts outward. Real GNP shifts upward immediately. Inflation starts in Year 3. As the price level rises, aggregate demand falls and
output begins to recede toward equilibrium. In 9 years, output is back to equilibrium but
the economy overshoots because expected inflation is positive at that point. The approach to equilibrium is again a spiral.

raises output, in the way described by the IS-LM model. But higher output
means inflation. After inflation gets started, expected inflation begins to
catch up with it. As the price level rises, aggregate demand falls. Eventually,
the economy gets back to equilibrium, with output equal to potential and
inflation at zero. In the new equilibrium, the only effect of the increase in
aggregate demand is to raise the price level. The path of the economy in response to an increase in aggregate demand is shown in the inflation-output
diagram of Figure 16–3.

The path starts at equilibrium in Year 1. There is no inflation and output
is at potential. In Year 2, the outward shift in aggregate demand raises output sharply. Because the price level does not respond immediately, output
increases by the full amount of the shift in aggregate demand. For the next
nine years, a series of increases in the price level depresses aggregate demand. At first, through Year 5, inflation gets worse each year, as expected
inflation catches up with actual inflation. From then on, inflation gradually
dissipates because output is less and less above potential. In year 10, output
is back to its potential level. However, expected inflation is still positive.
Further price increases depress aggregate demand below potential, and the

economy enters a very slight recession. The spiral approaches equilibrium rapidly thereafter.

EXAMPLE 4: AN OIL PRICE SHOCK

In the 1970s, the U.S. economy was twice battered by large and sudden increases in oil prices. Both sent the economy into periods of stagflation. We can trace out the reaction of the complete model to a one-time increase in materials prices, Z. Suppose Z is 2.5 percent in Year 2 and returns to zero for the indefinite future. The path of inflation and output is shown in Figure 16–4.

In Year 2, inflation jumps up to 2.5 percent from the contribution of oil prices to total costs and from the feedback through wages. The higher price level depresses output; the economy is in a state of stagflation. The recovery from stagflation proceeds as in Figure 16–2. At first, expected inflation dominates the deflation that is associated with output that is below potential. The price level rises some more and output falls even further below po-

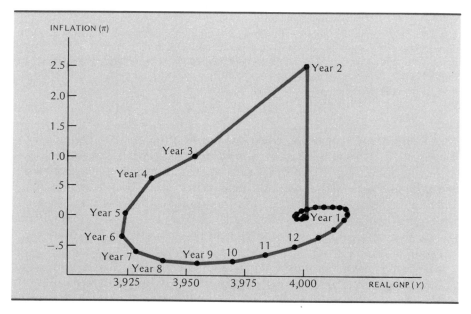

Figure 16–4.   AN OIL PRICE SHOCK (EXAMPLE 4).
The economy starts at equilibrium in Year 1. In Year 2, inflation jumps up to 2.5 percent because of the 1 percent increase in total costs from the higher oil price. In Year 3, the level of output is much lower because the price level is higher. In Years 4, 5, and 6, the price level is even higher and output even lower because of expected inflation. Starting in Year 7, a recovery takes place because the price level begins to fall. Around Year 12, output is back to potential. The economy overshoots slightly on its way back to equilibrium.

tential. As expected inflation subsides and deflation from low output dominates, aggregate demand begins to recover. The recovery overshoots a little and the economy experiences a little boom on the way to equilibrium.

16.5 Inflation-Output Loops in the United States, Germany, and the United Kingdom

How well does this model work as an explanation of the record of inflation and output fluctuations in modern economies? Before proceeding with policy analysis in the next chapter it is important to check whether the theory is consistent with experience.

The four inflation-output diagrams of the previous section (Figures 16–1, 16–2, 16–3, and 16–4) provide a fascinating and reasonably accurate way for us to confront the theory with the facts. In all the cases we considered— (1) recovery from a demand-deficient recession, (2) recovery from stagflation, (3) a boom, and (4) an oil price shock—the model economy was displaced from its long-run potential. In each case the return path to potential displays a striking characteristic that is clear in the diagrams: The path is a **counterclockwise loop** because the economy tends to spiral back to potential in a counterclockwise fashion.

Do inflation and output actually behave this way? Since real-world economies are constantly being shocked by many events, it is difficult to separate out isolated episodes like the special shocks in the model economy. Nevertheless, inflation and output fluctuations do display such counterclockwise loops. They are not so smooth and circular as in the model economy, but they are there nonetheless.

In Figure 16–5 we show inflation and output pairs in the United States for each of the years from 1971 through 1986. Even at a quick glance two big loops are evident: one from 1971 through 1976, and another from 1976 through 1986. The first loop involves the monetary-induced boom of 1971–72, the oil price shock of 1974, and the recession of 1975. The second loop occurred under very similar circumstances: a boom in 1977–78 followed by another oil shock in 1979—this time related to the revolution in Iran, a major oil producer—and a subsequent large recession in the early 1980s. In both cases expected inflation first rose and then fell. Note that the second loop started at a higher rate of expected inflation.

This type of output and inflation fluctuation is not unique to the United States economy. Figure 16–6 shows the data for a similar period in Germany. Again there are two loops.

The same picture is shown in Figure 16–7 for the United Kingdom. Here the loops are harder to see, but again two are evident. The first loop involved a very large increase in inflation and a small drop in output following the 1973 oil shock. Hence, the loop was standing up and skinny, though leaning slightly to the left. The second loop, centering around the 1979 oil

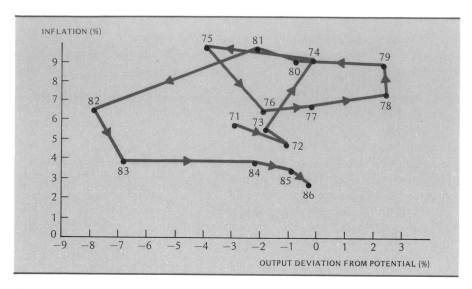

Figure 16–5.   INFLATION-OUTPUT LOOPS IN THE UNITED STATES, 1971–86.
During the 1971–86 period there were two big loops in the United States. The second loop started from a higher rate of expected inflation. Source: *Economic Report of the President,* 1985, Tables B–2 and B–3.

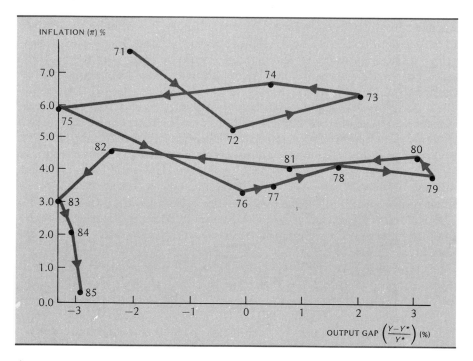

Figure 16–6.   INFLATION-OUTPUT LOOPS IN GERMANY, 1971–85.
In Germany there were two loops during the 1971–85 period, and they appear flatter than those for the United States. Source: *International Financial Statistics,* International Monetary Fund, various issues.

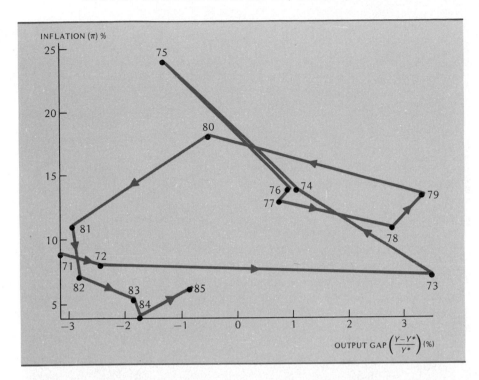

Figure 16–7. INFLATION-OUTPUT LOOPS IN THE UNITED KINGDOM, 1971–85. There are two loops here too, but they are much less evident and seem to have changed their orientation. Both were skinny, but the first was leaning up and the second was lying down. Source: *International Financial Statistics,* International Monetary Fund, various issues.

shock, had the opposite characteristic: a large drop in output and a much smaller fluctuation in inflation. Hence the second loop was again skinny, but now lying down on its side. (Note the vertical scale is compressed for the U.K. compared to the U.S. and especially Germany.)

Overall, the model is consistent with the dynamic movements of inflation and output. While these graphical tests focusing on loops may appear overly simplistic, they are confirmed by more accurate statistical regression techniques and we believe they capture the essence of the theory and the facts.

Why Are Output Fluctuations in Japan So Small?

During the last 15 years, fluctuations in real output in Japan have been much smaller than in the United States and the other countries discussed in this chapter. As illustrated in the figure below, real GNP fluctuations in Japan are so small compared to those in the United States that actual GNP in Japan behaves much like smoothly trending potential GNP for the United States. Compared to the United States, the Japanese economy completely avoided the boom in GNP for the late 1970s as well as the bust of the early 1980s.

What might explain this difference? The theory of aggregate demand and price adjustment described in this chapter offers one possible explanation. If prices and wages adjust very quickly to demand—that is, if the coefficient f in the price adjustment equation is large, then relatively small fluctuations in output will be capable of stabilizing inflation. For example, if the response (f) of prices and wages is high, then the effect of a price shock like that in Example 4 and Figure 16–4 would result in only a small drop in output. Similarly, a boom resulting from a monetary expansion like that in Example 3 and Figure 16–3 would be relatively small.

In Japan, wages and prices do seem to be more sensitive to demand conditions than in the United States. One reason is that a significant fraction of wage payments comes in the form of bonuses that can be easily adjusted. Another reason for the greater sensitivity of wages is that most wage changes are synchronized in the spring quarter in the *shunto* as described on page 423 in Chapter 15.

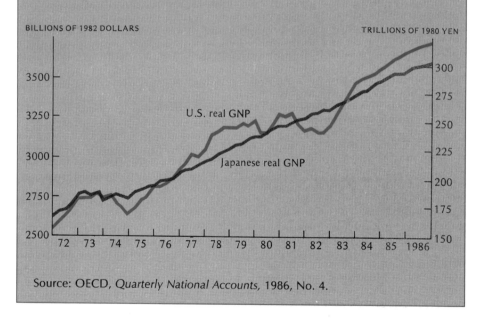

Source: OECD, *Quarterly National Accounts*, 1986, No. 4.

Review and Practice

MAJOR POINTS

1. A model of price adjustment must incorporate the response of wages to excess demand and to expected inflation.

2. Expected inflation has forward-looking features and backward-looking features. Expectations and contracts are both part of the micro underpinnings of the expected inflation term.

3. A simple model of price adjustment can be derived by combining wage adjustment with markup pricing behavior. The model of price adjustment is the same as in the model of Chapter 6 except that the coefficients of the model can change.

4. No simple mechanical formula is satisfactory as a model of expected inflation. Any such model would be inconsistent with actual inflation behavior if policy or the economic environment changed.

5. The accelerationist or natural rate hypothesis holds that, in the long run, unemployment will equal the natural rate regardless of how high inflation is, as long as it is steady.

6. A model that combines aggregate demand with price adjustment implies that inflation and output will fluctuate or spiral as the economy returns to potential after a shock.

7. During the 1970s and 1980s the United States and other countries went through economic fluctuations that displayed such spirals of counterclockwise loops.

KEY TERMS AND CONCEPTS

Expected inflation

Accelerationist hypothesis

Indexing

Expectations of future labor market conditions

Stagflation

Inflation-output loops

Markup pricing

Consistent model of expected inflation

Oil shock to price setting

wage-price spiral

QUESTIONS FOR DISCUSSION AND REVIEW

1. What are the three elements included in the price-adjustment equation?

2. How is expected inflation related to forward-looking behavior? To staggered wage setting?

3. Why might the total effect of an increase in materials prices be greater than the effect portrayed in the markup equation?

4. How can you determine potential output from the price-adjustment equation?

5. Why does a one-year stimulus cause inflation to remain higher for many years?

6. Trace out the effects over time of an increase in materials prices, assuming that output is held constant.

7. What happens if policy tries to hold the output above the natural rate for an extended period?

8. What are the three relationships that make up the unified model that shows how the economy moves over time?

9. Explain why the economy approaches equilibrium in a spiral in the inflation–real GNP diagram.

PROBLEMS

Numerical

1. Example 1 of Section 16.3 looked at the inflation effects of a one-time stimulus to output. In this problem we show how such effects vary with different models of inflationary expectations. Consider the following alternatives to Equation 16–2:
   (i) $\pi^e = \pi_{-1}$; (ii) $\pi^e = .9\pi_{-1}$; (iii) $\pi^e = .5\pi_{-1} + .5\pi_{-2}$; (iv) $\pi^e = .33\pi_{-1} + .33\pi_{-2} + .33\pi_{-3}$.
   a. For each of these expressions find the inflation effects of a one-time 3 percent stimulus to output. Calculate the inflation rate for years 1 through 10.
   b. Estimate the long-run rate of inflation in each case.
   c. Based on your calculations and the calculations shown in Table 16–1, explain how inflation varies with (i) the sum of the coefficients in the expression for π^e, and (ii) the weight given to recent inflation compared to more distant inflation in the expression for π^e.
   d. Do any of the expressions for inflationary expectations given above lead to systematic errors in forecasting inflation? If so, which ones? If not, explain the relationship between expected and actual inflation when fiscal and monetary policy are used to keep output at potential. Is one expression for expected inflation more likely to prevail than another?

2. In this problem we consider the behavior of the economy following a demand deficient recession. We look at how the recovery is influenced by the model used for inflationary expectations. Suppose the economy starts off with output at potential $(Y = Y^* = 4000)$, $\pi = 0$, and $P = 1$. Aggregate demand is given by Equation 16–3; price adjustment is given by Equation 16–1 with $f = .25$. In year 1 the money supply is reduced from 600 to 570, creating a recession.
   a. Calculate the path of inflation, the price level, and output for years 1 through 6 assuming (i) $\pi^e = .4\pi_{-1} + .2\pi_{-2}$, and (ii) $\pi^e = \pi_{-1}$. In performing your calculations compute P as $(1 + \pi_{-1})P_{-1}$.
   b. For which model of expectations does the return to potential output take longer? For which model will there be more overshooting?
   c. We assumed here that the value taken by f in the price adjustment equation was the same for both models in inflationary expectations. Explain why in reality the value of f might differ from one model to the other. (Hint: In Chapter 15 we discussed the relationship between f and the length of the business cycle.)

3. In this problem we look at how the recovery from an oil price shock is affected by the model used for inflationary expectations. Let the model of the economy and its initial conditions be the same as in Problem 2. Note that the money supply will remain at 600. In year 1 let $Z = .025$.
   a. Calculate the path of inflation, the price level, and output in years 1 through 6 under each of the models for π^e given in Part a of Problem 2.
   b. In each case, how long does it take inflation to first return to zero? Analyze the factors that cause inflation to fall in each case.
   c. In which case is the fall in output greater? How do you explain this result?

4. Reconsider the oil price shock of Problem 3, only now suppose that the aim of policy makers is to keep inflation equal to zero in every year possible. This is achieved by manipulating the money stock.
   a. Assuming that the oil price shock was unexpected, can anything be done about the rate of inflation in year 1? Why or why not?
   b. Suppose π^e is always equal to zero. Find the values of M chosen by policy makers each year during and following the oil shock.

c. Now assume that π^e is given alternately by π_{-1} and $.5\pi_{-1}+.5\pi_{-2}$. Repeat the calculations from Part b for each case.

d. Is $\pi^e=0$ reasonable given the goals of policy? Use this example to explain the importance of policy makers maintaining their credibility.

Analytical

1. Explain why the inflation output loops in Section 16.4 are vertical at the point where inflation equals zero. Would the same be true if the money supply was increasing each year?

2. In this problem we consider the policy actions underlying Example 1 of Section 16.3.
   a. Assuming that the natural rate of unemployment is 6 percent, what is the unemployment rate in year 1 and year 2 onward?
   b. Diagram the actions taken by policy makers in year 1 and year 2 onward on an aggregate demand graph.
   c. Again, diagram the actions of policy makers each year on an IS-LM graph assuming that (i) all policy actions consist of fiscal policy, and (ii) all policy actions consist of monetary policy. Explain why your diagram in Part b does not depend on the nature of the policy action taken.

3. Describe the behavior of investment and interest rates during the boom described in Example 1 of Section 16.4 assuming that the boom was created by an exogenous increase in investment. How do interest rates and investment behave during and following an oil price shock?

4. What is the correlation between output and interest rates implied by the inflation-output loops of Section 16.4? What assumption is made about monetary policy in constructing these loops? Are the predictions of the model consistent with the data presented in Chapter 1?

5. Suppose that agents use all available information to make unbiased, but not error-free, forecasts of inflation. In that case, we can say that

$$\pi_t=\pi^e_t+e_t$$

where e_t is a forecast error whose average value is zero.
   a. What does this relationship between π and π^e imply about the average value of the output gap? (Hint: Use the price-adjustment equation.)
   b. Suppose now that π^e was formed such that π^e always differed from π by a constant, e. Using the price-adjustment equation, show that the accelerationist hypothesis doesn't hold.

PART IV

Macroeconomic Policy Evaluation

17

Designing and Maintaining a Good Macro Policy

As WE have seen, modern macroeconomic theory incorporates new ideas about rational expectations and price adjustment into traditional Keynesian and monetarist frameworks. What are the policy implications of this theory? This chapter begins with a review of the principal features. After examining the problem of matching policy instruments to targets and the problem of uncertainty in implementing policy, we go on to apply these principles to macroeconomic policy problems in the United States. In the next chapter we extend this to the world economy.

17.1 General Principles of Macro Policy Analysis

Much of our discussion of the recent developments in macroeconomics—rational expectations, policy rules, time inconsistency, theories of wage rigidities, the nature of economic fluctuations—has been technical. It is important not to lose sight of the central ideas by focusing too much on the technical details. The central ideas are summarized in the following five propositions.[1]

[1] This discussion is related to that in John B. Taylor, "An Appeal for Rationality in the Policy Activism Debate," In R. W. Hafer (ed.), *The Monetary and Fiscal Policy Debate: Lessons from Two Decades,* Roman and Allanheld, Totowa, N.J., Allanheld, 1986.

1. *When making decisions, people think about the future, and their expecta-*
tions of the future can be modeled by assuming that they have a sense of eco-
nomic fluctuations and use their information to make unbiased (but not
error-free) forecasts.

The notion that people make the most of the information available to
them when forecasting the future was originally proposed by John Muth in
1960 for use in microeconomic applications, such as the demand and supply
for agricultural commodities.[2] Farmers need to predict future prices in
order to know how much to grow. Muth suggested that we model a farmer's
expectations by simply assuming that the supply and demand model was
known to the farmer.

Whatever its value in agricultural economics, the idea seems reasonable
for macroeconomic applications. Many features of economic fluctuations
are recurrent from one business cycle to another; there are established statistical regularities. We have documented many of these regularities. Since
business cycles have been observed for hundreds of years, it makes sense to
assume that people have become familiar with them. Of course, in the face
of new, unprecedented events, people will make significant errors in trying
to look forward.

2. *Macroeconomic policy can be usefully described and evaluated as a policy*
rule, rather than by treating the instruments as exogenous and looking only
at one-time changes in these instruments.

Because people are forward-looking, their expectations of future policy
actions affect their current behavior and the state of the economy. Hence, in
order to evaluate the effect of policy on the economy we need to specify not
only current policy changes but also future policy changes. In other words,
we need to specify a contingency plan that describes how policy will react to
future events. Such a contingency is nothing more than a rule for policy.
The contingency plan could be as specific as a constant growth rate rule for
the money supply, but more generally it establishes a range of reactions depending on the state of the economy.

The rational expectations approach almost forces a macroeconomic ana-
lyst to think about policy as a rule or a strategy. Once you are working with a
rational expectations model you soon realize that you have little choice but
to specify policy as a rule. We will see in our policy evaluation study in the
latter part of this chapter that it is natural and convenient to specify policy as
a rule.

Note that the focus on rules does not mean that the effect of one-shot
changes in policy should never be calculated; such a calculation can be a

---

[2] John Muth, "Rational Expectations and the Theory of Price Movements," *Econometrica,*
Vol. 29, pp. 315–335, 1960.

useful exercise to help understand the workings of the model. We did this extensively in the previous chapter to see if our model was consistent with the facts.

In a famous critique of traditional policy evaluation, Robert Lucas of the University of Chicago argued in the early 1970s that traditional macro models, like the model of Chapters 4–6, could give incorrect answers to policy evaluation questions if expectations were forward-looking and there was a change in the policy rule.[3] Since these traditional models were based on adaptive backward-looking expectations, their parameters would change when the policy rule changed. This was the negative part of the critique, and it has clearly made policy analysts wary of using the traditional models. But there was also a positive side. The critique provided a general framework for modifying the traditional models; by stipulating policy as a rule it is possible to calculate by how much the parameters of the traditional models would change. An example of this was discussed in Chapter 16, where we showed how the sensitivity of inflation to recessions would diminish if business cycles became less prolonged, due, perhaps, to a change in policy. Similarly, the model of the expected inflation term in the price-adjustment equation (Equation 16–1) would change if monetary policy changed.

Some macroeconomists, such as Christopher Sims of the University of Minnesota, have argued that the focus on policy rules is irrelevant.[4] Sims argues that we rarely get big changes in rules anyway, so we might as well use conventional models for policy. Indeed there is a utopian flavor to the "policy rules" approach. The search is for big policy reforms that would improve economic welfare over a long period of time. The reforms would probably require changes in the policy-making institutions, or the creation of new institutions. Such reforms are by their very nature rare. But they do occur. The creation of the Federal Reserve System, the departure from the gold standard, and the shift to floating exchange rates are all examples. These reforms seem to have had substantial effects on the economy. A careful analysis of the effects of future policy reforms therefore seems quite relevant.

3. *In order for a particular policy rule to work well, it is necessary to establish a commitment to that rule.*

We briefly discussed the problem of time inconsistency in Chapter 7. The possibility that policy makers will find it tempting to change their plans in the future—be time inconsistent—is a reason for maintaining a commitment to a stated rule. The problem of time inconsistency was first pointed out in macroeconomics by Finn Kydland of Carnegie-Mellon University and

---

[3] Robert E. Lucas, "Econometric Policy Evaluation: A Critique," in Carnegie-Rochester Conference Series, *The Phillips Curve*, 1976, pp. 19–46.

[4] Christopher Sims, "Policy Analysis with Econometric Models," *Brookings Papers on Economic Activity*, Vol. 1, pp. 107–164, 1982.

Edward Prescott of the University of Minnesota, and independently by Guillermo Calvo of the University of Pennsylvania.[5]

In attempting to find optimal policies for economies where people are forward-looking, these researchers found that once policy makers began an optimal policy there was incentive in future periods for the policy makers to change the plan—to be inconsistent. Policy makers could make things better by being inconsistent. This was true even if the policy makers had the interests of the public in mind. One example close at hand is that of a teacher giving an examination. It is tempting to call off an examination after the students have studied and learned the material in a course in anticipation of the exam. Then the students do not have to sweat through the exam, and the teacher does not have to grade the exam papers. The government's patent laws provide a similar problem of inconsistency. Patent laws confer a temporary monopoly as a reward for inventions. Hence, they spur inventiveness. But the monopoly is undesirable: It would be tempting to remove patents when an invention is completed, so that the new product would be produced and marketed competitively. Another example from the government sphere is the construction of dams for flood plains. The government tells people not to build houses on a dangerous flood plain, because there will be no dams for flood control built. But when people move in anyway, the government will find it desirable to build the flood control project in order to protect them.

However, by being inconsistent the policy makers are likely to lose credibility; people would begin to assume that the policy makers will change the rules and this would lead to a new policy-making equilibrium that was generally inferior to the original policy plan of the policy makers. If the students began to expect that the exam would be called off, they probably would not study for it. The implication is that, to prevent this inferior outcome, it is better to maintain a firm commitment to a policy rule.

Returning to the patent example, a policy maker who had the discretion to award patents each year would indeed be tempted not to do so. By holding back the patent, the economic inefficiencies of a monopoly are avoided. Fortunately, reneging on patent promises does not occur in practice because it is so clear that future inventive activity would suffer. Instead, we have patent laws that limit such discretion. The time inconsistency research suggests that discretion should be limited for similar reasons in macroeconomic policy.

It is important to distinguish between **activist policy rules** and **discretionary policy.** Activist policy rules involve *feedback* from the state of the

---

[5] Finn Kydland and Edward Prescott, "Rules Rather than Discretion: The Inconsistency of Optimal Plans," *Journal of Political Economy,* Vol. 85, pp. 473–491, 1977; and Guillermo Calvo, "On the Time Inconsistency of Optimal Policy in a Monetary Economy," *Econometrica,* Vol. 46, pp. 1411–1428, 1979. Also see Stanley Fischer, "Dynamic Inconsistency, Cooperation, and the Benevolent Dissembling Government," *Journal of Economic Dynamics and Control,* Vol. 2, pp. 93–107, 1980.

economy to the policy instruments, but the feedback is part of the rule. Sometimes the term **passive policy rule** is used to refer to special rules without feedback, like the fixed growth rate rule for the money supply. An example of an activist policy rule is the following: If the unemployment rate rises by a certain amount next year, then the money supply will increase by a certain stated amount. Discretionary policy is formulated on a case-by-case and year-by-year basis with no attempt to commit to or even talk about future policy decisions in advance. Those in favor of discretionary policy disagree with the whole concept of a rule of the game approach, whether the rule is a feedback rule or a constant setting for the policy instruments. Activist and constant growth rate policy rules have much more in common with each other than do activist policy rules and discretionary policy. Both types of policy rules involve commitments and lead to the type of policy analysis suggested by the rational expectations approach.

4. *The economy is basically stable; after a shock the economy will eventually return to its normal trend paths of output and employment. However, because of rigidities in the structure of the economy, this return could be slow.*

The macro models we have looked at are *dynamic* systems continually disturbed by *shocks.* After each shock the economy has a tendency to return to the normal or natural growing level of output and employment, although there may be overshooting or a temporary cumulative movement away from normal. A smooth return is never observed in practice, however, because new shocks are always hitting the system. Since the economy is viewed as always being buffeted around the shocks, the equilibrium is really a random or stochastic equilibrium. The combination of the shocks and the dynamics of the model is capable of mimicking the actual behavior of business cycles surprisingly well, as we saw in the previous chapter. The properties of the random equilibrium are much like the actual behavior of business cycles.

The shocks can be due to many factors, but usually have been money shocks, demand shocks, or price shocks. The dynamics are due to many possible rigidities in the economy, but price-wage rigidities and slow adjustment of capital (including inventories) have been the most important empirically.

Because of these rigidities the impact of a shock to the economy takes time to sort itself out. Suppose, for example, that there is a shift in money demand with people wanting to hold more money at any level of income and interest rates. Eventually the price level will fall so that the real supply of money is effectively increased. But if there are wage and price rigidities this adjustment will take time: First the increase in money demand will cause an increase in interest rates; the higher level of interest rates will in turn depress demand for durables and have repercussions throughout the economy; depressed demand conditions will then begin to put downward pressure on prices; and the fall in prices then will begin to raise the real supply of money—this process will continue until the economy is back to its natural level of output and employment. The whole process could take more than a year.

Combined with these structural rigidities is the supposition that expectations are not restrained by similar rigidities. A shock can change expectations of inflation, exchange rates, and other variables overnight even though there are rigidities that cause the economy to take additional time to adjust fully to the shock. The expectations take account of the structural rigidities since these are part of the model. The combination of rigidities in the economy with perfectly flexible expectations is an essential feature of most rational expectations models.

There has been a tendency to get expectations assumptions mixed up with assumptions about how markets work. Hence, the comment that expectations might be rational in flexible auction markets but not in sticky wage labor markets is frequently heard. But there is no reason why expectations are not rational in both areas. Labor union staffs may spend more time predicting future wage and price inflation than the staffs of brokerage firms.

As we saw in Chapter 15, there has been much technical research on the effect of price and wage rigidities in rational expectations models. The important general feature of this research is that prices and wages have a forward-looking feature, whether they are sticky or not. When workers and firms set wages and prices they look ahead to the period during which the prices or wages will be in effect—to demand conditions, to the wages of other workers, and so on. This means that expectations of future policy actions will affect wage and price decisions, a property that is quite unlike models of wage and price rigidities with purely backward-looking expectations. The view that the economy will eventually return to normal—however slowly—after a shock is also inconsistent with the view that the economy stagnates permanently below potential.

> 5. *The objective of macroeconomic policy is to reduce the size (or the duration) of the fluctuations in output, employment, and inflation from normal levels after shocks hit the economy. The objective is to be achieved over a long period of time, which will in general include a larger number of business cycle experiences. Future business cycle fluctuations are not viewed as less important than the current one.*

By responding to economic shocks in a systematic fashion, economic policy can offset their impact or influence the speed at which the economy returns to normal. It thus can change the size of the fluctuations. How this should be done is a main area of disagreement among proponents of different policy rules.

From a technical viewpoint the disagreement can be addressed by inserting alternative policy rules into a rational expectations model and calculating how each rule affects the variance of output, employment, and inflation in the moving equilibrium that describes the business cycle fluctuations. We want to choose a policy that provides the best economic performance. One simple criterion is the minimization of the size of the fluctuations in output and inflation. Since in many models with price and wage rigidities there will be a trade-off between the reduction of output and inflation variability, it will usually be necessary to stipulate a welfare or loss function that reflects certain value judgments. Frequently one policy will so dominate another that the particular welfare weights do not matter much, however. This approach to policy will be featured later in this chapter.

The average rate of inflation can obviously be influenced by monetary policy, and it is important to choose a target rate that maximizes economic welfare. The objective of macroeconomic policy, however, is to keep the inflation rate close to this target rate—that is, to minimize fluctuations around the target, regardless of what the actual value of the target is. Alternatively, if a zero inflation target is appropriate, the objective of policy is to keep the price level near some target; the specific target value itself is much less important.

17.2 Instruments and Targets

Generally stated, the macro policy problem is one of choosing policy rules that describe how the *instruments* of policy should respond to economic conditions in order to improve the performance of the *target* variables. The instruments of macro policy are things like the monetary base or tax rates—or, more generally, monetary policy and fiscal policy. The targets of policy are the endogenous economic variables that we care about: inflation, unemployment, capital formation, and economic growth. Sometimes it is useful to distinguish between *intermediate* targets and *final* targets. For example, for the Fed, the money supply is an intermediate target while its instrument to control that target is the monetary base. The final targets for the Fed are real output and inflation.

To describe our objectives for the target variables it is necessary to define a **social welfare function** that summarizes the costs of having the target variables deviate from their desired levels. Such a social welfare function should reflect the tastes of individuals in society. If people do not like inflation, then deviations of inflation from zero should register as a loss of welfare in the social welfare function. In practice, it is very difficult to determine what the social welfare function actually is. Since people are different, we cannot just choose policy to improve the welfare of some representative individual.

Once a social welfare function has been specified, we can view the macro policy problem much like any other economic problem: We want to choose policy rules for the instruments to maximize the social welfare function. Analogously, in a consumption problem the consumer chooses a contingency plan for consumption—a decision rule—to maximize utility.

In most macro problems we are faced with the typical economic problem of scarcity. Whenever there is scarcity in economics we are faced with a *trade-off* between competing goals. In fact, scarcity is the most fundamental problem in economics. An important principle of optimal macro policy is that whenever there is a scarcity of instruments—that is, the number of instruments is less than the number of target variables—there is a trade-off between the different target variables. Jan Tinbergen, the Dutch economist who won the Nobel Prize for his work on macro modeling and on techniques for macro policy evaluation, established this important principle relating the number of instruments to the number of targets.[6] As long as the number of instruments is less than the number of targets, society is faced with a cruel choice between meeting one goal or another. The choice between inflation and unemployment is the best example of this type of cruel choice in macroeconomics, and we will consider it in detail later in this chapter. Another example that we will consider is the trade-off between money supply instability and interest rate instability.

It is very important to note that equality between the number of instruments and the number of targets is not sufficient for avoiding a cruel choice. In many cases the different instruments are not independent enough in their effects on the target variables. Again, the best example of this is the inflation-unemployment trade-off. A simple counting of instruments and targets could lead to the following type of incorrect reasoning: "We have two instruments, monetary policy and fiscal policy, and we have two target variables, inflation and unemployment. Thus there is no cruel trade-off. We can use monetary policy to control inflation and fiscal policy to control unemployment." This reasoning is wrong because it assumes that monetary and fiscal policies affect inflation and output in different and independent ways. In fact, we already know from our macro model that monetary and fiscal policies affect output and inflation in the same way—by shifting the aggregate demand curve. Unless one instrument can directly affect inflation without going through aggregate demand, we are left with a trade-off. For example, if monetary policy had a separate effect on expected inflation, or if tax policy could affect price setting, then there would be a separate channel.

17.3 Uncertainty and Timing Considerations

In practice, the target-instrument approach described above is too simple. It ignores the inherent uncertainty that exists in our understanding of the economy. If there is uncertainty about the effect of an instrument of policy on the economy, then we must be careful not to exploit that relationship too much. Very active use of an uncertain instrument can be risky. This is one of the central reasons for using less-active policies in practice.

[6] Jan Tinbergen, *On the Theory of Economic Policy,* Amsterdam, North-Holland, 1952.

When there are many instruments and uncertainty, the theory of economic policy tells us to use a mix of the instruments in a way that minimizes the risk. William Brainard of Yale University showed how the choice of instruments under uncertainty is much like the problem of choosing an optimal portfolio of common stocks.[7] Just as an individual should attempt to diversify a portfolio of stocks—"don't put all of your eggs in one basket"—policy makers should diversify their instruments, in order to reduce risk.

Another reason that macroeconomic policy-making is difficult is that its benefits do not occur at the same time as its costs. An expansionary monetary or fiscal policy, for example, involves balancing the short-term benefits of a stimulative move against the long-term costs of inflation the move will bring. Conversely, the costs of a contractionary policy occur in the short run and the benefits occur later and are perhaps drawn out over many years. We will start with a look at the benefits and costs. Then we will set up a framework within which policy makers can make an intelligent choice between expansion and contraction.

17.4 The Benefits of Full Employment and Price Stability

Macro policy makers should try to achieve the best combination of employment and inflation. The Employment Act of 1946 and the Humphrey-Hawkins Act of 1978 legislated this requirement, though without an enforcement provision. Chapter 16 showed the difficulties that policy makers face in dealing with unemployment and inflation. No policy can give the ideal of low unemployment and zero inflation, year after year. A policy that concentrates on low unemployment will permit a good deal of price instability; one that keeps prices on target will bring serious recessions and booms. Policy makers face a trade-off between unemployment stability and price stability.

Economic analysis deals with trade-offs of many types. For example, consider a consumer who cannot afford an expensive car and an expensive home—to buy a better car, the consumer will have to settle for a more modest home, and vice versa. Micro theory describes the consumer's preferences in terms of indifference curves. The consumer chooses the combination of car and house on the best indifference curve within the consumer's budget. The combination is at a point of tangency of an indifference curve and the line showing all the different combinations of car and house the consumer can afford.

We can look at the nation's choice between employment and price stability in the same way. Preferences give a set of indifference curves. The behavior of the economy, as described by the model of Chapter 16, gives the

[7] William Brainard, "Uncertainty and the Effectiveness of Policy," *American Economic Review, Papers and Proceedings*, Vol. 57, pp. 411–425, 1967.

set of different combinations of employment and price stability that can be achieved. We call the curve showing those combinations the **policy frontier.** The optimal policy is at the point of tangency of an indifference curve and the policy frontier.

The starting point for the analysis is to choose the two axes for the indifference curves and for the policy frontier. One axis has something to do with price stability and the other something to do with unemployment. For inflation, it seems clear that the desirable level is near zero. Large departures above zero have been the big problem in recent decades. Departures below zero were the problem in the depression of the 1930s and in some earlier contractions. There is no good reason to think that the cost of a positive error is any different from the cost of a negative error. In addition, it seems reasonable to suppose that *the marginal cost of an inflation or deflation error rises with the magnitude of the error.* A simple measure of the loss with these properties is the **squared error.**

This suggests that a good general summary of the inflation side of the performance of the economy is the average of the squared deviation of the inflation rate from its target, near zero. We will call this the **inflation loss.** If everything else is held the same, the ideal macro policy will keep the inflation loss at zero. In real life, the inflation rate cannot be kept exactly at zero, and the average inflation loss will be positive.

For the output-employment-unemployment side of the economy, the situation is a little different. For a number of reasons, the *natural* unemployment rate is probably not the *optimal* unemployment rate. Because of taxes and unemployment compensation that make the social cost of unemployment exceed the private cost, and because of monopoly power, it is likely that social welfare rises whenever unemployment drops below the natural rate. But, in the last chapter, we stressed that macro policy cannot influence the average rate of unemployment. It can only influence the fluctuations of unemployment around the natural rate. Consequently, macro policy makers should do what they can do: limit the fluctuations of unemployment about the natural rate. Based on this logic, we define the **unemployment loss** as the average squared departure of unemployment from the natural rate.

Social preferences about inflation and unemployment can be displayed in a family of indifference curves as shown in Figure 17–1. Note that the indifference curves bend in the opposite direction from the usual ones for the theory of the consumer. Consumer theory deals with things people like. Inflation and unemployment losses are things the public does not like, so the indifference curves have the opposite curvature. At the upper left end of each curve, the public is willing to trade quite a bit of added unemployment loss to reduce their inflation loss a little from its high level. At the lower end, they will accept only a small added amount of unemployment loss to reduce their inflation loss quite a bit. Curves closer to the origin are socially preferred because they involve lower amounts of both unemployment and inflation loss.

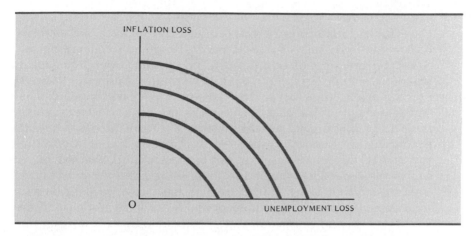

Figure 17–1.   SOCIAL PREFERENCES ABOUT INFLATION AND UNEMPLOYMENT.
Each indifference curve shows the locus of combinations of average inflation loss and average unemployment loss that the public finds equally acceptable. The curve that is farthest from the origin is the worst one. The public prefers curves that are closer to the origin.

WHY IS INFLATION UNDESIRABLE?

The American public has made it abundantly clear that inflation is unpopular. In 1976 and 1980, two presidents—Ford and Carter—were denied reelection soon after large bursts of inflation. Stringent anti-inflation policies in the early 1980s seem to have been politically acceptable, even though they brought on a pair of recessions. Whenever inflation rises above 10 percent per year, public opinion polls show that inflation is the number one economic problem, even when unemployment is high.

Though some specific economic costs of inflation have been identified, it is hard to quantify and assess them. The areas of economic costs include the following:

1. *"Shoe-Leather Costs" of Holding Money.* When inflation is high, currency and non-interest-bearing checking accounts are undesirable because they are constantly declining in purchasing power. People will make extra trips to the bank to avoid holding much money. These trips involve genuine economic costs, and these costs would be avoided with stable prices. One response to inflation has been the development of checking accounts that pay interest closer to market interest rates. This change in banking has reduced the cost of inflation because people do not have to spend so much time and effort transferring money between accounts.

2. *Tax Distortions.* Until recently the United States tax system was written entirely in current dollars. In 1985 the brackets for the personal in-

come tax were indexed, as we discussed in Chapter 11, and they will rise with the consumer price index. Bracket creep due to inflation has been eliminated. But many other parts of the tax system are not indexed, the presumption being that the purchasing power of the dollar is stable from one year to the next. For example, businesses take depreciation deductions that are based on the original dollar cost of plant and equipment investments. When inflation rages, the actual value of these deductions is much less than it should be, thanks to the declining purchasing power of the dollar. But this problem has been offset by speeding up the deductions. Even better, the tax law could be changed so that the deductions automatically rise along with the cost of living.

3. *Unfair Gains and Losses.* When inflation hits, some people gain and some lose. Retired people whose pensions are fixed in dollar terms lose. Homeowners gain because they can pay off their mortgages in less valuable dollars. In total, losses equal gains. In each transaction set in dollars, there is somebody paying who wins under inflation, and somebody losing exactly the same amount. The social loss occurs because inflation makes long-term transactions more unreliable. There seems to be no clear tendency for inflation to favor the rich over the poor or the poor over the rich. Gains and losses from inflation are more or less randomly distributed in this respect.

4. *Nonadapting Economic Institutions.* Certain standard economic practices have not adapted readily to inflation, and the public has suffered as a result. The most important is private retirement arrangements. The typical private pension plan pays its retirees a certain number of dollars per month when they retire. The number of dollars is based on their earnings in the last few years of work. In this respect, the pension keeps up with inflation. But once retirement starts, the amount of the pension is fixed in dollars. A pension that starts out at a generous level may dwindle to inadequacy as a result of inflation. One way retirement plans could adapt would be to build in an allowance for, say, 5 percent inflation. Payments would rise by 5 percent every year. They would start at a lower level than they do now, but keep up better with inflation. But no pension plan has made this simple adaptation.

Many of these costs are avoidable by apparently simple means. Shoe-leather costs have been cut by permitting banks to pay market interest rates on checking accounts. Changing the tax system to avoid distortions from inflation is not too difficult, and would be even easier if some other highly desirable tax reforms were instituted. Gains and losses could be avoided completely by linking payments and receipts to government price indexes, as many businesses do today in their transactions with other businesses. Better pension plans with cost-of-living indexation have been designed and put forward by a number of economists.

The public's negative view of inflation seems to come from sources other than these identifiable economic costs. One is the notion that the dollar is supposed to be a unit of purchasing power just as the yard is a unit of length. If the government decreased the length of the yard randomly by 5 or 10 percent each year, the public would be upset in a way that would also be out of proportion to the technical costs a changing unit of length would impose on us. It is a sign that the government is doing its job when its units of weights, measures, or purchasing power are reliable. Inflation is historically associated with the breakdown of government.

Perhaps another reason some people may be upset about inflation is that they do not take the same broad view as an economist, who sees inflation as a general rise in all prices and dollar incomes. Recall that, in a general inflation, wages and prices increase by the same amount. If wages increase less rapidly than prices, then something else in addition to inflation—like a drop in productivity—is affecting the economy. Someone who does not think about the economy in that way will not associate an increase in income with the increase in prices that goes with it. Such a person may imagine that the increase in income would have occurred even without the inflation. In that case, the inflation appears to diminish the purchasing power of the income, and so to be a loss. To put it another way, some people may not realize that both their incomes and the prices they pay will not rise as fast under an anti-inflation policy.

Costs of Inflation

1. There are some specific economic costs of inflation, but they are hard to quantify. These include:
   - Shoe-leather costs of conserving money holdings.
   - Distortions because much of the tax system is not indexed.
   - Capricious losses suffered by holders of dollar claims, though offset by surprise gains enjoyed by those paying fixed dollar debts.
   - Problems caused by the failure of retirement plans and other institutions to adapt to declining purchasing power.

2. People see inflation as a breakdown of the basic government responsibility to provide a stable unit of purchasing power.

3. Some people may not understand the relation between their own incomes and rising prices. To them, higher prices represent diminished real income.

COSTS OF OUTPUT LOSS AND UNEMPLOYMENT

There is less mystery about the output and unemployment losses, especially on the downside. As we noted in Chapter 11, when real GNP falls by a billion dollars, people see about half a billion dollars immediately in the form of reduced disposable income. Reduced corporate retained earnings account for part of the reduction. The remainder, hundreds of millions of dollars, takes the form of reduced tax revenue for federal, state, and local governments. The public suffers from this reduction as well, either in the form of cuts in government services or in the form of higher taxes later.

In addition to the obvious economic costs of lost output, there are other serious costs of a period of low output and high unemployment. Young workers are particularly likely to become unemployed. Many of them are working in low-wage jobs where part of the benefit is the training they are receiving. When they stop work, the loss includes not just what they were producing, which is included in GNP, but also the value of the training, which is not included in GNP. The experience of unemployment itself may have social costs beyond reduced GNP. Unemployed people may be more likely to turn to crime or to become physically or mentally ill.

The direct costs of lost GNP are overwhelming. In a typical recession, GNP falls below potential by around 5 percent for about two years. Total lost GNP is about 10 percent of one year's GNP, or over $300 billion at 1982 levels. There are about 100 million families in the United States, so the loss is about $3,000 per family. Some recessions are much deeper and involve even larger losses.

Of course, there are some benefits of lower employment and output that need to be evaluated. When people are not working as many hours on their jobs, they have more time for other pursuits. When jobs are hard to get, for example, more people go to school and fewer people quit school for work. The added education is a valuable use of time that offsets the lost GNP to a small extent. People with more time on their hands often do work on their own houses, another valuable use of time. But the offset to the lost GNP from alternative uses of work effort is probably a small fraction of the lost GNP. Because tax rates are high, the private value of time in the U.S. economy is much less than the social value. Further, as we mentioned in Chapter 13, labor supply functions are not very elastic with respect to wages. Consequently, the marginal value of a worker's time falls quickly if the worker is forced to work short hours.

Economists have thought less about the costs of episodes when GNP is above potential. The microeconomic argument supporting the idea that the costs are important is the following: The extra work effort needed to push GNP above potential is worth more than is the extra GNP. Instead of working as many hours as they do during a boom and consuming and investing the extra output, the public would be better off with less output and more time to spend with their children, on their houses, and in recreation. Again, because of high taxes, the private value of time is well below the social value of work, so there is at least a range where a boom is socially beneficial even though it is privately costly to workers to be working longer hours.

In terms of unemployment, there is little disagreement that the marginal social costs of unemployment are higher at higher rates of unemployment. Remember that it is not the overall level of the marginal social cost that matters, but the extent to which the marginal social cost of unemployment is higher in recessions than in booms. The value of the extra time at home that becomes available with higher unemployment is much lower for people who are already partly idle because of a recession than it is for people who are busy because of a boom. Consequently, keeping the variability of unemployment low is an important social goal.

Costs of Output Fluctuations and Unemployment

1. The marginal social cost of unemployment is higher when unemployment is high.

2. Because labor supply is inelastic, the marginal value of time in other uses falls if employment falls, and rises if employment rises above normal.

3. Because of these considerations, the economy is better off with stable output at its full-employment level, as against fluctuating output and employment.

17.5 The Policy Frontier between Inflation Loss and Unemployment Loss

In Chapter 7 we saw that, when aggregate demand shifts for some reason not related to macro policy, the shift can be offset through a policy that moves aggregate demand back to its original position. Then output and inflation will be back at their original levels as well. There is no need for aggregate demand shifts to cause either inflation losses or output-unemployment losses. Both can be avoided by a simple reversal of an aggregate demand shift.

In general, the best way to set up policy is to establish fixed rules for dealing with the foreseeable contingencies. One good fixed rule is to offset completely each aggregate demand disturbance. Another is to decide in advance how to deal with a shock that affects the price level. The choice of such a rule is a more complicated issue.

The price-adjustment equation from Chapter 16 is

$$\pi = f\frac{Y_{-1} - Y*}{Y*} + \pi_{-1} + Z. \tag{17-1}$$

Here we use the assumption that the expectations term is simply the lagged value of inflation, $\pi^e = \pi_{-1}$. But recall that alternative models of the expectations term may be more appropriate depending on the type of policy that is used. The last term in Equation 17–1, Z, represents price shocks, like increases in the price of oil.

In Figure 17–2 we show how policy might handle a price shock. The diagram shows the price-adjustment equation (17–1). Output is the horizontal axis and inflation is the vertical axis. Policy can try to offset the price shock by lowering output, or policy can keep output at potential and ignore the increase in inflation. Keeping output at potential is a policy that is *fully accommodative to inflation*. The more policy lowers output below potential, the *less accommodative to inflation* is the policy. Because of Okun's law, the policy that lowers output below potential raises unemployment above the natural rate. When output stays at potential, unemployment stays at the natural rate. Policy cannot keep both unemployment and prices stable.

We can characterize the policy alternatives in terms of a coefficient of response, g. If g is zero, the policy response keeps output at potential (and unemployment at the natural rate) and permits every shift of the price-adjustment schedule to translate into the same amount of inflation. With g equal to zero, there is no attempt to control inflation. Point C in Fig-

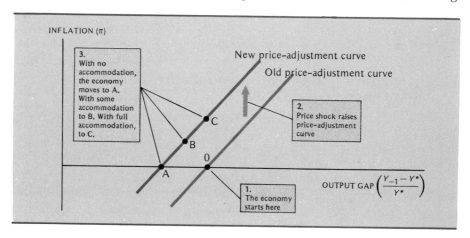

Figure 17–2.   ALTERNATIVE RESPONSES TO A POSITIVE PRICE SHOCK.
The economy starts in equilibrium with output at potential and inflation at zero. A positive price shock occurs, shifting the price-adjustment schedule upward. Policy can keep inflation at zero, which will require a decrease in output, as at point A. Or, it can tolerate an increase in inflation together with a smaller decrease in output, as at point B. A third alternative is to keep output at potential and let the shock raise inflation, as at point C.

ure 17–2 is the one chosen for $g = 0$. If g is greater than zero, the policy response always lowers output and raises unemployment, in order to stabilize inflation. The larger g is, the larger the reduction in output when an inflation shock occurs. In Figure 17–2, point A represents a very large value of g and point B represents an intermediate value. The coefficient g measures how accommodative policy is to inflation. For $g = 0$, policy is fully accommodative to inflation. Larger values of g represent less accommodative policies.

In mathematical form, the coefficient of response g is part of the policy response function. Thus:

$$\frac{Y - Y^*}{Y^*} = -g\pi. \tag{17–2}$$

In words, the output gap is reduced below zero if inflation rises above zero.

We can use the price-adjustment equation to find out how much inflation will be reduced by different choices of the response coefficient g. If we substitute the policy rule, Equation 17–2, into the price-adjustment equation, we get

$$\pi = (1 - fg)\pi_{-1} + Z. \tag{17–3}$$

When g is large, past inflation affects future inflation less, and the effects of a single price shock are more quickly withdrawn from inflation. Define k as $1 - fg$. The coefficient k measures how long and how much a price shock affects inflation. If g is zero (a fully accommodative policy), so that $k = (1 - fg) = 1$, then the price shock permanently raises the inflation rate by Z; in this situation the effects of the price shock are never withdrawn from inflation. If inflation was zero before the price shock, it will be permanently above zero after the price shock. If, at the other extreme, $k = 0$, then the effect of the price shock disappears after only one year. If k is in the intermediate range, between 0 and 1, then the effect of the price shock *gradually* disappears: Inflation is k times the price shock in the year after the shock, k^2 times the price shock in the second year, k^3 in the third year, and so on, eventually back to zero inflation. For example, if k is .8, and inflation is initially raised from zero to 10 percent because of the price shock, then inflation is 8 percent in the next year, 6.4 percent in the third year, 5.1 percent in the fourth year, 4.1 percent in the fifth year, and so on, eventually getting to zero inflation.

A policy that aggressively counters price shocks (with g large and k near zero) will incur large fluctuations in output and unemployment. This is clear from Equation 17–2. For example, suppose that the sensitivity of inflation f to output is .2. Then, to achieve a value of k equal to .8 we set g equal to 1. With these coefficients, now suppose that a positive shock initially raises inflation by 10 percent. With $g = 1$, then, according to the policy rule

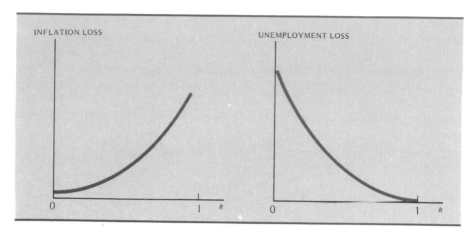

Figure 17–3. AVERAGE INFLATION AND UNEMPLOYMENT LOSSES FOR ALTERNA-
TIVE POLICIES.

For $k = 0$, policy changes unemployment enough to make price shocks disappear from
inflation after only one year. The average inflation loss is small, but the unemployment
loss is substantial. At $k = 1$, policy keeps unemployment at the natural rate and lets the
price shock influence actual inflation fully. Unemployment loss is at a minimum but inflation loss is high.

in Equation 17–2, this will reduce output below potential by 10 percent in
the period right after the shock. Eventually output will come back to potential as inflation declines. When g is large, the drop in output is large and, because of Okun's law, the rise in unemployment is large. On the other side, a
negative shock that lowers inflation by 10 percent will require output to rise
by 10 percentage points above potential if g is 1. According to Okun's law,
unemployment falls in this case. A policy that rolls completely with price
shocks (g equal to zero) will have a completely stable level of output and unemployment.

The implications of the choice of the coefficient k for inflation and unemployment losses are shown in Figure 17–3. Because the inflation loss and
unemployment loss are related to the squared deviations from normal, the
two curves sag as k is raised from zero.

There is another way we can depict the same trade-off. In Figure 17–4,
we draw a curve representing the policy frontier in a diagram where average unemployment loss is the horizontal axis and average inflation loss is the
vertical axis.[8]

---

[8] The idea of constructing policy frontiers in terms of the squared deviations of output and
inflation and choosing alternative policy rules to get to the best point on such a frontier was described in John B. Taylor, "Estimation and Control of a Macroeconomic Model with Rational
Expectations," *Econometrica*, Vol. 47 (September 1979), pp. 1267–1286; the model used in
that paper corresponds closely with that discussed in the text.

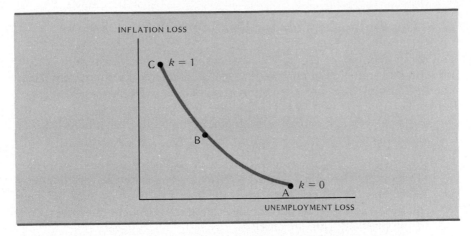

Figure 17–4. THE POLICY FRONTIER FOR UNEMPLOYMENT AND INFLATION LOSSES.

Every point on the frontier can be achieved by a policy that lets unemployment respond to inflation. At the upper left is the point of minimal unemployment loss and maximal inflation loss, corresponding to $k = 1$. At the lower right is the point of low inflation loss and high unemployment loss, corresponding to the other extreme, $k = 0$. The points marked A, B, and C are the same as in Figure 17–2.

The Inflation-Unemployment Policy Frontier

1. The optimal policy for dealing with a shift in aggregate demand is to reverse the shift through a compensating change in aggregate demand policy. In that case, the shift does not cause either an inflation loss or an unemployment loss.

2. A general policy for dealing with price-adjustment shocks is to let the actual amount of inflation be a fraction, k, of the amount of the shock. The rest of the shock is canceled through aggregate demand policy.

3. An aggressive anti-inflation policy has a low k close to 0.

4. There is a policy frontier defined by different values of k from zero to 1. The frontier shows the available combinations of average inflation loss and average unemployment loss. The frontier curves toward the origin.

17.6 The Optimal Policy for Dealing with Price Shocks

The policy frontier of Figure 17–4 shows the alternative combinations of inflation and unemployment loss that are available from different policies. The best policy will achieve a compromise between the two types of losses. Remember that the best policy is the one closest to the origin, that is, the one that achieves low values of both unemployment and inflation losses. Uncompromising policies are unattractive for two reasons.

1. A policy of strict price stability ($k = 0$, the point at the lower right-hand end of the policy frontier) involves a large amount of unemployment loss. It takes large movements of unemployment to keep inflation exactly at zero in the face of oil price shocks and other shifts in the price-adjustment process.
2. A policy of strict unemployment stability ($k = 1$, the point at the upper left-hand end of the policy frontier) involves a large amount of inflation loss. When an inflationary shock occurs, the policy does nothing to offset the shock. Not only does inflation jump upward in the year of the shock, but inflation is higher in future years as well, because the shock raises expected inflation.

The uncompromising policies are unsuitable because, in both cases, the trade-off set by the policy frontier strongly favors making at least a small compromise. From strict inflation stability, a small move toward the middle of the frontier gives a large payoff in reduced unemployment loss with only a small sacrifice of inflation loss. From strict unemployment stability, a small move to the middle gives a large payoff in reduced inflation loss with only a small sacrifice of unemployment loss.

To find the optimal compromise, we superimpose the policy frontier of Figure 17–4 on the family of social indifference curves from Figure 17–1. The best point on the frontier is the one tangent to the indifference curve closest to the origin, as shown in Figure 17–5.

In Chapter 16 we looked at the macro performance of the United States, Germany, and the United Kingdom for the 1970s and 1980s in terms of output-inflation loops (Figures 16–5, 16–6, and 16–7). In these diagrams inflation is the vertical axis and output is the horizontal axis. Recall that the flat loops represented large output fluctuations and small inflation fluctuations, performance corresponding to values of k near zero. The steep (standing-up) loops represented the reverse—large inflation fluctuations and small unemployment fluctuations, performance corresponding to values of k near 1. Therefore, according to this empirical evidence, Germany, with its flat loops during this period, followed a less accommodative policy: Output fluctuations were relatively large and inflation fluctuations were relatively small. The United Kingdom evidently changed its policy in a less accommodative direction from the early 1970s to the late 1970s and

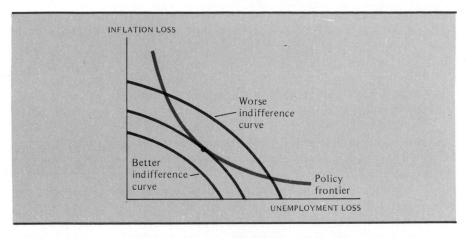

Figure 17–5. THE OPTIMAL POLICY FOR RESPONDING TO PRICE SHOCKS.
The colored line shows the policy frontier. At the upper left are policies that stabilize unemployment at the cost of higher average inflation loss. At the lower right are policies
that stabilize inflation at the cost of higher average unemployment loss. The optimal policy is in the middle, where the frontier is tangent to the indifference curve that is closest
to the origin of all the indifference curves that touch the policy frontier.

early 1980s. The orientation of its loops changed around the time that mar-
garet Thatcher became prime minister. The United States has had a policy
that falls between the others: more accommodative than Germany, and less
accommodative than the United Kingdom before Thatcher. There is not
much evidence that the overall accommodative stance of U.S. policy
changed during this period.

THE MESSAGE FOR POLICY MAKERS

It is not an easy matter to conduct macro policy in an optimal way. Our
analysis has reached two conclusions about the appropriate response to
shocks in the economy:

1. If the shock affects only aggregate demand, then a compensating
   change in aggregate demand policy (monetary or fiscal) will eliminate
   both the inflation loss and the unemployment loss.
2. If the shock affects the price-adjustment schedule, then the best policy
   divides its effects between inflation and unemployment according to
   the rule that the actual amount of inflation declines by a fraction k
   each year.

In general, to develop policy from our model, the policy maker needs to
be able to separate shocks into their aggregate demand and price-adjustment components and then figure out the magnitude of the response

needed to offset fully the aggregate demand shock and to offset partially the price-adjustment shock. Clearly some technical analysis is necessary to do this.

NOMINAL GNP TARGETING: A REASONABLE WAY TO EXPRESS POLICY?

There is another less technical way to express the optimal policy that may be useful to policy makers who also need to discuss economic policy with nonspecialists. The alternative begins with the observation that the optimal policy tends to stabilize nominal GNP. Suppose in some year a positive aggregate demand shock raises real GNP without much effect on prices. It shows up as above-normal growth of nominal GNP. A rule that calls for steady GNP would automatically offset aggregate demand shocks, just as our optimal policy recommends.

When a positive price-adjustment shock strikes, the optimal policy is to let part of the shock raise prices and part of the shock reduce output and raise unemployment. Keeping nominal GNP on a prescribed growth track does exactly that. Nominal GNP is the product of the price level and real GNP. If the price level jumps, real GNP must fall to keep nominal GNP growth at a prescribed rate. Keeping nominal GNP growth at a prescribed rate is a compromise policy of the type we just derived as optimal.

The degree of compromise in a policy that stabilizes nominal GNP seems to favor unemployment stability over price stability. The value of the coefficient of response g for a nominal GNP policy is 1. As we showed above, when $g = 1$, the value of k is .8 for the numerical example of price adjustment used here. Eighty percent of a price-adjustment shock is tolerated as a continued increase in inflation the year after it occurs. Twenty percent is extinguished by permitting output to fall. Thereafter, 20 percent of inflation is offset each year, by keeping output below normal.

Suppose the initial inflation impact from a shock is 10 percent. Under the fixed nominal GNP policy, real GNP falls by 10 percent, and inflation in the following year is reduced to 8 percent. From Okun's law, this means that unemployment rises by 3 percent in the first year.

If the public is so opposed to inflation that the optimal value of k is well below .8, then nominal GNP targeting is inappropriate—it gives excessive inflation losses that will not be made up, in the public's view, by the lower unemployment losses it will bring. Or, if the public cares less about inflation, nominal GNP targeting will bring excessive unemployment losses that will not be made up by its favorable influence on inflation losses. In either case it would be possible to change the policy goal and let nominal GNP respond to the price shock. If $k = .8$ is too large, then nominal GNP should be reduced when price shocks occur. If $k = .8$ is too small, then nominal GNP could be allowed to grow a bit when a price shock occurs. But the simplicity of a fixed nominal GNP may outweigh the benefits of modifying the path of nominal GNP in this way.[9]

If nominal GNP targeting were used explicitly in practice, the process might work in the following way: Each year the Fed and the administration would announce a target rate of growth of nominal GNP for the next two or three years. The announcement dates could occur at the same time as the Fed's money aggregate targets now occur, once in July with an update the following February (see Chapter 12). Then each month, as new information became available about the growth of nominal GNP, the Fed and the administration could adjust monetary and fiscal policy to eliminate errors. If growth was above target, for example, the Fed would contract the monetary base. The FOMC would instruct the open-market desk to sell government securities, which would reduce the monetary base and raise interest rates. If growth was below target, the Fed would expand the monetary base by raising the base and lowering interest rates.

Nominal GNP targeting should not be viewed as an alternative to the optimal policies described above. Rather, it is an easy and convenient way to talk about policy procedures and goals. For example, if there is a policy mistake that brings about a very high unemployment rate, then the optimal policy is to bring the economy back to normal quickly. There is no reason to hold output Y below potential Y^* if inflation is low. Holding nominal GNP growth to a fixed level might not allow for the economy to catch up and bring Y back to Y^*. But even in this case the policy makers should announce their intentions for nominal GNP.

What Would an Optimal Policy Have Been in 1979–86?

In the late 1970s inflation was high. A large price shock had hit the U.S. economy in 1978 and 1979, when a revolution in Iran overthrew the Shah early in 1979 and Iraq invaded Iran. The result was a substantial fall in world oil production and a dramatic increase in oil prices. The inflation shock was several percentage points and actual inflation rose about 2 percentage points. Then, in 1982, an adverse aggregate demand shock occurred. The demand for money shifted up —for given levels of income and interest rates, the public wanted to hold more money. Part of this shift may have come from financial deregulation, which permitted banks to offer more attractive terms on checking accounts.

[9] See Robert E. Hall, "Macroeconomic Policy under Structural Change," in *Industrial Change and Public Policy*, Federal Reserve Bank of Kansas City, 1983, pp. 85–111, and James Tobin, "Commentary," in *Industrial Change and Public Policy*, Federal Reserve Bank of Kansas City, 1983, pp. 113–122. A review of the alternative proposals is found in John B. Taylor, "What Would Nominal GNP Targeting Do to the Business Cycle?" *Carnegie-Rochester Conference Series on Public Policy*, Vol. 22 (1985), pp. 61–84.

With the policy actually pursued, the response of the economy to these two shocks is shown in the diagram. Nominal growth remained at a high level in 1979 but fell substantially in 1980. It resumed in 1981 and then fell drastically in 1982. A vigorous recovery then followed in 1983 and 1984, with more modest growth in 1985 and 1986.

What would an optimal policy have looked like? A reasonable set of targets for nominal GNP starting in 1979 is shown by the black line in the diagram. The decline is in accord with the optimal policy rule of k = .9, with underlying real growth.

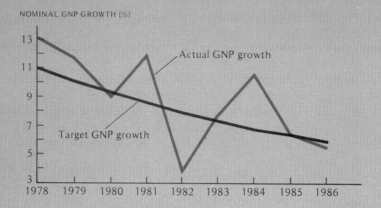

Nominal GNP growth was 1.4 percentage points above this target in 1979; an error of this magnitude is reasonable and would not have represented a failure of monetary policy. In 1980, nominal growth was almost exactly on target. In 1981, nominal growth was 3.1 percentage points above target. Such an error is outside the bounds of normal variation. In 1982, nominal GNP growth was 4.2 percent below target. Such an excessive contraction is clearly below the targets of the nominal GNP-based policy. Growth in 1983 was close to target, but growth in 1984 again exceeded the target. Some of this later fast growth was appropriate because of the mistake in 1982 which dropped real output too far below potential. Growth in 1985 and 1986 was close to target.

Judged by the nominal GNP targets, the policy for handling inflation and the oil price shock in 1979–80 was appropriate. This meant suffering—unemployment jumped and real GNP slumped. But any macro policy to reduce inflation would require some extra unemployment.

On the other hand, there was a policy error when the money demand shock occurred in 1982. Real output fell, unemployment rose, and inflation dropped faster than a smooth decline in nominal GNP growth would have implied. Keeping nominal GNP growth at 8 percent for 1982 would have offset the demand shock. The Fed's reaction appeared to be late. Not until late 1982 did the Fed ease policy. The reasons for the Fed's policy mistake are not clear. Possibly chairman Paul Volcker and the rest of the FOMC were still very concerned about a resurgence of inflation, or were not sure that money demand was shifting.

17.7 Changing the Policy Frontier

The policy we described in the previous section is optimal in the sense that it tells policy-makers how to make the best of a bad situation. But the policy does not make the situation good. We should spend at least as much effort thinking about how to move the policy frontier toward the origin as we spend thinking about choosing the best point on the frontier. If the frontier were closer to the origin, both inflation loss and unemployment loss would be lower.

STREAMLINE THE LABOR MARKET

The policy frontier lies far from the origin because wages do not respond quickly and vigorously to the situation in the labor market. When an inflation shock strikes, policy has to raise unemployment to get inflation back down. When wages are less responsive, a larger rise in unemployment is necessary. If wages could be made to adjust rapidly to surpluses and shortages of labor, then the average unemployment loss needed to keep inflation loss at a given level would be lower. The policy frontier would be closer to the origin.

Because the reasons for sluggish adjustment of wages are not well understood, it is not obvious what types of new policies would speed up the process. Some proposals include:

1. *Better Job Matching.* In the highly decentralized labor market of the United States, employers have trouble getting in touch with potential workers. There may be a large number of qualified people ready to work at a particular job at a low wage. If the employer cannot let them know about the job, it may be necessary to hire a nearby worker at a higher wage. Some kind of electronic job listing might make it possible to draw from a larger number of potential workers. Or, if there were better information available about the number of qualified job seekers, firms would be in a better position to tailor wage offers to the state of the market. Federal and state employment agencies have tried to perform this service for many years, however, and have found that employers are reluctant to list most types of jobs. Employers fear hav-

ing to deal with thousands of unqualified applicants if they list jobs publicly. Instead, they seem to prefer to look at smaller numbers of candidates located privately. There seems to be no basis to hope that the labor market could be significantly improved by expansion of public job listings.

2. *Eliminate Government Price and Wage Fixing.* Hundreds of government regulations have the effect of either fixing prices and wages directly or limiting the flexibility of businesses in setting prices and wages. The Davis-Bacon Act, for example, prevents contractors from cutting construction costs by taking advantage of slack conditions in markets for construction workers. Local governments regulate bus and taxi fares, so they cannot fall to accommodate the increased supply of drivers in times of higher unemployment. Many government regulations that limited price and wage flexibility have been abolished, however. Airlines are now free to adjust fares whenever market conditions change. Most restrictions on professionals publicizing their prices have been lifted. The scope for further reform in this area is limited.

3. *Reform Unemployment Compensation.* Unemployed workers receive unemployment benefits for up to 6 months after job loss. Consequently, their incentives to look for new work and to accept new jobs at lower wages are reduced. Unemployment compensation serves a vital purpose and should not be abolished, but certain types of reforms could improve incentives without making the unemployed suffer. The most important is to make employers pay more for benefits whenever possible. If an employer had to pay for benefits during a layoff, the employer might prefer to keep the worker at work and cut prices as necessary to sell the output. Publicly financed benefits create incentives to lay a worker off, produce less, and maintain a higher price when demand falls.

4. *Legislate the Share Economy.* Martin Weitzman of M.I.T. has proposed a structural reform of the labor market that he calls "the share economy," which has received a good deal of popular attention.[10] Under Weitzman's plan, the government would provide tax incentives to businesses to induce them to pay workers under a share system in place of existing wage systems. In a share system, part or all of a worker's earnings would be set as a share of the firm's revenue, rather than as a fixed hourly wage. The share system has two virtues, according to Weitzman. First, it automatically makes earnings respond to the state of the economy. Unemployment rises less during a recession in a share economy than in a wage economy. However, as we discussed in Chapter 15, an optimal labor contract should not link the wage to the success of the firm, but to the economy as a whole. Second, when com-

---

[10] Martin L. Weitzman, *The Share Economy,* Cambridge, Mass., Harvard University Press, 1984. The *New York Times* called Weitzman's plan "the best idea since Keynes" in a March 28, 1985, editorial.

pensation is set as a share of revenue, the firm faces no cost to add another worker. Weitzman foresees an economy where employers pursue the few remaining unemployed workers relentlessly, because their marginal products are above their costs of employment. But the workers already employed suffer wage loss every time the firm adds a new worker. Whether the economy would run more efficiently, taking all the effects of the share economy into consideration, is an open question.

IMPROVE INDEXATION

In Chapter 16 we saw that when wages are linked directly to prices through cost-of-living indexation the impact of outside price shocks is amplified—a price shock goes immediately into wages, then into costs, and finally into prices again, all within the same year. Although indexation prevents workers from being left behind by general inflation, it is harmful to the economy when wages rise in response to oil or other outside price shocks.

The ideal method of cost-of-living escalation would omit price increases that arise from imports and other materials costs. Though economists have suggested price indexes that would perform better than the CPI for wage indexation, nobody has started to use them for actual wage setting. It is not easy to persuade a skeptical employer or labor union that a new price index is superior to the tried and true consumer price index. Proposals to make much smaller changes in the indexes used for wage indexation have encountered stiff resistance. There are no grounds for optimism that wage setters will voluntarily adopt new indexation methods. Nor is it clear that the government can or should try to force changes in this area.

AVOID GOVERNMENT PRICE SHOCKS

Sometimes the government itself creates a shock in the price-adjustment process. An important example occurred in Britain in 1979. The government cut income taxes and substituted a value-added tax to raise the same revenue. Because the value-added tax is imposed on firms, it adds to costs just as does an increase in the price of a material input. The VAT is much like a sales tax. In terms of the price-adjustment model of Chapter 16, the value-added tax adds an inflationary impetus Z in the year that it goes into effect.

In Britain, the value-added tax shock and the oil price shock occurred simultaneously. The British economy suffered from more inflation and a larger reduction in output than did the U.S. economy, which suffered only from the oil price shock. If self-inflicted government price shocks can be kept to a minimum, the policy frontier will be closer to the origin.

Avoiding government price shocks need not prevent tax reform or other useful changes in the government's influence on the economy. For example, a value-added tax can be changed in a simple way that does not change its favorable properties as a tax—it could be instituted so that the cost falls on workers rather than on businesses. Then the switch to the tax will not create a price shock. Changes in all types of economic policies need to be designed with the harmful effects of macro price shocks in mind.

CONTROLS AND INCENTIVES

The reason the policy frontier is so far from the origin is that the government influences inflation only indirectly through its control of demand. If the government could simply dictate the price level, then there would be no need for either inflation losses or unemployment losses. Moreover, there need not be shortages or excess supplies in such an economy. The government could set the price level and the position of the aggregate demand schedule so as to have them intersect exactly at full employment.

Only once has the U.S. government tried to set prices and wages directly in peacetime. In the early 1970s, high inflation inherited from expansionary policies of the 1960s (partly related to the war in Vietnam) created a political uproar. From the summer of 1971 until the spring of 1974, a succession of price-wage control schemes were tried out under the Nixon administration. The professed goal was exactly what we just set out—to keep the economy at a point of full employment and low inflation.

The only point of agreement in evaluating our experience under price controls is that they involved a significant bureaucracy and a great deal of strife. Firms were supposed to follow government rules in setting prices. If their customers thought the rules were being violated, they could complain in Washington. Every wage change could also be reviewed in Washington. The result was a great accumulation of cases to be studied and ruled upon by the Cost of Living Council which was set up to administer the price and wage control program. Handling the wage cases was particularly important because the labor unions involved were politically powerful and because they could threaten to strike if the wage increase they had won was not approved.

Economists are still unsettled as to whether the Nixon controls had any important effect on inflation. Opponents of controls point to examples of shortages and other distortions from the controls. Proponents say that the Nixon program was exactly the wrong way to run controls and that a good system would work much better. Quite apart from the economic merit of controls, it does seem questionable whether the American political system can operate a system of controls for a sustained period. Just as wartime controls collapsed at the ends of World Wars I and II, growing political opposition brought a fairly speedy end to the Nixon controls.

Economists looking for a permanent policy to shift the inflation-unemployment policy frontier toward the origin have proposed systems based on incentives rather than controls. **Tax-based incomes policies** would reward businesses and workers who followed government guidelines for price and wage increases. Businesses would lose tax deductions for cost increases beyond the guideline rates and would pay extra taxes on revenue attributable to excess price increases. In the aftermath of a price shock, policy could get inflation back down by setting a low guideline for wage and price increases. The disincentive cost to taxpayers would be less than the cost of the unemployment that would result from achieving the same degree of disinflation through higher unemployment.

Since we do not have any practical experience with incentives, it is hard to know how well they would work. Any incentive program would have to be designed with great care. In 1978, President Carter submitted an incentive plan to Congress. In addition to specific incentives for individual price and wage setters, it offered workers a general assurance that the program could not hurt them. Labor had been concerned that they might be required to moderate their wage growth while businesses did nothing to cut price inflation. Carter's program included "real wage insurance." In the event that prices did rise more than wages, workers would have received income tax cuts large enough to make up their loss in real wages.

Only a few months after the real wage insurance proposal was made, real wages fell by several percentage points, thanks to an event that had nothing to do with the anti-inflation program. World oil prices almost tripled. That event was never contemplated in designing real wage insurance. Had real wage insurance gone into effect in 1978, huge tax cuts would have occurred quite accidentally in 1979 and 1980, when the federal budget was already in deficit. Fortunately, real wage insurance died in Congress and this accident never took place.

TRADE POLICY

One of the ways the government affects the variability of inflation is through trade policy. Generally, policies that restrict imports will raise inflation when they are imposed and lower inflation when they are removed. As we noted in Chapter 10, different protectionist policies can have very different effects on U.S. prices. Quotas have a strong and immediate effect on prices. Tariffs have a strong effect if they are not absorbed by foreign sellers. For example, an oil tariff would immediately raise the U.S. price of oil, because it is unlikely that OPEC would choose to lower its price to U.S. purchasers in response to the tariff. On the other hand, a tariff on Japanese cars might well be absorbed by Japanese auto makers, just as they absorbed most of the impact of the appreciating yen in the 1985–87 period.

Each time a protectionist measure is imposed or tightened, it gives a one-time shock to inflation. If a tariff is on a single important product, such as oil, it can cause a perceptible shock to total inflation. An equal but negative shock will occur if the tariff is taken off. Stabilization policy would be significantly more difficult and less successful if protectionist measures are imposed and removed in order to satisfy other goals, such as protecting ailing domestic industries, fostering energy conservation, or reducing the trade deficit.

Improving the Policy Frontier

1. Policies for streamlining the labor market could push the inflation-unemployment frontier toward the origin. The same amount of inflation loss would be achieved with less unemployment loss if inflation responded more vigorously to unemployment.

2. Public job placement has not been very successful. Reduced government price and wage fixing might be a small help. Reform in unemployment compensation would also improve the frontier a little.

3. Controls on prices and wages are another option, but in practice they have been difficult to administer and have not had a lasting impact on inflation.

4. The government should be careful not to create unnecessary price shocks.

Review and Practice

MAJOR POINTS

1. The general policy implication of recent research in macro is that policy should be formulated as a rule or contingency plan.

2. Macroeconomic policy can be logically formulated and evaluated using the target and instrument framework. A social welfare function could be used to represent goals for the target variables.

3. Much as in most areas of economics, trade-offs are widespread in macroeconomics. As long as the number of instruments is scarce we will face a tough trade-off between the goals of the target variables.

4. Uncertainty in the models leads to less active use of the policy instruments.

5. High inflation is bad because it causes people to hold too little money. It is also difficult to adjust the tax system to be neutral to inflation. Inflation also sometimes brings higher uncertainty, which can interfere with efficient resource allocation. Deflation is undesirable for similar reasons.

6. Variations in unemployment are undesirable because the social costs of periods of high unemployment outweigh the benefits of periods of low unemployment.

7. Indifference curves between inflation loss and unemployment loss curve away from the origin. Higher indifference curves represent poorer macroeconomic performance.

8. Policy rules describe how accommodative the monetary policy makers are to inflation. More accommodative policy results in better output performance, but worse inflation performance.

9. A rule of keeping nominal GNP constant is a good way to characterize an optimal macroeconomic policy.

10. The only type of policy move that could improve both inflation and unemployment performance would be an inward shift of the policy frontier, but unfortunately the prospects seem limited for this type of policy.

KEY TERMS AND CONCEPTS

Lucas critique	Discretionary policy
Social welfare function	Shoe-leather cost of inflation
Time inconsistency	Marginal social cost of unemployment
Model uncertainty	Inflation loss
Commitment to a policy	Unemployment loss
Final targets	Social indifference curve
Intermediate targets	Policy frontier
Scarcity of instruments	Policy rule
Policy trade-offs	Accommodation of inflation shock
Activist policy	Nominal GNP target

QUESTIONS FOR DISCUSSION AND REVIEW

1. If the purpose of the final exam is to motivate students to study, why will the instructor not cancel the final at the last minute, after all studying has occurred, in order to save everybody's time and effort?

2. What is the basic argument against discretionary policy?

3. If the effect of a policy instrument is uncertain, will policy makers be more or less aggressive in the use of the instrument than they would be under certainty?

4. Give some of the reasons that both inflation and deflation are undesirable.

5. Explain why both high and variable unemployment are undesirable. Why does the policy frontier deal just with the variability and not with the level of unemployment?

6. Explain the consequences for unemployment and inflation if policy makers fully accommodate a price shock. Repeat for zero accommodation and for 50 percent accommodation.

7. Describe the axes of the policy frontier diagram and how to find points on the frontier.

8. How should policy makers choose the best point on the frontier?

9. How much accommodation of price shocks occurs if nominal GNP targets are followed?

10. List some of the proposals that have been made to shift the policy frontier inward.

11. Trace out the effects of a restrictive quota on auto imports.

PROBLEMS

Numerical

1. Calculate the value of k that corresponds to the policy of keeping nominal GNP at a given level in the year that a price shock occurs. Assume that f equals 1. Assume that the economy starts in equilibrium, with $Y = Y^*$, $\pi = 0$, and $P = 1$. Then an inflationary shock of 10 percent, $Z = .1$, occurs. Compute the change in the price level, using Equation 17–1. Compute the change in output from Equation 17–2. Show that the percentage change in real GNP plus the percentage change in the price level equals zero, the percentage change in nominal GNP.

2. An economy has an aggregate demand schedule $Y = 2,067 + 3.221(M/P)$. It starts at potential ($Y = Y^* = 4,000$) with a money stock of 600. Then it is hit by an inflation shock of $Z = .1$. Policy uses a value of k of .9. Assume that $f = .25$. Compute the change in the money stock necessary to achieve the policy. Also compute the change in P and Y. Repeat the calculations for $k = .1$. Explain the differences.

3. The purpose of this exercise is to illustrate the trade-off between inflation and unemployment. However, we focus on the output gap rather than on unemployment because the two are so closely related due to Okun's law. Suppose that the policy rule

$$(Y - Y^*)/Y^* = -g\pi \qquad \text{(Policy Rule)}$$

is substituted into the price-adjustment equation to get

$$\pi = (1 - .2g)\pi_{-1} + Z. \qquad \text{(Inflation)}$$

a. Starting from $Y = Y^*$ and from $\pi = 0$ (zero percent inflation), use the second equation to calculate the effect on inflation for Years 1 through 10 of a price shock $Z = .1$ (a 10 percent shock to the price level). Set $g = .5$.

b. Using the values of inflation that you calculated in Part a, calculate the value of the GNP gap, $(Y - Y^*)/Y^*$, for all 10 years using the policy rule.

c. Plot the values of inflation and the output gap for all 10 years on two time series diagrams (put the variable on the vertical axis and the year on the horizontal axis).

d. Plot the values of output and inflation on a diagram with inflation on the vertical axis and output on the horizontal axis (like Figure 16–5 of Chapter 16).

e. Calculate the average squared loss for inflation. That is, square each value of inflation (π^2) for all 10 years, sum up the squares, and divide by 10. Calculate the average squared loss for the output gap in the same way. Now repeat the calculations in Parts a through d and the inflation loss and output loss for $g = .1$ and $g = .9$. You should now have three pairs of inflation loss and output loss, one for each of the three values of the policy rule (g). Plot the three pairs on a diagram with average inflation loss on the vertical axis and average output loss (output gap) on the horizontal axis. Comment on the position of the three points. Is a trade-off between inflation loss and output loss evident? Compare your diagram with that of Figure 17–4. (Note that the output gap loss and the unemployment loss will occupy similar relative positions because of Okun's law.)

4. The purpose of this exercise is to illustrate that a "stochastic" dynamic model with shocks can lead to business cycle fluctuations. Suppose that the income identity is

$$Y = C + I + G,$$

where $G = 750$. Consumption is equal to

$$C = 80 + .63Y_{-1},$$

and investment is a random variable given by

$$I = 650 + (7 - \text{Number from a roll of a pair of dice}) \text{ times } 93.$$

a. Roll a pair of dice twenty times, and record the number for each roll. Use the investment function to calculate investment for each roll. This gives 20 years of stochastic investment. Investment in Year 1 is the first roll and investment in Year 20 is the last roll. Plot the values of investment on a time series chart with investment on the vertical axis and the year on the horizontal axis. The values should look random, with investment fluctuating around 650.

b. Now use the values of investment for the 20 years to calculate income Y. Substitute the consumption function into the income identity. Start with Y_{-1} equal to 4,000 and with investment equal to the value that you calculated for Year 1. Then calculate the second year's income by substituting in income for the first year for Y_{-1} and investment in the second year. Do the same thing for the third year and so on through Year 20.

c. Plot the resulting values of income Y for the 20 years with the year on the horizontal axis. The average value should be near 4,000 but you should see some prolonged fluctuations around this average value that look like business cycles. Compare the prolonged nature of the fluctuations of Y with that of the random but less prolonged fluctuations of investment I. Calculate the average time between peaks for each series. Unless your dice are loaded, the average time between peaks for income will be longer than that for investment. Try to explain why.

5. Suppose that price-adjustment and inflationary expectations are given by Equations 16–1 and 16–2 respectively. Policy is given by Equation 17–2 with $g{=}0$. Initially there is an oil price shock of 2.5 percent ($Z{=}.025$).
   a. Calculate inflation and expected inflation for years 1 through 4. Are expectations rational?
   b. Is the monetary authority using a constant money stock target, a constant nominal GNP target, or neither? Explain your answer.

Analytical

1. Derive the aggregate demand schedule for the case where the Fed maintains nominal GNP at a given target level.

2. In Chapter 5 at the end of Section 5.5 there is a quote from President Reagan criticizing the Fed (p. 116). Given the discussion of optimal policy in this chapter, comment on the validity of this statement.

3. In Chapter 12 we showed how monetary policy affects the economy with a lag. What are the implications of these lags for our suggestions about optimal policy

in this chapter? What do lags in the effect of money imply for nominal GNP targeting?

4. Compare monetary aggregate targeting by the Fed (as described in Chapter 12) with targeting nominal GNP. Prepare a brief argument in favor of each type of targeting, listing advantages and disadvantages.

5. Using the IS-LM method, show what the Fed must do to the money supply to reduce output by a certain percentage when there is a price shock. Could the same actions be undertaken by fiscal policy? Why might a mix of monetary and fiscal policies be used to reduce output after a price shock?

6. Suppose that in response to a large and unexpected oil price shock the Fed acts to keep output at potential. Inflationary expectations are given by the expression $\pi^e = .9\pi_{-1}$. Prices are sticky and price adjustment is given by an equation like 16–1. The change in the money stock, prices, and output for the first 4 years are:

Year	%ΔM	%ΔP	%ΔY
1	10	10	0
2	9	9	0
3	8.1	8.1	0
4	7.3	7.3	0

a. How large was the oil price shock?
b. An economist writing for a popular newsweekly comments: "The Fed is up to its old tricks again, fueling inflation with money stock growth." The economist goes on to note that every time the Fed increases the money supply by X percent it leads to an increase in prices of X percent, just as predicted by the classical model. Is this economist right; that is, has inflation over the last 4 years been caused by increases in the money stock?
c. The economist ends his column with an admonition to the Fed to stick to a constant money stock rule. This, he asserts, will give us noninflationary full employment. If the Fed had held the money stock constant over the last 4 years, would output have remained constant? Diagram the path the economy would have followed using an output-inflation loop.

7. Suppose that as a result of the Fed's policy rule, inflation is given by Equation 17–3, where the parameter k lies between 0 and 1. Sketch the output-inflation loop for the case of an oil price shock. Is there overshooting as in the output-inflation loops of Chapter 16? Why or why not?

8. In the June 4, 1979, issue of *Fortune,* an article by Herbert Stein, a former chairman of the Council of Economic Advisers, appeared that argued, "The idea that we need to get beyond the day-to-day, or even year-to-year, management of economic policy has been gaining more and more recognition. . . . The idea still has no operational effect on policy, however. Someone in authority has to take a step. The President and the Chairman of the Federal Reserve Board could describe what they regard as the desirable path of GNP for, say, the next five years. They could declare their intention, insofar as it lies within their power, to manage fiscal and monetary policy to stay on that path, and return to it if the economy strayed off. . . . Such an initiative would not prevent anyone from changing his mind. I am not proposing a constitutional amendment." Write a short essay evaluating Stein's proposal. Why would policy makers want to change their minds? What good is the proposal if they probably will? Why is Stein reluctant to propose a constitutional amendment?

18

◆━━━━━━━━━━━━━━━━━━━━━━━━━━━━━━━━◆

Macroeconomic Policy in the World Economy

TOTAL WORLD trade, measured by the dollar value of imports to all countries, was over $2 trillion in the mid-1980s—more than a tenfold increase since 1960. During this same period U.S. exports as a percentage of GNP doubled, from about 5 percent to about 10 percent; in Britain these exports are now over 25 percent of GNP. Each day, throughout the world, several hundred billion dollars in financial assets are traded in the interbank foreign exchange market. These large international trade and financial movements indicate how closely the world's economies—including the U.S. economy—are now linked together.

We saw in Chapter 10 that changes in U.S. macroeconomic policy can have significant effects on foreign trade and on the exchange rate. An expansionary fiscal policy, for example, increases demand for imports from abroad and thereby increases aggregate demand in other countries as well as in the United States. An expansionary fiscal policy also raises interest rates in the United States, and this causes the dollar to appreciate. An appreciated dollar reduces demand for U.S. exports and induces U.S. consumers and firms to import goods from abroad, rather than purchase goods produced at home. This further stimulates aggregate demand in other countries, while it reduces the stimulus to the U.S. economy. Hence, an expansionary fiscal policy crowds out spending not only in interest-sensitive capital goods industries, but also in export industries and in import-competing industries.

This chapter extends our analysis of international macroeconomic issues in two ways. First, we broaden our focus to consider macroeconomic policy and economic fluctuations in the world economy as a whole rather than in the United States in particular. To do this we need to consider policies of fixed exchange rates, since many countries in the world still follow such policies. Second, we examine the effects of macroeconomic policy in a classical model with perfectly flexible wages and prices. As with the domestic economy, the classical model is useful for examining long-run international issues such as the effects of steady inflation.

You should be familiar with the ideas about international finance that we introduced in Chapter 10. If you feel that you are a bit rusty, or if material in the last two paragraphs seems unfamiliar, you might want to review that chapter.

18.1 The International Monetary System

We begin by describing the international monetary system as it exists in the world today. An international monetary system is a set of rules for each country's monetary authority that stipulates how exchange rates are to be determined. Like the rules of a domestic monetary system, international monetary rules can be either explicit or implicit. In the current system, some of the rules are stipulated explicitly in international agreements, but many have been adopted less formally by individual countries. The rules can stipulate that exchange rates be **fixed**, or that they be **floating**, or that they be **managed**, with policy makers attempting to "lean against the wind" in order to smooth out exchange rate fluctuations.

Our present international system evolved during the 1970s. The system is still in a state of flux. We will see that a number of European countries maintain fixed exchange rates among themselves, even though they all have floating exchange rates with the United States. Japan has a floating exchange rate, but the Bank of Japan has an active role in setting the value of the yen. Many Latin American and Caribbean countries fix their exchange rates to the dollar, and many African countries fix their currencies to the French franc.

To understand the current international monetary system and how it might change in the future, it is necessary to study how the system evolved during the 1970s from the Bretton Woods System of fixed exchange rates to the more flexible and varied system that we have now. An examination of the Bretton Woods period is also useful for understanding monetary policy in those countries that still maintain fixed exchange rates today.

THE BRETTON WOODS SYSTEM

From the end of World War II until the early 1970s the world economy operated under a system of fixed exchange rates. This system evolved out of an agreement between major trading nations at an international conference at Bretton Woods, New Hampshire, in 1944. The key economists participating in this conference were John Maynard Keynes, representing the United Kingdom, and Harry Dexter White of the U.S. Treasury. Their choice of fixed rather than freely floating exchange rates was based on the feeling that floating exchange rates were partly responsible for the poor performance of the world economy during the 1920s and the 1930s, compared with the better performance during a previous period of fixed exchange rates before World War I. However, they also recognized the need to change exchange rates under certain circumstances, and they therefore created a system that allowed for limited flexibility.

According to the Bretton Woods System, each country agreed to fix, or **peg**, the exchange rate for its currency in terms of the dollar. The numerical value of this fixed exchange rate—for example, $2.80 per British pound sterling—was called the **par value**. Each country agreed to intervene in currency markets to keep the exchange rate within 1 percent above and 1 percent below its par value. The range between the **upper intervention point** of plus 1 percent and the **lower intervention point** of minus 1 percent was called the **intervention band** (see Figure 18–1). Intervention was carried out by each country's monetary authority, usually the central bank of the country. Each monetary authority would purchase dollar securities to keep its currency from appreciating, and, conversely, would sell dollar se-

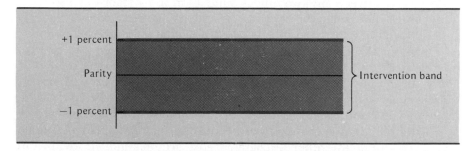

Figure 18–1.   INTERVENTION BAND OF A FIXED EXCHANGE RATE SYSTEM.
The central bank enters the foreign exchange market when the exchange rate reaches the lower limit and offers to buy as much of its currency at that price as traders want to sell so as to prevent the currency from falling below the lower limit. Similarly, the central bank enters the foreign exchange market when the exchange rate reaches the upper limit and offers to sell as much of its currency as traders want to buy at that price so as to prevent the exchange rate from rising above the upper limit.

curities to keep its own currency from depreciating. The dollar was the **intervention currency** for all countries. As with any other commodity, the price of foreign exchange would stay within the intervention band as long as the monetary authorities were willing and able to sell unlimited quantities of the currency at the upper intervention point and to buy unlimited quantities of the currency at the lower intervention point.

The Bretton Woods System was an organized and systematic way to stabilize exchange rates by applying the principle discussed in Chapter 10, Section 10.8. When economic forces threaten to make a country's currency rise in relation to the dollar, that country is to make an expansionary shift in its monetary policy. The expansionary shift generally had the particular form of purchasing dollar securities by issuing domestic reserves. Similarly, when a depreciation would otherwise occur, the central bank would contract by selling dollar securities and reducing domestic reserves, a form of contractionary monetary policy.

The dollar securities of foreign central banks under the Bretton Woods System constituted their foreign *reserves.* When a central bank was preventing an appreciation of its currency by purchasing dollar securities, there was a *reserve inflow* or *balance of payments surplus.* This was generally considered a favorable sign for that economy. When the central bank was defending its currency by selling dollar securities, there was a *reserve outflow* or a *balance of payments deficit.* A deficit could last only as long as the central bank had a stock of reserves of dollar securities. After the stock ran out, the bank would have to turn to other restrictive measures, or cease its policy of stabilizing the exchange rate. Balance of payments deficits were a matter of great publicity and concern under the Bretton Woods System.

With all countries pegging their exchange rates to the dollar, the exchange rate between any two other countries in the system was also fixed. To see this, suppose that the Bank of England maintained a par value for the British pound of exactly $4.00, and that the Bank of France maintained a par value for the French franc of $.25. Then the exchange rate between pounds and francs could not deviate from 16 francs per pound or, equivalently, .0625 pound per franc. If it did, then private international currency traders could make enormous profits by selling in one market and buying in another. A fixed exchange rate system in N countries requires that only $N - 1$ independent exchange rates need to be maintained by the monetary authorities. All other exchange rates are maintained by private currency traders.

As a rule, exchange rates are quoted in terms of foreign currency units per domestic currency unit. For example, 16 francs per pound would be the rate quoted in London, while .0625 pound per franc would be the rate quoted in Paris. When the franc appreciates from .0625 pound to .125 pound in Paris, the pound depreciates from 16 francs to 8 francs in London. One exception to this rule is that the sterling exchange rate in the United States is usually quoted in terms of dollars per pound. Thus, one would hear that the dollar fell from $2.00 per pound to $2.25! Another exception is the Canadian dollar.

As part of the Bretton Woods agreement, two international monetary institutions were created. The **International Monetary Fund** (IMF) was set up to provide relatively short-term loans to countries in order to help them support their currencies during temporary periods of balance of payments difficulty. In the 1960s the IMF was authorized to create its own deposit money called Special Drawing Rights, which can be used for international payments between countries in place of the dollar. The other institution is known as the International Bank for Reconstruction and Development (or the **World Bank**). It was set up to make longer-term loans to developing countries. Today, the IMF and the World Bank are deeply involved in advising developing countries that are in debt to banks in the United States and other Western countries and policing their macroeconomic policies.

The original par values of the Bretton Woods agreement were based on the concept of purchasing power parity, which we discussed in Chapter 10. Under purchasing power parity, the price of similar goods in two different countries should be about the same. Hence, if an 8-ounce jar of jam costs $1.50 in New York City and £.5 in London, then purchasing power parity would imply that the exchange rate should be $3.00. Of course, the actual purchasing power parity calculations at Bretton Woods were based on the average price of many commodities and services, not just jam.

INFLATION DIFFERENTIALS AND PARITY ADJUSTMENTS

If inflation is higher in one country than in another, then the exchange rate implied by purchasing power parity will change. Recalling the jam example, if the United States had an inflation rate of 10 percent while the British had an inflation rate of 20 percent, then after one year jam would cost $1.65 in New York City and £.60 in London; according to purchasing power parity the dollar would appreciate from $3.00 to $2.75—roughly a 10 percent appreciation. More generally, purchasing power parity indicates that *the exchange rate should appreciate by the difference between the foreign inflation rate and the domestic inflation rate.*

The economists and diplomats who drew up the Bretton Woods agreement knew that international differences in inflation and productivity growth could cause the original par values to get out of line, with undesirable consequences. A higher inflation rate in Britain—with no adjustment of the exchange rate—would make British goods relatively expensive and cause a balance of trade deficit, because British imports would increase and British exports would decrease. The reduced demand for British pounds sterling would put downward pressure on the currency and the Bank of England would be forced to sell more and more dollar reserves in order to maintain the fixed exchange rate.

To improve the balance of payments without a change in the exchange rate, the British would have no choice but to contract their economy with a program of tight monetary and fiscal policies. This would reduce the demand for imports, and it would also lower inflation in Britain, thereby making British exports more competitive and further reducing the demand for imports. These developments would improve the balance of payments. Note, however, that to restore purchasing power at the existing exchange rate the British price level would have to *fall*. This would require a period of painful deflation.

To prevent this type of situation, the designers of the Bretton Woods System permitted adjustments in the par values in cases where a "fundamental" imbalance would persist. These relatively infrequent parity adjustments were called **devaluations** when the exchange rate was lowered and **revaluations** when the exchange rate was raised. These terms are usually used instead of appreciation and depreciation for changes in par values in a fixed exchange rate system. *Markets* cause a currency to depreciate; the *government* devalues the currency. During the Bretton Woods period there were two instances where the British pound was devalued: first, from $4.00 to $2.80 in September 1949, and, second, from $2.80 to $2.40 in November 1967.

In practice, devaluations and revaluations did not occur as often as they needed to, given the differences in inflation rates. Devaluations were frequently postponed because they seemed to represent defeat for the government in power. The credibility of the government's commitment to maintain parity was an important part of the system. To convince the markets that the country was committed to its pledge to maintain parity, the finance ministers would often put their own word and that of the government on the line. Once their commitment was widely publicized, it became difficult to devalue for this would seem like a broken promise.

Revaluations were also difficult. When a currency increases in value domestic producers are made less competitive relative to foreign producers. This reduces profits and employment in the export industries and in the industries that compete with foreign imports. Since a revaluation requires deliberate action on the part of the government, it is easy to blame the government for the loss of jobs and profits.

The most serious problem with the Bretton Woods System was that it was even more difficult to devalue the dollar. This problem led to the breakdown of the system starting in 1971. Under the Bretton Woods System the only way that the dollar could be devalued was for all countries to revalue their currencies against the dollar. The United States's part in the Bretton Woods agreement was a commitment to exchange the dollar for gold at a price of $35 per ounce. As inflation in the United States began to increase in the 1960s it became more and more difficult for the United States to maintain this commitment. For one thing, the general inflation made gold a bargain at $35 per ounce. But, more important, as prices rose in the United States relative to many of its trading partners, the demand for U.S. products fell compared with foreign products. United States expenditures abroad rose and foreign expenditures in the United States declined, leading to lower net exports, which was worsened by heavy U.S. military expenditures abroad. To maintain parity of their currencies with the dollar, foreign monetary authorities had to buy up the dollar debt that was flowing out of the United States to pay for these expenditures. By 1971 dollar securities held by foreign monetary authorities were over three times the amount of gold at Fort Knox. It had by that time become clear that the United States could not maintain its commitment.

Various stopgap measures were enacted during the 1960s to remedy the situation. An interest equalization tax was enacted to make it more costly to invest in foreign securities. A program to discourage firms from making direct investments abroad was run by the United States Department of Commerce. Export industries were given support by the Export-Import Bank, which made low-interest loans to foreigners who bought U.S. products. But despite all these efforts the current-account deficits of the United States continued. The competitive position of U.S. industries remained unfavorable. By almost all calculations the dollar was overvalued and would remain so unless the United States introduced severe contractionary policies to reduce inflation, or the rest of the world enacted expansionary policies to increase inflation.

THE DEVALUATION OF THE DOLLAR AND THE COLLAPSE OF BRETTON WOODS

On August 15, 1971, the Nixon administration ended the United States commitment to sell gold at $35 dollars per ounce. This in itself would not cause a devaluation of the dollar, unless all other countries agreed to shift their par values with the dollar. Such action would require difficult multilateral negotiations. Rather than going in empty-handed to such a multilateral negotiation with all other countries, the U.S. administration unilaterally enacted a special 10 percent tariff on imports, which would be eliminated only when its major trading partners agreed to revalue their currencies relative to the dollar. The multilateral negotiations took place at the Smithsonian Institution in Washington in December 1971, at which most countries agreed to revalue by various amounts. So the United States strategy worked. Of course, it will never be known whether the United States needed to take such strong unilateral action to get what it wanted.

After the realignment of parities further efforts were made to reform the Bretton Woods System to prevent such problems in the future. The main goal of the United States during this period was to get more freedom to

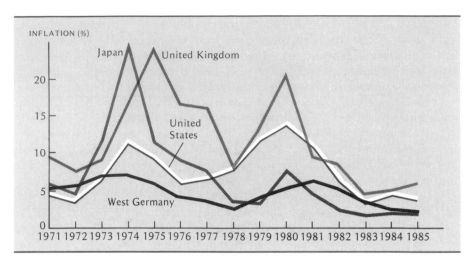

Figure 18–2.   INFLATION RATES, 1971–85.
The inflation rate increased in most countries in 1973–74. The increase was larger in Japan and the United Kingdom than in the United States and West Germany. The timing of the increase was also different in different countries. These discrepancies put additional pressures on existing exchange rate parities. Source: *Economic Report of the President,* 1987, Table B–106.

conduct its own domestic macroeconomic policy. Floating exchange rates seemed to offer this possibility, but there was no agreement on this point either within or outside the government.

World events had more to do with how the system evolved from the Smithsonian agreement than any formal reform effort. In 1973–74 the price of oil increased fourfold and inflation accelerated. The acceleration was worse for some countries than for others, as shown in Figure 18–2. With widely different inflation rates in different countries, the Smithsonian parities were soon abandoned as countries found it increasingly difficult to maintain them. The 1974–75 recession, which hit all countries (see Figure 18–3), put additional pressure on existing parities.

The desire of different countries to choose their own macroeconomic policies in response to the 1974–75 recession meant that exchange rates would have to shift further. Eventually most currencies began to float with no set parities, although there were considerable interventions aimed at preventing large movements. The world had emerged from the 1973–74 inflation and the 1974–75 recession with an essentially floating exchange rate system. It was not until January 1976 at an international conference in Jamaica that the IMF agreements were changed to reflect the reality of the floating exchange rate system. At that time the countries also agreed to abandon gold as a part of the international monetary system.

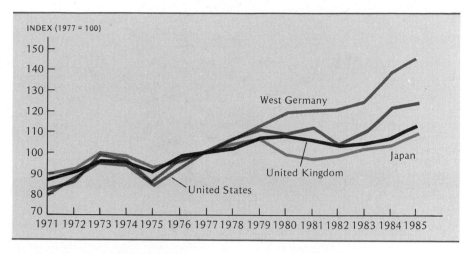

Figure 18–3. INDUSTRIAL PRODUCTION IN FOUR COUNTRIES, 1959–85.
The 1973–74 recession hit all countries, but some countries chose different monetary
and fiscal policies in response to it. This put additional pressure on exchange rate parities.
Source: *Economic Report of the President,* 1987, Table B–106.

THE CURRENT SYSTEM

Some economists think of the current international monetary system as a
"non-system." There is certainly a lot of variety, as a glance at Table 18–1,
which gives some of the different types of exchange rate arrangements used
as of October 1986, will show. Five countries not listed in the table peg their
currency to some other single currency.

In the current system the U.S. dollar fluctuates against other countries.
In 1978 the United States intervened heavily to stop a depreciation of the
dollar that was accelerating as U.S. inflation got worse. This intervention
was soon reduced after a temporary halt to the dollar's fall, but the dollar
continued to depreciate. When the Reagan administration came into office
in 1981, it declared formally that the United States would not intervene in
foreign exchange markets at all. By that time the dollar had begun to appreciate. After some pressure from European governments in 1983, the
United States agreed to intervene to "prevent disorderly markets"; this simply meant that the foreign exchange desk of the Fed in New York would attempt to smooth out day-by-day exchange rate fluctuations.

In September 1985, at a famous meeting at the Plaza Hotel in New York,
the United States, Germany, Japan, Britain, and France made a joint commitment to lower the value of the dollar and to intervene to stabilize the
four currencies against the dollar. Since then intervention has occurred.
But none of the countries was willing to make exchange rate stabilization

Table 18-1. EXCHANGE RATE POLICIES IN SELECTED COUNTRIES

Independently Floating	European Monetary System	Crawling Peg	Pegged to Dollar	Pegged to French Franc
Australia	Belgium	Brazil	Barbados	Cameroon
Bolivia	Denmark	Chile	Egypt	C. African Rep.
Canada	France	Colombia	Ethiopia	Chad
Japan	W. Germany	Madagascar	Iraq	Congo
Lebanon	Ireland	Portugal	Nicaragua	Gabon
New Zealand	Italy	Somalia	Panama	Mali
Philippines	Luxembourg		Paraguay	Niger
Nigeria	Netherlands		Peru	Senegal
S. Africa			Syria	Togo
United Kingdom			Venezuela	
United States				
Uruguay				

Managed Floating	Pegged to Special Drawing Right	Pegged to Other Composites of Currencies	Limited Flexibility Against Dollar
Argentina	Burma	Algeria	Afghanistan
China, P.R.	Iran	Austria	Qatar
Ecuador	Jordan	Finland	Saudi Arabia
Greece	Kenya	Hungary	
Iceland	Libya	Kuwait	
India	Rwanda	Malaysia	
Indonesia	Seychelles	Norway	
Israel	Vietnam	Poland	
Korea		Romania	
Mexico		Singapore	
Pakistan		Sweden	
Spain		Thailand	
Turkey		Tunisia	
Yugoslavia		Zimbabwe	

Source: *International Financial Statistics,* International Monetary Fund, December 1986, p. 20 (selected countries).

the exclusive goal of monetary policy. The 1985 agreement was followed by a much larger appreciation of some of the currencies than was anticipated at the Plaza. In early 1987 the United States, Japan, and other countries intervened very heavily in foreign-exchange markets in order to prevent the dollar from appreciating.

As Table 18-1 indicates, some countries—usually those with relatively high inflation rates—have a **crawling peg** system under which the currency is indexed to a domestic price index or some other indicator; the currency then appreciates or depreciates relative to the dollar according to how much that indicator moves. Brazil has one of the oldest crawling peg systems.

Eight European countries belong to a subsystem called the **European Monetary System** (EMS), and maintain a fixed exchange rate among themselves. The EMS was created in 1979, when the countries each agreed to

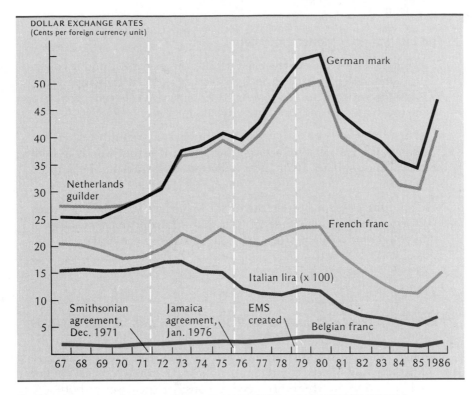

Figure 18–4.   FIVE CURRENCIES IN THE EUROPEAN MONETARY SYSTEM.
Since 1979 the currencies in the system have been fixed to each other (with occasional adjustments), but collectively they float against the dollar. The chart shows how five of the currencies move together in synchrony against the dollar. The other countries show the same pattern. Source: *Economic Report of the President*, 1987, Table B–105.

keep their currency within a fixed band around a par value set in terms of a composite unit (called the European Currency Unit) consisting of the currencies in the subsystem. The currencies are fixed within these limits among themselves, but as a group they jointly fluctuate against the dollar and against the currencies of other countries. Figure 18–4 shows how the exchange rates of five of these countries move against the dollar. The Italian lira has been the weakest of the currencies, and now has a wider intervention band than the others.

Most of the countries in the world—about 90—operate with their exchange rates fixed to a single currency or to a composite of currencies. About 30 countries peg their exchange rate to the dollar. Of course, the currencies of these countries fluctuate against other countries' currencies in the world just as the dollar does. Another 40 countries peg their exchange rate to a composite including the IMF's Special Drawing Right.

The International Monetary System

1. From the late 1940s to the early 1970s, the major economies operated under the Bretton Woods System, with fixed exchange rates. Each central bank aimed to keep the value of its currency within a narrow band around its dollar exchange rate.

2. When inflation rates vary across countries, a system of fixed exchange rates ultimately breaks down. The Bretton Woods System was abandoned in 1971 after inflation worsened in the United States.

3. Under the current system, the dollar floats freely; U.S. policy does little to control its movements. The major European currencies are fixed relative to each other but float relative to the dollar.

ALTERNATIVE MODELS: MACRO POLICY ANALYSIS IN THE WORLD

We have seen that the current international monetary system has a mixture of floating and fixed exchange rate policies. To analyze macro policy in the world economy we therefore need to consider the cases of both a *fixed* exchange rate and a *floating* exchange rate. Finally, we need to consider the two different assumptions about prices: *sticky* (predetermined but gradually adjusting) as in the dynamic model of Chapter 16, and *perfectly flexible* as in the classical model of Chapter 13.

18.2 Macro Policy in an Economy with Sticky Prices: The Case of a Fixed Exchange Rate

Many countries still operate under a fixed exchange rate rule of one kind or another. In this section we show how monetary and fiscal policies in these countries differ from those in a country with a floating exchange rate. We begin by assuming that the price level is predetermined in the short run; this is the same assumption that we used in the discussion of floating exchange rates in Chapter 10.

We showed in Chapter 10 that devoting monetary policy to the goal of holding the exchange rate at the prescribed level means that monetary policy cannot be used for domestic goals. The central bank must adopt a monetary policy that makes the LM curve a horizontal line. That is, the central bank must hold the domestic interest rate at the world rate. If it permitted the domestic rate to exceed the world rate, a large capital inflow would occur. Under a floating rate, that inflow could be discouraged by expectations of depreciation. However, if the central bank is successful in preventing exchange rate changes, there can't be expectations of depreciation. Hence, a nation with a fixed exchange rate has to keep its interest rate at the world rate.

CENTRAL BANK ACTIVITIES WITH FIXED RATES

Table 18–2 shows the balance sheets of the central bank of the home country with the fixed exchange rate. On the asset side of the balance sheet are securities that the central bank has purchased. A similar balance sheet for the central bank was presented in Chapter 12. Here, there are two types of securities: domestic and foreign. Domestic securities are denominated in domestic currency—these may be government bonds or even loans to private firms. The value of domestic securities held by a central bank is frequently called **domestic credit.** Domestic credit is the total credit that the central bank has extended to the home economy, whether to the government or to the private sector. Foreign securities are denominated in foreign currency. Most frequently these are bonds issued by foreign governments. Foreign securities are **foreign reserves.**

Table 18–2.   BALANCE SHEET OF THE CENTRAL BANK WITH FOREIGN RESERVES

Assets	Liabilities
Domestic credit	Currency
Foreign reserves	Bank reserves

Recall that the monetary base is defined as currency plus bank reserves. Because assets must equal liabilities, we know that domestic credit plus foreign credit equals the monetary base. That is,

$$\text{Monetary base} = \text{Domestic credit} + \text{Foreign reserves.} \qquad (18–1)$$

We will assume that the central bank follows the policy for setting the exchange rate of buying foreign reserves whenever the currency threatens to appreciate and selling foreign reserves if it threatens to depreciate. Now suppose that the central bank wants to increase the money supply in order to stimulate the economy. It purchases government bonds in the open market—an open-market purchase—causing domestic credit to rise. This means that the monetary base and the money supply will tend to increase. This increase in the money supply will tend to exert downward pressure on the interest rate. But the interest rate cannot be reduced, at least not by much or for very long. Capital will flow out of the country and the currency will start to depreciate as soon as the interest rate begins to fall below the world interest rate. The logical implication of our previous analysis is that the interest rate stays close to the world interest rate unless depreciation occurs.

How does the central bank prevent depreciation? As foreign-denominated bonds begin to look more attractive relative to domestic bonds, the central bank must provide the increased demand for foreign exchange by selling foreign reserves in order to prevent the exchange rate from depreciating. It does this by entering the foreign exchange market and selling its foreign reserves for domestic currency at the fixed exchange rate. In other words, foreign reserves decrease. The decrease in foreign reserves lowers the monetary base and offsets the previous effect of the open-market operation. In fact, since the interest rate does not fall, we know that the decrease in foreign reserves must be exactly equal to the increase in domestic credit. This keeps the money supply from increasing.

In the case of an open-market sale, the same channels keep the money supply from falling. The upward pressure on interest rates leads the central bank to buy foreign reserves, which increases the money supply. Because of the commitment to maintain the exchange rate at parity, the central bank is thwarted in its attempt to change the money supply. The money supply is essentially out of the control of the central bank in a small country whose capital market is linked to world markets. Monetary policy cannot be used for domestic purposes.

Now suppose that there is an expansionary fiscal policy—an increase in government spending. This increase in government spending does not increase the interest rate if the central bank is fixing the exchange rate, because the money supply automatically increases.

STERILIZED INTERVENTION

A central bank normally responds to a potential depreciation of its currency by selling foreign reserves. Then the money supply contracts, the interest rate rises, and the potential depreciation is offset. However, it is possible for the central bank to sell foreign reserves and buy domestic credit at the same time in the same amount. Such a move is called a *sterilized intervention*. From Table 18–2, it is apparent that a sterilized intervention has no effect on the assets of the central bank. Thus it has no effect on the monetary base and no effect on the domestic economy.

Under modern conditions with highly integrated capital markets, it is unlikely that a sterilized intervention has much effect. A central bank would have to sell a huge volume of foreign reserves to defend its currency against a threatened depreciation. Its ability to make such a move is limited by its stock of foreign reserves. After the stock is exhausted, the bank would have to revert to normal monetary contraction.

CAPITAL OR EXCHANGE CONTROLS

Capital controls, such as restrictions on the amount of foreign currency that domestic residents can purchase, would permit the domestic interest rate to be different from the world rate. In fact, capital controls are still being used in many small countries for exactly this reason. Although they would enable monetary policy to be more effective, capital controls have the disadvantage that they reduce the efficiency of international capital markets. Economic efficiency requires that different types of capital be allocated according to their after-tax rate of return. Although there are already many taxes in the world that distort the allocation of capital, adding additional taxes would probably distort the allocation even further.

One of the consequences of fixed exchange rates is the likely need for capital controls. As we mentioned in the previous section, the United States used capital controls in the 1960s when it had a fixed exchange rate under the Bretton Woods System. The interest equalization tax and the voluntary programs to discourage foreign investment were efforts to reduce the demand for foreign-denominated securities. James Tobin, on the other hand, has argued that similar taxes or controls should be enacted now so that capital does not move so quickly or by as much. Tobin argues that we should "throw some sand" into the excessively efficient international financial system so that monetary policy can regain some control.[1]

Fixed Exchange Rates in an Economy with Sticky Prices

1. With the high capital mobility and no expected change in the exchange rate, the domestic interest rate will be the same as the world interest rate.

2. Under fixed rates, the central bank loses control of the domestic interest rate. The bank must act to keep the domestic interest rate equal to the world rate.

3. Fixed exchange rates can also be achieved with capital controls, but these interfere with the efficient allocation of capital.

18.3 Macro Policy in a Classical Open Economy

In Chapter 13 we examined the effects of monetary policy in a classical model with perfectly flexible wages and prices. Although prices and wages

---

[1] James Tobin, "A Proposal for International Monetary Reform," *The Eastern Economic Journal*, Vol. 4, pp. 153–159, 1978.

are sticky in the real world, the classical model is a useful benchmark for calculating the long-run effects of policy when prices and wages have fully adjusted. In the classical model an increase in the rate of growth of the money supply causes the inflation rate to increase by the same amount and leaves output unchanged. The same is true of the long-run effects for a model with sticky wages and prices.

In this section we examine the behavior of a classical open economy. We consider the case of both fixed and floating exchange rates.

A SMALL CLASSICAL ECONOMY WITH A FIXED EXCHANGE RATE

For a small country, the world price level, P_w, is unaffected by monetary policy in the home country. Let us assume that monetary policy abroad is not changing and that P_w is constant. Purchasing power parity says that the price of goods at home and abroad should be about the same when stated in equivalent currency units. In algebraic terms,

$$PE = P_w, \tag{18--2}$$

where P is the domestic price level and E is the exchange rate. Deviations from purchasing power parity cannot last for long in a flexible-price model. If home goods become cheaper because of a drop in home prices, then increased demand for home goods will quickly drive up home prices again. Similarly, an increase in home prices will reduce demand for home goods and home prices will fall back down again.

As we noted in Chapter 13, in a classical economy monetary policy controls the price level directly; it has no effect on output. Equation 18–2 shows what price level, P, is needed to achieve an exchange rate E given the world price level P_w. Thus, the central bank has to devote itself single-mindedly to a single target for the price level. It cannot use monetary policy for another goal. The situation is similar to the one for fixed rates and sticky prices, where the central bank has to adhere to an interest-rate target.

Figure 18–5 shows the aggregate demand curve for the home country. The vertical line at potential output Y^* indicates that output cannot deviate from potential. This is the primary implication of the classical model. The intersection of the aggregate demand curve and the vertical line at potential is shown to occur at $P = P_w/E$, the value implied by purchasing power parity. The economy is at rest at this intersection.

Now suppose the central bank tries to increase the money supply. The aggregate demand curve will begin to shift up. Since output is unchanged, the price level will begin to rise. As it does there will be a reduced demand for home goods. As fewer home goods are purchased and more foreign goods are purchased there will be downward pressure on the exchange rate. To maintain the exchange rate, the central bank will have to sell its foreign ex-

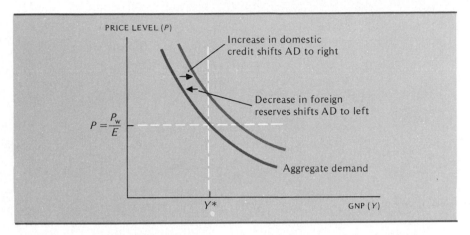

Figure 18–5. MONETARY POLICY IN A SMALL CLASSICAL ECONOMY WITH FIXED EXCHANGE RATES.
The domestic price level is determined by world prices. Any increase in domestic credit that shifts the aggregate demand curve to the right is offset by a decrease in foreign reserves that shifts the aggregate demand curve to the left.

change reserves. As we saw in the last section, the reduction in reserves will reduce the monetary base and the money supply. This reduction will move the aggregate demand curve back down until it is at the original intersection.

In effect, the central bank has lost control of the money supply just as in the fixed-price model. The original increase in the money supply is offset by an equal decline as the central bank supports the currency. The reverse case of a reduction in money growth is analogous.

An important practical question concerns the reaction of a country with fixed exchange rates to an increase in world prices. Suppose that foreign prices rise as a result of inflationary policies abroad. If P_w goes up and E is fixed we know that the domestic price level must rise. But the economy is always at full employment, so this means that aggregate demand must increase. By pegging the exchange rate the monetary authority will automatically increase the money supply to accommodate the increase in domestic prices. As world prices rise the relative price of home goods will fall, and the relative price of imports will rise. This will increase the demand for the home country's goods and put upward pressure on the home currency. The central bank must then buy foreign securities in order to keep its own currency from appreciating. As the central bank's holdings of foreign reserves rise, the monetary base will increase. Hence, the money supply increases, and will continue to increase until the aggregate demand curve rises to the new intersection point with the higher domestic price level. This is shown in Figure 18–6.

Some evidence of how an increase in world prices can lead to an expan-

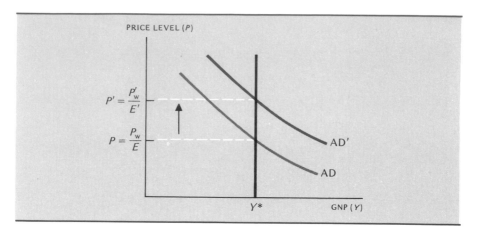

Figure 18–6. AN INCREASE IN WORLD PRICES FACED BY AN ECONOMY WITH FIXED EXCHANGE RATES.
The increase in world prices raises domestic prices. The domestic monetary authority automatically accommodates the increase by increasing its foreign reserves in order to keep the exchange rate from rising.

sion of the domestic money supply in this way can be obtained by looking at West Germany in the late 1960s and early 1970s before the end of Bretton Woods. The increase in world prices was partly due to the expansionary policies in the United States relating to the war in Vietnam. Compared to the United States, West Germany is relatively small. Figure 18–7 shows how the monetary base increased in Germany during this period. Starting around 1969 the German central bank's (the Bundesbank's) holdings of foreign reserves increased sharply. This led to a similar sharp increase in the monetary base. Almost all of the increase in the monetary base during this period was due to the Bundesbank's foreign exchange operations.[2]

We now consider how a long-run steady increase in prices—a steady inflation—fits into the model of a small country with a classical economy and a fixed exchange rate. Suppose that the world price level is increasing at the rate π_w. This could be the result of inflationary monetary policy in the world. Suppose the growth rate of output in the home country is $\Delta Y/Y$. Then we know from the results of the closed-economy classical model (Chapter 13) that inflation in the home country is equal to

$$\pi = \Delta M/M - \Delta Y/Y + \Delta V/V, \qquad (18-3)$$

where M is the money supply and V is velocity.

Purchasing power parity with a fixed exchange rate implies that the rate of inflation at home must equal the rate of inflation in the world. That is, π

---

[2] This discussion is based on Ronald I. McKinnon, *Money in International Exchange: The Convertible Currency System,* New York, Oxford University Press, 1979.

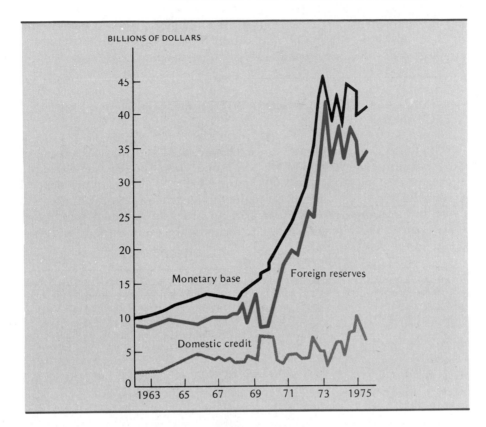

Figure 18–7. THE EFFECT OF FOREIGN RESERVES ON THE MONETARY BASE: GERMANY, 1962–75.
An increase in world prices led to an increase in the demand for German goods. As the Bundesbank prevented the Deutschemark from appreciating, it increased its holdings of foreign reserves and the monetary base expanded by about the same amount. Source: H Cleveland and B. Brittain, *The Great Inflation: A Monetarist View*, National Planning Association, 1976, p. 36.

$= \pi_w$. From Equation 18–3, this means that the rate of money growth in the home country must be

$$\Delta M/M = \Delta Y/Y + \pi_w - \Delta V/V. \qquad (18–4)$$

That is, the rate of domestic money growth is determined by three factors: the growth rate of output, the growth rate of velocity, and the foreign inflation rate. All three are unaffected by monetary policy in the home country: They are exogenous. Hence, the central bank has no control over money growth. If the central bank reduces the rate of growth of domestic credit, there must be an increase in the rate at which it accumulates foreign reserves. The increased foreign reserve accumulation will require persistent balance of payments surpluses, as we saw in the saving-investment accounting identities of Chapter 2. When the rate of domestic credit growth is low, the surplus will be large. The implication is that a lower rate of domestic credit growth will cause a balance of payments surplus.

A SMALL CLASSICAL ECONOMY WITH A FLOATING EXCHANGE RATE

With floating exchange rates, the exchange rate E can adjust as a result of the increase in money. Suppose that the money supply increases and that the aggregate demand curve shifts up (Figure 18–8). According to the classical model, the price level will rise. Since the foreign price level is fixed, this will cause the exchange rate to depreciate in order to maintain purchasing power parity. The currency will depreciate by the same amount as the increase in the money supply.

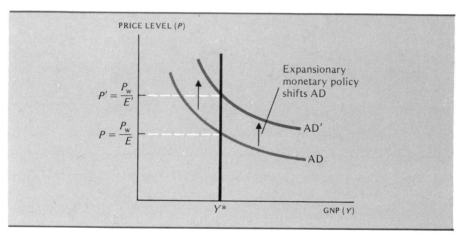

Figure 18–8. AN EXPANSIONARY MONETARY POLICY IN A CLASSICAL ECONOMY WITH A FLOATING EXCHANGE RATE.
The exchange rate depreciates and the price level rises. Real GNP is unchanged.

WORLD INFLATION WITH FLOATING EXCHANGE RATES

One of the most important properties of a floating exchange rate system is that it permits different countries to have different inflation rates. Inflation at home need not be equal to the inflation rate in other countries because depreciation of the currency will preserve purchasing power parity. As long as the rate of depreciation of the currency is equal to the difference between the home inflation rate and the foreign inflation rate, purchasing power parity will be satisfied. That is,

$$\pi - \pi_w = -\Delta E / E. \tag{18-5}$$

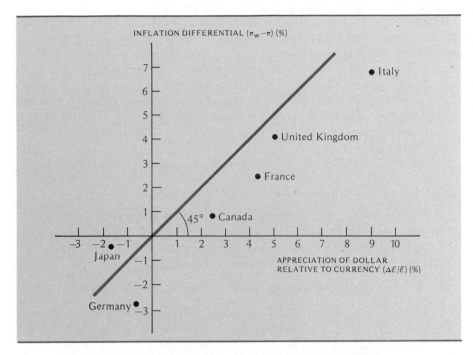

Figure 18–9. INFLATION DIFFERENTIALS AND APPRECIATION OF THE DOLLAR RELATIVE TO SIX COUNTRIES, 1972–85.
The inflation rates are measured by the consumer price index in each country. The rates of inflation and appreciation are annual averages for the 13-year period. When the inflation differential is high, appreciation of the dollar against that country's currency is high. Source: *Economic Report of the President*, 1987, Tables B–105 and B–106.

How accurate is this equation as a description of the long-run behavior? In Figure 18–9 the inflation differentials and exchange rate appreciations between six economies and the United States are shown for the 13-year period from 1972 to 1985. The difference between inflation in each country (π_w) and inflation in the United States (π) is shown on the vertical axis. The rate of appreciation ($\Delta E / E$) of the dollar against each of the corresponding currencies is on the horizontal axis. The 45-degree line is then the relation between inflation differentials and exchange rate depreciation implied by Equation 18–5. The actual inflation rates and exchange rate behavior come very close to the theoretical prediction. West Germany has had the strongest currency and the lowest inflation rate compared to the United States. Italy is at the other extreme, with a comparatively weak currency and a high inflation rate compared to the United States. This relation between inflation and exchange rate behavior is even more striking for countries with very high inflation rates. For example, during this same 13-year period, the difference between the inflation rate in Argentina and that in the United States was about 50 percent per year. The Argentine peso depreciated by 48 percent per year against the dollar during that period.

The freedom that a floating exchange rate gives to countries in determining their own inflation rates is a mixed blessing according to some economists. They feel that discipline rather than freedom is needed because of the tendency for many countries' political systems to generate too much inflation. For a small country it might be better to peg its currency to one of its trading partners that has a relatively low inflation rate. As long as the exchange rate is maintained the small country will then eventually also have a low inflation rate.

Open Economies with Completely Flexible Prices

1. In a small open economy with flexible prices and a fixed exchange rate, the central bank has to adjust the money stock as necessary to keep the exchange rate at par. The domestic price level is determined by the world price level and the fixed exchange rate.

2. A large open economy can influence the world price level.

3. In an open economy (large or small) with floating exchange rates, monetary policy is unconstrained. A monetary expansion raises the domestic price level and lowers the international value of the currency.

4. Under floating exchange rates, each country has its own inflation rate. Exchange rates will depreciate as needed to preserve purchasing power parity.

18.4 International Macro Policy Coordination

We have examined the effects of macroeconomic policy in a number of circumstances relevant to the conditions of the international monetary system today. The results show consistently that monetary policy is not very useful for domestic stabilization purposes in an economy with a fixed exchange rate. If capital is mobile, as it seems to be in most advanced countries without exchange controls, the central bank has little direct control over the money supply if it must support a fixed exchange rate. Moreover, a small country with a fixed exchange rate is essentially forced into adopting price stability goals that are identical to the country that it pegs its currency to.

Floating exchange rates offer much more freedom to use monetary policy for domestic stabilization purposes. That freedom can be a mixed blessing if the country's political system requires external discipline when it comes to monetary policy.

Floating exchange rates, however, do not completely insulate one economy from the effects of macroeconomic policies in other countries. In principle, therefore, international coordination of macro policies might be useful. The optimal macro policy that we discussed for the United States in Chapter 17 might be different if the effects of U.S. policy on other countries were taken into account, or if the effects of other countries' policies on the United States were taken into account.

Macro policy making in the world economy can be thought of as a game. Each country is a player in the game. The objective of policy makers in each country might be the same as those we discussed in Chapter 17. Each country has a social welfare function that includes output stability and price stability. Policy makers choose their instruments to minimize a combination of each type of loss (see Figure 17–1). But if there is an interaction among countries, then the choice of a policy rule in one country will affect the social welfare function in the other country. Country 1 might improve its macroeconomic performance by worsening Country 2's macroeconomic performance. But if Country 1 does so, Country 2 might retaliate, or at least watch out for itself, with harmful side effects for Country 1. This would be a **noncooperative policy choice.** A **cooperative policy choice,** on the other hand, is one in which each country agrees to use a policy rule that doesn't have an adverse effect on the other country, in exchange for getting the same treatment from the other country. Some international coordination or discussion about policies, like that at Bretton Woods after World War II, would probably be necessary for this cooperative outcome.

In recent years there has been an annual international summit meeting among the leaders of seven large industrial countries that interact with each other: Canada, France, Germany, Italy, Japan, the United Kingdom, and the United States. One of the stated purposes of these summit meetings is to discuss macro policy. The amount of actual international coordination that goes on varies from meeting to meeting. Under the Carter administration there was much effort by the United States to get other countries to expand. In the first term of the Reagan administration, when contractionary policies were enacted in the United States to reduce inflation, these types of coordination efforts were abandoned. However, during President Reagan's second term there was more discussion about coordination.

Are the gains from coordination large? How different would optimal policies look if countries cooperated, rather than acting independently? For example, should countries be less or more accommodative to inflation than calculations like those in Chapter 17 indicated?[3] Or perhaps countries

[3] Macroeconomic research on this question is just beginning. See Koichi Hamada, "Macroeconomic Strategy and Coordination under Flexible Exchange Rates," in Rudiger Dornbusch and Jacob A. Frenkel (eds.), *International Economic Policy: Theory and Evidence,* Baltimore, Johns Hopkins, 1979, pp. 292–324; Gilles Oudiz and Jeffrey Sachs, "Macroeconomic Policy Coordination among the Industrialized Countries," *Brookings Papers on Economic Activity,*

should use their monetary policies to reduce the size of the fluctuations in the exchange rate as well as of the inflation rate and the unemployment rate.[4]

We saw in Chapter 10 that changes in the United States money supply have effects on the exchange rate. A monetary contraction raises the exchange rate and a monetary expansion lowers the exchange rate. What are the effects of these changes abroad? What might foreign macro policy-makers do about these changes? Consider the case of a dollar appreciation associated with tight U.S. monetary policy or a loose U.S. fiscal policy. Obviously, an appreciation of the dollar is a depreciation of other currencies. A depreciation in the rest of the world has two effects that must be considered by policy makers.

First, the depreciation increases aggregate demand in the rest of the world. The depreciation is like an aggregate demand shock that increases net exports in the rest of the world—the aggregate demand curve shifts to the right. According to our optimal policy analysis, the appropriate response of policy makers in the rest of the world is to offset this shift by effecting tighter fiscal or monetary policy. Policies should be coordinated to get this result, but since the effect of the U.S. policy can be offset by the appropriate choice of policies abroad, there is no loss in world welfare on this account.

The second effect cannot be offset so easily, however. *The depreciation of the foreign currency will raise the price of imported products in the rest of the world.* Recall that the price shock term (Z) in the inflation equation in Chapter 17 was due to changes in the price of inputs to production, such as oil. If the exchange rate depreciates, then the price that firms pay for these products rises. For example, Japan Airlines will have to pay 2.5 billion more yen for a $50 million Boeing 747 jet made in Seattle if the yen depreciates from 150 yen per dollar to 200 yen per dollar. The second effect of the U.S. monetary policy is thus to create a price shock in the rest of the world.

As we already know, a price shock presents a cruel choice to policy makers: Inflation must rise, unemployment must rise, or both must rise. The magnitude of the inflation or unemployment depends on how much accommodation is built in to policy in the rest of the world. Some loss, however, is inevitable. This effect of the U.S. policy, therefore, does result in a loss in welfare in the rest of the world and opens the possibility of cooperation. A cooperative policy would be one in which both the United States and other countries are more accommodative to inflation than they otherwise would be. This would make monetary policy less contractionary in the face of a price shock at home and would therefore have smaller harmful effects

Number 1, pp. 1–64, 1984; and John B. Taylor, "International Coordination in the Design of Macroeconomic Policy Rules," *European Economic Review,* Vol. 26, 1985.

[4] See Ronald I. McKinnon, *An International Standard for Monetary Stabilization,* Washington, D.C., The Institute for International Economics (distributed by M.I.T. Press), 1984.

abroad. In return, other countries would agree to be more accommodative to inflation in their countries. Although it is clear that optimal cooperative policies should be more accommodative than noncooperative policies, the difference could be small. Since our historical experience with flexible exchange rates is still fairly short, there is unfortunately little empirical evidence about the size of the difference between the policies.

The Annual Economic Summits

Each year the leaders of seven large western countries get together at summit meetings to discuss economic policy. There were surprising similarities between economic conditions at the times of the two economic summit meetings held in Bonn, West Germany, in 1978 and again seven years later in 1985. At the first Bonn summit, a Democratic president, Jimmy Carter, represented the United States and a Social Democratic chancellor, Helmut Schmidt, represented Germany. Seven years later these two leaders had been replaced by a Republican president, Ronald Reagan, and a Christian Democrat chancellor, Helmut Kohl. In 1978 the position of the United States was that Germany and Japan should expand fiscal policy. This would reduce the U.S. trade deficit and stimulate the world economy. In the U.S. view, Germany and Japan were far below potential and could afford to expand. Both countries were reluctant to do so. Germany and Japan were more concerned about inflation than was the United States. Nevertheless, a bargain was struck: Germany and Japan would expand in exchange for a new U.S. energy policy.

In the intervening years, President Reagan came into office and there was much less talk from the United States about coordination of macro policy. The United States did not want further expansion in the other countries because of the high rate of inflation and the U.S. intention to contract monetary policy. In the U.S. view, the other countries needed to contract as much as the United States. In the summits in the early 1980s other countries had complained about the tight monetary policy in the United States, so any coordination would have probably required more monetary ease in the United States—a change in policy that was not wanted by the United States at that time.

However, by the 1985 Bonn summit the United States was again in a position of asking Germany and Japan to expand their fiscal policies. The dollar was still very high and foreign expansion would help to bring it down. Moreover, the U.S. administration felt that the other countries were far below potential and could afford to expand without an increase in inflation. The United States was close to potential and could probably not expand too rapidly.

> Seven years of fluctuations in output and inflation had brought the international partners back to a similar spot. At the 1986 summit in Tokyo the positions of each country were about the same as in Bonn. By 1986, however, the Japanese had begun an active policy to stimulate their economy. At the 1987 summit in Venice the Germans continued to be reluctant to stimulate their economy for fear of inflation.

Review and Practice

MAJOR POINTS

1. Each country has a choice between letting the open market determine the world value of its currency or using monetary policy to peg the value at a particular fixed rate. Today, the United States lets the dollar float but many other countries maintain fixed rates.

2. A country that fixes its exchange rate has to dedicate monetary policy to that task. It cannot use monetary policy for domestic goals.

3. With fixed rates, the domestic interest rate equals the world interest rate.

4. Fixed rates also enhance the effect of fiscal policy, because the interest rate movements that limit the effect in a closed economy are absent or small in an open economy linked to world capital markets.

5. A floating exchange rate allows monetary policy to pursue domestic goals. With fully flexible prices, a change in monetary policy brings a change in the price level and an equal change in the exchange rate.

KEY TERMS AND CONCEPTS

Open economy	Intervention
Floating exchange rate	European Monetary System
Fixed exchange rate	Capital and exchange controls
Bretton Woods System	Sterilization
Devaluation and revaluation	Policy coordination

QUESTIONS FOR DISCUSSION AND REVIEW

1. Compare the Bretton Woods System with the European Monetary System.

2. How has Japanese monetary policy changed since the collapse of the Bretton Woods System?

3. Why is it important to distinguish between large and small economies in discussing the international aspects of economic policy?

4. Why does high capital mobility cause equalization of interest rates under fixed exchange rates?

5. Explain why monetary policy cannot be used for domestic goals when the exchange rate is fixed. Consider fixed, fully flexible, and gradually adjusting prices.

6. Why is the response of GNP to government purchases higher under a policy of a fixed rather than a floating exchange rate?

7. What determines the price level in a small country with completely flexible prices and a fixed exchange rate?

8. How did the Vietnam War raise the German price level?

9. What determines the price level in a country with completely flexible prices and a floating exchange rate?

PROBLEMS

Numerical

1. Consider a macro model of a small open economy consisting of the following equations:

$$Y = C + I + G + X$$
$$C = 80 + .63\ Y$$
$$I = 750 - 2{,}000\ R$$
$$M = (.1625\ Y - 1{,}000\ R)P$$
$$X = 500 - .1\ Y - 100\ (EP/P_w),$$

where government spending G equals 750. Suppose that the exchange rate is *fixed* at $E = 1$, that the world interest rate $R_w = .05$, and that both price levels P and P_w are predetermined at 1.0. (Note that the domestic interest rate R must equal .05.)

a. Explain why M rather than R is an endogenous variable in this model in contrast to the macro model in Chapters 5 and 10.
b. Find the values of Y, C, I, X, and M that are predicted by the model.
c. Suppose that government spending G increases by \$50 billion. Calculate what happens to the endogenous variables Y, C, I, X, and M. What mechanism brings about the change in the money supply? Is there any crowding out of investment or net exports by the fiscal policy expansion? Why or why not?

2. Suppose that prices in the small open economy in Problem 1 are determined by

$$\pi = 2\left(\frac{Y_{-1} - Y^*}{Y^*}\right),$$

where $Y^* = \$4{,}000$ billion is potential GNP and $\pi = (P - P_{-1})/P_{-1}$ is the rate of inflation. Suppose that $G = 750$, $E = 1$, $R = R_w = .05$, $P_w = 1.0$. As in Problem 1, start out with a price level $P = 1.0$, but now let prices adjust after the first period.

a. Calculate the responses of Y, C, I, X, M, and P to a permanent increase in G of \$10 billion. Give the numerical values in the first 4 years. Plot accurately the values for each variable against time for the first 4 years and then sketch what happens after the fourth year.
b. Is there any crowding out of investment or net exports after the first year? Why or why not?

3. Suppose now that the equations in Problem 1 refer to a small classical open economy in which the price level P is perfectly flexible, Y is always equal to potential output, and $Y^* = \$4,000$ billion. Calculate what happens when government spending G increases by $10 billion. How do your results compare with the long-run results in Problem 2?

4. Consider a model of a world economy consisting of only two countries.

$$
\begin{aligned}
Y &= C + I + G + X & Y_w &= C_w + I_w + G_w + X_w \\
C &= 80 + .63\,Y & C_w &= 80 + .63\,Y_w \\
I &= 750 - 2{,}000\,R & I_w &= 750 - 2{,}000\,R_w \\
M &= (.1625\,Y - 1{,}000\,R)P & M_w &= (.1625\,Y_w - 1{,}000\,R_w)P_w \\
R &= R_w \\
X &= -X_w = 100 - .1(Y - Y_w) - 100(EP/P_w)
\end{aligned}
$$

The notation is the same as that used in the text except that the subscript w means the other country (the world). (Note that net exports from one country must equal the negative of net exports of the other country.) Suppose that the price levels P and P_w are both predetermined at 1.0 and that the exchange rate E is fixed at 1.0.

a. Calculate the values of output, investment, consumption, government spending, net exports, and the money supply M_w if $G = 750$, $G_w = 750$, and $M = 600$.
b. Calculate what happens to these same variables if M increases by $50 billion, to $650 billion. Explain why the money supply M_w in the other country changes.
c. Calculate what happens to these same variables if G increases by $50 billion but M and G_w do not change.
d. Find a policy for the home country to follow to keep Y unchanged when G_w increases by $10 billion.

Analytical
1. Consider a small open economy with sticky prices under a fixed exchange rate. Explain why the aggregate demand curve is vertical. What determines the level of output at which the curve is vertical?

2. Consider again the economy described in Question 1. Explain why an increase in government spending will increase output by the same amount as in the simple spending balance model of Chapter 4.

3. In a small open economy with a fixed exchange rate, suppose that actual GNP is below potential GNP. Inflation is low and the objective is to bring the economy back to potential.

a. Illustrate this situation with an IS-LM diagram.
b. Describe a policy that can bring about the desired objectives. Would the policy be any different if investment was very sensitive to the interest rate?

4. Describe what happens in a small classical open economy with a fixed exchange rate when the price level abroad falls. Illustrate your answer with an IS-LM diagram.

5. Explain why aggregate demand shocks need not lead to a policy conflict between countries while a price shock might. (Hint: Take account of the effect of the exchange rate on prices.)

6. Explain why a depreciation of the exchange rate could have an inflationary impact in one country and a deflationary impact in other countries.

Appendix: "Overshooting" of Exchange Rates with Sticky Prices and Rational Expectations

In Chapter 10 we based our theory of real exchange rate determination on rational expectations. We argued that the real exchange rate eventually returns to purchasing power parity, and that people rationally expect this return. This expectation theory enabled us to relate the *level* of the real exchange rate to the rate of appreciation or depreciation of the real exchange rate. Since the rate of depreciation is equal to real interest rate differentials, this led to an explicit relation between the real interest rate and the real exchange rate.

In recent years there has been considerable discussion among open-economy macroeconomists about **exchange rate overshooting.** Overshooting usually refers to a situation where the nominal exchange rate E overshoots its long-run value after an unanticipated but permanent increase in the money supply.[5] This occurs essentially because the exchange rate can move freely while prices cannot because they are sticky. In this appendix we show why overshooting may occur.

We consider a small country that takes as given the world interest rate and the world price level and within which a permanent unanticipated increase in the money supply occurs. According to our analysis of the classical model, the permanent increase in the money supply will eventually raise the domestic price level and *depreciate* the currency by the same amount. In addition, in the long run, output will return to potential and all other real variables will return to normal.

In the short run, an increase in the money supply should reduce the domestic interest rate. For this to occur, however, there must be an expected appreciation of the currency. How do we get an expected appreciation when we know that in the long run the exchange rate will depreciate? As illustrated in Figure 18–10, this can occur if the exchange rate first **overshoots** its long-run value and then appreciates up toward that value. The initial sharp fall in the exchange rate will be unexpected, because the money supply increase was unanticipated. After that jump down, the exchange rate is then expected to move up again smoothly.

Now that we have calculated how the exchange rate behaves, we can complete our investigation of the effect of the money supply increase. As is illustrated in Figure 18–11, the aggregate demand curve shifts to the right. Since output is greater than potential, the price level begins to rise. Since the price level rises more slowly than the exchange rate falls at the point of impact, the real exchange rate (PE/P_w) falls and home goods are in greater demand than foreign goods. This stimulates exports from the home country. The price level will continue to rise until the aggregate demand curve shifts back to its original position. By then the economy has returned to potential.

The same general results can occur for a large country whose policies affect the rest of the world. Again suppose that the money supply is increased in the large home country. As the real exchange rate moves in favor of the home country, the demand for exports from the rest of the world will decline. This will reduce aggregate demand abroad. On the other hand, there will be a decline in interest rates, which will stimulate aggregate demand abroad. These two factors work in opposite directions. A third factor is the effect of decreased costs of imports from the home country because of the depreciation of the exchange rate. Lower import prices in the rest

---

[5] The paper by Rudiger Dornbusch, "Expectations and Exchange Rate Dynamics," *Journal of Political Economy,* Vol. 84, pp. 1161–1176, 1976, led to much of the discussion of overshooting.

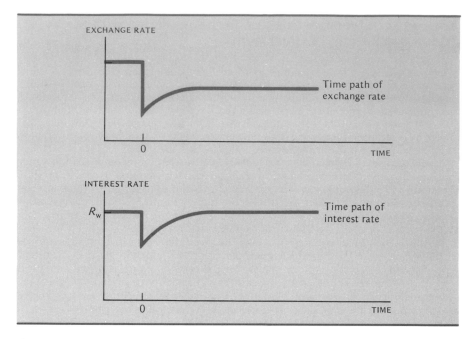

Figure 18–10.   OVERSHOOTING: THE EXCHANGE RATE DEPRECIATES SHARPLY AND THEN GRADUALLY APPRECIATES.
When the money supply increases at Time 0, the exchange rate unexpectedly falls below its new long-run value. The subsequent appreciation is expected and permits the domestic interest to remain below the world interest rate. The rate of change of the exchange rate declines as it gets closer to its long-run value.

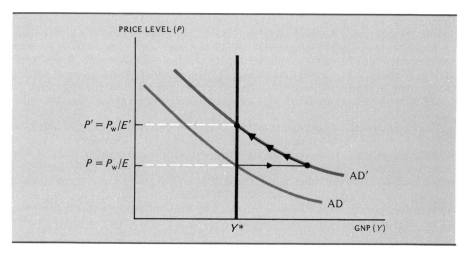

Figure 18–11.   MONETARY POLICY WITH EXCHANGE RATE OVERSHOOTING.
Monetary expansion shifts aggregate demand from AD to AD'. Through the process of price adjustment, the economy reaches a new equilibrium at a higher price level, P', and a correspondingly lower exchange rate, E'.

of the world will lower world prices. If the world money supply is left unchanged, then *real* money balances in the rest of the world will rise and this will tend to lower interest rates in the rest of the world even further. However, the total effect on the rest of the world can be either positive or negative depending on the magnitude of the various effects.

Index